A

HISTORY

OF THE

UNITED STATES OF AMERICA,

ON A PLAN

ADAPTED TO THE CAPACITY OF YOUTH,

AND DESIGNED

TO AID THE MEMORY BY SYSTEMATIC ARRANGEMENT AND

INTERESTING ASSOCIATIONS.

BY

CHARLES A. GOODRICH.

ILLUSTRATED BY ENGRAVINGS AND COLORED MAPS.

TO WHICH ARE ADDED

THE CONSTITUTION OF THE UNITED STATES,

AND

THE DECLARATION OF INDEPENDENCE.

REVISED FROM FORMER EDITIONS,

AND BROUGHT DOWN TO THE PRESENT TIME.

1852.

British Library Cataloguing-in-Publication Data
A catalogue record for this book is available from the
British Library

Charles A. Goodrich

Reverend Charles Augustus Goodrich was born in 1790. An American author and Congregational minister, he popularized the motto, 'a place for everything and everything in its place.' Goodrich attended Yale University in his youth, where he studied theology and graduated in 1812. Four years later, he became formally ordained and was appointed pastor of the First Congregational Church in Worcester, Massachusetts.

In 1820, Goodrich moved to Berlin, Connecticut, America, and in 1848 he moved again to Hartford, Connecticut. Goodrich continued to work as a pastor in Hartford and was also a member of the Connecticut Senate (the upper house of the Connecticut General Assembly, which had thirty six members, each representing a district with around 100,000 inhabitants). As well as this hefty workload, Goodrich also aided his brother, Samuel Goodrich (who published under the name of 'Peter Parley') in writing books for children. Charles Goodrich was the author of several books himself, passionate about the subjects of history, teaching the young and religion. He penned (among others): *View of Religions* (1829), *History of the United States of America* (1852-5), *Family Tourist* (1848), *Family Sabbath-Day Miscellany* (1855), *Geography of the Chief Places mentioned in the Bible* (1855), *Greek Grammar* (1855), and the *Child's History of the United States* (1855).

As has already been noted, Goodrich is also known for having the first printed citation of the epigram: 'Have a place for everything, and keep everything in its proper place.' The phrase was published in an article called 'Neatness' which Goodrich published in *The Ohio Repository* (Canton, Ohio), in December 1827. The idea that everything should have, and be kept in its place has subsequently appeared in many texts. In 1841 the phrase was used in a modified version in an item headed 'Brother Jonathan's Wife's Advice to her Daughter on her Marriage', in the *Hagerstown Mail,* Maryland: 'A place for everything and everything in time are good family mottos.' In *Masterman Ready, or the Wreck of the Pacific,* in 1842, Frederick Marryat wrote, 'In well-conducted man-of-war everything is in its place, and there is a place for everything.'

Charles Augustus Goodrich died on 4th June 1862, aged seventy-two.

THE ARMS OF THE UNITED STATES,
AND OF THE SEVERAL STATES OF THE AMERICAN UNION.

INDEX TO MAPS.

PREFACE.

THE School History herewith presented to the public has undergone such alterations as nearly to justify the announcement of it as a new work. The original division into periods, however, has been retained; the experience of teachers, for more than twenty years, having decided that, in this respect, it scarcely admits of improvement. And, in confirmation of the correctness of this judgment, it may be stated that every School History of the United States, published since the date of Goodrich's first edition, has been written, without exception, it is believed, upon the same general plan; and, in some instances, so nearly identical with his, as in the estimation of some to justify a question of legality.

The following are the principal alterations and improvements now introduced:

1. Upon the recommendation of an experienced teacher, the two sizes of type used in former editions are dispensed with; and all matters by way of explanation, or in respect to which simply reading is deemed sufficient, are reduced to notes.

2. The individual and separate history of the several colonies founded prior to the "French and Indian War," declared in 1756, is given to that period; and thence unitedly, as their histories from that time naturally blend together.

3. As to chronology, the New Style has been adopted in relation to all events prior to 1751, the time when the English Parliament adopted the Gregorian reformation.

4. A manifest improvement the author thinks he has made in his mode of treating the several administrations; namely, by giving the pupil an early and distinct ENUMERATION of the principal events by which each one was distinguished.

5. The author anticipates the approbation of intelligent and experienced teachers for one feature of the work, if for no other, — the omission of minor events, which would serve to embarrass and discourage the pupil, while an attempt is made to give due prominence to such events as are of obvious importance, and which should be firmly riveted in the memory. This want of discrimination has often sadly marred our historical school-books.

6. A series of questions is now appended to the volume. It is scarcely necessary to add — what every author has found a source of no small perplexity — that, in regard to the date of numerous events in our history, authorities differ, and so widely, sometimes, as to render it difficult, if not impossible, to determine the precise truth. Should positive errors be discovered, the author will esteem it a favor to be informed, that the needful corrections may be made.

CHARLES A. GOODRICH.

Hartford, 1852.

1*

INTRODUCTION.

The study of History presents the following advantages :

1. It sets before us striking instances of virtue, enterprise, courage, generosity, patriotism ; and, by a natural principle of emulation, incites us to copy such noble examples. History also presents us with pictures of the vicious ultimately overtaken by misery and shame, and thus solemnly warns us against vice.

2. History, to use the words of Professor Tytler, is the school of politics. That is, it opens the hidden springs of human affairs ; the causes of the rise, grandeur, revolutions and fall of empires ; it points out the influence which the manners of a people exert upon a government, and the influence which that government reciprocally exerts upon the manners of a people ; it illustrates the blessings of political union, and the miseries of faction, — the dangers of unbridled liberty, and the mischiefs of despotic power.

3. History displays the dealings of God with mankind. It calls upon us often to regard with awe his darker judgments ; and, again, it awakens the liveliest emotions of gratitude for his kind and benignant dispensations. It cultivates a sense of dependence on him, strengthens our confidence in his benevolence, and impresses us with a conviction of his justice.

4. Besides these advantages, the study of History, if properly conducted, offers others,— of inferior importance, indeed, but still not to be disregarded. It chastens the imagination, improves the taste, furnishes matter for reflection, enlarges the range of thought, strengthens and disciplines the mind.

5. To the above it may be added, that the History of the United States should be studied, 1. Because it is the history of our own country. 2. Because it is the history of the first civil government ever established upon the genuine basis of freedom. 3. Because it furnishes lessons upon the science of civil government, social happiness, and religious freedom, of greater value than are to be found in the history of any other nation on the globe. 4. Because it presents uncommon examples of the influence of religious principle. 5. Because an acquaintance with it will enable a person better to fulfil those duties which, in a free government, he may be called to discharge.

GENERAL DIVISION.

THE History of the United States of America may be divided into Sixteen Periods, each distinguished by some striking characteristic, or remarkable circumstance.

PERIOD FIRST extends from the Discovery of America by Columbus, 1492, to the first permanent English settlement in America, at Jamestown, Virginia, 1607, and is distinguished for DISCOVERIES.

PERIOD SECOND extends from the Settlement of Jamestown to the " French and Indian War," 1756, and is distinguished for SETTLEMENTS.

PERIOD THIRD extends from the French and Indian War, 1756, to the commencement of the American Revolution, in the Battle of Lexington, 1775, and is distinguished for the FRENCH AND INDIAN WAR.

PERIOD FOURTH extends from the Battle of Lexington, 1775, to the disbanding of the American Army at West Point, New York, 1783, and is distinguished for the WAR OF THE REVOLUTION.

PERIOD FIFTH extends from the Disbanding of the Army, 1783, to the Inauguration of George Washington as President of the United States, under the Federal Constitution, 1789, and is distinguished for the FORMATION AND ESTABLISHMENT OF THE FEDERAL CONSTITUTION.

PERIOD SIXTH extends from the Inauguration of President Washington, 1789, to the Inauguration of John Adams, 1797, and is distinguished for WASHINGTON'S ADMINISTRATION.

PERIOD SEVENTH extends from the Inauguration of President Adams, 1797, to the Inauguration of Thomas Jefferson, 1801, and is distinguished for ADAMS' ADMINISTRATION.

PERIOD EIGHTH extends from the Inauguration of President Jefferson, 1801, to the Inauguration of James Madison, 1809, and is distinguished for JEFFERSON's ADMINISTRATION.

PERIOD NINTH extends from the Inauguration of President Madison, 1809, to the Inauguration of James Monroe, 1817, and is distinguished for MADISON's ADMINISTRATION, and the late WAR WITH GREAT BRITAIN.

PERIOD TENTH extends from the inauguration of President Monroe, 1817, to the Inauguration of John Quincy Adams, 1825, and is distinguished for MONROE's ADMINISTRATION.

PERIOD ELEVENTH extends from the Inauguration of President Adams, 1825, to the Inauguration of Andrew Jackson, 1829, and is distinguished for ADAMS' ADMINISTRATION.

PERIOD TWELFTH extends from the Inauguration of President Jackson, 1829, to the Inauguration of Martin Van Buren, 1837, and is distinguished for JACKSON's ADMINISTRATION.

PERIOD THIRTEENTH extends from the Inauguration of President Van Buren, 1837, to the Inauguration of William Henry Harrison, 1841, and is distinguished for VAN BUREN's ADMINISTRATION.

PERIOD FOURTEENTH extends from the Inauguration of President Harrison, 1841, to the Inauguration of James K. Polk, 1845, and is distinguished for HARRISON AND TYLER's ADMINISTRATIONS.

PERIOD FIFTEENTH extends from the Inauguration of President Polk, 1845, to the Inauguration of Zachary Taylor, 1849, and is distinguished for POLK's ADMINISTRATION.

PERIOD SIXTEENTH includes the brief administration of President Taylor, from his Inauguration, 1849, to his death, 1850; and thence from the Inauguration of President Fillmore, 1850, to ——

UNITED STATES.

PERIOD I.

DISTINGUISHED FOR DISCOVERIES.

EXTENDING FROM THE DISCOVERY OF SAN SALVA-
DOR BY COLUMBUS, 1492, TO THE FIRST PERMANENT
ENGLISH SETTLEMENT, AT JAMESTOWN, VIRGINIA,
1607.

I. COLUMBUS. — 1. The honor of first making known to the
inhabitants of Europe the existence of a WESTERN CONTINENT
belongs to SPAIN, as a nation, and to CHRISTOPHER COLUMBUS, a
native of Genoa, as an individual.*

2. Columbus was born about the year 1435 or 1436. His
father was a reputable and meritorious man; by occupation, a
wool-comber, long resident in the city of Genoa. Columbus was

---

* Previous to the discovery of America, several of the nations of Europe
had long been engaged in attempting to find a passage to India by water.
The rich merchandise of that country, before the discovery of the passage
around the Cape of Good Hope, by the Portuguese, in 1497, had been conveyed to Europe over the Red Sea, and across the Isthmus of Suez ; thence
over the Mediterranean Sea to the different parts of Europe ; and it was to
find an easier passage that Columbus made his voyage of discovery.

After the discovery had been made, other nations laid claim to this honor;
and thus attempted to deprive the Genoese navigator, as well as the Spanish
nation, of the merit to which they were justly entitled.

The only nations, however, which appear to have had even the semblance
for such a claim, were the WELSH and NORWEGIANS.

In regard to the WELSH, no well-founded claim appears to exist, beyond the
discovery and attempted settlement of the islands in the Atlantic called the
AZORES; and even these are doubtful. There is stronger reason for believing
that the NORTHMEN, in the beginning of the 10th century, discovered Newfoundland or Labrador, and even visited the shores of Rhode Island and

the eldest of four children, having two brothers, Bartholomew and Diego, and one sister. His early education was limited; but he diligently improved the advantages which the means of his father enabled him to enjoy. After spending a short time at the University of Pavia, he returned to his father, whom he assisted in wool-combing. His enterprising disposition, however, prompted him to more active employment; and, at the age of fourteen years, we find him entering upon a seafaring life.

3. Having spent some time in the service of a distant relation, who followed the seas, he repaired to Lisbon. He was at this time about thirty-four years of age ; a tall, well-formed, vigorous man ; enterprising in his disposition, and uncommonly dignified in his manners. Taking up his residence, for a time, at Lisbon, he became acquainted with and married the daughter of a distinguished navigator, Bartholomew Perestrello, the former governor of Porto Santo, an island in the vicinity of Madeira.

4. The father of his wife being dead, Columbus resided with his mother-in-law, who gave him the privilege of examining the charts and journals of her deceased husband. These made Columbus acquainted with many facts and suggestions touching the enterprise in which the Portuguese were engaged, namely, the discovery of a passage to the East Indies, by doubling the southern extremity of Africa.

5. To a mind like that of Columbus, this subject was invested with the deepest interest ; and the more he read and reflected upon the figure of the earth, the stronger was his belief, not only that a western passage to India was practicable, but that a large body of land lay west of the Atlantic, designed to balance the lands lying in the eastern hemisphere.

6. In this latter opinion he was strengthened by various discoveries in the Atlantic, such as pieces of carved wood, and trunks of huge pine-trees, which had been noticed, after long westerly winds ; but, especially, by the well-established fact, that the bodies of two men had been cast upon one of the Azores Islands, whose features differed from those of any known race of people.

7. Having matured the plan of a voyage, with the above object in view, he first offered to sail under the patronage of his countrymen, the Genoese ; but they rejected his proposal. He

Massachusetts. It is claimed, also, that they attempted to colonize the country. While there is no certain record of these events, historical writers treat the claims in favor of the Northmen with respect. But these cannot detract from the honor of the great Genoese navigator. His was a discovery not of chance, but of calculation.

next applied to the Portuguese. The king and his advisers, however, long detained him; and, meanwhile, availing themselves of his explanations, secretly despatched a vessel to make the proposed discovery, but without success. Thus being disappointed in this application also, and despairing of assistance from Henry VII. of England, — to whom he had sent his brother Bartholomew, but who, being captured by pirates, did not reach England for some time, — he next repaired to Spain.

8. By what route, or by what means, Columbus reached Spain, is uncertain. The first trace we have of him in this country is as a stranger, on foot, and in humble guise, stopping at the gate of the convent of Santa Maria de Rabida, not far from the little seaport of Palos, and asking of the porter a little bread and water for a child, — his son Diego, whom his deceased wife had left to him. While receiving this humble refreshment, the prior of the convent, happening to pass by, was struck with the appearance of the stranger; and observing, from his air and accent, that he was a foreigner, entered into conversation with him, and soon learned the particulars of his story, and entered warmly into his views and plans. Through the prior's influence, the enterprising navigator was enabled to lay his plans before Ferdinand and Isabella, then on the united thrones of Castile and Arragon.*

9. For a time, these sovereigns were deaf to his application; but, at length, the queen undertook the enterprise, in behalf of the crown of Castile; and, to defray the expense of the outfit and voyage, offered to part with her royal jewels. The necessary funds being thus provided, a fleet, consisting of three small vessels, was soon ready for the voyage. Two of these were light barks, called caravals, not superior to river and coasting craft of more modern days. These were open, without deck in the centre, but built high at the prow and stern, with forecastles and cabins for the accommodation of the crew. The names of these vessels were the Pinta and Nina. The ship of Columbus, the Santa Maria, was decked, and of larger dimensions. On

---

* Spain, which had long been in possession of the Romans, was invaded by the VANDALS, and other tribes from the north, in the 5th century; these tribes were subdued by the VISIGOTHS, or WESTERN GOTHS. During the 8th century, the MOORS or SARACENS invaded and conquered a great part of the country; but the Goths retained a portion, and afterwards founded several distinct kingdoms, the most considerable of which were Castile and Leon, Arragon and Navarre. In 1496, Ferdinand, King of Arragon, married Isabella, Queen of Castile and Leon, and thus they united the two kingdoms. Navarre was subsequently conquered in 1521, and Spain was thus formed into one monarchy.

board this fleet were ninety mariners, together with various private adventurers, — in all, one hundred and twenty persons.

10. On Friday, the 13th of August, 1492, the squadron of Columbus set sail from Palos, steering in a south-westerly direction for the Canary Islands, whence it was his intention to strike due west.

11. Passing over many incidents in their outward voyage, — the storms and tempests which they encountered — the delusive appearances of land — their hopes and their fears — their excitement, and then their dejection — the murmurs, and even mutinous spirit, of the crew, and the happy expedients of Columbus to raise their courage, and to keep burning within them the spirit of the enterprise, — we arrive at the 20th of October, at which time the indications of land were so strong, that, at night, Columbus ordered a double watch on the forecastle of each vessel, and promised to the first discoverer of the long-looked-for land a doublet of velvet, in addition to the pension of thirty crowns which had been offered by Ferdinand and Isabella.

12. The greatest animation now prevailed throughout the ships; not an eye was closed that night. As evening darkened, Columbus took his station on the top of the castle or cabin, on the high poop of his vessel. However he might carry a cheerful and confident countenance during the day, it was to him a time of the most painful anxiety. And now, when wrapped by the shades of night from observation, he maintained an intense and unremitting watch. Suddenly, about ten o'clock, he beheld, he thought, a light glimmering at a distance. Fearing that his hopes might deceive him, he called to Pedro Gutierrez, gentleman of the king's bed-chamber, and demanded whether he saw a light in that direction; the latter replied in the affirmative.

13. Columbus, yet doubtful, called Roderigo Sanchez, of Segovia, and made the inquiry. By the time the latter had ascended the round-house, the light had disappeared. They saw it once or twice afterwards, in sudden and passing gleams, as if it were a torch in the bark of a fisherman, rising and sinking with the waves. So transient and uncertain were these gleams, that few attached any importance to them. Columbus, however, considered them as certain signs of land; and, moreover, that the land was inhabited.

14. They continued their course until two in the morning, when a gun from the Pinta gave the joyful signal of land. It was first descried by a mariner, named Roderigo de Friana; but the reward was afterwards adjudged to the admiral, for having previously perceived the light. The land was now clearly seen

about two leagues distant; whereupon they took in sail, and laid to, waiting impatiently for the dawn.

15. The morning at length arrived, — October 12th, or N. S. October 21, — and before the delighted Spaniards lay a level and beautiful island, called by the natives GUANAHANI, but to which Columbus gave the name of SAN SALVADOR. This island, known on English maps by the name of CAT ISLAND, was several leagues in extent, of great freshness and verdure, and was covered with trees, like a continual orchard.

16. Columbus, in a rich dress, and with a drawn sword, soon after landed with his men, with whom, having kneeled and kissed the ground with tears of joy, he took possession of the island, in the name of Queen Isabella, his patron. On landing, the Spaniards were surprised to find a race of people quite unlike any that they had ever seen before. They were of a dusky copper-color, naked, beardless, with long black hair, floating on their shoulders, or bound in tresses round their heads. The natives were still more surprised at the sight of the Spaniards, whom they considered as the children of the sun, their idol. The ships they looked upon as animals, with eyes of lightning and voices of thunder.

17. Having spent some time in an examination of this island, he proceeded to visit several others not far distant; and at length, on the 7th of November, came in sight of the Island of

Cuba, and not long after fell in with the Island of Hispaniola, or San Domingo.

18. Having spent some time in examining the country, and in traffic with the natives, Columbus set sail on his return. He was overtaken by a tremendous storm ; during which he enclosed in a cake of wax a short account of his voyage and discovery, which he put into a tight cask, and threw it into the sea, hoping that, if he perished, it might fall into the hands of some navigator, or be cast ashore, and thus the knowledge of his discovery be preserved to the world. But the storm abated, and he arrived safe in Spain, March, 1493.

19. For this discovery, which laid the foundation for all subsequent discoveries in America, Columbus was entitled to the honor of giving name to the New World. But he was robbed of it by the address of Americus Vespucius. This adventurer was a Florentine, who sailed to the New World in 1499, with one Alonzo Ojeda, who had accompanied Columbus in his first voyage. On his return, he published so flattering an account of his voyage, that his name was given to the continent, with manifest injustice to Columbus.

20. After this, Columbus made a second and third voyage ; in the latter of which he discovered the continent, near the mouth of the river Orinoco. This was August 10th, 1498. Yet he was ignorant, at the time, that the land in question was anything more than an island.

21. During this third voyage, Columbus was destined to experience severe afflictions. After his departure from Spain, having been appointed governor of the New World, his enemies, by false representations, persuaded the king to appoint another in his place. At the same time, the king was induced to give orders that Columbus should be seized and sent to Spain. This order was executed with rigid severity ; and the heroic Columbus returned to Spain in irons !

22. On his arrival, he was set at liberty by the king ; but he never recovered his authority. Soon after his return from a fourth voyage, finding Isabella, his patroness, dead, and himself neglected, he sunk beneath his misfortunes and infirmities, and expired at Valladolid on the 30th of May, 1506, or 1507. His last words were, " Into thy hands, O Lord, I commend my spirit."

23. The body of Columbus was deposited in the convent of St. Francisco, but was afterwards removed to a monastery at Seville, where, for a time, it rested, with the remains of his son, Diego. The bodies of both, however, were afterwards removed

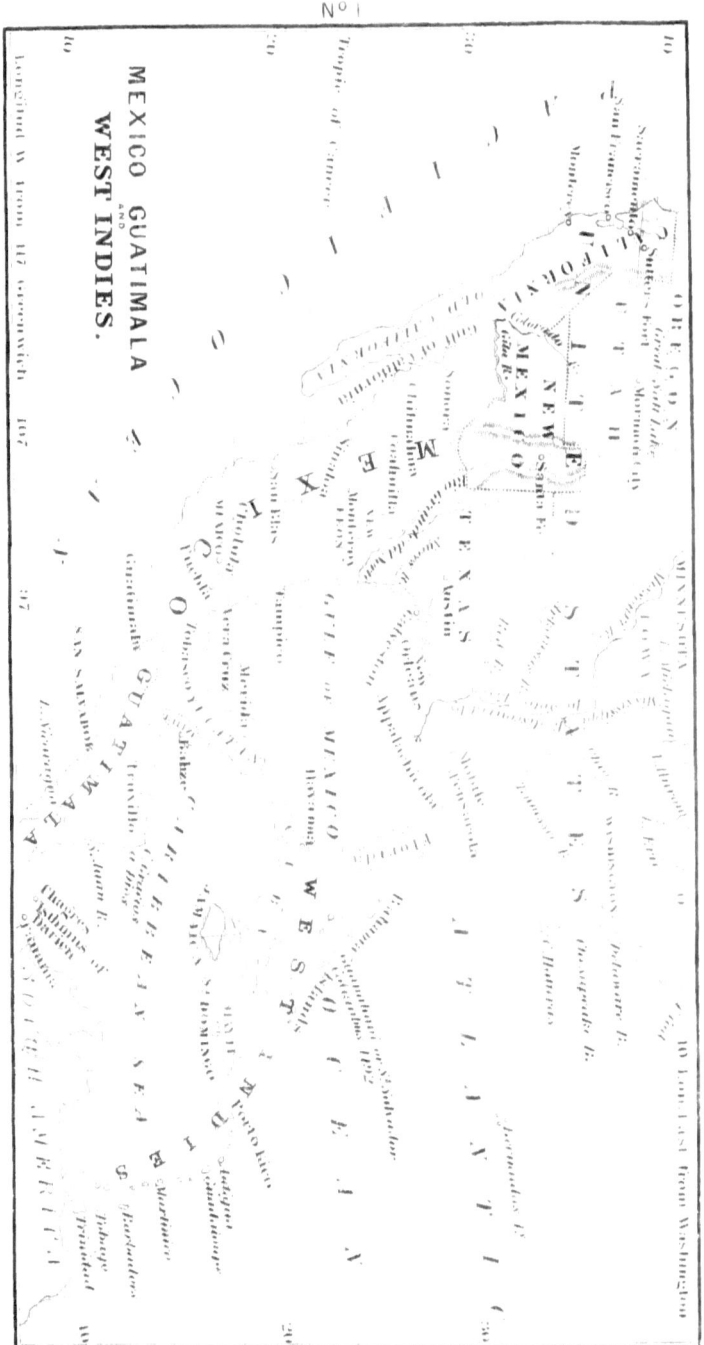

MEXICO GUATIMALA AND WEST INDIES.

to Hispaniola, and here again disinterred, and conveyed to Havana, in the island of Cuba, where in peace they now repose.

24. We shall conclude this notice of the great pioneer to this western world, in the eloquent language of the author to whom we have been indebted for the principal incidents in the life of this illustrious man.* "He (Columbus) died in ignorance of the real grandeur of his discovery. Until his last breath, he entertained the idea that he had merely opened a new way to the old resorts of opulent commerce, and had discovered some of the wild regions of the East. He supposed Hispaniola to be the ancient Ophir, which had been visited by the ships of Solomon; and that Cuba and Terra Firma were but remote parts of Asia. What visions of glory would have broken upon his mind, could he have known that he had indeed discovered a new continent, equal to the whole of the old world in magnitude, and separated by two vast oceans from all the earth hitherto known by civilized man!"

II. JOHN CABOT. — When the discovery of Columbus was announced, the civilized nations of Europe became eager to share with Spain the honors and advantages of further discoveries in the New World. As early as May, 1497, John Cabot, a Venetian by birth, but then a resident in England, accompanied by his son, Sebastian, a young man, sailed under the patronage † of Henry VII., King of England, on a voyage of discovery; and on the 24th of June O. S., or July 3d N. S., fell in with land, to which he gave the name of PRIMA VISTA (First Seen), and which, until a recent date, was judged to be the Island of Newfoundland, but which is now believed to have been the coast of Labrador. During this same voyage, however, it is thought he discovered the Island of Newfoundland; immediately following which, elated with his success, he returned to England.

III. SEBASTIAN CABOT. — In 1498, Sebastian Cabot, in company with three hundred men, made a second voyage; during which he explored the continent from Labrador to Virginia, and, according to some authorities, to Florida. After several other voyages, he returned to England, during the reign of Edward VI., and, as a reward for his eminent services, was created Grand Pilot of the kingdom.

IV. JOHN VERRAZANI. — 1. The French attempted no dis-

---

* Irving's Columbus.

† The commission granted Cabot is the oldest American state paper of England, bearing date March 5, O. S. 1496, although he did not sail till the year following.

coveries on the American coast until 1524. But this year, John Verrazani, a Florentine navigator of celebrity, sailed with a squadron of four ships, fitted out by Francis I. Of these ships, three were soon compelled to return, and Verrazani proceeded with a single vessel.

2. He reached the American coast about the latitude of Wilmington, Delaware, whence, after a southern exploration, he proceeded northerly, along the coast, landing at several points in New Jersey and New York, as interest or curiosity prompted. Near New York the voyagers kidnapped and bore away an Indian child. In Newport harbor, Rhode Island, Verrazani anchored for fifteen days, whence he proceeded north, exploring the coast as far as Newfoundland. To the whole region thus discovered by him he gave the name of NEW FRANCE, which, however, was afterwards applied only to Canada, and which name it held while in possession of the French.

3. The following year, this enterprising navigator, during a second voyage to America, by means of some unknown disaster, was lost, with all his crew.

V. JAMES CARTIER. — 1. In 1534, James Cartier, under a commission from the King of France, made a voyage to America, in which he visited the Island of Newfoundland, and discovered the Gulf of St. Lawrence. The following year, during a second voyage, he proceeded up the Gulf of St. Lawrence, to the Isle of Orleans, and thence as far as Montreal. Here he found a large Indian settlement, by the inhabitants of which he was well treated. This Indian settlement was called Hochelaga. Cartier gave it the name of Mount Royal, from a mountain in the neighborhood. From this circumstance the island and city of Montreal derive their name. He spent the winter at the Isle of Orleans, and in the spring returned to France.

2. In 1540, Cartier again visited America, with the intention of forming a settlement. He built a fort at some distance from the Isle of Orleans; but, in the following spring, not having received anticipated supplies, he set sail, to return to France with his colony. At Newfoundland, he met with three ships and two hundred persons, on their way to the new settlement. Cartier proceeded on his voyage to France. The other ships continued their course to the fort which Cartier had left. After passing a distressing winter, the whole party, abandoning the settlement, in the spring returned to France.

VI. FERDINAND DE SOTO. — 1. In the spring of 1541, six years from the discovery of the river St. Lawrence, another equally important river — the Mississippi — was discovered.

This honor belongs to Ferdinand de Soto, a Spaniard, who, having projected the conquest of Florida from the natives, arrived from Cuba, 1539, with a considerable force. He traversed the country to a great distance, and, in the spring of 1541, first discovered the Mississippi, five or six hundred miles from its mouth.

2. The object of Soto, in traversing so wide an extent of country, appears to have been to search for gold. The summer and winter of 1539 he spent in Florida. In 1540, he began his tour north-east, and, having crossed the Altamaha, Savannah, and Ogechee rivers, he turned westerly, and, crossing the Alleghanies, proceeded southwardly as far as Mobile and Pensacola. The winter of this year he spent with the Chickasaws. The following spring, he made the important discovery above mentioned.

3. The next year, 1542, Soto died on the banks of the Mississippi river, May 21, in the bosom of whose waters he was buried. Under the guidance of a successor whom Soto had appointed, his followers wandered about the country, in an ineffectual effort to penetrate to Mexico. During these wanderings, they once more came upon the Mississippi, a short distance above Red river. Here they encamped, and proceeded to build several large boats, on which they embarked, July 12th, 1543, and in seventeen days reached the Gulf of Mexico; whence continuing their voyage, in the following September they reached a Spanish settlement at the mouth of the river Panuco, in Mexico.

VII. SIR WALTER RALEIGH. — 1. In 1584, Sir Walter Raleigh, under a commission from Queen Elizabeth of England, despatched two small vessels, commanded by Amidas and Barlow, to the American coast.* On their arrival, they entered Pamlico Sound, now in North Carolina, and thence proceeded to Roanoke, an island near the mouth of Albemarle Sound. Here

---

* Previously to the above voyage, under the auspices of Sir Walter Raleigh, two unfortunate attempts had been made by his brother-in-law, Sir Humphrey Gilbert, to effect a settlement in the New World. Both, however, proved ineffectual; and during the last, while Sir Humphrey was returning to England, his vessel was shipwrecked, and all on board perished. Not discouraged by the unfortunate issue of the enterprises of Gilbert, Raleigh fitted out an expedition, as we have above stated, in 1584. The report brought back by Amidas and Barlow induced Sir Walter, in 1585, to attempt a settlement at the Island of Roanoke. This colony was, in a short time, reduced to great distress, and, in 1586, returned with Sir Francis Drake to England. The following year, however, another colony was sent out, consisting of one hundred and fifty adventurers. These, most unfortunately, were neglected, in respect to supplies; and when, at length, a vessel was despatched to inquire into their state, not a vestige of them remained.

2*

they spent several weeks in trafficking with the natives, but effected no settlement. On their return to England, they gave so splendid a description of the beauty and fertility of the country, that Elizabeth bestowed upon it the name of VIRGINIA, as a memorial that the happy discovery had been made under a virgin queen.

VIII. BARTHOLOMEW GOSNOLD. — 1. In 1602, Bartholomew Gosnold, in a voyage from Falmouth to the northern part of Virginia, discovered the promontory in Massachusetts Bay, which, since his time, has been known by the name of Cape Cod, from the circumstance of his taking a great number of cod-fish at that place.

2. Gosnold was the first Englishman who, abandoning the circuitous route by the Canaries and West Indies, came in a direct course to this part of the American continent. He was but seven weeks in making the passage. After the discovery of Cape Cod, coasting south-west, he discovered two islands, one of which he named Martha's Vineyard, and the other Elizabeth Island. On the western part of this latter island it was concluded to settle, and a fort and storehouse were accordingly erected; but, before Gosnold left the place, discontents arising among those who were to form the colony, it was thought expedient to abandon the settlement, and to return to England. The homeward voyage occupied but five weeks.*

IX. STATE OF THE COUNTRY. — 1. As we are now about to enter upon a period which will exhibit our ancestors as inhabitants of this New World, it will be interesting to know what was its aspect, when they first landed upon its shores.

2. North America was almost one unbroken wilderness. From the recesses of these forests were heard the panther, the catamount, the bear, the wild-cat, the wolf, and other beasts of prey. From the thickets rushed the buffalo, the elk, the moose, and the carrabo; and, scattered on the mountains and plains, were seen the stag and fallow deer. Numerous flocks of the feathered tribe enlivened the air, and multitudes of fish filled the rivers, or glided along the shores. The spontaneous productions of the soil, also, were found to be various and abundant. In all parts of the land grew grapes, which historians have likened to the ancient grapes of Eshcol. In the south were found mulberries,

---

* There were various other voyages of discovery undertaken by navigators, previous to the settlement of North America; but the foregoing are the principal which relate to the history we are proposing to write. An account of others, while out of place in these pages, would serve only to oppress the memory of our pupils.

plums, melons, cucumbers, tobacco, corn, peas, beans, potatoes, squashes, pumpions, &c. Acorns, walnuts, chestnuts, wild cherries, currants, strawberries, whortleberries, in the season of them, grew wild in every quarter of the country.

X. ABORIGINES. — 1. The country was inhabited by numerous tribes or clans of Indians. Of their number, at the period the English settled among them, no certain estimate has been transmitted to us. They did not probably much exceed one hundred and fifty thousand within the compass of the thirteen original states.*

2. In their physical character, the different Indian tribes, within the boundaries of the United States, were nearly the same. Their persons were tall, straight, and well proportioned. Their skins were red, or of a copper brown ; their eyes black ; their hair long, black, and coarse. In constitution, they were firm and vigorous, capable of sustaining great fatigue and hardship.

3. As to their general character, they were quick of apprehension, and not wanting in genius. At times they were friendly, and even courteous. In council, they were distinguished for gravity and eloquence ; in war, for bravery and address. When provoked to anger, they were sullen and retired ; and when determined upon revenge, no danger would deter them, — neither absence nor time could cool them. If captured by an enemy, they never asked life ; nor would they betray emotions of fear, even in view of the tomahawk or of the kindling fagot.

4. They had no books or written literature, except rude hieroglyphics ; and education among them was confined to the arts of war, hunting, fishing, and the few manufactures which existed among them, in most of which every male was more or less instructed. Their language was rude, but sonorous, metaphorical, and energetic, and well suited to the purposes of public speaking. Their arts and manufactures were confined to the construction of wigwams, bows and arrows, wampum, ornaments, stone hatchets, mortars for pounding corn ; to the dressing of skins, weaving of coarse mats from the bark of trees, or a coarse sort of hemp, &c.

5. Their agriculture was small in extent, and the articles they cultivated were few in number. Corn, beans, peas, potatoes, melons, and a few others of a similar kind, were all. Their skill in medicine was confined to a few simple prescriptions and operations. Both the cold and warm bath were often applied, and a considerable number of plants were used with success. For some

---

* This is the estimate of Dr. Trumbull.

diseases they knew no remedy; in which case they resorted to their powow, or priest, who undertook the removal of the disease by means of sorcery.   It may be remarked, however, that the diseases to which the Indians were liable were few, compared with those which prevail in civilized society.

6. The employments of the men were principally hunting, fishing, and war.   The women dressed the food, took charge of the domestic concerns, tilled their narrow and scanty fields, and performed almost all the drudgery connected with their household affairs.

7. The amusements of the men were principally leaping, shooting at marks, dancing, gaming, and hunting, in all of which they made the most violent exertions.   Their dances were usually performed round a large fire.   In their war-dances they sung or recited the feats which they or their ancestors had achieved; represented the manner in which they were performed, and wrought themselves up to an inexpressible degree of martial enthusiasm.   The females occasionally joined in some of these sports, but had none peculiar to themselves.

8. Their dress was various.   In summer they wore little besides a covering about the waist; but in winter they clothed

themselves in the skins of wild beasts.   They were exceedingly fond of ornaments.   On days of show and festivity, their sachems wore mantles of deer-skin, embroidered with white beads or copper; or they were painted with various devices. Hideousness was the object aimed at in painting themselves. A chain of fish-bones about the neck, or the skin of a wild-cat, was the sign of royalty.

9. For habitations, the Indians had weekwams, or wigwams, as pronounced by the English. These originally consisted of a strong pole, erected in the centre, around which, at the distance of ten or twelve feet, other poles were driven obliquely into the ground, and fastened to the centre pole at the top. Their coverings were of mats, or barks of trees, well adjusted, so as to render them dry and comfortable.

10. Their domestic utensils extended not beyond a hatchet of stone, a few shells and sharp stones which they used for knives, stone mortars for pounding corn, and some mats and skins, upon which they slept. They sat, and ate, and lodged, on the ground. With shells and stones they scalped their enemies, dressed their game, cut their hair, &c. They made nets of thread twisted from the bark of Indian hemp, or of the sinews of the moose and deer. For fish-hooks, they used bones which were bent.

11. Their food was of the coarsest and simplest kind, — the flesh, and even the entrails, of all kinds of wild beasts and birds; and, in their proper season, green corn, beans, peas, &c. &c., which they cultivated, and other fruits, which the country spontaneously produced. Flesh and fish they roasted on a stick, or broiled on the fire. In some instances they boiled their meat and corn by putting hot stones in water. Corn they parched, especially in the winter; and upon this they lived, in the absence of other food.

12. The money of the Indians, called wampum, consisted of small beads wrought from shells, and strung on belts, and in chains. The wampum of the New England Indians was black, blue, and white. That of the Six Nations was of a purple color. Six of the white beads, and three of black or blue, became of the value of a penny. A belt of wampum was given as a token of friendship, or as a seal or confirmation of a treaty.

13. There was little among them that could be called society. Except when roused by some strong excitement, the men were generally indolent, taciturn, and unsocial. The women were too degraded and oppressed to think of much besides their toils. Removing, too, as the seasons changed, or as the game grew scarce, or as danger from a stronger tribe threatened, there was little opportunity for forming those local attachments, and those social ties, which spring from a long residence in a particular spot. Female beauty had little power over the men; and all other

pleasures gave way to the strong impulses of public festivity, or
burning captives, or seeking murderous revenge, or the chase, or
war, or glory.

14. War was the favorite employment of the savages of North
America. It roused them from the lethargy into which they
fell when they ceased from the chase, and furnished them an
opportunity to distinguish themselves, — to achieve deeds of
glory, and taste the sweets of revenge. Their weapons were
bows and arrows headed with flint or other hard stones, which
they discharged with great precision and force. The southern
Indians used targets made of bark; the Mohawks clothed themselves with skins, as a defence against the arrows of their enemies. When they fought in the open field, they rushed to the
attack with incredible fury; and, at the same time, uttered their
appalling war-whoop. Those whom they had taken captive they
often tortured with every variety of cruelty, and to their dying
agonies added every species of insult. If peace was concluded
on, the chiefs of the hostile tribes ratified the treaty by smok-
ing, in succession, the same pipe, called the calumet, or pipe of
peace.

15. The government of the Indians, in general, was an absolute monarchy, though it differed in different tribes. The will
of the sachem was law. In matters of moment, he consulted his
councillors; but his decisions were final. War and peace, among
some tribes, seem to have been determined on in a council formed
of old men, distinguished by their exploits. When in council,
they spoke at pleasure, and always listened to the speaker with
profound and respectful silence.

16. When propositions for war or peace were made, or
treaties proposed to them by the colonial governors, they met
the ambassadors in council, and, at the end of each paragraph or
proposition, the principal sachem delivered a short stick to one
of his council, intimating that it was his peculiar duty to remember that paragraph. This was repeated, till every proposal was
finished; they then retired, to deliberate among themselves.
After their deliberations were ended, the sachem, or some councillors to whom he had delegated this office, replied to every paragraph, in its turn, with an exactness scarcely exceeded in the
written correspondence of civilized powers. Each man actually
remembered what was committed to him, and, with his assistance, the person who replied remembered the whole.

17. The religious notions of the natives consisted of traditions,
mingled with many superstitions. Like the ancient Greeks,
Romans, Persians, Hindoos, &c., they believed in the existence

of two gods: the one good, who was the superior, and whom they styled the Great or Good Spirit; the other, evil. They worshipped both; and of both formed images of stone, to which they paid religious homage. Besides these, they worshipped various other deities, — fire, water, thunder, — anything which they conceived to be superior to themselves, and capable of doing them injury. The manner of worship was to sing and dance round large fires. Besides dancing, they offered prayers, and sometimes sweet-scented powder. In Virginia, the Indians offered blood, deer's suet, and tobacco. Of the creation and the deluge they had distinct traditions.

18. Marriage among them was generally a temporary contract. The men chose their wives agreeably to fancy, and put them away at pleasure. Marriage was celebrated, however, with some ceremony, and, in many instances, was observed with fidelity; — not unfrequently it was as lasting as life. Polygamy was common among them. Their treatment of females was cruel and oppressive. They were considered by the men as slaves, and treated as such. Those forms of decorum between the sexes, which lay the foundation for the respectful and gallant courtesy with which women are treated in civilized society, were unknown among them. Of course, females were not only required to perform severe labor, but often felt the full weight of the passions and caprices of the men.

19. The rites of burial, among the Indians, varied but little throughout the continent. They generally dug holes in the ground, with sharpened stakes. In the bottom of the grave were laid sticks, upon which the corpse, wrapped in skins and mats, was deposited. The arms, utensils, paints, and ornaments of the deceased, were buried with him, and a mound of earth raised over his grave. Among some tribes in New England, and among the Five Nations, the dead were buried in a sitting posture, with their faces towards the east. During the burial they uttered the most lamentable cries, and continued their mourning for several days.

20. The origin of the Indians is involved in much obscurity. The opinion best supported is, that they originated in Asia, and that at some former period, not now to be ascertained, they emigrated from that country to America, over which, in succeeding years, their descendants spread. This opinion is rendered the more probable by the fact, that the figure, complexion, dress, manners, customs, &c. &c., of the nations of both continents, are strikingly similar. That they might have emigrated from the eastern continent is evident, since, in latitude 66°, the two con-

tinents are not more than forty miles distant from each other; and between them are two islands less than twenty miles distant from either shore.

XI. REFLECTIONS. — 1. We shall find it pleasant and profitable occasionally to pause in our history, and consider what instruction may be drawn from the portion of it that has been perused. In the story of Columbus, we are introduced to a man of genius, energy, and enterprise. We see him forming a new, and, in that age, a mighty project; and, having matured his plan, we see him set himself vigorously about its execution. For a time he is either treated as a visionary or baffled by opposition. But, neither discouraged nor dejected, he steadily pursues his purpose, surmounts every obstacle, and at length spreads his sails upon the unknown waters of the Atlantic. A kind Providence auspiciously guides his way, and crowns his enterprise with the unexpected discovery of a new world.

2. While we admire the lofty qualities of Columbus, and look with wonder at the consequences which have resulted from his discovery, let us emulate his decision, energy, and perseverance. Many are the occasions, in the present world, on which it will be important to summon these to our aid; and by their means many useful objects may be accomplished, which, without them, would be unattained. But, while we thus press forward in the career of usefulness, while we aim to accomplish for our fellow-men all the amount of good in our power, let us moderate our expectations of reward here, by the consideration that Columbus died the victim of ingratitude and disappointment.

3. Another consideration, of still deeper interest, is suggested by the story of Columbus. We, who live to mark the wonderful events which have flowed from his discovery, within the short space of three centuries, cannot but advert with awe to HIM who attaches to the actions of a single individual a train of consequences so stupendous and unexpected. How lightly soever, then, we may think of our conduct, let us remember that the invisible hand of Providence may be connecting with our smallest actions the most momentous results to ourselves and others. With respect to Americus Vespucius, it may be observed, that, although he deprived Columbus of the merited honor of giving his name to the New World, and gained this distinction for himself, still his name will ever remain stigmatized, as having appropriated that to himself which fairly belonged to another.

UNITED STATES.

PERIOD II.

DISTINGUISHED FOR SETTLEMENTS.

EXTENDING FROM THE FIRST PERMANENT ENGLISH SETTLE-
MENT, AT JAMESTOWN, VIRGINIA, 1607, TO THE DECLARA-
TION OF WAR BY ENGLAND AGAINST FRANCE, 1756, CALLED
"THE FRENCH AND INDIAN WAR."

I. VIRGINIA.

1. PRIOR to the year 1607, a period of one hundred and
fifteen years from the discovery of San Salvador by Columbus,
several attempts were made to effect settlements in various parts

of North America; but none had proved successful. In the
month of May of this year, a colony from England, consisting
of one hundred and five persons, arrived in Virginia; and, on

3

a beautiful peninsula in James river, began a settlement, which they called JAMESTOWN. This was the first permanent settlement effected by Europeans in the United States.*

2. This place was called Jamestown, in honor of James I. of England, who, in 1606, claiming the country lying between the 34th and 45th degrees of north latitude, — that is, from the mouth of Cape Fear river, one hundred and fifty miles northeast from Charleston, in South Carolina, to Halifax, the capital of Nova Scotia, — divided it into two nearly equal parts, and granted it to two companies, called the LONDON† and PLYMOUTH ‡ Companies. The southern part, called SOUTH VIRGINIA, he conveyed to the " London Company ;" and the northern part, called NORTH VIRGINIA, to the " Plymouth Company."

3. The first settlement of Virginia was commenced under the auspices of the " London Company." The expedition was commanded by Captain Christopher Newport ; but the government of the colony was framed in England, before it sailed. It was to consist of a council of seven persons, with a president, to be elected by the council from their number. Who composed it was unknown at the time the expedition sailed, their names being carefully concealed in a box, which was to be opened after their arrival.

4. The original intention of the colony was to form a settlement at Roanoke ; but, being driven by a violent storm north

---

* A sufficient reason may be assigned for the failure of the several attempts to effect permanent settlements in North America ; namely, that they were undertaken upon individual responsibility, with bad calculations, and intrusted, in most instances, to men of mercenary views. And, as to the sovereigns of Europe, they were too much occupied with affairs at home, to engage in speculations abroad. Besides, no prince or statesman in Europe appears to have foreseen the advantages of planting colonies in this northern continent. Had it contained mines of gold and silver, like South America, they would have contended with one another for the prize. But it seems not to have been conceived how numerous and hardy colonies could give such strength, opulence and grandeur, to empires, as could never be derived from the gold and other rich productions of the southern regions.

† The London Company consisted of Sir Thomas Gates, Sir George Somers, Richard Hackluyt, Edward Maria Wingfield, &c. These were authorized to make a settlement at any place between the 34th and 41st degrees of latitude ; and in them was vested the right of property in the land, extending fifty miles each way from their place of habitation, and reaching one hundred miles into the country.

‡ The Plymouth Company consisted of Thomas Hanham, Raleigh Gilbert, William Parker, George Popham, and others, principally inhabitants of Bristol, Plymouth, and the eastern parts of England. To this company was granted the lands between the 38th and 45th degrees of latitude. They were vested with the right of property in lands to the same extent as in the southern colony : neither company, however, were to form settlements within one hundred miles of the other.

of that place, they discovered the entrance of Chesapeake Bay, the capes of which they named Charles and Henry. Entering this, they at length reached a convenient spot upon which to commence a settlement. The code of laws, hitherto cautiously concealed, was now promulgated; and, at the same time, the council appointed by the company in England was made known. It consisted of Bartholomew Gosnold, John Smith, Edward Wingfield, Christopher Newport, John Ratcliffe, John Martin, and George Kendall. Mr. Wingfield was chosen president.

5. Among the most enterprising and useful members of this colony, and one of its magistrates, was Capt. John Smith,*

---

* John Smith had been apprenticed to a merchant in his youth; but, being of a roving turn, he quitted his master, and, although at this time but thirteen years of age, he travelled in France, whence he proceeded to the Netherlands, Egypt and Germany, and at length entered the service of the Emperor of Austria, who was engaged in a war with the Turks.

The regiment in which he served was engaged in several hazardous enterprises, in which Smith exhibited a bravery admired by all the army; and when Meldrick left the imperial service for that of his native prince, Smith followed.

At the siege of Regal, he was destined to new adventures. The Ottomans deriding the slow advance of the Transylvania army, the Lord Turbisha despatched a messenger with a challenge, that, for the diversion of the ladies of the place, he would fight any captain of the Christian troops.

The honor of accepting this challenge was determined by lot, and fell on Smith. At the time appointed, the two champions appeared in the field on horseback, and, in the presence of the armies, and of the ladies of the insulting Ottoman, rushed impetuously to the attack. A short but desperate conflict ensued, at the end of which Smith was seen bearing the head of the lifeless Turbisha in triumph to his general.

The fall of the chief filled his friend Crualgo with indignation, and roused him to avenge his death. Smith, accordingly, soon after received a challenge from him, which he did not hesitate to accept; and the two exasperated combatants, upon their chargers, fell with desperate fury upon each other. Victory again followed the falchion of Smith, who sent the Turk headlong to the ground.

It was now the turn of Smith to make the advance. He despatched a message, therefore, to the Turkish ladies, that, if they were desirous of more diversion of a similar kind, they should be welcome to his head, in case their third champion could take it.

Bonamalgro tendered his services, and haughtily accepted the Christian's challenge. When the day arrived, the spectators assembled, and the combatants entered the field. It was an hour of deep anxiety to all: as the horsemen approached, a deathlike silence pervaded the multitude. A blow from the sabre of the Turk brought Smith to the ground; and, for a moment, it seemed as if the deed of death was done. Smith, however, was only stunned. He rose like a lion when he shakes the dew from his mane for the fight, and, vaulting into his saddle, made his falchion "shed fast atonement for its first delay." It is hardly necessary to add that the head of Bonamalgro was added to the number.

In a general battle, in which Smith was subsequently engaged, he was wounded and taken prisoner. On his recovery, he was sold as a slave, and was taken to Constantinople. He was required to wait upon the lady of his

whose devotion to the interests of the colony was as signal and
unremitted, as his life had been replete with danger and suffering. But for his spirit of patriotism and self-denial, it is certain that its existence would have been short-lived. Before the
arrival of the colony, his colleagues in office, becoming jealous
of his influence, arrested him on the absurd charge that he
designed to murder the council, usurp the government, and
make himself king of Virginia. He was, therefore, rigorously
confined during the remainder of the voyage.

6. On their arrival in the country, he was liberated, but could
not obtain a trial, although, in the tone of conscious integrity, he
repeatedly demanded it. The infant colony was soon involved
in perplexity and danger. Notwithstanding Smith had been
calumniated, and his honor deeply wounded, his was not the
spirit to remain idle when his services were needed. Nobly dis-
daining revenge, he offered his assistance, and, by his talents,
experience, and indefatigable zeal, furnished important aid to
the infant colony.* Continuing to assert his innocence, and to

---

master, who, captivated by his fine appearance, sent him, in the absence of
her husband, to the care of her brother, who resided near the Sea of Asoph.

But he, being of a cruel disposition, treated Smith with so much inhumanity, that, one day, in a fit of desperation, he killed his new master, and
fled into Russia. From this country, he travelled through Germany, France,
and Spain ; and, at length, returned once more to England.

At this time, the settlement of America was occupying the attention of
many distinguished men in England. The life of Smith, united to his fond-
ness for enterprises of danger and difficulty, had prepared him to embark
with zeal in a project so novel and sublime as that of exploring the wilds of
a newly-discovered continent.

He was soon attached to the expedition about to sail under Newport, and
was appointed one of the magistrates of the colony sent over at that time.

* When the affairs of the colony had become somewhat settled, the active
spirit of Smith prompted him to explore the neighboring country.   In an
attempt to ascertain the source of Chickahominy river, he ascended in a
barge as far as the stream was uninterrupted. Designing to proceed still
further, he left the barge in the keeping of the crew, with strict injunctions
on no account to leave her, and, with two Englishmen and two Indians, left
the party. But no sooner was he out of view, than the crew, impatient of
restraint, repaired on board the barge, and, proceeding some distance down
the stream, landed at a place where a body of Indians lay in ambush, by
whom they were seized.

By means of the crew, the route of Smith was ascertained, and a party of
Indians were immediately despatched to take him. On coming up with
him, they fired, killed the Englishmen, and wounded himself. With great
presence of mind, he now tied his Indian guide to his left arm, as a shield
from the enemies' arrows, while, with his musket, he despatched three of
the most forward of the assailants.

In this manner, he continued to retreat towards his canoe, while the
Indians, struck with admiration of his bravery, followed with respectful cau-

demand a trial, the time at length arrived when his enemies could postpone it no longer. After a fair hearing of the case, he

tion. Unfortunately, coming to a miry spot, he sunk, so as to be unable to extricate himself, and was forced to surrender.

Fruitful in expedients, to avert immediate death, he presented an ivory compass to the chief, whose attention was arrested by the vibrations of the needle. Taking advantage of the impression thus made, partly by signs and partly by language, he excited their wonder still more, by telling them of its singular powers.

Their wonder seemed soon to abate, and their attention returned to their prisoner. He was now bound and tied to a tree, and the savages were preparing to direct their arrows at his breast. At this instant, the chief holding up the compass, they laid down their arms, and led him in triumph to Powhatan, their king.

Powhatan and his council doomed him to death ; and at length he was led out to execution. His head was laid upon a stone, and a club presented to Powhatan, who claimed the honor of becoming the executioner. The savages in silence were circling round, and the giant arm of Powhatan had

already raised the club to strike the fatal blow, when, to his astonishment, the young and beautiful Pocahontas, his daughter, with a shriek of terror, rushed from the throng, and threw herself upon the body of Smith. At the same time, she cast an imploring look towards her furious but astonished father, and, in all the eloquence of mute but impassioned sorrow, besought his life.

The remainder of the scene was honorable to Powhatan. The club of the chief was still uplifted ; but a father's pity had touched his heart, and the eye that had at first kindled with wrath was now fast losing its fierceness. He looked round as if to collect his fortitude, or perhaps to find an excuse for his weakness in the pity of the attendants. A similar sympathy had melted the savage throng, and seemed to join in the petition which the weeping Pocahontas felt, but durst not utter, " My father, let the prisoner live." Powhatan raised his daughter, and also the captive, from the earth.

was honorably acquitted of the charges alleged against him, and soon after took his seat in the council.

7. The colony, thus commenced, soon experienced a variety of calamities, incidental, perhaps, to infant settlements, but not the less painful and discouraging. Inefficiency and a want of harmony marked the proceedings of the council. Provisions were scarce, and of a poor quality. The neighboring tribes of Indians became jealous and hostile ; and, more than all, sickness spread among them, and carried a large proportion of their number to an early grave, among whom was Captain Gosnold, the projector of the enterprise.

8. The condition of the colony, however, was, at length, somewhat improved, by the arrival of Captain Newport (who had been despatched to England), with a supply of provisions, and an additional number of men. Captain Nelson, who had sailed with Newport, also soon after arrived, with additional emigrants and provisions. With these accessions, the colonists now amounted to two hundred men. This number was still further increased, before the end of 1608, by the arrival of seventy colonists, among whom were many persons of distinction.

9. Early in the year 1609, the London Company, not having realized their anticipated profit from their new establishment in America, obtained from the king a new charter, with more ample privileges. Under this charter, Thomas West, otherwise called Lord De la War, was appointed governor for life. The company, under their new act of incorporation, was styled " The Treasurer and Company of Adventurers and Planters for the First Colony in Virginia." They were now granted in absolute property what had formerly been conveyed only in trust, — a territory extending from Point Comfort two hundred miles north and south, along the coast, and throughout the land from sea to sea.

Shortly after, Powhatan dismissed Captain Smith, with assurances of friendship ; and the next morning, accompanied with a guard of twelve men, he arrived safely at Jamestown, after a captivity of seven weeks.

In 1609, circumstances having arisen to interrupt the friendly dispositions of Powhatan towards the colony, he plotted their entire destruction. His design was to attack them unapprized, and to cut them off at a blow.

In a dark and stormy night, the heroic Pocahontas hastened alone to Jamestown, and disclosed the inhuman plot of her father. The colony were thus put on their guard, and their ruin averted.

It may be interesting to add, concerning Pocahontas, that some time after this she was married to an English gentleman of the name of Rolfe, with whom she visited England. She embraced the Christian religion, and was baptized by the name of Rebecca. She left one son, who had several daughters, the descendants of whom inherited her lands in Virginia, and are among the most respectable families in that state.

10. Lord De la War, being appointed governor of the colony, but not being able to leave England, immediately despatched to America nine ships and five hundred men, under command of Sir Thomas Gates, his lieutenant, and Sir George Somers, his admiral. Eight of these ships arrived in safety at Jamestown, in the month of August; but that on board of which was Sir Thomas and other officers, being wrecked on the Bermudas, did not arrive till May of the following year; and then in two small vessels, which meanwhile they had built.

11. At the time Sir Thomas and the other officers arrived, the colony had become reduced to circumstances of great depression. Captain Smith, in consequence of a severe accidental wound, had some time before returned to England; and his departure was the signal for insubordination and idleness. Moreover, the Indians refused the usual supplies of provisions; in consequence of which, famine ensued, during which the skins of the horses were devoured, the bodies of the Indians whom they had killed, and even the remains of deceased friends. Of five hundred persons, sixty only remained. At this juncture, the shipwrecked from Bermuda arrived. An immediate return to England was proposed; and, with that intent, they embarked. But just as they were leaving the mouth of the river, Lord De la War appeared, with supplies of men and provisions, and they were persuaded to return. By means of his judicious management, the condition of the colony soon wore a better aspect, and for several years continued to prosper.

12. It was unfortunate, however, that ill health obliged Lord De la War, in March, 1611, to leave the administration. He was succeeded by Sir Thomas Dale, who arrived in May. Hitherto, no right of property in land had been established, but the produce of labor was deposited in public stores, and shared in common. To remedy the indolence and indifference growing out of such a system, Sir Thomas assigned to each inhabitant a lot of three acres as his own, and a certain portion of time to cultivate it. The advantages of this measure were soon so apparent, that another assignment, of fifty acres, was made, and, not long after, the plan of working in a common field was abandoned.

13. The year 1619 forms a memorable epoch in the history of Virginia, a provincial legislature being at this time introduced, in which the colonists were represented by delegates chosen by themselves. This colonial assembly — the first legislature to which the people of America sent representatives — was convoked by Sir George Yeardly, the governor-general of the colony, and met at Jamestown, on the 29th of June. Before this, the col-

onists had been ruled rather as soldiers in garrison, by martial law ; but now they were invested with the privileges of free-men. They were divided into eleven corporations, each of which was represented in the assembly.

14. The following year, the colony received a large accession to their number. Eleven ships arrived, with twelve hundred and sixty settlers. Nearly one thousand colonists were resident here before. In order to attach them still more to the country, one hundred and fifty respectable young women were sent over, to become wives to the planters. These were sold at the price, at first, of one hundred, and afterwards, one hundred and fifty, pounds of tobacco, which was worth, at the time, three shillings per pound. Debts incurred for the purchase of wives were recoverable before any others.

15. Accessions to the colony of a different character were also made. By order of King James, one hundred persons who had rendered themselves obnoxious to government by their crimes were sent to the colony by way of punishment. This, perhaps designed for its benefit, as the exiles were chiefly em-ployed as laborers, was ultimately prejudicial to its prosperity. During the year 1620, slave-holding was introduced into the colony. A Dutch ship from Africa, touching at Jamestown, landed twenty negroes for sale. These were purchased by the planters ; and slavery was thus introduced into the country.

16. In 1622, the Virginia colony, which for some time had enjoyed great prosperity, and had received frequent accessions, experienced a stroke which proved nearly fatal. The successor of Powhatan, of a proud, revengeful spirit, and extremely hostile to the colony, concerted a plan to cut them off at a blow ; and, on the 1st of April, it was so far put in execution, that three hundred and forty-seven of the colony — men, women, and chil-dren — were butchered almost in the same instant.*

---

* The chief by whom this massacre was planned, and under whom it was executed, was Opecancanough, the successor of Powhatan. The whole sur-rounding Indian population had been enlisted by this artful chief ; and yet they visited the English settlements, and even purchased arms and borrowed boats to enable them to accomplish their savage purpose.

"On the morning of the fatal day, as also the evening before, they came, as at other times, into the houses of the English, with deer, turkeys, fish, and other things to sell. At mid-day, the hour appointed, the blow fell ; and, in the work of death, neither sex nor age was spared. So quick was the execution, that few perceived the weapon or the blow which despatched them.

"Jamestown and some of the neighboring places were saved by the dis-closure of a Christian Indian, named Chanco, who was confidentially informed of the design by his brother, on the morning of the 1st of April." As soon

17. In 1624, the London Company, which had settled Virginia, was dissolved by an act of King James I., under pretext of the calamities which had befallen the colony, and the dissensions which had agitated the company. Their charter was taken away, and the government of the colony assumed by the crown. The king himself appointed the governor, in whom, with twelve councillors, the powers of government were vested.

18. The London Company, thus dissolved, consisted of gentlemen of liberal views, who had expended more than one hundred thousand pounds of their fortunes in this first attempt to plant an English colony in America; and more than nine thousand persons had been sent from the mother country to people this new settlement. At the time of the dissolution of the company, scarcely two thousand survived.

19. The dissolution of the charter was an arbitrary act on the part of the king; and not less arbitrary and odious were his subsequent regulations. Under these the people suffered till 1636, at which time, inflamed to madness by the oppressive conduct of Sir John Harvey, the then governor, they seized him, and sent him prisoner to England. Their conduct in this was so displeasing to the king, Charles I., successor of James I., that he sent Harvey back. But, in 1639, the king appointed Sir William Berkley to succeed him, with instructions again to allow the Virginians to elect representatives. For this privilege they were so grateful, that they continued faithful to the royal cause, even after Cromwell had usurped the government. This loyalty brought upon them the vengeance of Parliament, in 1652, at which time a fleet was despatched to reduce them to submission. At this time, Governor Berkley was obliged to retire.

20. About the time of Cromwell's death, but before that event, the Virginians proclaimed Charles II., and invited Berkley to resume his authority. On the accession of Charles, he confirmed Berkley in his office. But, from this time, the conduct of the governor was odious and oppressive. Agents were sent to England, to lay their grievances at the foot of the throne; but agents were unsuccessful, and, at length, the discontent of the people ripened into a formidable insurrection, known by the name of "Bacon's Rebellion."

---

as the English had time to recover themselves, they rose to avenge the death of their slaughtered friends, and succeeded in driving far into the wilderness such as they could not destroy. But, by means of the calamities which fell upon the English, their settlements were reduced from eighty to eight; and by the year 1624, out of nine thousand persons who had been sent from England, but eighteen hundred existed in the colony.

21. This Bacon (Nathaniel) was an Englishman, who, soon after his arrival, had been appointed a member of the council. He was young, of commanding person, and distinguished for ambition, energy and enterprise. The colony, at this time, being engaged in war with the Susquehannah Indians, Bacon despatched a messenger to Governor Berkley, requesting a commission to proceed against them. This, for a time, was refused; in consequence of which, great animosity arose between Berkley and Bacon; and, at length, the former publicly denounced Bacon as a rebel, although previously he had given him the required commission. Hearing of this denunciation, Bacon, instead of marching against the Indians, proceeded to Jamestown, wreaking his vengeance upon all who opposed him. Finding it in vain to withstand him, the governor fled across the bay, and the council dispersed, leaving Bacon in possession of supreme power.

22. At length, the governor, with a small force, under command of Major Robert Beverly, recrossed the bay, to oppose the malecontents. Civil war had now commenced. Jamestown was burnt by Bacon's followers; various parts of the colony were pillaged, and the wives of those that adhered to the governor's party were carried to the camp of the insurgents. In the midst of these commotions, Bacon died. The malecontents, thus left to reflection, began to disperse. Two of Bacon's generals surrendered and were pardoned, and the people quietly returned to their homes. Upon this, Berkley resumed the government, and peace was restored. This rebellion forms an era of some note in the history of Virginia, and its unhappy effects were felt for thirty years. During its continuance, husbandry was almost entirely neglected, and such havoc was made among all kinds of cattle that the people were threatened with famine. Sir William Berkley, after having been forty years governor of Virginia, returned to England, where he soon after died.

23. It may be proper to add, that some historians take a more favorable view of Bacon's character and conduct than is here presented. It must be admitted that the administration of Berkley, in many of its measures, was arbitrary and severe; — fines and confiscations, and even executions, were frequent; and, moreover, no printing-presses were allowed in the province. It is not to be concealed that the people were grievously oppressed; but Bacon's conduct was condemned by the council, of which he was a member; and by them, also, he was declared a " rebel."

24. In 1679, some time after the death of Berkley, Lord Culpepper came over as governor, with certain laws prepared in con-

formity to the wishes of the ministry of England, and designed
to be enacted by the assembly in Virginia. One of those laws
provided for raising a revenue for the support of government.
It made the duties perpetual, and placed them under the direction of his majesty. Out of the duties, Culpepper dishonestly
took, as his salary, two thousand pounds, and one hundred and
sixty pounds, in addition, for house-rent. On presenting these
laws to the assembly, Culpepper informed them that, in case they
were passed, he had instructions to offer pardon to all who had
been concerned in Bacon's rebellion; but if not, he had commissions to try and hang them as rebels, and a regiment of soldiers
on the spot to support him. Thus threatened, the assembly
passed the laws. From this period to the occurrence of the
French War, no events are to be found, in the history of
Virginia, of sufficient importance to be noticed in the present
pages.

II. MASSACHUSETTS.

1. The name " MASSACHUSETTS " is supposed to have been
derived from a tribe of Indians in the neighborhood of Boston;
and the tribe itself, according to Roger Williams, was so called
from the " Blue Hills of Milton."

2. The territory now so denominated was originally a part
of North Virginia, which had been conveyed, by charter of
James I., in 1606, to the " Plymouth Company," as South Virginia had been to the " London Company." *

3. Soon after the above grant, the " Plymouth Company "
despatched a vessel to explore the country, and, not long after,
sent a colony of one hundred planters, under George Popham
and Raleigh Gilbert, to form a settlement. These landed, Aug.
21, at the mouth of the Sagadahock, since called the Kennebec.
The two ships returned to England in December, leaving forty-
five of the colonists in the plantation, which received the name
of Fort St. George. But the hardships of the colony, during
the following winter, were so severe, that in the spring the settlement was abandoned, and the survivors returned to England.

4. In 1614, Captain John Smith, distinguished in the early
history of Virginia, sailed, with two ships, for North Virginia,
for the purposes of trade and discovery. During the voyage, he
explored the coast from Penobscot to Cape Cod, giving names to
several important points of land, which, for the first time, were

---

* For further account of these companies, see p. 26.

now discovered. On his return, he presented a map of the country, which he had projected, to Prince Charles, afterwards Charles I., and to which the latter, "in the warmth of his admiration," gave the name of NEW ENGLAND.

5. The flattering representations of Captain Smith regarding the country revived the slumbering interests of the "Plymouth Company," and induced them to form new plans for its settlement. Smith himself was appointed admiral of the country, for life; and after some years a new charter was obtained from the king, — the old "Plymouth Company" being dissolved, — and a new company formed, by the title of the "Council of Plymouth," to which was granted, in absolute right, all the territory between the fortieth and the forty-eighth degrees of north latitude, extending from the Atlantic to the Pacific, and comprising more than a million of square miles, with all the privileges and authority originally granted to the "Plymouth Company."

6. This charter bore date November 13, 1620, and was the basis of the several grants subsequently made of the New England territory. Yet the settlement of that territory was destined to be commenced, in the first instance, without any patent from the "Council of Plymouth," or from the king, and, indeed, without their knowledge or concurrence. To the history of this first New England colony we now proceed.

I. PLYMOUTH COLONY. — 1. During the same month (November, 1620) that the above charter was granted by James to the "Council of Plymouth," a colony of pilgrims, consisting of one hundred and one persons, arrived from England, and, after spending some time in exploring the coast, landed, on the 21st of December, at a place since called "FOREFATHERS' ROCK," and began the first permanent settlement in New England, calling it PLYMOUTH.*

2. The persons composing this colony, and, indeed, the first settlers of New England, were principally from the counties of Nottinghamshire, Lancashire, and Yorkshire. In these counties there prevailed, about the year 1602, an extensive revival of religion. The new converts, wishing to worship God in a manner more simple than was observed in the established church, but not being allowed to do it while they continued members of it, agreed upon a separation from it; and, for the sake of peace and more liberty of conscience, resolved upon a removal to the states of Holland, which, at that time, granted a free toleration to different denominations of Protestants. The leader of these emi-

* Or New Plimouth, as it was then written.

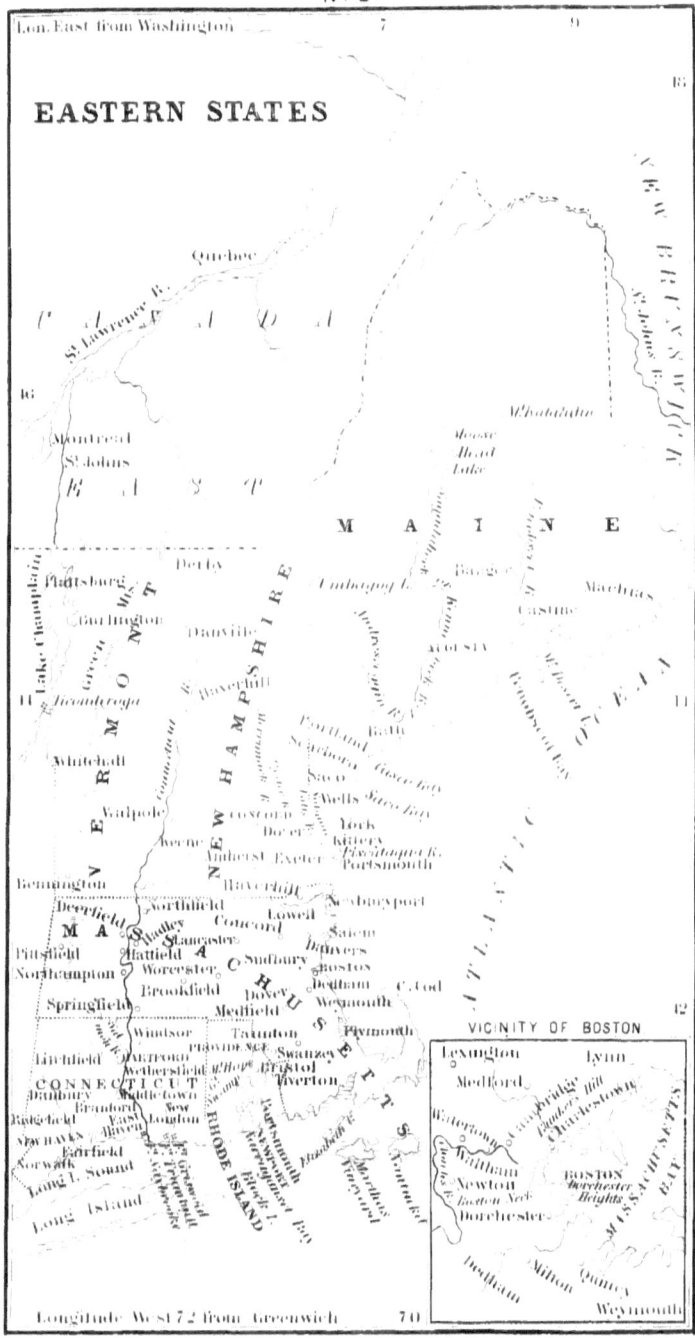

EASTERN STATES

VICINITY OF BOSTON

Longitude West 72 from Greenwich

grants, in the year 1607, was an able and pious man, Mr. John Robinson, who, with his congregation, prepared for their removal to Amsterdam; but they found the ports and harbors carefully watched, strict orders being given not to suffer them to depart. Twice they attempted to embark, but were discovered and prevented. At another time, having got on board a ship, with their effects, the ship-master sailed a little distance, and then returned and delivered them to the resentment of their enemies.

3. The next year, they made another attempt, in which, after the severest trials, they succeeded. Yet, when only a part of their number were on board, and while the women and children were in a bark, approaching the ship, the Dutch captain, apprehensive of danger to himself, hoisted sail, and, with a fair wind, directed his course to Holland. The passengers used every effort to persuade him to return, but in vain. They saw their wives and children fall into the hands of merciless enemies, while unable to afford them any relief. They had none of their effects, not even a change of clothes, on board.

4. Moreover, a storm arose, which raged seven days without intermission. By its violence, they were driven to the coast of Norway. On a sudden, the sailors exclaimed, "The ship has foundered! she sinks! she sinks!" The seamen trembled in despair; the pilgrims looked up to God, and cried, "Yet, Lord, thou canst save; yet, Lord, thou canst save." To the astonishment of all, the vessel soon began to rise, rode out the storm, and at length reached its destined port. After some time, all their friends who had been left arrived safely in Holland.

5. After remaining a number of years in Holland, first at Amsterdam, and then at Leyden, this little flock found their situation, on many accounts, unpleasant. The immoralities of their neighbors were dangerous to the rising generation; the difficulties of procuring a comfortable living induced not a few of their sons to enter the Dutch armies; and at no distant day, there was reason to apprehend, their posterity would become incorporated with the people of the country, and their church become extinct. These considerations, added to the more powerful motive, the hope of laying the foundation for the extensive advancement of the kingdom of Christ in the western wilderness, induced them to remove to America. Previous to their final determination, as their governing maxim always was, "In all thy ways, acknowledge God, and he shall direct thy paths," they set apart a day for fasting and prayer, to seek direction from God.

6. Their original plan contemplated a settlement in South Vir-

4

ginia, on lands owned by the London Company; but the king not being willing " to tolerate them in their religious worship by his public authority under his seal," they concluded to form a partnership with certain " merchant adventurers " of London. The terms of this partnership were hard upon these pilgrims; but, as there was to be no interference with their civil and religious rights, the articles were agreed upon.*

7. They now began to prepare themselves for their momentous enterprise. For this purpose, they procured two vessels, the Speedwell and the Mayflower. The Speedwell, of sixty tons, they purchased in Holland, with the intention of keeping her for their accommodation in America. The Mayflower, of one hundred and eighty tons, they hired at London.

8. All things being in readiness for their departure from Leyden, they kept a day of solemn humiliation and prayer. On the 1st of August, the pilgrims repaired to Delfthaven, a place about twenty miles from Leyden, and two miles from Rotterdam. Here they were to embark. To this port they were kindly attended by many of their brethren and friends from Amsterdam, as well as from Leyden. Leaving Delfthaven, they sailed for Southampton, at which place they were joined by the rest of their company from London, in the Mayflower. On the 15th of August, 1620, both vessels set sail for the New World; but before proceeding far, the Speedwell sprung a-leak, and at Plymouth, whither they put in, she was condemned as not seaworthy. Under these circumstances, a part of the emigrants were dismissed, and the rest were taken on board of the Mayflower.

9. With one hundred and one passengers,† this vessel sailed from Plymouth, September 16th. For two months they were tossed and driven upon the tempestuous ocean ; till, at length, on the 19th of November, they had the happiness to descry the bleak and dreary shores of Cape Cod. But they were still

---

* The copartnership was for seven years. The shares were two pounds each. Each person sixteen years of age must take one share, and every ten pounds put in by any one was accounted an additional share. At the end of seven years, all the possessions of the colony, with everything gained by them, were to be equally divided among the adventurers, merchants as well as pilgrims. Such was the essence of the copartnership on the grounds of which alone the pilgrims could find friends to help them get to America. And it proved a sad business for the colony, keeping it in a constant state of embarrassment.

† It will be pleasant to the learner, we trust, to know the names of those who came over in the Mayflower. The following is a list of the men, with the number of persons in their several families set opposite their names. One individual died on the passage, and one was born, whom they named

remote from the place selected for a habitation, it being their intention to settle near the mouth of the Hudson.   Toward that river they now bent their course.   But the wintry season induced them to relinquish their design, and seek the nearest resting-place.   They, therefore, turned back, and, after two days, November 21st, anchored in Cape Cod harbor, between Cape Cod and Plymouth.

10. Before landing, having devoutly given thanks to God for their safe arrival, they formed themselves into a body politic, forty-one signing a solemn contract, according to the provisions of which they were to be governed.   Mr. John Carver was elected governor for one year.   Government being thus established, sixteen men, well armed, with a few others, were sent on shore, to procure wood and make discoveries ; but they returned at night, without having found any person or habitation.   The company, having rested on the Lord's day, proceeded, on Monday 23d, to make further discovery of the country.

11. On Wednesday, Miles Standish and sixteen armed men, in searching for a convenient place for settlement, saw five or six Indians, whom they followed several miles; but, not overtaking them, were constrained to lodge in the woods.   The next day they discovered heaps of earth, which proved to be Indian graves.   In different heaps of sand they also found baskets of corn, a quantity of which they carried away.   This providential discovery gave them seed for a future harvest, and preserved the infant colony from famine.   Before the close of the month Mrs. Susannah White became the mother of an infant son, who was called Peregrine, the first child of European extraction born in New England.

OCEANUS.   The names in small capitals indicate those who died before the end of March, 1621:

Mr. John Carver, . . . 8	EDWARD TILLY, ... 4	JAMES CHISTON, ... 3
William Bradford, . . . 2	JOHN TILLY, ... 3	JOHN CRACKSTON, ... 2
Mr. Edward Winslow, . . 5	Peter Brown, ... 1	John Billington, ... 4
Mr. William Brewster, . 6	RICHARD BRITTERIDGE, . 1	MOSES FLETCHER, ... 1
Mr. Isaac Allerton, . . . 6	George Soule, ... †	JOHN GOODMAN, ... 1
Capt. Miles Standish, . . 2	RICHARD CLARK, ... 1	DECORY PRIEST, ... 1
John Alden, ... 1	Richard Gardiner, . . . 1	THOMAS WILLIAMS, . . . 1
Mr. Samuel Fuller, . . . 2	Francis Cook, ... 2	Gilbert Winslow, ... 1
MR. CHRISTOPHER MARTIN,4	THOMAS ROGERS, ... 2	EDMUND MARGESON, . . . 1
MR. WM. MULLINS, . . . 5	THOMAS TINKER, ... 3	JOHN ALLERTON, ... 1
MR. WILLIAM WHITE, . . 5	JOHN RIDGDALE, ... 2	THOMAS ENGLISH, ... 1
Mr. Richard Warren, . . 1	EDWARD FULLER, ... 3	Edward Dotey, ... †
John Howland, ... *	JOHN TURNER, ... 3	Edward Leister, ... ‡
Mr. Stephen Hopkins, . . 8	Francis Eaton, ... 3	

* Howland was servant of Governor Carver.
† Soule was servant of Governor Winslow.
‡ Dotey and Leister were servants of Mr. Hopkins.

12. From this time, the 16th of December, they were employed for several days in searching for a proper place on which to settle. On the night of the 18th they reached a small island, on which they spent Saturday and the Sabbath. The day following, the 21st, they sounded the harbor, and found it fit for shipping;

went on shore, and explored the adjacent land, where they saw various corn-fields and brooks; and judging the situation to be convenient for a settlement, they returned with the welcome intelligence to the ship. This marks the era of the LANDING OF THE PILGRIM FATHERS, on what has been appropriately styled "FOREFATHERS' ROCK."

13. In a few days the Mayflower was safely riding in the harbor. As a matter of high importance, a platform for their ordnance was erected on a hill, commanding an extensive prospect of the plain beneath, and of the neighboring bay. Preparations were also begun for the erection of habitations for the settlers. A division of the company was made into nineteen families, to each of which was assigned a suitable lot for house and garden. A house about twenty feet square was erected and used in common. This, for a time, besides a place of rendezvous, served as a MEETING-HOUSE.* In 1622, however, a timber fort

* When the pilgrims first left for America, it was the wish of Mr. Robinson to accompany them; but, as a great part of his church still remained at Leyden, he was persuaded to remain and minister to them, until the way was prepared for the removal of church and pastor. Mr. William Brewster,

was erected, with flat roof and battlements, on which their cannon were mounted, and a watch was kept. This also was their house of worship.

14. Difficulties and discouragements, however, gathered round these servants of God. Many soon fell sick, by reason of want and exposure. Winter set in before their habitations were comfortably prepared. Death, too, swept many to an untimely grave. Six died in December, eight in January, seventeen in February, thirteen in March; and of these forty-four, nineteen had subscribed the great compact on board the Mayflower. The burying place selected was but a short distance above " Forefathers' Rock." Those early graves, however, are lost from present knowledge, having been levelled by the pilgrims, and sowed, for the purpose of concealing them from the Indians, " lest, by counting the number of the dead, they should ascertain the weakness of the living."

15. Fortunately for the colony, the neighboring Indians offered them no serious molestation during the time of their severest trials; nor for several months did they approach sufficiently near to hold any intercourse. In March, however, 1621, the way was prepared for the negotiation of a treaty in the ensuing autumn, through Governor Carver, with Masassoit, the great sachem of the neighboring Indians. This treaty " of friendship, commerce, and mutual defence," was kept inviolate for over fifty years, until the breaking out of King Philip's War, in 1675; and not only gave general peace to the colony, but laid the foundation for the colony's intimate and amicable correspondence with the neighboring tribes.*

who had been Robinson's assistant came over as minister to those who embarked on board the Mayflower, and occupied the first meeting-house ever erected in New England. Mr. Robinson himself never removed, although he often contemplated it; and a reason assigned for his not fulfilling his design was the unwillingness of the " merchant adventurers " to furnish him a passage. His death occurred March 1st, 1625.

* The person chiefly instrumental in bringing this event to pass was Samoset, a sagamore or chief of the country lying at the distance of about five days' journey. He was the first visitant of the colony at Plymouth, and greatly surprised the inhabitants, by calling out, as he entered their village, " Welcome, Englishmen! welcome, Englishmen! " He had conversed with the English fishermen who had come to the eastern coast, and had learned some of the language. He informed the colony that the place where they were settled was called by the Indians *Patuxit;* that, five years before, a plague had swept off all the natives from the place, — that there was neither man, woman nor child, remaining. Providence had thus singularly prepared the way for the colonies to take possession of the land, without molesting a single owner.

Samoset, having been treated with hospitality by these strangers, was

4*

16. The manner in which Canonicus, the proud and powerful chief of the Narragansets, was awed into submission, is at once an evidence of his cowardice and of the sagacity of Governor Bradford. Canonicus, in token of his hostile bearing towards the colony, sent to Plymouth a bundle of arrows wrapped in a rattlesnake's skin. Nothing daunted, Bradford filled the skin with powder and shot, and returned it. Upon seeing this, the courage of Canonicus cooled. He did not choose to accept the challenge; and hence, skin, powder and shot, were brought back to the governor.

17. In 1623, fears were entertained for the safety of the colony, by reason of an anticipated famine. From the third week in May to the middle of July, no rain fell. The corn withered under the heat of a scorching sun. The Indians prophesied famine for the colony, and a consequent easy triumph over them. In this extremity, a public fast was observed, with great solemnity, — the first voluntary fast ever kept on these western shores. The morning of the fast was cloudless, and the day proved intensely hot. But, as evening approached, clouds collected, and rain descended in moderate but refreshing showers; the languishing crops revived, and a bountiful harvest succeeded. In token of the general gratitude, a day of public thanksgiving was ordered, — the second such day ever observed in New England, — the first having been observed after the first harvest had been gathered by the fathers.*

18. The partnership convention of the colonists with the "London Adventurers" had, from the commencement, proved

---

disposed to cultivate a further acquaintance with them; and, on his third visit, was accompanied by Squanto, a native of the country, who had been carried away, in 1614, by one Hunt, and sold into Spain, but had been taken to London, whence he had returned to America.

They informed the English that Masassoit, the greatest sachem of the neighboring Indians, was near, with a guard of sixty men. Mutual distrust prevented, for some time, any advances from either side. But Squanto, who was, at length, sent to Masassoit, returned, saying that the sachem wished the English to send some one to confer with him. Mr. Edward Winslow was accordingly sent, bearing suitable presents to the chief. These proving acceptable, Masassoit left Mr. Winslow in the custody of his men as a hostage, and ventured to the English, by whom he was hospitably entertained, and with whom he concluded the treaty already noticed.

* Before the appointment of this first thanksgiving, the governor sent out a "fowling expedition," that for their thanksgiving dinners, and for the festivities of the week they might have "more dainty and abundant materials than ordinary." This was the week in which Masassoit and ninety of his men were entertained. Labor was suspended, and the English employed themselves in military exercises before their visitants. The annual New England custom of Thanksgiving dates back, it may be seen, to the first year of our forefathers' arrival.

unprofitable and embarrassing. The former were compelled to effect loans of the adventurers at ruinous rates of interest; while the latter, receiving few or no returns for investments, grew discouraged, and in several instances acted in opposition to the interests of the colony, especially in refusing the venerable pastor Robinson a passage to America.

19. In 1627, however, an end was put to the partnership, the colonists purchasing the interests of the "London Merchants" for eighteen hundred pounds, two hundred of which were to be paid yearly. Upon this, the colonists became the sole proprietors of the land on which they had settled, a patent for which having been procured from the "Council of Plymouth" in 1621, during the existence of the partnership. An equitable division of the property, which before was in common stock, was now made by the colonists among themselves.

20. It may here be added, that the colony was never incorporated by the king. The government was at first formed and conducted according to a voluntary compact, entered into before landing. Till the year 1624, it consisted of a governor and one assistant only. From this period, five were annually chosen, the governor having a double vote. The number of assistants was afterwards increased to seven. The laws of the colony were enacted, and the affairs of government conducted, by these officers, for near twenty years. In 1639 the towns for the first time sent deputies. The colony continued distinct near seventy years, until 1691, when, by charter of William and Mary, it was united to the colony of Massachusetts and the Province of Maine.

II. COLONY OF MASSACHUSETTS BAY. — 1. In 1628 the foundation was laid for another colony in New England, by the name of the "COLONY OF MASSACHUSETTS BAY," — several enterprising men at that time purchasing of the "Council of Plymouth" a tract of land for the purpose of settling it.* During the same year, the purchasers sent one Mr. John Endicot, with one hundred colonists, to begin a settlement, which they effected at SALEM, previously called by the Indians NAUMKEAK.

2. The settlement of Massachusetts Bay, like the colony of Plymouth, was commenced by non-conformists, for the purpose of enjoying greater religious liberty in matters of worship. Among the most active in this enterprise were Mr. Endicot and

---

* These were Sir Henry Roswell, Sir John Young, Thomas Southcoat, John Endicot, and Simon Whetcomb, of Dorchester.

Mr. White; the latter a pious and active minister of Dorchester, in England.

3. The tract purchased extended three miles north of the Merrimack river, and three miles south of Charles river, and east and west from the Atlantic to the South Sea, or Pacific Ocean.

4. In 1629 the Massachusetts Company obtained a charter from the king, being incorporated by the name of " The Governor and Company of Massachusetts Bay, in New England." Mr. Endicot, being in the country, was appointed the first governor. In June, two hundred additional settlers arrived, bringing with them horses, sheep and goats, and large stores of necessaries. A part of these emigrants, not being pleased with the situation of Salem, commenced the settlement of Mishawum, or Charlestown.

5. The following year, 1630, it being judged reasonable that a colony should be ruled by men residing in the plantation, the proprietors agreed that the charter and powers of government, conferred by it, should be transmitted from London to the colony in America. Accordingly, this was done, the officers of government being in the first instance chosen by the company in England. The excellent John Winthrop was chosen governor, and Thomas Dudley deputy governor ; Isaac Johnson, Sir Richard Saltonstall, and others, to the number of eighteen, were chosen assistants.

6. Governor Winthrop was accompanied to Massachusetts by nearly three hundred families, or fifteen hundred souls, many of whom were distinguished for their " quality," as well as their intelligence and piety. This company designed to settle at Charlestown ; but the prevalence of a fatal sickness previous to their arrival, imputed to the badness of the water, induced many of the emigrants to form other settlements, some at Dorchester, others at Roxbury and Watertown. Governor Winthrop, with some of the most distinguished gentlemen of the company, hearing of an excellent spring of water at Shawmut, established themselves there, and erected a few cottages. This was the commencement of Boston, which for a short time was denominated by the English Tri-Mountain.

7. On the arrival of Governor Winthrop, who continued from this time to his death the head and father of the colony, he found the plantation in a distressed and suffering state. In the preceding autumn the colony contained about three hundred inhabitants ; eighty of these had died, and a great part of the survivors were in a weak and sickly state. Their supply of corn

was not sufficient for more than a fortnight, and their other provisions were nearly exhausted.

8. In addition to these evils, they were informed that a combination of various tribes of Indians was forming for the utter extirpation of the colony. Their strength was weakness, but their confidence was in God, and they were not forsaken. Many of the planters who arrived this summer, after long voyages, were in a sickly state, and disease continued to rage through the season. By the close of the year, the number of deaths exceeded two hundred. Among these were several of the principal persons in the colony. Mr. Higginson, the venerable minister of Salem, spent about a year with that parent church, and was removed to the church in glory. His excellent colleague, Mr. Skelton, did not long survive him. Mr. Johnson, one of the assistants, and his lady, who was a great patroness of the settlement, died soon after their arrival. Of the latter an early historian observes, " She left an earthly paradise, in the family of an earldom, to encounter the sorrows of a wilderness, for the entertainments of a pure worship in the house of God ; and then immediately left that wilderness for the heavenly paradise." *

9. The succeeding winter commenced in December with great severity. Few of the houses which had been erected were comfortable, and the most of them were miserable coverings. Unused to such severities of climate, the poor people suffered severely from the cold. Many were frozen to death. The inconveniences of their accommodations increased the diseases which continued to prevail among them. But their constancy had not yet been brought to the last trial. During the continuance of the severe season, their stock of provisions began to fail. Those who wanted were supplied by those who possessed, as long as any remained. A poor man came to the governor to complain, and was informed that the last bread of his house was in the oven. Many subsisted upon shell-fish, ground-nuts, and acorns, which, at that season, could not have been procured but with the utmost difficulty.

---

* Isaac Johnson, one of the five undertakers of this expedition (Governor Winthrop, Deputy Governor Dudley, Sir Richard Saltonstall, and Mr. Revelle, being the other four), died September 30. Governor Winthrop says, " He was a holy man and wise," and that he died in " sweet peace." His estate was larger than that of any other emigrant. He was a principal founder of Boston. He was buried in his own lot, which is the present burying-place near the Stone Chapel, in that city. His wife, Lady Arabella, was the daughter of the Earl of Lincoln. She died at Salem, soon after her arrival. No monument, it is said, designates her grave. Of those who accompanied Governor Winthrop, two hundred, at least, died before December. About one hundred persons, disappointed and discouraged, returned in the same ships to England.

10. In consideration of their perilous condition, the sixth day of February was appointed a day of public fasting and prayer, to seek deliverance from God. On the fifth of February, the day before the appointed fast, the ship Lion, which had been sent to England for supplies, arrived laden with provisions. She had a stormy passage, and rode amidst heavy drifts of ice after entering the harbor. These provisions were distributed among the people according to their necessities, and their appointed fast was exchanged for a day of general thanksgiving.

11. Early in 1631, two important rules were adopted at a meeting of the electors in General Court, namely, 1. That the freemen alone should have the power of electing the governor, deputy governor and assistants. 2. That those only should be made freemen who belonged to some church within the limits of the colony. This latter rule would not be tolerated at the present day. It was repealed in 1665. The design of it, however, was good, originating in a desire to retain civil influence, as the order avowed, among " good and honest " men.

12. In 1634, a still more important change was effected in the mode of legislation. The settlements had become so numerous and extended, that the freemen could not, without great inconvenience, meet and transact the public business in person. It was therefore ordered that the whole body of the freemen should be convened only for the election of the magistrates, who, with deputies to be chosen by the several towns, should have the power of enacting the laws. " Thus," observes Mr. Bancroft, " did the epidemic of America break out in Massachusetts, just fifteen years after its first appearance in Virginia. The trading corporation had become a representative democracy."

13. " For ten years from this time, a discussion was had as to the relative powers of the assistants and deputies. Both received office at the hands of the people ; but the former were elected by the freemen of the colony, the latter by the towns. The two bodies used to meet in convention ; but the assistants claimed and exercised the right of a separate negative vote on all joint proceedings." At last, in 1644, a remedy was found for this long and disturbing evil, by dividing the court in their consultations, — the magistrates and the deputies each constituting a separate branch, and each possessing a negative on the proceedings of the other.* Thus commenced the separate existence of

---

* This was the second House of Representatives in the American colonies ; the first was convened at Jamestown, in Virginia, by Governor Yeardly, June, 1619.

the democratic branch of the Legislature, or House of Representatives.*

14. In the autumn of 1635, Roger Williams was banished from the colony, for publishing novel opinions, which were deemed seditious and heretical, both by ministers and magistrates. He seems to have denied the right to possess the lands of the Indians by virtue of any patent from the king, or any deed from a company, without their consent.† He also maintained that an oath should not be tendered to an unregenerate man ; and, that no Christian could lawfully pray with such an one, though it were a wife or child. But while on these and other points Mr. Williams was over scrupulous, and even at fault, the principal accusation against him, and the chief cause of his banishment, was his distinguishing doctrine, that the civil power has no control over the religious opinions of men, — a doctrine which at the present day no man would venture to deny, and which shows that in this respect Mr. Williams was far in advance of the age.

15. The banishment of Mr. Williams was doubtless a great wrong. But it is not necessary to impeach the motives of the pilgrim fathers. They acted from a sincere but misdirected desire to uphold the government and the church, both of which they truly believed in danger. Soon after his banishment, Mr. Williams removed, and laid the foundation of Rhode Island.

16. During the same year, 1635, three thousand new settlers were added to the colony ; among whom were Reverend Hugh Peters, a minister of great energy and popular eloquence, and Henry Vane, afterwards Sir Henry Vane, a young man distinguished for his intelligence and integrity.‡ By his correct deportment and winning manners, the latter so won upon the colonists, that the year following they elected him governor ; an " unwise choice," says Mr. Bancroft ; " for neither the age nor the distinction of Vane entitled him to the honor."

---

* Bancroft's United States.

† Mr. Williams strongly contended that the king was guilty of grievous wrong in selling or giving away the lands of the Indians ; and so he wrote him. But it should be remembered that the pilgrims acted generally on the very principle which Mr. Williams advocated. They did purchase the lands of the Indians, — often, indeed, for a trifling compensation, as it seems to us ; but such as satisfied the Indians.* Doctor Dwight states "that until Philip's War, in 1675, not a foot of ground was claimed or occupied by the colonists on any other score but that of fair purchase."

‡ Vane was at this time only twenty-five years of age. On his return to England, both he and Peters acted a conspicuous part in the civil wars of that country. Peters was, some time, chaplain to Oliver Cromwell. Both he and Vane were ultimately accused of high treason, convicted, and executed.

* Knowles' Memoir of Roger Williams.

17. And the colonists soon had reason to repent their choice. During his administration, the celebrated Anne Hutchinson, a woman of great eloquence and enthusiasm, advanced certain mystical doctrines, one of which was the monstrous doctrine that the elect saints might be assured of their salvation, however vicious their lives might be. Many embraced her views and supported her cause ; among whom were Governor Vane, and Messrs. Cotton and Wheelright, two distinguished clergymen. Governor Winthrop, and a majority of the churches, however, deemed her sentiments heretical and seditious. Great excitement for a time prevailed among the people ; conferences were held, fasts observed ; and, at length, a general synod was called, by which her opinions were condemned, and she and some of her adherents were banished from the colony. Failing of being reëlected, Governor Vane returned the following year to England. Mrs. Hutchinson sought an asylum among the Dutch, near New York, where she and her family, except one daughter, were some time afterwards massacred by the Indians.

18. As many of the pilgrims were persons of liberal education, they were able to appreciate the importance of learning to the rising commonwealth, as among its surest safeguards. As early as 1636, therefore, the General Court had laid the foundation of a public school or college, by the appropriation of four hundred pounds ; and which. the next year, was located at Newtown. In 1638, Reverend John Harvard, a pious minister of Charlestown, dying, left to the institution upwards of three thousand dollars. In consideration of this liberal benefaction, the General Court gave to the institution the name of " Harvard College ; " and, in memory of the place where many of the first New England settlers had received their education, that part of Newtown in which the college was located received the name of " Cambridge." " As early as 1647, Massachusetts required by law that every township which had fifty householders should have a school-house and employ a teacher, and that such as had one thousand freeholders should have a grammar-school."

19. The next event of importance in our history is the union of the colonies of Massachusetts, Plymouth, Connecticut and New Haven, by the name of THE UNITED COLONIES OF NEW ENGLAND. The articles of this confederation, which had been agitated for three years, were signed May, 1643. To this union the colonies were strongly urged by a sense of common danger from the Indians (a general combination of whom was expected), and by the claims and encroachments of the Dutch at Manhattan, New York.

20. By these articles, each colony retained its distinct and separate government. No two colonies might be united into one, nor any colony be received into the confederacy, without the consent of the whole. Each colony was to elect two commissioners, who should meet annually, and at other times if necessary, and should determine " all affairs of war and peace, of leagues, aids, charges, and numbers of men for war," &c. Upon notice that any colony was invaded, the rest were immediately to despatch assistance.

21. This union subsisted more than forty years, until the charters of the colonies were either taken away or suspended, by James II. and his commissioners. In 1648 Rhode Island petitioned to be admitted to this confederacy, but was denied, unless she would be incorporated with Plymouth, and lose her separate existence. This she refused, and was consequently excluded. The effects of this union on the New England colonies were, in a high degree, salutary. On the completion of it, several Indian sachems, among whom were the chiefs of the Narraganset and Mohegan tribes, came forward and submitted to the English government. The colonies, also, became formidable, by means of it, to the Dutch. This union was also made subservient to the civil and religious improvement of the Indians.

22. Prior to this period, Mr. Mayhew and the devoted John Eliot had made considerable progress towards civilizing the Indians, and converting them to Christianity. They had learned the Indian language, and had preached to the Indians in their own tongue. Upon a report in England of what these men had done, a society was formed for propagating the Gospel among the Indians, which sent over books, money, &c., to be distributed by the commissioners of the United Colonies. The Indians, at first, made great opposition to Christianity; and such was their aversion to it, that, had they not been overawed by the United Colonies, it is probable they would have put to death those among them who embraced it. Such, however, were the ardor, energy and ability, of Messrs. Mayhew and Eliot, aided by the countenance and support of government, and blessed by Providence, that, in 1660, there were ten towns of converted Indians in Massachusetts. In 1695 there were not less than three thousand adult Indian converts in the islands of Martha's Vineyard and Nantucket.

23. With the history of Massachusetts the early history of New Hampshire and of the Province of Maine is intimately connected. As early as 1641, the settlements which existed in the former were incorporated with Massachusetts; and in 1652, the

5

inhabitants in the latter were, at their own request, taken under her protection. As early as 1626, a few feeble settlements were commenced along the coast of Maine; but, before they had gathered much strength, the "Plymouth Council" granted to several companies portions of the same territory, from the Piscataqua to the Penobscot. These conflicting patents gave rise, in after years, to long and angry litigation.

24. In 1639 Sir Ferdinand Gorges, who had obtained a royal charter of the province, first established a government over it, and the following year a General Court was held in Saco. His death occurring in 1649, the officers whom he had appointed deserted it, upon which the inhabitants found it necessary to provide for themselves, and accordingly sought the jurisdiction of Massachusetts.

25. In 1664 a royal fleet, destined for the reduction of the Dutch colonies on the Hudson, arrived in Boston, on board of which were four commissioners,—Colonel Nichols, commander of the fleet, Sir Robert Carr, George Cartwright, and Richard Maverick,—authorized and directed to look after the colonies of his majesty, and to proceed to settle the peace and security of the country. King Charles entertained no good will towards them, and the measure was considered a hostile one.

26. The conduct of the commissioners was exceedingly arbitrary and offensive. Under pretext of executing their commission, they received complaints against the colonies from the Indians; required persons, against the consent of the people, to be admitted to the privileges of freemen, to church membership, and full communion; heard and decided in causes which had already been determined by the established courts; and gave protection to criminals. After involving the colonies in great embarrassment and expense (although little attention was paid to their acts), they were recalled, and the colonies enjoyed a season of peace and prosperity, till the breaking out of King Philip's War.

27. The year 1675 was distinguished for a memorable war in New England with the Indians, called KING PHILIP'S WAR; by which the peace of the colonies was greatly disturbed, and their existence, for a time, seriously endangered.* For several years

---

* Massachusetts was the principal theatre of this war; but other portions of New England experienced a measure of its horrors, especially New Hampshire. For several years previous to its occurrence, the colonies had enjoyed unusual peace and tranquillity. Mr. Bancroft estimates the white population in New England, at this time, at fifty-five thousand; of which he assigns seven thousand to Plymouth, fourteen thousand to Connecticut,

previous to the opening of the war, the Indians had regarded the English with growing jealousy. They saw them increasing in numbers, and rapidly extending their settlements. The prospect before them was humbling to the haughty descendants of the original lords of the soil.

28. The principal exciter of the Indians was Philip, sachem of the Wampanoags, son and successor of Masassoit, who, fifty years before, had made a treaty with the colony of Plymouth. (Page 41.) The residence of Philip was at Mount Hope, in Bristol, Rhode Island. The immediate cause of the war was the execution of three Indians by the English, whom Philip had excited to murder one Sausaman, an Indian missionary. Sausaman, being friendly to the English, had informed them that Philip, with several tribes, was plotting for their destruction. The execution of these men roused the anger of Philip, who armed his men and commenced hostilities. Their first attack was made on the 4th July, upon the people of Swanzey, in Plymouth colony, as they were returning from public worship, on a day of humiliation and prayer, appointed under an apprehension of an approaching war. Eight or nine persons were killed.

29. The country being immediately alarmed, the troops of the colony repaired to the defence of Swanzey, where, being joined by troops from Boston, they attacked Philip's forces, killing several. Philip left Mount Hope the same night; marking his route, however, with the burning of houses and the scalping of the defenceless inhabitants. It being known that the Narragansets favored the cause of Philip, he having sent his

---

twenty-two thousand to Massachusetts proper, four thousand to each of the colonies Maine, New Hampshire, and Rhode Island. "Haverhill, on the Merrimack," he says, "was a frontier town; from Connecticut, emigrants had ascended the river as far as the rich meadows of Deerfield and Northfield; but to the west, Berkshire was a wilderness; Westfield was the remotest plantation. Between the towns on Connecticut river and the cluster of towns near Massachusetts Bay, Lancaster and Brookfield were the solitary settlements of Christians in the desert. The colonies, except Rhode Island, were united; the government of Massachusetts extended to the Kennebec, and included more than half the population of New England; the confederacy of the colonies had been renewed, in anticipation of dangers." The number of Indians in all New England, west of the St. Croix, the same writer estimates at forty-five or fifty thousand. Of these, twelve thousand are supposed to have dwelt in Massachusetts and Plymouth, and only four thousand in New Hampshire. Connecticut and Rhode Island were quite populous. The number in Maine, also, was considerable. Great efforts had been made, especially in Massachusetts, by the English, to instruct and evangelize the Indians, by Eliot and the Mayhews. And at one time, it is said, that a larger proportion of the Massachusetts Indians could read and write than recently of the inhabitants of Russia.

women and children to them for protection, the Massachusetts forces, under Captain Hutchinson, proceeded into their country, either to renew a treaty or give them battle. Fortunately, a treaty was concluded, and the troops returned.

30. On the 27th of July, news arrived that Philip was in a swamp at Pocasset, now Tiverton. The Massachusetts and Plymouth forces immediately marched to that place, and the next day charged the enemy in their recesses. As the troops entered the swamp, the Indians continued to retire. The English in vain pursued, till night, when the commander ordered a retreat. Many of the English were killed, and the enemy took courage. It being impossible to encounter the Indians with advantage in the swamps, it was determined to starve them out; but Philip, apprehending their design, contrived to escape, with his forces, to the Nipmucks, in Worcester county, whom he induced to assist him. This tribe had already commenced hostilities against the English; but, in the hope of reclaiming them, Captains Wheeler and Hutchinson were sent to treat with them. But the Indians, having intimation of their coming, lurked in ambush for them, and fired upon them, killing some and mortally wounding others, of whom Captain Hutchinson was one.

31. The remainder fled to Quaboag, Brookfield, closely pursued by the Indians, who burnt every house excepting the one

in which the inhabitants had taken refuge. This, also, at length, they surrounded, and "for two days continued to pour a storm of musket-balls upon it; with long poles they next thrust against it brands and combustibles; they shot arrows of fire; they loaded a cart with flax and tow, and, with long poles fastened together, they pushed it against the house. Destruction seemed inevitable. But when the house was kindling, and the savages stood ready to destroy the first that should open the door to escape, a torrent of rain descended, and suddenly extinguished the kindling flames." At length, Major Willard came to their relief, raised the siege, and destroyed a considerable number of the assailants.

32. During the month of September, Hadley, Deerfield, and Northfield, on Connecticut river, were attacked, and several inhabitants killed, and many buildings consumed. Captain Lathrop, with several teams, and eighty young men, having been sent to Deerfield to transport a quantity of grain to Hadley, were suddenly attacked by nearly eight hundred Indians, while stopping at Muddy Brook to gather grapes. Resistance was in vain; seventy of these young men fell, and were buried in one grave. Captain Mosely, then at Deerfield, hearing the report of the guns, hastened to the spot, and attacked the Indians, killed ninety-six, and wounded forty, losing but two of his number.

33. Early in October, the Springfield Indians concerted a plan with the hostile tribes, to burn that town. Having, under cover of night, received two or three hundred of Philip's men into their fort, they set fire to the town. The plot, however, was discovered so seasonably, that troops from Westfield arrived in time to save the town, excepting thirty-two houses, which had been previously consumed. Soon after hostilities were commenced by Philip, the Tarrenteens began their depredations in New Hampshire and the Province of Maine. They robbed the boats and plundered the houses of the English. In September, they fell on Saco, Scarborough and Kittery, killing between twenty and thirty of the inhabitants, and consigning their houses, barns and mills, to the flames.

34. Elated with these successes, they next advanced towards the Piscataqua, committing similar outrages at Oyster River, Salmon Falls, Dover and Exeter. Before winter, sixty of the English, in that quarter, were killed, and nearly as many buildings consumed.

35. Notwithstanding the Narragansets had pledged themselves, by their treaty, not to engage in the war, it was discovered that they were taking part with the enemy. Upon this, Governor Winslow, of Plymouth, with about one thousand eight

5*

hundred troops from Massachusetts and Connecticut, and one hundred and sixty friendly Indians, commenced their march from Pettysquamscot, on the 29th of December, through a deep snow, towards the enemy, who were in a swamp some fifteen miles distant. In the middle of this swamp, on a rising ground, stood the fortress of the Indians, — a work of strength, composed of palisades, and surrounded by a hedge sixteen feet thick. One entrance only led to the fort, through the surrounding thicket. Upon this the English providentially fell, and, without waiting to form, rushed impetuously towards the fort. The English captains entered first. The resistance of the Indians was gallant and warlike. But at length the English were compelled to retreat.

36. At this crisis, some Connecticut men, on the opposite side of the fort, discovering a place destitute of palisades, instantly sprang into the fort, fell upon the rear of the Indians, and, aided by the rest of the army, after a desperate conflict, achieved a complete victory. Six hundred wigwams were now set on fire, and an appalling scene ensued. Deep volumes of smoke rolled up to heaven, mingled with the dying shrieks of mothers and infants, which, with the aged and infirm, were consumed in the flames. The Indians were estimated at four thousand; of whom seven hundred warriors were killed, and three hundred died of their wounds; three hundred were taken prisoners, and as many women and children; the rest, except such as were consumed, fled. The victory of the English, complete as it was, was purchased with blood. Six brave captains fell, — Davenport, Gardiner, Johnson, Gallop, Siely, and Marshall; eighty of the troops were killed or mortally wounded, and one hundred and fifty were wounded who recovered.

37. From this defeat the Indians never recovered. They were not yet, however, effectually subdued. During the winter they continued their savage work of murdering and burning. The towns of Lancaster,* Medfield, Weymouth, Groton, Spring-

---

* Pen can scarcely describe the distresses of the people of Lancaster, during this savage visitation. Forty-two persons sought shelter under the roof of Mary Rowlandson; and after a hot assault, the Indians succeeded in setting the house on fire. "Quickly," Mrs. Rowlandson says, "it was the dolefulest day that mine eyes ever saw. Now the dreadful hour is come. Some in our house were fighting for their lives; others wallowing in blood; the house on fire over our heads, and the bloody heathens ready to knock us on the head, if we stirred out. I took my children to go forth; but the Indians shot so thick, that the bullets rattled against the house as if one had thrown a handful of stones. We had six stout dogs, but none of them would stir. * * * The bullets flying thick, one went through my side, and through my poor child in my arms!" The brutalities of an Indian

field, Northampton, Sudbury, and Marlboro,' in Massachusetts, and of Warwick and Providence, in Rhode Island, were assaulted, and some of them partly, and others wholly, destroyed. The success of the Indians, during the winter, had been great; but, on the return of spring, the tide turned against them. The Narraganset country was scoured, and many of the natives were killed, among whom was Canonchet, their chief sachem.*

38. On the 22d of August, 1676, the finishing stroke was given to the war in the United Colonies, by the death of Philip. After his flight from Mount Hope, he had attempted to rouse the Mohawks against the English. To effect this purpose, he killed, at various times, several of that tribe, and charged it upon the English. But, his iniquity being discovered, he was obliged hastily to flee, and returned to Mount Hope. Tidings of his return being brought to Captain Church, a man who had been of eminent service in this war, and who was better able than any other person to provide against the wiles of the enemy, he immediately proceeded to the place of Philip's concealment, near Mount Hope, accompanied by a small body of men. On his arrival, he placed his men in ambushes round the swamp, charging them not to move till daylight, that they might distinguish Philip, should he attempt to escape. Such was his confidence of success, that, taking Major Sandford by the hand, he said, " It is scarcely possible that Philip should escape." At that instant, a bullet whistled over their heads, and a volley followed.

39. The firing proceeded from Philip and his men, who were now in view. Perceiving his peril, the savage chief hastily seized his powder-horn and gun, and fled; but, directing his course towards a spot where an Englishman and an Indian lay concealed, the former levelled his gun; but, missing fire, the Indian drew, and shot him through the heart. Captain Church

---

massacre followed. Mrs. Rowlandson was taken captive, with one poor wounded babe. She adds, " Down I must sit in the snow, with my sick child, the picture of death, in my lap. Not the least crumb of refreshment came within either of our mouths from Wednesday night to Saturday night, except a little cold water." Little do the mothers of the land at the present day know of the " sorrows of woman of a former generation."

* Canonchet was a savage, but he had the courage and fortitude of a hero. "We will fight to the last man," said the gallant chieftain, " rather than become servants to the English." When taken prisoner near the Black-stone, a young Englishman began to question him. " Child," said he, " you no understand war; I will answer your chief." His life was offered him, if he would procure a treaty of peace; he refused the offer with disdain. " I know," said he, " the Indians will not yield." When condemned to death, his only reply was, " I like it well; I shall die before I speak anything unworthy of myself."

ordered him to be beheaded and quartered. The Indian who
executed this order pronounced the warrior's epitaph : " You
have been one very great man. You have made many a man
afraid of you. But so big as you be, I will now chop you to
pieces."

40. Thus fell a savage hero and patriot, — of whose trans-
cendent abilities our history furnishes melancholy evidence.
The advantage of civilized education, and a wider theatre of
action, might have made the name of Philip of Mount Hope as
memorable as that of Alexander or Cæsar. After the death
of Philip, the war continued in the Province of Maine, till the
spring of 1678. But westward, the Indians, having lost their
chiefs, wigwams and provisions, came in singly, by tens and
by hundreds, and submitted to the English. Thus closed a
melancholy period in the annals of New England, during which
six hundred men had fallen, twelve or thirteen towns had been
destroyed, and six hundred dwelling-houses consumed. Every
eleventh family was houseless, and every eleventh soldier had
sunk to his grave. So costly was the inheritance which our
fathers have transmitted to us !

41. In 1677 a controversy which had subsisted for some
time between the colony of Massachusetts and the heirs of Sir
Ferdinando Gorges, relative to the Province of Maine, was
decided in England, and the colony adjudged to Gorges' heirs.
Upon this, Massachusetts purchased the title, for one thousand
two hundred pounds sterling, and the territory, from that time
till 1820, was a part of Massachusetts. The claim of Massachusetts to the province was founded upon her patent of 1628,
which was construed as including the latter. (See page 43.)
The claim of Gorges' heirs, on the other hand, was founded upon
a charter to Gorges, in 1639, of all the lands from the Piscataqua to the Sagadahoc, styled the Province of Maine. In 1652
the province was taken under the jurisdiction of Massachusetts,
and was erected into a county, by the name of Yorkshire, and
was represented in the General Court, at Boston. In 1692 the
territory was incorporated with Massachusetts; and, although
repeated efforts were made by a portion of the inhabitants to
effect a separation, the connection continued till 1818, when a
separation took place, and March 16, 1820, Maine became an
independent State of the Union.

42. Two years after the above decision in regard to the Province of Maine, — namely, in 1679, — an order was issued by the
crown for the separation of New Hampshire from the jurisdic-

tion of Massachusetts,* and its erection into a royal province, over which was established the FIRST ROYAL GOVERNMENT IN NEW ENGLAND. The form of government prescribed by the king ordained a president and council to govern the province, with an assembly, &c.; the assembly to be chosen by the people, the president and council to be appointed by the crown. The colony had been under the jurisdiction of Massachusetts since 1640, — nearly forty years, — the patent holders having that year agreed to surrender the jurisdiction of the territory to Massachusetts.

43. In the year 1684, June 28, an event highly interesting to the colony of Massachusetts occurred in England. This was a decision, in the high court of chancery, that she had forfeited her charter, and that henceforth her government should be placed in the hands of the king. Before King Charles had time to adjust the affairs of the colony, he died, and was succeeded by James II. Soon after his accession, similar proceedings took place against the other colonies. Rhode Island submitted, and relinquished her charter. Plymouth sent a copy of her charter to the king, with an humble petition that he would restore it. Connecticut voted an address to his majesty, in which she prayed him to recall the writ that had been filed against her, and requested the continuance of her charter.

44. The petitions and remonstrances of the colonies were, however, of no avail. After all their hardships and dangers in settling a wilderness, they had no other prospect before them but the destruction of their dearest rights, and no better security of life, liberty and property, than the capricious will of a tyrant. In pursuance of this cruel policy, two years after the charter of Massachusetts was vacated, King James commissioned and sent out Sir Edmund Andros as Governor of all New England, Plymouth excepted.

45. On his arrival at Boston, December 30th, 1686, he entered upon his administration; which, at the commencement, was comparatively auspicious. But in a few months the fair prospect was changed. Among other arbitrary acts, restraints were laid upon the freedom of the press, and marriage contracts. The liberty to worship after the Congregational mode was threatened, and the fees of all officers of government were exorbitantly and oppressively enhanced.

46. The condition of the New England colonies was now dis-

---

* The separation actually took place in 1780.

tressing, and, as the administration of Andros was becoming still more severe and oppressive, the future seemed to promise no alleviation. But Providence was invisibly preparing the way for their relief. In November, 1688, William, Prince of Orange, who married Mary, daughter of James II., landed at Torbay, in England, and, compelling James II. to leave the kingdom, assumed the crown, — being proclaimed February, 1689, to the general joy of the nation.

47. Under the sudden impulse of their feelings, on the news of the revolution in England, the inhabitants of Boston imprisoned Andros and fifty of his associates, and sent them to England to answer for mal-administration, at the same time reëstablishing their former mode of government.

48. On leaving England, James fled to Louis XIV., King of France, who espoused his cause. This kindled the flames of war between the two countries, which extended to their colonial possessions in America, and which continued from 1690 to the peace of Ryswick, in 1697. This is commonly known as "KING WILLIAM'S WAR."

49. The opening of this war was signalized by the most shocking barbarities, perpetrated by different parties of French and Indians upon settlements in the northern colonies. In July, 1689, Major Waldron and twenty of the garrison at Dover village, in New Hampshire, were surprised and murdered, and twenty-nine captives taken to Canada, most of whom were sold to the French. In 1690, February 18, three hundred French and Indians fell upon Schenectady,* a village on the Mohawk, and burnt it. Salmon Falls, a settlement on the east side of the Piscataqua, in Maine, was destroyed in the following March; and in May, Casco, a fort and settlement also in Maine, shared a similar fate. Roused by these proceedings of the French, the colony of Massachusetts resolved to attack the enemy in turn. Accordingly, an expedition, consisting of seven vessels and eight hundred men, under command of Sir William Phipps, sailed, in

---

* The circumstances attending the burning of Schenectady were of the most tragical kind. The season was cold, and the snow so deep that it was deemed impossible for an enemy to approach. The attack was made in the dead of the night. Not a sentinel was awake to announce the approaching danger. Care had been taken, by a division of the enemy, to attack almost every house in the same moment. When the preparations were ready, the appalling war-whoop was begun; houses were broken open and set on fire; men and women were dragged from their beds, and, with their sleeping infants, were inhumanly murdered. Sixty persons perished in the massacre, thirty were made prisoners, while the rest of the inhabitants, mostly naked, fled through a deep snow, either suffering extremely, or perishing in the cold.

May, for the reduction of Port Royal, in Nova Scotia, which was easily and speedily effected.

50. In the latter part of the same year, an expedition was planned by the colonies of New York, Connecticut, and Massachusetts unitedly, for the reduction of Montreal and Quebec. Two thousand troops, furnished by the two former colonies, were to proceed to the attack of Montreal, by way of Lake Champlain, while a naval armament furnished by Massachusetts, under command of Sir William Phipps, with a similar number of troops, should invest Quebec. But the troops destined for Montreal, not being supplied either with boats or provisions sufficient for crossing the lake, were obliged to return. The naval expedition did not reach Quebec until October. After spending several days in consultation, the landing of the troops was effected, and they began their march for the town. At the same time, the ships were drawn up; but the attack, both by land and water, was alike unsuccessful. The troops were soon after reëmbarked; and the weather, proving tempestuous, scattered the fleet and terminated the expedition. The success of the expedition had been so confidently anticipated, that provision had not been made for the payment of the troops; there was danger, therefore, of a mutiny. In this extremity, Massachusetts issued bills of credit, as a substitute for money; the first emission of the kind in the American colonies.

51. In 1692, King William, who had refused to restore to Massachusetts her former charter, granted a new one, almost the only privilege of which it allowed the people was the right of choosing their representatives.* But it greatly extended the limits of the province, embracing, besides the former territory, Plymouth, Maine, and Nova Scotia.

52. To render the new charter the more acceptable, Sir William Phipps, who was a native of the colony, was appointed governor; and on the 24th of May, 1692, he arrived in Boston with the new charter. No opposition was made by the inhabitants to the new government, whatever regret was felt at the loss of their former charter.

53. Among the first acts of the new governor and his council was the institution of a court to try certain persons in the

---

* The king reserved to himself the right of appointing the governor, lieutenant-governor, and secretary, of the colony, and of repealing the laws within three years after their passage. The Legislature was now composed of three branches, — a governor, representatives, and a council, — the last to be chosen by the representatives, subject to the negative of the governor. The restrictions imposed by the charter were grievous, and served to alienate the people from the mother country.

colony accused of WITCHCRAFT. A law punishing this supposed crime with death existed in England, and under it many had been tried and executed; a belief in the existence of such evil possessions was current on both sides of the water.

54. The first suspicion of witchcraft in the New England colonies began at Springfield, Massachusetts, as early as 1645. Several persons were, about that time, tried and executed, in Massachusetts; one at Charlestown, one at Dorchester, one at Cambridge, and one at Boston. For almost thirty years afterwards, the subject rested. But, in 1687 or 1688, it was revived in Boston; four of the children of John Goodwin uniting in accusing a poor Irish woman with bewitching them. Unhappily, the accusation was regarded with attention, and the woman was tried and executed. Near the close of February, 1692, the subject was again revived, in consequence of several children in Danvers, then a part of Salem, beginning to act in a peculiar and unaccountable manner. Their strange conduct. continuing for several days, their friends betook themselves to fasting and prayer. During religious exercises, it was found that the children were generally decent and still; but after service was ended, they renewed their former inexplicable conduct. This was deemed sufficient evidence of witchcraft.

55. At the expiration of some days, the children began to accuse several persons in the neighborhood of bewitching them. Unfortunately, they were credited, and the suspected authors of the spells were seized and imprisoned. From this date, the awful mania rapidly spread into the neighboring country, and soon appeared in various parts of Essex, Middlesex, and Suffolk. Persons at Andover, Ipswich, Gloucester, Boston, and several other places, were accused by their neighbors and others. For some time, the victims were selected only from the lower classes. But, at length, the accusations fell upon persons of the most respectable rank. In August, Mr. George Burroughs, some time minister in Salem, was accused, brought to trial, and condemned. Accusations were also brought against Mr. English, a respectable merchant in Salem, and his wife; against Messrs. Dudley and John Bradstreet, sons of the then late Governor Bradstreet; against the wife of Mr. Hale, and the lady of Sir William Phipps. The evil had now become alarming. One man, named Giles Corey, had been pressed to death for refusing to put himself on a trial by jury; and nineteen persons had been executed, more than one-third of whom were members of

the church. One hundred and fifty were in prison, and two hundred were accused.

56. At length a conviction began to prevail that the proceedings had been rash and indefensible. A special court was held on the subject, and fifty who were brought to trial were acquitted, excepting three, who were afterwards reprieved by the governor. These events were followed by a general release of those who had been imprisoned. " Thus the cloud," says the late President Dwight, " which had so long hung over the colony, slowly and sullenly retired; and, like the darkness of Egypt, was, to the great joy of the distressed inhabitants, succeeded by serenity and sunshine." *

57. For several years, the war with the French and Indians continued, and atrocities of the most barbarous kind were committed. In 1694, Oyster River, a settlement not far from Portsmouth, New Hampshire, was attacked, and nearly one hundred persons either killed or carried away captive. In March, 1697, Haverhill, Mass., was assaulted by a body of savages, and forty of the inhabitants were either murdered or taken prisoners. But, at length, September 20th of the same year, a treaty was concluded at Ryswick, a town in the west of Holland, which put an end to hostilities between France and England, and which restored countries, forts and colonies, to their former proprietors.†

---

* We who live to look back upon this scene are wont to contemplate with wonder the seeming madness and infatuation, not of the weak, illiterate, and unprincipled, but of men of sense, education, and fervent piety. Let us consider, however, that, at this period, the actual existence of witchcraft was taken for granted, and that doubts respecting it were deemed little less than heresy. The learned Baxter, who lived at this time in England, where the same notions on this subject prevailed, pronounced the disbeliever in witchcraft an "obdurate Sadducee;" and Sir Matthew Hale, one of the brightest ornaments of the English bench, repeatedly tried and condemned those as criminals who were accused of witchcraft.

In conclusion, it may be remarked that no people on earth are now more enlightened on this subject than are the people of America. Nothing of a similar kind has since existed, and probably never will exist. Stories of wonder, founded upon ancient tradition, or upon a midnight adventure, sometimes awe the village circle on a winter's night; but the succeeding day chases away every ghost, and lulls every fear. It becomes the present generation to advert with gratitude to their freedom from those delusions which distressed and agitated their ancestors, rather than to bestow invectives upon them, since they could plead, in palliation of their error, the spirit of the age in which they lived.

† King William's War, which was thus brought to a close, had been marked by atrocities, on the part of the French and Indians, until then unknown in the history of the colonies.

The details of individual sufferings which occurred, were they faithfully

58. The peace of Ryswick proved of short duration, when England and France were again involved in war. Three principal causes operated to produce hostilities: 1. The acknowledgment by France of Charles Edward, commonly known as the Pretender, to the throne of England, on the death of his father,

---

recorded, would excite the sympathies of the most unfeeling bosom. One instance only can we relate.

In an attack, by a body of Indians, on Haverhill, Massachusetts, in the winter of 1697, the concluding year of the war, a party of the assailants approached the house of a Mr. Dustan. Upon the first alarm, he flew from a neighboring field to his family. Seven of his children he directed to flee, while he himself went to assist his wife, who was confined to the bed with an infant a week old. But before she could leave her bed, the savages arrived.

In despair of rendering her assistance, Mr. Dustan flew to the door, mounted his horse, and determined, in his own mind, to snatch up and save the child which he loved the best ; but, upon coming up to them, he found it impossible to make a selection. He determined, therefore, to meet his fate with them; to defend and save them from their pursuers, or die by their side.

A body of Indians soon came up with him, and, from short distances, fired upon him and his little company. For more than a mile, he continued to retreat, placing himself between his children and the fire of the savages, and returning their shots with great spirit and success. At length, he saw them all safely lodged, from their bloody pursuers, in a distant house.

As Mr. Dustan quitted his house, a party of Indians entered it. Mrs. Dustan was in bed; but they ordered her to rise, and, before she could completely dress herself, obliged her and her nurse, a Mrs. Teff, to quit the house, which they plundered and set on fire.

In these distressing circumstances, Mrs. Dustan began her march, with other captives, into the wilderness. The air was keen, and their path led alternately through snow and deep mud, and her savage conductors delighted rather in the infliction of torment than the alleviation of distress.

The company had proceeded but a short distance, when an Indian, thinking the infant an incumbrance, took it from the nurse's arms, and violently terminated its life. Such of the other captives as began to be weary, and incapable of proceeding, the Indians killed with their tomahawks. Feeble as Mrs. Dustan was, both she and her nurse sustained, with wonderful energy, the fatigue and misery attending a journey of one hundred and fifty miles.

On their arrival at the place of their destination, they found the wigwam of the savage who claimed them as his personal property to be inhabited by twelve Indians. In the ensuing April, this family set out, with their captives, for an Indian settlement still more remote. The captives were informed that, on their arrival at the settlement, they must submit to be stripped, scourged, and run the gauntlet between two files of Indians. This information carried distress to the minds of the captive women, and led them promptly to devise some means of escape.

Early in the morning of the 10th of May, Mrs. Dustan awaking her nurse and another fellow-prisoner, they despatched ten of the twelve Indians, while asleep. The other two escaped. The women then pursued their difficult and toilsome journey through the wilderness, and at length arrived in safety at Haverhill. Subsequently, they visited Boston, and received, at the hand of the General Court, a handsome consideration for their extraordinary sufferings and heroic conduct.

James II., when the latter kingdom had settled the crown on Anne, second daughter of James. 2. The attempt of Louis XIV. to destroy the balance of power in Europe, by placing Philip of Anjou, his grandson, on the throne of Spain. And, 3. Certain pretensions by the French king to privileges in America, denied as rightfully his by the English crown. For these and other reasons, England declared war against France, which continued from 1702 to the peace of Utrecht, April 11, 1713. This is commonly known as "QUEEN ANNE'S WAR."

59. The whole weight of this war, in America, unexpectedly fell on New England. The geographical position of New York particularly exposed that colony to a combined attack from the lakes and sea; but just before the commencement of hostilities, a treaty of neutrality was concluded between the Five Nations and the French governor in Canada. The local situation of the Five Nations, bordering on the frontiers of New York, prevented the French from molesting that colony. Massachusetts and New Hampshire were thus left to bear the chief calamities of the war.

60. The declaration of war was immediately followed by incursions of French and Indians from Canada into these colonies, who seized every opportunity of annoying the inhabitants by depredation and outrage.*

---

* On Tuesday, March 11th, 1704, at daybreak, four hundred and fifty French and Indians, under command of the infamous Hextel de Rouville, fell upon Deerfield, Massachusetts. Unhappily, not only the inhabitants, but even the watch, were asleep. They soon made themselves masters of the house in which the garrison was kept. Proceeding thence to the house of Mr. Williams, the clergyman, they forced the doors, and entered the room where he was sleeping.

Awaked by the noise, Mr. Williams seized his pistol, and snapped it at the Indian who first approached; but it missed fire. Mr. Williams was now seized, disarmed, bound, and kept standing, without his clothes, in the intense cold, nearly an hour.

His house was next plundered, and two of his children, together with a black female servant, were butchered before his eyes. The savages, at length, suffered his wife and five children to put on their clothes, after which he was himself allowed to dress, and prepare for a long and melancholy journey.

The whole town around them was now on fire. Every house, but the one next to Mr. Williams', was consumed. Having completed their work of destruction, in burning the town and killing forty-seven persons, the enemy hastily retreated, taking with them one hundred of the inhabitants, among whom were Mr. Williams and his family.

The first night after their departure from Deerfield, the savages murdered Mr. Williams' servant; and, on the day succeeding, finding Mrs. Williams unable to keep pace with the rest, plunged a hatchet into her head. She had recently borne an infant, and was not yet recovered. But her husband was not permitted to assist her. He himself was lame, bound, insulted,

61. In the spring of 1707, Massachusetts, Rhode Island and New Hampshire, despatched an armament against Port Royal, in Nova Scotia. The expedition, consisting of one thousand men, sailed from Nantucket in twenty-three transports, under convoy of the Deptfort man-of-war, and the Province galley. After a short voyage, they arrived at Port Royal; but March, the commander of the expedition, though a brave man, being unfit to lead in an enterprise so difficult, little was done beyond burning a few houses and killing a few cattle.

62. In 1710, another attempt was made to reduce the place, in connection with a fleet from England, under command of Colonel Nicholson. New England furnished five regiments of troops. The armament left Boston in September, and on the 12th October demanded a surrender of the place. The garrison, being weak and dispirited, surrendered on the 13th, upon which the name of the place was changed to Annapolis, in honor of Queen Anne; and from this time Acadia, or Nova Scotia, became a dependency of the British crown.

63. The following year, a plan was projected for the conquest of Canada, in pursuance of which an armament, under Sir Hovenden Walker, arrived in Boston, July 6th. Additional forces were promptly raised by the colonies; and at length, August 10th, the whole force, consisting of fifteen men-of-war, forty transports, and nearly seven thousand troops, departed for the object in view. Shortly after the departure of the fleet, General Nicholson proceeded from Albany towards Canada, at the head of four thousand men, furnished by the colonies of Connecticut, New York, and New Jersey.

64. The fleet reached the St. Lawrence in safety, but, in ascending that river, eight or nine British transports were lost, and nearly one thousand men. Upon this disaster, the fleet sailed directly for England, and the provincial troops returned home. General Nicholson, who had advanced to Lake George, hearing of the fate of the naval expedition on the St. Lawrence, abandoned the enterprise. The failure of the expedition was

threatened, and nearly famished; but what were personal sufferings like these, and even greater than these, to the sight of a wife, under circumstances so tender, inhumanly butchered before his eyes ! Before the journey was ended, seventeen others shared the melancholy fate of Mrs. Williams.

On their arrival in Canada, it may be added, Mr. Williams was treated with civility by the French. At the end of two years, he was redeemed, with fifty-seven others, and returned to Deerfield, where, after twelve years' labor in the Gospel, he entered into his rest. A little daughter of Mr. Williams, it is related, continued to reside with the Indians for many years, and, at length, was married to a Mohawk chief.

unjustly imputed by the mother country to New England; nor did the colonies receive any credit for their vigorous exertions in raising men and fitting out the fleet.

65. Two years later, April 11th, 1713, a treaty concluded at Utrecht, a city of Holland, put an end to "Queen Anne's War." After the peace was known in America, the eastern Indians sent in a flag, and sued for peace. The Governor of Massachusetts, with his council, and that of New Hampshire, met them at Portsmouth, and entered into terms of pacification.

66. After enjoying a state of comparative peace and prosperity for nearly thirty years following "Queen Anne's War," the news of war between France and England again reached the American shores, — hostilities being declared by the former March 15th, and by the latter April 9th, 1744. This is commonly called "KING GEORGE'S WAR." It originated in disputes regarding the kingdom of Austria.

67. The most important event of this war in America was the seizure and capture of Louisburg. After the peace of Utrecht, in 1713, the French had built Louisburg, on the Island of Cape Breton, and fortified it at an expense of five and a half millions of dollars. The works had been twenty-five years in building, and were of such strength that the place was sometimes regarded as "the Gibraltar of America."

68. Impressed with the importance of rescuing this fortress from the French, as it furnished a convenient retreat to such privateers as annoyed those engaged in the fisheries, Governor Shirley, of Massachusetts, in January, 1745, communicated a plan to the Legislature which he had formed for its reduction. The measure was adopted only by a majority of a single voice, so serious were the objections urged against it. Connecticut, New Hampshire and Rhode Island, raised their respective quotas of troops; New York furnished artillery, and Pennsylvania provisions. The troops numbered four thousand, and the naval force consisted of twelve ships and vessels.

69. The coöperation of Commodore Warren, then in the West Indies, was expected; and when at the moment their hopes were likely to be disappointed in regard to his aid, — he having excused himself from any concern in the enterprise, — he joined the expedition with his fleet at Canso. On the 11th of May the combined forces appeared off Louisburg, and effected a landing at Gabarus Bay, the enemy being, until this moment, ignorant that an attack was meditated.

70. After several preliminary movements, a siege was commenced, and for fourteen nights they were occupied in drawing

6*

cannon towards the town, over a morass, in which oxen and horses could not be used. Incredible was the toil. By the 31st of May, several batteries had been erected, one of which mounted five forty-two pounders. These batteries did great execution.

71. Meanwhile, Commodore Warren captured the Vigilant, a French ship of seventy-four guns, and with her five hundred and sixty men, and large quantities of military stores. By this capture the English added to their military supplies, and seriously lessened the strength of the enemy. Shortly after, the number of the English fleet was considerably augmented by the arrival of several men-of-war. A combined attack by sea and land was now determined on, and fixed for the 29th of June. Before the arrival of the appointed time, however, the enemy desired a cessation of hostilities; and, on the 28th of June, after a siege of forty-nine days, the city of Louisburg and the Island of Cape Breton were surrendered to his Britannic majesty.

72. Thus successfully terminated a daring expedition, which had been undertaken without the knowledge of the mother country. The acquisition of the fortress of Louisburg was as useful and important to the colonies, and to the British empire, as its reduction was surprising to that empire and mortifying to the court of France. Besides the stores and prizes which fell into the hands of the English, — estimated at little less than a

N° 3

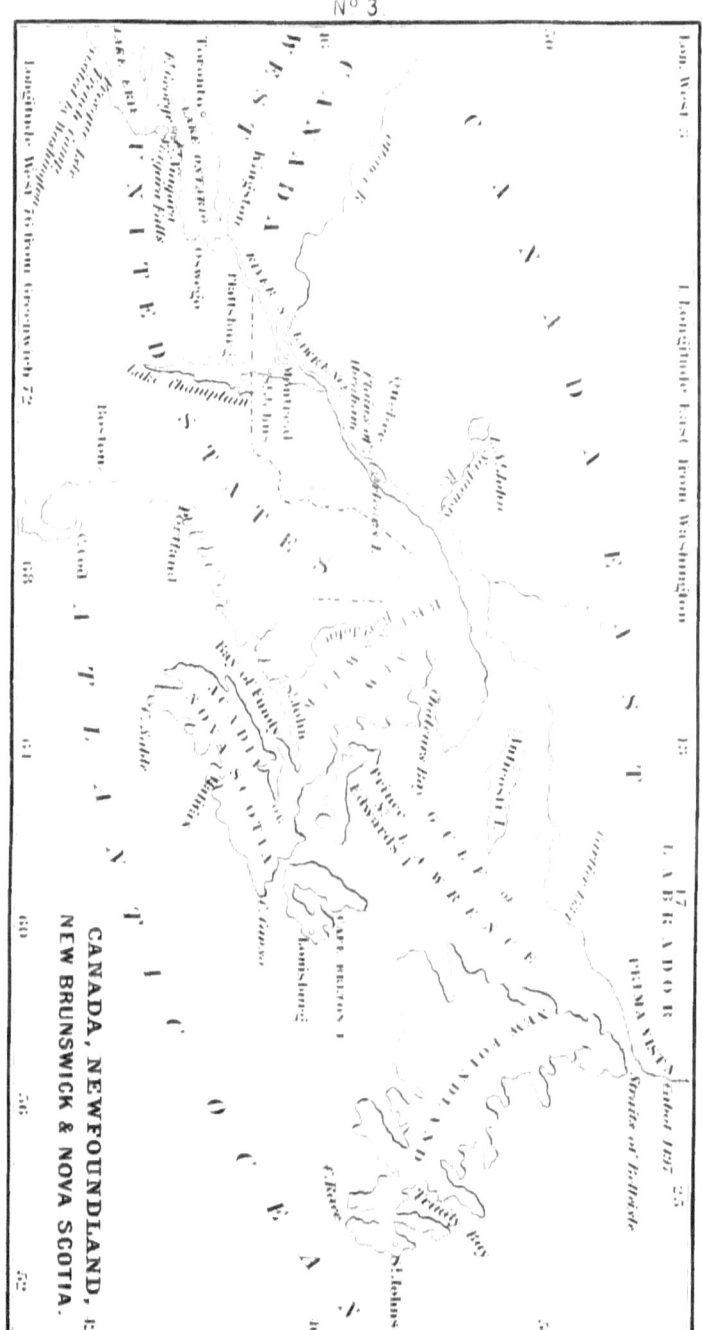

CANADA, NEWFOUNDLAND,
NEW BRUNSWICK & NOVA SCOTIA.

million sterling, — security was given to the colonies in their fisheries, Nova Scotia was preserved, and the trade and fisheries of France nearly ruined.

73. The capture of Louisburg roused the court of France to revenge. Under the Duke D'Anville, a nobleman of great courage, an armament was despatched to America, in 1746, consisting of forty ships-of-war, fifty-six transports, with three thousand five hundred men, and forty thousand stands of arms for the use of the French and Indians in Canada. The object of this expedition was to recover possession of Cape Breton, and to attack the colonies. But several ships of this formidable French fleet were damaged by storms; others were lost, and one forced to return to Brest, on account of a malignant disease among her crew. Two or three only of the ships, with a few of the transports, arrived at Chebucto, now Halifax. Here the admiral died, through mortification, or, as some say, by poison. The vice-admiral came to a similar tragical death, by running himself through the body. That part of the fleet that arrived sailed with a view to attack Annapolis; but a storm scattered them, and prevented the accomplishment of this object.

74. In April, 1748, preliminaries of peace were signed between France and England, at Aix-la-Chapelle, a city in the western part of Germany, soon after which hostilities ceased. The definitive treaty was signed in October. Prisoners on all sides were to be released without ransom, and all conquests made during the war were to be mutually restored.

III. MAINE. — 1. Maine was so called, as early as 1639, from Meyne, in France, of which Henrietta Maria, Queen of France, was at that time proprietor. Maine is not generally reckoned as a distinct colony or province, her history being long blended with that of Massachusetts, where the pupil will find an account of its first settlement, &c.

2. As early as 1626 a few feeble settlements were commenced along the coast of Maine; but, before they had gathered much strength, the Council of Plymouth granted to several companies portions of the same territory, from the Piscataqua to the Penobscot, which grants, in after years, were the source of serious controversies.

3. But in 1639 Sir Ferdinand Gorges secured to himself a distinct charter of all the land from Piscataqua to Sagadahock, which received the name of the Province of Maine. Soon after this, he formed a system of government for the province, and incorporated a city near the mountain Agamenticus, in York, by the name of Georgeana; but neither the province nor city

flourished. In 1652, the province was taken under the jurisdiction of Massachusetts, by the request of the people of Maine;
and continued in this connection till near 1820, when it became
a separate and independent state.

4. It would exceed our limits to examine the different grants
of territory which were made, at different times, of the State of
Maine. In 1652, at the time the province was taken under the
jurisdiction of Massachusetts, it was made a county, by the
name of Yorkshire. It had the privilege of sending deputies to
the General Court, at Boston. Massachusetts laid claim to the
province, as lying within her charter of 1628; and, after various
controversies, the territory was incorporated with her in 1692.
In 1786, 1787, 1802, and 1816, efforts were made by a portion
of the people of Maine to become separate from Massachusetts
proper; but to this a majority of the inhabitants were averse.
In 1818, however, this measure was effected; and on the 16th
of March, 1820, the district, by an act of Congress, became an
independent state.

5. The early settlements in Maine suffered untold calamities
from savage cruelty. In different years, Salmon Falls, Casco,
Berwick, Wells, and other places, were laid waste, their inhabitants murdered, or led into a captivity worse than death. But
if Maine early drank deep of the cup of affliction, that cup has
passed away, and for many years she has been increasing rapidly
in population, wealth, and moral strength.

III. NEW HAMPSHIRE.

1. NEW HAMPSHIRE derives her beautiful name from Hampshire, a county in England, and was first applied to the territory
in 1629, in honor of Captain John Mason, Governor of Portsmouth, in Hampshire, England, and also proprietor of the territory now so called.

2. At an earlier year, however, — namely, 1622, — this same
Captain Mason, Sir Ferdinand Gorges, and others, had obtained
of the "Council of Plymouth" a grant of land partly in Maine
and partly in New Hampshire, which they called LACONIA. In
the spring of 1623 they sent two small parties of emigrants to
settle it. Some of these commenced the settlement of Little
Harbor, on the west side of the Piscataqua river, a short distance
from the present site of Portsmouth; the others planted themselves at Cocheco, afterwards called Dover, further up the river.
The principal employment of these new settlers was fishing and
trade.

3. In 1629, the Reverend John Wheelright, a former patron of Anne Hutchinson (p. 48), purchased of the Indians the territory lying between the Merrimack and the Piscataqua rivers. He afterward laid the foundation of Exeter. During the same year, this tract of country, which was a part of the grant to Gorges and Mason, was conveyed to Mason alone, and now received the name of New Hampshire. By him the first house was erected at Portsmouth, in 1631.

4. In 1641, the several settlements in New Hampshire formed a coalition with Massachusetts, whose protection they enjoyed nearly forty years. In 1680, however, the territory was separated from that colony, by order of the king, and constituted a royal province, to be governed by a president and council, appointed by the crown, and a house of representatives, elected by the people (p. 57). No change of land titles was effected.

5. The first legislative assembly under the royal charter was held in March, 1680. It consisted of eleven members. A declaration in the code of laws passed by this assembly gave great umbrage to the king, indicating, as he thought, an unwarrantable spirit of independence. "No act, imposition, law, or ordinance," the declaration proceeded to say, "shall be imposed upon the inhabitants of the province, but such as shall be made by the assembly, and approved by the president and council." This is said to have been twelve years in advance of a similar enactment in Massachusetts. Thus early did a spirit of liberty and independence germinate among the granite hills of New Hampshire, and give promise of fruit which came to full maturity in after years.

6. Robert Mason, grandson and heir of John Mason, having himself been appointed one of the council, arrived in New Hampshire in 1681, and, by virtue of his claim to the territory, assumed the title of "Lord Proprietor," and demanded that leases should be taken out under him. His claims and demands, however, were resisted in the courts of law; and although judgments were obtained against landlords in the province, so universal and determined was the hostility of the people to Mason, that they could not be enforced.

7. For several years, the same governor presided over Massachusetts and New Hampshire. At the time of the revolution in England, however, in 1689, when Andros was seized and imprisoned in Massachusetts, the people of New Hampshire, assuming the government, again placed themselves under the jurisdiction of that colony. This was in 1690. In 1692, a

separation was again effected, and a royal government reëstablished. In 1699, the two provinces were once more united, and the Earl of Bellamont was appointed governor of both.

8. In 1691, Samuel Allen purchased of the heirs of Mason all their titles to lands in New Hampshire, and for several years grievously annoyed the people, by the prosecution of these purchased claims. In 1715, however, his heirs, not being able to substantiate them, gave up the controversy, upon which a descendant of Mason revived his claims, alleging a defect in the conveyance of Allen; but, at length, this long and unhappy controversy was terminated, the heirs of Mason consenting to take only the unoccupied portions of the province, and releasing all others.

9. In 1741, the final separation of the two provinces, Massachusetts and New Hampshire, took place, at which time a separate governor was appointed for each.*

---

* In the early Indian wars, during which the New England colonies suffered unnumbered cruelties, the New Hampshire settlements experienced their full share of massacre and blood. An account of these will be found in our colonial sketches of Massachusetts, with whose history that of New Hampshire has been necessarily blended. The details of the attack upon Dover, in 1689 (see p. 58), have been reserved to this place, and may be taken as a specimen of the barbarities often practised by the Indians, in the early annals of the country.

The principal citizen of Dover, at this time, was Major Waldron, a man of cruel bearing towards the Indians, and who, on that account, was most obnoxious to them.

Having decided upon their plan of attack, their next object was to allay suspicion, which they did effectually by a most kind and respectful behavior. On the night of the awful tragedy, some of their squaws had obtained permission to sleep in the fortified houses of the town.

At length the inhabitants retired to rest;—silence and quiet pervaded the town. The doors were now softly opened, and the signal given. The Indians had stealthily reached their posts. They rushed into Major Waldron's house like tigers, and made for his apartment.

Meanwhile, awakened by their savage yells, Waldron arose, and seizing his sword, drove them back. Again they returned to the charge, and while he was attempting to get his other arms, a blow from a tomahawk felled him to the floor. Next, he was taken into the hall, and being placed in a chair, was set upon a table, where he was treated with insult and indignity.

After feasting upon such provisions as the house afforded, each of the savages, approaching Major Waldron, gave him a deep knife-gash across his breast, saying, as he did it, "I cross out my account."

Meanwhile, the tortured man grew momentarily weaker and weaker; and when, at length, he was ready to fall, an Indian held his own sword under him, upon which falling, his earthly miseries were soon at end.

Similar barbarities were enacted at other houses in the village; yet it is said that a woman was spared, for her kindness to an Indian, shown him thirteen years before. What strange contrarieties sometimes meet in the same human breast!

IV. CONNECTICUT.

I. COLONY OF CÓNNECTICUT. — 1. Connecticut derives its name from its principal river, called by the Indians QUON-EII-TA-CUT, and which, in their language, signified "the long river."

2. Robert, Earl of Warwick, was the first proprietary of the soil of Connecticut, under a grant from the "Plymouth Council," in 1630. It was next held by Lords Say and Seal, and Lord Brooke and others, to whom the earl transferred it in 1631. The patent included that part of New England which extends from Narraganset river one hundred and twenty miles, on a straight line, near the shore, towards the south-west, as the coast lies, towards Virginia, and within that breadth, from the Atlantic Ocean to the South Sea, or the Pacific. This is the original patent of Connecticut.

3. During this latter year, Mr. Winslow, Governor of Plymouth, at the instance of Wahquimacut,* a sachem near the Connecticut, visited the river and the fertile valley through which it passes, and, after his return, decided to take measures to commence a settlement on its banks.

4. Meanwhile, the Dutch at New York, who had become acquainted with the river about the same time,† intending to anticipate the people of Plymouth, erected a fort, or house, at Hartford, in 1633, and planted two cannon. In October of the same year, William Holmes, who commanded the Plymouth expedition, proceeded in a vessel, with his party, for Connecticut, bearing a commission from the Governor of Plymouth, and a chosen company, to accomplish his design. On reaching the Dutch fort, Holmes was forbid proceeding, at the hazard of being blown to pieces; but, being a man of spirit, he coolly informed the garrison that he had a commission from the Governor of Plymouth to go up the river, and that go he should. They poured

---

* Wahquimacut, the sachem here mentioned, made a journey to Plymouth and Boston, earnestly soliciting the governors of each of the colonies to send men to form settlements upon the river. He represented the country as exceedingly fruitful, and promised that he would supply the English, if they would make a settlement there, with corn, annually, and give them eighty beaver-skins. He urged that two men might be sent to view the country. Had this invitation been accepted, it might have prevented the Dutch claim to any part of the lands upon the river, and opened an extensive trade in hemp, furs, and deer-skins, with all the Indians upon it, and far into Canada.

The Governor of Massachusetts treated the sachem and his company with generosity, but paid no further attention to his proposal. Mr. Winslow, the Governor of Plymouth, judging it worthy of attention, himself made a journey to Connecticut, discovered the river and the lands adjacent.

† Bancroft gives the Dutch credit for the prior discovery of the river.

out their threats, but he proceeded, and landing on the west side of the river, erected his house below the mouth of the little river, in Windsor. The house was covered with the utmost despatch, and fortified with palisades. The Dutch, considering Holmes and his men intruders, sent, the next year, a band of seventy men to drive them from the country; but finding them strongly posted, they relinquished the design.

5. In the autumn of 1635, a company, consisting of sixty men, women and children, from the settlements of Newtown and Watertown, in Massachusetts, commenced their journey through the wilderness to Connecticut river. On their arrival, they settled at Windsor, Wethersfield, and Hartford. They commenced their journey on the 25th of October; but, as a wide wilderness spread before them, filled with swamps and rivers, hills and mountains, they were so long on their journey, and so much time was spent in passing the river, and in getting over their cattle, that, after all their exertions, winter came upon them before they were prepared.

6. By the 25th of November, Connecticut river was frozen over, and the snow was so deep, and the season so tempestuous, that a considerable number of the cattle driven from Massachusetts could not be brought across the river; but they wintered even better than those which were brought over. Yet a considerable number perished. The loss of the Windsor settlers, in cattle, was estimated at near two hundred pounds sterling. The sufferings of the people for want of food, during the winter, were often severe. After all the help they were able to obtain from hunting and the Indians, they were obliged to subsist on acorns, malt, and grains.*

---

* It being impracticable to transport much provision or furniture through a pathless wilderness, they were put on board several small vessels, which were either cast away or did not arrive. Several vessels were wrecked on the coast of New England, by the violence of the storms.

About the 10th of December, provisions generally failed in the settlements on the river, and famine and death looked the inhabitants in the face. Some of them, driven by hunger, attempted their way, in this severe season, through the wilderness, from Connecticut to Massachusetts. Of thirteen, in one company, who made this attempt, one, in passing the rivers, fell through the ice, and was drowned. The other twelve were ten days on their journey, and would all have perished, had it not been for the assistance of the Indians. Such was the general distress, early in December, that a considerable part of the new settlers were obliged to abandon their habitations. Seventy persons — men, women, and children — determined to go down the river to meet their provisions, as the only expedient to preserve their lives. Not meeting with the vessels which they expected, they all went on board the Rebecca, a vessel of about sixty tons. This, two days before, was frozen in, twenty miles up the river; but by the falling of a timely rain, together with

7. During the same month in which the emigrants commenced their journey to Connecticut, John Winthrop, son of the Governor of Massachusetts, arrived at Boston with a commission as Governor of Connecticut, under Lords Say and Seal, and Lord Brook, the proprietors, and with authority to erect a fort at the mouth of the river of that name. Accordingly, soon after his arrival, he despatched a bark of thirty tons, with twenty men, to take possession of Connecticut river, and to build a fort at its mouth. This was accordingly erected, and called Saybrook Fort, as the settlement or colony was called Saybrook colony, and which continued independent till 1644. A few days after their arrival, a Dutch vessel from New Netherlands appeared, to take possession of the river; but, as the English had already mounted two cannon, their landing was prevented.

8. The next June, 1636, the Reverend Messrs. Hooker and Stone, with a number of settlers from Dorchester and Watertown, removed to Connecticut. With no guide but a compass, they made their way one hundred miles, over mountains, through swamps and rivers. Their journey, which was on foot, lasted a fortnight, during which they lived upon the milk of their cows. They drove one hundred and sixty cattle. This party chiefly settled at Hartford. Mr. Hooker and Mr. Stone became the pastors of the church in that place, and were both eminent as men and ministers.

9. The year 1637 is remarkable, in the history of Connecticut, for a war with the Pequots, a tribe of Indians, whose principal settlement was on a hill, in the present town of Groton. Prior to this time, the Pequots had frequently annoyed the infant colony, and in several instances had killed some of its inhabitants. In March of this year, the commander of Saybrook Fort, with twelve men, was attacked by them, and three of his party killed. In April, another portion of this tribe assaulted the people of Wethersfield, as they were going to their fields to labor, and killed six men and three women. Two girls were taken captive by them, and twenty cows were killed. In this perilous state of the colony, a court was summoned at Hartford, May 11th. After mature deliberation, it was determined that war should be commenced against the Pequots. Ninety men, nearly half the fencible men of the colony, were ordered to be raised; forty-two from Hartford, thirty from Windsor, and eighteen from Wethersfield.

10. With these troops, together with seventy river and

the tide, the ice became so broken that she was enabled to get out. She ran, however, upon the bar, and the people were forced to unlade her to get her off. She was reladed, and in five days reached Boston.

Mohegan Indians, Captain Mason, to whom the command of the expedition was given, sailed down the river Connecticut to Saybrook. Here a plan of operations was formed, agreeably to which, on the 5th June, about the dawn of day, Captain Mason surprised Mystic, one of the principal forts of the enemy, in the present town of Stonington. On their near approach to the fort, a dog barked, and an Indian, who now discovering them, cried out, " O wanux! O wanux!" Englishmen! Englishmen!

11. The troops instantly pressed forward, and fired. The destruction of the enemy soon became terrible; but they rallied, at length, and made a manly resistance. After a severe and protracted conflict, Captain Mason and his troops being nearly exhausted, and victory still doubtful, he cried out to his men, " We must burn them!" At the same instant, seizing a firebrand, he applied it to a wigwam. The flames spread rapidly on every side; and as the sun rose upon the scene, it showed the work of destruction to be complete. Seventy wigwams were in ruins, and between five and six hundred Indians lay bleeding on the ground, or smouldering in the ashes.

12. But, though the victory was complete, the troops were now in great distress. Besides two killed, sixteen of their number were wounded. Their surgeon, medicines and provisions, were on board some vessels, on their way to Pequot harbor, now New London. While consulting what should be done in this emergency, how great was their joy to descry their vessels standing directly towards the harbor, under a prosperous wind! Soon after, a detachment of nearly two hundred men, from Massachusetts and Plymouth, arrived to assist Connecticut in prosecuting the war.

13. Sassacus, the great sachem of the Pequots, and his warriors, were so appalled at the destruction of their fort, that they fled towards Hudson's river. The troops pursued them as far as a great swamp in Fairfield, where another action took place, in which the Indians were entirely vanquished. This was followed by a treaty with the remaining Pequots, about two hundred in number, agreeably to which they were divided among the Narragansets and Mohegans. Thus terminated a conflict, which, for a time, was eminently distressing to the colonies. This event of peace was celebrated, throughout New England, by a day of thanksgiving and praise.

II. NEW HAVEN COLONY. — 1. During the expedition against the Pequots, the English became acquainted with Quinipiac, or NEW HAVEN; and the next year, 1638, the settlement of that town was commenced. This, and the adjoining towns, soon after settled, were distinguished by the name of the COLONY OF NEW HAVEN.

2. Among the founders of this colony, which was the fourth in New England, was Mr. John Davenport, for some time a distinguished minister in London. To avoid the indignation of the persecuting Archbishop Laud, he fled, in 1633, to Holland. Hearing, while in exile, of the prosperity of the New England settlements, he meditated a removal to America. On his return to England, Mr. Theophilus Eaton, an eminent merchant in London, with Mr. Hopkins, afterwards Governor of Connecticut, and several others, determined to accompany him. They arrived in Boston in June, 1637.

3. Though the most advantageous offers were made them by the government of Massachusetts, to choose any place within their jurisdiction, they preferred a place without the limits of the existing colonies. Accordingly, they fixed upon New Haven as the place of their future residence; and on the 28th of April they kept their first Sabbath in the place, under a large oak-tree, where Mr. Davenport preached to them.

4. The following year, January 24, 1639, the three towns on Connecticut river, Windsor, Hartford and Wethersfield, finding themselves without the limits of the Massachusetts patent, assembled by their freemen at Hartford, and formed themselves into a distinct commonwealth, and adopted a constitution. This constitution, which has been much admired, and which, for more than a century and a half, underwent little alteration, ordained that there should annually be two general assemblies,— one in April, the other in September. In April, the officers of government were to be elected by the freemen, and to consist of a governor, deputy-governor, and five or six assistants. The towns were to send deputies to the general assemblies. Under this constitution, the first governor was John Haynes, and Roger Ludlow the first deputy-governor.

5. The example of the colony of Connecticut, in forming a constitution, was followed, the next June, by the colony of New Haven. The planters assembled in a large barn. Among other rules, it was established that none but church-members should vote, or be elected to office; that all the freemen of the colony should annually assemble and elect its officers; and that the word of God should be the only rule for ordering the affairs of the commonwealth.

6. In October following, the government was organized, when Mr. Eaton was chosen governor. To this office he was annually elected, till his death, in 1657. No one of the New England

colonies was so much distinguished for good order and internal tranquillity as the colony of New Haven. Her principal men were eminent for their wisdom and integrity, and directed the affairs of the colony with so much prudence, that she was seldom disturbed by divisions within, or by aggressions from the Indians from without. Having been bred to mercantile employments, the first settlers belonging to this colony were inclined to engage in commercial pursuits; but in these they sustained several severe losses, and, among others, that of a new ship of one hundred and fifty tons, which was foundered at sea in 1647, and which was freighted with a valuable cargo, and manned with seamen and passengers from many of the best families in the colony. This loss discouraged, for a time, their commercial pursuits, and engaged their attention more particularly in the employments of agriculture.

7. The Dutch at New Netherlands (New York) early proved themselves troublesome neighbors to the Connecticut colonies. Besides claiming the soil as far east as Connecticut river, they plundered the property of settlers adjoining their territory, insti- gated the Indians to hostilities, supplied them with arms, and otherwise disturbed their peace. These were among the causes which induced these colonies to unite with the other New Eng- land colonies in the memorable confederacy of 1643, an account of which we have given in another place, p. 48.

8. In 1644, the little colony of Saybrook, which till now had been independent, was united with Connecticut; she having purchased the soil and jurisdiction of George Fenwick, one of the proprietors, for about two thousand pounds.

9. In 1650, Governor Stuyvesant concluded a treaty of amity and partition, at Hartford, between the Dutch and English. By this treaty the former relinquished all claim to the territory, except the land which they then occupied. A divisional line was also established, and pledges exchanged to abide in peace.

10. The harmony of the two people, however, was not of long duration. A war broke out between England and Holland, in 1652, taking advantage of which, and notwithstanding his pledge, Stuyvesant, it was understood, was plotting the overthrow of the English. Ninigret, the famous sachem of the Narragansets, and the wily and implacable enemy of the colonies, spent the winter of 1652–3 in New York with the Dutch governor. The colonies became alarmed.

11. A meeting of the commissioners was called, and a majority decided upon war against the Dutch; but, Massachusetts refusing to furnish her quota, hostilities were prevented. Con-

necticut and New Haven, indignant at the course pursued by Massachusetts, applied to Cromwell, then Protector of England, for aid ; and, in 1654, four or five ships were despatched to reduce the Dutch. Peace, however, was concluded between Holland and England before the·fleet arrived. During this year the Legislature of Connecticut sequestered the Dutch houses, lands, and property of all kinds, at Hartford, from which time the latter prosecuted no further claims in New England.

12. Charles II. was restored to the throne in 1660 ; after which, Connecticut, expressing her loyalty, applied for a charter. It was in the king's heart to deny her request; but, providentially, as it were, her agent, Governor Winthrop, when about to urge her petition, presented to the monarch a ring which had belonged to Charles I., and by him had been given to his grandfather. This act of courtesy so won the heart of the king, that he not only gave a liberal charter to the colony, but confirmed the very constitution which the people had adopted. The date of this charter was May 30th, 1662. Under this the people of Connecticut lived and flourished till the adoption of the present constitution, in 1818, a period of one hundred and fifty-six years.

13. This charter included New Haven, and most of the territory of Rhode Island. But the former utterly refused * to be united, and in that opposition persisted till 1665, when a reluctant consent was obtained, and the two were made one. In 1663, Charles conferred a charter on Rhode Island and Providence Plantations, which, however, as it included a portion of territory already granted to Connecticut, laid the foundation for a controversy between the two colonies, which lasted near sixty years.

14. From the calamities in which the war of Philip, in 1675, involved the New England colonies, Connecticut was comparatively exempted ; yet, she promptly responded to demands made upon her for aid in that dark period of New England history. Her captains were brave,— her soldiers unyielding. In the terrible swamp-fight (p. 54) with the Narragansets, December 29th, 1675, her troops suffered more than those of either Massachusetts or Plymouth, and were compelled to return home.

15. On the 30th of December, 1686, Sir Edmund Andros, "glittering in scarlet and lace," landed at Boston, as Governor of all New England. In the autumn of 1687, Andros, attended by some of his council, and a guard of sixty troops, went to Hart-

---

* As evidence of the opposition which existed, it may be stated that Rev. Mr. Pierson, the minister of Branford, and almost all his people, were so dissatisfied with the charter, that they removed to Newark, New Jersey.

7*

ford, and entering the House of Assembly, then in session, demanded the charter of Connecticut, and declared the colonial government to be dissolved. Reluctant to surrender the charter, the assembly protracted its debates till evening, when the charter was brought in and laid on the table. Upon a preconcerted signal, the lights were at once extinguished, and a Captain Wadsworth, seizing the charter, hastened away, under cover of night, and secreted it in the hollow of an oak. The candles, which had been extinguished, were soon relighted, without disorder; but the charter had disappeared. Sir Edmund, however, assumed the government, which was administered in his name, until the dethronement of James II., in 1789, and the elevation of the Prince of Orange, as William III.

16. On this event, Connecticut spurning the government which Andros had appointed, and "which," as Mr. Bancroft says, "they had always feared it was a sin to obey," the secreted charter was taken from its hiding-place, May 19th, "discolored, but not effaced;" the assembly was convened, and the records of the colony were once more opened.

17. Not long after, another encroachment upon the rights of the colony was attempted, but nobly resisted. In 1692, Colonel Fletcher was appointed Governor of New York, with a commission to take command of the militia of Connecticut. As this was a power which the charter had reserved to the colony, the demand of the colonel was denied. In the autumn of 1693, Fletcher repaired to Hartford, intending to enforce his commission. The Legislature was in session. The demand was repeated, and refused. The Hartford companies were then ordered to assemble, before which Fletcher directed his commission to be read.

18. But presently nothing could be heard but the noise of the drums, which Captain Wadsworth, the senior officer of the companies, commanded to be beaten. "Silence!" exclaimed Fletcher, and his aid read on. "Drum, drum, I say!" repeated Wadsworth. "Silence!" once more cried Fletcher. "Drum, drum!" said Wadsworth, at the same time turning to Fletcher, upon whom his eye-balls glared with fire and indignation, adding, "Sir, if I am interrupted again, I will make the sun shine through you in a moment!" This was enough. The crest of the haughty colonel instantly fell, and soon after he and suite departed for New York. On a representation of the affair to the king, he decided that the command of the militia, in time of peace, should be with the governor; but, in case of war, a determinate number should be placed under the orders of Fletcher.

From this time, the history of Connecticut blends with the general history of the colonies.

V. RHODE ISLAND.

1. RHODE ISLAND was so called from a fancied resemblance to the ancient Island of Rhodes, in the Mediterranean.

2. Roger Williams, having been banished from Massachusetts, as related page 47, visited Ousamequin, sachem of Pokanoket, whose residence was at Mount Hope, near the present town of Bristol (Rhode Island). From him he obtained a grant of land in the town of Seekonk, and here made preparations to erect a house; but, being informed by the Governor of Plymouth that he was within the limits of that colony, he resolved to move. Accordingly, about the middle of June, 1636, he embarked in a canoe, with five others, and proceeded down the Narraganset river to a spot near the mouth of the Moshassuck. This he selected as a place of settlement, which, in grateful remembrance of the mercies of God, he called PROVIDENCE.

3. This was within the jurisdiction of the Narraganset Indians. The sachems were Canonicus, and his nephew, Miantinomo. These he visited, and received a verbal cession of land, which, two years afterwards, was formally conveyed to him by deed.

4. In the course of two years, Mr. Williams was joined by a number of friends from Massachusetts, with whom he shared the land he had obtained, reserving to himself only two small fields, which, on his first arrival, he had planted with his own hands.

5. And here, in this community, was presented the first example the world ever saw of perfect religious toleration, — every one permitted to hold such religious opinions, and to worship God after that manner he pleased, without fear and molestation. The honor of this arrangement belongs to Mr. Williams.

6. He was careful, nevertheless, to provide for the maintenance of the civil peace. All the settlers were required to sign a covenant to submit themselves to all such orders or agreements as should be made for the public good; only, however, IN CIVIL THINGS. This simple instrument, combining the principles of a pure democracy and of unrestricted religious liberty, was the basis of the first government of Rhode Island.

7. The government of the town being thus placed in the hands of the inhabitants, the legislative, judicial, and executive functions were exercised for several years by the citizens, in town-meeting. Two deputies were appointed, from time to time, whose duty it was to preserve order, to settle disputes, to call

town-meetings, to preside in them, and to see that their resolutions were executed.

8. In 1638, William Coddington and eighteen others, being persecuted in Massachusetts for their religious tenets, followed Mr. Williams to Providence. By his advice, they purchased* of Canonicus and Miantinomo Aquetneck (now Rhode Island) and other islands in Narraganset Bay, and began the settlement of Portsmouth, on the northern part of the island. Soon after, another settlement was commenced, on the south-western side, by the name of Newport. Both towns were considered as belonging to the same colony, which received the name of the Rhode Island Plantation.

9. In imitation of the form of government† which existed for a time among the Jews, the inhabitants elected Mr. Coddington to be their magistrate, with the title of Judge; and a few months afterward, they elected three elders to assist him. This form of government continued till March 12, 1640, when they chose Mr. Coddington governor, Mr. Brenton deputy-governor, with a treasurer, secretary and three assistants. No other change as to the form of government took place till the charter was obtained.

10. At the time of the union of the New England colonies in their confederacy of 1643, the proposal of the Providence and Rhode Island Plantations to join it was refused, on the ground that they had no charter; whereupon, the following year, Roger Williams proceeded to England, and obtained from Parliament a free charter of incorporation, by which the two plantations were united under one government. In 1663 a royal charter was granted to them by Charles II. This charter constituted an assembly, consisting of a governor, deputy-governor, and ten assistants, with the representatives from the several towns, all to be chosen by the freemen. In 1686, Andros, being made Governor of New England, dissolved the charter of Rhode Island, and appointed a council to assist him in governing the colony. Three years after, William, Prince of Orange, ascended the throne of England, and Andros was seized and imprisoned; upon

---

* The consideration given was forty fathom of white beads. The natives then residing on Aquetneck received ten coats and twenty hoes to remove before the next winter.

† The following instrument was signed by Mr. Coddington and his associates: "We whose names are underwritten do swear solemnly, in the presence of Jehovah, to incorporate ourselves into a body politic, and, as he shall help us, will submit our persons, lives and estates, unto our Lord Jesus Christ, the King of kings and Lord of Hosts, and to all those most perfect and absolute laws of his, given us in his holy word of truth, to be guided and judged thereby."

which, the freemen assembled at Newport, and, having resumed their charter, restored all the officers whom Andros had displaced.

VI. NEW YORK.

1. NEW YORK (originally called New Netherlands) was so named in honor of the Duke of York and Albany, to whom the territory was granted on its conquest from its first settlers, the Dutch.

2. On the 13th of September, 1609, a vessel called the Crescent came to anchor within Sandy Hook,* about seventeen miles from the present city of New York. It was the first vessel ever within those waters.† Her commander, Henry Hudson, was an English captain in the service of the Dutch East India Company, and on a voyage for discovering a northern passage to India; but, failing in this, he proceeded along the shores of Newfoundland, and thence southward, as far as Chesapeake and Delaware Bays. Thence returning, he was exploring the coast, with the hope of finding a passage THROUGH the continent to the Pacific, when he came to anchor as above mentioned. Having here spent a week, he passed through the Narrows, ‡ and " went sounding his way above the Highlands," till at last the Crescent had sailed some miles above the city of Hudson, and a boat had advanced a little beyond Albany.§

3. Having employed ten days in this manner, and in frequent intercourse with the Indians resident on the banks of the river, Hudson descended on the 14th of October, and sailed for England, "leaving once more to its solitude" the stream which in after years was to bear his name.‖ In November, he reached England, whence he forwarded to his Dutch employers "a brilliant account" of his discoveries; but the English monarch,

---

* Sandy Hook is an island, five miles long, on the eastern coast of New Jersey, and seventeen miles south of New York.

† Except the ship under command of John Verrazani, nearly a century previous. (See page 16.)

‡ The entrance to New York harbor. It is about one mile wide, and nine miles below the city. It has Long Island on the east, and Staten Island on the west.

§ Bancroft.

‖ Hudson was destined never more to visit the noble river which bears his name. In a subsequent voyage to the northern seas, in search of a path to the Pacific, his provisions failed, and his crew became mutinous. In their discontent, they seized Hudson, his son, and seven others, and threw them into a shallop, and set them adrift. The carpenter requested to share his master's fate. Nothing more was ever heard of this noble man ; and it seems probable that, in some wild storm, he and his companions found a watery grave.

James I., forbade his return to Holland, lest the Dutch, by virtue of his having sailed under their patronage, should lay claim to the country.

4. The Dutch, as feared, did lay claim to it; and the following year the East India Company fitted out a ship with various merchandise, bound for the newly-discovered river, to trade with the natives. The enterprise was successful, and other voyagers succeeded. Several rude hovels were erected on the island, called by the natives MANHATTAN; and here, in 1613, Captain Argall, when on his return, with his fleet, from an expedition against the French at Port Royal, found several Dutch traders.

5. But he promptly demanded a surrender of the place to the English crown, as properly constituting a part of Virginia. The surrender was reluctantly made; but, on his retirement, the Dutch continued their residence, and during the following year, 1614, constructed a rude fort on the southern part of the island, which was the beginning of NEW AMSTERDAM, afterward New York. In 1615, a settlement was begun near the present site of Albany, to which the name of FORT ORANGE was given. The country received the name of NEW NETHERLANDS.

6. Notwithstanding the claim of Argall, in 1613, to the territory of New Netherlands, as belonging to the English crown, the Dutch held possession of it till 1664, the English meanwhile neglecting further pretensions to it.

7. In 1621, the Dutch republic of Holland granted to the Dutch West India Company — a corporation then recently formed — a territory whose boundaries were not accurately defined; but which the latter construed as including the lands between Delaware river on the south, and Connecticut river on the north.* The foregoing boundaries, therefore, included, besides New York, the present States of Delaware, New Jersey, a considerable part of Connecticut, and Long Island; and to these several territories the Dutch subsequently laid claim, and these claims, in after years, involved them in serious and very troublesome disputes.

8. Small settlements, in addition to those at New Amsterdam and Albany, were early begun, — in New Jersey, in Delaware, on the west end of Long Island; and a trading-house, or fort, at Hartford, on the Connecticut river, which Bancroft says the Dutch had discovered a little previous to the erection of the trading-house, by Holmes, at Windsor.

9. The first governor of New Netherlands, appointed by the West India Company, was Peter Minuits, who arrived at New

---

* Some writers make this grant much more extensive.

Amsterdam in 1625; and with him came a company who settled at Brooklyn, Long Island. Under him were several officers, or functionaries, as an OPPER-KOOPMAN, or chief merchant, an ONDER-KOOPMAN, a KOOPMAN, and an assistant.

10. During the administration of Governor Minuits, the foundation was laid for the manors of New York; some of which remain to this day, and which, on account of rents demanded from those who improve the leased lands belonging to those manors, are at this present time the cause of sad disturbances in that state. In 1629, the above West India Company, in order to give an impulse to colonization in their territory, allowed persons who should within four years undertake to plant colonies, consisting of certain specified numbers, to select lands miles in extent,* which should descend to their posterity forever. Of this privilege several availed themselves. Such were called lords of the manor, or patroons,— that is, patrons. By these patroons, Wouter Van Twiller was despatched as an agent, to inspect the condition of the country, and to purchase the lands of the Indians previous to settlement, — a condition specified by the West India Company. It was also recommended that a minister and schoolmaster should be provided.

11. In 1633, disturbances arising in the colony, Minuits was recalled, and Wouter Van Twiller, the former agent, succeeded him. A few months before his arrival, the Dutch, who had discovered Connecticut river, had erected a trading-house, or fort, where Hartford stands, as noticed in our history of Connecticut. (See page 71.) Under Van Twiller, the interests of the colony considerably advanced; although the controversy occasioned by the encroachments of the English on the eastern end of Long Island and western part of Connecticut began.

12. In 1638, Van Twiller gave place to Sir William Kieft, a man of enterprise and ability, but impetuous and imperious. From this time, the history of the Dutch is little less than a chronicle of struggles and contentions with English, Swedes, and Indians.

13. About the same time that Kieft began his administration, a colony of Swedes, under ex-Governor Minuits,† arrived, and formed a settlement on Christiana Creek, near Wilmington, in the present State of Delaware. To this movement Kieft remon-

---

* Sixteen miles, unless they lay on both sides of a river, in which case they might extend eight miles on each bank, and stretch into the country as far as the situation required.

† Minuits, on being removed from office among the Dutch, offered the benefit of his experience to the Swedes.

strated; but the Swedes gradually extended their settlements, at length occupying the territory from Cape Henlopen to the Falls of Delaware, opposite Trenton. This territory was called New Sweden.

14. But the Dutch were destined to troubles far more serious. For some time dishonest traders had overreached the Indians of Long Island and New Jersey, and they sought revenge. In 1640, they ruined the settlement on Staten Island. In consequence of this, the Dutch fitted out a roving expedition, south of the Hudson, against the Indians; but it proved fruitless. At length, a Hollander was killed by the son of a chief. The Indians expressed their grief, but refused to surrender the murderer. Kieft was inexorable, and united with a party of Mohawks, just then arrived from the north, in an expedition of blood and death against the neighboring tribes.

15. In the stillness of a dark winter's night (February, 1643) the united forces crossed the Hudson, and the work of destruction began. Nearly a hundred of the savages, men, women and children, perished in the carnage. No sooner was it discovered by the surrounding tribes that the Dutch united with the Mohawks in this midnight attack, but they were seized with the frenzy of revenge. And their revenge was seemingly full. Villages were laid waste; the farmer was murdered in his field, and his children swept into captivity. It was on this occasion that the celebrated Anne Hutchinson, who was banished from Massachusetts, perished, with her family. (See page 48.) So greatly were the Dutch pressed, and so imminent became their danger, that they were compelled to sue for peace. Fortunately, that peace-maker, Roger Williams, then in Manhattan, on his way to England, interfered, and a truce between the contending parties was effected.

16. But harmony and confidence were not restored. The Indians found themselves not satisfied. They thirsted for further revenge, and the war was renewed. The Dutch, however, had no competent leader. They therefore engaged the services of Captain John Underhill, one of the bravest men of his day, but who had been banished from Massachusetts for his religious eccentricities. With one hundred and twenty men, Underhill met and attacked and routed the Indians, on Long Island, and at Strickland Plains, and Horseneck.

17. At length, after the war had continued two years, both Dutch and Indians became weary of the contest. At this time, the Mohawks stepped in, and claimed sovereignty over all the tribes in the neighborhood of Manhattan; and through their

influence, these tribes now (1645) made peace with the Dutch. Such was the joy diffused through the colony, at this event, that a general thanksgiving was observed.

18. To Kieft, the author of much of the blood which had been shed, a long infamy attached. His conduct was reprobated both at home and abroad. Deprived of his office, he embarked, some time after, for Europe, in a richly-laden ship; but ere he reached his destination, his vessel was engulfed in the briny waters, and the guilty Kieft perished.

19. The fourth and last governor of New Netherlands was Peter Stuyvesant, who succeeded Kieft in 1647. He was a brave officer, who had served as viceroy in one of the West India Islands; a scholar of some learning, and, withal, an honest man. His policy toward the Indians was marked by kindness; in consequence of which, a more peaceable disposition prevailed among them.

20. But the controversy of the Dutch with other parties still continued. In 1650, Stuyvesant went to Hartford, to demand a full surrender of the lands on Connecticut river. After several days spent in controversy, it was agreed that Long Island should be divided: the Dutch claims to extend to Oyster Bay, thirty miles east of the city; and on the main land as far as Greenwich, near the present boundary between the States of New York and Connecticut. The lands on the Connecticut river the Dutch were compelled to relinquish, excepting those of which they then held actual possession; and these were some time after sequestered.

21. On the Delaware, the Swedes made strenuous efforts to maintain their power; but in 1655 Stuyvesant sailed, with six hundred men, for their reduction, and in this enterprise he was successful. The Swedish power was annihilated. Some of the colonists, with their governor, Rising, returned to Europe; others removed to Maryland and Virginia. The rest, taking the oath of allegiance to Holland, continued on their lands, under Dutch rule.

22. In 1663, a sudden irruption was made by the Indians upon the village of Esopus, now Kingston, ninety miles above New York, on the Hudson. Sixty-five of the inhabitants were either killed or made captives. But the Indians suffered greatly, in return, by means of a force sent up from New Amsterdam, which laid waste their fields, and killed many of their warriors. In December, a truce was proclaimed, and the captives taken by the Indians were released. In the following May a treaty of peace was concluded.

8

23. But the government of the Dutch over New Netherlands was now drawing to a close. The English had never ceased to regard the territory as belonging to them, by virtue of its discovery by Hudson, as an Englishman, but still more on the ground of the first discovery of the continent, by Cabot. In 1664, therefore, Charles II., King of England, disregarding all other claims, made a grant, to his brother James, then Duke of York, of the whole territory from Connecticut river to the shores of the Delaware, including, therefore, besides a part of Connecticut, New York, New Jersey and Delaware.

24. The duke was not slow to assert his claim. He fitted out a squadron, consisting of four frigates and three hundred men, under command of Sir Robert Nichols, who forthwith sailed for New Amsterdam. On entering the harbor, Stuyvesant addressed him a letter, desiring to know the reason of his approach. To this Nichols replied the next day, by a summons to surrender. Stuyvesant, determining on a defence, refused to surrender; but, at length, finding himself without the means of resistance, and that many of the people were desirous of passing under the jurisdiction of the English, he surrendered the government into the hands of Colonel Nichols, who promised to secure to the governor and inhabitants their liberties and estates, with all the privileges of English subjects.

25. The jurisdiction of the territory having thus passed into the hands of the English, New Amsterdam was changed to New York, and Fort Orange received the name of Albany. About the same time, the Swedes on Delaware Bay and river capitulated to Sir Robert Carr, an associate of Nichols; thus completing the subjection of New Netherlands to the British crown. As to New Jersey, the duke had already conveyed his interest to others, as will be noticed in its proper place. Long Island, notwithstanding that it had been long before granted to the Earl of Sterling, the duke purchased; and it became, and has since continued, a part of New York.

26. Colonel Nichols now assumed the government, in the name of the Duke of York, and continued in office for a little more than three years. His administration was marked by moderation, yet the people were allowed no representation, but he himself exercised both legislative and executive power. Contrary to all right, however, the titles to lands held by the Dutch they were compelled to renew at exorbitant charges, which went to the profit of the governor.

27. Nichols resigned to Governor Lovelace, in 1667, whose administration corresponded, in its essential features, to that of

his predecessor; but a remonstrance of the people to taxation without representation he ordered to be burnt by the common hangman.

28. In 1672, during the administration of Lovelace, war was declared by England against Holland; upon which, in the following year, a small Dutch squadron was sent against New York. Lovelace being absent at the time of its arrival, August 9th, the city was surrendered, by Captain Manning, without firing a gun, or otherwise attempting to defend the place. For this he was tried, condemned, and cashiered. Peace was restored in February of the following year; and early in November, New York, to which the old title of New Netherlands had been once more given, was again restored to the English, as were New Jersey and Delaware, which had submitted temporarily to Dutch rule.

29. To remove all controversy respecting his title to the lands granted him while they were in possession of the Dutch, the Duke of York took out a new patent, and appointed Sir Edmund Andros governor, who entered upon the duties of his appointment in October, 1674. But his administration was arbitrary and severe. He admitted the people to no share in legislation, but ruled them by laws to which they had never given their assent.

30. Connecticut also experienced the weight of his oppression and despotism. That part of her territory west of Connecticut river, although long before granted to the colony of Connecticut, was included in the grant to the Duke of York. By virtue of this grant, Andros now claimed jurisdiction over the territory, and in July, 1675, made an attempt, with an armed force, to take possession of Saybrook Fort. The Governor and Council of Connecticut, having notice of his design, despatched Captain Bull to defend the fort. On the arrival of Andros at the mouth of the river, after making a show of force, he invited Captain Bull to a conference. This was granted; but no sooner had he landed, than he attempted to read his commission and the duke's patent. This Captain Bull firmly and positively forbid; and Sir Edmund, finding the colony determined, at all events, not to submit to his government, relinquished his design, and sailed for Long Island.

31. 1682. — This year, an important change was effected in respect to the "Territories," as the present State of Delaware was then called, — namely, a transfer of them, by the Duke of York, to William Penn, from which time, till the American Revolution, they remained attached to Pennsylvania, or were under her jurisdiction.

32. On the return of Andros to England, Colonel Thomas Dongan, who, as well as the duke, was a Roman Catholic, was appointed governor, and arrived in the colony in 1683, with instructions to call an assembly, to consist of a council of ten, and of eighteen representatives, elected by the freeholders. On the accession of the Duke of York to the throne, under the title of James II., he refused to confirm to the people the privileges granted them while he was duke. No assembly was permitted to be convened, printing-presses were prohibited, and the more important provincial offices were conferred on Papists.

33. In 1688, New York and New Jersey were added to the jurisdiction of New England, and the arbitrary Andros was appointed captain-general of the whole. At the same time, Dongan was removed, and Francis Nicholson, who had been lieutenant-governor under him, was appointed governor under Andros.

34. Such was the position of affairs, when, in 1689, news of the flight of James II., and of the accession of William and Mary to the throne, arrived. Andros, as has been related, was seized in Boston, and imprisoned. This was joyful intelligence to the people of New York, who immediately rose in open rebellion to the existing government.

35. Immediately upon this, one Jacob Leisler and forty-nine others seized the fort at New York, and held it for William and Mary. Nicholson and his officers made what opposition they were able; but, being overpowered, he, the council and magistrates, of whom Colonel Bayard was at the head, retired to Albany. While affairs were in this posture, a letter from the Lords Carmathen and Halifax arrived, directed "To Francis Nicholson, Esq., or, in his absence, to such as, for the time being, take care for preserving the peace and administering the laws," &c. Accompanying this letter was another, of a subsequent date, vesting Nicholson with the chief command. As Nicholson had absconded, Leisler construed the letter as directed to himself, and from that time assumed the title and authority of lieutenant-governor. The southern part of New York generally submitted to him; but Albany refusing subjection, Milborn, his son-in-law, was sent to demand the surrender of the fort; but failing, he returned without accomplishing his object.

36. On the 29th of March, 1691, Colonel Sloughter arrived at New York, in the capacity of king's governor. Nicholson and Bayard, who had been imprisoned by Leisler, were released. The latter now surrendered the fort, and, with Milborn, his son-in-law, was apprehended, tried for high treason, and condemned.

Their immediate execution was urged by the people; but the governor, fearful of consequences, chose to defer it. To effect their purpose, an invitation was given him by the citizens to a sumptuous feast, and, while his reason was drowned in intoxication, a warrant for their execution was presented to him, and signed. Before he recovered his senses, the prisoners were no more. Measures so violent greatly agitated the existing parties; but, in the end, the revolution which had taken place restored the rights of Englishmen to the colony. Governor Sloughter convoked an assembly, which formed a constitution. This, among other provisions, secured trials by jury; freedom from taxation, except by the consent of the assembly; and toleration to all denominations of Christians, excepting Roman Catholics.

37. It may be added, in this place, that the civil history of New York, from this period to the French War, presents few events of special interest to the young. The governors who succeeded Sloughter, during the above interval, were Fletcher, 1692;* the Earl of Bellamont, 1698; Lord Cornbury, 1702; Hunter, 1710; Burnet, 1720; Montgomery, 1731; Crosby, 1732; Clark, 1736;† George Clinton, 1743. In general, these governors were strongly attached to the interests of the crown, and often apparently more solicitous to subserve their own selfish purposes than to advance the permanent welfare of the colony. Hence, collisions frequently arose between them and the colonial assemblies, which disturbed the general peace, and retarded the prosperity of the colony.

VII. NEW JERSEY.

1. NEW JERSEY was so named, in 1664, at the time of its conquest by the English from the Dutch, in honor of Sir George Carteret, who had been governor of the Isle of Jersey, in the

---

* P. 78, where an account is given of Fletcher's visit to Connecticut.

† During Governor Clark's administration, the supposed discovery of a negro plot occasioned great excitement in the city of New York; and in the progress of the commotion and alarm, many negroes were arrested and imprisoned. When the time of trial arrived, no lawyer could be found to defend them; consequently, their cause suffered, and, of the accused, fourteen were sentenced to be burned, eighteen to be hung, and seventy-one to be transported. Two whites were at the same time convicted, and suffered death, as concerned with them.

But when the alarm was over, and calm judgment came to take the place of heat and prejudice, many persons came to doubt the justice or propriety of the course pursued. That some of the negroes had been guilty of firing the city, there was too much evidence to doubt; but serious doubts were entertained as to any extensive plot or combination among them. At least, the evidence of it was too vague and uncertain to justify such summary proceedings.

8*

British Channel, and to whom, with Lord Berkley, the Duke of York conveyed the territory.

2. Until the above year, the territory continued under the jurisdiction of the Dutch, at New Netherlands. In March of that year, Charles II. conveyed the whole territory to his brother, the Duke of York, who, in July, sold the tract called New Jersey to Carteret and Berkley, about three months prior to its reduction by Colonel Nichols.*

3. The first settlement in New Jersey was probably about the year 1620, at Bergen, a village a few miles west of New York. Fort Nassau, five miles from Camden, was built in 1623, but was deserted not long after. A few other settlements were made in the territory, but the settlement of Elizabethtown, in 1664, by persons from Long Island, is generally fixed upon as the era of colonization.

4. The following year, 1665, Philip Carteret, appointed governor by the proprietors, arrived at Elizabethtown, which he made the seat of government. He brought with him a constitution for the colony, which ordained a free assembly, consisting of a governor, council, and representatives; the latter to be chosen by each town. The legislative power resided in the assembly; the executive, in the governor and council.

5. The liberal provisions of this constitution, in connection with the fertility of the soil and salubrity of the climate, soon induced emigrants, chiefly from New England and New York, to form settlements within the territory. And, for some years, these settlements enjoyed an unusual exemption from the hardships and sufferings to which most of the other early colonies were subjected.

6. On the occurrence of war between Holland and England, in 1672, New York was taken by the former, and again brought under Dutch government. New Jersey and Delaware also submitted. All, however, was returned to the English during the following year.

7. In 1674, Lord Berkley made a conveyance of his half to John Fenwick, in trust for Edward Billinge and his assigns. Billinge, being in debt, presented his interest in the province to his creditors, William Jones and others being appointed trustees to dispose of the lands.

8. In the year 1676, the province of New Jersey was divided into East and West Jersey. In this division Carteret took

---

* The grant to the duke was made March 22, and the sale to Carteret and Berkley July 4. The articles of capitulation were signed September 8. Surrender of the whole territory, October 11.

East Jersey, the government of which he retained; and the trustees of Billinge, West Jersey. The Duke of York, though he had conveyed away his powers of government, when he sold the province to Berkley and Carteret, in 1664, unjustly claimed West Jersey, as a dependency of New York. These claims of the duke, Sir Edmund Andros, his governor in America, attempted to assert, and actually extended his jurisdiction over the province. But, at length, through the discontent and remonstrances of the citizens, the subject was referred to commissioners, who decided against the Duke of York; upon which, in 1680, he relinquished his claims to the proprietors.

9. In 1682, Carteret, disgusted with the people, sold his right to East Jersey to William Penn and others, who immediately sold one half of it to the Earl of Perth and his associates. Robert Barclay, the celebrated author of "The Apology for the Quakers," was the next year made Governor of East Jersey. In 1688, both the Jerseys and New York were annexed to New England, in which connection they continued till the accession of William and Mary to the throne of England, in 1689. "A government under the proprietors of both the Jerseys had become extremely disagreeable to the inhabitants, who, from various causes, became so uneasy, that the proprietors surrendered the government of East and West Jersey to the crown in 1702."

10. The two provinces were now united into one, and annexed to New York, under the government of Lord Cornbury. The people were allowed a House of Representatives, consisting of twenty-four members; but the governor and council, consisting of twelve members, were appointed by the crown.

11. From this time to 1738 the province continued under the Governors of New York; but in that year an application made as early as 1728 for a separation from New York was granted, and Lewis Morris was appointed royal governor of the province.

VIII. DELAWARE.

1. DELAWARE was so called, in 1703, from Delaware Bay, on which it lies, and which received its name from Lord De la War, who died on board a vessel, while descending the bay.

2. The first settlement effected within the bounds of Delaware was by a number of Swedes and Finns, who arrived from Sweden in 1638, in charge of Peter Minuits, the first Governor of New York, who, after leaving the Dutch (page 83), undertook to lead a colony to America, according to a plan originally devised by the celebrated Gustavus Adolphus, King of Sweden.

On his arrival, Minuits, with his colony, settled on Christiana Creek, near Wilmington, and there built a fort. The territory extending from Cape Henlopen to the Falls of Trenton received the name of New Sweden. (Page 84.)

3. The Dutch, at New Netherlands, however, laid claim to the territory, and mutual contests subsisted for a long time between them and the Swedes. Governor Kieft, by way of keeping them in check, rebuilt Fort Nassau, about five miles south from Camden, on the eastern bank of the Delaware, which was first erected in 1623, but, being neglected, had fallen to decay. The Swedish governor, John Printz, on the other hand, by way of retaining his position and gaining the ascendency over the Dutch, established himself at Tinicum, a few miles below Philadelphia, where he not only erected an elegant mansion for himself, but built a fort for the defence of the colony. Another fort was erected at Lewistown.

4. In 1651 Governor Stuyvesant built Fort Casimir, on the present site of Newcastle, five miles from Christiana. To this Printz protested; and his successor, Governor Rising, under guise of making a friendly visit to the commandant, rose upon the garrison, and, with the aid of thirty men, took possession of the fort.

5. Indignant at such an act of treachery, Governor Stuyvesant reported the outrage to the home government, which ordered him forthwith to bring the usurpers to submission. Accordingly, in 1655, he sailed from New York with six hundred troops, and, in a brief space of time, reduced the forts at Newcastle and Christiana, and, subsequently, all others belonging to the Swedes. Upon this, a portion of the latter, taking the oath of allegiance to Holland, remained on their estates; a few removed to Maryland and Virginia; the rest, among whom was Governor Rising, were sent to Europe. (Page 85.)

6. From this time until 1664 the territory remained in possession of the Dutch; but on the conquest of New Netherlands by the English, an expedition was sent against it, under Sir Robert Carr, to whom it surrendered, and was united to New York. In 1682, however, the Duke of York sold the town of Newcastle, and the country twelve miles around it, to William Penn, and, some time after, the territory between Newcastle and Cape Henlopen. These tracts, then known by the name of "Territories," constitute the present State of Delaware. Until 1703, they were governed as a part of Pennsylvania; but, at that time, they had liberty from the proprietor to form a separate and distinct assembly; the Governor of Pennsylvania, however,

still exercising jurisdiction over them, until the era of the Revolution.

7. In that momentous struggle, Delaware "acted well her part." The Delaware regiment greatly signalized itself for its energy and efficiency in the continental army.

IX. MARYLAND.

1. MARYLAND was so called in honor of Henrietta Maria, Queen of Charles I., in his patent to Lord Baltimore, June 30, 1632.

2. Sir George Calvert, whose title was Lord Baltimore, was a Roman Catholic nobleman. Finding the laws against the Roman Catholics in England severe, he resolved to emigrate to Virginia, in the hope of enjoying a liberty of conscience which was not permitted in England during the reign of James the First. But he was disappointed. The Virginians proved nearly as intolerant as those he had left; and he felt compelled to seek another asylum.

3. This he proposed to find in a territory on both sides of Chesapeake Bay, then inhabited only by natives; and which having sufficiently explored, he returned to England, for the purpose of procuring a patent of it. From Charles I., who succeeded James I., he readily received a grant of the territory; but he died before the patent was completed.

4. It was, however, subsequently made out, in 1632, in favor of Cecil Calvert, son of Sir George, who inherited his father's title, and who now came into possession of the country from the Potomac to the fortieth degree of north latitude. This grant covered the land which had long before been granted to Virginia, as what was now granted to Lord Baltimore was in part subsequently given to William Penn. In consequence of these arbitrary acts of the crown, long and obstinate contentions arose between the descendants of Penn and Lord Baltimore.

5. In 1633, Lord Baltimore appointed his brother, Leonard Calvert, governor of the province, who, with about two hundred planters, mostly Roman Catholics, left England near the close of this year, and arriving, in 1634, at the mouth of the river Potomac, purchased of the Indians Yoamaco, a considerable village, where they formed a settlement by the name of Saint Mary's.

6. Several circumstances contributed to the rapid growth and prosperity of Maryland. Her people were exempted from hostilities from the Indians, having satisfied them in the purchase of their land; the soil was fertile, and the seasons mild. But, more than all, their charter conferred on them more ample privi-

leges than had been conferred on any other colony in America. It secured to emigrants equality in religious rights, and civil freedom ; and it granted the privilege of passing laws, without any reservation on the part of the crown to revoke them. Even taxes could not be imposed upon the inhabitants without their consent.

7. At first, when few in number, the freemen assembled in person, and enacted the necessary laws ; but, in 1639, it was found expedient to constitute a "house of assembly." This consisted of representatives chosen by the people, of others appointed by the proprietor, and of the governor and secretary, who sat together. In 1650, the legislative body was divided into an upper and lower house ; the members of the former being appointed by the proprietor, those of the latter by the people.

8. Few of the colonies escaped intestine troubles, nor did Maryland form an exception. In 1635, a rebellion broke out, chiefly caused by one William Clayborne. This man, under license of the king to trade with the Indians, had formed a settlement on the Island of Kent, nearly opposite Annapolis ; and when the grant was made to Lord Baltimore, he refused to submit to his authority, and attempted to maintain his possession by force of arms. His followers, however, were taken prisoners, and he himself fled. The Maryland assembly confiscated his estate, and declared him guilty of treason.

9. Early in 1645, Clayborne once more returned to Maryland, and, heading a party of insurgents, overthrew the government. Calvert, the governor, was compelled to take refuge in Virginia. The revolt, however, was suppressed the following year, and Calvert resumed his office.

10. In 1649, the assembly of the colony reiterated in solemn form the original and fundamental principles of religious toleration of Lord Baltimore, in an act that no one professing faith in Jesus Christ should be molested on account of such belief, or in the free exercise of his religion ; and, that any one who should reproach another on account of his religious creed should pay a fine to the person thus abused. Thus religious toleration was established by law ; and its benign influence was early perceived. Maryland presented an asylum for all who felt themselves religiously oppressed ; and hither came Puritans from the south, and churchmen from the north, and found a welcome reception, and the largest liberty.

11. In 1651, Parliament, having triumphed over King Charles I., appointed commissioners, of whom Clayborne, the enemy of

Maryland, was one, "to reduce and govern the colonies within the Bay of Chesapeake." This gave rise to a civil war in Maryland, between the Catholics, who adhered to the proprietor, and the Protestants, who sided with the Parliament. At first, Stone, the lieutenant of the proprietor, was removed; but was soon restored, on his consenting to acknowledge the authority of Parliament. But, in 1654, the commissioners again visited Maryland, and required him to surrender the government.

12. The next assembly which convened, which was entirely under the influence of the Protestant and now victorious party, ordained that no person professing the Catholic religion was entitled to the protection of the laws. Early the following year, 1655, civil war commenced. Having organized a military band, Stone assumed the government, intending to maintain his position by force; but the Protestant party resisted, and, at length, a battle ensued, in which the Catholics were defeated, with a loss of fifty killed. Stone was taken prisoner, and was executed, with four others, men of note in the province.*

13. At the Restoration, in 1660, Lord Baltimore was once more restored to his rights, and Philip Calvert appointed governor. A general pardon was extended to all political offenders, and the former mild and liberal principles of the proprietor once more held sway in Maryland.

14. Towards the close of the year 1675, Cecil, Lord Baltimore, the founder of Maryland, died, and was succeeded by his son Charles, both in his honors and estates. For more than forty years, Cecil Calvert, in presiding over the province as its proprietor, had displayed the highest regard for the rights and happiness of others. He deserved well of posterity, and his name will be long honored and revered by the people of Maryland. In integrity, benevolence and practical wisdom, the son strongly resembled the father.

15. On the accession of William and Mary to the throne of England, 1689, the tranquillity of Maryland was again interrupted. A rumor was fabricated, and industriously circulated, that the Catholics had combined with the Indians to cut off the Protestants of the colony. This roused the latter in their own defence, and to the assertion of the rights of the king and queen. An association was formed and armed for these purposes, which the Catholics attempting to subdue by force, failed, and were compelled to relinquish the government into the hands of the former.

---

* Some authorities say that Stone and his associates were only long imprisoned.

16. And in their hands it continued till 1691, when the king, in the exercise of sovereign power, wrested the province from Lord Baltimore, and erected it into a royal government. And in the further exercise of sovereignty, the following year, he sent Sir Lionel Copley as royal governor, to take charge of the province. Under him religious toleration was disallowed, and the Church of England's forms of worship were established and supported by law.

17. But in 1716 this great wrong was rectified. The heir of Lord Baltimore, although an infant, was reëstablished in his rights ; the proprietary form of government was restored ; and thus matters continued till the war of the Revolution, when the people formed a constitution for themselves, and no longer recognized the claims of the quondam proprietor to either jurisdiction or property.

X. PENNSYLVANIA.

1. PENNSYLVANIA was so called in 1681, after William Penn, the founder of Philadelphia.

2. This William Penn was the son of Sir William Penn, an admiral in the British navy, who rendered important services to the nation, on account of which, and by way of recompense, Charles II. granted to the son the territory of Pennsylvania, so naming it after Penn himself.

3. This patent encroached on the territory of Lord Baltimore in Maryland one whole degree, or sixty-nine miles and a half; and on the north, nearly three hundred miles, across the whole territory conveyed to Connecticut in 1631,* and confirmed by the royal charter of 1662. Hence arose contentions between the colonies of Pennsylvania and Connecticut, about boundaries, that were not settled till a century after. Within a short time from the date of the grant by King Charles to Penn, two other conveyances were made to him, by the Duke of York. One was a bill of sale of Newcastle, and a territory of twelve miles around it. The other was a bill granting a tract south of the former, as far as Cape Henlopen. These two deeds embraced the whole State of Delaware, known at that time by the name of the "Territories."

4. Penn himself was a Quaker, or member of the Society of Friends ; a man of large and liberal views, and of great benevolence and integrity of purpose. And now, having obtained possession of a valuable territory, he was desirous of founding a

---

* See page 71.

colony where civil and religious liberty might be enjoyed, and the people of which might dwell together in the bonds of peace.

5. To the Swedish settlements already existing in the territory he gave the assurance that they should in no wise be molested in their religion or laws. He desired their welfare, and they might seek it in their own way.

6. As it was Penn's object and interest to forward the settlement of his territory, he issued an invitation to purchasers, offering them land on the liberal condition of one thousand acres for twenty pounds, or at an annual rent of one penny per acre. Many persons, chiefly Quakers, were induced to purchase; and, in the fall of the same year, three ships, with settlers, sailed for Pennsylvania. In one of these ships came over the agent and deputy-governor of the proprietor, William Markham, to superintend the affairs of the colony, and to establish a good understanding with the Indians. At the same time, Penn addressed a letter to the latter, residing on the territory, assuring them of his pacific disposition, and his determination, should difficulties arise between them and the emigrants, to have them settled on principles of equity.

7. The next year, Penn published a form of government, by which the supreme power was lodged in a general assembly, to consist of a governor, council, and house of delegates : the council and house to be chosen by the freemen; the proprietor and governor to preside, and to have a treble voice in the council, which was to consist of seventy-two members. It was also agreed that every person of good moral character, professing his faith in Christ, should be a freeman, and capable of holding any office; and that none who believed in one God should be molested in his religion, or be compelled to attend or maintain religious worship.

8. In November,* Penn, with two thousand planters, mostly Quakers, arrived at Newcastle, which was a part of the "Territories." Upon this tract he found settled, as already noticed, about three thousand Dutch, Swedes and Finns. He proceeded to Chester, where, in December, he convoked an assembly ; but, so few delegates appearing, he ordered that, instead of seventy-two, three members only should constitute the council, and nine the house of assembly. This assembly annexed the Territories to

---

* That was a beautifully simple letter in which Penn took leave of his family. To his wife he said, " Live low and sparingly till my debts are paid." Yet for his children, he adds : " Let their learning be liberal ; spare no cost, for by such parsimony all is lost that is saved. Let my children be husbandmen and housewives."

9

the province, adopted a frame of government, and enacted a body of laws.

9. Markham having, according to instructions, secured the assent of the neighboring Indians to the form of a treaty, Penn, some weeks after his arrival, met a numerous delegation of these tribes, to ratify the same. This was one of the most interesting scenes in our colonial history. The spot selected for the transaction was beneath a large elm-tree, at Shaxamaxon, since Kensington, the north-east suburb of Philadelphia, on the Delaware. On his arrival at the spot, attended by a few friends, the simple children of the forest gathered around him, and he thus addressed them : "We meet on the broad pathway of good faith and good will ; no advantage shall be taken on either side, but all shall be openness and love. I will not call you children ; for parents sometimes chide their children too severely : nor brothers only ; — brothers differ. The friendship between me and you, I will not compare to a chain ; for the rains may rust, or the falling tree might break. We are the same as if one man's body were to be divided into two parts, — we are all one flesh and blood."

10. Touched by this warm-hearted and generous address, the Indians accepted the presents which followed, and, in return, gave the belt of wampum. And to this they added, "We will live in love with William Penn and his children, as long as the moon and the sun shall endure." "And now," says Mr. Bancroft, "the simple sons of the forest, returning to their wigwams, kept the history of the covenant by strings of wampum ; and long afterwards, in the cabin, would count over the shells on a clean piece of bark, and recall to the memory, and repeat to their children or to strangers, the words of William Penn." And it is remarkable that all this was accomplished so kindly, so gently, when the more northern colonies of New England had just been embroiled in a long and disastrous war with Indian tribes. But Penn was eminently bent on peace, and he had the advantage of the sad experience of others. The result of and the reward of his kindness and integrity was, "that not a drop of Quaker blood was ever shed by an Indian."

11. A few months after Penn's arrival, he commenced the city of Philadelphia, or "Brotherly Love," — a name in keeping with all his other transactions. The land being a part of the tract owned by the Swedes, who had already erected a church there, he purchased it of them. The growth of the city was rapid, numbering, at the close of a year, nearly a hundred houses

and cottages, and at the expiration of the second year, two thousand five hundred inhabitants.

12. Pennsylvania had a more rapid and prosperous settlement than any of the other colonies. This was doubtless owing, in part, to its healthful climate and fruitful soil; partly to the fact, that the great obstacles of settlement had been overcome by the other colonies; and, partly, to the religious tolerance, mildness and equity, which characterized its laws and their administration.

13. In 1683, Penn convened a second assembly, which was held in Philadelphia; and, at the request of the freemen and delegates, granted them a second charter, by which eighteen persons were to form a council, and thirty-six the assembly. At this time it was ordained, " that, to prevent law-suits, three arbitrators, to be called peace-makers, should be chosen by the county courts, to hear and determine small differences between man and man; that children should be taught some useful trade; that factors wronging their employers should make satisfaction, and one-third over; that all causes of rudeness, cruelty and irreligion, should be repressed; and that no man should be molested for his religious opinions." To these wholesome regulations Pennsylvania was indebted for her great prosperity and rapid settlement.

14. In 1684, Penn returned to England, leaving the administration of the government in the care of five commissioners. Soon after, James II. abdicated the throne. For this monarch Penn felt a sincere regard, and continued, even after his expulsion from the throne, to administer the colonial government in his name. This exciting the displeasure of William, successor of James, his friends caused Penn to be imprisoned several times; and the government of the colony was taken from him, and given to Colonel Fletcher, Governor of New York. But, some time after, the charges of disloyalty to William having been proved to be unfounded, he was permitted to resume the exercise of his rights, whereupon he appointed William Markham to be his deputy-governor.

15. In 1699, Penn made a second visit to Pennsylvania. Finding discontents had crept in, in relation to the government, he humanely prepared a new charter, on still more liberal principles. This was offered November 7th, 1701, and accepted, on the same day, by the people of Pennsylvania; but the " Territories," now Delaware, declining, they were allowed a distinct assembly, under the same governor. The assembly was first convened in 1703.

16. Having thus settled affairs, Penn again returned to Eng-

land, leaving the executive authority to be exercised by a deputy-governor. Discontentment, however, again appeared, and at times the deputy-governors became quite obnoxious to the people. Still, the colony prospered; — they lived in great harmony with the Indians, and increased in numbers and wealth. At length, about the commencement of the Revolutionary War, the people formed a new constitution, by which the proprietor was excluded from all participation in the government; and, by way of discharging all quit-rents due from the inhabitants, he was allowed about five hundred and eighty thousand dollars.*

XI. CAROLINAS.

1. CAROLINA (North and South) was so called by the French, in 1563 or 1564, in honor of Charles IX., King of France (Carolus, in Latin, meaning Charles), under whose patronage the coast was discovered.

2. The territory thus named afterwards included the lands between the 30th and 36th degrees of north latitude, and extended from the Atlantic Ocean to the South Sea, or Pacific Ocean. In 1663, this defined territory† was conveyed, by Charles II., King of England, who claimed it by virtue of Cabot's discovery, to Lord Clarendon, Sir William Berkley, Sir George Carteret, and four others,‡ with ample powers to settle and govern it. Bancroft says they begged the country, under pretence of "a pious zeal for the propagation of the Gospel;" and their sole object was the increase of their own wealth and dignity.

3. Between 1640 and 1650, before the above grant to Clarendon and others, a settlement had been begun by planters from Virginia, near the mouth of the Chowan, on the northern shore of Albemarle Sound. This settlement was placed, by Governor Berkley, of Virginia, under the superintendence of William Drummond. The little plantation received the name of the ALBEMARLE COUNTY COLONY, in honor of the Duke of Albemarle, one of the proprietors.

4. In 1665, a second permanent settlement was effected, near the mouth of the Clarendon or Cape Fear river, by emigrants from the Island of Barbadoes. This was called the CLARENDON COUNTY COLONY. It had a similar constitution with the more

---

* William Penn died in England, in 1718. He left his interest in Pennsylvania and Delaware to his surviving sons, John, Thomas and Richard, who continued to hold the same, and to administer the government, by agents or deputies, till the American Revolution.
† The territory included, also, the present State of Georgia.
‡ The four others were the Duke of Albemarle, Lord Craven, Lord Ashley, and Sir John Colleton.

northern colony. Sir John Yeamans was the first governor. Both of the above settlements, or colonies, were within the present limits of NORTH CAROLINA.

5. In 1670, a third colony was founded, called the CARTERET COUNTY COLONY, after Sir George Carteret. The colonists were accompanied by Governor Sayle, who had previously explored the coast. The ships which bore the emigrants first entered the harbor of Port Royal, near Beaufort; but, not being pleased with the place, they not long after sailed into Ashley river, and laid the foundations of Old Charleston. In 1680, this settlement was abandoned for Oyster Point, on which was commenced the present city of Charleston. This was the commencement of SOUTH CAROLINA.

6. During the administration of Governor Sayle, a form of government was prepared for these colonies, at the request of the celebrated Lord Shaftesbury, acting in behalf of the proprietors, by the still more celebrated John Locke. It proposed a court, to consist of the proprietors, one of whom was to be elected president for life; also, an hereditary nobility, and a parliament, the latter to consist of the two former, and representatives from each district. All were to meet in one apartment, and to have an equal voice. This ill-contrived and absurd plan of government was attempted to be applied in practice, but it was found to be impracticable. In Albemarle county, it caused an insurrection. It was therefore abandoned, and the former proprietary government restored.

7. In the year 1671, Governor Sayle dying, Sir John Yeamans, Governor of Clarendon, was appointed to succeed him. In consequence of this, and the little prosperity of the colony, chiefly arising from the barrenness of its soil, the inhabitants of this latter settlement, within a few years, removed to that of Charleston, and the three governments, consequently, were reduced to two. Being widely separated, the distinctive names of North and South Carolina began to be used in respect to them.

I. NORTH CAROLINA COLONY. — 1. The progress of the Albemarle or North Carolina Colony was long retarded by domestic dissensions. An insurrectionary state of the inhabitants arose out of an attempt to enforce Mr. Locke's plan of government; — taxes were enormous, and commercial restrictions embarrassing. In 1677, in attempts by the officers to enforce the revenue laws against a smuggler from New England, the people rose upon the government, and imprisoned the president of the colony and six members of the council, and, having done this, assumed the prerogative of governing themselves.

9*

2. In 1683, the proprietors sent over Seth Sothel, one of their number, hoping through him to restore quiet and contentment. But he only increased existing disorders. For six years, the inhabitants endured his injustice and oppression, and then seized him, and, after trying him, banished him from the colony. What must that officer of a government be, of whom an historian remarks, " The dark shades of his character were not relieved by a single ray of virtue " ?

3. Philip Ludwell, of Virginia, succeeded the infamous and exacting Sothel, and redressed the wrongs he had done. Under him, and his successor, Sir John Archdale, in 1695, a Quaker, and an excellent man, order was restored to the colony. Emigrants began to flock in, and various other portions of the territory, in the course of a few years, were settled. Liberal assignments of land were made them by the proprietors, and here many, who had fled from religious persecutions, or the devastations of war, in foreign lands, found a peaceful and grateful asylum. This was particularly true of a company of French Protestants, who arrived in 1707, and settled on the river Trent, a branch of the Neuse, and of a large number of Germans, who fled from persecution in 1710, and planted themselves in the same part of the province. These were a great accession to the strength and numbers of the colony, which, though of sixty years' standing, remained exceedingly small.

4. But the inhabitants of this colony were destined soon to experience a sad, and, to many, a fatal calamity. The Indian tribes on the sea-coast, once numerous and powerful, were fast dwindling before the enterprise of the colonists. To the more inland tribes, especially the Tuscaroras and the Corees, this was an indication not to be mistaken that the days of their prosperity were fast numbering. Grieved and exasperated at the prospect before them, they now combined with other tribes to utterly exterminate the new settlers. This purpose they attempted to carry into effect; and so successful were they, that in one night (October 2, 1711) they massacred one hundred and thirty persons belonging to the settlements along the Roanoke river and Pamlico Sound.

5. A few, escaping, hastened to South Carolina, for assistance. Governor Craven immediately despatched to their aid nearly a thousand men, under Colonel Barnwell. On his arrival, he defeated the enemy in several actions; and, at length, pursued them to their fortified town, which capitulated, and peace was concluded.

6. But it proved of short duration. The Indians renewed

their hostilities, and the assistance of the southern colony was again involved. In response, Colonel Moore set forth for the hostile territory, with a competent force, — forty white men, and eight hundred friendly Indians. They reduced the fort of the Tuscaroras, and with it took eight hundred prisoners. Broken and disheartened by this defeat, the tribe, in 1713, migrated north, and became the sixth nation of the great Iroquois Confederacy, — sometimes called the FIVE, and, after this event, the SIX Nations. In 1715, a treaty was concluded with the Corees.

7. In 1719, the proprietary government, which had continued from the settlement of the colony till now, was terminated, in consequence of difficulties between the inhabitants and the proprietors. Their charter was vacated by the crown, and royal government substituted. Ten years after, 1729, the proprietors surrendered their right to the government, and interest in the soil, to the king; upon which the province was divided into North and South Carolina, and their governors and councils were appointed by the crown.

II. SOUTH CAROLINA COLONY. — 1. The foundation of the Carteret or Southern Colony, in Carolina, was laid by Governor Sayle, and emigrants accompanying him, in the settlement of Old Charleston, in 1670. (See page 101.) Sayle falling a victim to some disease of the climate early the following year, Sir John Yeamans, then Governor of Clarendon Colony, was appointed his successor. On being transferred, he drew after him a considerable portion of the latter colony.

2. The progress of the southern colony was, from the commencement, more rapid than that of the northern. Several circumstances contributed to this. The soil was more feasible and fertile. Many Dutch families from New York, dissatisfied with the transfer of their home to the English, in 1664, were ready to find a home here; and, in 1671, ship-loads of them were transported by the proprietors to Carolina, free of expense, and liberal grants of land were made them. They chiefly concentrated at a place called Jamestown, west of the Ashley river, where they were, from time to time, enforced by emigrants from Holland. The profanity and licentiousness of the court of Charles II. also drove not a few Puritan refugees across the Atlantic, a considerable number of whom settled in Carolina.

3. In 1680, the people of Old Charleston, attracted by the more pleasant location of a point of land between the rivers Ashley and Cooper, called "Oyster Point," removed thither, and there laid the foundation of the present city of Charleston, which, from that time, has had the honor of being the capital of the colony and state.

4. They were, however, immediately afterward, annoyed, and the safety of the place even endangered, by the hostile and predatory conduct of the Westoes, a powerful tribe of Indians in the neighborhood. Retaliatory measures became necessary; numbers of the Indians were shot; and others, who were captured, were sent into slavery, in the West Indies. Fortunately, peace was made with them the following year.

5. In 1686, soon after the revocation of the edict of Nantes, by Louis XIV., a large number of Huguenots, or French Protestants, came over, and settled in the colony. To the English settlers, who were Episcopal, these refugees, being of so different a faith, were by no means welcome; and they were quite disposed to drive them from the colony, notwithstanding the latter had been introduced by the proprietors under an assurance of enjoying the rights of citizenship.

6. About this time, James Colleton, a brother of Sir John, was appointed governor, under an expectation that he would be able to reduce the people to a proper submission to proprietary authority, to which they had for a long time seemed averse. But his arbitrary conduct, in excluding refractory members from the colonial assembly, and in attempting to collect rents claimed by the proprietors as due, drove the people to open resistance. The public records were seized, the colonial secretary imprisoned, the governor defied, and, at length, banished from the colony.

7. In 1690, that notable person, Seth Sothel, who, for his corrupt conduct, had been driven from North Carolina in disgrace (page 102), appeared in the province, and was allowed by the people to assume the government. But, impelled by his avarice to acts of meanness and oppression, as formerly, at the expiration of two years he was banished from the colony. Next, Philip Ludwell was appointed by the proprietors as the person to teach the South Carolinians submission and good manners; but they were too turbulent, as he thought, and he became glad, at no distant day, to retire.

8. In 1695, John Archdale, the Quaker, was appointed governor, with power to redress all grievances. The people had long complained against their rulers, and had quarrelled among themselves. Archdale, by a wise and conciliatory course, restored harmony, and removed the causes of civil dissatisfaction. He introduced a more republican form of government, thus restoring to the people rights and privileges which had been monopolized by the proprietors, or their agents.

9. One difficulty, however, still remained, and which he was

compelled to leave to the "softening influence of time" to remove. This was the jealousy and antipathy, already alluded to, of the English Episcopalians against the French Protestants. The latter, it was contended, could not legally hold real estate in the colony; that the French ministers could not lawfully solemnize marriages; and the children of the refugees must be debarred inheriting the property of their fathers.

10. But these animosities and differences found an end. When, at length, the inoffensive and even exemplary lives of these exiles were observed by the English, and also their uniform and liberal efforts to sustain and advance the interests of the colony, prejudice and opposition yielded; and, in a few years, the colonial assembly gladly extended to them all the rights of citizens and freemen.*

11. Soon after the declaration of war, in 1702, by England against France and Spain, called "Queen Anne's War," Governor Moore proposed to the assembly of the colony an expedition against the Spanish settlement of St. Augustine, in Florida. To this the more considerate of the assembly were opposed; but, the enterprise being approved by a majority, nearly ten thousand dollars were appropriated for the object, and twelve hundred troops raised, one-half of whom were Indians. With the forces above named, and some merchant vessels, impressed as transports, Governor Moore sailed for St. Augustine. The design was for Colonel Daniel, an enterprising officer, to proceed by the inland passage, and to attack the town by land, with a party of militia and Indians; while Moore was to proceed by sea, and take possession of the harbor. Daniel advanced against the town, entered and plundered it, before the governor's arrival. The Spaniards, however, retired to the castle, with their principal riches, and with provisions for four months.

12. The governor, on his arrival, could effect nothing, for want of artillery. In this emergency, Daniel was despatched to Jamaica, for cannon, mortars, &c. During his absence, two large Spanish ships appearing off the harbor, Governor Moore hastily raised the siege, abandoned his shipping, and made a precipitate retreat into Carolina. Colonel Daniel, having no intelligence that the siege had been raised, on his return, stood in for the harbor, and narrowly escaped the ships of the enemy. In

---

* It is a complimentary remark, due to South Carolina, which Mr. Bancroft makes, namely : "Religious bigotry never disgraced South Carolina. If full hospitality was, for a season, withheld, the delay grew out of a controversy in which all Carolina had a common interest ; and the privileges of citizen were conceded, so soon as it could be done, by Carolinians themselves."

consequence of this rash and unfortunate enterprise, the colony was loaded with a debt of nearly thirty thousand dollars, which gave rise to the first paper currency in Carolina, and was the means of filling the colony with dissension and tumult.

13. The failure of this expedition was soon after, in a measure, compensated by a successful war with the Apalachian Indians, who, in consequence of their connection with the Spaniards, became insolent and hostile. Governor Moore, with a body of white men and Indian allies, marched into the heart of their country, and compelled them to submit to the English. All the towns of the tribes between the rivers Altamaha and Savannah were burnt, and between six hundred and eight hundred Indians were made prisoners.

14. In 1704, Sir Nathaniel Johnson succeeded Governor Moore; and now, under his influence, a long-cherished object of the proprietors was accomplished. This was the establishment of the Church of England forms of worship as the religion of the province, and the exclusion of dissenters from all participation in the government. But, in 1706, these laws of exclusion or disfranchisement were repealed, by direction of the English Parliament, which decided that they were inconsistent with the laws of England. But the acts establishing the Church of England religion continued in force, until they were abrogated by the Revolution.

15. In 1706, while yet Queen Anne's War continued, a French and Spanish squadron, consisting of a French frigate and four armed sloops, appeared before Charleston, with a design of annexing Carolina to Florida; but, by the prompt and energetic efforts of the governor, seconded by Colonel Rhett and the inhabitants, this issue was averted.*

---

* When, at length, the enemy had passed the bar, he sent a summons to the governor to surrender. Four hours were allowed him to return his answer. But the governor informed the messenger that he did not wish one minute. On the reception of this answer, the enemy seemed to hesitate, and attempted nothing that day.

The day succeeding, a party of the enemy, landing on James Island, burnt a village by the river's side. Another party landed at Wando Neck. The next day both these parties were dislodged; the latter party being surprised, and nearly all killed or taken prisoners.

This success so animated the Carolinians, that it was determined to attack the enemy by sea. This was attempted with a force of six vessels, under command of Rhett; but, on his appearance, the enemy weighed anchor, and precipitately fled.

Some days succeeding, Monsieur Arbuset appeared on the coast with a ship of force, and landed a number of men at Sewee Bay. Rhett sailed out against him; and, at the same time, Captain Fenwick crossed the river, marching to attack the enemy by land. After a brisk engagement, Fen-

16. In 1715, the province came near the verge of ruin, by reason of a combination of the Yamassees and other Indian tribes—stretching from Cape Fear to Florida—against them. The 15th of April, 1715, was fixed upon as the day of their general destruction. Owing, however, to the wisdom, despatch and firmness of Governor Craven, and the blessing of Providence, the calamity was, in a measure, averted, and the colonies saved, though at the expense, during the war, of near four hundred of the inhabitants. The Yamassees were expelled the province, and took refuge among the Spaniards, in Florida.

17. 1719. — The people of Carolina, having been long disgusted with the management of the proprietors, were resolved, at all hazards, to execute their own laws, and defend the rights of the province. A subscription to this effect was drawn up, and generally signed. On the meeting of the assembly, a committee was sent, with this subscription, to the governor, Robert Johnson, requesting him to accept the government of the province, under the king, instead of the proprietors. Upon his refusal, the assembly chose Colonel James Moore governor, under the crown; and on the 21st of December, 1719, the convention and militia marched to Charleston fort, and proclaimed Moore governor, in his majesty's name.

18. The Carolinians, having thus assumed the government, in behalf of the king, referred their complaints to the royal ear. On a hearing of the case, the privy council adjudged that the proprietors had forfeited their charter. From this time, therefore, the colony was taken under the royal protection, under which it continued till the American Revolution. This change was followed, in 1729, by another, nearly as important. This was an agreement, between the proprietors and the crown, that the former should surrender to the crown their right and interest, both to the government and soil, for the sum of seventeen thousand five hundred pounds sterling. This agreement being carried into effect, the province was divided into North and South Carolina, each province having a distinct governor, under the crown of England.

XII. GEORGIA.

1. GEORGIA received its name, in 1732, in honor of George II., King of England.

2. The territory of Georgia was originally included in the Carolina patent granted to Lord Clarendon and his associates,

wick took the enemy on land prisoners, and Rhett succeeded in capturing the ship.

but it was a region wild and unoccupied, except by savage tribes, at the time the proprietors surrendered their interest in it to the crown, in 1729 (page 107). It was competent, therefore, for the king to re-grant it to whom he pleased. But, at the same time, Spain laid claim to it, as constituting a part of Florida.

3. In 1732, several gentlemen in England, at the head of whom was James Oglethorpe, a member of the British Parliament, and greatly distinguished for his philanthropic views, concerted a plan for planting a colony in America, for the indigent and persecuted in Britain ; where the one class might find relief from poverty, and the other from persecution.

4. George II., in token of his approbation of the enterprise, granted to a corporation, "in trust for the poor," the said territory of Georgia, which was to be apportioned gratuitously among the settlers. Liberal donations were made by the charitable, to defray the expenses of the first company of settlers to the new province.

5. In November of the same year, these, consisting of one hundred and sixteen in number, embarked from England, under the kind and enterprising Oglethorpe ; and, after touching at Charleston, they landed, in February, on the banks of the Savannah. For several days the people were employed in erecting a fortification, and in felling the woods, while the general marked out the town. This was begun on YAMACRAW BLUFF, to which was given the name Savannah, after the Indian name of the river. The fort being completed, the guns mounted, and the colony put in a state of safety, the next object of Oglethorpe's attention was to treat with the Indians for a share of their possessions.

6. In pursuance of this object, he collected fifty chiefs, before whom he spread his wants and wishes, in regard to the purchase of territory. He then distributed presents ; upon which, Tomochichi, in the name of the Creeks, made a speech to him. Among other things, he said, "Here is a little present ;" and then gave him a buffalo's skin, painted on the inside with the head and feathers of an eagle, and desired him to accept it, "because the eagle signified SPEED, and the buffalo, STRENGTH. The English," he proceeded to say, "are swift as a bird, and as strong as a beast ; since, like the first, they fly over the vast seas, and, like the second, nothing can withstand them. The feathers of the eagle are SOFT, and signify LOVE ; the buffalo's skin is WARM, and signifies PROTECTION : he hoped, therefore, that they would love and protect their families."

7. In treating with these and other Indians, Oglethorpe was

greatly assisted by an Indian woman whom he found at Savannah, by the name of Mary Musgrove. She had resided among the English, in another part of the country, and was well acquainted with their language. She was of great use, therefore, to Oglethorpe, as an interpreter, for which service he gave her a hundred pounds a year.*

---

* Among those who came over with Oglethorpe was a man by the name of Thomas Bosomworth, who was the chaplain of the colony. Soon after his arrival at Savannah, he married the above-mentioned Mary Musgrove. Unhappily, Bosomworth was at heart a bad man. He was distinguished for his pride, and love of riches and influence. He was also artful and intriguing ; yet, on account of his profession, he was, for a time, much respected by the Indians.

At one of the great councils of the Indians, Bosomworth induced the chiefs to crown Malatche, one of the greatest among them, Empress of all the Creeks. After this, he persuaded his wife to call herself the eldest sister of Malatche; and she told the Indians that one of her grandfathers had been made king, by the Great Spirit, over all the Creeks. The Indians, believing what Mary told them, for they had become very proud of her since Oglethorpe had been so kind to her, acknowledged her for their queen. Upon this, they called a great meeting of the chiefs, and Mary made them a long talk. She told them that the whites were their enemies, and had done them much injury ; that they were getting away the lands of the Indians, and would soon drive them from all their possessions. Said she, " We must assert our rights ; we must drive them from our territories ! Let us call forth our warriors ; I will head them. Stand by me, and the houses which they have erected shall smoke in ruins !" The spirit of Queen Mary was contagious. Every chief present declared himself ready to defend her to the last drop of his blood.

After due preparation, the warriors were called forth. They had painted themselves afresh, and sharpened anew their tomahawks for the battle. Their march was now commenced. Queen Mary, attended by her infamous husband, the real author and instigator of all their discontent, headed the savage throng. Before they reached Savannah, their approach was announced. The people were alarmed. They were few in number, and though they had a fortification and cannon, they had no good reason to hope that they should be able to ward off the deadly blow which was aimed against them.

By this time, the savages were in sight of Savannah. At this critical moment, an Englishman, by the name of Noble Jones, a bold and daring man, rode forth, with a few spirited men, on horseback, to meet them. As he approached them, he exclaimed, in a voice like thunder, " Ground your arms ! ground your arms ! Not an armed Indian shall set his foot in this town."

Awe-struck at his lofty tone, and perceiving him and his companions ready to dash in among them, they paused, and soon after laid down their arms. Bosomworth and his queen were now summoned to march into the city ; the Indian chiefs were also allowed to enter, but without their arms. On reaching the parade-ground, the thunder of fifteen cannon, fired at the same moment, told them what they might expect, should they persist in their hostile designs. The Indians were now marched to the house of the president of the council, in Savannah. Bosomworth was required to leave the Indians, while the president had a friendly talk with them.

In his address to them, he assured them of the kindness of the English, and demanded what they meant by coming in this warlike manner. In

8. The colony, for many reasons, did not flourish. In their regulations for its management, the trustees enacted that all lands granted by them to settlers should revert back, in case of the failure of male succession; although certain privileges were to be allowed to widows and daughters. At the same time, all trade with the Indians was prohibited, unless by virtue of special license. The use of negroes and the importation of rum were absolutely forbidden. In all this, the trustees were actuated by the purest motives, — by principles of humanity, and a regard to the health and morals of the inhabitants; — but the system of regulations was unfitted to the condition of the poor settlers, and was highly injurious to their increase and prosperity.

---

reply, they told the president that they had heard that Mary was to be sent over the great waters, and they had come to learn why they were to lose their queen. Finding that the Indians had been deceived, and that Bosomworth was the author of all the trouble, and that he had even intended to get possession of the magazine, and to destroy the whites, the council directed him to be seized and thrown into prison. This step Mary resented with great spirit. Rushing forth among the Indians, she openly cursed Oglethorpe, although he had raised her from poverty, and declared that the whole world should know that the ground she trod upon was her own.

The warlike spirit of the Indians being thus likely to be renewed, it was thought advisable to imprison Mary also. This was accordingly done. At the same time, to appease the Indians, a sumptuous feast was made for the chiefs by the president, who, during the better state of feeling which seemed to prevail, took occasion to explain to them the wickedness of Bosomworth, and how, by falsehood and cunning, he had led them to believe that Mary was really their queen — a descendant of one of their great chiefs. "Brothers," said he, "this is not true; Queen Mary is no other than Mary Musgrove, whom I found poor, and who has been made the dupe of the artful Bosomworth, and you, brothers, the dupes of both."

The aspect of things was now pleasant. The Indians were beginning to be satisfied of the villany of Bosomworth, and of the real character of Mary; but, at this moment, the door was thrown open, and, to the surprise of all, Mary burst into the room. She had made her escape from prison, and, learning what was going on, she rushed forward, with the fury of a tigress. "Seize your arms!" exclaimed she, "seize your arms! remember your promise, and defend your queen!" The sight of their queen seemed to bring back, in a moment, all the original ardor of the enterprise. In an instant, every chief seized his tomahawk, and sprang from the ground, to rally at the call of their queen.

At this moment, Capt. Jones, who was present, perceiving the danger of the president and the other whites, drew his sword, and demanded peace. The majesty of his countenance, the fire of his eye, the glittering of his sword, told Queen Mary what she might expect, should she attempt to raise any higher the feverish spirits of her subjects. The Indians cast an eye towards her, as if to inquire what they should do. Her countenance fell. Perceiving his advantage, Jones stepped forward, and, in the presence of the Indians, seized Mary, and conducted her back to prison. A short imprisonment so far humbled both Bosomworth and Mary, that each wrote a letter, confessing what they had done, and promising, if released, that they would conduct with more propriety in future.

9. Emigrants, however, continued to arrive. The first adventurers being poor and unenterprising, a more active and efficient race was desirable. To induce such to settle in the colony, eleven towns were laid out in shares of fifty acres each, one of which was offered to each new settler. Upon this, large numbers of Swiss, Scotch and Germans, became adventurers to the colony. Within three years from the first settlement, one thousand four hundred planters had arrived. To aid the colony, Parliament made several grants of money ; individuals also gave considerable sums for the same purpose. Owing, however, to the impolitic regulations of the trustees, the colony maintained only a feeble existence.

10. When Oglethorpe had satisfactorily arranged the affairs of his little colony, he visited England, taking with him Tomochichi, his queen, and several other Indians. In 1736, he once more returned to Georgia, with a reïnforcement of three hundred emigrants. He was accompanied by the celebrated John Wesley, who came on a mission, to preach to the colonists, and convert the Indians. But while he made some proselytes among the former, he made, it is said, more enemies. After a residence of two years, he returned to England, where he laid the foundation of that large and still growing denomination, the Methodists.

11. Two years afterwards, he was succeeded by the famous George Whitefield. The object of this great man was to establish an orphan house in Georgia, where poor children might be properly provided for, and instructed in the principles of religion. He often crossed the Atlantic, and both in England and America was the instrument of converting thousands. His orphan asylum did not flourish. At length he died, at Newburyport, Massachusetts.

12. In 1740, General Oglethorpe, having been appointed commander-in-chief of the forces of South Carolina and Georgia, projected an expedition against St. Augustine. Aided by Virginia and Carolina, he marched, at the head of more than two thousand men, for Florida ; and, after taking two small Spanish forts, Diego and Moosa, he sat down before St. Augustine. Captain Price, with several twenty-gun ships, assisted by sea ; but, after all their exertions, the general was forced to raise the siege, and return, with considerable loss.

13. Two years after, 1742, the Spaniards invaded Georgia, in turn. A Spanish armament, consisting of thirty-two sail, with three thousand men, under command of Don Manuel de Monteano, sailed from St. Augustine, and arrived in the river Altamaha. General Oglethorpe was, at this time, at Fort Simons. Finding

himself unable to retain possession of it, having but about seven hundred men, he spiked his cannon, and, destroying his military stores, retreated to his head-quarters at Frederica.   On the first prospect of an invasion, General Oglethorpe had applied to the Governor of South Carolina for assistance ; but the Carolinians, fearing for the safety of their own territory, and not approving of General Oglethorpe's management in his late expedition against St. Augustine, declined furnishing troops, but voted supplies.

14. In this state of danger and perplexity, the general resorted to stratagem. A French soldier belonging to his army had deserted to the enemy.   Fearing the consequences of their learning his weakness, he devised a plan by which to destroy the credit of any information that the deserter might give.   With this view, he wrote a letter to the French deserter in the Spanish camp, addressing him as if he were a spy of the English.   This letter he bribed a Spanish captive to deliver, in which he directed the deserter to state to the Spaniards that he was in a weak and defenceless condition, and to urge them to an attack.

15. Should he not be able, however, to persuade them to this, he wished him to induce them to continue three days longer at their quarters, in which time he expected two thousand men and six British men-of-war, from Carolina.   The above letter, as was intended, was delivered to the Spanish general, instead of the deserter, who immediately put the latter in irons.   A council of war was called, and, while deliberating upon the measures which should be taken, three supply-ships, which had been voted by Carolina, appeared in sight.   Imagining these to be the men-of-war alluded to in the letter, the Spaniards, in great haste, fired the fort, and embarked, leaving behind them several cannon, and a quantity of provisions.   By this artful but unjustifiable expedient, the country was relieved of its invaders, and Georgia, and probably a great part of South Carolina, saved from ruin.

16. In 1743, Oglethorpe, the founder, friend and protector, of the colony, returned to England, to visit it no more.   He left it in a state of tranquillity ; but it had never flourished.   The emigrants were poor and inefficient.   They were prohibited slave labor, and were cut off from a free title to the land they cultivated. At length, the trustees finding the colony continue to languish, and wearied themselves with the complaints of the colonists, they surrendered their charter to the crown ; and from this time Georgia was and continued to be a royal province, till the Revolution, which unbound the fetters of all.

NOTES.

1. The period of settlements, now reviewed, extending from 1607 to 1756, embraces one hundred and forty-nine years; during which fifteen colonies were planted in America, namely, Virginia, Plymouth, Massachusetts Bay, New Hampshire, Connecticut, New Haven, Rhode Island, New York, New Jersey, Delaware, Maryland, Pennsylvania, North and South Carolina, and Georgia.

2. Thirteen of these colonies were settled within a period of fifty-six years; that is, between 1607, the date of the settlement of Virginia, and 1663, the commencement of the Carolinas. During the next sixty-nine years, only one colony was planted, — that of Georgia, in 1732.

3. But, of these colonies, Plymouth and Massachusetts Bay were early united, as were New Haven and Connecticut, — the one taking the name of Massachusetts, the other the name of Connecticut.* Thus, at the close of the period of settlements, there were thirteen colonies, the oldest of which was one hundred and forty-nine years, and the youngest twenty-four.

4. The greater number of these colonies were settled by emigrants from England : yet New York was first colonized by the Dutch ; Maryland, by Roman Catholics ; Pennsylvania, by Quakers ; Delaware, by Swedes and Finns ; while in others, and, indeed, in all, at length, were to be found representatives from most of the European nations, especially the Germans, French and Scotch.

5. The inhabitants of these several colonial settlements, therefore, for many years, exhibited as great a variety as to character, religion, manners, customs, as the respective nations whence they emigrated. Yet the people of these communities, it is believed, lived in general in great peace and harmony among themselves ; — partly, it may have been, from necessity ; but, in greater part, from the kindly impulses of their nature. They had a common country, and now a common interest.

MANNERS OF THE COLONISTS, CUSTOMS, MODE OF LIVING, &c. — 1. In Virginia, the manners of the colonists were those of the less rigid English, rendered still more free and voluptuous by the influence of a softer climate and a more prolific soil. Stith, indeed, says of the first settlers of this colony, that some emigrated " to escape a worse fate at home ; " and others, to repair

---

* The little colony founded at Saybrook in 1635 was united with Connecticut in 1644.

10*

fortunes by emigration which had been ruined by excess. But many persons of high character were among the emigrants; and amidst the licentiousness of the Virginia colony were found, at the close of this period, a good deal of that frankness, hospitality, taste and refinement, which distinguish the people of the south at this day.

2. Beverly says, " that they were so courteous to travellers as to need no other recommendation but their being human beings; and that the poor planters who had only one bed would often sit up, or lie upon a form or couch, all night, to make room for a weary traveller to repose himself after his journey."

3. Most of the earliest emigrants to Virginia were in humble circumstances, and were single men; or, if they had wives, they left them for a time at home, fearing the dangers of a long voyage and a new climate. When, at length, the colonists were in some measure established, there was a great dearth of women for wives; one hundred and fifty were sent over at one time. Those who carried over good testimonials as to character soon found husbands; and Beverly says, nothing was more common than for a man " to buy a deserving wife at the price of one hundred pounds, and then to think he had a bargain."

4. The Virginians never suffered from want, as did some of the northern colonists. Their climate was milder, and the soil far more fertile. Indeed, living was often too cheap for good morals or manners. An early writer says he remembered the time when five pounds, left by a charitable testator to the poor of the parish he lived in, lay nine years before the executors could find one poor enough to accept the legacy; but, at last, it was given to an old woman. In those days, the disabled from accident or sickness were kept at the public charge at some " charitable planter's house."

5. The habitations of the first settlers were, of course, only rude dwellings; but, as years passed, great improvement took place in the style and comfort of building. Before the close of the period, many houses, spacious, airy and commodious, were erected of brick. The governor's house is spoken of as having been " very beautiful."

6. The Virginians, from the earliest settlement of the colony, loved good living; and they had the means of indulging their taste. Their beef and mutton were not equal to those of England. But it was good, and cheap, seldom commanding more than one or two pence per pound. Beverly puts down the price of some articles, which shows the reason why there were so many " lazy" among the colonists. It cost nothing to live.

" Largest Poulets," six pence ; capons, eight pence ; chickens, three or four shillings a dozen ; turkeys, fifteen pence ; deer, five to ten shillings.   " Bread," he adds, " in gentlemen's houses, is generally made of wheat ; but the poorer sort of people greatly prefer pone, or oppone, the Indian name for hominy."

7. The clothing of the colonists was nearly all procured from England, although they had the materials, or might have had them, near home.   A writer says of their sheep, " that they sheared them only to cool them ;" and, " that, to the eternal reproach of their laziness," they imported even their " bowls and birchen brooms."   But it is to be remembered that when, at length, they would have manufactured many necessary articles, they were forbidden by the government in England.

8. Among the NEW ENGLAND colonies, there existed much that was quite in contrast with what we have recorded of the Virginians.   They were more strict in their notions, and consequently more rigid in their manners.   If they had no greater faith in the Scriptures, they moulded their government and shaped private character and morals upon a more severe and literal construction of them.   They had not the means of external show, or sumptuous living, as had their southern brethren ; — they did not covet them.   They studied simplicity of manners, taste, living.   Yet they were patriotic, industrious, and public-spirited ; and, though of a grave and reflecting exterior, they often showed that shrewd inquisitiveness, and keen relish of a jest, which are still characteristic of the New Englanders.

9. The laws of the colonies throw great light on the views and manners of the people of that age.   Take several laws of the MASSACHUSETTS COLONY : one, in 1639, prohibiting the drinking of healths ; another, in 1651, prohibiting " persons whose estate did not exceed two hundred pounds wearing gold or silver lace, or any bone lace above two shillings per yard ;" and requiring the selectmen to take notice of the " apparel " of the people, especially their " ribbands and great boots."   And one Mr. Josias Plaistowe, for stealing corn from the Indians, was to be called only Josias, and not Mr., as formerly.   Sergeant Perkins was doomed to carry forty turfs to the fort for being drunk ; and Robert Shorthose, for swearing in a certain manner, was sentenced to have his tongue put into a cleft stick, and to stand so for the space of half an hour, — a punishment it were well if all profane swearers were subject to in these days.

10. The laws and regulations of the TOWN OF HARTFORD and of

the COLONY OF CONNECTICUT show a similar watchfulness over the interests, manners and morals, of the community. In 1635, it was ordered by the town that every religious meeting should be guarded by a certain number of men, well armed with guns and powder and ball. Every freeman who neglected to attend town-meeting was fined sixpence, unless he had a good excuse. Boys playing in the time of public services, whether in the house or outside, were to be punished publicly before the assembly. And, in 1643, it was ordered that the watch should ring a bell every morning, before daybreak, passing through the street from Master Moodey's (Wyllys Hill) to John Pratt's; and that at least one person should be up within one quarter of an hour after, in every house.

11. In 1647, the colony of Connecticut ordered that no person under twenty years of age should use any tobacco, without a certificate from a physician; and no others, although addicted to its use, unless they were ten miles from any house, and then not more than once a day. And this regulation was made while the Virginians were raising all the tobacco they were able, deriving a revenue from it for the support of government, and paying their ministers with it for preaching, and attending funerals, and solemnizing marriages.

12. The laws and regulations of the COLONY OF NEW HAVEN were of a similar minute and vigilant tenor. In 1639, the colony resolved that they would be governed by the rules of the Scriptures; and that church-members only should act in the civil affairs of the plantation. In the same year it was ordered that one Broomfield should be set in the stocks for profaning the Lord's day, and stealing wine from his master, which he drank and gave to others. Persons were often whipped and dismissed from the plantation for being disorderly; or set in the stocks, or imprisoned, for misdemeanors or personal differences, which, at the present day, would attract no attention, or which would be left to be settled by the parties themselves.

13. These matters are sometimes referred to, in these days, by way of reproaching our ancestors, as being puritanic, over-scrupulous and austere. But there is little just cause for the censure. Most of them were eminent for their piety, wisdom, and love of order. At first, they had no written code of laws, and, therefore, were compelled to consider grievances as they occurred, each one to be decided upon as the case then presented itself; and the history of these transactions went on to the public records in the quaint and simple language of the day. There they still exist, food for the captious and the sarcastic; but evi-

dence, while the world shall last, of the paternal character of the ministry and magistracy of those earlier days, and their strenuous efforts to order themselves and the community according to the dictates of religion and a good conscience.

14. In the COLONY OF NEW YORK, the manners of the colonists, until the conquest by the English in 1664, were strictly Dutch, — the same steadfast pursuit of wealth, the same plodding industry, the same dress, air and physiognomy, which are given as characteristic of Holland, were equally characteristics of the inhabitants of New Amsterdam. After the English became the owners of the territory, the manners of the Dutch were more or less modified by intercourse with them; but they did not blend readily, and the differences were long to be observed.

15. The manners and customs of the Dutch were, doubtless, as singular and laughable as those of the New England colonies. The gable-end of their houses invariably faced on the street. They had large doors and small windows on every floor. The date of their erection was curiously designated by iron figures on the front, and on the top of the roof was a fine-looking little weather-vane.

16. The family always entered the gate, and most generally lived in the kitchen. The front door was never opened, except on special occasions, such as a marriage, a funeral, or a New Year's day. The grand parlor was, of course, washed and sanded once a week, even if no one had stepped into it during the week. The sand on the floor was stroked into angles, and curves, and other figures, with the broom.

17. In the kitchen, near the chimney, the old burgher would sit for hours in perfect silence, puffing his pipe, and looking into the fire with half-shut eyes, thinking of nothing on earth; while his "goede vrowe," on the opposite side, would sew, or knit, or mend stockings; the young folks, meanwhile, listening to some old crone of a negro, who would entertain them with stories about New England witches, ghosts, and such like.

18. A well-regulated family always rose at day-break, dined at eleven, and went to bed about sun-down. At tea-parties, they commonly assembled at three o'clock in the afternoon, and returned at six. The tea-table was crowned with a huge earthen dish, well stored with slices of fat pork, cut up into morsels, and swimming in fat. Sometimes the table was graced with immense apple-pies, or saucers full of preserved peaches. Doughnuts, or "oly koeks" were seldom forgotten. Such is the humor-

ous, and yet, for the most part, truthful account of the Dutch in New York, furnished by one of their own writers.*

19. These peculiarities are observable, to some extent, in Dutch settlements, even to the present time. Within the remembrance of the author, the following occurrence took place. He was seated at the tea-table, while on a visit at a fine old Dutch gentleman's, when the mistress of ceremonies said to him, "Sir, do you stir or bite?" "Stir or bite! Madam, pardon me, I do not understand you." " O," she replied, smiling, " some persons prefer to stir the sugar in the tea ; others, to bite the sugar and sip the tea." Upon this, the old burgher remarked, that this was modern custom, but that at an earlier day the practice was to suspend a large lump of sugar directly over the tea-table, by a string from the ceiling, so that it could be swung round from mouth to mouth.

20. In other colonies peculiarities might be noticed, as those of the Finns in Delaware, the Roman Catholics in Maryland, and the Quakers in Pennsylvania ; but, before the close of the period, the peculiarities of the several classes became less distinct by intercourse with the others, and every succeeding generation seemed to exhibit less strikingly those traits which distinguished the preceding. The elegant varieties of life were more tolerated, and the refinements of polished society appeared among the higher classes.

RELIGION. — 1. The colony of Virginia, from its earliest existence, was exclusively devoted to the Church of England ; though, for several years, its unsettled state prevented that attention to a religious establishment which afterwards the subject received.

2. In 1621, the Virginia Company ordered a hundred acres of land, in each of the boroughs, and two hundred pounds sterling, to be raised, as a standing and certain revenue, out of the profits of each parish, to make a living. This stipend was thus settled : — That the minister shall receive, yearly, five hundred pounds of tobacco, and sixteen barrels of corn, which were collectively estimated at two hundred pounds sterling. In 1642, the assembly passed a law, prohibiting all, but those who had been ordained by English bishops, from preaching.

3. In 1650, during the time of Governor Berkley, the religion of the Church of England was confirmed, and provision made for the support of the ministers. The maintenance of a minister was put at sixteen thousand pounds of tobacco, which, as valued

---

* Knickerbocker's New York.

at that time, at ten shillings per hundred, was about eighty pounds sterling.   But, in addition, he had a dwelling-house and glebe; also, four hundred pounds of tobacco, or forty shillings, for a funeral sermon, and two hundred pounds of tobacco, or twenty shillings, for performing marriage by license, or five shillings when the banns were proclaimed.   The tobacco destined for the minister was brought to him well packed, in hogsheads, prepared for shipping.

4. The special object of the New England planters, in settling the country, was the enjoyment of their religious opinions, and the free exercise of religious worship, without molestation. Early attention was, therefore, paid to the gathering of churches, and the regulation of religion.   They were Calvinists in doctrine, and Congregational in discipline.   Each church maintained its right to govern itself.   They held to the validity of Presbyterian ordination, and the expediency of synods on great occasions. From the commencement, they used ecclesiastical councils, convoked by particular churches, for advice, but not for the judicial determination of controversies.   In each of the churches, there were a pastor, teacher, ruling elder, and deacons.   The pastor's office consisted principally in exhortation; upon the teacher devolved the business of explaining and defending the doctrines of Christianity.   The business of the ruling elder was to assist the pastor in the government of the church.

5. Early provision was made for the support of the ministry. On the arrival of the colonists of Massachusetts Bay at Charlestown, before landing, a court of assistants was held, and the first question proposed was, How shall the ministers be maintained? The court ordered that houses be built, and salaries be raised for them, at the public charge.   Their two ministers, Mr. Phillips and Mr. Wilson, were granted a salary, — the former thirty pounds per annum, and the latter twenty pounds, until the arrival of his wife.   After the settlement of the several colonies, all persons were obliged by law to contribute to the support of the church.   Special care was taken that all persons should attend public worship.   In Connecticut, the law obliged them to be present on the Lord's day, — on all days of public thanksgiving, appointed by civil authority, — on penalty of five shillings for every instance of neglect.

6. In 1637, the first synod convened in America sat at Newtown, Massachusetts, and was composed of all the teaching elders in the country, and messengers of the several churches.   Magistrates, also, were present, and spoke as they thought fit.   The object of calling this synod was to inquire into the opinions of

that very extraordinary woman, Anne Hutchinson, who held public lectures in Boston, and taught doctrines considered heretical. The whole colony was agitated, and divided into parties. The synod, after a session of three weeks, condemned eighty-two erroneous opinions, which had become disseminated in New England.

7. The DUTCH REFORMED CHURCH was introduced into New York with the first settlers, and was generally embraced by the Dutch population of that colony. The first church was erected, within the fort, in 1642. It was seventy-two feet long, and fifty-two broad, and cost about two thousand dollars, to be paid for "in beaver, cash, or merchandise." It was covered with "slate, split of oak wood," — that is, with oak shingles, which, by rain and wind, soon resembled slate. To this church the town-bell was removed, where it was rung to tell when to retire, when to leave off work, and when to stop selling "ardent liquor," and when to send home people from the taverns. This was at nine o'clock in the evening.

8. The ROMAN CATHOLICS first came to America in 1632. They settled in Maryland, and now constitute a respectable and numerous portion of the inhabitants of that state. The first BAPTIST CHURCH in America was formed at Providence, in 1639, under the celebrated Roger Williams. Their sentiments spreading into Massachusetts, in 1651, the General Court passed a law against them, inflicting banishment for persisting in the promulgation of their doctrines.

9. In 1656, the QUAKERS making their appearance in Massachusetts, the Legislature of that colony passed severe laws against them. No master of a vessel was allowed to bring any one of this sect into its jurisdiction, on penalty of one hundred pounds. Other still severer penalties were inflicted upon them in 1657, such as cutting their ears, and boring their tongues with a hot iron, &c. They were at length banished, on pain of death ; and, for refusing to go, were executed, in 1659. Without intending to justify these severities toward the Baptists, Quakers, and other sectaries, it is still proper to state, as some apology for them, that the conduct of the leaders of these sects was often calculated, and no doubt designed, to provoke persecution. They sought improper occasions to inculcate their peculiar tenets, departed unnecessarily from the decencies of social intercourse, and rudely inveighed against established and cherished opinions. In this way, the peace of the colonies was disturbed, and that unanimity of religious sentiment which had hitherto existed was broken. Our forefathers sought to avert these evils by the

arm of civil power, not yet having learnt that persecution is a ready way to propagate the sentiments of the persecuted.

10. In the year 1646, a synod met at Cambridge, which, by adjournment, protracted its session to 1648, when it dissolved. This synod composed and adopted the "Cambridge Platform,' and recommended it, together with the Westminster Confession of Faith, to the General Court and to the churches. In this synod were present the ministers and churches of Connecticut and New Haven, who united in the form of discipline which it recommended. This, in connection with the ecclesiastical laws, was the religious constitution of Connecticut, until the compilation of the Saybrook Platform, a period of about sixty years.

11. In 1681, Penn began to colonize Pennsylvania. Being himself a Quaker, he followed the views and tenets of that sect in many of his regulations, especially in prohibiting an appeal to arms. Quaker worship was instituted, with all the peculiarities which distinguish that sect; yet it was a fundamental principle of Penn, that no one acknowledging his belief in one God, and living peaceably in society, should be molested for his opinions or practices. Episcopacy was introduced into New York in 1693; into New Jersey and Rhode Island, in 1702; into South Carolina, in 1703, by law; in Connecticut, in 1704.

12. In 1708, the Saybrook Platform was formed by a synod composed of Congregational ministers, under authority of the Legislature of Connecticut. About the year 1737, a revival of religion very extensively prevailed in New England. At this time, great numbers united themselves to the church, and testified, by their conduct through life, the genuineness of their profession. The celebrated Whitefield came to America about the year 1740, and produced great religious excitement by his singular powers of pulpit eloquence. He did not found any peculiar sect in this country, although he gave rise to that of the Calvinistic Methodists in England.

13. It may be remarked, in conclusion, that, as years revolved, and the various religious sects became more established, religious bigotry and intolerance abated; and before the close of the period religious persecution had ceased in all the colonies, and the rights of conscience were generally recognized.

TRADE AND COMMERCE. — 1. At first the colonies had but little trade with any nation, except England, and even that was on a limited scale. They imported all their merchandise, and made such returns as they were able in tobacco, peltry, and, after a time, in beef, pork, grain, and fish.

2. During the first thirty years of the colony of Virginia, their

11

exports were confined to tobacco. But the price of it fell, at length, from three shillings and sixpence per pound, to twenty shillings per hundred; in consequence of which, a trade was opened with the frontier Indians and the Five Nations. The skins of the deer, elk and buffalo, and the furs of the otter, hare, fox, muskrat and beaver, were procured for rum, hatchets, blankets, &c. These skins and furs were exported to England. English grain and Indian corn were also exported to a considerable extent. Although the Virginians owned a few vessels, the greater part of the trade was carried on by English vessels, during this period. They brought to the colony English manufactures, and took tobacco, furs, skins, grain, tar, pitch, &c., in return. The Virginians also carried on some trade with Canada. The principal article of export from New England, during this period, was peltry, which was procured of the Indians for goods of small value. In 1639, a fishing trade was begun at Cape Ann; and in 1641, three hundred thousand codfish were sent to market.

3. The first vessel directly from the West Indies was a Dutch ship of one hundred and sixty tons, which arrived at Marblehead, 1635. The first American vessel that made a voyage to the West Indies was a pinnace of thirty tons, in 1636. The ship Desire, of Salem, made a voyage, in 1638, to New Providence and Tortuga, and returned laden with cotton, tobacco, salt, and negroes. This was the first introduction of African slaves into New England. The first importation of indigo and sugar from the West Indies, mentioned in our accounts, was made in 1639. In 1642, a Dutch ship exchanged a cargo of salt for plank and pipe-staves, the first exports of lumber from New England. The next year, eleven ships sailed for the West Indies with lumber.

4. But at length, as the population and enterprise of the colonies increased, they desired to engage more in trade and commerce. This, however, began to excite the jealousy of the mother country, and laws were at various times passed by Parliament designed to keep them in safe subjection to England, and dependent upon her. Hats were prohibited being exported; mills for slitting and rolling iron were forbidden; and they were required to procure articles in England which they could have procured twenty per cent. cheaper in other markets. But, notwithstanding those restrictions, trade and commerce gradually and steadily increased. To England the colonies exported lumber of all sorts, hemp, flax, pitch, tar, oil, rosin, copper ore, pig and bar iron, whale-fins, tobacco, rice, fish, indigo, flax-seed, beeswax, raw silk, &c. They also built many vessels, which were sold in the mother country.

5. But the importation of goods from England, in consequence of the restrictive policy of the British government, was all along in excess of the colonial efforts, and a balance was yearly to be provided for. How was it done ? By gold and silver, obtained chiefly from the West India settlements, to which they exported lumber, fish of an inferior quality, beef, pork, butter, horses, poultry and other live stock, an inferior kind of tobacco, corn cider, apples, cabbages, onions, &c. They built also many small vessels, which found a ready market. The cod and whale fisheries were becoming considerable ; they were principally carried on by New England. The codfish were sold in Spain, France, England, the West Indies, &c. ; and the money obtained for them aided the colonies in paying the balance of trade against them in England.

AGRICULTURE. — 1. Early attention was paid to agriculture. The first business of the settlers was to clear the forests, and supply themselves with food from the soil. But the fertility of the earth taught them soon to look to agriculture as a source of wealth, as well as of subsistence. It, therefore, became the leading object of industry in the colonies. The method adopted by the first settlers to clear the land was slow and laborious, compared with the present modes. They used generally to cut down the trees, and dig up the stumps, before tillage. Tobacco was early cultivated in Virginia, and soon began to be exported. The year after the colony landed, the people gathered corn of their own planting, the seed of which they received of the Indians. Vineyards were attempted, and experienced vine-dressers were sent over for the purpose of attending them. Flax, hemp, barley, &c., were cultivated to a considerable extent. Rye was first raised in Massachusetts in 1633. Ploughs were early introduced into the country.

2. Neat cattle were first introduced into New England by Mr. Winslow, in 1624. In 1629, one hundred and forty head of cattle, with horses, sheep and goats, were imported into Massachusetts Bay. In a few years, they became so numerous as to supply all the wants of the inhabitants. In 1623, the cattle in Virginia had increased to above one thousand head. New York raised considerable beef and pork for exportation, and in 1678 there were exported from the province sixty thousand bushels of wheat. From this time, agriculture continued to receive more and more attention. As other colonies were settled, immense forests were cleared, and more enlightened modes of husbandry were introduced. Before the close of the period, the colonies not only raised a sufficient supply of food for their own use, but their

exports became great.   Wheat and other English grain were the principal products of the middle colonies; grain, beef, pork, horses, butter, cheese, &c., were the chief products of the northern colonies; tobacco, wheat and rice, were the principal products of the south.   In the south, also, large numbers of swine ran wild in the forests, living upon mast.   These were taken, salted down, and exported to a considerable extent.

ARTS AND MANUFACTURES. — 1.   The colonists, at first, being chiefly occupied in gaining a subsistence, and, in protecting themselves against their enemies, had occasion for few articles beyond the necessaries and comforts of life.   Arts and manufactures, therefore, received but little encouragement, beyond the construction of such articles, and even those were principally imported.

2.   In 1620, one hundred and fifty persons arrived in Virginia, from England, for the purpose of manufacturing silk, iron, potash, tar, pitch, glass, salt, &c.; but they did not succeed.   In 1673, Chalmers says of New England, " There be five iron works, which cast no guns; no house in New England has above twenty rooms; not twenty in Boston have ten rooms each; a dancing-school was set up here, but put down; a fencing-school is allowed. There be no musicians by trade.   All cordage, sail-cloth and mats, come from England; no cloth made there worth four shillings per yard; no alum, no copperas, no salt, made by their sun."

3.   The first buildings of the settlers were made of logs and thatched, or were built of stone.   Brick and framed houses were soon built in the larger towns, and afterwards in the villages.   The frames and brick were, however, in some instances, imported. The first mill in New England was a wind-mill, near Watertown; but it was taken down in 1632, and placed in the vicinity of Boston.   Water-mills began to be erected the next year.   The first attempt to build a water-craft in New England was at Plymouth, in 1626.   A house-carpenter sawed their largest boat into two parts, and lengthened it five or six feet, built a deck, and rigged it into a convenient vessel, which did service for seven years.   The first vessel built in Massachusetts was a bark, in 1631, called THE BLESSING OF THE BAY.   In 1633, a ship of sixty tons was built at Medford.   In 1636, one of one hundred and twenty tons was built at Marblehead.   In 1641, a ship of three hundred tons was launched at Salem, and one of one hundred and sixty tons at Boston.   From this time, ship-building rapidly extended in the northern colonies.

4.   The first printing in New England was executed in 1639, by one Day.   The proprietor of the press was a clergyman, by

the name of Glover, who died on his passage to America. The first article printed was the Freeman's Oath, the second an almanac, and the third an edition of the Psalms. John Eliot, the celebrated missionary, having translated the Bible into the Indian language, had it printed at Cambridge, in 1664. The mode of travelling considerable distances was on foot, or on horseback, there being no carriages for that purpose, and the roads from one village to another being only narrow foot-paths, through forests.

5. Before the close of the period, notwithstanding the obstacles interposed by Great Britain to the arts and manufactures in the colonies, they made some progress. The coarser kinds of cutlery, some coarse cloths, both linen and woollen, hats, paper, shoes, household furniture, farming utensils, &c., were manufactured to a considerable extent; not sufficient, however, to supply the inhabitants. All these manufactures were on a small scale. Cloths were made, in some families, for their own consumption.

6. The art of printing made considerable progress during this period. A newspaper, the first in North America, called "The Boston Weekly News-Letter," was established in 1704. Before the close of this period, ten others were established, — four in New England, two in New York, two in Pennsylvania, one in South Carolina, and one in Maryland. The number of books published was also considerable, although they were executed in a coarse style, and were generally books of devotion, or for the purposes of education.

POPULATION. — 1. The population of the English American colonies, in 1701, was estimated by Dr. Humphreys as follows:

Massachusetts,	70,000	New York,	30,000
Connecticut,	30,000	The Jerseys,	15,000
Rhode Island,	10,000	Pennsylvania,	20,000
New Hampshire,	10,000	Maryland,	25,000
		Virginia,	40,000
New England,	120,000	North Carolina,	5,000
Mid. and S. Colonies,	142,000	South Carolina,	7,000
Total,	262,000		142,000

2. In 1755, the close of the period, the estimate was this:

New Hampshire,	30,000	New York,	100,000
Massachusetts Bay,	220,000	The Jerseys,	60,000
Rhode Island and Providence Plantations,	35,000	Pennsylvania,	250,000
		Maryland,	85,000
Connecticut,	100,000	Virginia,	85,000
New England,	385,000	North Carolina,	45,000
Mid. and S. Colonies,	661,000	South Carolina,	30,000
		Georgia,	6,000
Total,	1,046,000		661,000

11*

According to Dr. Franklin, not more than eighty thousand of these were foreigners; the rest were American born. Emigration, therefore, had nearly ceased.

EDUCATION. — 1. Scarcely had the American colonists opened the forests, and constructed habitations, before they directed their attention to the object of education. Moneys were collected for the establishment of a college at Henrico, for the education of Indian children; and about the same time, the Virginia Company appropriated ten thousand acres of land for the same purpose, and also for the foundation of a seminary for English scholars. In 1621, a school was endowed at Charles City for the benefit of all the colony. As they did not flourish, in 1692 their funds were given to William and Mary's College.

2. Still more attentive to education were the northern colonies. In 1636, a General Court of Massachusetts Bay appropriated the sum of four hundred pounds towards the commencement of a college. In 1637, the college was located at Newtown, which, not long after, was called Cambridge, in memory of Cambridge, in England, where many of the colonists had received their education. Mr. John Harvard, a worthy minister, dying at Charlestown, about this time, bequeathed nearly eight hundred pounds to the college; in consideration of which legacy, it was called after him. In 1642 was held the first commencement, at which nine were graduated. To this institution the plantations of Connecticut and New Haven contributed funds from the public purse; and for a time sent to it such of their youth as they wished to be educated. Private subscriptions were also made from the United Colonies, to aid the institution.

3. Great attention was also paid, by all the colonies, to the subject of common schools. As a specimen of the arrangements common to the New England colonies, we may notice those of Connecticut. By her first code, in 1639, only six years from the time the first house was erected within the colony, it was ordered that every town consisting of fifty families should maintain a good school, in which reading and writing should be well taught, and that in every county-town a good grammar-school should be instituted. Large tracts of land were appropriated by the Legislature as a permanent support of these schools, and the selectmen of every town were required to see that all heads of families instructed their children and servants to read the English tongue well.

4. Yale College, in Connecticut, was commenced in 1700, eleven of the principal ministers in the neighboring towns, who had been appointed to adopt such measures as they should deem

expedient on the subject of a college, agreeing to found one in the colony. The next year, the Legislature granted them a charter. The college was begun at Saybrook, where was held the first commencement, in 1702. In 1717, it was removed to New Haven, where it became permanently established. It was named after the Honorable Elihu Yale, Governor of the East India Company, who was its principal benefactor. The college at Princeton, New Jersey, called "Nassau Hall," was first founded by charter from John Hamilton, Esq., President of the Council, about the year 1738, and was enlarged by Governor Belcher, in 1747.

5. In respect to colonies settled at a later period, some attention was paid to the education of children and youth; but far less than their true interests demanded, and less than would have been done, had they more fully appreciated the blessings of learning.

REFLECTIONS. — 1. At the commencement of this period, our history presented us with a continent over whose surface an interminable wilderness had for ages cast its deep and solemn shade. If we approach the shore, and look through the gloom that gathers over it, the scenes which strike the eye are Indians at their war-dance, or, perhaps, flames curling round some expiring captive, or wild beasts mangling their prey. Passing from this point of time to the close of our period, the prospect is greatly changed. We now see smiling fields and cheerful villages, in the place of dismal forests; instead of beasts of prey, we see grazing herds; instead of the kindling fagot, we witness the worship of Jesus Christ; and instead of the appalling war-whoop, we listen to the grateful songs of David. In the beautiful words of Scripture, the wilderness has begun to blossom as the rose, and the desert is becoming vocal with the praises of God.

2. And how is it that so wonderful a change has been brought to pass? The answer is easy. Our fathers were men of extraordinary energy, wisdom, enterprise, and hardihood. Yet, what then? Without the smiles and constant influence of a benign Providence working in their favor, and mysteriously establishing their strength and security, they had never accomplished such wonders, especially when exercised for years with trial, danger, and misfortune.

3. Look at them. Through cold and storm, through sickness and famine, many of them for years made their way; and then they are visited by cruel and desolating wars, in which they bear the burdens of the mother country; — they fight her battles, sustain her oppressions; and yet they advance in popu-

lation, extend their commerce, enlarge their boundaries, and lay wider and deeper the foundations of a future nation.

4. And, while we look back, with admiration, upon the hardy spirit which carried our ancestors through scenes so trying, and enabled them to reap prosperity from the crimsoned fields of battle and bloodshed, let us be thankful that our lot is cast in a happier day; and that, instead of sharing in the perils of feeble colonies, we enjoy the protection and privileges of a free and powerful nation.

5. In addition to the reflection subjoined to the account which we have given of the "Salem witchcraft," we may add another, respecting the danger of popular delusion. In that portion of our history, we see a kind of madness rising up, and soon stretching its influence over a whole community. And such, too, is the pervading power of the spell, that the wise and ignorant, the good and bad, are alike subject to its control, and, for the time, alike incapable of judging or reasoning aright. Now, whenever we see a community divided into parties, and agitated by some general excitement, — when we feel ourselves borne along, on one side or the other, by the popular tide, — let us inquire whether we are not acting under the influence of a delusion which a few years — perhaps a few months, or days — may dispel and expose. Nor, at such a time, let us regard our sincerity, or our consciousness of integrity, or the seeming clearness and certainty of our reasonings, as furnishing an absolute assurance that, after all, we do not mistake, and that our opponents are not right.

6. Another reflection, of some importance, and one that may serve to guard us against censuring too severely the wise and good, is suggested by this account of the "Salem witchcraft." It is this, — that the best men are liable to err. We should not, therefore, condemn, nor should we withhold our charity from, those who fall into occasional error, provided their characters are, in other respects, such as to lay claim to our good opinion.

UNITED STATES.

PERIOD III.

DISTINGUISHED FOR THE FRENCH AND INDIAN WAR.

EXTENDING FROM THE DECLARATION OF WAR BY ENG-
LAND AGAINST FRANCE, 1756, TO THE COMMENCEMENT
OF HOSTILITIES BY GREAT BRITAIN AGAINST THE AMER-
ICAN COLONIES, IN THE BATTLE OF LEXINGTON, 1775.

1. Up to the opening of this period, the history of the several colonies has properly been kept distinct. From this date forward, they are to act more or less together ; and, consequently, their history blends.

2. For years, however, that history is little more than a costly and sanguinary struggle with French and Indians, in which they become involved by reason of their connection with the mother country, who declares war against France ; and her American colonies must sustain her in it on this side the water, as they had done in her previous contests, to the loss of thousands of their citizens, and the great impoverishment of their treasuries. The colonies had now enjoyed peace but about eight years,*

---

* The treaty of Aix la Chapelle was negotiated in 1748 (see p. 67), and terminated a war, which, though it lasted but a few years, involved the New England colonies and New York in an expense of not less than a million pounds sterling. Massachusetts alone is said to have paid half this sum, and to have expended nearly four hundred thousand pounds in the expedition against Cape Breton. The expenses of Carolina, for the war in that quarter, were not less in proportion.

To supply the deficiency of money, bills of credit were issued to the amount of several millions. The bills issued by Massachusetts, during two or three years of the war, amounted to between two and three millions currency; while, at the time of their emission, five or six hundred pounds were equal to one hundred pounds sterling. Before the complete redemption of these bills, says Dr. Trumbull, in those colonies where their credit was best supported, the depreciation was nearly twenty for one.

when, on the 17th of May, 1756, England made formal declaration of war against France, which was reciprocated by the latter power, June 9th.

3. In narrating the principal events of the French and Indian War, we shall have occasion to notice :

1754. {
The causes which led to it ;
The circumstances which opened it ;
The expedition of Washington against Fort du Quesne ;
Albany plan of union between the colonies.
}

1755. {
Conquest of Nova Scotia ;
Defeat of General Braddock ;
Battle of Lake George ;
Expedition against Niagara.
}

1756. {
Formal declaration of war by England against France ;
Failure of expeditions against Niagara and Crown Point ;
Fall of Fort Oswego.
}

1757. {
Attempted reduction of Louisburg ;
Loss of Fort William Henry.
}

1758. {
Reduction of Louisburg ;
Failure of expedition against Ticonderoga ;
Capture of Fort Frontenac ;
Occupation of Fort du Quesne ;
Treaty with Mohawks, Senecas, &c.
}

1759. {
Surrender of Ticonderoga ;
    "   " Crown Point ;
    "   " Niagara ;
Siege and capture of Quebec.
}

1760. {
Battle of Sillsery ;
French siege of Quebec ;
Surrender of Montreal ;
And the rest of Canada.
}

1763.   Treaty of peace.

4. The general cause, leading to this war, known as the " FRENCH AND INDIAN WAR," was alleged encroachments of the French upon the frontier English colonial settlements. These settlements extended along the ocean from Newfoundland to

---

The losses sustained by the colonies, in the fall of many of their bravest men, during this and the last Indian war, were severely felt. From 1722 to 1749, a period of twenty-seven years, the losses of Massachusetts and New Hampshire equalled the whole increase of their numbers; whereas, in the natural course of population, their numbers would have more than doubled.

Florida. On the other hand, the French had extended themselves from the mouth of the St. Lawrence to Montreal ; had built forts and trading-houses on Lake Ontario ; had settled New Orleans ; and, having discovered the valley of the Mississippi, they decided to connect their southern and northern settlements by a chain of posts along the line of that river and the Ohio, to Ontario ; and, by so doing, to hold territory which they, indeed, claimed by virtue of occupation and exploration, but to which the English laid claim on account of Cabot's early discovery. Thus these two powers were at issue, and upon the tired and impoverished colonies falls the brunt of the war.

5. The circumstance which served to open the war was the alleged intrusion of the OHIO COMPANY upon the territory of the French. This company consisted of a number of influential men, from London and Virginia, who had obtained a charter grant of six hundred thousand acres of land, on and near the river Ohio, for the purpose of carrying on the fur trade with the Indians, and of settling the country. The Governor of Canada had early intelligence * of the transactions of this company ; and, fearing that their plan would deprive the French of the advantages of the fur trade, and prevent communications between Canada and Louisiana, he addressed a letter to the Governors of New York and Pennsylvania, claiming the country east of the Ohio to the Alleghanies, and forbidding the further encroachments of the English traders.

6. The Ohio Company, thus threatened, appealed to the Lieutenant-governor of Virginia, Dinwiddie, who laid the subject before the assembly, which ordered a messenger to be despatched to the French commandant on the Ohio, to demand the reasons of his hostile conduct, and to summon the French to evacuate the forts which they had recently built in that region.

7. The person intrusted with this service was GEORGE WASHINGTON, who, at the early age of twenty-one, thus stepped forth in the public cause, and began that line of services which ended in the independence of his country. The service to which Washington was appointed was both difficult and dangerous; the place of his destination being above four hundred miles distant, two hundred of which lay through a wilderness, inhabited only by

---

* As yet, the Pennsylvanians had principally managed the trade with the Indians. But, being now about to be deprived of it by the Ohio Company, which was opening a road to the Potomac, they excited the fears of the Indians, lest their lands should be taken from them, and gave early intelligence to the French of the designs and transactions of the company.

Indians. He arrived in safety, however, and delivered a letter
from Governor Dinwiddie to the commandant.* Having received
a written answer, and secretly taken the dimensions of the fort,
he returned.   The reply of the commandant to Governor Dinwiddie was, that he had taken possession of the country under
the direction of the Governor-general of Canada, to whom he
would transmit his letter, and whose orders only he would
obey.

8. The British ministry, on being made acquainted with the
conduct of the French, instructed the Virginians to resist their
encroachments by force.   Accordingly, a regiment was raised in
Virginia, which was joined by an independent company from
South Carolina ; and, with this force, Washington, early in April,
1754, commenced his march towards the Great Meadows, lying
within the disputed territories, for the purpose of expelling the
French.

9. On his arrival at the Great Meadows, having erected a
small stockade fort, afterwards called Fort Necessity, he proceeded with his force, increased to nearly four hundred men,
towards the French Fort du Quesne (du-Kane), the present site
of Pittsburg, with the intention of dislodging the enemy.
Hearing, however, that the enemy was approaching, he retired to
Fort Necessity, where, not long after, he was attacked by nearly
fifteen hundred troops from Fort du Quesne, under command of
M. de Villiers. After an engagement of several hours, De Villiers demanded a parley, and offered terms of capitulation.
These terms were rejected ; but, during the night, July 4th,
articles were signed, by which Washington was permitted, upon
surrendering the fort, to march with his troops, unmolested, to
Virginia.   Such was the beginning of open hostilities, which
were succeeded by a series of other hostilities, characterized by
the spirit and manner of war, although the formal declaration of
war was not made until 1756, two years after, as already
mentioned.

10. The British ministry, perceiving war to be inevitable,
recommended to the British colonies in America to unite in some
scheme for their common defence. Accordingly, a convention
of delegates from Massachusetts, New Hampshire, Rhode Island,
Connecticut, Pennsylvania, Maryland, with the lieutenant-governor and council of New York, was held at Albany, in 1754, and

---

* The commandant was M. de St. Pierre; he was occupying a fort which
the French called Venango, on the site of the present village of Franklin,
the chief town of Venango country.

a plan * of union adopted, resembling, in several of its features, the present constitution of the United States. But the plan met with the approbation neither of the provincial assemblies nor the king's council. By the former it was rejected, because it gave too much power to the crown; and by the latter, because it gave too much power to the people.

CAMPAIGN OF 1755.† — 1. Early in the spring of 1755, preparations were made by the colonies for vigorous exertions against the enemy. Four expeditions were planned: — one against the French in Nova Scotia, a second against the French on the Ohio, a third against Crown Point, and a fourth against Niagara.

2. The expedition against Nova Scotia, consisting of three thousand men, chiefly from Massachusetts, was conducted by Generals Monckton and Winslow. With these troops they sailed from Boston, May 20th, and on the 1st of June arrived at Chignecto, in the Bay of Fundy. After being joined by three hundred British troops, and a small train of artillery, they proceeded against Fort Beau Se-jour, which, after four days' invest-

---

* According to this plan, a grand council was to be formed, of members chosen by the provincial assemblies, and sent from all the colonies; which council, with a governor-general, appointed by the crown, and having a negative voice, should be empowered to make general laws, to raise money in all the colonies for their defence, to call forth troops, regulate trade, lay duties, &c. &c.

The plan, thus matured, was approved and signed, on the fourth of July, — the day that Washington surrendered Fort Necessity, and twenty-two years before the Declaration of Independence, — by all the delegates, excepting those from Connecticut, who objected to the negative voice of the governor-general.

One circumstance, in the history of this plan, deserves here to be recorded, as evincing the dawning spirit of the Revolution. Although the plan was rejected by the provincial assemblies, they declared, without reserve, that, if it were adopted, they would undertake to defend themselves from the French, without assistance from Great Britain. They required but to be left to employ their supplies in their own way, to effect their security and predominance.

The mother country was too jealous to trust such powers with the Americans; but she proposed another plan, designed to lay a foundation for the perpetual dependence and slavery of the colonies. This plan was, that the governors, with one or more of their council, should form a convention to concert measures for the general defence, to erect fortifications, raise men, &c. &c., with power to draw upon the British treasury, to defray all charges; which charges should be reimbursed by taxes upon the colonies, imposed by acts of Parliament. But to allow the British government the right of taxation, to lay the colonies under the obligation of a debt to be thus liquidated, to subject themselves to the rapacity of king's collectors, we scarcely need say was a proposal which met with universal disapprobation.

† For the principal events of the campaign of 1755, the pupil is referred to page 130; and the teacher should question him as to those events, and the events of every subsequent campaign of the war.

12

ment, surrendered.   The name of the fort was now changed to that of Cumberland.   From this place General Monckton proceeded further into the country, took other forts in possession of the French, and disarmed the inhabitants.   By this successful expedition, the English possessed themselves of the whole country of Nova Scotia, a part of which the French claimed; its tranquillity was restored, and placed upon a permanent basis.

3. The French force in Nova Scotia being subdued, a difficult question occurred, respecting the disposal of the inhabitants. Fearing that they might join the French in Canada, whom they had before furnished with intelligence, quarters and provisions, it was determined to disperse them among the English colonies. Under this order, nearly two thousand miserable occupants of a sterile soil, and yet attached to it, and so loyal as to refuse to take the oath of allegiance to the King of England, were driven on board the British shipping, and dispersed among the English colonies.

4. The expedition against the French on the Ohio was led by General Braddock, a British officer, who commenced his march from Virginia in June, with about two thousand men, for Fort du Quesne.   Leaving Colonel Dunbar to follow, within the heavy baggage, he selected twelve hundred troops, and pressed forward.   When at the distance of some twelve or fourteen miles from the fort, he was warned by his officers to guard against surprise ; but, too self-confident to receive advice, he urged forward his troops, and, on the 9th of July, when within seven miles of the fort, he was suddenly attacked by a body of French and Indians.   Although the enemy did not exceed five hundred, yet, after an action of three hours, Braddock, under whom five horses had been killed, was mortally wounded, and his troops defeated,* with the loss to the English army of sixty-four out of eighty-five officers, and nearly half the privates.

---

* De Haas, in his History of Western Virginia, maintains, as an unquestionable point of history, that Braddock was shot by one of his own men, by the name of Tom Fausett.   Braddock had issued a foolish yet positive order, that none of the troops should protect themselves behind trees.   Regardless of this, Joseph Fausett, a brother of Tom, had so posted himself ; which Braddock perceiving, rode up, and struck him down with his sword. Tom saw his brother fall, and immediately drew up his rifle, and shot Braddock in the back.   The ball was stopped, in its passage through the body, by a coat of mail in front.   Tom Fausett is said to have died in 1828, at the great age of one hundred and fourteen years.   The sash of General Braddock (in which he was borne from the field) was presented, in 1846, by a gentleman of New Orleans, into whose possession it had come, to General Taylor.   It was composed of red silk, and the date of its manufacture was interwoven, " 1707."   The blood of General Braddock had left marks upon it of deep discolorations.

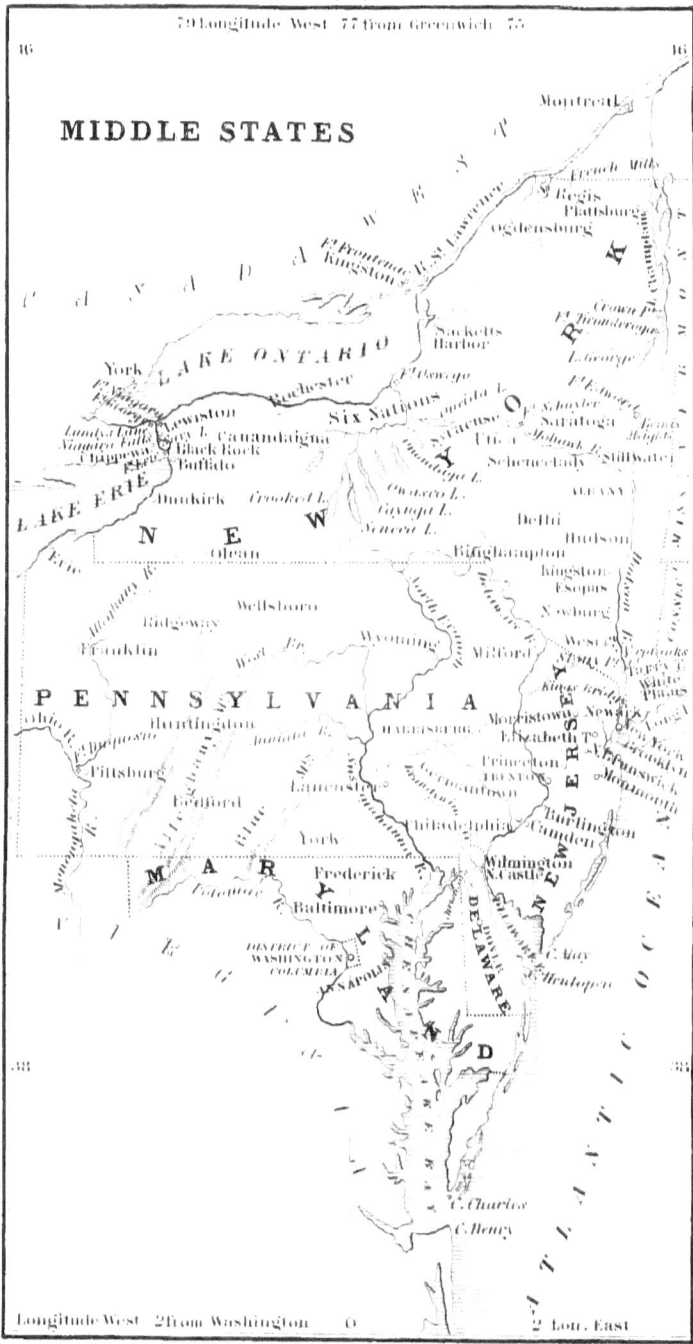

5. A remarkable event in the history of this affair remains to be told. General Braddock held the provincial troops in great contempt. Consequently, he kept the Virginians, and other provincials who were in the action, in the rear. Yet, although equally exposed with the rest, far from being affected with the fears that disordered the regular troops, they stood firm and unbroken, and, under Colonel Washington, covered the retreat of the regular troops, and saved them from total destruction. The retreat of the army, after Braddock was wounded, was precipitate. No pause was made until the rear division, under Colonel Dunbar, was met. This division, on its junction with the other, was seized with the same spirit of flight; and both divisions proceeded to Fort Cumberland, a distance of nearly one hundred and twenty miles from the place of action. Had the troops, even here, recovered their spirits and returned, success might still have crowned the expedition. At least, the army might have rendered the most important service to the cause, by preventing the devastations and inhuman murders perpetrated by the French and Indians, during the summer, on the western borders of Virginia and Pennsylvania. But, instead of adopting a course so salutary and important, Colonel Dunbar, leaving the sick and wounded at Cumberland, marched with his troops to Philadelphia.

6. The expedition against Crown Point was conducted by General William Johnson, a member of the council of New York; and although it failed as to its main object, yet its results diffused exultation through the American colonies, and dispelled the gloom which followed Braddock's defeat. The army under Johnson arrived at the south end of Lake George the latter part of August. While here, intelligence was received that a body of the enemy, two thousand in number, had landed at Southbay, now Whitehall, under command of Baron Dieskau, and were marching towards Fort Edward, for the purpose of destroying some provisions and military stores. At a council of war, it was resolved to detach a party to intercept the French and save the fort. This party consisted of twelve hundred men, commanded by Colonel Ephraim Williams, of Deerfield, Massachusetts. Unfortunately, this detachment was surprised by Dieskau, who was lying in ambush for them. After a most signal slaughter, in which Colonel Williams, and Hendrick, a renowned Mohawk sachem, and many other officers, fell, the detachment was obliged to retreat.

7. The firing was heard in the camp of Johnson; and, as it seemed to approach nearer and nearer, it was naturally conjectured

that the English troops were repulsed. The best preparations which the time allowed were made to receive the advancing foe. Dieskau, with his troops, soon appeared, and commenced a spirited attack. They were received, however, with so much intrepidity,—the cannon and musketry did so much execution among their ranks,— that the enemy retired in great disorder, having experienced a signal defeat, rendered still more severe by a mortal wound received by Dieskau, by which he fell into the hands of the English.*

8. The expedition against NIAGARA was committed to Governor Shirley, of Massachusetts, whose force amounted to two thousand five hundred men. But the season was too far advanced, before his preparations were completed, to effect anything of importance. After proceeding to Oswego, on Lake Ontario, the army being poorly supplied with provisions, and the rainy season approaching, the expedition was abandoned, and the troops returned to Albany. Thus ended the campaign of 1755.

CAMPAIGN OF 1756.—1. In the spring of 1756, Governor Shirley was succeeded by General Abercrombie, until the arrival of the Earl of Loudon, commander-in-chief of all his majesty's forces in America. The hostilities of the two preceding years

---

* Few events of no greater magnitude leave stronger impressions than resulted from the battle of Lake George. Following, as it did, the discomfiture of Braddock, it served to restore the honor of the British arms, and the tone of the public mind.

At the time it was meditated to send a detachment, under Colonel Williams, to intercept Dieskau, the number of men proposed was mentioned to Hendrick, the Mohawk chief, and his opinion asked. He replied, "If they are to fight, they are too few. If they are to be killed, they are too many." The number was accordingly increased. General Johnson proposed to divide the detachment into three parties. Upon this, Hendrick took three sticks, and, putting them together, said to him, "Put these together, and you cannot break them ; take them one by one, and you will break them easily." The hint succeeded, and Hendrick's sticks saved many of the party, and probably the whole army, from destruction.

Among the wounded of the French, as already stated, was the Baron Dieskau. He had received a ball through his leg; and, being unable to follow his retreating army, was found by an English soldier, resting upon the stump of a tree, with scarcely an attendant. Dieskau, apprehensive for his safety, was feeling for his watch, in order to give it to the soldier, when the man, suspecting that he was feeling for a pistol, levelled his gun, and wounded him in the hips. He was carried to the camp, and treated with great kindness. From the camp he was removed to Albany and New York, whence, some time after, he sailed for England, where he died. He was a superior officer, possessed of honorable feelings, and adorned with highly polished manners. One stain, however, attaches to his character. Before his engagement with Colonel Williams' corps, he gave orders to his troops neither to give nor take quarter.

had been carried on without any formal proclamation of war; but on the 17th of May, as already stated, war was declared by Great Britain against France, and, soon after, by France against Great Britain, in turn.

2. The plan of operations for the campaign of 1756 embraced the attack of NIAGARA and CROWN POINT, still in possession of the French. Both these places were of great importance: the former being the connecting link in the line of fortifications between Canada and Louisiana; and the latter commanding Lake Champlain, and guarding the only passage, at that time, into Canada. But, important as they were, the reduction of neither was this year accomplished, nor even attempted, owing, chiefly, to the great delays of those who held the chief command. Troops were raised for the expedition against Crown Point, amounting to seven thousand, the command of whom was assigned to Major-general Winslow, of Massachusetts. But his march was delayed by obstacles ascribed to the improvidence of Abercrombie.

3. After the mortal wound received by Dieskau at the battle of Lake George, the Marquis de Montcalm, an able and enterprising officer, succeeded to the command of the French forces. In the month of August, this officer, with eight thousand regular troops, Canadians and Indians, invested the fort at Oswego, on the south side of Lake Ontario, — one of the most important posts held by the English in America, — and in a few days took it. On the receipt of this intelligence, Lord Loudon, who entered upon the command, despatched orders to General Winslow, on his march towards Crown Point, not to proceed. The fall of the fort at Oswego was most unfortunate for the English; and their loss of men made prisoners, and munitions of war, peculiarly severe.

4. By the capture of this post, the enemy obtained the entire command of the Lakes Ontario and Erie, and of the whole country of the Six Nations. Sixteen hundred men were made prisoners, and one hundred and twenty pieces of cannon were taken, with fourteen mortars, two sloops-of-war, and two hundred boats and batteaux. After this disastrous event, all offensive operations were immediately relinquished, although it was then three months to the time of the usual decampment of the army. Thus, through the inactivity of a man whose leading trait was indecision, not one object of the campaign was gained.

CAMPAIGN OF 1757. — 1. Notwithstanding the failure of the campaign of 1756, the British Parliament made great preparations to prosecute the war of 1757. In July, an armament of

12*

eleven ships-of-the-line and fifty transports, with more than six thousand troops, arrived at Halifax, destined for the reduction of Louisburg. The colonies having been raising men for an expedition against Ticonderoga and Crown Point, their disappointment was great to learn, from the orders of Lord Loudon, that these troops were to be employed against Louisburg. But they were obliged to submit; and his lordship proceeded to join the armament at Halifax. So dilatory were their measures, however, that, before they were ready to sail, Louisburg was reinforced by a fleet of seventeen sail, and with troops to make it nine thousand strong. On the reception of this intelligence, the expedition was abandoned.

2. While weakness and indecision were thus marking the councils of the English, the French continued to urge on their victories. Montcalm, still commander of the French in the north, finding the troops withdrawn from Halifax for the reduction of Louisburg, seized the occasion to make a descent on Fort William Henry, situated on the north shore of Lake George, and garrisoned by three thousand men. With a force of nine thousand, he laid siege to it, and, at the expiration of six days, took it, thus securing the command of the lake, and of the western frontier.*

3. The defence of Fort William Henry was so gallant, that Colonel Munroe, with his troops, was admitted to an honorable capitulation. The capitulation, however, was most shamefully broken. While the troops were marching out at the gate of the fort, the Indians attached to Montcalm's party dragged the men from their ranks, and, with all the inhumanity of savage feeling, plundered them of their baggage, and butchered

* The defence of the fort against such numbers reflected the highest honor upon its brave commander, Colonel Munroe. Six days was the enemy kept at bay with unabated resolution, in full expectation of assistance from General Webb, who lay at Fort Edward, only fifteen miles distant, with an army of four thousand men.

The character of General Webb continues sullied by his unpardonable indifference to the perilous situation of his brethren in arms at Fort William Henry. It deserves to be known, that Sir William Johnson, after very importunate solicitations, obtained leave of General Webb to march, with as many as would volunteer in the service, to the relief of Munroe.

At the beat of the drums, the provincials, almost to a man, sallied forth, and were soon ready and eager for the march. After being under arms almost all day, what were their feelings when Sir William, returning from head-quarters, informed them that General Webb had forbidden them to march!

The soldiers were inexpressibly mortified and enraged; and their commander did himself no common honor in the tears he shed, as he turned from his troops, and retired to his tent.

them in cold blood. Out of a New Hampshire corps of two hundred, eighty were missing. It is said that efforts were made by the French to restrain the barbarians; but the truth of the assertion may well be doubted, when it is considered that Montcalm had at least seven thousand French in command, and yet these barbarians were not restrained.

CAMPAIGN OF 1758.—1. In 1758, the celebrated Pitt, Lord Chatham, was placed at the head of the administration, and breathed a new soul into the British councils, reviving the energies of the colonies, weakened and exhausted by a series of ill-contrived and unfortunate expeditions. The tide of success now turned in favor of the English, who continued, with some few exceptions, to achieve one victory after another, until the whole of Canada surrendered to the British arms. Upon coming into office, Pitt addressed a circular to the colonial governors, in which he assured them of the determination of the ministry to send a large force to America, and called upon them to raise as many troops as the number of inhabitants would allow. To this call the colonies promptly responded, Massachusetts, Connecticut and New Hampshire, unitedly, raising fifteen thousand men, who were ready to take the field in May.

2. Three expeditions were proposed: — the first against Louisburg; the second against Ticonderoga; the third against Fort du Quesne.

3. On the expedition against LOUISBURG, Admiral Boscawen sailed from Halifax, May 28th, with a fleet of twenty ships-of-the-line, eighteen frigates, and an army of fourteen thousand men, under the command of Brigadier-general Amherst, next to whom in command was General Wolfe. On the 26th of July, after a vigorous resistance, this important fortress was surrendered, and with it more than five thousand prisoners, and large munitions of war. At the same time, St. Johns, with Cape Breton, fell into the hands of the English, who now became masters of the coast from the St. Lawrence to Nova Scotia. The surrender of this fortress was a more signal loss to France than any which she had sustained, since the commencement of the war. It greatly obstructed her communications with Canada, and was powerfully instrumental in hastening the subjugation of that country to the British crown.

4. The expedition against TICONDEROGA was conducted by General Abercrombie, now commander-in-chief in America, Lord Loudon having returned to England. An army of sixteen thousand men, nine thousand of whom were provincials, followed his standard, besides a formidable train of artillery. Having

passed Lake George, the army proceeded, with great difficulty, towards the fortress. Unfortunately, Abercrombie trusted to others, who were incompetent to the task, to reconnoitre the ground and intrenchments of the enemy; and, without a knowledge of the strength of the places, or of the proper points of attack, issued his orders to attempt the lines, without bringing up a single piece of artillery. The army advanced to the charge with the greatest intrepidity, and for more than four hours maintained the attack with incredible obstinacy. After the loss of nearly two thousand in killed and wounded, the troops were summoned away. The retreat was as unhappy as the attack had been precipitate and ill-advised. Had the siege been prosecuted with prudence and vigor, the reduction of the place would have been easily accomplished, without such a waste of human life, as the garrison amounted to but little more than three thousand men.*

5. After his repulse, Abercrombie retired to his former quarters on Lake George. Here, anxious in any way to repair the mischief and disgrace of defeat, he consented, at the solicitation of Colonel Bradstreet, to detach him, with three thousand men, against Fort Frontenac, on the north-west side of the outlet of Lake Ontario. With these troops, mostly provincial, Bradstreet sailed down the Ontario, landed within a mile of the fort, opened his batteries, and in two days forced this important fortress to surrender. Nine armed vessels, sixty cannon, sixteen mortars, and a vast quantity of ammunition, &c. &c., fell into his hands.

6. To dispossess the French at Fort du Quesne, the bulwark of their dominion over the western regions, was a third expedition contemplated this year. This enterprise was intrusted to General Forbes, who left Philadelphia in July, but did not arrive at Du Quesne till late in November. The force collected for the attack amounted to eight thousand effective men. An attack, however, was needless, the fort having been deserted by

---

* The passage of Abercrombie across Lake George, on his way with his army to Ticonderoga, was effected by means of one thousand and thirty-five boats. The splendor of the military parade on the occasion was eminently imposing. Dr. Dwight thus describes it :

"The morning was bright and beautiful ; and the fleet moved with exact regularity, to the sound of fine martial music. The ensigns waved and glittered in the sunbeams, and the anticipation of future triumph shone in every eye. Above, beneath, around, the scenery was that of enchantment. Rarely has the sun, since that luminary was first lighted up in the heavens, dawned on such a complication of beauty and magnificence." How greatly did all this parade, and all the anticipation indulged, add to the mortification of the defeat which followed !

the garrison the evening before the arrival of the army. In honor of Mr. Pitt, its name was now changed to Pittsburg.

7. Another event of this year concurred in bringing to pass the fortunate issues of the next. This was a treaty of peace and friendship with the Six Nations, and other tribes inhabiting between the Apalachian Mountains, the Alleghanies, and the lakes. This treaty was concluded at Easton, sixty miles from Philadelphia.*

CAMPAIGN OF 1759. — 1. The campaign of 1759 having for its ultimate object the conquest of Canada, three separate forces were raised: one, under General Amherst, for the reduction of TICONDEROGA and CROWN POINT, and thence to proceed to Quebec by Lake Champlain and the St. Lawrence; a second, under General Prideaux, to proceed against NIAGARA, and thence to Montreal; while a third, under Wolfe, was to ascend the St. Lawrence for the siege of QUEBEC, there to be joined by Amherst and his forces. On the 22d of July, Amherst reached Ticonderoga; soon after which it surrendered, the principal part of the garrison having retired to Crown Point. Having strengthened Ticonderoga, the army next proceeded against that also, of which they took quiet possession, the enemy having fled before their arrival. On the arrival of General Prideaux at Niagara, July 6, the fort was immediately invested: on the 24th, a general battle took place, which decided the fate of Niagara, and placed it in the hands of the English.†

2. While the English troops were achieving these important victories, General Wolfe was prosecuting the most important enterprise of the campaign, namely, the reduction of Quebec. Embarking at Louisburg with eight thousand men, under convoy of Admirals Saunders and Holmes, he landed with his troops, in June, on the Island of Orleans, below Quebec. After several fruitless attempts to reduce the place, Wolfe decided to avail himself of a project said to have been suggested by General

---

* The managers of the treaty, on the part of Great Britain, were the Governors of Pennsylvania and New Jersey, Sir William Johnson, four members of the council of Pennsylvania, six members of assembly, and two agents from New Jersey.

The tribes represented on this occasion, and with which the treaty was made, were the Mohawks, Oneidas, Onondagoes, Cayugas, Senecas, Tuscaroras, Nanticoques, and Conays, the Tuteloes, Chugnuts, Delawares, Unamies, Minisinks, Mohicans, and Wappingers. The whole number of Indians, including women and children, present, amounted to five hundred.

† Four days previous to this battle, that able and distinguished officer, General Prideaux, was killed, by the bursting of a cohorn. The command devolved on Sir William Johnson, who successfully put in execution the plans of his lamented predecessor.

Townshend, of ascending a precipice of from one hundred and fifty to two hundred feet, by which he would reach the Plains of Abraham, and thus gain access to the enemy in a less fortified spot.

3. Accordingly, the troops were transported up the river about nine miles. On the 12th of September, one hour after midnight, Wolfe and his troops left the ships, and in boats silently dropped down the current, intending to land a league above Cape Diamond, and there ascend the bank leading to the station he wished to gain. Owing, however, to the rapidity of the river, they fell below the intended place, and landed a mile, or a mile and a half, above the city. The operation was a critical one, as they had to navigate, in silence, down a rapid stream, and to find a right place for landing, — which, amidst surrounding darkness, might be easily mistaken. Besides this, the shore was shelving, and the banks so steep and lofty as scarcely to be ascended, even without opposition from an enemy.

4. About an hour before day, the army began to ascend the precipice, the distance of one hundred and fifty or two hundred feet almost perpendicular ascent, above which spread the Plains of Abraham. By daylight, September 13th, this almost incredible enterprise had been effected; the desired station was attained, the army was formed, and ready to meet the enemy. To Montcalm this intelligence was most surprising. The impossibility of ascending the precipice he considered certain, and therefore had taken no measures to fortify its line. But no sooner was he informed of the position of the English army, than, perceiving a battle no longer to be avoided, he prepared to fight. Between nine and ten o'clock, the two armies, about equal in numbers, met face to face.

5. The battle now commenced. Inattentive to the fire of a body of Canadians and Indians, one thousand five hundred of whom Montcalm had stationed in the corn-fields and bushes, Wolfe directed his troops to reserve their fire for the main body of the French, now rapidly advancing. On their approach within forty yards, the English opened their fire, and the destruction became immense. The French fought bravely, but their ranks became disordered, and, notwithstanding the repeated efforts of their officers to form them, and to renew the attack, they were so successfully pushed by the British bayonet, and hewn down by the Highland broad-sword, that their discomfiture was complete.

6. During the action, Montcalm was on the French left, and Wolfe on the English right; and here they both fell, in the critical moment that decided the victory. Early in the battle, Wolfe received a ball in his wrist, but continued to encourage

his men. Shortly after, another ball penetrated his groin; but this wound, although much more severe, he concealed, till a third bullet pierced his breast. He was now obliged, though reluctant, to be carried to the rear of the line. General Monckton succeeded to the command; but, being immediately wounded, was conveyed away, upon which the command devolved upon General Townshend. Montcalm, fighting in front of his battalion, received a mortal wound about the same time, and General Jennezergus, his second in command, fell near his side.

7. Wolfe died in the field, before the battle was ended; but he lived sufficiently long to know that the victory was his. While leaning on the shoulder of a lieutenant, who kneeled to support him, he was seized with the agonies of death: at this moment was heard the distant sound, "They fly — they fly!" The hero raised his drooping head, and eagerly asked, "Who fly?" Being told that it was the French — "Then," he replied, "I die happy," and expired.* The result of this battle, so fatal to the heroic Wolfe, and yet so honorable to the British arms, was the capture of a thousand prisoners, and the death of a thousand French troops. The loss of the English scarcely exceeded six hundred, in killed and wounded. Five days after, the city capitulated: the inhabitants were to enjoy their civil and religious rights, and remain neutral during the war. The city was garrisoned under command of General Murray. The capture of Quebec, which soon followed, important as it was, did not immediately terminate the war. The French in Canada had still a powerful army, and some naval force above the city.

CAMPAIGN OF 1760. — 1. In the ensuing spring, 1760, Monsieur Levi approached Quebec, from Montreal, assisted by six frigates, for the purpose of recovering it from the English. General Murray, who commanded the English garrison, marched to meet him, with only three thousand men; and, on the 28th of April, after a bloody battle, fought at Sillsery, three miles above the city, the English army was defeated, with the loss of one thousand men, the French having lost more than double

---

* "This death," says Professor Silliman, "has furnished a grand and pathetic subject for the painter, the poet and the historian; and, undoubtedly, considered as a specimen of mere military glory, it is one of the most sublime that the annals of war afford."

Montcalm was every way worthy of being the competitor of Wolfe. In talents, in military skill, in personal courage, he was not his inferior. Nor was his death much less sublime. He lived to be carried to the city, where his last moments were employed in writing, with his own hand, a letter to the English general, recommending the French prisoners to his care and humanity. When informed that his wound was mortal, he replied, "I shall not, then, live to see the surrender of Quebec."

that number. The English retreated to Quebec, to which the French now laid siege. About the middle of May, an English squadron arrived with reinforcements, soon after which the French fleet was taken and destroyed, and the siege was raised.

2. The attention of General Amherst was now directed to the reduction of Montreal, the last fortress of consequence in the possession of the French. To effect this, he detached Colonel Haviland, with a well-disciplined army, to proceed to Lake George, Crown Point, and Lake Champlain; General Murray was ordered from Quebec, with such forces as could be spared from the garrison, while General Amherst himself proceeded, with ten thousand men, by Lake Ontario, down the river St. Lawrence. Generals Amherst and Murray arrived at Montreal on the 6th of September, and were joined by Haviland on the day succeeding. While preparing to lay siege to the place, the commander of Montreal, M. de Vaudreuil, perceiving that resistance would be ineffectual, demanded a capitulation. On the 8th, Montreal, Detroit, Michilimackinac, and all the other places within the government of Canada, were surrendered to his Britannic majesty.

3. Thus ended a war which, from the first hostilities, had continued six years, and during which much distress had been experienced, and many thousand valuable lives lost. Great and universal was the joy of the colonies at the successful termination of a contest so long and severe; and public thanksgivings were generally appointed, to ascribe due honor to HIM who had preserved to them their existence and liberties.

4. While the troops were thus employed in the conquest of Canada, the colonies of Virginia and South Carolina suffered invasion and outrage from the Cherokees, a powerful tribe of savages on the west. But, in 1761, they were signally defeated by Colonel Grant, and compelled to sue for peace.

5. The conquest of Canada having been achieved, in 1763 a definitive treaty, the preliminaries of which had been settled the year before, was signed at Paris, and soon after ratified by the Kings of England and France; by which all Nova Scotia, Canada, the Isle of Cape Breton, and all other islands in the gulf and river St. Lawrence, were ceded to the British crown.

UNITED STATES.

PERIOD IV.

DISTINGUISHED FOR THE WAR OF THE REVOLUTION.

EXTENDING FROM THE COMMENCEMENT OF HOSTILITIES BY GREAT BRITAIN, AGAINST THE AMERICAN COLONIES, IN THE BATTLE OF LEXINGTON, 1775, TO THE DISBANDING OF THE AMERICAN ARMY, AT WEST POINT, 1783.

1. " THE Revolution in America," the first blood of which was shed in the battle of Lexington, Massachusetts, on the 19th of April, 1775, was an extraordinary event, and at the time of its occurrence was unlooked for, both by the government and nation of Great Britain. That the colonies had long been dissatisfied with the conduct of England towards them, and that this dissatisfaction was gradually increasing, was well known ; but the statesmen on the other side supposed that they should be able to secure the submission of the colonies to whatever line of policy they might choose to adopt.

2. But they little understood the American character. The colonists had, indeed, filial feelings towards the mother country. That was their " home ; " and, aside from the treatment they met with, they had no desire or intention of becoming independent. Had the British statesmen shown kindness towards them, they might have preserved the bond of union ; but, by means of neglect, of acts of oppression, of restriction upon commerce, and abusive taxation, they hastened the very event which they so much deplored. Let us advert to some of the remote and proximate causes of the Revolution. These were :

13

A love of liberty inherited from the Pilgrim Fathers.	Stamp act. Writs of assistance.
Forms of government adopted in the colonies.	Arrival and conduct of royal officers and troops.
Neglect of the mother country.	Affray of the 5th March, 1770.
Early measures of oppression.	Introduction and destruction of
Restrictions on commerce.	tea.
Prohibition of manufactures.	First Continental Congress.
Unjust taxation.	Massachusetts Provincial As-
Transportation of Americans to England for trial.	sembly.

3. At the era of this great event, thirteen colonies had been planted. These were Virginia, Massachusetts, New Hampshire, Connecticut, Rhode Island, New York, New Jersey, Delaware, Pennsylvania, Maryland, North and South Carolina, and Georgia. Different objects were proposed in the establishment of these colonies. Some had pecuniary profit in view. They hoped for returns for capital advanced. The northern colonies, on the other hand, came on their own concern, at their own expense, and for the enjoyment of religious freedom, of which they were deprived at home.

4. Now, was it to be expected that such persons would tamely consent to have that liberty abridged? If many of the Pilgrim Fathers had such love of liberty, would not their descendants be likely to have? The spirit of liberty does not easily die; especially among a people where everything tends to strengthen their physical frame, and increase their moral courage. Felling forests, resisting savages, building towns, were quite likely to make the young, ardent and ambitious, think of and long for independence.

5. In the next place, the forms of government adopted by the colonists conduced to independence. Three forms of government existed, — charter, proprietary, and royal. The charter governments were confined to New England; the proprietary governments were those of Maryland, Pennsylvania, the Carolinas, and the Jerseys. The others were royal governments, or those immediately subject to the crown.

6. Setting aside the royal governments, where the spirit of liberty might be supposed to be kept in check, look at the others. As early as 1619, only twelve years from its settlement, a provincial legislature, in which the colonists were represented, was introduced into Virginia (p. 31). In Plymouth (p. 39) and in Massachusetts (p. 46), the colonies organized

their bodies politic and social upon principles of perfect equality. In 1639, only three years after the commencement of the Connecticut colony, it formed a system of government which most admirably provided for the rights of all (p. 75). Maryland, Pennsylvania and the Carolinas, did essentially the same.

7. The very first principles, then, of the colonies, were anti-monarchical, and in favor of and tending to liberty. And this early spirit was never lost to them. It continued unabated, and, indeed, strengthened, until at last it ended in a broad, irresistible current against British oppression.

8. The neglect of Britain contributed to the same result. Excepting Georgia, all the thirteen colonies were established, and had attained to considerable strength, without the slightest aid from the treasury of England. Neither the crown nor the Parliament paid one dollar towards purchasing the soil of the Indians. The whole expense fell upon the colonists. The settlement of Massachusetts Bay cost two hundred thousand pounds. Lord Baltimore expended forty thousand pounds in settling Maryland. Virginia cost the first settlers immense wealth. The same was true of the original planters of Connecticut.

9. This they could have borne. But what shall be said of the conduct of England, during those long, fierce, and bloody Indian wars, declared on her account? In not one did she furnish any pecuniary aid whatever, and seldom any troops. She erected no fortifications, and manifested no sympathy; hundreds died, — nay, thousands, — some from famine, some through hardship and fatigue, and others by the arrow and tomahawk. But she heeded it not. Her wars were carried on by the colonies, and then they were left to pay the expenses. The natural consequences of such a policy are obvious. Teach a child to walk early, and he will soon decline your aid. Send a son abroad to take care of himself, and he will soon require no parental assistance. The colonists, neglected as they were, soon learned the important fact, that they could take care of themselves.

10. But that which more directly tended to hasten the Revolution than all other causes was parliamentary measures of oppression. These consisted of restrictions upon commerce, prohibitions to carry on manufactures, writs of assistance, various plans for taxation, and laws by which to send persons to England for trial; the object of all which was either to enrich the mother country, or to keep the colonies in subjection.

11. Writs of assistance were orders issued by the Superior

Court of the province, requiring sheriffs and other civil officers to assist the person to whom they were granted in breaking open and searching every place, even private dwellings, if suspected of containing prohibited goods. The first application of the kind was made by the deputy collector of Salem, in 1760. The power of the court to grant such writs being called into question, a trial was had in the old town-house in Boston. Mr. Gridley, a distinguished lawyer, appeared for the crown ; Mr. Thatcher and Mr. Otis, for the merchants. The judges were five in number, of whom Lieutenant-governor Hutchinson was one, and the president of the bench. The room was filled with deeply anxious citizens.

12. Mr. Gridley opened the case, and maintained " that the Parliament of Great Britain was the sovereign legislator of the British empire." That body had ordered these writs, and hence no more was to be said. Mr. Thatcher followed, and Mr. Otis succeeded him. The elder President Adams was present. " Otis," said he, in after times, " was a flame of fire." " To my dying day," said Otis, raising his voice in tones of thunder, — " to my dying day, I will oppose, with all the powers and faculties God has given me, all such instruments of slavery on the one hand, and villany on the other."

13. The occasion was intensely exciting. The liberties of the people were in danger. Their very dwellings — those sanctuaries where every man should feel safe for himself and for his effects — were in jeopardy. So thought the vast throng then gathered ; " and they retired," says Mr. Adams, " each apparently ready, as I was, to take arms against writs of assistance." The court adjourned without coming to a decision. These writs were afterwards, in a few instances, granted, but were exceedingly unpopular. In Connecticut, it is said, they were never issued.

14. Before the peace of 1763, the subject of taxing the colonies had been wisely let alone. If money was wanted of them, the Parliament of England had been content to ask for it, and the colonial legislatures had supplied it with a willing hand. But, now, a different and oppressive policy was begun. The first act, the avowed purpose of which was a revenue from the colonies, passed the Parliament, September 29th, 1764, the preamble to which began thus : — " Whereas, it is just and necessary that a revenue be raised in America, for defraying the expenses of defending, protecting, and securing the same, we, the Commons," &c. The act then proceeds to lay a duty on " clayed sugar, indigo, coffee, &c. &c., being the produce of a colony not under the dominion of his majesty."

15. This act the colonies did not approve, because it recognized

a right to tax them while unrepresented in Parliament; whereas it was a fundamental law of all right government, — so they thought, — that taxation and representation were inseparable. Without such representation, their property might be taken from them, and no voice to remonstrate. This claim, of the right to tax, on the one side, and the denial of it, on the other, was the very hinge on which the Revolution turned.

16. In 1765, the policy thus begun was followed up by the passage of the famous stamp act. This ordained that instruments of writing, such as deeds, bonds, notes, &c., among the colonies, should be null and void, unless executed on stamped paper, for which a duty should be paid to the crown.*

---

* This act consisted of fifty-five specific duties, laid on as many different instruments, in which paper was used. For a diploma or certificate of a college degree, two pounds were charged; for a license for selling wine, twenty shillings; for a common deed, one shilling and sixpence; for a newspaper, one half-penny to a penny; pamphlets, one shilling per sheet; advertisements, two shillings; almanacs, fourpence.

Such a measure had been suggested during the administrations of Walpole and Pitt. Said Walpole, "I will leave the taxation of America to some of my successors, who have more courage than I have;" and said Pitt, "I will never burn my fingers with an American stamp act."

When the bill was brought in, the ministers, and particularly Charles Townshend, exclaimed:

"These Americans, — our own children, — planted by our care, nourished by our indulgence, protected by our arms, until they have grown to a good degree of strength and opulence, — will they now turn their backs upon us, and grudge to contribute their mite to relieve us from the heavy load which overwhelms us ?"

Colonel Barré caught the words, and, with a vehemence becoming a soldier, rose and said:

"Planted by your care ! — No ! your oppression planted them in America. They fled from your tyranny into a then uncultivated land, where they were exposed to almost all the hardships to which human nature is liable, and, among others, to the savage cruelty of the enemy of the country, — a people the most subtle, and, I take upon me to say, the most truly terrible, of any people that ever inhabited any part of God's earth; and yet, actuated by principles of true English liberty, they met all these hardships with pleasure, compared with those they suffered in their own country, from the hands of those that should have been their friends.

"They nourished by your indulgence ! — They grew by your neglect. As soon as you began to care about them, that care was exercised in sending persons to rule over them, in one department and another, who were, perhaps, the deputies of the deputies of some members of this house, sent to spy out their liberty, to misrepresent their actions, and to prey upon them; men, whose behavior, on many occasions, has caused the blood of these sons of liberty to recoil within them; men promoted to the highest seats of justice, some of whom, to my knowledge, were glad, by going to foreign countries, to escape the vengeance of the laws in their own.

"They protected by your arms ! — They have nobly taken up arms in your defence; have exerted their valor, amidst their constant and laborious industry, for the defence of a country whose frontiers, while drenched in blood, its interior parts have yielded, for your enlargement, the little savings of

13*

17. On the arrival of the news of the stamp act in America, a general indignation spread through the country, and resolutions were passed against the act, by most of the colonial assemblies.* In June, Massachusetts recommended the meeting of a Colonial Congress, to consult for the general safety. To this recommendation eight colonies acceded, namely, Rhode Island, Connecticut, New York, New Jersey, Pennsylvania, Delaware, Maryland, and South Carolina, — commissioners from each of which met those from Massachusetts at New York, on the first Tuesday of October, 1765. This was the first general meeting of the colonies. Timothy Ruggles, a commissioner from Massachusetts, was chosen president. In their declaration, they acknowledged their allegiance to his majesty, and their willingness to render due honor to the rightful authority of Parliament; but they claimed that they had interests, rights and liberties, as the natural-born subjects of his majesty; and that, as they could not be represented in Parliament, that body had no right to impose taxes on them, without their consent. They declared

their frugality and the fruits of their toils, And, believe me, — remember I this day told you so, — that the same spirit which actuated that people at first will continue with them still."

The night after this act passed, Dr. Franklin, who was then in London, wrote to Charles Thompson, afterwards secretary of the Continental Congress, "The sun of liberty is set; the Americans must light the lamps of industry and economy." To which Mr. Thompson answered, " Be assured we shall light torches quite of another sort;" thus predicting the convulsions which were about to follow.

* The Assembly of Virginia was the first public body that met, after the news of the act reached America. Towards the close of the session, seven resolutions, chiefly relating to the rights and privileges of the colonies, were introduced into the House of Burgesses, by Patrick Henry, a young man highly distinguished for his moral courage, and bold and manly eloquence.

The debate on these resolutions was animated, and even violent. Nothing like them had ever transpired in America. They evinced a settled purpose of resistance, and conveyed to the ministry of Great Britain a lesson which, had they read with unprejudiced minds, might have saved them the fruitless struggle of a seven years' war. There were those in the House of Burgesses who strongly opposed the resolutions; but the bold and powerful eloquence of Henry bore them down, and carried five of them, though only by a majority of one ; the others were not adopted. In the heat of the debate, he boldly asserted that the king had acted the part of a tyrant; and, alluding to the fate of other tyrants, he exclaimed, " Cæsar had his BRUTUS, Charles I. his CROMWELL, and George III." — here pausing a moment, till the cry of " Treason, treason!" resounding from several parts of the house, had ended, — he added, " may profit by their example; if this be treason, make the most of it ! "

The next day, in the absence of Mr. Henry, the fifth resolution was rescinded; but that, with the others passed, had already gone forth to the world. By the friends of freedom they were received with enthusiasm, and served to raise still higher the justly indignant feelings of a people whose rights were disregarded.

the stamp act, and other acts of Parliament, to have a manifest tendency to subvert the rights and liberties of the colonists. This Congress adjourned on the 25th of October; their proceedings having been approved by all the members, except Mr. Ruggles, of Massachusetts, and Mr. Ogden, of New Jersey.

18. The stamp act came into operation on the first day of November. But on that day not a single sheet, of all the bales of stamps, could have been found in the colonies of New England, New York, New Jersey, Pennsylvania, Maryland, and the two Carolinas. They had either been committed to the flames, had been re-shipped to England, or were safely guarded by the opposition, into whose hands they had fallen. A general suspension of all business which required stamped paper was the consequence. The printers of newspapers only continued their occupation; alleging, for excuse, that if they had done otherwise, the people would have given them such an admonition as they little coveted. None would receive the gazettes coming from Canada, as they were printed on stamped paper. The courts of justice were shut; even marriages were no longer celebrated; and, in a word, an absolute stagnation in all the relations of social life was established.*

---

* It would scarcely be possible to convey an adequate idea of the feelings of opposition to this odious act which pervaded the friends of liberty in America. As might be expected, these feelings were manifested in various riotous proceedings, which not only cannot be justified, but which mar the sublime beauty of a people steadily asserting the rights given them by the God of nature.

One morning, about the middle of August, there were discovered two effigies hanging on the branch of an old elm, in the southern part of Boston; one of which was designed to represent a stamp-officer, — the other a jack-boot, out of which rose a horned head, appearing to look round.

The novelty of the spectacle soon attracted a multitude to the spot, which continued to increase all day. Towards evening, the effigies were taken down, placed on a bier, and carried in funeral procession through several streets, — a host following, and shouting, "Liberty and property forever! — no stamps!" At length, arriving in front of a house owned by one Oliver, which they supposed was intended for a stamp-office, they demolished it to its very foundations.

From this, they proceeded to his dwelling; but finding Oliver had fled, they destroyed his fences, broke open the doors of his dwelling, and greatly injured his furniture. On the following day, apprehensive of a second visit from this lawless multitude, Oliver gave public notice that he had forwarded to England his resignation as a stamp-officer. This becoming known by the populace, which had assembled to renew the last night's assault, they gave three cheers for Oliver, and departed without doing further damage.

They next proceeded to the mansion of Lieutenant-governor Hutchinson, who, with his family, had barely time to escape. It was now midnight. The work of destruction commenced; and, by four o'clock in the morning, "one of the best-finished houses in the colony had nothing remaining but the bare walls and floors." The rioters carried off between four and five thousand dollars, a large quantity of plate, family pictures and

19. About this time, associations were formed in the colonies, under the title of Sons of Liberty, the object of which was, by every practicable means, to oppose the unjust and arbitrary measures of the British government.   Added to this, societies were instituted, including females as well as males, the members of which resolved to forego all the luxuries of life, rather than be indebted to the commerce of England.   These societies denied themselves the use of all foreign articles of clothing ; carding, spinning and weaving, became the daily employment of women of fashion ; sheep were forbidden to be used as food, lest there should not be found a sufficient supply of wool ; and to be dressed in a suit of homespun was to possess the surest means of popular distinction. And so true were these societies to their mutual compact, that the British merchants and manufacturers soon began to feel the necessity of uniting with the colonies in petitioning Parliament for a repeal of the obnoxious law.

20. Fortunately for the interests both of the colonies and of Great Britain, a change took place, about this time, in the administration of England, by which Mr. Pitt, and other friends of America, came into power.   To this new ministry it was obvious that measures must be taken either to repeal the odious statute, or compel America to submit by force of arms.   The former being deemed the wiser course, a motion was made in Parliament to that effect ; and though the debate on the question was long and angry, it was at length carried ; but only by accompanying the repealing act by one called the declaratory act, the language of which was that Parliament have, and of right ought to have, power to bind the colonies in all cases whatsoever.

21. It was during the debate on the general question that Mr. Pitt, the invariable friend of the colonies, delivered his famous speech on American liberty ; in which he declared it to be his opinion that the kingdom had no right to tax the colonies ; that he rejoiced that they had resisted, and he hoped that they would resist to the last drop of their blood.   On learning this vote, the transports of the people were ungovernable.   Impressed with the conviction that they owed their deliverance to Mr. Pitt, their gratitude knew no bounds ; when he appeared at the door, in the language of Burke, " they jumped upon him, like children on a long absent father.   They clung to him as captives about

clothing.   Nothing was spared.   But, as destruction, and not plunder, was the object of the mob, the street in front of the house, the next morning, was found strewed with the money, plate and rings.

The opposition of the friends of liberty in other places was manifested by proceedings of a similar kind.

their redeemer. All England joined in his applause." In the House of Peers the opposition to the motion was still obstinate. Some of the dukes, and the whole bench of bishops, were for forcing the Americans to submit, with fire and sword.

22. The satisfaction of the colonies, on the repeal of the stamp act, was sincere and universal. Elevated with the idea of having removed an odious and oppressive burden, and believing, notwithstanding the declaratory act of Parliament, that the right to tax the colonies was at length surrendered, better feelings were indulged; commercial intercourse was revived, and larger importations of goods were made than ever. On the meeting of the House of Representatives of Massachusetts, a vote of gratitude to the king, and of thanks to Mr. Pitt, the Duke of Grafton, and others, was passed by that body. By the House of Burgesses, in Virginia, it was resolved to erect a statue in honor of the king, and an obelisk in honor of all those, whether of the House of Peers or of the Commons, who had distinguished themselves in favor of the rights of the colonies.

23. The enemies of American liberty in England had no intention, however, of surrendering their favorite project of taxing the colonies. In 1767, another plan was introduced into Parliament, namely, an imposition of duties on glass, paper, pasteboard, painter's colors, and tea. Mr. Pitt being unable, by reason of indisposition, to raise his voice against it, the bill passed both houses without much opposition, and received the royal assent. At the same time were passed two other acts, — the one establishing a new board of custom-house officers in America, and the other restraining the Legislature of the province of New York from passing any act whatever, until they should furnish the king's troops with several required articles.

24. These three acts reached America at the same time, and again excited universal alarm. The first and second were particularly odious. The new duties were only a new mode of drawing money from the colonies; and the same strong opposition to the measure was exhibited which had prevailed against the stamp act. Several of the colonies, through their colonial assemblies, expressed their just abhorrence of these enactments, and their determination never to submit to them.*

---

* Soon after the establishment of the new board of custom-house officers, at Boston, under the above act, a fit occasion presented itself for an expression of the public indignation. This was the arrival at that port, in May, 1768, of the sloop Liberty, belonging to Mr. Hancock, and laden with wines from Madeira.

During the night, most of her cargo was unladen, and put into stores ; on

25. The public excitement was soon after increased by the arrival in the harbor of two regiments of troops, under the command of Colonel Dalrymple. These were designed to assist the civil magistrates in the preservation of peace, and the custom-house officers in the execution of their functions. On the day after its arrival, the fleet was brought to anchor near Castle William. Having taken a station which commanded the town, the troops, under cover of the cannon of the ships, landed without molestation, and, to the number of upwards of seven hundred men, marched, with muskets charged, bayonets fixed, martial music, and the usual military parade, on to the common. In the evening, the selectmen of Boston were required to quarter the two regiments in the town; but they absolutely refused. A temporary shelter, however, in Faneuil Hall, was permitted to one regiment.

26. The next day, the state-house, by order of the governor, was opened for the reception of the soldiers; and after the quarters were settled, two field-pieces, with the main guard, were stationed just in its front. Everything was calculated to excite the indignation of the inhabitants. The lower floor of the state-house, which had been used by merchants as an exchange, the representatives' chamber, the court-house, Faneuil Hall, were all filled with soldiers. Guards were placed at the doors of the state-house, through which the council must pass, in going to their chamber. The common was covered with tents. Soldiers were constantly marching and countermarching to relieve the guards. The sentinels challenged the inhabitants as they passed. The Lord's day was profaned, and the devotion of the sanctuary disturbed by the sound of drums and other military music.

27. In February, 1769, Parliament went a step beyond all that had preceded, in an address to the king, requesting him to give orders to the Governor of Massachusetts to take notice of such as might be guilty of treason, that they might be sent to England and tried there. A measure more odious to the people

---

the following day, the sloop was entered at the custom-house, with a few pipes only. A discovery being made of these facts, by the custom-house officers, the vessel was seized, and by their order removed alongside of the Romney, a ship-of-war then in harbor. The conduct of the custom-house officers, in this transaction, aroused the indignant feelings of the Bostonians, who unwarrantably attacked the houses of the officers, and even assaulted their persons. No prosecutions, however, could be sustained, from the excited state of public feeling. Finding themselves no longer safe in town, the officers prudently sought protection on board the Romney, and subsequently retired to Castle William.

of America, or more hostile to the British constitution, could not be named, than for a man to be torn from his country, to be tried by a jury of strangers.

28. During the session of Parliament, in 1770, a bill was introduced abolishing duties imposed by the act of 1767 on all the articles, except tea. This partial suspension of the duties served to soften the feelings of the Americans; but the exception in relation to tea, it was quite apparent, was designed as a salvo to the national honor, and an evidence that the British ministry were unwilling to relinquish the right of Parliament to tax the colonies.

29. While affairs were in this posture, an event occurred which produced great excitement, especially in Massachusetts. This was an affray, on the evening of the 5th of March, 1770, between several of the citizens of Boston, and a number of British soldiers stationed at the custom-house. The quarrel commenced on the 2d inst., at Gray's rope-walk, between a soldier and a man employed at the rope-walk. The provocation was given by the citizen, and a scuffle ensued, in which the soldier was beaten. On the 5th, the soldiers, while under arms, were insulted, and dared to fire. One of them, who had received a blow, fired at the aggressor; and a single discharge from six others succeeded. Three of the citizens were killed, and five dangerously wounded. The town was instantly thrown into the greatest commotion; the bells were rung, and the general cry was, "To arms!" In a short time, several thousands of the citizens had assembled, and a scene of blood must have ensued, but for the promise of Governor Hutchinson, that the affair should be settled to their satisfaction in the morning. Captain Preston, who commanded the soldiers, was committed with them to prison. Upon their trial, the captain and six soldiers were acquitted; two were convicted of manslaughter. For several subsequent years, the evening of the day on which this outrage was committed was commemorated by the citizens of Boston; and the event gave occasion for addresses the most warm and patriotic, serving to waken up and increase the spirit of the Revolution.

30. During the summer of 1772, another event occurred, which presented a fresh obstacle to a reconciliation between America and the mother country. This was the destruction, by the people of Rhode Island, of a British armed schooner, called the Gaspee, which had been stationed in that colony to assist the board of customs in the execution of the revenue and trade laws. The destruction of the vessel grew out of an odious requisition of

her commander, upon the masters of packets, navigating the bay, to lower their colors on passing the schooner. On the 9th of June, this requisition was made on the captain of the Providence packet, as she was sailing into the harbor of Newport. Upon his refusal, a shot was fired from the schooner, which immediately made sail in chase. By dexterous management of the master of the packet, he led the schooner on to a shoal, where she grounded, and remained fast. At night, a number of fishermen, headed by several respectable merchants of Providence, made themselves masters of her, and set her on fire. When the knowledge of this event came to the governor, a reward of five hundred pounds was offered for the discovery of the offenders, and the royal pardon to those who would confess their guilt. Commissioners were appointed also to investigate the offence, and bring the perpetrators to justice. But, after remaining some time in session, they reported that they could obtain no evidence, and thus the affair terminated.

31. In 1773, an important measure was adopted by most of the colonies, namely, the appointment of committees of correspondence and inquiry, in various parts of their respective territories, by means of which a confidential and invaluable interchange of opinions was kept up between the colonies, and great unity of sentiment was thereby promoted. This measure had its origin in Boston, in an assembly of whose citizens a committee was appointed to address the several towns in the colony, and to urge upon them the importance of an unanimous expression of their feelings with regard to the conduct of the British ministry. These proceedings being communicated to the House of Burgesses, in Virginia, that body passed a resolution appointing a committee of correspondence and inquiry, whose business it was to obtain the most early and authentic intelligence of the proceedings of the British government in relation to the colonies, and to maintain a correspondence with the other colonies touching all affairs of mutual interest. Similar committees of correspondence and inquiry were appointed by the different colonial assemblies, and a confidential interchange of opinion was thus kept up between the colonies, and which served greatly to produce unity of sentiment and harmony of action.

32. During these movements, a plan was devised by the British Parliament to introduce tea into the colonies; little of which had, for some time, been imported, from a determination not to pay the existing duty upon it. To enable the East India Company to export their teas, which had greatly accumulated in their warehouses, the British minister introduced a bill into Par-

liament, allowing the company to export their teas into America, with a drawback of all the duties paid in England. As this would make the tea cheaper in America than in Great Britain, it was presumed that the Americans would pay the small duty upon it, which was only three pence. On the passage of this bill, therefore, the company made a shipment of large quantities of tea to Charleston, Philadelphia, New York and Boston. But, before its arrival, the resolution had been formed by the inhabitants of those places that it should not even be landed. The cargo destined for Charleston was, indeed, landed and stored, but was not permitted to be offered for sale. The vessels which brought tea to Philadelphia and New York were compelled to return to England, without even having made an entry at the custom-house.

33. It was designed by the leading patriots of Boston to make a similar disposition of the cargoes expected at that place ; but, on their arrival, the consignees were found to be the relations or friends of the governor, and they could not be induced to resign their trust. Several town-meetings were held, at which spirited resolutions were passed, among which was one, that no considerations would induce the inhabitants to permit the landing of the tea.

34. It was in this state of things that the citizens of Boston again assembled ; and while the discussions were going on, a

captain of a vessel was despatched to the governor to request a passport. At length, he returned to say, that the governor refused. The meeting was immediately dissolved. A secret plan had been formed to mingle the tea with the waters of the ocean. Three different parties soon after sallied out, in the costume of Mohawk Indians, and precipitately made their way to the wharves. At the same time, the citizens were seen in crowds directing their course to the same place, to become spectators of a scene, as novel as the enterprise was bold. Without noise, without tumult, the tea was taken from the vessel by the conspirators, and expeditiously offered as an oblation " to the watery god."

35. Intelligence of these proceedings being communicated, in a message from the throne, to both houses of Parliament, that body, by way of retaliation, passed a bill (March 7th, 1774), called the " Boston Port Bill," by which that port was precluded from the privilege of landing or discharging, or of loading and shipping goods, wares and merchandise. A second bill followed, essentially altering the charter of the province, — making the appointment of the council, justices, judges, &c., dependent upon the crown, or its agent. To these was added a third, authorizing and directing the governor to send any person indicted for murder, or any other capital offence, to another colony, or to Great Britain, for trial.

36. On the arrival of these acts, the town of Boston expressed its views in the following vote : " That it is the opinion of this town, that, if the other colonies come into a joint resolution to stop all importation from Great Britain and the West Indies, till the act for blocking up this harbor be repealed, the same will prove the salvation of North America and her liberties." Copies of this vote were transmitted to each of the colonies ; and as an expression of their sympathy with the people of Boston in their distress, the House of Burgesses, in Virginia, ordered that the day on which the Boston port bill was to take effect should be observed as a day of fasting and prayer.*

37. During these transactions in Massachusetts, measures had been taken to convene a Continental Congress. On the 4th of September, 1774, deputies from eleven colonies met at Philadelphia, and elected Peyton Randolph, the then late speaker of

---

* The words Whigs and Tories were about this time introduced, as the distinguishing names of parties. By the former was meant those who favored the cause of Boston, and were zealous in supporting the colonies against the Parliament ; by the latter was meant the favorers of Great Britain.

the Virginia assembly, president, and Charles Thompson secretary. During its session, this body agreed upon a declaration of their rights; recommended the non-importation of British goods into the country, and the non-exportation of American produce to Great Britain, so long as their grievances were unredressed. They also voted an address to his majesty, and likewise one to the people of Great Britain, and another to the French inhabitants of Canada.*

38. On the 5th of October following, General Gage summoned a meeting of the provincial assembly; but, before that period arrived, judging their meeting inexpedient, he counteracted the writs of convocation. The assembly, however, to the number of ninety, met at Salem, where, the governor not attending, they adjourned to Concord. Here, having chosen John Hancock president, they adjourned to Cambridge, where they drew up a plan for the immediate defence of the province, by enlisting men, appointing general officers, &c. In November, this assembly again met, and resolved to equip twelve thousand men, to act in any emergency; and to enlist one-fourth part of the militia as minutemen. At the same time, a request was forwarded to Connecticut, New Hampshire and Rhode Island, jointly to increase this army to twenty thousand men.

39. On the opening of the following year (January 7th), Lord Chatham, Mr. Pitt, after a long retirement, resumed his seat in the House of Lords, and introduced a conciliatory bill, the object of which was to settle the troubles in America. But the efforts of this venerable and peace-making man wholly failed, the bill not only being rejected by a large majority, but its rejection was

---

* The Congress of 1774 has justly been celebrated, from that time to the present; and its celebrity will continue while wisdom finds admirers, and patriotism is regarded with veneration. Both at home and abroad, they were spoken of in terms of the highest admiration. Abroad, the Earl of Chatham, in one of his brilliant speeches, remarked of them : "History, my lords, has been my favorite study; and in the celebrated writings of antiquity have I often admired the patriotism of Greece and Rome; but, my lords, I must declare and avow, that, in the master states of the world, I know not the people or senate who, in such a complication of difficult circumstances, can stand in preference to the delegates of America assembled in General Congress at Philadelphia." At home, they were celebrated by a native and popular bard, in an equally elevated strain:

"Now meet the fathers of this western clime ;
Nor names more noble graced the rolls of fame,
When Spartan firmness braved the wrecks of time,
Or Latian virtue fanned the heroic flame.

"Not deeper thought the immortal sage inspired,
On Solon's lips when Grecian senates hung ;
Nor manlier eloquence the bosom fired,
When genius thundered from the Athenian tongue."

followed, the next day, by the passage of a bill to restrain the trade of the New England provinces, and to forbid their fishing on the banks of Newfoundland. Soon after, restrictions were imposed upon the middle and southern colonies, with the exception of New York, Delaware, and North Carolina. This bill, designed to promote disunion among the colonies, happily failed of its object.

40. We have thus given a succinct account of the system of measures adopted by the ministry of England toward the American colonies, after the peace of 1763, — measures most unfeeling and unjust, but which no petitions, however respectful, and no remonstrances, however loud, could change. Satisfied of this, justice permitted the people, and self-respect and self-preservation loudly summoned them, to resist by force. The crisis, therefore, had now arrived ; the signal of war was given, and the blood shed at Lexington opened the scene.

PRINCIPAL EVENTS OF 1775.

Battle of Lexington.
Reduction of Ticonderoga.
Battle of Bunker's Hill.
Capitulation of St. Johns and Montreal.

Repulse at Quebec,— Death of Montgomery.
Cessation of Royal Government in the Colonies.

1. Learning that a large quantity of military stores had been collected by the Americans at Concord, General Gage,* the king's governor, detached Lieutenant Smith and Major Pitcairn, with eight hundred grenadiers, to destroy them. Meanwhile, the greatest precaution was taken by Governor Gage to prevent the intelligence of this expedition from reaching the country. Officers were dispersed along the road, to intercept expresses who might be sent from Boston. But the precaution proved ineffectual. The alarm was given, and was rapidly spread by means of church-bells, guns, and volleys.

2. On reaching Lexington, on the morning of the 19th of April, some seventy of the militia had assembled, and were under arms. On seeing them on the parade, near the church, Major Pitcairn rode up to them, and, with a loud voice, cried out, " Disperse, disperse, you rebels ! throw down your arms, and

---

* General Thomas Gage was born about the year 1721. He entered the army young. He succeeded Governor Hutchinson as Governor of Massachusetts Bay. He took strong and decided measures, and hastened the Revolution. In October, 1775, he resigned his command to Sir William Howe. His death occurred in 1788.

disperse!" The sturdy yeomanry not immediately obeying his
orders, he approached nearer, discharged his pistol, and ordered
his soldiers to fire; upon which, eight were killed, and several
wounded. From Lexington, the detachment proceeded to Concord, and destroyed the stores. After killing several of the militia, who came forth to oppose them, they retreated to Lexington,

with some loss, the Americans firing upon them from behind
walls, hedges, and buildings.

3. Fortunately for the British, a reinforcement of nine hundred men, some marines, and two field-pieces, here came to their
assistance; but, being greatly annoyed by the patriots, they continued their retreat to Bunker's Hill, in Charlestown, and the
day following crossed over to Boston. The British lost, in killed
and wounded, during their absence, two hundred and seventy-
three. The loss of the Americans amounted to eighty-eight,
killed, wounded, and missing. Thus flowed the first blood of
the Revolution, — shed wantonly, but which was poured out
freely on the altar of American liberty; firing the bosoms of
thousands, as the intelligence spread, and rousing them to defend
their country against British tyranny and oppression.

4. It was at once decided to be important to secure the fortresses at Ticonderoga and Crown Point. Accordingly, a number of volunteers, from Connecticut and Vermont, under command of Colonels Ethan Allen and Benedict Arnold, marched
against Ticonderoga, and, on the 10th of May, took it by sur-

14*

prise, the garrison being asleep. On the arrival of Allen, he demanded the surrender of the fort. "By what authority?" asked the commander. "I demand it," said Allen, "in the name of the great Jehovah, and of the Continental Congress."

The summons was instantly obeyed, and the fort was, with its valuable stores, surrendered. The capture of Crown Point soon followed.

5. In June following (17), a still more memorable event occurred, — THE BATTLE OF BUNKER'S HILL, as it is commonly called; or of Breed's Hill, where the battle was actually fought, — a high eminence in Charlestown, within cannon-shot of Boston. The evening preceding, a detachment of one thousand Americans was ordered to make an intrenchment on Bunker's Hill; but, by some mistake, they proceeded to Breed's Hill, and, by the dawn of day, had thrown up a redoubt eight rods square and four feet high. On discovering this redoubt in the morning, the British commenced a severe cannonade upon it from several ships and floating batteries, and from a fortification on Copp's Hill, in Boston, which was continued until afternoon. The Americans, however, urged on their defences, and, during the forenoon, lost but a single man. Between twelve and one o'clock, three thousand British, under command of Major-general Howe and Brigadier-general Pigot, crossed Charles river, with an intention to dislodge the Americans. As they advanced, the British commenced firing at some distance from the redoubt;

but the Americans reserved their fire until the enemy were within twelve rods. They then opened, and the carnage was terrible. The British retreated in precipitate confusion, but were rallied, and again led to the attack. The Americans now suffered them to approach within six rods, when their fire mowed them down in heaps, and again they fled.

6. Unfortunately for the Americans, their ammunition now failed; and, on the third charge of the British, they were obliged

to retire. The British lost in this engagement two hundred and twenty-six killed, — among whom was Major Pitcairn, who first lighted the torch of war at Lexington, — and eight hundred and twenty-eight wounded. The Americans lost one hundred and thirty-nine killed, and of wounded and missing there were three hundred and fourteen. Among the killed was the lamented General Warren.

7. The horrors of the scene were greatly increased by the conflagration of Charlestown, effected, during the heat of the battle, by order of General Gage. By this wanton act of barbarity, two thousand people were deprived of their habitations, and property to the amount of one hundred and twenty thousand pounds sterling perished in the flames. Wanton, however, as the burning was, it wonderfully enhanced the dreadful magnificence of the day. To the volleys of musketry and the roar of cannon, — to the shouts of the fighting and the groans of the dying, — to the dark and awful atmosphere of smoke, enveloping the whole peninsula, and illumined in every quarter by the streams of fire

from the various instruments of death, — the conflagration of six hundred buildings added a gloomy and amazing grandeur. In the midst of this waving lake of flame, the lofty steeple, converted into a blazing pyramid, towered and trembled over the vast pyre, and finished the scene of desolation. To the Ameri-

cans the consequences of this battle were those of a decided victory. They learned that their enemies were not invincible. At the same time, they were made to feel the importance of stricter discipline and greater preparations. As the result of the battle spread, the national pulse beat still higher, and the arm of opposition was braced still more firmly.

8. On the 10th of May, a second session of the Continental Congress was held at Philadelphia. As military opposition to Great Britain was now resolved upon by the colonies, and had actually commenced, it became necessary to fix upon a proper person to conduct that opposition. The person unanimously selected by Congress was GEORGE WASHINGTON, a member of their body from Virginia.* Following the appointment of Gen-

---

* The honor of having suggested and advocated the choice of this illustrious man is justly ascribed to the elder President Adams, at that time a member of the Continental Congress. The army was at this time at Cambridge, Massachusetts, under General Ward. As yet, Congress had not adopted the army, nor had it taken any measures to appoint a commander-in-chief. These points could with safety be neglected no longer. This Mr. Adams clearly saw, and by his eloquence induced Congress to appoint a day when the subject should be discussed.

eral Washington was the appointment of four major-generals, Artemas Ward, Charles Lee, Philip Schuyler, and Israel Putnam; and eight brigadier-generals, Seth Pomeroy, Richard Montgomery, David Wooster, William Heath, Joseph Spencer, John Thomas, John Sullivan, and Nathaniel Greene.

9. On his arrival at Cambridge, on the second of July, Washington was received with joyful acclamations by the American army. He found it, consisting of fourteen thousand men, stretched from Roxbury to Cambridge, and thence to Mystic river, a distance of twelve miles; while the British forces occupied Bunker and Breed's Hill, and Boston Neck.

10. The attention of the American commander was immediately directed to organizing his undisciplined forces; and while so employed, Generals Schuyler and Montgomery proceeded with one thousand men to the investment of St. Johns, the first British port in Canada (one hundred and fifteen miles north of Ticonderoga). On reaching St. Johns, the health of Schuyler failing, he returned to the latter place, while Montgomery took possession of the former important post on the 3d of November. Next, he proceeded to Montreal, which having capitulated without resistance, he continued his route towards Quebec. Before his arrival, however, Colonel Arnold, who had been despatched by

---

The day was fixed. It came. Mr. Adams went in, took the floor, urged the measure of adopting the army; and, after debate, it passed. The next thing was to get a lawful commander for this lawful army, with supplies, &c. All looked to Mr. Adams, on this occasion; and he was ready. He took the floor, and went into a minute delineation of the character of General Ward, bestowing on him the epithets which then belonged to no one else. At the end of this eulogy, he said, "But this is not the man I have chosen." He then portrayed the character of a commander-in-chief such as was required by the peculiar situation of the colonies at that juncture; and after he had presented the qualifications in his strongest language, and given the reasons for the nomination he was about to make, he said, "Gentlemen, I know these qualifications are high; but we all know they are needful, at this crisis, in this chief. Does any one say that they are not to be obtained in the country? I reply, they are: they reside in one of our own body, and he is the person whom I now nominate — GEORGE WASHINGTON, of Virginia!"

Washington, who sat on Mr. Adams' right hand, was looking him intently in the face, to watch the name he was about to announce; and, not expecting it would be his own, he sprang from his seat, the moment he heard it, and rushed into an adjoining room, as quickly as though moved by a shock of electricity.

An adjournment was immediately moved and carried, in order to give the members time to deliberate on so important a measure. The following day, Washington was unanimously appointed commander-in-chief of the American forces; and, on presenting their commission to him, Congress unanimously adopted the resolution, "that they would maintain and assist him, and adhere to him, with their lives and fortunes, in the cause of American liberty."

Washington, with one thousand men, from Cambridge, had reached that capital by the way of the river Kennebec,* and had already ascended the Heights of Abraham, where the brave Wolfe had ascended before him; but he had retreated some twenty miles distant, and was here awaiting the arrival of Montgomery.

11. As soon as a junction had been effected between these generals, they proceeded to lay siege to the city. At the expiration of a month, finding no prospect of success, the plan was adopted of scaling the walls. For this purpose, two attacks were made, at the same time, in different quarters of the town. The attempt, however, proved unsuccessful; and, to the great grief of the Americans, fatal to the brave Montgomery.† He fell while forcing a barrier; and with him fell two distinguished officers, Captain McPherson, his aid, and Captain Cheeseman. Upon this repulse, Arnold retired a short distance from Quebec, where, in an encampment, he passed a rigorous winter. On the return of spring, 1776, finding his forces inadequate to the reduction of Quebec, he retired. By the 18th of June, the Americans, having been compelled to relinquish one post after another, had wholly evacuated Canada.

12. During this same year, Virginia, through the indiscretion of Lord Dunmore, the royal governor, was involved in difficulties little short of those to which the inhabitants of Massachusetts were subjected. From the earliest stages of the controversy

---

* Seldom was there an expedition attempted, during the American war, in which more hardship was endured. In ascending the Kennebec, the troops were constantly obliged to work against an impetuous current, and often to haul their batteaux up rapid currents and over dangerous falls. Nor was their march through the country, by an unexplored route of three hundred miles, less difficult or dangerous. They had swamps and woods, mountains and precipices, alternately to surpass. Added to their other trials, their provisions failed; and, to support life, they were obliged to eat their dogs, cartouch-boxes, clothes, and shoes. While at the distance of one hundred miles from human habitations, they divided their whole store, about four pints of flour to a man. At thirty miles' distance, they had baked and eaten their last pitiful morsel. Yet the courage and fortitude of these men continued unshaken. They were suffering in their country's cause, — were toiling for wives and children, were contending for the rights and blessings of freedom. After thirty-one days of incessant toil through a hideous wilderness, they reached the habitations of men.

† Richard Montgomery was born in the north of Ireland, in 1737. He possessed an excellent genius, which was matured by a fine education. He entered the army of Great Britain, and was with Wolfe at the surrender of Quebec, in 1759. But he espoused the cause of freedom; and in that cause he fell, deplored by all. In 1818, New York, his adopted state, removed his remains to her own metropolis, where a monument has been erected to his memory.

with Great Britain, the Virginians had been in the foremost rank of opposition ; and, in common with other provinces, had taken measures for defence. These measures the royal governor attempted to thwart, by the removal of guns and ammunition, stored by the people in a magazine. The conduct of the governor roused the inhabitants, and occasioned intemperate expressions of resentment. Apprehending personal danger, Lord Dunmore retired on board the Fowey man-of-war, from which he issued his proclamation, instituting martial law, and proffering freedom to such slaves as would repair to the royal standard. Here, also, by degrees, he equipped and armed a number of vessels ; and, upon being refused provisions by the provincials from on shore, he proceeded to reduce the town of Norfolk to ashes. The loss was estimated at three hundred thousand pounds sterling. Nearly six thousand persons were deprived of their habitations. In like manner, the royal governors of North and South Carolina thought it prudent to retire, and seek safety on board men-of-war. Royal government generally terminated this year throughout the country, the king's governors, for the most part, abdicating their governments, and taking refuge on board the English shipping.

PRINCIPAL EVENTS OF 1776.

Evacuation of Boston.	Execution of Hale.
Defence of Fort Moultrie.	British Occupation of N. York.
Declaration of Independence.	Battle of White Plains.
Occupation of New York by Washington.	Retreat of Washington.
Arrival of Royal Troops.	Surrender of Forts Washington and Lee.
Failure of Negotiations.	Battles of Trenton and Princeton.
Battle on Long Island.	

1. In the spring of 1776, General Washington proposed the expulsion of the British army from Boston, by direct assault. But, in a council of war, it was judged expedient rather to take possession of and fortify Dorchester Heights, which commanded the harbor and British shipping. Accordingly, in the evening of the 4th of March, a covering party of eight hundred, followed by a working party of twelve hundred, with intrenching tools, took possession of the heights, unobserved by the enemy ; and, by morning, had constructed fortifications, which completely sheltered them. The English admiral, on examining the works, declared that, if the Americans were not dislodged from their

position, his vessels could no longer remain in safety in the harbor. It was determined, therefore, by the British, to evacuate Boston; and, on the 17th of March, the troops, under command of Lord William Howe, successor of General Gage, sailed for Halifax.*

2. While affairs were proceeding thus at the north, a plan was devised for the reduction of Charleston, South Carolina, by the united forces of General Clinton from New York, and a large squadron, directly from England, having on board two thousand five hundred troops, under Sir Peter Parker. Charleston had been fortified; and a rude fort erected on Sullivan's Island, six miles below, and commanding the channel leading to the town. The garrison of the fort consisted of only about four hundred men, under command of Colonel Moultrie. On the fort were mounted twenty-six cannon, of eighteen and nine pounders. On the 28th of June, a strong force, under General Clinton, advanced against the fort; while the British squadron, consisting of two fifty-gun ships, and four frigates, each of twenty-eight guns, besides smaller vessels, commenced a bombardment, which continued from eleven o'clock in the morning till seven in the evening. But, to the great mortification of the British, they were repulsed, with signal injury to their shipping, and with the loss of nearly two hundred men, while the loss of the Americans was but ten killed and twenty-two wounded. By this repulse of the British, the Southern States obtained a respite from the calamities of war for two years and a half.†

---

* The rear guard of the British was scarcely out of the town, when Washington entered it on the other side, with colors displayed, drums beating, and all the forms of victory and triumph. He was received by the inhabitants with demonstrations of joy and gratitude. Sixteen months had the people suffered the distresses of hunger, and the outrages of an insolent soldiery.

The town presented a melancholy spectacle at the time the army of Washington entered. One thousand five hundred loyalists, with their families, had just departed on board the British fleet, tearing themselves from home and friends, for the love of the royal cause. Churches were stripped of pews and benches for fuel, shops were opened and rifled of goods to clothe the army, and houses had been pillaged by unfeeling soldiery.

† The fort on Sullivan's Island was a square pen, constructed by Colonel Moultrie, of palmetto logs. General Lee, who was appointed to the command at the south, arrived just after the fort was finished; and, in derision, called it a "Slaughter Pen," and requested Governor Rutledge to have it immediately evacuated. This, however, the latter declined, and Moultrie determined to stand the siege.

The day of attack was bright and beautiful. The wind being fair, the British fleet came proudly on, and one after another took the stations assigned them. Never, perhaps, were hopes brighter or more sanguine than those of the British. Like Prescott at the battle of Bunker's Hill, however, Moultrie directed the men to wait his orders. At length, these orders came. The

3. During these transactions in the south, the Continental Congress was in session, deeply engaged in discussing, among other important subjects, that of declaring America free and independent. Pursuant to the general wish, on the 8th of June, Richard Henry Lee, of Virginia, introduced a resolution to that effect, and supported it, as did others, with great force. On the 11th, a committee was appointed to draft a declaration, consisting of Thomas Jefferson, John Adams, Benjamin Franklin, Roger Sherman, and Robert R. Livingston.

4. Mr. Jefferson and Mr. Adams, standing at the head of the committee, were requested by the other members to act as a sub-committee to prepare the draft ; and Mr. Jefferson drew up the paper. The honor of it, therefore, belongs to Mr. Jefferson. Some changes were made in it on the suggestion of other members of the committee; and others by Congress, while it was under discussion. But none of them altered the general character of the instrument. While Mr. Jefferson was the author of the declaration itself, Mr. Adams was its great supporter on the floor of Congress. This was the unequivocal testimony of Mr. Jefferson. "John Adams," said he, on one occasion, "was our Colossus on the floor: not graceful, not elegant, not always fluent in his public addresses, he yet came out with a power, both of thought and of expression, that moved us from our seats." And at another time he said, "John Adams was the pillar of its support on the floor of Congress; its ablest advocate and defender against the multifarious assaults which were made against it."

5. On the arrival of the day assigned, the subject was resumed ; and, on the 4th of July, 1776, upon the report of the foregoing

fire on both sides was terrible. But the old "Slaughter Pen" held out, and dealt death and destruction on every side. Lee, from a distance, watched Moultrie's movements, and was amazed. Moultrie himself, after the first onset, lighted his pipe, and rolled forth volumes of smoke, while his guns rolled forth their balls amid volumes of fire.

Among Moultrie's garrison was a Sergeant Jasper. In the warmest of the contest, the flag-staff of the fort was shot away, and fell to the outside of the ramparts, on the beach. To recover it was a most perilous enterprise. But, nothing daunted, Jasper leaped upon the beach, and, running the entire length of the ramparts, picked it up amidst a shower of balls, and placed it again upon the parapet. On visiting the fort, a few days after, Governor Rutledge took his sword from his side, and presented it to Jasper, as a reward for his heroic conduct ; following this, the accomplished Mrs. Elliot presented a pair of elegant colors to the regiment of Moultrie. These colors were, at a subsequent day, at the siege of Savannah. There, as at Fort Moultrie, they were shot down ; and, in an attempt to replace them, Jasper was mortally wounded. Yet, while he still lived, he sent the sword presented to him to his father, and to Mrs. Elliot this message : "Tell her that I lost my life supporting the colors which she presented to my regiment."

committee, thirteen confederate colonies dissolved their allegiance to the British crown, and declared themselves free and independent, under the name of the thirteen United States of America. This declaration was ordered to be handsomely engrossed on parchment; and, on the 2nd of August, 1776, was signed by all the members then present, and by some who were not members on the 4th of July.* It was then published abroad, and was everywhere received with transports of joy. The ensigns of royalty were now destroyed, public processions were made, bells were rung, cannon were fired, with other suitable demonstrations of public exultation.

6. On taking possession of Boston, following the evacuation of it by the British (p. 168), Washington proceeded to place it in a posture of defence; which having accomplished, early in April he moved, with his main army, to New York, in anticipation of an attempt on the part of the British to occupy it themselves. For greater security, he stationed a considerable force at

---

* A signature to this instrument was an act of serious concern. In England, it would be regarded as treason, and expose any man to the halter or the block. This the signers well knew; yet they proceeded to the transaction, prepared, if defeat should follow, to lead, without repining, in the way to martyrdom. The only signature, on the original document, which exhibits indications of a trembling hand, is that of Stephen Hopkins; but he had been afflicted with the palsy. In this work of treason, John Hancock led the way, as President of the Congress; and by the force with which he wrote, he seems to have determined that his name should never be erased. The pen with which these signatures were made has been preserved, and is now in the cabinet of the Massachusetts Historical Society.

The number who signed the Declaration was fifty-six; and the average length of their lives was about sixty-five years. Four of the number attained to the age of ninety years and upwards; fourteen exceeded eighty years; and twenty-three, or one in two and a half, reached threescore and ten. The longevity of the New England delegation was still more remarkable. Their number was fourteen, the average of whose lives was seventy-five years. Who will affirm that the unusual age to which the signers, as a body, attained, was not a reward bestowed upon them for their fidelity to their country, and the trust which they in general reposed in the overruling providence of God? Who can doubt the kindness of that Providence to the American people, in thus prolonging the lives of these men, till the principles for which they had contended, through a long series of years, had been acknowledged, and a government been founded upon them?

Of this venerable body not a single one survives. They are now no more. They are no more, as in 1776, bold and fearless advocates of independence. They are dead. But how little is there of the great and good which can die! To their country they yet live, and live forever. They live in all that perpetuates the remembrance of men on earth; in the recorded proofs of their own great actions, in the offspring of their own great interest, in the deep-engraved lines of public gratitude, and in the respect and homage of mankind. They live in their example; and they live emphatically, and will live, in the influence which their lives and efforts, their principles and opinions, now exercise, and will continue to exercise, on the affairs of men, not only in our own country, but throughout the civilized world.

Brooklyn, on Long Island, while the remainder took post in the city itself. Washington's aggregate number now was seventeen thousand men.

7. As to the design of the British general the patriot chief was not mistaken; for, in June, General Howe * arrived from Halifax, and on the 2d of July took possession of Staten Island. Soon after, he was joined by his brother, Admiral Howe, from England, and by the forces under Clinton,† from the south, making in all the formidable force of twenty-four thousand veteran troops. The object of this movement was, besides keeping possession of New York, to command the Hudson, and thus to communicate with Canada, and also to separate the eastern and western colonies from acting in concert.

8. While the armies were in this relative position, Admiral and General Howe addressed a letter to "George Washington, Esq.," informing him that they were commissioned by the home government to settle existing difficulties between Great Britain and her colonies; but, as the letter did not recognize the official title of Washington, he declined receiving it. Their powers, however, it was subsequently ascertained, were altogether inadequate to the important object proposed.

9. Having thus failed in their attempts at negotiation, the British generals decided upon a direct and powerful attack of the Americans on Long Island, now under command of General Putnam. This attack was made on the 27th of August, and resulted in the loss to the Americans of one thousand men, while the loss of the British did not much exceed four hundred. The American Generals Sullivan, Sterling and Woodhull, were among the prisoners. In the heat of the engagement, General Washington crossed over to Brooklyn; and, on seeing some of his best troops slaughtered or taken, he uttered, it is said, an exclamation of anguish. But, deep as his anguish was, and much as he wished to succor his troops, prudence forbade the calling in of his forces from New York, as they would by no means have sufficed to render his army equal to that of the English.

10. After the sad repulse at Brooklyn, perceiving the occupation of his position on Long Island to be of no probable importance, Washington withdrew his troops to New York, and soon after evacuated the city; upon which, on the 15th of Sep-

---

* Sir William Howe was a fine figure, — full six feet high, and admirably well proportioned. In person he strongly resembled Washington. His manners were polished, graceful, and dignified.

† Sir Henry Clinton was short and fat, with a full face, prominent nose, and animated countenance. In his manners he was polite and courtly, but more formal and distant than Howe.

tember, the British entered it.   Seldom, if ever, was a retreat conducted with more ability and prudence, or under more favorable auspices, than that of the American troops from Long Island.   The necessary preparations having been made, at eight in the evening of the 29th the troops began to move in the greatest silence.   But they were not on board their vessels before eleven.   A violent north-east wind, and the ebb tide, which rendered the current very rapid, for a time prevented the passage; but, fortunately, the wind suddenly veered in their favor, and enabled them to reach the opposite side.   About two o'clock in the morning, a thick fog (and, at that season of the year, extraordinary) covered all Long Island, whereas the air was perfectly clear on the side of New York.   Notwithstanding the entreaties of his officers, Washington remained the last upon the shore.   It was not till the next morning, when the sun was already high, and the fog dispelled, that the English perceived the Americans had abandoned their camp, and were sheltered from pursuit.

11. On retiring from New York, Washington occupied, for a short time, the heights of Harlem; but, finding his position, at that point, too hazardous, he removed, and, with a part of his forces, took post at White Plains.   The British followed, and on the 28th of October a partial engagement ensued, during which several hundreds fell on both sides, but neither party could claim a decided advantage.

12. About the time that Washington and his army took post at Harlem, it was deemed important to ascertain the state of the British army on Long Island.   For this purpose, Captain Nathan Hale, a young officer of liberal education and accomplished manners, volunteered his services.   He entered the British army in disguise, and obtained the information desired; but, on his return, he was apprehended, and sent to General Howe, who delivered him to the cruel Marshal Cunningham, by whom he was ordered to execution without a trial.   He was not allowed a Bible, nor the attendance of a minister.   His last observation, at the place of execution, was, " that he only lamented that he had but one life to lose for his country."

13. Although not defeated, Washington wisely removed his forces to North Castle, about five miles further north.   As the British general indicated an intention of attacking the American posts on the Hudson, with a view to penetrating into New Jersey, Washington, leaving three thousand troops with Colonel Magraw, for the defence of Fort Washington, crossed the Hud-

SOUTHERN & WESTERN STATES.

son, and joined General Greene, in his camp, at Fort Lee.* On the 16th of November, the former of these fortresses was attacked by a strong force; and although the defence made by Colonel Magraw was resolute, he was compelled to surrender to the enemy, one thousand of whom, however, had been killed in the assault. Two days after, Lord Cornwallis † crossed the Hudson, with six thousand men, and proceeded against Fort Lee. Fortunately, the garrison had opportunity to escape, and effected a junction with Washington, who, meanwhile, had retreated to Newark, on the south side of the Passaic.

14. Finding Newark, however, too near his triumphant foe, Washington next retreated to Brunswick, on the Raritan, and Lord Cornwallis on the same day entered Newark. The retreat was still continued from Brunswick to Princeton, from Princeton to Trenton, and from Trenton to the Pennsylvania side of the Delaware, the pursuit being urged with so much rapidity that the rear of the American army, while engaged in demolishing the bridges which they had crossed, was often within sight and shot of the van of the enemy, employed in building them up.

15. This retreat through New Jersey was made under circumstances of the deepest depression. The Americans had just lost the two forts, Washington and Lee, and with the former nearly three thousand men. Numbers of the militia were daily claiming to be discharged; and even the regular troops, as if struck with despair, deserted in bodies. This left the army of Washington so reduced, that it scarcely amounted to three thousand men; and even these were poorly fed, were without tents to shelter them from the inclemency of the season, and in the midst of a population even hostile to the republic. Added to this, numbers of the leading characters, both in New Jersey and Pennsylvania, were changing sides, and making peace with the enemy. This example became pernicious, and the most prejudicial effects were to be apprehended from it. But, in the midst of so much adversity, Washington did not seem to despair of the public safety. On the contrary, as darkness hovered around, he trimmed more care-

---

* Fort Washington was on the east bank of the Hudson, eleven miles above New York. Fort Lee was on the west side of the Hudson, and ten miles from the city. It stood on a rocky summit, three hundred feet above the river.

† In person, Lord Cornwallis was short and thick set, but not so corpulent as Sir Henry Clinton. He had a handsome nose; his hair, when young, was light, and rather inclined to sandy; but at the time of his leaving, as the pupil will learn, after the battle of Yorktown, it had become somewhat gray. He winked badly with one eye. He was uncommonly easy and affable in his manners. He was a great friend to his country's cause, and a most determined foe to America.

15*

fully the lamp of hope ; and while the hearts of others sunk in
despondency, he manifested the greater firmness, constancy, and
fortitude.

16. The object next aimed at by the British general was the
occupation of Philadelphia ; and the only obstacle which prevented it was the position of Washington, on the Pennsylvania
side of the Delaware. While waiting for the freezing of that
river, to allow him to cross, the British general placed about
four thousand German troops along the river from Trenton to
Burlington, while strong detachments were stationed at Princeton and New Brunswick. The remainder of the British army
were scattered about the villages of New Jersey.

17. In this state of things, Washington conceived the plan
of re-crossing the Delaware, and of attacking the German troops
stationed at Trenton so suddenly as not to allow them the assistance of the main body. Accordingly, on the night of the 25th
of December, the American troops detached for this service,
consisting of two thousand four hundred men, arrived in the

dusk of the evening at the bank of the river. The passage by
the troops and artillery, it was expected, would be effected before
midnight. But the cold was so intense, and the river so
obstructed with floating ice, that the landing of the artillery was
not accomplished, until four in the morning. An immediate and
precipitate march was made towards Trenton, with the hope of

reaching it before day.   But a thick fog setting in, so retarded their march, that they did not reach Trenton until eight o'clock; yet, at this late hour, the Hessians had no suspicion of the approach of the enemy.   Incapable, therefore, of making any defence, and hemmed in on all sides, they were obliged to surrender, to the number of nearly one thousand.   Some thirty or forty were killed, among whom was a Colonel Rahl, the commanding officer.

18. To the American cause, the success at Trenton was as auspicious as it was mortifying to the British.   To regain the ground lost, Cornwallis forthwith concentrated his forces at Princeton; and, on the 2d of January, 1777, marched out to the attack of Washington, who had again crossed the Delaware, and had taken post at Trenton.   That night the British encamped not far distant, elated at the prospect of a victory the ensuing morning.

19. The morning came, but Washington and his troops were gone.   He had projected another bold enterprise, which was to proceed under cover of night to Princeton, where Cornwallis had left a portion of his troops, and give them battle.   Accordingly, renewing his camp-fires, and while they were burning brightly, he withdrew; and, at sunrise, unexpectedly fell in with two British regiments, upon which a spirited contest ensued.   The Americans fought well; but just as they were giving way, Washington himself headed the main body, and led them to the attack.   His bravery gave impulse to his troops, and the enemy were put to rout.   Instead of pursuing them, however, he hastened forward to Princeton, where was stationed another regiment.   Of this he made three hundred prisoners, while the remainder sought safety in flight.   The loss of the Americans was not severe in numbers, but several valuable officers were killed and wounded.   Among the former was the brave General Mercer; among the latter, Lieutenant James Monroe, in after years President of the United States.

20. The victories of Trenton and Princeton were of signal importance to the American people, and especially to the inhabitants of New Jersey, who had long suffered from the presence of the British, and from their exactions, and even brutalities. They were highly gratified, and their courage greatly revived. Soon after, the royal army retired to winter quarters at New Brunswick, and Washington to Morristown, where his army was generally inoculated with the small-pox.   Thus closed the campaign of 1776.

PRINCIPAL EVENTS OF 1777.

Arrival of Marquis de La-fayette.	Occupation of Philadelphia.
Assistance rendered by France.	Battle of Germantown.
Burning of Danbury.	Invasion of Burgoyne.
Rencontre at Ridgefield.	Battle of Bennington.
Movement of British Army.	Battles of Saratoga and Still-water.
Battle of Brandywine.	Surrender of Burgoyne.

1. The spring of 1777 opened with a pleasing event, in the history of the American struggle. This was the arrival, in April, of the young, ardent, distinguished Marquis de Lafayette, intent on joining the American standard. During the preceding year, Dr. Franklin, Silas Dean and Arthur Lee, had been commissioned to proceed to France to solicit a loan of money of the French government, and an acknowledgment of the independence of the United States. Dr. Franklin arrived in Paris in December, and was cordially received, as the worthy representative of a people struggling for liberty. Through his efforts, the French government secretly favored the Americans, allowing arms to be taken from the public arsenals, and prizes taken by American privateers to be sold in French and West India ports.

2. The necessities of the United States being thus brought before the people of France, excited their sympathy, while the noble character of Washington called forth their admiration. Several French officers were thus prompted to offer their services to the Americans, and Lafayette among the number. At his own expense, he hired a vessel to transport him to the United States, and of Washington solicited permission to serve without pay ; but Congress, in token of their estimation of his generous conduct, invested him with the commission of Major-general.

3. During the same month, a large quantity of public stores were burnt at Danbury, in Connecticut, by General Tryon, with two thousand men, from New York, together with eighteen dwellings. Three of the inhabitants were wantonly murdered, and thrown into the flames. After accomplishing their object, the enemy retreated to their shipping on the sound. In a rencontre with some militia, headed by General Wooster, he received a mortal wound. At Ridgefield, General Arnold attacked them with great spirit, with a small militia force. In this latter place they burnt several houses. Before reaching the sound, they had

incurred a loss of nearly three hundred men. The loss of the Americans did not exceed one hundred. In testimony of their sense of the heroic conduct of Wooster and Arnold, Congress voted a monument to the former, and a properly caparisoned horse to the latter.

4. Towards the close of May, the American army, augmented to nearly ten thousand men, moved from their winter encampment at Morristown, and took post at Middlebrook, about ten miles from New Brunswick, the encampment of the British. For a time, the movements of General Howe indicated an intention of attacking Washington ; but, on ascertaining the strength of the American posts, he suddenly changed his purpose, and having concentrated his army at Staten Island, embarked, with eighteen thousand men, on the 23d of July, and put forth to sea.

5. Penetrating his design, Washington immediately put his army in motion towards Philadelphia, to prevent, if possible, its occupation by Howe ; and had already advanced beyond Wilmington, when the British army, which, proceeding up the Chesapeake, had landed at the head of Elk river, in Maryland, was announced as approaching. His superior strength admonished Washington to withdraw across the Brandywine ; but here he decided to make a stand for the defence of Philadelphia.

6. On the morning of the 11th of September, the armies engaged, and continued the contest nearly the entire day. In the sequel, the Americans were compelled to retreat, first to Chester, whence they proceeded to Philadelphia. In the above battle, several foreign officers distinguished themselves ; among whom were Count Pulaski, a Polander, and Lafayette, the latter of whom was wounded, while endeavoring to rally the fugitives.

7. Not considering the battle of Brandywine as decisive, Congress, then in session in Philadelphia, recommended Washington to risk another engagement. Accordingly, on the 16th, he recrossed the Schuylkill, and advanced against the British at Goshen. But a violent storm occurring, the armies were compelled to defer the contest. Soon after, Washington abandoned Philadelphia, and took post at Pottsgrove, thirty-five miles north-west. An easy access to Philadelphia being now presented, Howe entered it on the 26th, stationing his army at Germantown, some six miles distant, — Congress having adjourned to Lancaster.

8. Immediately after the occupation of Philadelphia, the attention of General Howe was drawn to the reduction of some forts on the Delaware, which rendered the navigation of that river

unsafe to the British. Accordingly, a part of the royal army was detached for that purpose, which coming to the knowledge of Washington, he seized the opportunity to attack the remainder, at Germantown.

9. This attack, which occurred on the 4th of October, resulted, after a severe action, in the repulse of the Americans, with a loss double that of the British. The latter now removed to Philadelphia, where they continued a long time inactive, while Washington, retreating, took post at Skippack, eleven miles from Germantown. The repulse of the Americans at Germantown caused deep chagrin to Washington; and the more, because the commencement of the battle was apparently so auspicious to the Americans. The ultimate failure of the latter was attributed to the inexperience of a part of the troops, and to embarrassments arising from a fog, which increased the darkness of the night. Congress, however, expressed their approbation of Washington's plan of attack, and highly applauded the courage and firmness of the troops.

10. While such was the progress of military operations in the Middle States, important events were taking place in the north. It has already been noticed (p. 162) that, in May, 1775, Ticonderoga and Crown Point had been taken by surprise, by Colonels Allen and Arnold; that, in the ensuing fall, General Montgomery had reduced the fort of St. Johns (p. 165), captured Montreal, and made an ineffectual though desperate assault upon Quebec. On the return of spring, the American army gradually retired up the St. Lawrence, and, after a loss of one post and another, in June, 1776, entirely evacuated Canada (p. 166).

11. In the spring of 1777, it was settled in England that an invasion of the States should be attempted from the north, and a communication formed between Canada and New York. Could such a plan have been executed, it would obviously have precluded intercourse between New England and the more southern states. The execution of the plan was committed to General Burgoyne,* who left Canada with seven thousand

---

* General John Burgoyne was the natural son of Lord Bingley. He was appointed to a command in America, in 1775. He was a very pompous man, and wrote such pompous addresses that he excited the ridicule of the Americans, by whom he was called " *Chrononhotonthologos.*" After the battle of Stillwater, some one composed the following :

   " Burgoyne, unconscious of impending fate,
      Could cut his way through woods, but not through GATES."

After his surrender, he returned to England. He died in 1792.

troops, besides a powerful train of artillery, and several tribes
of Indians; and on the 1st of July, invested Ticonderoga.
The American garrison at this time amounted to three thousand
men, under command of General St. Clair.

12. Deeming this force inadequate to maintain the post,
especially as Burgoyne had taken possession of Mount Defiance,
which commanded Ticonderoga, and not having provisions to
sustain the army for more than twenty days, St. Clair suddenly
abandoned the fort, and, by a circuitous route, — first into Vermont
and thence to the Hudson, — joined General Schuyler, commanding the main army of the north. After this junction, the
whole army continued to retire to Saratoga and Stillwater, and at
length took post on Van Shaick's Island, in the mouth of the
Mohawk, on the 18th of August.

13. After taking possession of Ticonderoga, (abandoned by St.
Clair,) Burgoyne, with the great portion of his troops, proceeding
up the lake, destroyed the American flotilla, and a considerable quantity of baggage and stores, at Skeensborough. Having
halted at this place for nearly three weeks, he proceeded to Fort
Edward, on the Hudson, where he arrived only on the 30th of
July, his way having been obstructed by Schuyler's army, which
felled trees across the road, and demolished the bridges, while
on their retreat.

14. While at this latter place, a detachment of his army, consisting of five hundred English and one hundred Indians, under
Colonel Baum, who had been despatched to seize a magazine of
stores at Bennington, in Vermont, was totally defeated, by a
party of Vermont troops, called Green Mountain Boys, and a
detachment of New Hampshire militia, under command of General Stark. Baum, on his arrival near Bennington, learning that
the Americans were strongly intrenched at that place, halted,
and despatched a messenger to General Burgoyne, for a reinforcement. General Stark, now on his march, with a body of
New Hampshire militia, to join General Schuyler, receiving
intelligence of Baum's approach, altered his movement, and collected his force at Bennington. Before the expected reinforcement could arrive, Stark, having added to his New Hampshire
corps a body of Vermont militia, determined to attack Baum in
his intrenchments. Accordingly, on the 16th of August, an
attack was made, which resulted in the flight of Baum's detachment, at the moment in which the reinforcement of troops,
despatched by General Burgoyne, arrived. With the assistance of
these, the battle was now renewed, but ended in the discomfiture
of the British forces, and with a loss on their part of about seven

hundred in killed and wounded, among whom was Colonel Baum himself. The loss of the Americans was about one hundred. This battle at Bennington greatly revived the courage of the Americans, and as greatly disappointed the hopes of Burgoyne, as it served materially to embarrass and retard his movements.

15. The situation of this general was now seriously perplexing. To retreat was to abandon the object of his expedition; to advance seemed replete with difficulty and danger. This latter step, however, at length, appearing the most judicious, on the 14th of September he passed the Hudson, and advanced upon Saratoga and Stillwater. On the 19th, an obstinate though indecisive engagement ensued between the two hostile armies, to which night only put an end, and in which the British loss exceeded that of the Americans.

16. On the 7th of October, the battle was renewed, by a movement of General Burgoyne towards the left of the Americans, by which he intended to effect his retreat to the lakes. The battle was extremely severe; and darkness only put an end to the effusion of blood. During the succeeding night, an attempt was made by the royal army to retreat to Fort Edward; but, while preparing to march, intelligence was received that this fort was already in possession of the Americans. No avenue to escape now appeared open. Worn down with constant toil and watching, and having ascertained that there were but three days' provisions, a council of war was called, which unanimously resolved to capitulate to General Gates, who had succeeded General Schuyler, and under whom this signal victory was achieved. Preliminaries were soon after settled, and the army, consisting of five thousand seven hundred effective men, surrendered prisoners of war, on the 17th of October.

17. Immediately after, General Gates despatched Colonel Wilkinson to announce the grateful intelligence to Congress. On being introduced, he said, "The whole British army has laid down arms at Saratoga. Our sons, full of vigor and courage, expect your orders. It is for your wisdom to decide where the country may still have need of their services."

18. It would be difficult to describe the joy which the news of the surrender of Burgoyne excited among the Americans; and this joy was, not long after, greatly increased, by an acknowledgment of the independence of America at the court of France,*

---

* For more than a year, commissioners from Congress, at the head of whom was Dr. Franklin, had resided at the court of France, urging the above important measure. But the success of the American struggle was yet too

and the conclusion of a formal treaty of alliance and commerce between the two countries, — an event highly auspicious to the interests of America. The treaty was signed February 6th ; — "neither of the contracting powers to make war or peace, without the formal consent of the other."

19. The Declaration of Independence, in 1776, did not make the States, in fact, free and independent. For that, they had yet to fight. Indeed, it formed no real bond of union, and for some time none existed between them. One common sentiment with regard to the war, however, kept them together. But something more was necessary. In November (the 15th), 1777, Congress adopted "Articles of Confederation," which for some time had been maturing, and which were afterwards ratified by several of the state Legislatures. These articles authorized Congress to carry on war ; to make peace ; to manage affairs with foreign nations. They were also to decide the number of men and the amount of money to be raised, and to assign to each state its proportion. But here their power ended. They could make no general laws, and could lay no direct taxes. These powers, the states reserved to themselves. In consequence of these reservations, supplies of men and money were often delayed, to the great detriment of the cause.

20. During the following winter, the British army continued to occupy Philadelphia, while the Americans had their winter quarters at Valley Forge, on the Schuylkill, fifteen miles from the former place. With the royalists the winter passed in the enjoyment of all the conveniences which an opulent city could afford. Not so with the patriots ; — their only shelter were rude huts. Provisions nearly failed ; comfortable clothing was deficient. Many, for want of shoes, were compelled to walk barefoot on the frozen ground ; and few, if any, had even blankets for the night. Nearly three thousand were, at one time, incapable of bearing arms.

---

doubtful for that country to embroil herself in a war with Great Britain. The capture of the British army at Saratoga seemed to increase the probability that the American arms would finally triumph, and decided France to espouse her cause. The aid which France brought to the Americans was of great importance. It is even doubtful whether the colonies, without her contributions of money, navy, troops, would have been able to resist the British powers ; at least, the struggle must have been greatly prolonged. To this intervention France was inclined, by her own hostility to England, whom she delighted to see humbled, especially by a people struggling for independence.

Holland acknowledged the independence of the United States in 1782; Sweden, in February, 1783 ; Denmark, in the same month ; Spain, in March ; Russia, in July.

16

PRINCIPAL EVENTS OF 1778.

Evacuation of Philadelphia.
Battle of Monmouth.
Massacre at Wyoming.

1. On the opening of the spring, 1778, in consequence of the alliance of France and America, orders were issued by the British general to evacuate Philadelphia, and concentrate the royal force in the city and harbor of New York. Pursuant to this order, the British, now under command of Sir Henry Clinton, left Philadelphia, and on the 18th of June passed the Delaware into New Jersey.

2. Washington immediately quitted his camp, and hung upon the retreating enemy, watching a favorable opportunity to offer battle. On the 27th, the British army encamped on some high grounds in the neighborhood of Freehold court-house, in the county of Monmouth.

3. On the morning of the 28th, General Lee was ordered to take command of five thousand troops, and to proceed to an attack. This honor he at first declined, upon which it was tendered to Lafayette; but, at length, Lee decided to assume the command himself, and led forth his troops to the onset.

4. The morning was clear and hot. Before noon, the mercury of the thermometer had reached ninety-six. Man and beast panted for breath. Water was needed at every step. Moreover, it was the Sabbath, that day when the hum of life is ordinarily hushed, and when men are commonly with their families in the house of God.

5. Lee gave pursuit; but suddenly the British army wheeled, as if to charge upon him, and he ordered a hasty retreat. Washington was behind. When apprized of the flight of Lee, he vaulted into his saddle, and, putting spurs to his horse, was soon amid the scene of confusion. He bent on Lee a face of fearful expression, and in thunder tones demanded, "Sir, I desire to know what is the reason, and whence arises this disorder and confusion?" The rebuke was terrible. Wheeling his steed, he rallied the retreating forces, which, under his courageous bearing, wheeled, and formed in splendid style. This done, Washington, approaching Lee, exclaimed, "Will you, sir, command in that place?" He replied, "Yes." "Well," continued the chief, "I expect you to check the enemy immediately." "Your orders shall be obeyed," said the stung commander, "and I will not be the first to leave the field." The battle, upon this, opened with

renewed fury, and Washington hurried back to bring his own division into the field.

6. From that time, all did their duty. Few such days were seen during the Revolutionary War. The tongues of the soldiers, for the want of water, swelled so greatly, as not to be retained in the mouth. For twelve long hours were the respective armies that day engaged. Not a few died from sun-stroke, and still more from fatigue. The cry for "water, water!" from the wounded and the dying, was sufficient to affect the stoutest heart.

7. At length the sun went down, and darkness closed the contest. Both armies slept that night in sight of each other, on the field of battle. With the morning light, Washington had decided to renew the battle; but, when morning came, the enemy had retired.* On the following day, finding his foe gone, he took up his line of march, and by easy stages moved towards the Hudson, disappointed that the enemy had escaped him; yet conscious that, if he did not enjoy all the advantages of a decided victory, he had suffered no defeat. On retiring from the field of Monmouth, the British army proceeded to Sandy Hook, and thence, by their fleet, to New York. Washington led his army to White Plains, where he continued till late in the autumn, when he went into winter quarters at Middlebrook, in New Jersey.

8. Early in July, a scene of shocking barbarity was witnessed in the retired and peaceful valley of Wyoming, in Pennsylvania. A force of Tories and Indians, to the number of sixteen hundred, led by Colonel John Butler, and the famous Indian chieftain, Brant, attacked the inhabitants, slew nearly four hundred who came out to oppose them, and, having surprised their wives and children, they shut them up in the houses and barracks, where they perished in one general conflagration. This, however, was only a prelude to other enormities committed in that once happy valley. All the settlements were desolated by fire and sword.

---

* Lee, deeply irritated by the reprimand of Washington, subsequently addressed two passionate letters to him, demanding reparation. By order of Washington, he was arrested and tried by a court-martial, by which he was found guilty of misconduct on the field of battle, and of disrespect to the commander-in-chief. He was suspended from command for one year; but he never again joined the army, but died, just before the close of the war, in Philadelphia, in seclusion. It has sometimes been charged upon Washington that on the occasion of rebuking Lee he was profane. But the charge is without proof. Lafayette, who was near Washington at the time, afterward said, that it was not so much the expression itself, as the manner in which it was uttered, that stung Gen. Lee. That manner was terrible. The wrath of Washington was without disguise.

PRINCIPAL EVENTS OF 1779.

Surrender of Savannah to the British.

Predatory Excursion of General Tryon to Horseneck.

Expedition of same to Maritime Parts of Connecticut.

Reduction of Stony Point.

Failure of Attempt to recapture Savannah.

Depreciation of Paper Currency.

1. Hitherto the conquest of the states had been chiefly attempted by offensive operations in the north. But, following the events already noticed, the Southern States became the principal theatre of the war, during its continuance ; and, as Georgia was one of the weakest, she was marked out as the first object of attack.

2. In November of 1778, Colonel Campbell was sent from New York, by General Clinton, with two thousand men, for the reduction of Savannah. Late in December, the troops were landed in the vicinity of the city, at that time under the care of General Robert Howe, with six hundred regular troops and a few hundred militia, under his command. This force being wholly inadequate to the defence of the city, Howe was compelled to surrender it ; but only at the end of a spirited engagement.

3. In February, 1779, Governor Tryon, with fifteen hundred men, proceeded from Kingsbridge, thirteen miles above New York, into Connecticut, as far as Horseneck, a part of Greenwich, where he plundered the inhabitants, and destroyed their salt-works. General Putnam, happening to be in that vicinity, hastily collected a small number of men, whom he employed at firing upon the enemy, with a couple of field-pieces, from the high ground near the meeting-house. At length, however, a detachment of the enemy was ordered to charge upon Putnam and his men. Ordering the latter to make good their retreat to a neighboring swamp, he himself put spurs to his horse, and plunged down the precipice at the church. This was so steep as to have artificial stairs, composed of nearly one hundred stone steps, for the accommodation of worshippers ascending to the sanctuary. On the arrival of the dragoons at the brow of the hill, they paused, thinking it too dangerous to follow the steps of the adventurous hero. Before any could go round the hill, and descend, Putnam had escaped, uninjured by the many balls which were fired at him in his descent. But one touched him, and that only passed through his hat.

4. In July, another predatory excursion was projected by Tryon, at the head of two thousand six hundred men, against

the maritime parts of Connecticut. During the expedition, New Haven was plundered; East Haven, Fairfield, Norwalk, and Green's Farms, were reduced to ashes.*

5. While Tryon was thus rendering his name infamously conspicuous in acts of plundering, burning and rapine, the Americans were engaged in some of the boldest enterprises of the war. Of this number was the reduction of Stony Point, a fortress on the Hudson, forty miles above New York, on the 15th of July.

6. At this time, this was a strong-hold of the enemy, well garrisoned, with abundant stores, and formidable defensive preparations. Washington, however, decided to hazard its reduction. The enterprise was committed to General Wayne, who, with a strong detachment of active infantry, set out towards

---

* In an account of the devastations made by the English in this expedition, which was transmitted to Congress, it appeared that at Fairfield there were burnt two houses of public worship, fifteen dwelling-houses, eleven barns, and several stores; at Norwalk, two houses of public worship, eighty dwelling-houses, sixty-seven barns, twenty-two stores, seventeen shops, four mills, and five vessels. In addition to this wanton destruction of property, various were the acts of brutality, rapine and cruelty, committed on aged persons, women, and prisoners. At New Haven, an aged citizen, who labored under a natural inability of speech, had his tongue cut out by one of the royal army. At Fairfield, the deserted houses of the inhabitants were entered; desks, trunks, closets and chests, were broken open, and robbed of everything valuable. Women were insulted, abused and threatened, while their apparel was taken from them. Even an infant was robbed of its clothes, while a bayonet was pointed at the breast of its mother.

16*

the place, at noon. His march of fourteen miles, over high mountains, through deep morasses, and difficult defiles, was accomplished by eight o'clock in the evening.

7. At the distance of a mile from the Point, Wayne halted, and formed his men into two columns, putting himself at the head of the right. Both were directed to march in order and silence, with unloaded muskets and fixed bayonets. At midnight, they arrived under the walls of the fort. An unexpected obstacle now presented itself; the deep morass, which covered the works, was, at this time, overflowed by the tide. The English opened a tremendous fire of musketry and of cannon loaded with grape-shot; but neither the inundated morass, nor a double palisade, nor the storm of fire, could arrest the impetuosity of the Americans; they opened their way with the bayonet, prostrated whatever opposed them, scaled the fort, and the two columns met in the centre of the works. The English lost upwards of six hundred men, in killed and prisoners. The conquerors abstained from pillage, and from all disorder, — a conduct the more worthy, as they had still present in mind the ravages and butcheries which their enemies had so recently committed in Connecticut.

8. Early in September, Count d'Estaing* with a French fleet, arrived on the coast of Georgia, with a view to the reduction of Savannah. Before the arrival of General Lincoln, who was expected to aid, the count had sent "a haughty summons" to Prevost, the English commander, to surrender. The latter requested a day to consider the proposition; which being incautiously granted, was fatal to the expedition, as Prevost, besides strengthening his position, received a large reinforcement. He therefore rejected the overture.

9. Upon this, siege was laid to the city, and was continued for a month, when an assault was made, on the 9th of October, which resulted in a marked repulse of the combined army. D'Estaing and Pulaski, the brave Polander, were wounded, — the latter mortally. The loss of the Americans, in killed and wounded, was nearly one thousand. Here, too, the brave Jasper fell, grasping the standard from which floated the flag presented by Mrs. Elliot to the regiment of Moultrie, after the brave defence of Fort Moultrie, and which was now the winding-sheet of the brave-hearted Jasper (p. 169). Immediately following

---

* Count D'Estaing was a native of France, and descended from an ancient family. During the American war, he was vice-admiral. He was an officer of courage, but not distinguished for his skill. He suffered death by the guillotine, in 1793, for opposing the French Revolution.

this repulse, D'Estaing retired from the American coast, while Lincoln retreated into South Carolina.

10. The campaign of 1779 was remarkable, on the part of the Americans, for nothing, except their want of enterprise and energy. Nearly every scheme undertaken proved a failure. This resulted, in part, doubtless, from their disappointment as to anticipated assistance from France. The French fleet accomplished little or nothing ; and consequently the Americans grew despondent and inactive.

11. But there existed another, perhaps, still more potent reason for their feeble exertions. This was the daily depreciation of their bills of credit. The first issue of these bills by Congress was in June, 1775, and then to the amount of two millions. By the year 1780, the amount in circulation was two hundred millions, and the depreciation fifty or sixty for one. In after years, the depreciation was several hundreds for one. Several causes combined to sink this paper currency. But the two principal reasons were the extensive counterfeits of it by the enemy, and the general want of confidence that it would ever be redeemed.

12. With such a currency, it was impossible to carry on a war with energy. On the part of the Americans, therefore, the campaign of 1779 was spiritless and inefficient. On the part of Great Britain, although no very splendid victories had been achieved, preparations on a most liberal scale were made for the future. Parliament voted to raise eighty thousand seamen, and thirty-five thousand additional troops; while the House of Commons voted one hundred millions of dollars.

PRINCIPAL EVENTS OF 1780.

Capitulation of Charleston to the British.	Hard Winter, and Sufferings of the American Army.
Battle of Camden.	Arrival of French Fleet and Troops.
Wanton Conduct of the British at Connecticut Farms.	Treachery of Arnold.

1. Towards the close of 1799, General Clinton sailed from New York, with ten thousand troops, destined for the reduction of Charleston ; the small American force at which point was still under the command of General Lincoln. On the first of April, 1780, Clinton commenced erecting batteries, within eight hundred yards of the American works.

2. On the 9th, the British fleet, under Admiral Arbuthnot,

succeeded in passing Fort Moultrie, and anchored within cannon-shot of the city. Meanwhile, Lincoln, urged on by Governor Rutledge and other prominent citizens, had attempted to fortify the place; but his force and preparations were wholly inadequate, as was at length proved, the batteries of the besiegers obtaining a decided superiority. A capitulation became necessary; according to the terms of which, the whole American force, with all the inhabitants, and a large park of artillery, were surrendered to the British, on the 12th of May. A humiliating condition was imposed upon the vanquished; — the garrison was to march out and deposit their arms in front of the works, but they were not permitted to beat an American march. Eighteen months after, this was remembered at Yorktown, when to Cornwallis was administered a similar and retaliatory humiliating cup.

3. Charleston having thus surrendered, measures were adopted for reëstablishing royal authority over the province. With that view, several expeditions were sent into the country, which succeeded in their plans of subduing all to the royal standard. This accomplished, in June, Clinton embarked, with a large body of his troops, for New York, leaving Lord Cornwallis in command of the southern forces.

4. On the fall of Charleston, Lincoln was superseded in command by General Gates, the hero of Saratoga. The force placed at his disposal amounted to four thousand, of whom scarcely one thousand were regular troops; the rest being North Carolina, Maryland or Virginia militia.

5. On learning the approach of this force, Lord Rawdon, commander on the frontier, concentrated his army — two thousand in number — at Camden, situated one hundred and twenty miles north-west from Charleston, where, soon after, he was joined by Cornwallis. In this neighborhood, near Sander's Creek, eight miles from Camden, the hostile forces met, on the 16th of August.

6. The first onset decided the fate of the battle. A large body of the Virginia militia, under a charge of the British infantry with fixed bayonets, threw down their arms and fled. A considerable part of the North Carolina militia followed their unworthy example. But the continental troops evinced the most unyielding firmness, submitting only when forsaken by their brethren-in-arms, and when overpowered by numbers. In this battle, the brave Baron de Kalb, second in command, at the head of the Marylanders, fell, covered with wounds, which he survived only a few days. De Kalb was a German by birth, and had formerly served in the armies of the French. In consideration

of his distinguished merit as an officer and soldier, Congress resolved that a monument should be erected to his memory at Annapolis. The battle of Camden was exceedingly bloody, and had the effect to spread a deep gloom over the face of American affairs. But, if Cornwallis was the victor, the British cause had reached its culminating point. Elated with their successes, the victors grew insolent and rapacious, — the Americans, resolute and determined.

7. While the campaign of 1780 was thus filled up with important events, in the southern department, it passed away, in the Northern States, in successive disappointments, and reiterated distresses. In June, a body of five thousand of the enemy, under General Kniphausen,* entered New Jersey, and, in addition to plundering the country, wantonly burnt several villages. On the arrival of this body at Connecticut Farms, a small settlement containing about a dozen houses and a church, they burnt the whole. At this place there resided a Presbyterian minister, by the name of Caldwell, who had taken a conspicuous part in the cause of freedom, and who had, of course, incurred the deep displeasure of General Kniphausen. Hoping, however, that the general's resentment would be confined to himself, and not extend to his wife and children, who had been guilty of no crime, on the approach of the enemy, he hastily withdrew. Colonel Drayton had previously withdrawn the militia from the place, that there might be no pretext for enormities ; but the British soldiers did not wait for pretexts to be cruel. Mrs. Caldwell was shot, in the midst of her children, by a villain, who walked up to the window of the room in which she was sitting, and took deliberate aim with his musket. This atrocious act was attempted to be excused as an accident, as a random shot ; but the attempt at palliation served only to increase the crime.

8. Besides these predatory incursions, by which the inhabitants suffered alarm, distress and destruction of property, they suffered greatly, also, from the constantly diminishing value of their paper currency, and from unfavorable crops. The situation of General Washington —often, during the war, embarrassing — had been distressing through the winter, in his encampment at Morristown. The cold was more intense than it had ever before been known to be in this climate, within the memory of the oldest inhabitant. The winter, to this day, bears the distinctive

---

* General Kniphausen commanded the German troops, or Hessians, as they were sometimes called, from Hesse, a territory in Germany, from whence they came. He was a fine-looking officer, nearly six feet in stature.

epithet of the " hard winter." The army suffered extremely ;
and often had Washington the prospect before him of being
obliged to break up his encampment, and disband his soldiers.

9. The return of spring brought little alleviation to their
distress. Great disorder pervaded the departments for supplying
the army. Abuses crept in; frauds were practised; and, notwithstanding the poverty of the country, economy, on the part of
the commissioners, was exiled. In May, a committee from Congress visited the army, and reported to that body an account of
the distresses and disorders conspicuously prevalent. In particular, they stated, " that the army was unpaid for five months ;
that it seldom had more than six days' provisions in advance,
and was, on several occasions, for sundry successive days, without meat; that the medical department had neither sugar,
coffee, tea, chocolate, wine, nor spirituous liquors of any kind ;
and that every department of the army was without money,
and had not even the shadow of credit left."

10. But, under all this tide of evils, there appeared no disposition, in public bodies, to purchase their relief by concession.
On the contrary, they seemed to rise in the midst of their distresses, and to gain firmness and strength by the pressure of
calamity.

11. Fortunately for the Americans, as it seemed, M. de
Ternay arrived at Rhode Island, July 10th, from France, with
a squadron of seven sail-of-the-line, five frigates, and five
smaller armed vessels, with several transports, and six thousand
men, all under command of Lieutenant-general Count de
Rochambeau. Great was the joy excited by this event, and
high-raised expectations were indulged from the assistance of so
powerful a force against the enemy. But the British fleet in
our waters was still superior ; and that of the French, and the
French army, were, for a considerable time, incapacitated from
coöperating with the Americans, by being blocked up at Rhode
Island.

12. The fortress of West Point, sixty miles north of New
York, from its position, and especially from its commanding the
Hudson, was of great importance to the Americans. Of this
fortress, General Arnold had solicited and obtained the command ; soon after which, he treacherously entered into negotiations with Sir Henry Clinton, to make such a disposition of
the forces in the fortress as that the latter might easily take
possession of it by surprise. Fortunately, this base plot was
seasonably discovered, to prevent the ruinous consequences that
must have followed.

13. The agent employed by General Clinton, in maturing the plan with General Arnold, was Major John Andre, at that time adjutant-general of the British army, an officer extremely young, but high-minded, brave and accomplished. He was transported, in a vessel called the Vulture, up the North river, as near to West Point as was practicable, without exiting suspicion. On the 21st of September, at night, a boat was sent to bring him to the shore. On its return, Arnold met him at the beach, without the posts of either army. Their business was not finished, till too near the dawn of day for Andre to return to the Vulture. He, therefore, lay concealed within the American lines. During the day, the Vulture found it necessary to change her position; and Andre, not being able to get on board, was compelled to attempt his return to New York by land.

14. Having changed his military dress for a plain coat, and received a passport from Arnold, under the assumed name of John Anderson, he passed the guards and outposts, without suspicion. On his arrival at Tarrytown, a village thirty miles north of New York, in the vicinity of the first British posts, he was met by three militia soldiers, — John Paulding, David Williams, and Isaac Van Wert. He showed them his passport, and they suffered him to continue his route. Immediately after this, one of these three men, thinking that he perceived something singular in the person of the traveller, called him back. Andre asked them where they were from. " From down below," they replied, intending to say from New York. Too frank to suspect a snare, Andre immediately answered, " And so am I."

15. Upon this, they arrested him, when he declared himself to be a British officer, and offered them his watch, and all the gold he had with him, to be released. But, poor and obscure as these soldiers were, they were not to be bribed. Resolutely refusing his offers, they conducted him to Lieutenant-colonel Jameson, their commanding officer. Jameson injudiciously permitted Andre — still calling himself Anderson — to write to Arnold, who immediately escaped on board the Vulture, and took refuge in New York. Washington, on his way to headquarters, from Connecticut, where he had been to confer with Count de Rochambeau, providentially happened to be at West Point, just at this time. After taking measures to insure the safety of the fort, he appointed a board, of which General Greene was president, to decide upon the condition and punishment of Andre. After a patient hearing of the case, in which every feeling of kindness, liberality, and generous sympathy,

was strongly evinced, the board, upon his own confession, unanimously pronounced Andre a spy, and declared that, agreeably to the laws and usages of nations, he ought to suffer death.

16. Major Andre had many friends in the American army; and even Washington would have spared him, had duty to his country permitted. Every possible effort was made by Sir Henry Clinton in his favor; but it was deemed important that the decision of the board of war should be carried into execution. When Major Andre was apprized of the sentence of death, he made a last appeal, in a letter to Washington, that he might be shot, rather than die on a gibbet. To this request it was deemed necessary to give a denial; and, on the 2d of October, this unfortunate young man expired on the gallows, while foes and friends universally lamented his untimely end.

17. As a reward to Paulding, Williams and Van Wert, for their virtuous and patriotic conduct, Congress voted to each a farm in Westchester county of the value of five hundred pounds, an annuity of two hundred dollars, and a silver medal, on one side of which was a shield, with this inscription, — "Fidelity," — and on the other, the following motto — "Amor patriæ vincit," — the love of country conquers.

18. Arnold, the miserable wretch whose machinations led to the melancholy death of Andre, escaped to New York, where, as the price of dishonor, he received the commission of brigadier-general, and the sum of ten thousand pounds sterling. This

last boon was the grand secret of Arnold's fall from virtue. He had involved himself in debt, from which he saw no hope of extricating himself, but by bartering his honor and sacrificing his country for British gold.*

* That Washington's sympathy was deeply enlisted for Andre, admits of no doubt. And it seems highly probable that, could Arnold have been brought to justice, his victim might have escaped. To accomplish an object so desirable, Washington devised the following plan, which, though it ultimately failed, evinced the kindness of his heart towards Andre, and his deep sense of the villany and treachery of Arnold.

Having matured the plan, Washington sent to Major Lee to repair to headquarters, at Tappan, on the Hudson. "I have sent for you," said General Washington, "in the expectation that you have some one in your corps who is willing to undertake a delicate and hazardous project. Whoever comes forward will confer great obligation upon me personally ; and, in behalf of the United States, I will reward him amply. No time is to be lost : he must proceed to-night. I intend to seize Arnold, and save Andre." Major Lee named a sergeant-major of his corps, by the name of Champe, a native of Virginia, a man of tried courage, and inflexible perseverance. Champe was sent for by Major Lee, and the plan proposed. This was for him to desert, to escape to New York, to appear friendly to the enemy, to watch Arnold, and, upon some fit opportunity, to seize him, and conduct him to a place on the river, where boats should be in readiness to bear them away.

For a time, Champe objected ; but at last he accepted the service. It was now eleven o'clock at night. With his instructions in his pocket, the sergeant returned to camp, and, taking his cloak, valise and orderly-book, drew his horse from the picket, and, mounting, put himself upon fortune. Scarcely had half an hour elapsed, before Captain Carnes, the officer of the day, waited upon Lee, and informed him that a dragoon, it was believed, had deserted. Lee, hoping to conceal the flight of Champe, complained of fatigue, and told the captain that it was probably a mistake. Carnes, however, was not thus to be quieted ; and he withdrew, to assemble his corps. On examination, it was found that Champe was absent. The captain now returned, and acquainted Lee with the discovery, adding that he had detached a party to pursue the deserter, and begged the major's written orders.

After making as much delay as practicable, Lee delivered his orders. "Bring him alive," said he, "that he may suffer in the presence of the army ; but kill him if he resists, or if he escapes after being taken." A shower of rain falling soon after Champe's departure, enabled the pursuing dragoons to take the trail of his horse, — his shoes, in common with other horses of the army, being made in a peculiar form, and each having a private mark, which was to be seen in the path. Middleton, the leader of the pursuing party, left the camp a few minutes past twelve, so that Champe had the start of but little more than an hour. During the night, the dragoons were often delayed in examining the road ; but, on the coming of morning, the impression of the horse's shoes was so apparent, that they pressed on with rapidity. Some miles above Bergen, a village three miles north of New York, on the opposite side of the Hudson, on ascending a hill, Champe was descried, not more than half a mile distant. Fortunately, Champe descried his pursuers at the same moment ; upon which, putting spurs to his horse, he was able to reach a place on the river, in which were some British galleys at anchor. Throwing himself from his horse, he gave a plunge, and succeeded in reaching one of these galleys, on board of which he was safe from his pursuers. These now, having recovered the sergeant's horse and cloak, returned to camp. On their appearance with the well-known horse, the soldiers made the air resound with acclamations that the scoundrel was killed. The agony of Lee,

17

PRINCIPAL EVENTS OF 1781.

Revolt of Pennsylvania Troops.	Battle of Ninety-Six.
Depredations of Arnold in Virginia.	Execution of Hayne.
	Battle of Eutaw Springs.
Battle of Cowpens.	Recovering of Charleston.
Remarkable Retreat of General Greene.	Arnold's Expedition against New London.
Engagement at Guilford Courthouse.	Siege of Yorktown, and Surrender of Cornwallis.
Battle of Hobkirk's Hill.	

1. The year 1781 opened with an event which, for a time, seriously endangered the American cause. This was the revolt of the whole Pennsylvania line of troops, at Morristown, to the

for a moment, was past description, lest the faithful Champe had fallen. But the truth soon relieved his fears, and he repaired to Washington, to impart to him the success, thus far, of his plan.

Champe soon found means to communicate to Lee an account of his adventures ; but, unfortunately, he could not succeed in taking Arnold, before the execution of Andre. Ten days before he brought his project to a conclusion, Lee received from him a communication, appointing the third subsequent night for a party of dragoons to meet him at Hoboken, opposite New York, when he hoped to deliver Arnold to the officers. Champe had enlisted into Arnold's legion, from which time he discovered that it was his custom to return home about twelve every night, and that, previously to going to bed, he always visited the garden. During this visit, the conspirators were to seize him, gag him, and bear him off, as if conveying a drunken soldier to the guard-house.

number of thirteen hundred. The occasion of this mutiny was want of pay, clothing and provisions. Upon examination of the grievances of the troops, by a committee from Congress, their complaints were considered just, and measures were immediately adopted for their relief; upon which, those whose time of service had not expired cheerfully returned to camp.

2. General Wayne, who commanded these troops, had used every exertion to quiet them, but in vain. In the ardor of remonstrance, he cocked his pistol, and turned towards them; when, instantly, a hundred bayonets were directed towards him, and the men cried out, " We love you, we respect you; but you are a dead man, if you fire. Do not mistake us; we are not going to the enemy. On the contrary, were they now to appear, you should see us fight under your orders, with as much resolution and alacrity as ever." Leaving the camp, the mutineers proceeded in a body to Princeton, whither Sir Henry Clinton despatched agents, with offers of large reward, to induce them to

When the day arrived, Lee, with a party of accoutred horses, left the camp for the appointed rendezvous, which they reached about midnight; and here they remained hour after hour, until, there being no longer any hope of Champe's approach, they returned to the camp. In a few days, Lee received an anonymous letter from Champe's patron and friend, informing him that, on the day preceding the night fixed for the execution of the plot, Arnold, most unfortunately, had removed his quarters to another part of the town; and that the American legion, consisting chiefly of American deserters, had been transferred from their barracks to one of the transports. Thus it happened that John Champe, instead of crossing the Hudson that night, was safely deposited on board one of the fleet of transports, from whence he never departed, until the troops under Arnold landed in Virginia. Some time after, he effected his escape, and, at length, again joined the American army.

His appearance excited extreme surprise among his former comrades, which was not a little increased, when they saw the cordial reception he met with from the late Major, now Lieutenant-colonel Lee. His story was soon known to the corps, which reproduced the love and respect of officers and soldiers, heretofore invariably entertained for the sergeant, heightened by universal admiration of his late daring and arduous attempt. Champe was introduced to General Greene, who complied with the promise made by the commander-in-chief; and, having provided the sergeant with a good horse, and money for his journey, sent him to General Washington, who munificently anticipated every desire of the sergeant, and presented him with a discharge from further service, lest, in the vicissitudes of war, he should fall into the hands of the enemy, when, if recognized, he was sure to die on a gibbet.

We shall only add, that when General Washington was called by President Adams, in 1798, to the command of the army prepared to defend the country against French hostility, he sent to Lieutenant-colonel Lee, to inquire for Champe, being determined to bring him into the field, at the head of a company of infantry. Lee sent to Loudon county, Virginia, where Champe settled after his discharge from the army; when he learned that the gallant soldier had removed to Kentucky, where he soon after died.*

* Lee's Memoirs.

espouse the British cause.   But these soldiers loved their country's cause too well to listen to proposals so reproachful.   They
were suffering privations which could no longer be sustained;
but they spurned, with disdain, the offer of the enemy.   They
also seized the agents of the British, and nobly delivered them
up to General Wayne, to be treated as spies.

3. In the midst of these troubles, news arrived of great depredations in Virginia, by Arnold, at the head of sixteen hundred
men, and a number of armed vessels.   Large quantities of
tobacco, salt, rum, &c., were destroyed.   In this manner did
Arnold show the change of spirit which had taken place in his
breast, and his fidelity to his new engagements.   Upon receiving
news of these depredations, a French squadron, from Rhode
Island, was sent to cut off Arnold's retreat.   Ten of his vessels
were destroyed, and a forty-four gun ship captured.   Shortly
after, an engagement took place, off the capes of Virginia, between
the French and English squadrons, which terminated so far to
the advantage of the English that Arnold was saved from falling
into the hands of his exasperated countrymen.

4. Following the unfortunate battle of Camden (p. 188),
General Gates was removed, and General Greene appointed his
successor.   Next to Washington, Greene was the ablest commander in the Revolutionary army.   He combined much of that
great man's sound judgment and caution, while he was distinguished, perhaps, even more than Washington himself, for
promptness of action in times of emergency.   On assuming the
command, Greene found the army reduced to two thousand men,
of whom one-half were militia, and not more than eight hundred
fit for service.   His officers, however, had few equals, and no
superiors.   These were Morgan, Lee, Marion, Sumpter and
Colonel Washington, whose heroic achievements have justly
placed them high on the rolls of fame.

5. The first measure of Greene was unusual; he separated
his forces, small as they were, into several divisions, and stationed
them at different points, under Morgan, Marion, &c.   For this
he has been censured, as contrary to military rule; but the
sequel proved the wisdom of the measure.   It served to perplex
Cornwallis, who scarcely knew what movement to make, or whom
first to attack.

6. At length, however, he decided to begin with Morgan, who
was stationed at Cowpens, near the northern boundary of South
Carolina.   For this object, Colonel Tarleton * was despatched,

---

* Colonel Tarleton was distinguished for his military courage and enterprise. He was below the middle size, stout, strong, with large legs, but

with eleven hundred men, to assail him in front, while Cornwallis, with the main army, would attempt to cut off his retreat.

7. On the approach of Tarleton, Morgan retired ; but a contest became inevitable. The first onset of Tarleton was terrible, and the Americans gave way ; but, at this critical moment, Colonel Washington gave orders to his bugler to sound a charge. It was nobly done. Morgan had time to rally his repulsed forces, and now sped on to victory. It was a brief and sanguinary scene, but the achievement was nearly as brilliant as any during the war.

8. Upon receiving intelligence of Tarleton's defeat, Cornwallis abandoned the invasion of North Carolina, and marched in pursuit of Morgan. Greene, suspecting his intentions, hastened, with his army, to join him ; which having been effected, the united force directed their march towards Guilford court-house,* which Greene had appointed as the rendezvous of his army.

9. This was a perilous undertaking. It was the season of winter, and the soldiers were nearly destitute of shoes, blankets and provisions. But there was no safe alternative. Accordingly, Greene commenced the retreat ; but the British urged the pursuit with such rapidity, that they reached the Catawba on the evening of the same day on which the Americans had crossed it ; and, before the next morning, a heavy fall of rain had rendered it impassable. A passage, at length, being effected, the pursuit was continued. By expeditious movements, the Americans crossed the Yadkin the second and third days of February, and secured their boats on the north side ; the British were again close in their rear, and were only prevented crossing through by the want of boats, and by a sudden and remarkable rise of the waters. This second interposition of Heaven served to confirm the Americans in the belief that their cause was favored by God.

10. The passage of the Yadkin being thus effected, Greene proceeded to Guilford court-house ; where, having been joined by the remainder of his army, he continued his retreat towards Virginia, still hotly pursued by Cornwallis. In their route, it was necessary to pass the Dan ; and here was their point of greatest danger. Cornwallis was near at hand, and, like Pharaoh of old, was bent on destruction.

11. They reached the banks. The deep waters were rolling before them. No time was to be lost. Lee's legion and Washington's horsemen were stationed in the rear, to keep in check the

uncommonly active. His eye was small, dark and piercing. His age was about twenty-five.

* Guilford court-house, now Greensborough, the capital of Guilford county, Virginia, is about eighty miles north-west from Raleigh.

17*

enemy, should he appear. About noon, a messenger announced the joyful tidings, that the army was safe on the opposite shore. Greene himself had not yet crossed. He had delayed, through anxiety for the safety of Lee, Washington, and their comrades.

12. These now came dashing to the river side, and were soon making the passage. The last boat left the shore, as the British van reached the banks. This was the climax of disappointment, especially after a pursuit of two hundred and fifty miles. But it was an hour of intense joy to Greene and his army. Here Cornwallis abandoned the pursuit, and, turning south, established himself at Hillsborough, thirty-five miles north-west of Raleigh.

13. Meanwhile, Greene's army being augmented, by reinforcements from Virginia, to forty-four hundred, he re-crossed the Dan into Carolina, and proceeding to Guilford court-house, awaited the approach of the enemy. On the 15th of March, Cornwallis appeared, with his army, and an engagement ensued. At first, the Carolina militia retreated, in disorder; but the regular troops stood their ground, for a time, with great firmness. At length, however, Greene felt compelled to order a general retreat, which left the field in possession of the enemy. But, if the result was a victory to the British, it was such as caused Fox to exclaim, when announced in the British House of Commons, "Another such victory will ruin the British army."

14. Following this battle, Cornwallis retired to Wilmington, and thence, after a halt of nearly three weeks, proceeded to Virginia. Meanwhile, Greene decided to lead back his forces into South Carolina, and to fall on the line of British posts, between Ninety-Six and Charleston. It was a bold and hazardous experiment; but, the decision once made, he took up his line of march, and in twelve days encamped on Hobkirk's Hill, a little more than a mile from Camden, where the British were strongly intrenched.

15. Here, on the 25th, Rawdon drew out his forces, and appeared in battle array. The Americans were engaged cooking their food, of which for twenty-four hours they had been destitute. For a moment, there was confusion; but, abandoning their meal, as Greene did his coffee, they stood in the order of battle. The action opened with promise to the Americans; but, at the critical moment, the Gunby regiment, mistaking the order of their leader (this was their apology), began to retreat.*

---

* This was the regiment which, at Guilford, had displayed great bravery, and upon which Greene now depended, perhaps, more than all others. In the din of arms, it was said, they did not understand the order of their leader.

16. Greene marked the movement with anguish; but, in a moment, he sped his charger among them, — headed them, — rallied them; — but it was too late. There was more fighting, but the battle was lost to the Americans. The killed, wounded and missing, were about equal on both sides.

17. Following the battle of Hobkirk's Hill, otherwise known as the battle of Camden, Greene proceeded to Ninety-Six, one hundred and forty-seven miles north-west from Charleston, a post of great natural strength, and strongly fortified. After prosecuting the siege of this place nearly four weeks, intelligence arrived of the rapid approach of Lord Rawdon, with large reinforcements. Notwithstanding this, Greene determined on an assault. This was made on the 18th of June; and, although made with admirable firmness, the Americans failed, and were compelled to raise the siege.

18. Rawdon followed Greene some fifteen or twenty miles, on his retreat, when, returning to Ninety-Six, he ordered its evacuation, while he himself proceeded to Charleston. His army took post at Eutaw Springs. Leaving Colonel Stewart in command of the British forces under him, Rawdon soon returned to England.

19. Before sailing, however, an event occurred which reflected great dishonor upon Lord Rawdon, and still more upon Colonel Balfour, the commandant at Charleston. This was the execution of Colonel Isaac Hayne, who, to escape imprisonment, had, on the surrender of Charleston, given in his adhesion to the British authorities; but subsequently, for good and sufficient reasons, as he thought, again taken up arms with the patriots. Being taken and brought before Balfour, he was condemned to death. It is said that Lord Rawdon, for a time, endeavored to shield him, but was finally persuaded to sanction his execution.*

---

* At the commencement of the war, Colonel Hayne was residing in the vicinity of Charleston, on a plantation, blessed with an ample fortune, a lovely family, and possessing a character of exalted worth. Animated with a zealous patriotism, he entered with ardor into the defence of Charleston. On the surrender of that city, he had the choice of becoming a British subject, or going into imprisonment. He chose the former, out of regard to his family, which was on his plantation, languishing with small-pox; and his decision was sanctioned by his friends. At length, the fortune of war changed, and the British were compelled to act on the defensive. Although Colonel Hayne had been assured that he should not be called to take up arms against his country, these assurances were forgotten, and he, with others, was summoned to the British standard. To this he could not consent; and, besides, feeling released·from an obligation which the British had themselves violated, he once more joined the cause of his countrymen; and, while acting as colonel of a regiment, he was taken prisoner, and confined in a dungeon. He had no trial, it is said, but was sentenced to death by Balfour. The

20. On the approach of the hot season, General Greene returned, with his forces, to the high hills of Santee.* Early in September, he approached the enemy, under Colonel Stewart, at Eutaw Springs. Here, on the 8th, occurred the battle of that name. The Americans were the first to commence the contest. The militia did themselves great credit. Indeed, both armies contended with a perseverance commensurate with the prize at stake. While, in the sequel, neither could claim a decided victory, the advantages rested with Greene. At the close of the battle, the belligerent armies united in burying their dead! What a contrast to the spectacle exhibited a few hours before!

21. The battle of Eutaw Springs was the last general engagement in the south. Soon after, the British concentrated themselves at Charleston. Here, for months, they were hemmed in and watched by the faithful and persevering Greene. But, at length, their situation became so distressing, that they determined to evacuate the city. This was carried into effect on the 13th of December, 1781. At three o'clock of the same day, Greene entered the city in triumph, when he was met with the exulting and welcoming shouts of an emancipated and rejoicing people, — "God bless you! God bless you!"

22. Green merited it all. He loved his country, and most faithfully did he serve her. Washington said of him, — and it was all true, — "Could he but promote the interests of his country in the character of a corporal, he would exchange, without a murmur, his epaulets for the knot."

23. We left Cornwallis moving from Wilmington towards Virginia (p. 198). In less than a month he reached Petersburg (May 20), where he found the troops of General Phillips, who had died a few days before his arrival.

24. Early in the spring, General Washington had detached the Marquis de Lafayette, with three thousand men, to coöperate with the French fleet, in Virginia, in the capture of Arnold, who was committing depredations in that state. On the failure of this expedition, Lafayette marched back as far as the head of Elk river. Here he received orders to return to Virginia, to oppose the British. On his return, hearing of the advance of Cornwallis towards Petersburg, twenty miles below Richmond,

---

royal governor and others petitioned for his pardon; and his children, in the habiliments of mourning for a mother, appeared, and plead, with outstretched hands, for the life of a father; — but all in vain. Lord Rawdon sanctioned the stern decree.

* These hills are east of the Wateree river, some twenty miles from Camden.

he hastened his march, to prevent, if possible, the junction of Cornwallis with the troops under General Phillips. In this, however, he failed.

25. One great object of Cornwallis now was to bring Lafayette to an engagement. Prudence, however, forbade the latter to run the hazard of a contest with an enemy of more than twice his force. He therefore continued to retreat. For a time, Cornwallis employed himself in destroying vast stores of public and private property, in the vicinity of James river; and then, crossing that river, after several movements, proceeded to Portsmouth. This he intended as a permanent post; but, not approving of it for that purpose, he concentrated his forces at Yorktown, on the south side of York river, which he immediately commenced fortifying. Gloucester Point, on the opposite side, was held by some six hundred men, under Colonel Tarleton.

26. The campaign for 1781 had, for its grand object, the siege of New York, by the combined forces of the Americans, under Washington, and the French, under Count de Rochambeau,* to be aided by a French fleet expected on the coast, under command of Count de Grasse. In prosecution of this plan, the French troops left Rhode Island, and joined Washington, who had concentrated his forces at Kingsbridge, fifteen miles above New York.

27. While all movements were being directed to the above enterprise, the plan of Washington was suddenly changed, by intelligence that the fleet under De Grasse would soon arrive in the Chesapeake, but would not proceed to New York. Cornwallis, therefore, now became Washington's object; and the combined troops, therefore, amounting to twelve thousand, took up their march from New York, and on the 30th of September appeared before Yorktown.†

28. The Count de Grasse, already arrived, had so blocked up James and York rivers as to prevent the escape of Cornwallis

---

* Count de Rochambeau was born in 1725. At sixteen, he entered the army. In 1780, he came, as Lieutenant-general, to America, at the head of six thousand troops. He was a fine officer. After the Revolution, he was made a Marshal by Louis XVI. He narrowly escaped death under the tyranny of Robespierre, during the French Revolution. In 1803, he was presented to Bonaparte, who gave him a pension. His death took place in 1809.

† No movement, during the war, was more felicitously accomplished than the above of Washington, in withdrawing his troops from New York, while the British general was kept in utter ignorance of his object. The latter, supposing it a feint, to draw him to a general engagement, remained at his ease; nor were his suspicions awakened until Washington and his troops were some distance on their way towards Virginia.

by sea, and a force of two thousand French troops from the fleet having joined Lafayette at Williamsburg, cut off all his hope, if he indulged any, of retreating into the Southern States.

29. While the combined armies were advancing to the siege of Yorktown, an excursion was made from New York, by General Arnold, against New London, in his native state. The object of this expedition seems to have been to draw away a part of the American forces, Sir Henry Clinton knowing but too well that, if they were left at liberty to push the siege of Yorktown, the blockaded army must inevitably surrender. This expedition was signalized by the greatest atrocities. Fort Trumbull, on the west, and Fort Griswold, on the east side of the river Thames, below New London, were taken, and the greater part of that town was burnt.

30. At Fort Trumbull, little or no resistance was made; but Fort Griswold was defended, for a time, with great bravery and resolution. After the fort was carried, a British officer, entering, inquired who commanded. Colonel Ledyard answered, "I did, but you do now," at the same time presenting his sword. The officer immediately plunged the sword into his bosom. A general massacre now took place, as well of those who surrendered as of those who resisted, which continued until nearly all the garrison were either killed or wounded. Sixty dwelling-houses, and eighty-four stores, in New London, were reduced to ashes.

31. Much as Washington deplored the conduct of Arnold, he could not be diverted from his now one great object. The fall of Cornwallis involved the termination of the war. With this in view, there was no wavering of purpose, and no interruption of toil.

32. We shall not enter into the details of this siege. It commenced on the evening of the 9th of October, and was opened by the American batteries upon the town, at the distance of six hundred yards. From that time, night and day, the grand object was pursued, — one steady advance of the besiegers was effected. On the 16th, nearly one hundred pieces of heavy ordnance were, at the same time, pouring their terrible contents upon the walls and fortifications of the British, and with such effect as to level them, and dismount nearly every gun.

33. One only hope now remained for Cornwallis. This was an attempt to retreat by way of Gloucester Point; but, as if Providence had decided here to terminate this long and distressing war, a storm arose on the night of the 16th, the time appointed for the attempted escape, and dispersed his boats, after one division had crossed the river. No alternative now remained

but to capitulate. On the 19th, the posts of York and Gloucester were surrendered, — the British army, to Washington; the
British fleet, to De Grasse.*

34. Five days after the surrender of Cornwallis, Sir Henry
Clinton made his appearance off the capes of Virginia, with a
reinforcement of seven thousand men; but, receiving intelligence
of his lordship's fate, he returned to New York. Cornwallis, in
his despatches to Sir Henry, more than hinted that his fall had
been produced by a too firm reliance on promises that no pains
were taken to fulfil. Clinton had promised Cornwallis that this
auxiliary force should leave New York on the 5th of October;
but, for reasons never explained, it did not sail until the 19th,
the very day that decided the fate of the army.

35. Nothing could exceed the joy of the American people at
this great and important victory over Lord Cornwallis. Exultation broke forth from one extremity of the country to the other.
To the unanimous acclaim of the people Congress joined the
authority of its resolves. It addressed thanks to the generals,
officers, and soldiers, — presented British colors, — ordered the
erection of a marble column, — and went into procession to
church, to render public thanksgiving to God for the recent
victory. The 30th of December was appointed as a day of
national thanksgiving.

36. The fall of Cornwallis may be considered as substantially

---

* General Lincoln was appointed, by the commander-in-chief, to receive
the submission of the royal army, in the same manner in which, eighteen
months before (p. 188), Cornwallis had received that of the Americans at
Charleston.

The spectacle was impressive and affecting. The road through which the
captive army marched was lined with spectators, French and American. On
one side, the commander-in-chief, surrounded with his suite, and the American staff, took his station; on the other side, opposite to him, was the Count
de Rochambeau, in the like manner attended.

The captive army approached, moving slowly in column, with grace and
precision. Universal silence was observed amidst the vast concourse, and
the utmost decency prevailed, exhibiting an awful sense of the vicissitudes
of human life, mingled with commiseration for the unhappy.

Every eye was now turned, searching for the British commander-in-chief,
anxious to look at the man heretofore so much the object of their dread. All
were disappointed. Cornwallis, unable to bear the humiliation of marching
at the head of his garrison, constituted General O'Hara his representative on
the occasion.

The post of Gloucester, falling with that of York, was delivered up, the
same day, by Lieutenant-colonel Tarleton.

At the termination of the siege, the besieging army amounted to sixteen
thousand. The British force numbered seven thousand one hundred and
seven, of which only four thousand and seven, rank and file, are stated to
have been fit for duty. The artillery surrendered consisted of one hundred
and sixty pieces, the greater part of which were brass.

closing the war. A few posts of importance were still held by the British, — New York, Charleston, and Savannah, — but all other parts of the country, which they had possessed, were recovered into the power of Congress. A few skirmishes alone indicated the continuance of war. A part of the French army, soon after the capture of Cornwallis, reëmbarked, and Count de Grasse sailed for the West Indies. Count Rochambeau cantoned his army for the winter, 1782, in Virginia; and the main body of the Americans returned, by the way of the Chesapeake, to their former position, on the Hudson.

PRINCIPAL EVENTS OF 1781-3.

Appointment of Peace Commissioners.

Cessation of Hostilities.

Farewell Orders of Washington.

Adieu to his Officers.

Resignation of his Commission.

Treaty of Peace.

1. From the 12th of December, 1781, to the 4th of March, 1782, motion after motion was made, in the British Parliament, for putting an end to the war in America. On this latter day, the commons resolved, " that the house would consider as enemies to his majesty, and to the country, all those who should advise or attempt the further prosecution of offensive war on the continent of North America."

2. On the same day, the command of his majesty's forces in America was taken from Sir Henry Clinton, and given to Sir Guy Carlton,* who was instructed to promote the wishes of Great Britain, for an accommodation with the United States. In accordance with these instructions, Carlton endeavored to open a correspondence with Congress; and, with this view, sent to General Washington to solicit a passport for his secretary. But this was refused, since Congress would enter into no negotiations, but in concert with his most Christian majesty.

3. The French court, on receiving intelligence of the surrender of Cornwallis, pressed upon Congress the appointment of commissioners for negotiating peace with Great Britain. Accordingly, John Adams, Benjamin Franklin, John Jay, and Henry Laurens, were appointed. These commissioners met Mr. Fitzherbert and Mr. Oswald, on the part of Great Britain, at Paris,

---

* Sir Guy Carlton was born in Ireland, in 1722. In 1748, he became Lieutenant-colonel. In 1759, he was at the siege of Quebec, under Wolfe. He was a distinguished man. In 1790, he was created Baron Dorchester. He died in 1808.

and provisional articles of peace between the two countries were signed, November 30th, 1782. The definitive treaty was signed on the 3d of September, 1783. Although the treaty was not signed until September, a state of peace had actually existed from the commencement of the year 1783. A formal proclamation of the cessation of hostilities was made, through the army, on the 19th of April; the eighth anniversary of the battle of Lexington. Savannah was evacuated by the British in July, New York in November, and Charleston in the following month.

4. The third of November was assigned by Congress for disbanding the army of the United States. On the day previous, Washington issued his farewell orders, and bade an affectionate adieu to the soldiers who had fought and bled by his side.* After mentioning the trying times through which he had passed, and the unexampled patience which, under every circumstance of suffering, his army had evinced, he passed to the glorious prospects opening before them and their country, and then bade them adieu in the following words: "Being now to conclude these his last public orders, to take his ultimate leave, in a short time, of the military character, and to bid a final adieu to the armies he has so long had the honor to command, he can only again offer, in their behalf, his recommendations to their grateful country, and his prayer to the God of armies. May ample justice be done them here; and may the choicest favor, both here and hereafter, attend those, who, under the divine auspices, have secured innumerable blessings for others! With these wishes, and this benediction, the commander-in-chief is about to retire from service. The curtain of separation will soon be drawn, and the military scene to him will be closed forever."

5. Soon after taking leave of the army, General Washington was called to the still more painful hour of separation from his officers, greatly endeared to him by a long series of common sufferings and dangers. The officers having previously assembled in New York for the purpose, General Washington now joined

---

* The disbanding of the army involved considerations of the deepest interest. Thousands were to be thrown out of service, — and what could they do ? Neither officers nor soldiers, for a long time, had received any pay; and the state of the public finances now rendered payment impossible. In this state, a very exciting appeal was made to the officers, in a letter, afterwards ascribed to John Armstrong, in which he recommended measures of redress, or a refusal to disband. It was an artful and even eloquent address; and, but for the firmness and prudence of Washington, it would have had its designed effect. The influence of that great man, however, prevailed. The officers decided, at a meeting which Washington called, and at which Gates presided, that they would do nothing which should tend to sully the glory they had acquired in their country's service.

18

them, and, calling for a glass of wine, thus addressed them : — " With a heart full of love and gratitude, I now take my leave of you. I most devoutly wish that your latter days may be as prosperous and happy as your former ones have been glorious and honorable." Having thus affectionately addressed them, he now took each by the hand, and bade him farewell. Followed by them to the side of the Hudson, he entered a barge, and, while tears rolled down his cheeks, he turned towards the companions of his glory, and bade them a silent adieu.

6. December 23d, Washington appeared in the hall of Congress, and resigned to them the commission which they had given him, as commander-in-chief of the armies of the United States. After having spoken of the accomplishment of his wishes and exertions, in the independence of his country, and commended his officers and soldiers to Congress, he concluded as follows : — " I consider it an indispensable duty to close the last solemn act of my official life, by commending the interests of our dearest country to the protection of Almighty God, and those who have the superintendence of them to his holy keeping. Having now finished the work assigned me, I retire from the great theatre of action ; and, bidding an affectionate farewell to this august body, under whose orders I have long acted, I here offer my commission, and take my leave of all the employments of public life."

7. Upon accepting his commission, Congress, through their president, expressed, in glowing language, to Washington, their high sense of his wisdom and energy in conducting the war to so happy a termination, and invoked the choicest blessings upon his future life. President Mifflin concluded as follows : — " We join you in commending the interest of our dearest country to the protection of Almighty God, beseeching him to dispose the hearts and minds of its citizens to improve the opportunity afforded them of becoming a happy and respectable nation. And, for you, we address to Him our earnest prayers, that a life so beloved may be fostered with all his care ; that your days may be as happy as they have been illustrious ; and that he will finally give you that reward which this world cannot give."

8. A profound silence now pervaded the assembly. The grandeur of the scene, the recollection of the past, the felicity of the present, and the hopes of the future, crowded fast upon all, while they united in invoking blessings upon the man, who, under God, had achieved so much, and who now, in the character of a mere citizen, was hastening to a long-desired repose at his seat, at Mount Vernon, in Virginia.

HISTORY OF THE NAVAL OPERATIONS, DURING THE AMERICAN REVOLUTION.

1. At the commencement of the Revolutionary struggle, the colonies had no naval force to aid their cause. But no sooner had the struggle commenced, than many brave and patriotic men began to digest plans, not for competing with the navy of Great Britain, but for cruising against her commerce. The seamen of the colonies were at home on the deep. They were bold, hardy, and adventurous.

2. The news of the battle of Lexington reached Machias, in Maine, May 9th, 1775. The people were roused, and ready to act in some way. At this time, there was lying in that port a British armed schooner, called the MARGARETTA. A plan was now devised to capture her. A sloop was manned with thirty men, and chase given after the schooner, the captain of which, suspecting some such design, had weighed anchor and put out to sea.

3. The sloop, being the better sailer, at length came up with the schooner. An action ensued, which was of short duration, but resulted in favor of the Americans. Twenty men, on both sides, were killed and wounded. Among the former was Captain Moore, commander of the schooner. Such was the first naval engagement in the war of the Revolution. It was wholly a private affair.

4. Before the subject of a naval force had received the attention of Congress, three of the colonies — Massachusetts, Rhode Island, and Connecticut — had provided each two vessels, fitted, armed and equipped, without the orders or advice of Congress.

5. But, in 1775, that body took the subject into serious consideration, authorizing a regular marine. Vessels were to be built in the four colonies of New England, in New York, Pennsylvania, Maryland, and Virginia. The following is a list of their names and respective rates, as ordered, as well as the colony where each was to be built, namely:

Name	Guns.	Colony	Name	Guns.	Colony
Washington,	32,	Pennsylvania.	Effingham,	28,	Pennsylvania.
Raleigh,	32,	New Hampshire.	Congress,	28,	New York.
Hancock,	32,	Massachusetts.	Providence,	28,	Rhode Island.
Randolph,	32,	Pennsylvania.	Boston,	24,	Massachusetts.
Warren,	32,	Rhode Island.	Montgomery,	24,	New York.
Maryland,	28,	Virginia.	Delaware,	24,	Pennsylvania.
Trumbull,	28,	Connecticut.			

6. Such was the design of Congress; but, for want of funds, — but more for want of materials to equip them, such as guns, anchors, rigging, &c., — but few of the above got to sea, in the service for which they were built. These were the Raleigh, Hancock, Boston, Warren, Providence, Maryland, and Randolph. The Congress and Montgomery were burnt on the Hudson, to prevent their falling into the hands of the British. The Washington and Effingham were burnt by the British themselves. The Delaware fell into their hands, at Philadelphia.

7. Such was the commencement of the American navy. Ezekiel Hopkins was placed at the head of it, with the title of "Commander-in-chief;" but his usual appellation was "Commodore." His pay was one hundred and twenty-five dollars per month. There were twenty-four naval officers appointed, with the rank of captain.

8. The flag used on board of some ships bore a device, representing a pine-tree, with a rattle-snake coiled at the root and ready to strike, with the appropriate motto, "Don't tread on me." Other vessels adopted the arms of the colony from which they sailed. In 1777, Congress adopted our present national colors.

9. Many of our naval officers were high-spirited and intelligent men. Those whose names have descended to us with greatest reputation were Commodore Hopkins; Captains Manly, Mugford, Jones, Barry, Barney, Waters, Young, Tucker, Talbot, Nicholson, — commander-in-chief after Hopkins, — Williams, Biddle, Robinson, Wickes, Rathburne, and Hacket.

10. Not a few of the commanders of the privateers were distinguished for their nautical skill. The privateers were numerous and successful. It has been estimated that during the war they captured not less than twelve hundred and ninety-seven vessels, not including those taken by public ships. It may be added, that generally the commanders of privateers were men of principle and humanity. Indeed, instances of the most magnanimous conduct among them might be given.

11. The records of engagements by the regular marine are nearly as abundant and circumstantial, as those of the American navy during the late war with Great Britain. But our limits will not allow us to enter into details of these exploits on the ocean. Spirited actions occurred between the Randolph and Yarmouth, the Raleigh and Druid, the Trumbull and Watt, the Congress and Savage, &c.; but, of all the naval engagements which occurred during the war, that between the Bon Homme Richard, of forty guns, and the Serapis, — the latter a British

frigate mounting forty-four guns, — was the most remarkable; and in the history of naval warfare has scarcely a parallel.

12. The Richard was commanded by that remarkable man, Paul Jones, whose history is a romance; the commander of the Serapis was Captain Pearson. The action occurred on the coast of Scotland, September 23d, 1779. It was commenced by a flotilla of French and American vessels, and two English frigates convoying a fleet of merchantmen. At half-past seven in the evening, the two frigates Bon Homme and Serapis came in contact, upon which Jones lashed them together. In this situation, the battle between them raged for more than two hours, each dealing out to the other the fire and thunder of its guns, as fast as they could be loaded.

13. At length, both ships were on fire, and the Richard on the point of sinking! In this awful moment, a sad mistake occurred. The Alliance, an American frigate, came up to Jones' assistance; but, in the darkness of the night, she poured her entire broad-side into the Richard, and caused sad destruction; but, soon perceiving her mistake, she joined her companion, and with such zeal that the Serapis was soon compelled to surrender. Both vessels were covered with the blood of their brave crews. Of three hundred and seventy-five men on board the Richard, three hundred were either killed or wounded; while the loss of the Serapis was one hundred and fifty, — nearly half her crew. On an examination of the Richard, it was found necessary to abandon her. The wounded were consequently removed to the Serapis, and, on the following day, the gallant ship settled slowly into the sea.

14. It belongs to this place to notice briefly an invention by David Bushnell, a native of Connecticut, in the year 1777, to blow up ships by means of torpedoes, as he called them. The torpedo bore a resemblance to two upper tortoise-shells, of equal sizes, placed in contact, and so large as to contain a man. It was fixed with glass windows, and with air-pipes and ventilators, so that the operator could breathe. Behind this sub-marine vessel was a powder magazine, made water-tight, and capable of holding one hundred and fifty pounds of powder. It was fitted with an apparatus for firing the powder; and could at any time be detached from the vessel, by turning a screw, and attached by other apparatus to the bottom of the intended victim.

15. With torpedoes of the above construction, Bushnell made several attempts to blow up British vessels in the American waters, — in none of which, however, was he entirely successful. But, in a single instance, a schooner was destroyed, and three

18*

men killed, and one badly injured. The men perceiving a line floating, and supposing it to be a fishing-line, drew it on board; when the machine attached to the end of it exploded, with the above result. It scarcely needs be added, that such a mode of warfare is too inhuman to be encouraged by civilized nations. But it is said that his failure cast a deep and permanent gloom over the mind of Bushnell.

NOTES.

MANNERS. — 1. At the commencement of the Revolution, the colonists of America were a mass of husbandmen, merchants, mechanics and fishermen, who were occupied in the ordinary avocations of their respective callings, and were entitled to the appellation of a sober, honest, and industrious set of people. Being, however, under the control of a country whose jealousies were early and strongly enlisted against them, and which, therefore, was eager to repress every attempt, on their part, to rise, they had comparatively little scope or encouragement for exertion and enterprise.

2. But, when the struggle for independence began, the case was altered. New fields for exertion were opened, and new and still stronger impulses actuated their bosoms. A great change was suddenly wrought in the American people, and a vast expansion of character took place. Those who were before only known in the humble sphere of peaceful occupation soon shone forth in the cabinet or in the field, fully qualified to cope with the trained generals and statesmen of Europe.

3. But, although the Revolution caused such an expansion of character in the American people, and called forth the most striking patriotism among all classes, it introduced, at the same time, greater looseness of manners and morals. An army always carries deep vices in its train, and communicates its corruption to society around it. Besides this, the failure of public credit so far put it out of the power of individuals to perform private engagements, that the breach of them became common; and, at length, was scarcely disgraceful. That high sense of integrity which had extensively existed before was thus exchanged for more loose and slippery notions of honesty and honor.

4. "On the whole," says Dr. Ramsay, who wrote soon after the close of this period, " the literary, political, and military talents of the United States, have been improved by the Revolution; but their moral character is inferior to what it formerly was. So great is the change for the worse," continues he, " that

the friends of public order are loudly called upon to exert their utmost abilities in extirpating the vicious principles and habits which have taken deep root during the late convulsions."

RELIGION. — 5. During the Revolution, the colonies being all united in one cause, — a Congress being assembled from all parts of America, — and more frequent intercourse between different parts of the country being promoted by the shifting of the armies, local. prejudices and sectarian asperities were obliterated, religious controversy was suspended, and bigotry softened. That spirit of intolerance which had marked some portions of the country was nearly done away.

6. But, for these advantages, the Revolution brought with it great disadvantages, to religion in general. The atheistical philosophy, which had been spread over France, and which would involve the whole subject of religion in the gloomy mists of scepticism, — which acknowledges no distinction between right and wrong, and considers a future existence as a dream, that may or may not be realized, — was thickly sown, in the American army, by the French; and, uniting with the infidelity which before had taken root in the country, produced a serious declension in the tone of religious feelings among the American people. In addition to this, religious institutions, during the war, were much neglected; churches were demolished, or converted into barracks; public worship was often suspended; and the clergy suffered severely from the reduction of their salaries, caused by the depreciation of the circulating medium.

TRADE AND COMMERCE. — 7. During the war of the Revolution, the commerce of the United States was interrupted, not only with Great Britain, but, in a great measure, with the rest of the world. The greater part of the shipping belonging to the country was destroyed by the enemy, or perished by a natural process of decay. Our coasts were so lined with British cruisers as to render navigation too hazardous to be pursued to any considerable extent. Some privateers, however, were fitted out, which succeeded in capturing several valuable prizes, on board of which were arms, and other munitions of war. During the last three years of the war, an illicit trade to Spanish America was carried on; but it was extremely limited.

AGRICULTURE. — 8. Agriculture was greatly interrupted, during this period, by the withdrawing of laborers to the camp, by the want of encouragement furnished by exportation, and by the distractions which disturbed all the occupations of society. The army often suffered for the means of subsistence, and the officers were sometimes forced to compel the inhabitants to furnish the soldiers food in sufficient quantities to prevent their suffering.

ARTS AND MANUFACTURES. — 9. The trade with England, during this period, being interrupted by the war, the people of the United States were compelled to manufacture for themselves. Encouragement was given to all necessary manufactures, and the zeal, ingenuity, and industry of the people, furnished the country with articles of prime necessity; and, in a measure, supplied the place of a foreign market. Such was the progress in arts and manufactures, during the period, that, after the return of peace, when an uninterrupted intercourse with England was again opened, some articles, which before were imported altogether, were found so well and so abundantly manufactured at home, that their importation was stopped.

POPULATION. — 10. The increase of the people of the United States, during this period, was small. Few, if any, emigrants arrived in the country. Many of the inhabitants were slain in battle, and thousands of that class called TORIES left the land, who never returned. Perhaps we may fairly estimate the inhabitants of the country, about the close of this period, 1784, at three millions two hundred and fifty thousand.

EDUCATION. — 11. The interests of education suffered, in common with other kindred interests, during the war. In several colleges, the course of instruction was, for a season, suspended; the hall was exchanged by the students for the camp, and the gown for the sword and epaulet. The number of colleges and academies in the United States, at the close of the period, is estimated at only twenty or twenty-five.

REFLECTIONS. — 12. The American Revolution is doubtless the most interesting event in the pages of modern history. Changes equally great, and convulsions equally violent, have often taken place; and the history of man tells us of many instances in which oppression, urged beyond endurance, has called forth the spirit of successful and triumphant resistance. But, in the event before us, we see feeble colonies, without an army, without a navy, without an established government, without a revenue, without munitions of war, without fortifications, boldly stepping forth to meet the veteran armies of a proud, powerful, and vindictive enemy. We see these colonies, amidst want, poverty and misfortune, supported by the pervading spirit of liberty, and guided by the good hand of Heaven, for nearly eight years sustaining the weight of a cruel conflict, upon their own soil. We see them at length victorious; their enemies sullenly retire from their shores, and these humble colonies stand forth enrolled on the page of history, a free sovereign, and independent nation. Nor is this all. We see a wise government springing up from the blood that was spilt ; and, down to our own time, shedding the choicest political blessings upon several millions of people.

13. What nation can dwell with more just satisfaction upon its annals than ours? Almost all others trace their foundation to some ambitious and bloody conqueror, who sought only by enslaving others to aggrandize himself. Our independence was won by the people, who fought for the natural rights of man. Other nations have left their annals stained with the crimes of their people and princes ; our annals shine with the glowing traces of patriotism, constancy and courage, amidst every rank of life and every grade of office.

14. Whenever we advert to this portion of our history, and review it, as we well may, with patriotic interest, let us not forget the gratitude we owe, as well to those who " fought, and bled, and died" for us, as to that benignant Providence who stayed the proud waves of British tyranny. Let us also gather political wisdom from the American Revolution. It has taught the world, emphatically, that oppression tends to weaken and destroy the power of the oppressor ; that a people united in the cause of liberty are invincible by those who would enslave them ; and that Heaven will ever frown upon the cause of injustice, and ultimately grant success to those who oppose it.

UNITED STATES.

PERIOD V.

DISTINGUISHED FOR THE FORMATION AND ESTAB-
LISHMENT OF THE FEDERAL CONSTITUTION.

EXTENDING FROM THE DISBANDING OF THE ARMY, 1783,
TO THE INAUGURATION OF GEORGE WASHINGTON, AS
PRESIDENT OF THE UNITED STATES, UNDER THE FED-
ERAL CONSTITUTION, 1789.

1. THE war of the Revolution was now closed. The British
troops had retired from the country. The American army was
disbanded. The great object of the colonies had been accomplished — they were FREE and INDEPENDENT. What further
could they expect? What more desire?

2. During the war, the American people had been looking
forward to the state to which they had now attained, as likely to
insure everything they wanted. But, in a short time, they
perceived their error. They were independent; but they had
no adequate bond of union among themselves, — they had no
federal constitution.

3. But they had the CONFEDERATION. True, they had that,
and under that they went through the war.* But it proved, as
it was called, "a rope of sand." By it, Congress had power to
declare war; to borrow money, or to issue bills of credit, to carry
it on. But it had no power to lay a tax of one cent for any
purpose whatsoever; and, therefore, it had no ability to pay the
debts incurred by the war. And yet, these debts now amounted
to more than forty millions of dollars. Congress could advise
the several states to raise money; but it could do no more.

4. What should be done? It was proposed that the states
should grant power to Congress to lay a duty of five per cent.
on all imported foreign goods, and that this revenue should be
applied to the discharge of the public debt. But Rhode Island

* See page 181.

would not agree; and, then, New York refused her consent. And the consequence was, that debt and interest remained unpaid, and the poor officers and soldiers could not get their dues, and were obliged to sell to speculators their certificates, for almost nothing.

5. Congress called upon the states to raise funds; if for no other purpose, at least, to pay the soldiers. But what could the Legislatures do? The people were poor, and the states had local debts to provide for. Some of the states attempted to lay taxes to support their credit, and satisfy their creditors. This, in Massachusetts, produced the memorable insurrection called "Shays' Insurrection," because headed by one Daniel Shays; and during which, one thousand five hundred or two thousand of the inhabitants in the north-western part of the state assembled, and demanded that the collection of debts should be suspended, and that the Legislature should authorize the emission of paper money for general circulation. So formidable was this gathering as to require an armed force of several thousand to suppress it.

6. At length, the conviction was general, that an evil existed for which some remedy must be found; either the articles of confederation must be amended, or a new constitution be framed.

7. In 1786, Virginia recommended a convention at Annapolis to establish a better system of commercial regulations. At this convention, only five states were represented; in consideration of which, they adjourned, to meet at Philadelphia the succeeding May, at the same time recommending to the several states to appoint delegates to that meeting, with power to revise the Federal system. Agreeably to the above recommendation, the several states of the Union, excepting Rhode Island, appointed commissioners, who convened at Philadelphia. Of this body, consisting of fifty-five members, George Washington, one of the delegates from Virginia, was unanimously elected president. The convention proceeded, with closed doors, to discuss the interesting subjects submitted to their consideration.

8. The first question discussed by the convention was, "whether the articles of confederation should be revised and amended." This, at length, being decided in the negative, the convention proceeded to the formation of a new constitution. After a session of about four months, a constitution was agreed on,* which,

---

* On several occasions during the deliberations of the convention, it was quite doubtful whether it would so far harmonize as to agree upon anything. On one question particularly it came near dissolving, — namely, whether the small states should have, as they demanded, an equal vote as the large

after being submitted to Congress, was sent to conventions of the people in the several states for their ratification. Among the states great diversity of opinion prevailed; and, for a time, it was doubtful whether the requisite number — nine states — would ratify it by the time appointed. But, at length, not only that number was attained, but all gave their assent, in the following order :

By Convention of Delaware, ...	December 7,	1787.
By Convention of Pennsylvania, . . .	December 12,	1787.
By Convention of New Jersey, ...	December 18,	1787.
By Convention of Georgia, ...	January 9,	1788.
By Convention of Connecticut, ...	June 9,	1788.
By Convention of Massachusetts, . . .	February 6,	1788.
By Convention of Maryland, ...	April 28,	1788.

states in the Senate ? At this interesting and solemn crisis, Dr. Franklin rose, and, addressing himself to the president, among other things, said : " Sir, how has it happened, that while groping so long in the dark, — divided in our opinions, and now ready to separate without accomplishing the great objects of our meeting, — that we have not hitherto once thought of humbly applying to the Father of Lights to illuminate our understandings ? In the beginning of the contest with Britain, when we were sensible of danger, we had daily prayer in this room for divine protection. Our prayers, sir, were heard ; and they were graciously answered. All of us who were engaged in the struggle must have observed frequent instances of a superintending Providence in our favor. To that kind Providence we owe this happy opportunity of consulting, in peace, on the means of establishing our future national felicity. And have we now forgotten that powerful friend ? or do we imagine that we no longer need its assistance ? I have lived, sir, a long time ; and, the longer I live, the more convincing proof I see of this truth, that God governs the affairs of men. And if a sparrow cannot fall to the ground without his notice, is it probable that an empire can rise without his aid ? We have been assured, sir, in the sacred writings, that except the ' Lord build the house, they labor in vain that build it.' I firmly believe this ; and I also believe that, without his concurring aid, we shall succeed in this political building no better than the builders of Babel ; we shall be divided by our little partial local interests ; our projects will be confounded, and we ourselves shall become a reproach and a by-word to future ages. And, what is worse, mankind may hereafter, from this important instance, despair of establishing government by human wisdom, and leave it to chance, war or conquest.

" I therefore beg leave to move that henceforth prayers, imploring the assistance of Heaven, and its blessings on our deliberations, be held in this assembly every morning before we proceed to business ; and that one or more of the clergy of this city be requested to officiate in that service."

This suggestion, it need scarcely be said, was favorably received by the convention; and, from that time, the guidance of divine wisdom was daily sought. As might be expected, greater harmony prevailed; the spirit of concession pervaded the convention; a motion was made for the appointment of a committee, to take into consideration both branches of the Legislature. This motion prevailing, a committee was accordingly chosen by ballot, consisting of one from each state; and the convention adjourned for three days.

On the meeting of the convention, after this adjournment, the above committee reported to the satisfaction of all, and the body proceeded to organize the legislative and other departments of the government.

By Convention of South Carolina, . . . May 23, 1788.
By Convention of New Hampshire, . . June 21, 1788.
By Convention of Virginia, ... June 26, 1788.
By Convention of New York, ... July 26, 1788.
By Convention of North Carolina, . . . November 21, 1788.
By Convention of Rhode Island, . . . May 29, 1790.

9. It may be added, that at the first session of Congress under the constitution, that body recommended the adoption of twelve amendments, chiefly relating to freedom of speech and of the press, the right of petition, trial by jury, bail, election of president, &c. Ten of these amendments were adopted by three-fourths of the Legislatures of the states. Subsequently, two others were added.

10. On the ratification of the constitution, the attention of the people was at once directed to General Washington, as the first President of the United States. The wishes of this great and good man were " to live and die in peace and retirement ;" but the nation demanded his services, and he obeyed. He was unanimously elected president, as well by Anti-Federalists as Federalists (for by these names the parties in favor of and against the constitution were called). John Adams was elected vice-president.

19

UNITED STATES.

PERIOD VI.

GEORGE WASHINGTON, Virginia, President.
Inaugurated at New York, April 30th, 1789; retired March 3d, 1797.

JOHN ADAMS, Massachusetts, Vice-president.

HEADS OF THE DEPARTMENTS.

Thomas Jefferson,	Virginia,	Sept. 26, 1789,	⎫ Secretaries of State.
Edmund Randolph,	Virginia,	Jan. 2, 1794,	⎬
Timothy Pickering,	Penn.,	Dec. 10, 1795,	⎭
Alexander Hamilton,	N. York,	Sept. 11, 1789,	⎫ Secretaries of Treas'y.
Oliver Wolcott,	Conn.,	Feb. 3, 1795,	⎭
Henry Knox,	Mass.,	Sept. 12, 1789,	⎫
Timothy Pickering,	Penn.,	Jan. 2, 1795,	⎬ Secretaries of War.
James McHenry,	Maryland,	Jan. 27, 1796,	⎭
Samuel Osgood,	Mass.,	Sept. 26, 1789,	⎫
Timothy Pickering,	Penn.,	Nov. 7, 1791,	⎬ Postmasters General.
Joseph Habersham,	Georgia,	Feb. 25, 1795,	⎭
Edmund Randolph,	Virginia,	Sept. 26, 1789,	⎫
William Bradford,	Penn.,	Jan. 27, 1794,	⎬ Attorneys General.
Charles Lee,	Virginia,	Dec. 10, 1795,	⎭

SPEAKERS OF THE HOUSE OF REPRESENTATIVES.

Frederick A. Muhlenberg,	Pennsylvania,	First Congress,	1789.
Jonathan Trumbull,	Connecticut,	Second do.	1791.
Frederick A. Muhlenberg,	Pennsylvania,	Third do.	1793.
Jonathan Dayton,	New Jersey,	Fourth do.	1795.

1. The inauguration of General Washington took place in the presence of the first Congress under the Federal Constitution, and an immense concourse of spectators, the Chancellor of the State of New York administering the oath of office. The ceremonies of the occasion being concluded, Washington entered the Senate-chamber, and delivered his first speech. In this, after expressing the reluctance with which he obeyed the call of his countrymen, and the diffidence with which he entered upon an office so full of responsibility, he proceeded: "It will be peculiarly improper to omit, in this first official act, my fervent sup-

plications to that Almighty Being who rules over the universe, who presides in the councils of nations." Immediately after his inaugural address, with the members of both houses, he attended divine service at St. Paul's chapel. Thus, in the commencement of his administration, did Washington, by every suitable means, acknowledge his sense of personal dependence upon divine wisdom, to guide with discretion the affairs of a nation committed to his care; thus did he set an example worthy of imitation by all who are elevated to places of authority and responsibility.

2. The acts and events which signalized his administration relate to a

System of Revenue.	Reëlection of Washington.
Regulation of Departments.	Difficulties with France.
Establishment of a Judiciary.	Insurrection in Pennsylvania.
Assumption of Debts.	Prohibition of the Slave-trade.
Removal of Seat of Government.	Jay's Treaty.
National Bank.	Admission of Tennessee.
Admission of Vermont.	Election of Mr. Adams.
Indian War.	Farewell Address.
Admission of Kentucky.	

I. SYSTEM OF REVENUE. — The first duty of Congress, under the Federal Constitution, was to provide a revenue for the support of government. For this purpose, duties were laid on imported merchandise, and on the tonnage of vessels. To encourage American shipping, higher tonnage-duties were imposed on foreign than on American vessels, and ten per cent. less duty on goods imported in American than in foreign vessels.

II. REGULATION OF DEPARTMENTS. — Three executive departments were created, designed to aid the president in the management of the government. They were styled Departments of War, of Foreign Affairs,* and of the Treasury. The heads of these departments were styled Secretaries. They were intended to constitute a council, to be consulted by the president at his pleasure; and their opinions on all important questions he was authorized to require in writing.

III. ESTABLISHMENT OF A JUDICIARY. — A national judiciary, also, was established during this first session of Congress, consisting of a Supreme Court, and Circuit and District Courts. The Supreme Court had one chief-justice, and five associate judges.

---

* Since called Department of State. The Navy Department was created subsequently. Aside from advising the president when called upon, the respective duties of these secretaries are indicated by the titles of their departments.

District Courts were to consist of one judge in each state; Circuit Courts, of a judge of the Supreme Court and the District judge. This system has remained nearly the same to the present time, except in the elder Adams' presidency; and then only for a short time, when the number of judges was increased. John Jay was the first chief-justice, and Edmund Randolph the first attorney-general.

IV. Assumption of Debts. — On the meeting of the second Congress, Mr. Hamilton, then Secretary of the Treasury, submitted a plan, as he had been requested to do, for maintaining the public credit. The foreign and domestic debt amounted to more than fifty-four millions of dollars; the debts of the states to twenty-five millions. These debts the secretary proposed that the general government should assume, as a measure of substantial justice and sound policy. To the assumption of the foreign debt there was little opposition; but a strong party opposed the assumption of the domestic debt, and the full payment of the state debts, particularly because that many of the original holders of the securities would receive no benefit, having been obliged, in their poverty, to sell them to speculators, for two or three shillings on the pound. On taking the vote in the House of Representatives, the plan of Mr. Hamilton was lost, by a majority of two. Fortunately, at this juncture, a question of deep interest was agitating the minds of northern and southern members. This was in relation to

V. The Removal of the Seat of Government. —The debates on this subject were almost as exciting as on the fiscal project of Mr. Hamilton. At length, a compromise was effected on this question, — the more important, as it led to a compromise in relation to the assumption of the state debts. It was understood that, should the seat of government be fixed for ten years at Philadelphia, and afterwards at a place to be selected on the Potomac, some of the members of the House of Representatives, from the Potomac, would withdraw their opposition to Mr. Hamilton. This was accordingly done, and his plans were adopted. This measure, in regard to assuming the debts aforesaid, laid the foundation of public credit upon such a basis, that government paper soon rose from two shillings and sixpence to twenty shillings on the pound; and, indeed, for a short time, was above par. Individuals, who had purchased certificates of public debt low, realized immense fortunes. A general spring was given to the affairs of the nation. A spirit of enterprise, of agriculture and commerce, universally prevailed; and the foundation was thus laid for that unrivalled prosperity which the United States, in subsequent years, enjoyed.

VI. NATIONAL BANK. — The next public measure adopted by Congress was a bill for the establishment of a national bank, on the recommendation of Mr. Hamilton. Mr. Jefferson and Mr. Randolph strongly opposed the project, as unconstitutional. After a long discussion, the bank was established by both houses, and approved by the president. The capital stock was ten millions of dollars; the duration of its charter was limited to 1811. It was located in Philadelphia, with the privilege of establishing branches in other places. This bill, however, with those relating to the finances of the country, the assumption of the state debts, the funding of the national debt, &c., contributed greatly to the complete organization of those distinct and visible parties, which, in their long and ardent conflict for power, have since shaken the United States to their centre.

VII. ADMISSION OF VERMONT. — 1. During the same session of Congress, Vermont, having adopted the constitution, was admitted into the Union. The name was given to the territory by the inhabitants, in their declaration of independence, January 16th, 1777, and was derived from the French words VERD, green, — and MONT, mountain.

2. Vermont was settled at a much later period than any other of the Eastern States. For many years, New York and New Hampshire laid claim to the territory; but, in 1777, the inhabitants denied the validity of the New Hampshire claim, and in 1789 they purchased the interest of New York, for thirty thousand dollars. A convention was soon after called, when it was resolved to join the Federal Union. The act of admission dates March 4th, 1791.

VIII. INDIAN WAR. — 1. As early as 1790, an Indian war broke out on the north-western frontiers. Pacific arrangements had been attempted by the president; in which failing, he despatched General Harmar to reduce the hostile tribes to submission. In October, Harmar, having destroyed several villages, and large quantities of corn, came to an engagement with the Indians, near Chillicothe, in which he was routed, with considerable loss.

2. Upon the failure of Harmar, the command was given to General St. Clair, then Governor of the North-western Territory. With a force of near two thousand men, St. Clair marched from Fort Washington, September, 1791, into the Indian country, and encamped in the western part of Ohio. Here, on the 4th of November, he was surprised, and defeated, with the loss of six hundred men.

19*

3. The further history of this war may here be detailed. General Wayne was appointed successor to St. Clair. In the autumn of 1793, he built Fort Recovery, near the spot where St. Clair was defeated, and spent the winter; the following summer, 1794, having erected Fort Defiance, on the Maumee, he moved down that river, and in August (20th), at the head of three thousand men, gained a complete victory over the hostile tribes. The following year, 1795, this painful war was brought to a close; a treaty being concluded with the Indians at Fort Greenville, situated on a western branch of the Miami, by which a large territory of land near Detroit, and west of Ohio, was ceded to the United States.

IX. ADMISSION OF KENTUCKY. — On the 1st of June, 1792, Kentucky was added, by act of Congress, as a state, to the Federal Union. She derives her name from her principal river. The territory was early known to the Indian traders, and was repeatedly visited by different individuals. But the first permanent settlement was made in 1775, by Colonel Daniel Boone and others, on the south side of the Kentucky, about eighteen miles south-east from Lexington. To this settlement was given the name of Boonsboro'. During the Revolutionary War, the inhabitants suffered severely from the Indians, incited by agents of the British government; but, in 1779, General Clarke overcame the Indians, after which the settlers enjoyed more security. For a time, Virginia extended her jurisdiction over Kentucky, and in 1779 erected it into a county; but in 1790 it became a separate state.

X. REËLECTION OF WASHINGTON. — Although Washington had determined to withhold himself from being again a candidate for the presidency, yet various considerations prevented the declaration of his wishes; and, on the meeting of the electors in the autumn of 1792, the choice again unanimously fell on him. Mr. Adams was reëlected vice-president.

XI. DIFFICULTIES WITH FRANCE.—1. The reëlection of Washington may be justly considered as among the most signal favors conferred on the American people. A revolution in France was in progress, remarkable for the political changes it was effecting and the sanguinary scenes which marked it. Monarchy had been abolished, Louis XVI. had fallen by the guillotine, a republic had been proclaimed, and the national convention had made proclamation of war against England, Holland, and Spain. This event excited the deepest interest in the United States. A large majority of the people, grateful for the aid that France had given us in our revolution, and devoted to the cause of liberty, were united in fervent wishes for the success of the French republic.

2. At the same time, the prejudices against Great Britain, which had taken deep root during the Revolution, now sprung forth afresh; and the voice of many was heard, urging the propriety of the United States making a common cause with France against Great Britain. It was the unanimous opinion of the cabinet, however, that a strict neutrality should be observed by the United States towards the contending powers. They were also unanimous in the opinion, that a minister from the French republic should be received, should one be sent. In accordance with the advice of his cabinet, the president issued his proclamation of neutrality, on the 22d of April, 1793.

3. As was anticipated, the republic of France recalled the minister of the crown, and appointed a minister of its own, Mr. Genet, to succeed him. His mission had for its object the enlisting of America in the cause of France, against Great Britain. Flattered by the manner in which he was received by the people, as well as by their professions of attachment to his country, Mr. Genet early anticipated the accomplishment of his object. Presuming too much upon this attachment, he was led into a series of acts infringing the neutrality proclaimed by the president.* He also attempted to rouse the people against the government, because it did not second all his views. At length, on the advice of his cabinet, the president solicited of the French republic the recall of Mr. Genet, and the appointment of some one to succeed him. Monsieur Fauchet was appointed, and was instructed to assure the American government that France totally disapproved of the conduct of his predecessor.

XII. Insurrection in Pennsylvania.—The summer of 1794 was signalized by an insurrection in the western counties of Pennsylvania, commonly known as the "Whiskey Insurrection." It had its origin in a dissatisfaction with a law of

---

* Mr. Genet, on his arrival in the country, landed at Charleston, South Carolina. He was received by the governor of that state, and by the citizens, with a flow of enthusiastic feeling, equalled only by that which had been evinced towards his nation at the conquest of Yorktown.

Soon after landing at Charleston, he began to authorize the fitting and arming of vessels in that port, enlisting men, and giving commissions to cruise and commit hostilities against nations with which the United States were at peace. Vessels captured by these cruisers were brought into port, and the consuls of France, under the authority of Genet, not yet recognized as a minister by the American government, assumed the power of holding courts of admiralty on them, of trying and condemning them, and of authorizing their sale.

Congress, enacted in 1791, by which a duty was imposed upon spirits distilled in the United States. The inhabitants of that part of Pennsylvania were chiefly foreigners, and consequently were less disposed to submit to the taxation necessary to the support of government. Strong opposition to the law was early manifested; and not a few outrages were committed upon the revenue officers while in the discharge of their duty, — such as "whipping, tarring, and branding." In August, the president issued his proclamation, commanding the insurgents to disperse. This not having the desired effect, a respectable body of militia was ordered out, under Governor Lee, of Maryland; on whose approach, the insurgents laid down their arms, solicited the clemency of the government, and promised future submission to the laws.

XIII. PROHIBITION OF THE SLAVE-TRADE. — 1. During the third Congress, a law was passed prohibiting the carrying on of the slave-trade from American ports. For fifty years prior to the settlement of Virginia, England had been engaged in the slave-trade. The first slaves — about twenty in number — were brought to Virginia, in 1619, by a Dutch ship. The importation of them gradually increased; and, although principally bought by the southern planters, slaves were soon found, in great numbers, in all the colonies. In 1784, they amounted to six hundred thousand; in 1790, they had increased to nearly seven hundred thousand. Opposition to the traffic appeared very early in the colonies; but it was countenanced and patronized by the English government, and thus introduced into and fastened upon the country, without the power, on the part of the colonies, to arrest it.

2. In Massachusetts, in 1645, a law was made, "prohibiting the buying and selling of slaves, except those taken in lawful war, or reduced to servitude by their crimes." In 1703, the same colony imposed a heavy duty on every negro imported; and, in a subsequent law on the subject, they called the practice "the unnatural and unaccountable custom of enslaving mankind." In Virginia, as early as 1699, attempts were made to repress the importation of slaves, by heavy duties. These, and other acts, show that the North American provinces would, if left to themselves, have put an end to the importation of slaves, before the era of their independence.

3. In 1778, Virginia abolished the traffic by law; Connecticut, Rhode Island, Pennsylvania, and Massachusetts, prohibited it before the year 1789. The Continental Congress passed a resolution against the purchase of slaves imported from

Africa, and exhorted the colonies to abandon the trade altogether. The third Congress of the United States, as stated
above, prohibited the trade by law. Thus we see, in the United
States, a very early and settled aversion to the slave-trade
manifesting itself; and, before European nations had consented
to relinquish it, several of the states had utterly prohibited it.

XIV. JAY'S TREATY. — 1. For some time, the relations subsist-
ing between the United States and Great Britain had been far from
amicable. The principal complaints were, on the one hand, the
non-delivery of the posts held by the latter within the American
lines, and the carrying off the slaves at the close of the war; on
the other, the interposition, by the states, of legal impediments
to the recovery of debts contracted before the war. Added to
these sources of trouble, Great Britain was accused of exciting
the hostility of the Indians on our northern frontier; of impress-
ing our seamen; and, still more recently, of capturing our
neutral vessels, retaliatory upon France, which had set the
example. For these reasons, a war between the United States
and England was now a probable event.

2. In the hope, however, of averting an issue so undesirable,
Chief Justice Jay was appointed envoy extraordinary to the
British court; where he had the good fortune to negotiate
a treaty, and which, on the 8th of March, 1795, was submitted
to the Senate. The main feature of this treaty respected indem-
nity for unlawful captures, which was provided for; but no
redress could be obtained for negroes carried away. The
obstructions to collecting debts were to cease, and the posts on
the frontiers were to be evacuated by the 1st of June, 1796.
Other stipulations were embraced, and the treaty was limited
to twelve years.

3. On the 24th of June, the Senate advised the ratification
of the treaty, by a vote of exactly two-thirds. It was well known
that the president was not entirely satisfied with it; but he had
determined to ratify it, if advised by the Senate. The cabinet
was divided. The country was also divided. Even the friends
of England were disappointed in its provisions, while her
enemies were loud in their complaints and threats. Boston, and
the other cities, passed condemnatory resolutions. In several
cities, mobs threatened personal violence to the supporters of the
treaty. Mr. Jay was burned in effigy; the British minister
was insulted; and Mr. Hamilton was stoned at a public meeting. Contrary to the opinions of its strong opposers, the treaty
settled the difficulties between the two countries, which were

becoming every month more formidable ; it even proved advantageous to the United States.

XV. Admission of Tennessee.— On the 1st of June, 1796, another accession was made to the Union, by the admission of Tennessee.   This state derives its name from its principal river, which the Indians fancied resembled a curved spoon.   The territory was originally included in the Carolinas.   On the division of those provinces, it fell to North Carolina, and by her was ceded, in 1789, to the United States.   In 1790, it was made a territorial government, under the title of " the Territory of the United States south of the Ohio."   It was first settled in 1765, by emigrants from North Carolina.

XVI. Election of Mr. Adams. — As the presidential term of Washington was now drawing to a close, he signified his intention to retire from the duties of public life.   During his administration, the people had become divided into two great political parties ; — at the head of one of which was Mr. Adams; at the head of the other, Mr. Jefferson.   The election was characterized by a zeal corresponding to the interest taken by the parties in their candidates, and their devotion to their respective political creeds.   The election resulted in the choice of Mr. Adams.

XVII. Farewell Address. — 1. Washington's administration terminated on the 3d of March, 1797.   Shortly before, he held his last formal levee.   It was an occasion of deep and solemn interest.   The distinguished of all parties and opinions were present, to honor the president, the hero, the statesman and the Christian.   To Washington the occasion was not less solemn and affecting.   It is said there were few smiles, but many tears, during the reception.

2. As he was about to retire forever from the theatre of public life, he felt it to be befitting him to express his views on some subjects connected, as he thought, with the vital interests and the future glory of his country.   These he embodied in a " Farewell Address," which, for purity of language, beauty of conception, and soundness of political sentiments, has never been equalled.   It can never be read but to be admired.   A single sentence only shall we cite : " The unity of government, which constitutes you one people, is dear to you.   It is justly so : for it is the mainspring in the edifice of your real independence ; the support of your tranquillity at home, — your peace abroad ; of your safety ; of your prosperity ; of that very liberty which you so highly prize."

UNITED STATES.

PERIOD VII.

JOHN ADAMS, Massachusetts, President.

Inaugurated March 4th, 1797; retired March 3d, 1801.

THOMAS JEFFERSON, Virginia, Vice-president.

HEADS OF THE DEPARTMENTS.

Timothy Pickering,	Penn.,	(continued in office),	} Secretaries of State.
John Marshall,	Va.,	May 13, 1800,	
Oliver Wolcott,	Conn.,	(continued in office),	} Secretaries of Treasury.
Samuel Dexter,	Mass.,	December 31, 1800,	
James McHenry,	Md.,	(continued in office),	
Samuel Dexter,	Mass.,	May 13, 1800,	} Secretaries of War.
Roger Griswold,	Conn.,	February 3, 1800,	
Benjamin Stoddert,	Md.,	May 21, 1798,	Secretary of the Navy.
Joseph Habersham,	Ga.,	(continued in office),	Postmaster General.
Charles Lee,	Va.,	(continued in office),	Attorney General.

SPEAKERS OF THE HOUSE OF REPRESENTATIVES.

Jonathan Dayton,	New Jersey,	Fifth Congress,	1797.
Theodore Sedgwick,	Massachusetts,	Sixth do.	1799.

1. THE condition of the country, on the accession of Mr. Adams, was one of great prosperity. At home, a sound credit had been established; an immense floating debt had been funded in a manner perfectly satisfactory to the creditors, and an ample revenue had been secured. Funds for the gradual payment of the debt had been provided, and a considerable part of it had been already discharged. The agricultural and commercial interests of the country were flourishing. The western Indians were pacified. War with England had been averted. In one quarter only was the horizon darkened; — our relations with France were still disturbed.

2. The principal events which distinguished the administration of Mr. Adams were :

Difficulties with France.	Removal of the Seat of Government.
Treaty with that Power.	
Death of Washington.	Election of Mr. Jefferson.

I. DIFFICULTIES WITH FRANCE. — 1. The misunderstanding between France and the United States, which had commenced during the administration of Washington (p. 222), not only extended into that of Mr. Adams, but, soon after his accession, assumed a still more formidable, and even warlike aspect. The French ministers who succeeded Mr. Genet (p. 223), Mr. Fauchet, and next Mr. Adet, insulted the administration, by accusing it of partiality towards the English, and hostility towards France. Notwithstanding this, several attempts were made to settle existing difficulties : first, by the appointment of Mr. Monroe as envoy to France ; and, upon his failure, through Mr. Pinckney. But the latter the French Directory refused to receive in his official capacity, and, by a written mandate, ordered him to leave the territories of the French republic.

2. Intelligence of these facts having been communicated to Mr. Adams, he summoned Congress to meet on the 15th of June, and, in his speech on that occasion, urged that body to repel this indignity of the French, in a manner worthy the nation. The president, however, was still desirous of peace ; and, upon his recommendation, three envoys were appointed to proceed to France, to adjust existing controversies. But their mission proved another failure.

3. Perceiving further negotiations to be in vain, Congress now proceeded to the adoption of vigorous measures for retaliating injuries which had been sustained, and for repelling still greater injuries which were threatened. Amongst these measures was the augmentation of the regular army. Of this army, and such other forces as might be raised, General Washington was appointed commander. A naval armament was also authorized, as were captures of French vessels-of-war. In short, every movement betokened war. Hostilities were, in fact, commenced, — the French frigate Insurgente capturing the American schooner Retaliation ; and the American frigate Constellation afterward capturing the Insurgente.

II. TREATY WITH FRANCE. — The bold and decided tone of the Americans, added to their preparations for prosecuting a war with vigor, — and, perhaps, more than all, the success of the Constellation in the above engagement with the Insurgente, — had the desired effect. Overtures for renewing the negotiations were received from the French Directory; which were immediately responded to by the president, by the appointment of Oliver Ellsworth, Chief Justice of the United States, and two other envoys extraordinary, for concluding a peace. On their arrival at Paris, they found the Directory overthrown, and the government in the hands of Napoleon Bonaparte, as First Consul. By him they were promptly received, and a treaty was concluded on the 30th of September, 1800; soon after which, the provisional army in America was, by order of Congress, disbanded.

III. DEATH OF WASHINGTON. — 1. The good and the great must die; and, at length, America was called to mourn the departure of the good and illustrious Washington. He did not live, much as he desired that event, to witness the restoration of peace; his death occurring at Mount Vernon, on the 14th of December, 1799, at the age of sixty-eight years. Believing, at the commencement of his complaint (an inflammatory affection of the wind-pipe), that its conclusion would be mortal, he economized his time, in arranging, with the utmost serenity, those few concerns which required his attention. To his physician he expressed his conviction that he was dying; "but," said he, "I am not afraid to die."

2. On the arrival of the news of his death at Philadelphia, Monday, Congress immediately adjourned. On the day succeeding, resolutions were adopted expressive of the grief of the members, and a committee was appointed to devise a mode by which the national feelings should be expressed. This committee, in their report, recommended that a marble monument be erected by the United States, at the city of Washington, to commemorate the great events of Washington's military and political life; that a funeral oration be delivered by a member by Congress; that the president be requested to write a letter of condolence to Mrs. Washington; and that it be recommended to the citizens of the United States to wear crape on the left arm for thirty days.

3. These resolutions passed both houses unanimously. The whole nation appeared in mourning. The funeral procession at the city of Philadelphia was grand and solemn, and the eloquent oration delivered on the occasion by General Henry Lee was heard with profound attention, and with deep interest. Throughout the United States, similar marks of affliction were exhibited. Funeral orations were delivered, and the best talents devoted to an expression of grief at the loss of "the man, first in war, first in peace, and first in the hearts of his fellow-citizens."

20

IV. Removal of the Seat of Government. — In 1800, agreeably to a resolution passed in Congress in 1790, the seat of government was transferred from Philadelphia to the city of Washington, in the District of Columbia.*

V. Election of Mr. Jefferson. — 1. The administration of Mr. Adams, through the whole course of it, was the subject of much clamor, especially by the Democratic party; but the measures which most contributed to destroy his popularity were the "Alien" and "Sedition" laws.

2. By the "alien law," the president was authorized to order any alien, whom "he should judge dangerous to the peace and safety of the United States, &c., to depart out of the territory, within such time" as he should judge proper, upon penalty of being "imprisoned for a term not exceeding three years," &c. The design of the "sedition law," so called, was to punish the abuse of speech, and of the press. It imposed a heavy pecuniary fine, and imprisonment for a term of years, upon such as should combine or conspire together to oppose any measure of government; upon such as should write, print, utter, publish, &c., "any false, scandalous, and malicious writing against the government of the United States, or either house of the Congress of the United States, or the president," &c.

3. On canvassing the votes of the electors for president, it was found that Mr. Jefferson and Mr. Burr had each seventy-three votes, Mr. Adams sixty-five, and C. C. Pinckney sixty-four. As the constitution provided that the person having the greatest number of votes should be president, and Mr. Jefferson and Mr. Burr having an equal number, it became the duty of the House of Representatives, voting by states, to decide between these two gentlemen.

4. As this was the first time that the election of president devolved upon Congress, a deep interest was taken in the subject. It was ordered that the doors should be closed during the ballotings, and that no adjournment should be had till a choice should be effected. On the first balloting, Mr. Jefferson had eight states, Mr. Burr six, and two divided; which result continued for thirty-five ballotings. The thirty-sixth resulted in the election of Mr. Jefferson. Mr. Burr, being the second on the list, was, of course, declared elected vice-president.

---

* The District of Columbia was originally a territory of ten miles square, on both sides of the Potomac, about one hundred and twenty miles from its mouth. The river ran through it diagonally, near the centre. It was ceded, in 1790, to the United States, by Maryland and Virginia, and is under the immediate government of Congress. It included the cities of Washington, Alexandria, and Georgetown. Alexandria has since been ceded to Virginia.

UNITED STATES.

PERIOD VIII.

THOMAS JEFFERSON, Virginia, President.
Inaugurated at Washington, March 4th, 1801 ; retired March 3d, 1809.

AARON BURR and GEORGE CLINTON, New York,
VICE-PRESIDENTS.

HEADS OF THE DEPARTMENTS.

James Madison,	Va.,	March 5,	1801,	Secretary of State.
Samuel Dexter,	Mass.,	(continued in office),		Secretaries of Treasury.
Albert Gallatin,	Penn.,	January 26,	1802,	
Henry Dearborn,	Mass.,	March 5,	1801,	Secretary of War.
Benjamin Stoddert,	Md.,	(continued in office),		Secretaries of the Navy.
Robert Smith,	Md.,	January 26,	1802,	
Joseph Habersham,	Ga.,	(continued in office),		Postmasters General.
Gideon Granger,	Conn.,	January 26,	1802,	
Levi Lincoln,	Mass.,	March 5,	1801,	Attorneys General.
John Breckenridge,	Ky.,	December 23,	1805,	
Cæsar A. Rodney,	Del.,	January 20,	1807,	

SPEAKERS OF THE HOUSE OF REPRESENTATIVES.

Nathaniel Macon,	North Carolina,	Seventh Congress,	1801.
Joseph B. Varnum,	Massachusetts,	Eighth	do.	1803.
Nathaniel Macon,	North Carolina,	Ninth	do.	1805.
Joseph B. Varnum,	Massachusetts,	Tenth	do.	1807.

1. THE commencement of Mr. Jefferson's administration was marked by the transfer of the most responsible and lucrative offices of the government to the Republican party; on the alleged ground that, hitherto, they had been held too exclusively by the Federal party. Internal taxes were abolished; and the former judicial system, which had been altered during Mr. Adams' administration, was restored.

2. The leading events in the presidential career of Mr. Jefferson will require us to notice :

The Admission of Ohio.
Purchase of Louisiana.
Murder of Hamilton.
Reëlection of Jefferson.
War and Peace with Tripoli.
Conspiracy and Trial of Burr.
War between France and England.

Attack on the Chesapeake.
Embargo.
British Orders in Council.
Milan Decree.
Non-intercourse.
Election of Mr. Madison.

I. ADMISSION OF OHIO. — In 1802, Ohio was admitted, by act of Congress, as an independent state, into the Union. It derived its name from the river Ohio, which sweeps the southeastern border of the state. The territory was claimed by Virginia, and held by her, although the charter of Connecticut, extending west to the Pacific Ocean, included a great part of it. In 1781, the Legislature of Virginia ceded to the United States the territory north-west of the river Ohio, excepting some few military tracts. In 1788, the first settlement was begun at Marietta, under General Rufus Putnam, from New England. Until 1795, the settlement of Ohio was retarded, by constant wars with the Indians. But, at that time, a general peace with the different tribes being effected, by General Wayne, under Washington (p. 222), the population of the territory rapidly increased by emigration from Europe, and still more from New England.

II. PURCHASE OF LOUISIANA. — In 1802, the Spanish governor of Louisiana closed the port of New Orleans against the United States. This was in direct violation of a treaty negotiated with Spain, in 1795, during the administration of Washington, securing to them the right of navigating the Mississippi from its source to the ocean, and the use of New Orleans as a place of deposit for three years, — and longer, if no other place of equal importance should be assigned. Great excitement consequently prevailed in Congress, and throughout the country, at this violation of treaty stipulations ; and a proposition was made to occupy the place by force. More prudent counsels, however, prevailed ; and the whole country of Louisiana was purchased of France (to which it had been secretly ceded by Spain), for fifteen millions of dollars. In December, 1803, the territory was transferred to the United States.

III. MURDER OF HAMILTON. — In July, 1804, occurred the death of General Alexander Hamilton, who fell in a duel fought with Aaron Burr, Vice-president of the United States. Burr had addressed a letter to General Hamilton, in which he demanded a denial or acknowledgment, on the part of the latter, of certain offensive political expressions, contained in a public paper. Hamilton, declining to give either, was challenged by Burr. Although averse, from principle, to this mode of settling personal controversies, in an evil moment Hamilton, actuated by a false sense of honor, accepted the challenge, and, on meeting his enemy, fell by means of his first fire. Among his personal and political friends, his death caused a deep sensation. The people of New York city, in which he resided, paid him extraordinary honors. Few men have shone with greater brilliancy in our country; few have been gifted with a more powerful eloquence, or have been more justly respected for their talents or attainments.*

IV. REËLECTION OF MR. JEFFERSON. — In the autumn of the above year, Mr. Jefferson was reëlected president. George Clinton, of New York, was chosen vice-president, in place of Colonel Burr.

V. WAR AND PEACE WITH TRIPOLI. — In June, 1805, a war, which had been continued for several years, between the United States and Tripoli, was concluded, and a treaty of peace negotiated by Colonel Lear, the authorized agent of the United States, by which the Tripolitan and American prisoners were exchanged, and the sum of sixty thousand dollars given to the Pacha.†

---

* It should be added, as a solemn dissuasive against a practice at war with reason, revelation, and all the dear and important relations of life, that Hamilton accepted the challenge, and repaired to the duelling-ground, contrary to the convictions of conscience and duty. In a paper written before the meeting, but in prospect of it, he wrote, "My religious and moral principles are strongly opposed to the practice of duelling;"—and yet he went. It is said that he did not fire at Burr. But, how foolish, and even wicked, to expose a life, so dear to his family and country, to be taken by a deliberate murderer! But Burr met his reward. From that fatal hour in which he laid Hamilton low, he was shunned by all classes, and for years roamed abroad, a fugitive from the land in which he was once honored.

† As early as 1803, a squadron, under Commodore Preble, had been sent to the Mediterranean, to protect the American commerce against the piratical Barbary powers. During the same year, Captain Bainbridge, in the Philadelphia, joined Commodore Preble, and, in chasing a cruiser into the harbor of Tripoli, grounded his vessel, and, with his crew, was taken prisoner. Shortly after, the Tripolitans got the Philadelphia afloat, and warped her into the outward harbor. In this situation, Lieutenant, afterwards Commodore Decatur, conceived the plan of attempting to set her on fire. This being approved by Commodore Preble, he selected twenty men, and an officer by the name of Morris; and, with these, and an old pilot concealed in the bottom of a small vessel, taken from the enemy, he proceeded, on the approach of night, towards the frigate. On reaching it, Decatur, with his

20*

VI. CONSPIRACY AND TRIAL OF BURR.—In the autumn of 1806, a project was detected, at the head of which was Colonel Burr, for revolutionizing the territory west of the Alleghanies, and of establishing an independent empire there, of which New Orleans was to be the capital, and himself the chief. Happily, however, government, being apprized of his designs, arrested him, while, as yet, he had few adherents, and before his standard was raised. He was brought to trial at Richmond, on a charge of treason committed within the district of Virginia; but, no overt act being proved against him in that state, he was released. In addition to this project, Colonel Burr had formed another,

companions, leaped on board, and in a few minutes swept the deck of every Tripolitan. Of fifty, not one reached the shore. The frigate was now set on fire, and while the flames rose, to spread consternation among the Tripolitans, they served to light the heroic Decatur and his band back in safety to the American squadron. Of the party, not one was killed, and but one wounded. This was a seaman, who saved the life of his commander. In the first desperate struggle on board the Philadelphia, Decatur was disarmed, and fell. A sabre was already lifted to strike the fatal blow, when this seaman, observing the perilous situation of his officer, reached forward, and received the blow of the sabre on his arm. In consequence of the burning of the Philadelphia, the sufferings of Commodore Bainbridge and his crew, as well as those of other Americans in captivity at Tripoli, were greatly increased. It happened that, some time before this, the then reigning bashaw of Tripoli, Jussuf, third son of the late bashaw, had murdered his father and eldest brother, and proposed to murder the second, in order to possess himself of the throne. But the latter, Hamet Caramelli, made his escape, and Jussuf, without further opposition, usurped the government. Hamet took refuge in Egypt. Here he was, on the arrival of an accredited agent of the United States, General Eaton, who revived his almost expiring hopes of regaining his rightful kingdom. Eaton had been consul for the United States up the Mediterranean, and was returning home when he heard the situation of Hamet. Conceiving a plan of liberating the Americans in captivity at Tripoli, by means of the assistance of Hamet, and, at the same time, of restoring this exile to his throne, he advised with Hamet, who readily listened to the project, and gave his coöperation. A convention was accordingly entered into between General Eaton, on the part of the United States, and Hamet, by which the latter stipulated much in favor of the Americans, and was promised to be restored to his throne. With a small force,—consisting of seamen from the American squadron, the followers of Hamet, and some Egyptian troops,—Eaton and Hamet, with incredible toil and suffering, passed the desert of Barca, and by assault took possession of Derne, the capital of a large province belonging to the kingdom of Tripoli. The success of Eaton struck the usurper Jussuf with terror. In this juncture, he proposed to Mr. Lear, the consul-general of America, then in the Mediterranean, to enter into negotiation. Mr. Lear accepted the proposal, and negotiated a treaty, although he knew of the success of Eaton and Hamet. Eaton and Hamet were consequently arrested in the prosecution of their purpose, and the unfortunate exile failed of his promised restoration to the throne. In 1805, Hamet visited the United States, with the expectation of obtaining some remuneration for his services from America, and for her failure in fulfilling her stipulations to him by General Eaton. A proposition to this effect was brought before Congress, but, after much discussion, it was rejected.

which, in case of failure in the first, might be carried on independently of it. This was an attack on Mexico, and the establishment of an empire there.

VII. FRANCE AND ENGLAND. — 1. For some time, a contest had been waging between these two powers. America being neutral, her vessels carried, from port to port, the productions of France and the manufactures of England. This was called "the carrying trade," and was proving a source of great wealth. On the 16th of May, 1806, the British government issued an order in council, declaring the ports and rivers from the Elbe, a river in Germany, to Brest, a town of France, to be in a state of blockade. By this order, American vessels, trading to these and intervening ports, were liable to seizure and condemnation; and, in numerous instances, such a fate befell them. In the following November, Bonaparte, by way of retaliation, issued a decree, at Berlin, declaring the British islands in a state of blockade, and prohibiting all commerce and correspondence with them.

2. In January, 1807, the British government retaliated upon Bonaparte, prohibiting all coasting trade with France. Thus, from the measures of these two rival powers, the commerce of the United States was seriously injured. In addition to this, there existed a controversy between the United States and England, in reference to the "right of search," so called. England claimed it as among her prerogatives to take her native-born subjects, wherever found, for her navy, and of searching American vessels for that purpose. Against this pretended right the American government had remonstrated, but hitherto in vain.

VIII. ATTACK ON THE CHESAPEAKE. — 1. At length, an event occurred, growing out of this pretended "right of search," which roused the indignation of the American people, and called for immediate executive notice. This was an attack upon the American frigate Chesapeake, Commodore Barron, off the capes of Virginia, by the British frigate Leopard, of fifty guns. The attack was occasioned by the refusal of Commodore Barron to surrender several seamen, who had deserted from the British armed ship Melampus, a short time previous, and had voluntarily enlisted on board the Chesapeake.

2. Being unsuspicious of danger, and unprepared for defence, the Chesapeake struck her colors, having been greatly damaged in her hull, rigging and spars, besides having three of her men killed and eighteen wounded, The men claimed (four in number) were now transferred to the Leopard. Upon investigation,

however, it was ascertained that three of them were Americans, and that the fourth had been impressed by the British, but had deserted.

3. In consequence of this outrage, the president issued his proclamation, in July, ordering all British vessels to leave the waters of the United States. At the same time, instructions were forwarded to Mr. Monroe, our minister in England, to demand satisfaction for the unauthorized attack upon the Chesapeake, and security against future impressment of seamen. But Mr. Canning, the British minister, objected to uniting these subjects; and Mr. Monroe not being authorized to treat them separately, Mr. Rose was despatched, by the English government, as envoy extraordinary to the United States, to adjust the difficulty which had arisen on account of the Chesapeake.*

IX. EMBARGO. — Before the arrival of Mr. Rose, Congress, which had been summoned by proclamation to meet in October, was engaged in putting the country in a posture of defence. Large appropriations of money were made for equipping the militia, completing fortifications, and increasing the navy. In addition to these defensive preparations, on the 22d of December an embargo was laid on all vessels within the jurisdiction of the United States.†

X. ORDERS IN COUNCIL. — In November, Great Britain issued her orders in council, which measure she declared to be in retaliation of the French decree of November, 1806. By these orders, all neutral nations were prohibited from trading with France or her allies, excepting upon the payment of a tribute to England.

XI. MILAN DECREE. — Scarcely had the news of the adoption of the above orders reached Milan, where Bonaparte

---

* This unhappy difficulty was not finally adjusted till 1811. Mr. Rose reached America December 25th; but, having no authority to negotiate until the president should recall his proclamation of July 2d, and the president declining to accede to such a preliminary, the negotiations, for the time, closed. In November, 1811, the British minister communicated to the Secretary of State that the attack on the Chesapeake was unauthorized by his majesty's government; that the officer at that time in command on the American coast had been recalled; that the men taken from the Chesapeake should be restored; and that suitable pecuniary provision should be made for those who suffered in the attack, and for the families of the seamen who fell. To these propositions the president acceded; but the question touching the right of search was left undecided.

† This measure was particularly obnoxious to the New England States. They deemed it both impolitic and oppressive. By means of it the large shipping interest of the United States was locked up. Many ships were, by this means, ultimately lost to their owners; besides that, meanwhile, they brought no income.

then was, than he issued, December 17th, a retaliatory decree, called the "Milan Decree," which confiscated any and every vessel, found in any of his ports, which had allowed herself to be searched by an English ship, or had paid the tribute demanded.

XII. NON-INTERCOURSE. — The embargo, contrary to expectation, had no effect upon the two belligerent powers, to modify their restrictive policy. The president, therefore, recommended a still more stringent course, — the repeal of the embargo, and the substitution of entire commercial non-intercourse. To this Congress acceded; and, in March, passed a law to that effect, with a proviso, however, that, should either of the hostile powers revoke its edicts, the president might renew the intercourse with the nation so revoking.

XIII. ELECTION OF MR. MADISON. — Such was the posture of things when Mr. Jefferson retired from office. Having declined a reëlection, Mr. Madison was chosen his successor, and George Clinton was reëlected vice-president.

UNITED STATES.

PERIOD IX.

JAMES MADISON, Virginia, President.

Inaugurated at Washington, March 4th, 1809; retired March 3d, 1817.

GEORGE CLINTON, N. Y., and ELBRIDGE GERRY, Mass., Vice-Presidents.

HEADS OF THE DEPARTMENTS.

Robert Smith,	Maryland,	March 6,	1809,	Sec's of State.
James Monroe,	Virginia,	Nov. 25,	1811,	
Albert Gallatin,	Penn.,	(continued in office),		
George W. Campbell,	Tennessee,	February 9,	1814,	Sec's of Treasury.
Alexander J. Dallas,	Penn.,	October 6,	1814,	
William Eustis,	Mass.,	March 7,	1809,	
John Armstrong,	New York,	January 13,	1813,	Sec's of War.
James Monroe,	Virginia,	Sept. 27,	1814,	
William H. Crawford,	Georgia,	March 3,	1815,	
Paul Hamilton,	S. Carolina,	March 7,	1809,	
William Jones,	Penn.,	January 12,	1813,	Sec's of the Navy.
Benj. W. Crowninshield,	Mass.,	December 17, 1814,		
Gideon Granger,	Conn.,	(continued in office),		Postmasters Gen.
Return J. Meigs,	Ohio,	March 17,	1814,	
Cæsar A. Rodney,	Delaware,	(continued in office),		
William Pinkney,	Maryland,	December 11, 1811,		Attorneys Gen.
Richard Rush,	Penn.,	February 10, 1814,		

SPEAKERS OF THE HOUSE OF REPRESENTATIVES.

Joseph B. Varnum,	Massachusetts,	Eleventh Congress,		1809.
Henry Clay,	Kentucky,	Twelfth	do.	1811.
Henry Clay,	Kentucky,	Thirteenth	do.	1813.
Langdon Cheves,	South Carolina,	Thirteenth	do.	1814.
Henry Clay,	Kentucky,	Fourteenth	do.	1815.

1. The condition of the country, on the accession of Mr. Madison, was in several respects gloomy and critical. The two great rival powers in Europe were still in hostile array against each other, and America was suffering under their and her own restrictions of commerce. And no light, from any quarter, as yet indicated any change for the better.

2. In April, Mr. Erskine, the British minister at Washington, informed the president that the British orders in council of November, 1807, would cease, in regard to the United States, on the 10th of June. Accordingly, as allowed by Congress, the latter issued his proclamation, renewing intercourse with England, from and after that day. But, as the British government denied the authority of Mr. Erskine to enter into any such stipulation, the president, on the 10th of August, renewed the nonintercourse act with Great Britain.

3. In March, 1810, Bonaparte issued his "Rambouillet decree" retaliating upon the act of Congress of 1809, which forbade French ships entering the ports of the United States. By this decree, all American vessels and cargoes, arriving in any of the ports of France, or of countries occupied by French troops, were ordered to be seized and condemned. On the 1st of May, Congress passed an act excluding British and French armed vessels from the waters of the United States; but, at the same time, providing, that, in case either of the above nations should modify its edicts before the 3d of March, 1811, so that they should cease to violate neutral commerce, commercial intercourse with the former might be renewed, but not with the latter. These conditions having been complied with by France, the president issued his proclamation, November 2d, resuming intercourse with that nation.

4. While the affairs of America, in relation to the belligerents, were in this posture, an unhappy engagement took place, May, 1811, on the coast of Virginia, between the American frigate President, commanded by Captain Rodgers, and a British sloop-of-war, the Little Belt, commanded by Captain Bingham. The latter had eleven men killed, and twenty-four wounded, while the President had only one wounded. A court of inquiry was ordered on the conduct of Captain Rodgers, which decided that it had been satisfactorily proved to the court that Captain Rodgers hailed the Little Belt first; that his hail was not satisfactorily answered; that the Little Belt fired the first gun, and that it was without previous provocation, or justifiable cause, &c. &c. The principal events and measures which subsequently signalized the administration of Mr. Madison were as follows:

1811.	1812.
	Declaration of War.
Admission of Louisiana.	Surrender of Hull.
Battle of Tippecanoe.	Capture of the Guerriere.
	Battle of Queenstown.

Capture of the Frolic.
Capture of the Macedonian.
Capture of the Java.

1813.

Battle of Frenchtown.
Capture of the Peacock.
Reëlection of Mr. Madison.
Capture of York.
Siege of Fort Meigs.
Loss of the Chesapeake.
Loss of the Argus.
Capture of the Boxer.
Perry's Victory.
Battle of the Thames.
Proposed Invasion of Canada.
Creek War.

1814.

Chippewa and Bridgewater.
Capture of Washington.
Defence of Baltimore.
War on the Coast of New England.
Engagement on Lake Champlain.
Hartford Convention.

1815–16.

Battle of New Orleans.
Treaty of Ghent.
Treaty with Algiers.
National Bank.
Admission of Indiana.
Election of Mr. Monroe.

I. ADMISSION OF LOUISIANA. — On the 30th of April, 1811, Louisiana was admitted into the Union, as an independent state. The name was given to the territory, which comprehended a vast tract, in honor of Louis XIV. of France, and was first discovered by Ferdinand de Soto, in 1541 (p. 17). After having been owned by several of the European powers, it was ceded by France to the United States, in 1803, for fifteen millions of dollars (p. 232). Several states have been formed out of the territory thus ceded.

II. BATTLE OF TIPPECANOE. — 1. This battle, fought on the 7th of November, 1811, was, doubtless, one of the most spirited and best fought actions recorded in the annals of Indian warfare. For several years the Indian tribes on the western frontier had exhibited a restless and hostile spirit, engendered by Tecumseh, and his brother, called the Prophet. The former was a bold and skilful warrior, sagacious in council and formidable in battle. The latter was cunning, cruel, cowardly, and treacherous.

2. In September, 1809, General Harrison, Governor of the North-west Territory, negotiated a treaty with the Miamies and other tribes, by which they sold to the United States a large tract of land on both sides of the Wabash. Tecumseh was not present at the treaty; but, on his return, he expressed great dissatisfaction at what had been done. His brother, who was present, made no objection. But, from this time, the Indians were guilty of deeds of depredation and murder.

3. In this state of things, General Harrison collected a large

force, and proceeded towards the Prophet's town; on reaching the neighborhood of which, the principal chiefs came out, and proposed a conference, — requesting Harrison and his men, with that view, to encamp for the night. They did so; but, apprehending treachery, the troops slept on their arms. Early on the following morning, November 7th, the Indians suddenly assailed the camp, and a bloody contest ensued. The loss on both sides was severe; but the Indians were repulsed. Tecumseh was not present, and the Prophet took no part in the engagement. The results of the battle were important; the Indians were humbled, and their plans defeated.

III. DECLARATION OF WAR.* — On the 4th of April, a bill declaring war against England passed the House of Representatives. On the 17th it received the sanction of the Senate, and on the 19th the president issued a proclamation of war. The principal grounds of war assigned by the president, in his message recommending that measure, and upon which the Democratic party, in Congress, acted in voting for it, were, summarily, — the impressment of American seamen by the British; the blockade of her enemy's ports, supported by no adequate force, in consequence of which the American commerce had been plundered in every sea, and the great staples of the country cut off from their legitimate markets; and the British orders in council. Against the declaration of war the representatives belonging to the Federal party presented a solemn protest, which was written with distinguished ability, and which denied the war to be

---

* The following are the orders in council, French decrees, and the consequent acts of the American government, with their respective dates, presented in one view:

1806, May 16th. — British blockade from the Elbe to Brest.
    "   November 21st. — Berlin decree.
1807, January 6th. — British order in council, prohibiting the coasting trade.
    "   November 11th. — The celebrated British orders in council.
    "   December 17th. — Milan decree.
    "   December 22d. — American embargo.
1809, March 1st. — Non-intercourse with Great Britain and France established by Congress.
    "   April 10th. — Mr. Erskine's negotiation, which opened the trade with England.
    "   June 19th. — Non-intercourse with Great Britain.
1810, March 18th. — Rambouillet decree.
    "   May 1st. — Act of Congress, conditionally opening the trade with England and France.
    "   November 2d. — President's proclamation, declaring the French decrees to be rescinded.
1812, April 4th. — American embargo.
    "   June 19th. — Proclamation of war by the United States against Great Britain.

" necessary, or required by any moral duty, or political expediency." The declaration was followed by an act of Congress,
giving the president authority to enlist twenty-five thousand
men, to accept of fifty thousand volunteers, and to call out one
hundred thousand militia, for the defence of the sea-coast and
frontiers.   Major-general Henry Dearborn, of Massachusetts,
was appointed commander-in-chief.   Among the brigadiers were
Generals Wilkinson, Bloomfield, Hampton, and Hull.

IV. SURRENDER OF GENERAL HULL. — 1. At the time of the
declaration of war, General Hull was Governor of Michigan, of
which Detroit was the capital.   On the 12th of July, with two
thousand regulars and volunteers, he crossed the Detroit river,
and encamped at Sandwich.   His ostensible object was an attack
upon Fort Malden, a British post, situated on the east bank of
the Detroit river.

2. Unfortunately, he here wasted nearly a month.   Meanwhile, Malden was reinforced, and Mackinaw, two-hundred and
seventy miles north-west from Detroit, — one of the strongest
posts in the United States, in that quarter, — was surprised by
British and Indians, and compelled to surrender.

3. This intelligence struck terror into General Hull, as it was
accompanied with a report that the victors were rapidly making
their way down the river.   Suddenly, to the great disappointment of his officers and men, who were anxiously waiting to be
led against Malden, Hull, on the night of the 7th of August,
re-crossed the river, and hastened to Detroit.

4. General Brock, the commander at Malden, now pursued
him, with a force of seven hundred British and six hundred
Indians.   On the appearance of the enemy, while the Americans
were anxiously awaiting orders to fire, what was their mortification to hear Hull direct a white flag to be hung out, in token of
his readiness to surrender!   Terms of capitulation were soon
agreed upon, by which the army, fort, territory, all were surrendered into the hands of the British.

5. The chief reason assigned by Hull for thus giving up the
fort was his own inferior force compared with that of the enemy ;
especially, the presence of a large Indian force, which, in case
of his defeat, would have rushed to indiscriminate slaughter.

6. Whether these views were well founded or not, the public
mind was altogether unprepared for an occurrence so disastrous
and mortifying.   Hull was, some time after, exchanged for thirty
British prisoners.   Subsequently, he was arraigned before a
court-martial, at Albany, on a charge of treason, cowardice, and
unofficer-like conduct.   On the first charge, the court declined

giving an opinion ; on the two last, he was sentenced to death, but was recommended to mercy, in consequence of his Revolutionary services, and his advanced age. The sentence was remitted by the president, but his name was ordered to be struck from the rolls of the army.

V. CAPTURE OF THE GUERRIERE. — On the 19th of August, three days after the unfortunate surrender of Detroit, that series of splendid naval achievements, for which this war was distinguished, was commenced by Captain Isaac Hull, of the United States' frigate Constitution, who captured the British frigate Guerriere, commanded by Captain Dacres. The American frigate was superior in force only by six guns. The action lasted but thirty-eight minutes, during which the Guerriere was so disabled as to require being burnt. The Constitution sustained so little injury as to be ready for action the following day.

VI. BATTLE OF QUEENSTOWN. — 1. Upon the declaration of war, the attention of General Dearborn was turned towards the invasion of Canada, for which purpose eight or ten thousand troops were collected at different points along the Canada line. These were distributed into three divisions, — one, under General Harrison, called the north-western army ; a second, under General Van Rensselaer, at Lewistown, called the army of the centre ; and a third, under the commander-in-chief, General Dearborn, in the neighborhood of Plattsburg and Greenbush, called the army of the north.

2. Early on the morning of the 13th of October, 1812, a detachment of about one thousand men, from the army of the centre, crossed the river Niagara, and attacked the British on Queenstown heights. These forces were divided into two columns, — one of three hundred militia, under Colonel Van Rensselaer ; the other of three hundred regulars, under Colonel Christie. These were to be followed by Colonel Fenwick's artillery, and afterwards the residue of the troops. Early after landing, Colonel Van Rensselaer was severely wounded, upon which the troops, under command of Captain Wool, advanced to storm the fort. Of this they gained possession ; but, at the moment of success, General Brock arrived from Fort George, with a reinforcement of six hundred men. These were gallantly driven back by the Americans, and, in attempting to rally them, the heroic Brock was killed.

3. General Van Rensselaer, who had previously crossed over, now returned to hasten the embarkation of the " tardy " militia. But what was his chagrin to hear more than twelve hundred

men, who, a little before, were panting for the battle, refuse to
embark, on the ground of scruples about invading a foreign territory, but, in truth, from fear; the wounded having been
unfortunately transported to the American shore, the sight of
savage wounds and flowing blood had cooled their ardor.   General Van Rensselaer urged, entreated, commanded, — but all in
vain.   Meanwhile, the enemy being reinforced, a desperate conflict ensued; but, in the end, the British were victorious.   Had
but a small part of the "idle men" passed over at the critical
moment, when urged by their brave commander, Revolutionary
history can tell of few nobler achievements than this would have
been.

VII. Capture of the Frolic. — On the 18th of October,
another naval victory was achieved, over an enemy decidedly
superior in force, and under circumstances the most favorable to
him.   This was the capture of the brig Frolic, of twenty-two
guns, by the sloop-of-war Wasp, off the coast of North Carolina.
A remarkable difference as to the manner of firing existed in the
case of these two vessels.   The English fired as their vessel rose,
so that their shot was either thrown away, or touched only the
rigging of the Americans.   The Wasp, on the contrary, fired as
she sunk, and every time struck the hull of her antagonist.   The
fire of the Frolic was soon slackened, and Captain Jones determined to board her.   As the crew leaped on board the enemy's
vessel, their surprise can scarcely be imagined, as they found no
person on deck, except three officers and the seaman at the
wheel.   The deck was slippery with blood, and presented a
scene of havoc and ruin.   The officers now threw down their
swords in submission; and Lieutenant Biddle, of the Wasp, leaped
into the rigging, to haul down the colors, which were still flying.
Thus, in forty-three minutes, ended one of the most bloody conflicts recorded in naval history.   Subsequently, on the same day,
both vessels were captured by a British seventy-four, the Poic-
tiers.

VIII. Capture of the Macedonian. — 1. The foregoing
achievement of Captain Jones was followed, on the 25th of October, by another, not much less splendid and decisive, by Commodore Decatur, of the frigate United States, of forty-four
guns, who captured the Macedonian, off the Western Isles, a
frigate of the largest class, mounting forty-nine guns, and
manned with three hundred men.   In this action, which continued an hour and a half, the Macedonian lost thirty-six killed,
and sixty-eight wounded: on board the United States, seven
only were killed, and five wounded.   The British frigate lost

her main-mast, main-top-mast, and main-yard, and was injured in her hull. The United States suffered so little that a return to port was unnecessary.

2. An act of generosity and benevolence, on the part of the brave tars of this victorious frigate, deserves to be honorably recorded. The carpenter, who was unfortunately killed in the conflict with the Macedonian, had left three small children to the care of a worthless mother. When the circumstance became known to the brave seamen, they instantly made a contribution among themselves, to the amount of eight hundred dollars, and placed it in safe hands, to be appropriated to the education and maintenance of the unhappy orphans.

IX. CAPTURE OF THE JAVA. — In December (29th) a second naval victory was achieved by the Constitution, — at this time commanded by Commodore Bainbridge, — over the Java, a British frigate of thirty-eight guns, but carrying forty-nine, with four hundred men, commanded by Captain Lambert, who was mortally wounded. This action was fought off St. Salvador, and continued nearly two hours, when the Java struck, having lost sixty killed and one hundred and twenty wounded. The Constitution had nine killed and twenty-five wounded. On the 1st of January, the commander, finding his prize incapable of being brought in, was obliged to burn her.

X. END OF THE CAMPAIGN. — Thus ended the year 1812. With the exception of the naval victories already mentioned, and others of the same kind, equally honorable to America, nothing important was achieved. Neither of the armies destined for the invasion of Canada had obtained any decisive advantage, or were in possession of any post in that territory. Further preparations, however, were making for its conquest. Naval armaments were collecting on the lakes, and the soldiers, in their winter quarters, were looking forward to "battles fought and victories won."

XI. CAMPAIGN OF 1813. — The military operations of the campaign of 1813 were considerably diversified, extending along the whole northern frontier of the United States. The location of the several divisions of the American forces was as follows: — The army of the west, under General Harrison, was placed near the head of Lake Erie; the army of the centre, under General Dearborn, between the Lakes Ontario and Erie; and the army of the north, under General Hampton, on the shores of Lake Champlain. The British forces in Canada were under the general superintendence of Sir George Prevost, under whom Colonels Proctor and Vincent had in charge the defence

21*

of the Upper Provinces, while the care of the Lower Provinces was committed to General Sheaffe.

XII. BATTLE OF FRENCHTOWN. — 1. On the opening of the year 1813, Michigan, which had been surrendered by General Hull (p. 242) to the British, was still held by them. The citizens of the western country, being anxious to regain possession of it, and with it the-fort of Detroit, General Harrison determined to undertake a winter campaign, with a view to its re-conquest. General Winchester, with about eight hundred troops, principally young men, from the most respectable families of Kentucky, proceeded in advance to Frenchtown, a village on the north bank of the river Raisin, twenty-five miles south-west from Detroit. A British party stationed there was attacked, routed and dispersed.

2. The Americans encamped on the field. On the morning of the 22d of January, a large force of British and Indians, under General Proctor, came suddenly upon them; and, though the Americans made a brave defence, it became necessary to surrender. To this, Winchester, who had been made prisoner, acceded, on a pledge of protection to the prisoners. This pledge Proctor gave, and marched back to Malden.

3. The Indians, however, after accompanying him some miles, turned back to the battle-ground, where, the following morning, the most inhuman butcheries were perpetrated. The wounded officers were killed, and scalped in the streets. The dead were stripped, and the houses fired. Those who were able to travel were conducted to Detroit to be ransomed at exorbitant prices, and others reserved for torture.

4. By this bloody tragedy all Kentucky was literally in mourning. Her brave and most respectable young men were murdered most inhumanly; and where they fell, there their remains lay until the ensuing autumn, beat by the storms of heaven, when their friends ventured to gather up their bleaching bones, and consigned them to the tomb.

XIII. CAPTURE OF THE PEACOCK. — On the 24th of February, an engagement took place, off the coast of South America, between the Hornet, Captain James Lawrence, and the British sloop-of-war Peacock, Captain William Peake. The action lasted but fifteen minutes, when the Peacock struck, and almost immediately sunk, carrying down nine of her crew, and three Americans. With a generosity becoming them, the crew of the Hornet divided their clothing with the prisoners, who were left destitute by the sinking ship. In the action, the Hornet received but a slight injury. The killed and wounded, on board the Peacock, were supposed to exceed fifty.

XIV. Reëlection of Mr. Madison. — On the 4th of March, 1813, Mr. Madison entered upon his second term of office as president, having been reëlected by a considerable majority over De Witt Clinton, of New York, who was supported by the Federal electors. George Clinton was elected vice-president; but his death occurring soon after, Elbridge Gerry was appointed to succeed him.

XV. Capture of York. — 1. On the 25th of April, General Dearborn embarked, with seventeen hundred men, on board a flotilla, under command of Commodore Chauncey, from Sacket's Harbor, for the purpose of attacking York, the capital of Upper Canada, the great depository of British military stores, whence the western posts were supplied. On the 27th, they arrived at the place of debarkation, about two miles west from the enemy's works. The British, under General Sheaffe, attempted to oppose the landing; but were thrown into disorder, and fled to their garrison.

2. General Pike, to whom was intrusted the command, having formed his men, proceeded towards the enemy's fortifications. On their near approach to the barracks, an explosion of a magazine, previously prepared for the purpose, took place, which killed about one hundred of the Americans, among whom was the gallant Pike. Pike lived, however, sufficiently long to direct his troops, for a moment thrown into disorder, " to move on." This they now did under Colonel Pearce, and proceeding towards the town, took possession of the barracks. On approaching it, they were met by the officers of the Canada militia, with offers of capitulation. At four o'clock, the troops entered the town.

XVI. Siege of Fort Meigs. — 1. At the time of the unfortunate battle of Frenchtown, General Harrison was on his march with reinforcements to General Winchester. Finding a further advance of no importance, he took post at the Rapids, where he constructed a fort, which, in honor of the Governor of Ohio, he named Fort Meigs. Here, on the first of May, he was besieged by General Proctor, with a force of two thousand, British and Indians. For nine days the siege was urged with great zeal; but, finding the capture of the place impracticable, on the 9th Proctor raised the siege, and retreated to Malden. General Harrison returned to Franklinton, in Ohio, leaving the fort under the care of General Clay. On the third day of the siege, an officer from the British demanded the surrender of the fort; to which Harrison characteristically replied, " Not, sir, while I have the honor to command."

2. On the 5th, intelligence was received of the approach of a

reinforcement of American troops, under General Clay, from Kentucky. Aided by these, a sortie was made upon the British, which proved so disastrous to both, that, for the three following days, hostilities were suspended, and prisoners exchanged. On the 9th, preparations were made to renew the siege; but, Tecumseh with his followers having deserted his allies the day before, suddenly the British general ordered it raised, and with his force retired.

3. In the latter part of July, General Proctor and Tecumseh, with four thousand British and Indians, again appeared at Fort Meigs, now under command of General Clay. After a few days, however, finding Clay ready to receive them, they retired, and proceeded against Fort Sandusky, garrisoned by one hundred and fifty men, under Major Croghan, a youth of twenty-one. On a demand to surrender, the gallant major replied that he would defend the place to the last extremity. And he did. On the 2d of August, a cannonade was opened upon the fort, and a breach made, when five hundred of the enemy attempted to carry the place by storm. But so terrible was the reception given them, that they fled, in confusion; and, soon after, the siege was raised, with the loss to the Americans of one killed and seven wounded, while the British in killed and wounded numbered one hundred and fifty.

XVII. Loss of the Chesapeake. — On the 1st of June, the American navy experienced no inconsiderable loss, in the capture of the Chesapeake, by the British frigate Shannon, off Boston harbor. Captain Lawrence had been but recently promoted to the command of the Chesapeake. On his arrival at Boston, to take charge of her, he was informed that a British frigate was lying off the harbor, apparently inviting an attack. Prompted by the ardor which pervaded the service, he resolved to meet the enemy, without sufficiently examining his strength. With a crew chiefly enlisted for the occasion, as that of the Chesapeake had mostly been discharged, on the first of June he sailed out of the harbor. The Shannon, observing the Chesapeake put to sea, immediately followed. At half past five, the two ships engaged. In a few minutes, every officer of the Chesapeake, who could take command of her, was either killed or wounded, and her rigging so cut as to become entangled with the Shannon. This gave an opportunity to the British to board her. Captain Lawrence, though severely wounded, still kept the deck. In the act of summoning the boarders, a musket-ball entered his body. As he was carried below, he issued a last heroic order, — "Don't give up the ship!" but it was too late to retrieve what was lost.

XVIII. LOSS OF THE ARGUS. — The tide of fortune still favored the British. On the 14th of August, the Argus, another of our national vessels, was captured by the Pelican. The Argus had been employed to carry out Mr. Crawford, as minister, to France. After landing him, she proceeded to cruise in the British Channel, and, for two months, greatly annoyed the British shipping. At length, that government was induced to send several vessels in pursuit of her. On the 14th of August, the Pelican, a sloop-of-war, of superior force, discovered her, and bore down to action. At the first broadside, Captain Allen fell, severely wounded; but remained on deck for some time, when it was necessary to carry him below. After a hard-fought action, the Argus was obliged to surrender.

XIX. CAPTURE OF THE BOXER. — On the 5th of September, victory again returned to the side of America, the British brig Boxer surrendering to the Enterprise, after an engagement of little more than half an hour, off the coast of Maine. The commanders of both vessels — the American Lieutenant Barrows, and the British Captain Blythe — fell in the action, and were interred beside each other, at Portland, with military honors.

XX. PERRY'S VICTORY ON LAKE ERIE. — During the summer, by the exertions of Commodore Perry, an American squadron had been fitted out on Lake Erie. It consisted of nine small vessels, carrying fifty-four guns. A British squadron had also been built and equipped, under the superintendence of Commodore Barclay. It consisted of six vessels, mounting sixty-three guns. On the 10th of September, Commodore Perry offered battle to Commodore Barclay, the latter having left the harbor of Malden for the purpose of accepting the challenge. In a few hours, the wind shifted, giving the Americans the advantage. Perry, forming the line of battle, hoisted his flag, on which was inscribed the words of the dying Lawrence, "Don't give up the ship!" Loud huzzas from all the vessels proclaimed the animation which this motto inspired. About noon, the firing commenced; after a short action, two of the British vessels surrendered, and the rest of the American squadron now joining in the battle, the victory was rendered decisive and complete. Commodore Perry gave intelligence of the victory to General Harrison, then at Fort Meigs, in the laconic but impressive words, — "We have met the enemy, and they are ours; — two ships, two brigs, one schooner, and one sloop."

XXI. Battle of the Thames. — 1. The victory of Perry was the more welcome, as, by means of it, the Americans became masters of Lake Erie, and the way was prepared to recover back the Territory of Michigan, which, with its forts, Malden and Detroit, were still in possession of Proctor. The first movement of Harrison, therefore, was against these forts. He had previously assembled a portion of the Ohio militia, which, with four thousand Kentuckians, under Governor Shelby, made a formidable force. On the 27th of September, the troops were received on board the fleet, and on the same day reached Malden. But, to their surprise, they found that fortress and the public storehouses burned. On the following day, the Americans marched in pursuit of Proctor and his troops; and, on the 29th, entered and took possession of Detroit.

2. Leaving Detroit on the 2d of October, Harrison and Shelby proceeded, with thirty-five hundred men, selected for the purpose; and, on the 5th, reached the place of Proctor's encampment, which was the Moravian village, on the Thames, about eighty miles from Detroit. The American troops were immediately formed in the order of battle, and the armies engaged with the most determined courage. In this contest, the celebrated Tecumseh was slain. Upon his fall, the Indians immediately fled. This led to the defeat of the whole British force, which surrendered, except about two hundred dragoons, which, with Proctor at their head, were enabled to escape. On this field of battle, the Americans had the pleasure to retake six brass field-pieces which had been surrendered by Hull; on two of which were inscribed the words, "Surrendered by Burgoyne, at Saratoga." Tecumseh, who fell in this battle, was, in several respects, the most celebrated Indian warrior who ever raised an arm against the Americans. He had been in almost every engagement with the whites since Harmar's defeat, although, at his death, he scarcely exceeded forty years of age.

XXII. Proposed Invasion of Canada. — 1. The fall of Detroit put an end to the Indian war in that quarter, and gave security to the frontiers. General Harrison now dismissed a great part of his volunteers, and, having stationed General Cass at Detroit, with about one thousand men, proceeded, according to his instructions, with the remainder of his forces, to Buffalo, to join the army of the centre. The result of the operations of the north-west, and the victory on Lake Erie, prepared the way to attempt a more effectual invasion of Canada.

2. General Dearborn having, some time before this, retired from the service, General Wilkinson was appointed to succeed

him as commander-in-chief, and arrived at Sacket's Harbor on the 20th of August. The first object of his instructions was the capture of Kingston, although the reduction of Canada, by an attack upon Montreal, was the ulterior aim of the campaign. The forces destined for the accomplishment of these purposes were an army of five thousand, at Fort George; two thousand, under General Lewis, at Sacket's Harbor; four thousand, at Platts-burg, under the command of General Hampton, which latter, proceeding by the way of Champlain, were to form a junction with the main body, at some place on the river St. Lawrence; and, finally, the victorious troops of General Harrison, which were expected to arrive in season to furnish important assist-ance.

3. On the 5th of September, General Armstrong, who had recently been appointed Secretary of War, arrived at Sacket's Harbor, to aid in the above project. The plan of attacking Kingston was now abandoned, and it was determined to proceed immediately to Montreal. Unexpected difficulties, however, occurred, which prevented the execution of the plan; and the American force, under Wilkinson, retired into winter quarters at French Mills. The forces of General Hampton, after pene-trating the country some distance, to join Wilkinson, retired again to Plattsburg, where he was succeeded by General Izard. The forces of General Harrison were not ready to join the expe-dition until the troops had gone into winter quarters.

XXIII. END OF THE CAMPAIGN OF 1813. — Thus ended a cam-paign which gave rise to a dissatisfaction proportioned to the high expectations that had been indulged of its success. Public opinion was much divided as to the causes of its failure, and as to the parties to whom the blame was properly to be attached.

XXIV. CAMPAIGN OF 1814 — CREEK WAR. — 1. Soon after the northern armies had gone into winter quarters, as noticed above, the public attention was directed to a war with the Creek Indians, who, being instigated thereto by the British govern-ment, had declared against the United States; and which proved exceedingly sanguinary during the year 1813, and until the close of the summer of 1814. At this latter date, General Jackson, who conducted it on the part of the Americans, hav-ing, in several rencounters, — as at Tallushatches, and at Tal-ladega, and then at Autossee, Emucfau, and other places, — much reduced them, signally defeated them, in the battle of Tohopeka, or Horse-shoe-bend. Following this, he concluded a treaty with them, August 9th, on conditions advantageous to the United States. Having accomplished this service, Jackson returned to Tennessee, and was soon after appointed to succeed General Wilkinson in the command of the forces at New Orleans.

2. The commencement of hostilities by the Creeks was an attack upon Fort Mimms, on the 30th of August, 1813, by six hundred Indians, who, taking the fort by surprise, massacred three hundred men, women and children, excepting seventeen, who, alone, effected their escape. On receipt of this intelligence, General Jackson, with two thousand Tennesseans, and five hundred under General Coffee, marched into the country of the Creeks, where occurred the battles already named. But the Creeks remained unsubdued. At length, they commenced fortifying Tohopeka, on the bend of Tallapoosa river. Against this fortified refuge of these infatuated savages General Jackson led his forces, and, in March, reduced it. Nearly six hundred of the Creeks were killed, and three hundred women and children made prisoners.

3. Their signal defeat put an end to the war. Shortly after, the remnant of the nation sent in their submission. Among these was the prophet and leader, Weatherford. In bold and impressive language, he said : " I am in your power. Do with me what you please. I have done the white people all the harm I could. I have fought them, and fought them bravely. There was a time when I had a choice ; I have none now, — even hope is ended. Once I could animate my warriors ; but I cannot animate the dead. They can no longer hear my voice ; their bones are at Tallushatches, Talladega, Emuefau, and Tohopeka. While there was a chance of success, I never supplicated peace ; but my people are gone, and I now ask it for my nation and myself."

XXV. CHIPPEWA AND BRIDGEWATER. — 1. During the winter of 1814, but few events of importance occurred on the northern frontier. Early in the spring, General Wilkinson proceeded from French Mills, his winter quarters, to Plattsburg, with a part of his army ; while the remainder, under General Brown, returned to Sacket's Harbor.

2. Near the last of March, Wilkinson penetrated into Canada, and attacked a body of British occupying a large stone mill, on the river La Cole. But he was repulsed, with considerable loss. At a subsequent day, he was tried by a court-martial for the above unfortunate issue ; and, though acquitted, he was removed from command, and was succeeded, as already stated, by General Izard.

3. For three months following, the armies of both nations

continued inactive, the world being occupied by the wonderful events then transpiring in Europe, — the abdication of Napoleon, his retirement to Elba, and the restoration of Louis XVIII. to the throne of France.

4. In the beginning of July, however, the contest was renewed by General Brown, who crossed over from Sacket's Harbor, and took possession of Fort Erie. At Chippewa, a few miles distant from Fort Erie, in a strong position, General Riall lay intrenched. On the 4th Brown approached these works, and on the 5th occurred the battle of Chippewa. The contest was obstinate and bloody; but, at length, the Americans were decidedly victorious.

5. Immediately after this defeat, General Riall retired to Burlington Heights. Here, Lieutenant-general Drummond, with a large force, joined him, and, assuming the command, led back the army towards the American camp. On the 25th, the two armies met at Bridgewater, near the cataract of Niagara; and a most desperate engagement ensued about sunset, and lasted till midnight. At length, the Americans were left in quiet possession of the field. The battle of Bridgewater, or Niagara, was one of the most bloody conflicts recorded in modern warfare. Generals Drummond and Riall were among the wounded, as were also Generals Brown and Scott. Unfortunately, the Americans, having no means to remove the British artillery which had been captured, were obliged to leave it on the field. On being apprized of this, the British forthwith returned, and took their artillery again in charge. Owing to this circumstance, the British officers had the hardihood, in their despatches to government, to claim the victory.

6. General Ripley, finding his numbers too much reduced to withstand a force so greatly his superior, deemed it prudent to return to Fort Erie. On the 4th of August, this fort was invested by General Drummond, with five thousand men, and for forty-nine days the siege was pressed with great zeal; but, at length, the British general was obliged to retire, without having accomplished his object.

XXVI. CAPTURE OF WASHINGTON. — While these events were transpiring in the north, the public attention was irresistibly drawn to the movements of the enemy on the seaboard. About the middle of August, a squadron of fifty or sixty British sail arrived in the Chesapeake, with troops destined for the attack of Washington, the capital of the United States. On the 23d of August, six thousand British troops, commanded by General Ross, forced their way to that place, and burnt the capitol,

22

president's house, and executive offices. Having thus accomplished an object highly disgraceful to the British arms, and wantonly burned public buildings, the ornament and pride of the nation, the destruction of which could not hasten the termination of the war, on the 25th they retired, and, by rapid marches, regained their shipping, having lost, during the expedition, nearly one thousand men.

XXVII. DEFENCE OF BALTIMORE. — The capture of Washington was followed, September 12th, by an attack on Baltimore, in which the American forces, militia and inhabitants, made a gallant defence. Being, however, overpowered by a superior force, they were compelled to retreat; but they fought so valiantly that the attempt to gain possession of the city was abandoned by the enemy, who, during the night of Tuesday, 13th, retired to their shipping, having lost, among their killed, General Ross, the commander-in-chief of the British troops.

XXVIII. WAR ON THE COAST OF NEW ENGLAND. — While the war was thus being waged in the vicinity of the capital, hostile movements were made in other quarters. A British fleet was dispersed along the coast of New England, — especially before the ports of New York, New London and Boston, — and succeeded in capturing large numbers of American coasters. In August, Commodore Hardy appeared before Stonington, Connecticut, which he proceeded to bombard for some days. Several attempts were made, by detachments from the fleet, to land; but they were as often repulsed by the militia of the vicinity.

XXIX. ENGAGEMENT ON LAKE CHAMPLAIN. — 1. The joy experienced in all parts of the United States, on account of the brave defence of Baltimore, had scarcely subsided, when intelligence was received of the signal success of the Americans at Plattsburg, and on Lake Champlain. The army of Sir George Prevost, amounting to fourteen thousand men, was compelled, September 11th, by General Macomb, to retire from the former; and the enemy's squadron, commanded by Commodore Downie, was captured by Commodore Macdonough, on the latter.

2. At this time, both the Americans and British had a respectable naval force on Lake Champlain; but that of the latter was considerably the superior, amounting to ninety-five guns, and one thousand and fifty men, while the American squadron carried but eighty-six guns, and eight hundred and twenty-six men. On the 11th of September, while the American fleet was lying off Plattsburg, the British squadron was observed bearing down upon it in order of battle.

3. Commodore Macdonough, ordering his vessels cleared for

action, gallantly received the enemy. An engagement ensued, which lasted two hours and twenty minutes. By this time, the enemy was silenced, and one frigate, one brig, and two sloops-of-war, fell into the hands of the Americans. Several British galleys were sunk, and a few others escaped. Previously to this eventful day, Sir George Prevost, with his army, arrived in the vicinity of Plattsburg. In anticipation of this event, General Macomb made every preparation which time and means allowed, and called in to his assistance considerable numbers of militia.

4. In the sight of these two armies, the rival squadrons commenced their contest. And, as if their engagement had been a preconcerted signal, and as if to raise still higher the solemn grandeur of the scene, Sir George Prevost now led up his forces against the American works, and began throwing upon them shells, balls, and rockets. At the same time, the Americans opened a severe and destructive fire from their forts. Before sunset, the temporary batteries of Sir George Prevost were all silenced, and every attempt of the enemy to cross from Plattsburg to the American works was repelled. At nine o'clock, perceiving the attainment of his object impracticable, the British general hastily withdrew his forces, diminished, by killed, wounded and deserted, two thousand five hundred. At the same time, he abandoned vast quantities of military stores, and left the inhabitants of Plattsburg to take care of the sick and

wounded of his army, and the " star-spangled banner " to wave in triumph over the waters of Champlain.

XXX. HARTFORD CONVENTION. — 1. The people of New England were generally opposed to the war, and during its progress that opposition became confirmed. Apprehending a crisis was forming which might involve the country in ruin, Massachusetts recommended a convention from the New England States. Although the measure was strongly opposed, delegates were appointed. This example was followed by Rhode Island and Connecticut. Vermont refused, and New Hampshire neglected to send.

2. On the 15th of December, these delegates, together with two elected by counties in New Hampshire, and one similarly elected in Vermont, met at Hartford. After a session of near three weeks, they published a report, in which, after dwelling upon the public grievances felt by the New England States particularly, and by the country at large in no small degree, they proceeded to suggest several alterations of the federal constitution, with a view to their adoption by the respective states of the Union.*

XXXI. BATTLE OF NEW ORLEANS. — 1. On the 8th of January, 1815, occurred this memorable battle. The British forces, amounting to twelve thousand, were commanded by General Packenham. The Americans consisted of about six thousand, chiefly militia, under command of General Jackson. The latter had been diligently employed for some time in preparations of defence. It was a bold enterprise, on the part of the British, to deliberately advance in solid columns over an even plain in front of the American intrenchments. When, at length, they were in reach of the batteries, a most destructive cannonade was opened upon them. Still the enemy continued to advance, until within reach of musketry and rifles, when the extended American line presented one sheet of fire. and poured in an unceasing tide of death.

* These alterations consisted of seven articles: — first, that representatives and direct taxes shall be apportioned to the number of free persons; — secondly, that no new state shall be admitted into the Union, without the concurrence of two-thirds of both houses; — thirdly, that Congress shall not have power to lay an embargo for more than sixty days; — fourthly, that Congress shall not interdict commercial intercourse, without the concurrence of two-thirds of both houses; — fifthly, that war shall not be declared without the concurrence of a similar majority; — sixthly, that no person, who shall be hereafter naturalized, shall be eligible as a member of the Senate or House of Representatives, or hold any civil office under the authority of the United States; and, seventhly, that no person shall be elected twice to the presidency, nor the president be elected from the same state two terms in succession. The conclusion of a treaty of peace with Great Britain, not long after, being announced, another convention was not called; and, on the submission of the above amendments of the constitution to the several states, they were rejected.

2. Being unable to stand the shock, the British became disorderly, and fled. In an attempt to rally them, General Packenham was killed. A second time they broke and fled. In a third but unavailing attempt to lead them again into action, Generals Gibbs and Kean were severely wounded — the former, mortally. The enemy, at length, sullenly retired, having lost in killed seven hundred, in wounded fourteen hundred, and prisoners·five hundred; while, strange to say, the loss of the Americans was only seven killed and six wounded.

XXXII. TREATY OF GHENT. — The blood poured out so freely at New Orleans might have been spared; a treaty of peace having been already signed at Ghent, on the previous 24th of December. But intelligence of this joyful event had not then transpired in America. The battle, however, served greatly to add honor to the American name; and from that day General Jackson was well and widely known as the " Hero of New Orleans." On the 17th of February, the treaty was ratified by the President and Senate.* Upon the subjects for which the war had been professedly declared, the treaty thus concluded was silent. It provided only for the suspension of hostilities, the exchange of prisoners, the restoration of territories and possessions obtained by the contending powers during the war, the adjustment of unsettled boundaries, and for a combined effort to effect the entire abolition of traffic in slaves.

XXXIII. TREATY WITH ALGIERS. — 1. The treaty with England was followed, on the 30th of June, by a treaty with the Dey of Algiers, concluded at Algiers, at that time, by William Shaler and Commodore Stephen Decatur, agents for the United States. The war which thus ended by treaty was commenced by the dey himself, in 1812; up to which time, from 1795, peace with him had been preserved by the United States, by the payment of an annual tribute.

2. In 1812, the American consul, Mr. Lear, was suddenly ordered to depart from Algiers, on account of the arrival of a cargo of naval and military stores, for the regency of Algiers, in fulfilment of treaty stipulations, which, the dey alleged, were not

* In 1813, the Emperor of Russia offered to mediate between the two countries; and Messrs. Gallatin, Bayard, and J. Q. Adams, were appointed commissioners, to proceed to Russia, to meet commissioners from England. The latter, however, declined the overture; but the Prince Regent offered a direct negotiation, either at London or Gottenburg. This being accepted, Messrs. Clay and Jonathan Russell were added to the already appointed commissioners. On the part of England, Lord Gambier, Henry Golbourn, and William Adams, were appointed. The place of meeting was subsequently changed to Ghent, in Flanders, where the commissioners met in August.

22*

such, in quantity or quality, as he expected. At the same time, depredations were commenced upon our commerce. Several American vessels were captured and condemned, and their crews subjected to slavery.

3. Upon a representation of the case, by the president, to Congress, that body formally declared war against the dey, in March. Soon after, an American squadron sailed for the Mediterranean, captured an Algerine brig and a forty-four gun frigate, and at length appeared before Algiers. The respectability of the American force, added to the two important victories already achieved, had prepared the way for the American commissioners to dictate a treaty upon such a basis as they pleased. Accordingly, the model of a treaty was sent to the dey, who signed it. By this treaty, the United States were exempted from paying tribute in future ; captured property was to be restored by the dey; prisoners to be delivered up, without ransom, &c. &c.

XXXIV. NATIONAL BANK. — In 1811, the former national bank expired. During the session of Congress 1815–16, a charter for a new bank, entitled " The Bank of the United States," with a capital of thirty-five millions of dollars, and to continue till 1836, was brought forward; and, after weeks of animated discussion, was passed, and April 10th received the signature of the president.

XXXV. ADMISSION OF INDIANA. — In December, 1816, Indiana was admitted into the Union. The name is derived from the word Indian. The French seem to have formed the first settlements in this territory; but the exact period is uncertain. During the war of 1812–14, Indiana was the scene of many Indian depredations, and many severe battles. Until 1801, it formed a part of the great north-western territory ; but at that date was erected into a territorial government.

XXXVI. ELECTION OF MR. MONROE. — Mr. Madison having signified his intention to retire at the expiration of his second term, James Monroe, of Virginia, was elected his successor ; and Daniel D. Tompkins, of New York, was chosen vice-president.

UNITED STATES.

PERIOD X.

JAMES MONROE, President.

Inaugurated at Washington, March 4th, 1817; retired March 3d, 1825.

DANIEL D. TOMPKINS, Vice-President.

HEADS OF THE DEPARTMENTS.

John Q. Adams,	Mass.,	March 5,	1817,	Sec'y of State.
William H. Crawford,	Georgia,	March 5,	1817,	Sec'y of Treasury.
Isaac Shelby,	Kentucky,	March 5,	1817,	} Sec's of War.
John C. Calhoun,	S. Carolina,	December 15, 1817,		
Benj. W. Crowninshield,	Mass.,	(continued in office),		
Smith Thompson,	New York,	November 30, 1818,		} Sec's of Navy.
Samuel L. Southard,	N. Jersey,	December 9, 1823,		
Return J. Meigs,	Ohio,	(continued in office),		} Postmasters Gen.
John M'Lean,	Ohio,	December 9, 1823,		
Richard Rush,	Penn.,	(continued in office),		} Attorneys Gen.
William Wirt,	Virginia,	December 14, 1817,		

SPEAKERS OF THE HOUSE OF REPRESENTATIVES.

Henry Clay,	Kentucky,	Fifteenth Congress,	1817.
Henry Clay,	Kentucky,	Sixteenth do.	1819.
John W. Taylor,	New York,	Sixteenth do.	1820.
Philip P. Barbour,	Virginia,	Seventeenth do.	1821.
Henry Clay,	Kentucky,	Eighteenth do.	1823.

1. THE elevation of Mr. Monroe to the presidency was an event highly auspicious to the interests of the nation. Besides having been employed for many years in high and responsible stations under the government, and therefore being well acquainted with the powers of the constitution, and the manner in which the government had been administered by his predecessors, he possessed a sound and discriminating judgment, and a remarkably calm and quiet temperament. In not a few of the qualities of his mind, he resembled Washington; and, like that great and good man, had the true interests of his country in view, in the acts and measures of his administration.

2. At the time of his accession, the country was beginning to recover from the effects of the late war. Commerce was reviving, and the manufacturers were hoping for more auspicious days. In every department of industry there was the commencement of activity; and, although the country had suffered too long and too seriously to regain at once her former prosperity, hopes of better times were indulged, and great confidence was reposed in the wise and prudent counsels of the new president.

3. A review of the principal measures and events during the presidency of Mr. Monroe will require us to notice the following topics :

Admission of Mississippi.	Admission of Maine.
Provision for Indigent Officers.	Reëlection of Mr. Monroe.
Admission of Illinois.	Admission of Missouri.
Seminole War.	Apportionment of Represent-
Convention with Great Brit-	atives.
ain.	Visit of Lafayette.
Cession of Florida.	Election of Mr. Adams.
Admission of Alabama.	

I. ADMISSION OF MISSISSIPPI. — The first European who visited the region of country of which the State of Mississippi was then a part was Ferdinand de Soto, in 1539 (p. 17). In 1683, M. de Salle visited the same region, and gave it the name of Louisiana, in honor of Louis XIV. of France. Over this undefined but vast extent of country, the French claimed jurisdiction; and, in 1716, they began a settlement at Natchez, and erected a fort. In 1763, they ceded the country east of the Mississippi to the English; and the latter ceded it to Spain in 1783. In 1798, the Spaniards abandoned it to the United States. In 1800, the territory lying between the western boundary of Georgia and the Mississippi river, and which, until now, had been claimed by Georgia, and called the "Georgia Western Territory," was erected by Congress into a distinct territorial government, by the name of the "Mississippi Territory." In December, 1827, this territory was divided, and the western portion of it admitted into the Union, as the "STATE OF MISSISSIPPI," the eastern forming the TERRITORY OF ALABAMA.

II. PROVISION FOR INDIGENT OFFICERS AND SOLDIERS. — Through the inability of the government, at the close of the Revolutionary War, the officers and soldiers, who had spent their strength and run the hazard of their lives, — who had exhausted their private fortunes, and subjected their families to incredible hardships, for the achievement of their country's independence,—were left without adequate compensation. They received certificates for bounty lands, and other dues; but these they were compelled to sell, and often nearly to sacrifice, to relieve the pressure of existing want,—the purchasers, in after years, when the government paid these certificates in full, amassing, in some instances, immense fortunes, the price of the toils and sufferings of those who fought the battles and achieved the freedom of their country. But, in 1818, Congress passed a law making provision, to a limited extent, for the surviving few of the officers and soldiers of the Revolution. It was a debt long due,—long acknowledged; but, though tardy in her payment of it, the government at length felt the justice of it, and measures were taken for their relief. Subsequently, this law was extended, so that the widows and children of the deceased officers and soldiers have been remembered. By these means, thousands and thousands have been made to rejoice.

III. ADMISSION OF ILLINOIS.—In 1818, Illinois adopted a state constitution, and in December following was admitted as a member of the Union. Illinois derives its name from its principal river, which, in the language of the Indians, signifies THE RIVER OF MEN. The first settlements, like those of Indiana, were made by the French, and were the consequence of the adventurous enterprises of M. de la Salle, in search of the Mississippi. The first settlements were the villages of Kaskaskia and Cahokia. In 1763, the country passed under British dominion. At the peace of 1783, Great Britain renounced her claims of sovereignty over this country, as well as the United States. Illinois remained a part of Indiana until 1809, when it received a territorial government.

IV. SEMINOLE WAR.—1. Within the southern limits of the United States, but mostly in Florida, lived a tribe or confederacy of Indians, called SEMINOLES. They consisted of fugitives from northern tribes, Creek Indians who were dissatisfied with the treaty General Jackson made with them in 1814, and negroes who had absconded from their masters. The resentments of this motley confederacy against the whites were, doubtless, fanned by foreign emissaries, of whom the most noted were two Englishmen, Alexander Arbuthnot and Robert C. Ambrister. At length, several outrages being committed by the Indians, the Secretary of War ordered General Gaines to remove, at his discretion, such Indians as were still on the lands ceded to the United States by the Creeks, in 1814. The execution of this order roused the Indians, who, in great numbers, invested

Fort Scott, where General Gaines was confined, with six hundred men.

2. In this posture of affairs, General Jackson was ordered, in December, to take the field, and to call on the governors of adjacent states for such forces as he might need. This order, however, he disobeyed, and invited to his standard a thousand volunteers from Tennessee. With these, and the forces already raised, he entered the Indian territory, which he overran without serious opposition.

3. Deeming it necessary, for the subjugation of the Seminoles, to enter Florida, General Jackson marched upon St. Marks, a feeble Spanish garrison, in which some Indians had taken refuge. Of this garrison he took possession, and occupied it as an American post. At St. Marks was found Alexander Arbuthnot, who was put in confinement. At the same time were taken two Indian chiefs, who were hung, without trial. St. Marks being garrisoned by American troops, the army marched to Suwaney river, on which they found a large Indian village, which was consumed; after which, the army returned to St. Marks, bringing with them Robert C. Ambrister, who had been taken prisoner on their march to Suwaney. During the halt of the army, for a few days, at St. Marks, a general court-martial was called, before which charges were made against Ambrister and Arbuthnot. Both were adjudged guilty; and the former was sentenced to be shot, — the latter to be hung. Subsequently, however, the sentence in respect to Ambrister was reconsidered, and he was sentenced to be whipped, and confined to hard labor. This decision General Jackson reversed, and ordered both to be executed, according to the first sentence of the court.

4. Next, General Jackson seized Pensacola, another Spanish possession, May 24th; and having sent the Spanish authorities and sloops to Havana, he established a new government, partly military, and in part of citizens of the province. The measures thus adopted by General Jackson, in the prosecution of this war, — particularly his appeal to the people of West Tennessee, his conduct in relation to the trial and execution of Arbuthnot and Ambrister, and his occupation of St. Marks and Pensacola, — excited strong sensations in the bosoms of a considerable portion of the American people. During the session of Congress in the winter of 1818-19, these subjects were extensively and eloquently debated. By the military committee of the house, a report was presented censuring the conduct of General Jackson, which, however, was not accepted; a report unfavorable to him

was also made in the Senate, but no discussion of its merits followed.

V. CONVENTION WITH GREAT BRITAIN. — In January, 1819, a convention between Great Britain and the United States — concluded at London, October, 1818 — was ratified by the President of the United States. By the first article of this convention, the citizens of the United States had liberty, in common with the subjects of Great Britain, to take fish on the southern, western, and northern coast of Newfoundland, &c. The second article established the northern boundaries of the United States from the Lake of the Woods to the Stony Mountains. By the fourth article, the commercial convention between the two countries, concluded at London in 1815, was extended for the term of ten years longer, &c. &c.

VI. CESSION OF FLORIDA. — On the 22d of February, following, a treaty was concluded at Washington, by John Quincy Adams and Luis de Onis, by which East and West Florida, with all the islands adjacent, &c., were ceded by Spain to the United States. By this treaty the western boundary between the United States and Spain was settled. A sum not exceeding five millions of dollars was to be paid by the United States out of the proceeds of sales of lands in Florida, or in stock, or money, to citizens of the United States, on account of Spanish spoliations and injuries.

VII. ADMISSION OF ALABAMA. — 1. On the 14th of December, 1819, a resolution passed Congress admitting ALABAMA — so called after her principal river — into the Union, on an equal footing with the original states. Alabama, though recently settled, appears to have been visited by Ferdinand de Soto in 1539. Some scattered settlements were made within the present State of Mississippi before the American Revolution; but Alabama continued the hunting-ground of savages until a much later period.

2. After the peace of 1783, Georgia laid claim to this territory; but, in 1802, she ceded it to the United States for one million two hundred and fifty thousand dollars. In 1800, the territory which forms the States of Mississippi and Alabama was erected into a territorial government. In 1817, this territory was divided, the western part forming the State of Mississippi, the eastern the territory of Alabama. The state constitution was adopted in July, 1819.

VIII. ADMISSION OF MAINE. — The following year, 1820, March 16th, Maine, hitherto under the jurisdiction of Massachusetts, was received into the Union as an independent state. For settlement and history of Maine, see page 50.

IX. REËLECTION OF MR. MONROE. — Mr. Monroe, whose second election to the presidency was nearly unanimous, entered upon his second term on the 4th of March, 1821. Mr. Tompkins was again elected vice-president.

X. ADMISSION OF MISSOURI. — 1. On the 10th of August, 1821, the president, by proclamation, declared Missouri — so called after the river of that name — to be an independent state, and a member of the Federal Union.

2. The first permanent settlements in Missouri appear to have been made at St. Genevieve and New Bourbon, which were founded soon after the peace of 1663. In the succeeding year, St. Louis, the capital of the state, was commenced. In 1762, Louisiana, which included the tract of country now known as Missouri, was secretly ceded by France to Spain; but the latter did not attempt to take possession of the country until some years after. Missouri remained in possession of Spain, through the war of the Revolution, until the cession of Louisiana to France, in 1801, by which latter power it was ceded to the United States, in 1803.

3. Upon the above cession of Louisiana, the district which now forms the STATE OF LOUISIANA was separated from the territory, and made a distinct government, by the name of the TERRITORY OF ORLEANS. In 1811, the territory of Orleans became a State, by the name of Louisiana. The remaining part of the original province of Louisiana, extending to the Pacific, was erected into a territorial government, and called Missouri. In 1818–19, application was made to Congress, by the people of this territory, to form a state constitution. A bill was accordingly introduced for the purpose, a provision of which forbade slavery or involuntary servitude. The bill, with this provision, passed the House of Representatives, but was rejected in the Senate; and, in consequence of this disagreement, the measure, for the time, failed. In the session of 1819–20, the bill was revived; and, after long and animated debates, a compromise was effected, by which slavery was to be tolerated in Missouri, and forbidden in all that part of Louisiana, as ceded by France, lying north of 36° 30′ north latitude, except so much as was included within the limits of the state. These provisions Missouri was obliged to accept, which she did, by her Legislature; and, upon this, the president issued the proclamation of admission.

XI. APPORTIONMENT OF REPRESENTATION. — The constitution has not limited the number of representatives, except providing that no more than one shall be sent for thirty thousand inhabitants. Public opinion seems generally to have decided that a numerous representation is an evil, by which not only the business of the nation is neglected in the conflicts of individual opinions, but the people are subjected to an unnecessary expense. The Congress that signed the Declaration of Independence consisted but of fifty-six members; and no deliberative assembly excelled them in industry and public virtue. The Congress that formed the Confederation consisted of forty-eight; that which formed the constitution consisted of only thirty-nine, and the first Congress under that constitution of but sixty-five. After the first census, the apportionment being one for every thirty-three thousand inhabitants, the house consisted of one hundred and five representatives. The same apportionment being continued under the second census, there were one hundred and forty-one representatives. The apportionment under the third census allowed one for thirty-five thousand; and the house consisted of one hundred and eighty-seven members. The ratio fixed upon by the Congress of 1822–23 was one for forty thousand; and the number of representatives was two hundred and twelve.

XII. VISIT OF LAFAYETTE. — 1. In the course of the summer of 1824, an event occurred which caused the highest sensations of joy throughout the Union. This was the arrival of the Marquis de Lafayette, the friend and ally of the Americans during the former war with Great Britain (p. 176), and who eminently contributed, by his fortune, influence, skill and bravery, to achieve the glorious objects of their Revolutionary struggle.

2. The visit of Lafayette to the United States occupied about a year; during which he visited each of the twenty-four States, and was everywhere hailed as a father. When the time arrived which he had fixed as the termination of his visit, a frigate was prepared at Washington, and named, in compliment to him, the Brandywine, to transport him to his native country.

3. On the 7th of September, about noon, he entered the spacious hall in the presidential mansion, where he was addressed by the chief magistrate of the nation in terms manly, patriotic, and affectionate. In a similar manner Lafayette replied, concluding as follows: — "God bless you, sir, and all who surround us. God bless the American people, each of their states, and the federal government. Accept this patriotic farewell of an overflowing heart; such will be its last throb, when it ceases to beat."

4. Then, taking an affectionate leave of each individual present, the general left the hospitable mansion of the president. He was attended to the vessel by the whole population of the district. All business was suspended, and the vast multitude which lined the shores witnessed his embarkation with a deep silence, highly

23

indicative of the feelings that the American people cherished towards Lafayette. In passing Mount Vernon, he landed to pay a farewell visit to the tomb of Washington, whence reëmbarking, a prosperous voyage soon safely landed him on his own paternal soil.

5. It may here be added, that, during the visit of this illustrious general, Congress passed a bill appropriating the sum of two hundred thousand dollars, and a complete township of land, as a partial remuneration of services rendered by him during the Revolutionary struggle of the country.

XIII. Election of Mr. Adams. — 1. During the presidency of Mr. Monroe, the country enjoyed a uniform state of peace and prosperity. By his prudent management of the national affairs, both foreign and domestic, he eminently contributed to the honor and happiness of millions ; and retired from office enjoying the respect, and affection, and gratitude, of all who were able duly to appreciate the blessings of having a wise ruler.

2. The subject of his successor was early introduced to the notice of the public, and the excitement of the several parties in the United States was both fostered and increased by the newspapers and public journals of the day. Besides Mr. Adams, Mr. Crawford, Secretary of the Treasury, Mr. Clay, Speaker of the House of Representatives, and General Jackson, a senator, were candidates for the office ; each of whom had their respective friends in the country, and among the Legislatures of the states, nearly all of which, by a public vote, declared in favor of some one of the candidates.

3. The electors, however, failed to make a choice, and the election devolved upon the House of Representatives. By the constitution, only the three highest on the list could be candidates for the office in the House of Representatives. Mr. Clay, therefore, was not voted for ; but is supposed, by his influence, to have determined the question in favor of Mr. Adams, in opposition to Mr. Crawford, who had been nominated by a caucus at Washington, and to General Jackson, who had received the highest vote by the electors.

UNITED STATES.

PERIOD XI.

JOHN QUINCY ADAMS, President.

Inaugurated at Washington, March 4th, 1825; retired March 9th, 1829.

JOHN C. CALHOUN, Vice-President.

HEADS OF THE DEPARTMENTS.

Henry Clay,	Ky.,	March 7,	1825,	Secretary of State.
Richard Rush,	Penn.,	March 7,	1825,	Secretary of Treasury.
James Barbour,	Va.,	March 7,	1825,	Secretaries of War.
Peter B. Porter,	N. Y.,	May 26,	1827,	
Samuel L. Southard,	N. J.,	(continued in office),		Secretary of the Navy.
John McLean,	Ohio,	(continued in office),		Postmaster General.
William Wirt,	Va.,	(continued in office),		Attorney General.

SPEAKERS OF THE HOUSE OF REPRESENTATIVES.

John W. Taylor,	New York,	Nineteenth Congress,	1825.
Andrew Stevenson,	Virginia,	Twentieth do.	1827.

1. The policy and views of Mr. Adams were in the main conformed to those of his immediate predecessor. No man, perhaps, better understood the interests of his country; no one could well be better skilled in every art of diplomacy and government. Yet the administration of Mr. Adams was destined to a formidable opposition. He was charged with having entered into a bargain with Mr. Clay, prior to the election, by which he was to be president, and Mr. Clay his principal secretary. But such a bargain was never proved, and, it is believed, never existed. It was unfortunate for Mr. Adams that he was not elected by the people, but held an office which a majority of the people had assigned to another, although that majority failed to elect a majority of electors who were in favor of his rival, General Jackson. The following are the principal topics upon which we propose to dwell, in noticing the administration of Mr. Adams, namely:

Controversy about Creek Lands. | " American System."
Fiftieth Anniversary of Inde- | Election of General Jackson.
pendence.

I. Controversy about Creek Lands. — This controversy was between Georgia and the United States government. The latter had agreed, as Georgia had relinquished her claims to Mississippi, to purchase for her the lands within her territory, owned and occupied by the Creeks, " whenever it could be peaceably done, upon reasonable terms." This agreement the government had in part fulfilled. Georgia demanded the fulfilment of the entire compact. But the Creeks declined selling their lands. The Governor of Georgia, however, had these lands surveyed, and distributed to the citizens by lottery. The general government interfered, to protect the Creeks. The difficulty became serious, and involved Georgia and the United States in perplexity. But, at length, the controversy was settled. The United States gave large annuities to the Indians ; whereupon, many agreed to move to a tract of land beyond the Mississippi, the expense of their removal and the first year's subsistence to be borne by the United States.

II. Fiftieth Anniversary of Independence. — 1. This was a day long to be remembered in the annals of the nation. The exultation of feeling throughout the country, that we had reached in safety the fiftieth anniversary of our independence, was great. The day was everywhere celebrated with more than the usual demonstrations of joy. But the most striking feature of the occasion was the simultaneous death of two ex-presidents of the United States, John Adams and Thomas Jefferson. The coincidence in their departure from life was certainly remarkable, more especially as having occurred at that particular juncture.

2. Both had been ministers abroad ; both vice-presidents, and both presidents ; both had lived to a great age ; both were early enlisted in their country's cause ; they were both members of the committee for preparing the Declaration of Independence ; they constituted the sub-committee appointed by the other members to make the draft. Mr. Jefferson was the author of the Declaration itself; Mr. Adams its great supporter on the floor of Congress (p. 169). Both were bold, ardent, unyielding patriots. Where others doubted, they were resolved ; where others hesitated, they pressed forward. These coincidences were surprisingly completed, as already mentioned, by their simultaneous

deaths on the anniversary of liberty, and only at an interval of a few hours.

III. "AMERICAN SYSTEM." — This is a phrase often used at the present day, and denotes that policy advocated by many of protecting home manufactures, by laying duties on foreign articles of the same kind. It began to be employed during the administration of Mr. Adams. No subject has given birth to more controversy. The principle of protection the south have generally opposed; also, importing merchants. In the east and north the farmers, manufacturers and mechanics, have generally been in favor of protection. In May, 1828, a bill for altering the tariff of duties on foreign articles was passed by Congress, but to the country at large the alteration furnished little satisfaction.

IV. ELECTION OF GENERAL JACKSON. — The administration of Mr. Adams, from its very commencement, met with a powerful opposition. The circumstance of his not having been elected by the people, united to the small majority by which he was elected to his office by Congress, was sufficient to call forth loud complaints, on the part of his opponents; and to justify, in their view, a more than usual watchfulness over his administration. Great pains were early taken to render him and his measures unpopular. When, therefore, the presidential election again approached, the claims to the presidency of the rival candidates, Mr. Adams and General Jackson, were urged with a zeal which had no previous parallel. Not only the public acts, but the private lives, of the candidates, were scanned by a most unwarrantable scrutiny, and their private characters most unjustifiably attacked. Mr. Adams was ably defended by his friends, and his administration shown to be free from extravagant expenditures, as was charged; but the popularity of General Jackson secured his election by even a greater majority than his most sanguine friends had predicted.

23*

UNITED STATES.

PERIOD XII.

ANDREW JACKSON, President.

Inaugurated at Washington, March 4th, 1829; retired March 3d, 1837.

J. C. CALHOUN and MARTIN VAN BUREN, Vice-presidents.

HEADS OF DEPARTMENTS.

Martin Van Buren,	New York,	March 6,	1829,	Sec's of State.
Edward Livingston,	Louisiana,	January 12,	1832,	
Louis M'Lane,	Delaware,	May 29,	1833,	
John Forsyth,	Georgia,	June 27,	1834,	
Samuel D. Ingham,	Pennsylvania,	March 6,	1829,	Sec's of Treasury.
Louis M'Lane,	Delaware,	January 13,	1832,	
William J. Duane,	Pennsylvania,	May 29,	1833,	
Roger B. Taney,	Maryland, (appointed in the recess; negatived by the Senate),			
Levi Woodbury,	New Hampshire,	January 27,	1834,	
John H. Eaton,	Tennessee,	March 9,	1829,	Sec's of War.
Lewis Cass,	Ohio,	December 30,	1831,	
John Branch,	North Carolina,	March 9,	1829,	Sec's of the Navy.
Levi Woodbury,	New Hampshire,	December 27,	1831,	
Mahlon Dickerson,	New Jersey,	June 30,	1834,	
William T. Barry,	Kentucky,	March 9,	1829,	Postmasters Gen.
Amos Kendall,	Kentucky,	March 15,	1836,	
John M. Berrien,	Georgia,	March 9,	1829,	Attorneys Gen.
Roger B. Taney,	Maryland,	December 27,	1831,	
Benjamin F. Butler,	New York,	June 24,	1834,	

SPEAKERS OF THE HOUSE OF REPRESENTATIVES.

Andrew Stevenson,	Virginia,	Twenty-first Congress,	1829.
Andrew Stevenson,	Virginia,	Twenty-second do.	1831.
Andrew Stevenson,	Virginia,	Twenty-third do.	1833.
John Bell,	Tennessee,	Twenty-fourth do.	1834.
James K. Polk,	Tennessee,	Twenty-fifth do.	1835.

1. THE condition of the United States, on the accession of General Jackson, was one of almost unexampled prosperity. The country was at peace with all nations; the national debt was in a course of rapid diminution; the treasury had within its vaults more than five millions of dollars; the revenue was annu-

ally exceeding, by a large surplus, the demands of the government; and the several branches of occupation — agriculture, commerce, and manufactures — were in a highly flourishing state.

2. A sketch of the more prominent measures and events of General Jackson's administration will require us to notice the following topics, namely :

Removals from Office.	Death of Lafayette.
National Bank.	Deposit and Distribution Act.
Georgia and the Cherokees.	Florida War.
Internal Improvements.	Admission of Arkansas.
Indian Hostilities.	Admission of Michigan.
Discontents in South Carolina.	Treasury Circular.
Reëlection of General Jackson.	Election of Mr. Van Buren.
Removal of the Deposits.	

I. REMOVALS FROM OFFICE. — 1. Immediately following his induction into office, General Jackson commenced a "work of reform," as he denominated it, and which he indicated, in his inaugural address, he should attempt, — namely, the removal of the then incumbents in office under the general government, and the appointment of his political friends. This he accomplished, in a brief time, to the number of hundreds, while the whole number removed by his predecessors was less than one hundred.* By the opposers of his administration, these removals, so numerous, and chiefly on party grounds, were strongly censured. He was charged with usurping an authority not conferred by the constitution, which, it was contended, only gave him the right to fill vacancies, either accidentally occurring, or caused by some official misconduct. It was further urged, that no preceding administration had made such radical changes; and that, even if such removals might be regarded as constitutional, such a precedent was both dangerous and inexpedient.

2. On the other hand, the friends of the president justified

---

* During Gen. Washington's administration, there were nine removals; of these, one was a defaulter.

In Mr. Adams' administration, there were ten removals; one of these was a defaulter.

In Mr. Jefferson's, there were thirty-nine.

In Mr. Madison's, there were five removals; of which three were defaulters.

In Mr. Monroe's, there were nine removals; of these, one was for dealing in slaves (Guinea), two for failures, one for insanity, one for misconduct, and one for quarrels with a foreign government.

In John Quincy Adams', there were two removals, both for cause.

his course. They maintained that he was " solely invested with the right of removal; that it was a discretionary right, for the exercise of which he was responsible solely to the nation; that that power was given to enable him, not only to remove incumbents for delinquency or incapacity, but with the view of reforming the administration of the government, and introducing officers of greater efficiency, or sounder principles, into its various departments."

3. On the assembling of Congress, these changes were the subject of much discussion in the Senate. A warm opposition was instituted, by the minority in that body against the whole course of the executive in relation to removals, both on the ground of their unconstitutionality and inexpediency. Many of those appointed were, however, confirmed; but several were rejected by strong votes.

II. NATIONAL BANK. — 1. In his first message, December, 1829, General Jackson took strong ground against the renewal of the charter of the United States Bank, which would expire in 1836. The bank had, as yet, asked no such renewal; but the subject being pressed upon the attention of Congress, by the president, thus early, it was referred to a committee, which reported that Congress had a constitutional right to charter a national bank, and that such a measure was expedient. In these views the Senate concurred with the committee, in opposition to the strongly expressed dissent of General Jackson.

2. In December, 1832, the president and directors of the bank formally petitioned for a renewal of their charter; and, in 1833, a bill passed both branches of Congress to that effect. But, soon after, it was returned by the president, with objections; and, not being repassed by a majority of two-thirds, the bank ceased to be a national institution, on the expiration of its charter, in 1836.

3. Although not unexpected to the country, the veto thus put upon the bill by the president gave great dissatisfaction to the friends of the bank, in every section of the United States. A general disturbance of the currency was predicted, as the necessary consequence. " We have arrived at a new epoch," said one of the advocates of the bank, on the floor of the Senate. " We are entering on experiments with the government and the constitution of the country, hitherto untried, and of fearful and appalling aspect."

III. GEORGIA AND THE CHEROKEES. — 1. One of the most embarrassing subjects which fell under the cognizance of the new administration related to the Indian tribes within the limits of the states, already admitted into the Union; but, especially, to the Cherokees, a powerful tribe within the limits of Georgia. This state laid claim to the territory occupied by the tribe; and, encouraged by the views of the executive, — namely, that he could not interpose to prevent a state from extending her laws over the tribes within her limits, — authorized an intrusion upon the Indian territory for the purpose of surveying it, and extending her jurisdiction over it. The state laws were accordingly attempted to be enforced. One George Tassel, a Cherokee, was arraigned for the murder of another Cherokee, tried and condemned, by the state authorities. Several missionaries were warned to quit the Indian territory; and, on refusal, were taken, and, for some time, imprisoned.

2. The case of the missionaries, however, was, at length, brought before the Supreme Court of the United States. The decision of that court, March 30, 1832, involved the question of jurisdiction over the country of the Cherokees. The claims of Georgia were set aside, by this decision, as unconstitutional; and her laws, by which the Indians had been deprived of their rights, and the missionaries confined and imprisoned, were pronounced null and void. This decision of the supreme judicial tribunal of the United States, however, was resisted by Georgia, and the missionaries continued in prison.

3. This unpleasant controversy was, at length, ended, by a letter addressed, January 8th, 1833, by the missionaries, to the Governor of Georgia, in which they informed him that they had forwarded instructions to their counsel to prosecute the case no further. Upon this, the governor issued his proclamation, remitting the further execution of the sentence, and discharging the missionaries from prison. We shall only add, that, in May, 1838, a military force, of several thousand men, under the command of General Scott, was assembled on the Cherokee territory, for the purpose of removing the nation to the territory assigned them, beyond the great river of the west, in accordance with the policy recommended by General Jackson, to remove all Indian tribes, within any of the states, to a location beyond the Mississippi.

IV. INTERNAL IMPROVEMENTS. — 1. During the administration of Washington and the elder Adams, no application was made of the public revenue to internal improvements. But, during the presidency of Mr. Jefferson, the internal improvement policy was begun, by an act passed in 1802, making appropriations for opening roads in the North-west Territory. This was followed by other similar appropriations. During Mr. Madison's administration, the appropriations were increased, and still further augmented while Mr. Monroe was in office. On the accession of Mr. Adams, the policy was still pursued ; and more appropriations were made for the above object, during his administration, than during those of all his predecessors.

2. On the accession of General Jackson, however, he manifested strong opposition to the policy, as unconstitutional and inexpedient; and accordingly vetoed several bills, which had passed both branches of Congress, making such appropriations.＊ Notwithstanding, however, the views of the executive, the houses re-passed several of these vetoed bills by decided majorities, thus showing that they considered such appropriations as an established policy of the country.

V. INDIAN HOSTILITIES. — During the spring of 1832, hostilities were commenced by the Sacs, Foxes and Winnebagoes, in the Wisconsin Territory, under the celebrated chief Black Hawk. This aggression created a necessity for the interposition of the executive, who ordered a portion of the troops, under Generals Scott and Atkinson, together with a detachment of militia from the State of Illinois, into the field. After a harassing warfare, prolonged by the nature of the country, and the difficulty of procuring subsistence, the Indians were defeated, and Black Hawk and the prophet were taken prisoners. Subsequently, a treaty was made with these tribes, by which a large tract of territory was ceded to the United States; and, for the purpose of making an impression upon Black Hawk and other chiefs, as to the power and resources of the states, they were taken to Washington, and through several of the larger cities of the Union.

VI. DISCONTENTS IN SOUTH CAROLINA.— 1. The year 1832 was distinguished for serious discontents in South Carolina, arising from dissatisfaction with the tariff of 1828. This tariff had been slightly modified in 1832 ; but the reduction of duties was less than South Carolina desired and expected. Great dissatisfaction, therefore, was the consequence. By her convention, held November 24th, at Columbia, the tariff laws were declared unconstitutional, and therefore null and void ; and her citizens, and the authorities of the United States, were forbidden to enforce the duties imposed by these acts.

2. This tone of menace naturally aroused the executive to corresponding energy and decision. He immediately issued a

---

＊ These were the Maysville Road bill, the Washington Turnpike, the Louisville and Portland Canal, and the road from Detroit to Chicago; and the Light-house bill, Harbor bill, &c.

proclamation, which will long be admired for its sound and able exposition of the principles of the constitution, for its breathings of a spirit of exalted patriotism, and its eloquent appeal to South Carolina herself, and to other states which were, perhaps, ready to join her standard, to remember the toil and blood which American liberty cost, the sacredness of the constitution, and the importance of the preservation of the Union. This able and judicious document of the president had no other effect, however, than to raise still higher the excitement in South Carolina. The Legislature authorized putting the state in a posture of defence, by raising troops, &c. Everything betokened a serious collision with the general government.

3. While the storm was apparently thus gathering strength, and was ready to burst in still greater violence upon the nation, two events occurred which served to allay it, and, indeed, were the harbingers of comparative peace and amity. The first of these was an affectionate appeal of the General Assembly of Virginia to the patriotism and magnanimity of South Carolina, expressed in a preamble and resolutions, as honorable to the "Ancient Dominion" as any act of her life, and worthy of her in the days of Patrick Henry and his contemporaries. The other event was the passage of a bill, introduced by Mr. Clay, termed the "compromise bill," which was designed as an act of pacification between the north and south, — a middle course between extremes ; and, although not entirely satisfactory, perhaps, to either party, it was accepted by both, and was the means, under Providence, of staying the risen storm. This bill provided for the gradual reduction of duties till 1843, when they were to sink to the level of twenty per cent.

VII. REËLECTION OF GENERAL JACKSON. — In the autumn of 1833, another presidential election occurring, the returns of the electoral votes exhibited a large majority in favor of General Jackson over Mr. Clay, the rival candidate. Martin Van Buren was elected vice-president.

VIII. REMOVAL OF THE DEPOSITS.— 1. By the laws of 1816, the public moneys were to be deposited with the United States Bank, subject to be removed only by the Secretary of the Treasury. As the president, however, had become hostile to the bank, he affected to believe that these moneys were no longer safe in the keeping of that institution. Accordingly, assuming the power, he directed Mr. Duane, the then secretary, to remove them to certain local banks ; which, however, the latter declining to do, that functionary was removed, and Roger B. Taney appointed in his place, who acceded to the wishes of the president.

2. Early in 1833, this removal attracted the attention of
Congress. Confidence as to the stability of the pecuniary institutions of the country began to be shaken, and predictions
of great derangement became prevalent. Two important resolutions were, therefore, introduced, and received the sanction
of the Senate: — that the reasons assigned by the secretary
for removing the public moneys were unsatisfactory, and that
such moneys as should be received after 1834 should be placed
with the United States Bank, in conformity to law. This
resolution, which gave great dissatisfaction to the president, as
reflecting upon him, remained on the Senate's journal till January
15th, 1837, when it was expunged, with great ceremony, by that
body, a majority of whom were, at this latter date, the friends
of the administration.

IX. Death of Lafayette. — On the 21st of June, the death
of this illustrious personage was announced to Congress, in a message from the president. This event occurred at La Grange, in
France, on the 20th of May. In his message, the president
spoke of him in terms of appropriate honor; of his character,
his love of liberty, his sacrifices in the cause of the Americans,
his efforts for the good of mankind. A joint select committee
of both houses reported a series of appropriate resolutions,
among which was one requesting the president to address a
letter of condolence to his surviving family, and another to
appoint John Quincy Adams to deliver, at the next session of
Congress, an oration on the life and character of this illustrious
man.

X. Deposit and Distribution Act. — As the United
States Bank was no longer the fiscal agent of the government,
for the reception and management of its funds, as it had been
for years, Congress provided by law for their deposit with certain banks in the several states. By means of this accession,
these banks were enabled, and by the president were encouraged,
to increase their loans to citizens and corporations; which they
did, to a most unjustifiable extent. Money, therefore, was
obtained with the greatest facility, and a spirit of speculation
promoted, which, in the issue, ruined thousands, and caused a
large loss to the government itself; the " pet " banks, as these
were called, being unable to restore their deposits to the government.

XI. Florida War. — 1. Towards the close of 1835, the
Seminole Indians, in Florida, commenced hostilities against the
settlements of the whites in their neighborhood. To this they
were incited by an attempt of the government to remove them

to lands west of the Mississippi, in accordance with a treaty executed in 1832, the validity of which the Indians denied. To this removal, Micanopy, the King of the Seminoles, and Osceola, their most distinguished warrior, were strongly opposed. It was his wish, the latter said, to rest in the lands of his fathers, and to have his children sleep by his side.

2. We shall not enter minutely into the history of this most sanguinary war. It was as savage and relentless as any recorded in American annals. Osceola bore himself with a spirit of determination and heroic bravery, only equalled by Philip of Pokanoket, in the earlier history of the country. He had been exasperated by an unjust imprisonment by General Thompson; and when, at length, he obtained his liberty, despite of all his promises, he rallied his forces, to mark his path with destruction.

3. In December, Major Dade and one hundred men, while marching to the aid of General Clinch, stationed at Fort Drane, about seventy miles south-west from St. Augustine, and who was in danger, were waylaid, and, with the exception of four, were all cut off at a blow; and the four were so horribly mangled that they subsequently died. About the same time, General Thompson, in the neighborhood of Fort King, sixty-five miles from St. Augustine, and with him two hundred and fifty men, were suddenly attacked while at dinner; and nearly one-half of the number was killed, among whom was General Thompson himself.

4. In May, 1836, several of the Creek towns and tribes joined the Seminoles, and from that time murders and devastations increased. The southern mail routes in Georgia and Alabama were infested by the Indians; steamboats, stages, towns, were attacked, and thousands compelled to fly for their lives.

5. At length, the Creeks, who had joined the Seminoles, were subdued, and were compelled to remove by thousands to the west of the Mississippi. But the Seminoles continued the war, which extended into the administration of Mr. Van Buren.

XII. ADMISSION OF ARKANSAS AND MICHIGAN. — 1. On the 15th of June, 1836, a resolution passed Congress admitting Arkansas into the Union, on an equal footing with the original states. And, on the same day, a similar resolution admitted Michigan, under certain conditions.

2. The first of these states has its name from its principal river; the second, from the lake on its borders. Arkansas was originally a part of the great Louisiana tract, as subsequently it

24

was comprehended in the territory of Missouri.   This being, at length, divided, the southern part was not long after formed into a territory, by the name of Arkansas.   In 1836, she rose to the dignity of an independent state.

3. The condition upon which Michigan was to be received into the Union was the assent of a convention of delegates, to be elected by the people of said state, to the boundaries of said state, as described in the act of admission.   A controversy had arisen between Ohio and Michigan as to the boundary line between those states, which was settled by the above act ; and to this the assent of Michigan was required.   This assent was subsequently given ; and her admission followed on that assent, January 26th, 1837.

XIII. TREASURY CIRCULAR. — On the 11th of July, an important circular was issued by the Secretary of the Treasury.   By this the receivers of public money were required, after the following 15th of August, to receive nothing but gold and silver for all governmental dues.   This was deemed, by a large portion of the people, as exceedingly arbitrary ; and, though sanctioned and doubtless suggested by the president, contributed to urge forward the disasters to the country which subsequently followed.

XIV. ELECTION OF MR. VAN BUREN. — In 1837, the presidential election resulted in the elevation to that distinguished office of Martin Van Buren, of New York.   Richard M. Johnson, of Kentucky, was chosen vice-president by the Senate, no choice having been effected by the people.

UNITED STATES.

PERIOD XIII.

MARTIN VAN BUREN, President.

Inaugurated at Washington, March 4th, 1837; retired March 3d, 1841.

RICHARD M. JOHNSON, Vice-president.

HEADS OF THE DEPARTMENTS.

John Forsyth,	Georgia,	(continued in office),	Secretary of State.
Levi Woodbury,	N. Hampshire,	(continued in office),	Sec'y of Treasury.
Joel R. Poinsett,	S. Carolina,	March 7, 1837,	Secretary of War.
Mahlon Dickerson,	New Jersey,	(continued in office),	Sec's of the Navy.
James K. Paulding,	New York,	June 30, 1838,	
Amos Kendall,	Kentucky,	(continued in office),	Postmasters Gen.
John M. Niles,	Connecticut,	May 25, 1840,	
Benjamin F. Butler,	New York,	(continued in office),	Attorneys General.
Felix Grundy,	Tennessee,	September 1, 1838,	

SPEAKERS OF THE HOUSE OF REPRESENTATIVES.

James K. Polk,	Tennessee,	Twenty-sixth Congress,	1837.
R. M. T. Hunter,	Virginia,	Twenty-seventh do.	1839.

1. PRIOR to the elevation of Mr. Van Buren to the presidency, he had been long in public life; and had been honored with several offices in his native state, and under the general government. His talents, learning and experience, though not greater than those of many others of his countrymen, were generally allowed to be adequate to his station. He had not, indeed, like all his predecessors, been connected more or less with the scenes of the Revolution, for he was born in the concluding year of the war. But, in the swiftly revolving years, it was evident that the time must soon come when others than the men of '76 would be called to the helm of government. On the day of Mr. Van Buren's inauguration, a long and elaborate farewell address by General Jackson to the people of the United States was circulated in Washington, and thence was extensively spread through the country.

2. In developing the administration of Mr. Van Buren, the following topics will be noticed :

Condition of the Country.	Internal Improvements.
Suspension of Specie Payments.	Difficulties in Maine.
Extra Session of Congress.	Border Troubles.
Resumption of Specie Payments.	Sub-Treasury Bill.
Seminole War.	Election of General Harrison.

I. CONDITION OF THE COUNTRY. — In less than a month after the accession of Mr. Van Buren, the pecuniary affairs of the country, seriously deranged as they had been during the latter part of General Jackson's administration, became visibly worse. During March and April, the failures in the city of New York were alone estimated to amount to nearly one hundred millions of dollars. Confidence, consequently, was destroyed. Not a few who retired at night in comparative affluence awoke in the morning bankrupt, and without a home.

II. SUSPENSION OF SPECIE PAYMENTS. — In this state of pecuniary embarrassment, Mr. Van Buren was earnestly solicited, by a delegation from New York, sent for that purpose, to rescind the "specie requiring circular," and to summon at once an extra session of Congress. But both these requests he saw fit to deny. Two days after the report of the above delegation to their constituents in New York, the banks in that city, without exception, ceased to redeem their notes in specie. This exciting and depressing intelligence travelled with unwonted speed, producing, in its progress, in all parts of the country, a similar suspension on the part of the banks.

III. EXTRA SESSION OF CONGRESS. — Although the president had declined convoking Congress, subsequent events early pressed that measure upon him. At his summons, therefore, that body met on the 4th of September, and closed its session on the 16th of October following. But it did little for the general relief, as had been solicited, confining its legislation to two measures, which had respect only to the interests and security of the government. One was the postponement to the 1st day of January, 1839, of the payment of the fourth instalment of the deposits with the states ; and the second was the issue of treasury notes to an amount not exceeding ten millions of dollars, reimbursable in one year, and of denominations of not less than fifty dollars.*

* In his message to Congress, at its extra session, the president assigned, as the causes of the pecuniary distress, over-action in business, arising from the excessive issues of bank paper, and other facilities for the acquirement

IV. RESUMPTION OF SPECIE PAYMENTS. — To the great joy of the whole country, especially commercial men, the banks, by previous concert, resumed the payment of specie, on the 13th of August, 1838. But, in October of the following year, the banks of Philadelphia again suspended; and in this they were followed by the banks of Pennsylvania generally, and the states south and west. The suspension of specie payments in May, 1836, was begun by the banks of New York, and the rest of the Union followed. In 1837, the banks of New York were required by law to resume. They naturally endeavored to induce other banks to do voluntarily what they were compelled to do by law. The public also were anxious for resumption. An effort was made to accomplish this object, and was effected, contrary, however, to the opinion of some of the ablest financiers of the country, who predicted a relapse. This prediction was verified in respect to the banks of Philadelphia and the south. The banks of New York and New England, with some few temporary exceptions, resolved to continue the payment of specie, which, with great effort, they were able to accomplish.

V. SEMINOLE WAR. — 1. The war with the Seminoles, in Florida, which commenced during the presidency of General Jackson, was continued during the greater part of Mr. Van Buren's administration, occasioning accumulated expense to the government, while the sickly character of the climate in which it was carried on proved generally fatal to the American soldiers engaged in it.

2. At length, a treaty was effected with the Indians, by General Jessup, by which they agreed upon a suspension of hostilities, and to their removal beyond the Mississippi. Through the influence of Osceola, however, this treaty was broken; whereupon General Jessup seized and confined him, although he had come to the American camp under protection of a flag. For this

---

and enlargement of credit; the contraction of a large foreign debt; investments in unproductive lands; vast internal improvements; and the great loss sustained by the commercial emporium of the nation in the fire of December, 1835. This calamity occurred during a season of intense cold, on the night of the 16th of December. Five hundred and twenty-nine buildings were consumed, and property to the amount of nearly twenty millions of dollars. Many of the insurance companies were ruined; but few mercantile houses failed, forbearance being practised by all, and mutual aid being rendered to a most commendable degree. To the opposition, these causes appeared altogether inadequate. They claimed that, prior to General Jackson's attempt to overthrow the bank, no people had enjoyed a better currency. "Our money system was nearly perfect. What a reverse!" said they; "and why has it come upon us? Who can doubt that, if the Bank of the United States had been re-chartered, if the public deposits had remained undisturbed, and the specie circular, or treasury order, had never been issued, the currency would at this time be sound, and the suspension of specie payments have been avoided?"

24*

violation of the flag, General Jessup was by many severely censured. But he pleaded, in justification, the treachery of the savage chief, and the necessity of his confinement to the security of
peace. Osceola never regained his liberty. After months of
confinement in Fort Moultrie, he ended his life by fever.

3. The capture of this brave Seminole chief did not, however,
terminate the war. Frequent encounters were had with the
Indians during the years 1838, 1839, and 1840. At length, in
December of the latter year, Colonel Harney, distinguished for
his knowledge of Indian warfare, penetrated into the recesses
of the everglades of Florida, where he succeeded in capturing a
considerable number of the enemy.

VI. INTERNAL IMPROVEMENTS. — During Mr. Van Buren's
administration, large sums were appropriated for internal improvements, although he was generally opposed, as was his
predecessor, to the policy. The expenditures were chiefly for
repairs of the Cumberland Road, and its continuance through the
States of Indiana and Illinois; and for light-houses, life-boats,
buoys, and monuments; the latter of which class of objects
would seem to be intimately connected with the interests of
navigation.

VII. DIFFICULTIES IN MAINE. — The north-eastern boundary
had long been a source of difficulty between the United States
and Great Britain. The question had seemed to be on the eve
of a decision by arms between the British authorities in New
Brunswick and the State of Maine. Armed bands had been sent
out, on both sides, to the territory in dispute. In this posture of
things, General Scott was deputed by the executive to repair
to the scene of contention; and, through his wise and conciliatory
policy, the public peace was preserved, although the question was
not yet settled. In 1839, Congress clothed the executive with
ample powers to defend the territory in dispute, should Great
Britain attempt to exercise exclusive jurisdiction over it. Meanwhile, an appropriation was made for sending a special minister
to England, should such a measure be deemed advisable, in the
opinion of the executive.

VIII. NORTHERN BORDER TROUBLES. — 1. The Canada rebellion, — so called, — which broke out during the years 1837–38,
strongly enlisted the sympathies of many Americans, especially in
the northern parts of the States of New York and Vermont.
They regarded it as the sacred cause of liberty and human rights.
In consequence of this, they assumed the name of patriots, and
formed associations called Hunters' Lodges, with the object of
aiding the insurgents in their efforts to establish the independence of Canada.

2. In the prosecution of this design, a daring party took possession of Navy Island, situated in Niagara river, about two miles above the falls, and within the jurisdiction of Upper Canada. This party increased to seven hundred, and were well supplied with provisions, and twenty pieces of cannon. They repeatedly fired upon the Canada shore, and upon passing boats.

3. At length, a small steamboat, called the Caroline, was hired by the insurgents to ply between Navy Island and Schlosser, on the American shore, to furnish them with the means of carrying on the war. In December, a detachment of one hundred and fifty Canadians in five boats, under cover of night, proceeded, with muffled oars, to Schlosser, where they cut the Caroline from her fastenings, and, setting her on fire, let her drift over the falls. A man by the name of Durfee was killed, and two or three more were reported to have been consumed in the steamboat. The Americans, in turn, were greatly excited, and a serious interruption of the peaceful relations of the two governments was prevented only by a prompt and admonitory proclamation of the president.

IX. SUB-TREASURY BILL. — In nearly every message of Mr. Van Buren, he had strongly recommended, and even urged the adoption of a new mode of keeping the public moneys; namely, by the appointment of independent sub-treasurers, to whom the custody of it should be confided,— subject, however, to the call of the Secretary of the Treasury. This was the great financial measure of his administration. At length, in 1840, Congress, which, until now, had rejected the measure, adopted it, to the great gratification of the president and his partisans ; but by the opposition it was long and strongly resisted and condemned.

X. ELECTION OF GENERAL HARRISON. — Mr. Van Buren was a candidate for reëlection in the canvass of 1840. But, during the progress of his administration, great political changes were effected. By not a few, even of his friends, his policy was doubted. His views in regard to banks and currency, according to which his administration had been shaped, had resulted, it was obvious, in a serious derangement of the monetary affairs of the nation, and great embarrassment among men of business. The political campaign, however, was most exciting. For months, the friends of the rival candidates, from Georgia to Maine, were engaged by night and by day. But, at length, the day of decision came. The freemen gathered to the polls, and cast their votes ; which, when collected, were in favor of electors a majority of whom gave their suffrages for William Henry Harrison, of Ohio, as the successor of Mr. Van Buren. John Tyler, of Virginia, was elected vice-president.

UNITED STATES.

WILLIAM HENRY HARRISON, President.

Inaugurated at Washington, March 4th, 1841; died April 4th, 1841.

JOHN TYLER, Vice-President.

HEADS OF THE DEPARTMENTS.

Daniel Webster,	Massachusetts,	March 5, 1841,	Secretary of State.
Thomas Ewing,	Ohio,	March 5, 1841,	Secretary of Treasury.
John Bell,	Tennessee,	March 5, 1841,	Secretary of War.
George E. Badger,	North Carolina,	March 5, 1841,	Secretary of the Navy.
Francis Granger,	New York,	March 5, 1841,	Postmaster General.
J. J. Crittenden,	Kentucky,	March 5, 1841,	Attorney General.

SPEAKERS OF THE HOUSE OF REPRESENTATIVES.

John White,	Kentucky,	Twenty-eighth Congress,	1841.
John W. Jones,	Virginia,	Twenty-ninth do	1843.

1. THE inaugural address of General Harrison was a clear, plain and comprehensive document; less stately than that of Washington, less philosophic than Jefferson's, and less terse than Mr. Madison's; but to the great body of the president's constituents it was very acceptable. In conclusion, the new president beautifully and forcibly alluded to the Christian religion, as intimately connected with, and essential to, the interests of the country. He said: " I deem the present occasion sufficiently important and solemn to justify me in expressing to my fellow-citizens a profound reverence for the Christian religion, and a thorough conviction that sound morals, religious liberty, and a just sense of religious responsibility, are essentially connected with all true and lasting happiness."

2. In one short month from the time he stood on the steps of the eastern portico of the capitol, lifting his hand to heaven, and swearing to be faithful to God and his country, General

Harrison was a pallid corpse in the national mansion. For such a bereavement the nation was in no wise prepared It came upon them with the suddenness of lightning, and as a thunderbolt from the hand of Almighty power. The mourning was sincere, as it was deep and universal. Even political opponents united to do the deceased president honor. Funeral processions were had in every principal city; and funeral orations were pronounced in his favor, or funeral discourses delivered by the ministers of religion, in which suitable admonitions were imparted to the people.

3. The legitimate successor, by the constitution, to the presidential chair, on the demise of General Harrison, was John Tyler, of Virginia, who had been elected to the office of vice-president at the time the former had succeeded to that of president, and who now entered upon the administration of the government.

JOHN TYLER, President.

Assumed the government, April 4th, 1841; retired March 3d, 1845.

[The cabinet of General Harrison continued in office under Mr. Tyler till September, when they all resigned, excepting Mr. Webster, who remained till the 8th of May, 1843, when the Department of State was temporarily filled by the Attorney General, Hugh S. Legaré.]

HEADS OF THE DEPARTMENTS.

Abel P. Upshur,	Va.,	January 2,	1844,	} Secretaries of State.
John C. Calhoun,	S. C.,	March 6,	1844,	
Walter Forward,	Penn.,	September 13, 1841,		}
John C. Spencer,	N. Y.,	March 3,	1843,	} Secretaries of Treasury.
George M. Bibb,	Ky.,	June 15,	1844,	
John C. Spencer,	N. Y.,	December 20, 1841,		}
James M. Porter,	Penn.,	March 8,	1843,	} Secretaries of War.
William Wilkins,	Penn.,	February 15,	1844,	
Abel P. Upshur,	Va.,	September 13, 1841,		
David Henshaw,	Mass.,	July 24,	1843,	
Thomas W. Gilmer,	Va.,	February 15,	1844,	Secretaries of the Navy.
John Y. Mason,	Va.,	March 14,	1844,	
Charles A. Wickliffe,	Ky.,	September 13, 1841,		Postmaster General.
Hugh S. Legaré,	S. C.,	September 13, 1841,		}
John Nelson,	Md.,	January 2,	1844,	} Attorneys General.
John Y. Mason,	Va.,	March 5,	1845,	

1. The bereavement which the nation had experienced seemed to demand from it a solemn recognition of a Divine Providence in the sad event. Accordingly, Mr. Tyler very properly appointed a day of public humiliation, fasting and prayer, to be observed throughout the land, in token of its sense of the divine

judgment, and as a means of securing the continuance of the divine favor. This was well received, and the day was religiously observed throughout our widely extended country.

2. In the room of an inaugural address, President Tyler made an official declaration, in a published document, of the principles and general course of policy which he intended should mark his administration. These, as summarily expressed, were generally satisfactory to his political friends. The principal measures and events of President Tyler's administration will be noticed in the following order:

Extra Session of Congress.	Repeal of Bankrupt Law.
Apportionment of Representatives.	Bunker Hill Monument.
	Explosion on board Steam-ship.
Exploring Expedition.	Treaty with China.
Settlement of North-eastern Boundary.	Annexation of Texas.
	Admission of Florida and Iowa.
Modification of the Tariff.	Election of Mr. Polk.

I. EXTRA SESSION OF CONGRESS. — 1. Previous to his decease, General Harrison had summoned an extra session of Congress, on the 31st of May, 1841. Several important measures were adopted during its session. First, a uniform system of bankruptcy throughout the United States. Many thousands of unfortunate debtors needed relief; and the object of the system was to absolve them from the claims of their creditors, on their relinquishment of all their property. A second measure adopted was the repeal of the sub-treasury law, enacted towards the close of Mr. Van Buren's administration. A third bill passed, providing for the distribution of the net proceeds of the public lands among the several states, according to their population.

2. But the great object of the extra session was the establishment of a national bank. Such an institution, it was thought by many, was greatly needed. But the president, having strong objections to it, vetoed two bills, both of which, but especially the latter, it was thought, would meet his approbation. These vetoes gave great dissatisfaction to the members of President Tyler's cabinet, all of whom, excepting Mr. Webster, resigned.

II. APPORTIONMENT OF REPRESENTATIVES. — The census of 1840 having shown a large increase of population in the United States, — exceeding thirty-two and a half per cent. for the last ten years, and amounting in the aggregate to a fraction more than seventeen millions, — Congress, at its session in 1841-42, made a new apportionment of representatives among the several States, adopting the ratio of one for every seventy thousand six hundred and eighty inhabitants.

III. Exploring Expedition.—During the month of June, 1842, an exploring expedition, fitted out by the general government, returned to the United States, having been absent nearly four years, and having sailed nearly ninety thousand miles. During their absence, they discovered, it was supposed, an antarctic continent. The number of sketches of natural scenery brought home was some five hundred; the number of portraits, about two hundred. Of birds, one thousand species, and twice that number of specimens, were collected, besides great numbers of fishes, reptiles, insects, shells, &c. This expedition was fitted out at great expense, and its results have proved highly honorable, both to the nation which projected and the officers who executed it. Several volumes, containing a history of the expedition, with its discoveries, scientific researches, &c., have been published at the national expense.

IV. Settlement of North-eastern Boundary.—The important event of defining and agreeing upon the north-eastern boundary of the United States took place in 1842; and the treaty with England on this subject, negotiated by Mr. Webster and Lord Ashburton, in behalf of the respective powers, was ratified by the Senate in August. The proper boundary between the United States and the British possessions, in that quarter, had been a matter of serious controversy and difficulty for nearly half a century, and on several occasions had well-nigh produced hostilities. Fortunately, Mr. Webster was still a member of the cabinet, and brought the weight of his character and official station to bear upon the question.

V. Modification of the Tariff.— 1. In 1842, a bill passed Congress making essential alterations in the tariff of 1836. The revenues of the United States are chiefly derived from duties laid on imported goods. It is necessary, therefore, that they should be so laid as to raise sufficient funds for the government. This is conceded by all parties; but a portion of the country would limit the tariff to the actual wants of the government, whatever should become of the manufacturing interest. On the other hand, this interest claims that, in fixing a tariff, respect should also be had to home industry; and that, if necessary to foster and protect it, the tariff should so far be discriminating and protective.

2. The tariff of 1842 was designed not only to raise revenue, but to protect such branches of manufacture as could not be sustained without it. Hence, the bill was powerfully sustained by its friends, and as strongly opposed by its enemies. It

passed both houses of Congress, but the president vetoed it. This was a severe trial to the friends of the measure; and, for a time, they were at a loss how to proceed. But, fortunately, a second bill was introduced, divested of several objectionable features of the former bill, and to this the president gave his sanction.

VI. REPEAL OF THE BANKRUPT LAW. — At the time the bankrupt law was passed (p. 286), there existed a strong sentiment in its favor, throughout the country. But dishonest men took advantage of it to defraud their creditors. Many concealed their property, at the same time declaring that they had none. This brought an otherwise good law into disrepute, and led to its early repeal.

VII. BUNKER HILL MONUMENT. — 1. In June, 1842, this noble monument having been completed, the event was celebrated with appropriate demonstrations of joy. The President of the United States and his cabinet were invited to honor the day and occasion. The celebration took place on the 17th, and an oration was pronounced by Daniel Webster. The scene was grand and imposing. Thousands were gathered to the spot once moistened by the blood of patriots; and grateful homage went up to Him, under whose fostering care the nation enjoyed a measure of prosperity unknown to any other nation on the globe.

2. But scarcely were the festivities of the occasion ended, when the melancholy intelligence was circulated, that Mr. Legaré, the Attorney General, and acting Secretary of State, had suddenly deceased at his lodgings, in Boston. He had followed the president, to mingle in the joys of the occasion; but sickness fell upon him, and in a brief space he was numbered with the dead. He sustained the reputation of a man of rare endowments, of great acquisitions, and exalted character.

VIII. EXPLOSION ON BOARD THE STEAMSHIP PRINCETON. — In March of the following year, a tragical event occurred on board of the United States steamship Princeton, during her return from an excursion down the Potomac, which deserves mention, as, besides others, two members of the cabinet were instantly deprived of life, by the bursting of one of her guns, — Mr. Upshur, the Secretary of State, and Mr. Gilmer, Secretary of the Navy.*

---

* Captain Stockton, the commander of the ship, had invited the president, secretaries with their families, and several members of Congress, to an excursion down the river. The day was fine; the company large and brilliant, — probably not less than four hundred, — of both sexes. During the passage, one of the large guns on board, called the "Peace-maker," carrying a ball of two

IX. TREATY WITH CHINA. — On the 10th of January, 1845, an important treaty between the United States and the Chinese empire was ratified by the Senate, by a unanimous vote. This treaty was concluded by Caleb Cushing, United States commissioner to China, and Tsiyeng, the governor-general, on the part of the Emperor Taow Kwang, at Hang-Hiya, on the 3d of July, 1844. By this treaty, our relations with China were placed on a new footing, eminently favorable to the commerce and other interests of the United States.

X. ANNEXATION OF TEXAS. — On the 1st of March, 1845, the president gave his signature to a joint resolution * for the annexation of Texas to the United States. This annexation had been for some time contemplated by the advocates of the measure ; and had actually been attempted by President Tyler, by treaty, in 1844, which, however, was rejected by the Senate. Now, the subject was brought forward in a different form, and was adopted by a majority of both Houses of Congress. But, while to the president and southern members, generally, it was a favorite object, to the north this mode of admitting a territory appeared unconstitutional, and fraught with serious consequences to the country. It was represented to be an act of injustice to Mexico, and likely to involve the United States in hostilities with that

---

hundred and twenty-five pounds, was fired several times, exhibiting the great power and capacity of that formidable weapon of war. The ladies had partaken of a sumptuous repast; the gentlemen had succeeded them at the table, and some of them had left it. The vessel was on her return up the river, opposite the fort, when Captain Stockton consented to fire another shot from the same gun, around and near which, to observe its effect, many persons had gathered, though by no means so many as had witnessed the previous discharge.

The gun was fired. The explosion was followed, before the smoke cleared away so as to observe its effect, by shrieks of woe, which announced a dire calamity. The gun had burst, three or four feet from the breech, and scattered death and desolation. Mr. Upshur, Secretary of State, Mr. Gilmer, recently appointed Secretary of the Navy, Commodore Kennon, one of its gallant officers, Virgil Maxey, lately returned from a diplomatic residence at the Hague, Mr. Gardiner, of New York, formerly a member of the Senate of that state, were among the slain. Besides these, seventeen seamen were wounded, several of them mortally. Others were stunned by the concussion, among whom were Captain Stockton, Colonel Benton, of the Senate, Lieutenant Hunt, of the Princeton, and W. D. Robinson, of Georgetown.

* To this resolution there were three conditions: — The 1st was, that Texas should adopt a constitution, and lay it before Congress, on, or before, the 1st day of January, 1846. 2. That all mines, minerals, fortifications, arms, navy, &c., should be ceded to the United States. 3. That new states might hereafter be formed out of the said territory. An amendment of Mr. Walker allowed the President of the United States, instead of proceeding to submit the foregoing resolutions to the republic of Texas, as an overture on the part of the United States for admission, to negotiate with that republic.

25

government; besides greatly augmenting the public debt of the country, and increasing the " area of slavery."

XI. Admission of Florida and Iowa. — On the 3d of March, 1845, the day that terminated the official career of Mr. Tyler, Con   s passed an act admitting the above two states into the Union   Florida was so called by Juan Ponce de Leon, as early as 1572, because it was discovered on Easter Sunday; in Spanish, Pascus Florida. Iowa derives its name from a tribe of Indians; and was so called in 1838, when it was first erected into a separate territorial government. For a further account of Florida, see p. 263.

XII. Election of Mr. Polk. — On the occurrence of a new presidential election, the rival candidates were James K. Polk, of Tennessee, and Henry Clay, of Kentucky. The strife between the adherents of each of these was eager and persevering; and for a time the issue appeared doubtful. But the close of the canvass showed that Mr. Polk, the Democratic nominee, had been elected. George M. Dallas, of Pennsylvania, was elected vice-president.

UNITED STATES.

PERIOD XV.

JAMES K. POLK, President.

Inaugurated at Washington, March 4th, 1845; retired March 3d, 1849.

GEORGE M. DALLAS, Vice-president.

HEADS OF THE DEPARTMENTS.

James Buchanan,	Pennsylvania,	March 5,	1845,	Secretary of State.
Robert J. Walker,	Mississippi,	March 5,	1845,	Secretary of Treasury.
William L. Marcy,	New York,	March 5,	1845,	Secretary of War.
George Bancroft,	Massachusetts,	March 10,	1845,	} Sec's of the Navy.
John Y. Mason,	Virginia,	Sept. 9,	1846,	
Cave Johnson,	Tennessee,	March 5,	1845,	Postmaster General.
John Y. Mason,	Virginia,	March 5,	1845,	} Attorneys General.
Nathan Clifford,	Maine,	Dec. 23,	1846,	
Isaac Toucey,	Connecticut,	June 21,	1848,	

SPEAKERS OF THE HOUSE OF REPRESENTATIVES.

John W. Davis,	Indiana,	Twenty-ninth Congress,	1845.
Robert C. Winthrop,	Massachusetts,	Thirtieth,	do.	1847.

THE events and measures which signalized the administration of Mr. Polk were the following :

Death of General Jackson.	Expedition of Doniphan.
Admission of Texas.	Reduction of Vera Cruz.
Difficulties with Mexico.	Battle of Cerro Gordo.
Division of Oregon.	Progress of the Army.
Commencement of Hostilities.	Contreras. — Churubusco.
Siege of Fort Brown.	Attempts at Peace.
Battle of Palo Alto.	Reduction of Chepultepec.
Battle of Resaca de la Palma.	Occupation of Mexico.
Fall of Monterey.	Treaty.
Proceedings of Congress.	Death of Mr. Adams.
Battle of Buena Vista.	Admission of Wisconsin.
Naval Operations.	Election of General Taylor.
Army of the West.	

I. Death of General Jackson. — 1. On the 8th of June, General Jackson, " the hero of New Orleans," breathed his last, at his residence, at the Hermitage, Tennessee, in the seventy-ninth year of his age. It is said that he died a Christian. He expressed his belief in the Gospel, and rested his hopes of pardon and acceptance with God on the merits of Jesus Christ. He took an affectionate leave of his family, expressing his hope that he should meet them in a better world.

2. General Jackson was, doubtless, no ordinary man. For many years he occupied a prominent place in the affairs of his country. Whatever may have been thought of the wisdom or constitutionality of some of his measures, all united in awarding to him the merit of honesty, and a true desire to promote the welfare of the nation. That he was ardent, and, withal, precipitate in his measures, and in a degree even obstinate, may be admitted, without any meditated wrong to his reputation. But, when death laid him in the grave, political differences were forgotten, and political opponents united in paying a high and well-merited tribute to his memory.

II. Admission of Texas. — 1. On the assembling of Congress, in December, President Polk informed that body that the terms of annexation which were offered by the United States to Texas had been accepted by her (p. 289) ; and that nothing, therefore, remained, to consummate that annexation, but the passage of an act to admit her into the Union on an equal footing with the original states.

2. In accordance with this suggestion, a joint resolution of admission was early introduced into Congress ; and, although great and weighty objections* were urged against a measure so novel in the history of the country, it received a large majority in both branches, with the privilege of sending two representatives to the National Assembly, when her population was insufficient to entitle her to one.

III. Difficulties with Mexico. — 1. In consequence of the foregoing measures of the American Congress in relation to Texas, while claimed by Mexico as her province, the Mexican minister demanded his passports, and left the country ; while, at a subsequent date, the American minister, Mr. Slidell, was refused a

* These objections were, in substance, as follows: — 1. That to enlarge the boundaries of our government, or the territory over which our laws are now established, would be to endanger the permanency of our institutions. 2. That the admission of Texas would extend and perpetuate slavery. 3. That it would lead to a collision with Mexico. 4. That the process of admission was unconstitutional.

reception and recognition as such, by the Mexican government. Thus, as had been predicted, a serious and open rupture with that power was apparently at hand.

2. At length, a single act of the president precipitated the predicted war. This was an order issued to General Taylor, to break up his camp at Corpus Christi, in Texas, where he had, for some time, been stationed, with a body of troops, and pass the river Nueces, claimed by Mexico as her boundary, taking post on the left bank of the Rio Grande, within the territory mutually claimed by Texas and Mexico.

IV. DIVISION OF OREGON. — 1. Prior to Mr. Polk's accession to the presidency, several attempts had been made by the governments of Great Britain and the United States to settle, by negotiation, questions in dispute between them, as to the proprietorship and occupation of Oregon, — all of which, however, had failed. In 1818, it was mutually agreed that the harbors, bays, &c., of that territory, should be open to the citizens of both countries, for ten years. In 1827, this agreement was continued, with the proviso that either party might rescind it, by giving the other party twelve months' notice. In subsequent years, other propositions were made, which failing, in 1845, upon the recommendation of the president, Congress authorized him to give the twelve months' notice.

2. Accordingly, in April, 1846, this notice was given; but, before it was delivered, the British minister informed the president that his government was ready to enter upon the settlement of the vexed question. This being acceded to, Mr. Packenham, on the part of the British government, and Mr. Buchanan, on that of the United States, compromised the difficulties, by a treaty negotiated at Washington.

3. By this treaty, the northern boundary of Oregon was fixed by a line of latitude 49 degrees, while to the British was ceded the whole of Vancouver's Island, and the joint navigation of the Colombia. The amicable settlement of this question was a subject of congratulation in both hemispheres, as, previously, indications were daily increasing of an approaching rupture.

V. COMMENCEMENT OF HOSTILITIES. — 1. Agreeably to orders, General Taylor moved from Corpus Christi, on the 8th of March, 1846, and on the 25th reached Point Isabel, a harbor on the Texas coast, nearest the mouth of the Rio Grande. Having here deposited a portion of his stores, under guard of Major Munroe, with four hundred and fifty men, he proceeded to the mouth of the Rio Grande, opposite the Spanish city, Matamoras.

2. Here he intrenched himself, and commenced a fort, to

25*

which he gave the name of Fort Brown, after its destined commander, and whose guns pointed to the heart of the city.   Meanwhile, the Mexicans industriously fortified Matamoras, while General Ampudia gave notice to General Taylor to break up his encampment, within twenty-four hours.

3. On the 24th of April, General Arista superseded Ampudia, and communicated to Taylor that he "considered that hostilities had commenced, and that he should continue them."   On the same day, Captain Thornton, who had been sent by General Taylor, with sixty-three dragoons, up the river, to reconnoitre, fell into an ambuscade, and was obliged to surrender, with the loss of sixteen killed and wounded.   Captain Thornton himself effected an escape, by an extraordinary leap of his horse ; but, subsequently, he was taken prisoner, and conducted to Matamoras. This was the first actual fight of the war.

VI. Siege of Fort Brown. —1. While these events were transpiring, General Taylor received intelligence that Point Isabel, thirty miles from Fort Brown, where his stores were deposited, was about being assailed.   To keep open communication with that point, and to guard his stores, were essential.

2. Accordingly, leaving Major Brown in command of the fort, with a competent garrison, he commenced his march, with the main body of his army, towards Point Isabel, leaving instructions that, in case the fort was attacked, information should be given by firing the eighteen-pounders at stated intervals.

3. For two days following the departure of the army, the fort remained unmolested ; but, on the third morning, the Mexicans opened a battery of seven guns, killing Sergeant Weigard, but otherwise effecting no material damage.   But, at length, the situation of the fort became critical, — Major Brown having been mortally wounded, — whereupon, the signal-guns were fired.

VII. Battles of Palo Alto and Resaca de la Palma. — 1. The signal-guns were heard by General Taylor, who left Point Isabel, on the evening of the 7th, with a force of two thousand men.   At the distance of seven miles he encamped, resuming his march early on the morning of the 8th.

2. In their progress, they, at length, reached a broad prairie, bounded by Palo Alto, a thick grove of dwarfish trees.   On either side of the American army were ponds of water, and beyond them chapparal, or thick entangled hedges.   Upon this prairie a large body of Mexicans were drawn up in battle array.

3. No time was lost on the part of the Americans.   The battle soon opened ; and, at the expiration of two hours, the

Mexican batteries began to slacken.   They were unable to stand before the terrible fire of Ringgold's, Churchill's, Duncan's and Ridgeley's guns.   They again formed in a new line, but in a few hours were compelled to retire.   Before doing so, however, they poured upon Ringgold's battery a tempest of balls.

4. The brave Captain Page fell, mortally wounded; and nearly at the same time the heroic Ringgold met a similar fate. Night now put an end to the contest.   The Mexicans left the field in disorder : the Americans sank exhausted upon the ground where they were.

5. At two o'clock on the following morning, the American army was summoned to renew its march towards Fort Brown. Towards evening, what was their surprise, on approaching a ravine, called Resaca de la Palma, or the Dry River of Palma, to discover the Mexican army occuping this well-selected spot, and again drawn up in order of a battle !

6. A vigorous action immediately ensued.   It was a shorter contest than at Palo Alto, but much more severe, and still more favorable to the American arms.*   Eight pieces of artillery were captured, three standards, and a large number of prisoners, among whom was the Spanish-Mexican General La Vega.   Following the battle, General Taylor continued his march to Fort Brown ; and, on the 18th, took possession of the city of Matamoras, on the opposite side of the river,

7. Shortly after the foregoing battles, — that is, on the 23d of May, — the Mexican government made a formal declaration of war against the United States.   This latter power made no such declaration ; but, on receiving from General Taylor an account of the first blood shed (April 24th), when Captain Thornton's party was waylaid, and a portion slain, the president announced to Congress, May 11th, that the Mexicans had "invaded our territory, and shed the blood of our citizens on its

---

* It was during this battle that the celebrated charge of Captain May occurred.   A Mexican battery, under command of General La Vega, was doing great execution, when May was ordered to take it.   ".I will do it," said he, at the same time wheeling his troops, and pointing them to the battery, pouring forth its terrific explosions.   "Remember your regiment ! men, follow ! "   He struck his charger, and bounded on before them, while a deafening cheer answered his call; and immediately the whole were dashing toward the cannons' mouths.   May outstripped them.   Wonderful was his escape, wonderful the escape of so many of his followers, exposed as they were to so fearful a fire.   At a single bound May's horse cleared the battery; the horses of a few others were equal to the leap; wheeling again, they drove the gunners off, and took possession of the battery, which they now employed against the enemy.   It was a bold, perilous enterprise, but greatly added to the issues of the day.

own soil." To this Congress responded in two ways: first, by declaring that "war existed by the act of Mexico;" and second, by authorizing the raising of fifty thousand volunteers for twelve months, and appropriating ten millions of dollars for carrying on the war.

VIII. FALL OF MONTEREY. — 1. Following the occupation of Matamoras, General Taylor prepared, by order of the government, to advance into the interior of Mexico. During these preparations, occupying more than three months, several Mexican villages — Reinosa, Weir, Revilla and Camargo — were taken possession of.

2. The latter part of August, the first division of the American army, under General Worth, took up its line of march towards Monterey, the capital of New Leon, some two hundred miles from Matamoras; soon after which, the other divisions followed, under command of General Twiggs and General Butler. On the 9th of September, the several divisions were concentrated at a place called Walnut Springs, three miles distant from Monterey.

3. This latter was a strongly fortified place, with a competent garrison, under command of General Ampudia. On the evening of the 19th of September, a reconnoissance of the fortifications was made, and on the following day the attack was commenced by the division of General Worth. On the 21st and 22d, the siege was continued. On the morning of the 23d, the streets of the upper part of the city became the scene of action; here, all that day, the battle raged, the Americans proceeding from house to house, and from square to square.

4. Early on the 24th, sensible of his critical position, Ampudia prepared to surrender. A suspension of hostilities was arranged for that purpose, and terms of capitulation were agreed upon. The Mexican forces were permitted to retire, and marched out with the honors of war. They consisted (besides forty-two pieces of mounted cannon) of seven thousand troops of the line, and two thousand irregulars. The American troops amounted to less than seven thousand. The loss of the latter was much less than that of the former.

5. General Taylor, at the same time, acceded to a proposal by Ampudia for an armistice, made on the ground that a peace might shortly be expected, through the influence of Santa Anna, who had superseded Paredes, as president of the Mexican republic. To this he was also inclined, from the want of provisions to supply and of troops to guard the Mexican army, should he retain them as prisoners. The armistice thus allowed

was to continue eight weeks, unless revoked by one or both of the interested governments. This the American government did, as early as was practicable.

IX. PROCEEDINGS IN CONGRESS. — 1. Besides providing for carrying on the war in Mexico, Congress, during its session of 1845–46, passed several important bills which it belongs to this place to mention: — one ·for protecting the rights of American citizens in Oregon ; a second, establishing a Smithsonian Institute, for the increase and diffusion of knowledge among men, from funds, to the amount of half a million of dollars, given for that purpose, in 1835, by James Smithson, Esq., a generous and philanthropic Englishman ; a third, reëstablishing the sub-treasury ; and a fourth, altering the tariff of 1842.

2. Until now, the tariff had been adjusted with reference to protecting the manufacturing interests of the country ; and hence discriminating and specific duties had been laid on imported articles, varying according to the necessity of protection. But, by the tariff of 1846, this system of protection was in a great measure abandoned, and an ad valorem duty, or a duty according to the value of the article, substituted. To this measure the Democratic party was pledged, while to the manufacturers of the country it prognosticated — so they thought — unavoidable ruin to many branches, although it might greatly enhance the revenues of the country, which it subsequently did.

X. BATTLE OF BUENA VISTA. — 1. The capture of Monterey having been effected, several months were occupied in various military movements, in the neighboring provinces. General Taylor proceeded to and took possession of Victoria, the capital of Tamaulipas ; General Worth, at the head of nine hundred troops, marched on Saltillo, the capital of Coahuila ; General Wool was ordered to proceed to Chihuahua (Chi-waw-waw), but, finding his proposed route to that province impracticable, he took post in the fertile region of Parras.

2. While thus relatively situated, intelligence reached General Worth that Santa Anna had concentrated a force of twenty-two thousand men at San Luis Potosi, with which he soon intended to make a descent upon him. As General Taylor was at Victoria, two hundred miles distant, General Worth despatched an express to General Wool, to hasten to his assistance. To this the latter responded by an immediate march to Agua Nueva, a distance of one hundred and fifty miles, in four days, and within twenty-one of Saltillo.

3. While at Victoria, the proposed expedition of General

Scott against Vera Cruz (hereafter noticed more fully) was communicated to General Taylor, accompanied by an order to transfer a large portion of his troops to the former. A similar requisition was made upon General Wool. With these orders these patriotic generals, of course, complied, painful as the withdrawal of so many soldiers must have been, in their present position.

4. The movements, also, of Santa Anna, were also communicated to General Taylor; who, having returned to Monterey, took with him three hundred men, and urged his march to the camp of Wool, at Agua Nueva. Their combined force, including officers, amounted to only four thousand six hundred and ninety men.

5. On the 21st of February (1847) the camp of Agua Nueva was broken up, and the army took post at Buena Vista, now placed in charge of General Wool, while General Taylor proceeded to Saltillo, eleven miles, to protect his military stores from a party of Mexicans, under General Minon. Meanwhile, Santa Anna, with his formidable army of more than twenty-two thousand troops, was pressing on to an attack.

6. The following morning, the 22d, memorable as the birthday of the Father of his Country, the American army was drawn up in order of battle, and skirmishing ensued. General Taylor arrived. A haughty summons from Santa Anna to surrender was communicated, to which the hero of Palo Alto gave a characteristic reply, "I beg leave to say that I decline your request." That day ended without a general battle, and the Americans remained under arms the following night.

7. Before sunrise of the 23d, the Mexicans opened the attack. No pen can adequately describe the contest which ensued. It was long, desperate, sanguinary. On the part of the Americans, it was fought at fearful odds. Several times, they were on the point of being overwhelmed. At length, a final, desperate assault was made by Santa Anna, with his concentrated forces, upon the American centre, commanded by General Taylor in person. The shock was tremendous; but, at the critical moment, the batteries of Bragg and Sherman appeared, and decided the contest.

8. The battle ceased only with the departing day. The Americans lay upon their arms, prepared to renew the battle on the following morning; but, during the night, the Mexicans withdrew, leaving their killed to be buried, and the wounded to be nursed by the victors. The loss of the latter bore no comparison to that of the Mexicans; yet, among the American

officers killed, were several of distinguished rank, — Colonels Hardin, McKee, and Yell, together with Captain George Lincoln, aid to General Wool, and Lieutenant-colonel Clay, son of the eminent statesman of that name.

9. The victory of Buena Vista secured to the Americans the quiet possession of the northern provinces of Mexico proper. Consequently, active operations in that quarter ceased ; and some months after, General Taylor, leaving General Wool in command at Monterey, returned to the United States, to receive the admiration and honor to which he was entitled.

XI. NAVAL OPERATIONS. — 1. Having followed the fortunes of General Taylor till his return to the United States, we next proceed to notice other movements during the year 1846. At the commencement of the war, Commodore Sloat was in the Pacific, with a squadron. On the 7th of July, he took possession of Monterey, on that coast ; and, on the 9th, Commodore Montgomery, in charge of a part of the squadron, took Francisco, a port to the north. On the 15th, Commodore Stockton arrived in a frigate, and, in connection with Colonel Frémont (who had been sent out by the government the year previous, and who had, with the aid of Americans, established an independent government round the Bay of Francisco and north), proceeded to Ciudad de los Angelos, the capital, of which Stockton assumed the government, in the name and by authority of the President of the United States.

2. The operations of the " Home Squadron " were confined to the capture of several maritime towns on the Gulf of Mexico, the most important of which were Tobasco and Tampico, — the former, by Commodore Perry, in October; the latter, by Commodore Conner, in November.

XII. ARMY OF THE WEST. — 1. The army so called was organized early after the commencement of the war, and the command of it given to General Kearney, with instructions to undertake the conquest of New Mexico and California.

2. In obedience to these orders, General Kearney left Fort Leavenworth in June, 1846, passing a southerly course across the Platte, the branches of the Kansas, along the Arkansas, and thence south-westerly to Santa Fé, the capital of New Mexico, which he reached on the 18th of August, having accomplished a march of nine hundred miles, through wild and uncultivated regions, in the space of fifty days.

3. Having taken peaceable possession of New Mexico, he organized a government, of which Charles Bent was constituted governor ; and then took up his line of march for California.

Soon after leaving Santa Fé, he was informed, by express, despatched by Colonel Frémont, that the conquest of California had already been achieved ; whereupon, ordering the return of the main body of his troops to Santa Fé, he proceeded, under escort of one hundred men, towards California ; and on the 14th of January, 1847, reached Los Angelos, where he met Commodore Stockton and Colonel Frémont.

4. General Kearney now claimed the government of the province, by virtue of his superior rank, and the authority of the executive. Commodore Stockton advocated the claims of Frémont. The latter refusing to obey the written orders of Kearney, he then proceeded to Monterey ; where, issuing his proclamation as governor, he declared California annexed to the United States.

5. At a subsequent date, Frémont was arrested by Kearney for disobedience to orders, and assumption of undelegated power. On his trial at Washington, the court-martial sentenced him to the loss of his commission. This the president offered to restore, which, however, was declined.

XIII. Expedition of Colonel Doniphan. — 1. Before leaving Santa Fé for California, General Kearney directed Colonel Doniphan to commence his march on Chihuahua, immediately on the arrival of recruits, momentarily expected, under Colonel Price. By a second order, given after Kearney's departure, Doniphan was instructed to march his regiment against the Navajo Indians, who inhabited wild and distant regions at the west, and whose chiefs had failed, contrary to their promise, to be present at a council held at Santa Fé to negotiate a peace.

2. Dividing his regiment into three bands, Doniphan assigned one to Major Gilpin, to pursue a northern route, a second to Colonel Jackson, to take a southerly direction, while with the third, under his immediate command, he would pursue a central course. It was a perilous enterprise; yet, after incredible hardships, and a march of hundreds of miles, it was accomplished, — the chiefs were convened at Ojo Oso, or the Bear Springs, when a treaty was made with them, on the 22d of November.

3. Doniphan next proceeded towards Chihuahua, where he expected to find General Wool ; but, on his route, he learned that Wool had abandoned the enterprise of reaching that province (p. 297). On approaching Chihuahua, he encountered an army of Mexicans, four thousand strong, come out to oppose his progress. These he utterly routed, with a force of one thousand men ; and, on the 2d of March, planted his standard on the citadel

of Chihuahua, a city of forty thousand inhabitants. The province also, with the city, fell into his possession.

4. Having here recruited his army, Doniphan proceeded by Parras to Saltillo, the head-quarters of General Wool, which he reached on the 22d of May. As their time of service terminated with May, he proceeded with his troops to New Orleans, by way of Camargo and the Rio Grande, where they arrived on the 15th of June, having accomplished, doubtless, the longest and most toilsome and perilous march — a distance of five thousand miles — recorded in the annals of American history.

XIV. REDUCTION OF VERA CRUZ. — 1. Although several places in the Mexican empire were in possession of the Americans, to its complete conquest it was deemed necessary to reach its capital, by way of Vera Cruz, a maritime place on the Gulf of Mexico, some two hundred miles south-easterly from the city of Mexico. Nearly opposite, and on an island, stood the Castle of San Juan d'Ulloa, a fortress long celebrated for its strength. The reduction of these — city and fortress — as preliminary to an advance on Mexico, was intrusted to General Scott.

2. The American force employed in this memorable siege amounted to thirteen thousand men, a considerable portion of whom had been detached from the forces of Generals Taylor and Wool (p. 298). The rendezvous of the invading army was the Island of Lesbos, one hundred and twenty-five miles from the city, from which they were conveyed by a squadron under Commodore Conner. The landing was effected on the 2d of March, and the city invested on the 13th.

3. The garrison refusing to surrender, a bombardment of the city was commenced on the night of the 18th. About the same time, two steamers and five schooners opened a brisk fire. On the 23d, at daylight, a naval battery of three thirty-two pounders and three eight-inch Paixhan guns, which the previous day had been transported from the ships, with incredible difficulty, a distance of three miles, over a sandy and difficult route, to a commanding height within seven hundred yards of the city, was prepared to open its terrible fire.

4. Early on the morning of the 26th, the work of destruction having been completed, the garrison offered to surrender. The fortress was surrendered at the same time, with five thousand prisoners (who were dismissed on parole), and five hundred pieces of artillery. Two American officers, Captains Alburtis and Vinton, and ten privates, were killed. Captain Swift died from over exertion.

5. During the assault, not less than six thousand seven hun-

26

dred shot and shells were thrown by the American batteries, weighing, in the aggregate, more than four hundred thousand pounds! "No power of language," says a writer, "can portray the sufferings, agony, despair, and helpless misery, which the inhabitants of Vera Cruz endured for five days and nights, previous to the cessation of hostilities." The number of killed and wounded can never be ascertained.

XV. BATTLE OF CERRO GORDO. — 1. Leaving a garrison at Vera Cruz, General Scott commenced his march towards the capital, by way of Jalapa, on the 8th of April; and, in a few days, the American army reached a mountain-pass called Cerro Gordo, some sixty miles from Vera Cruz. Here Santa Anna had strongly intrenched himself, having fortified several mountain ridges. His force amounted to twelve thousand, while the American troops did not exceed eight thousand five hundred.

2. Finding a front attack of these fortified heights impracticable, General Scott took advantage of a new road, which was discovered and cut by his troops, and by which he was able to reach the rear of the enemy's camp. On the 17th of April, General Scott issued his general order for the operations of the following day. That day arrived, and his plans were carried out. One height after another was taken, until the whole were in possession of the Americans. More than a thousand Mexicans fell, and three thousand were made prisoners, among whom were four generals.

3. Notwithstanding the boast of Santa Anna, previous to the battle, that he would die in the contest, rather than "the Americans should proudly tread the imperial capital of Azteca," he fled on a mule taken from his carriage, which was left behind, as was also his cork limb, his leg having been lost in a battle some years before.

XVI. PROGRESS OF THE ARMY. — 1. Following the battle of Cerro Gordo, the army resumed its march. Jalapa was surrendered, without resistance; as was also the fortress of Perote, some fifty miles distant from Jalapa, and which, next to the castle at Vera Cruz, was considered the strongest in Mexico. Here large military stores fell into possession of the Americans.

2. Next, an advance was made upon Puebla, a walled and fortified city of some seventy or eighty thousand inhabitants, who received the invaders without resistance. In this city General Scott rested his army, while Santa Anna proceeded towards the capital.

XVII. CONTRERAS — CHURUBUSCO. — 1. On the 7th of August, General Scott resumed his march towards the metropolis.

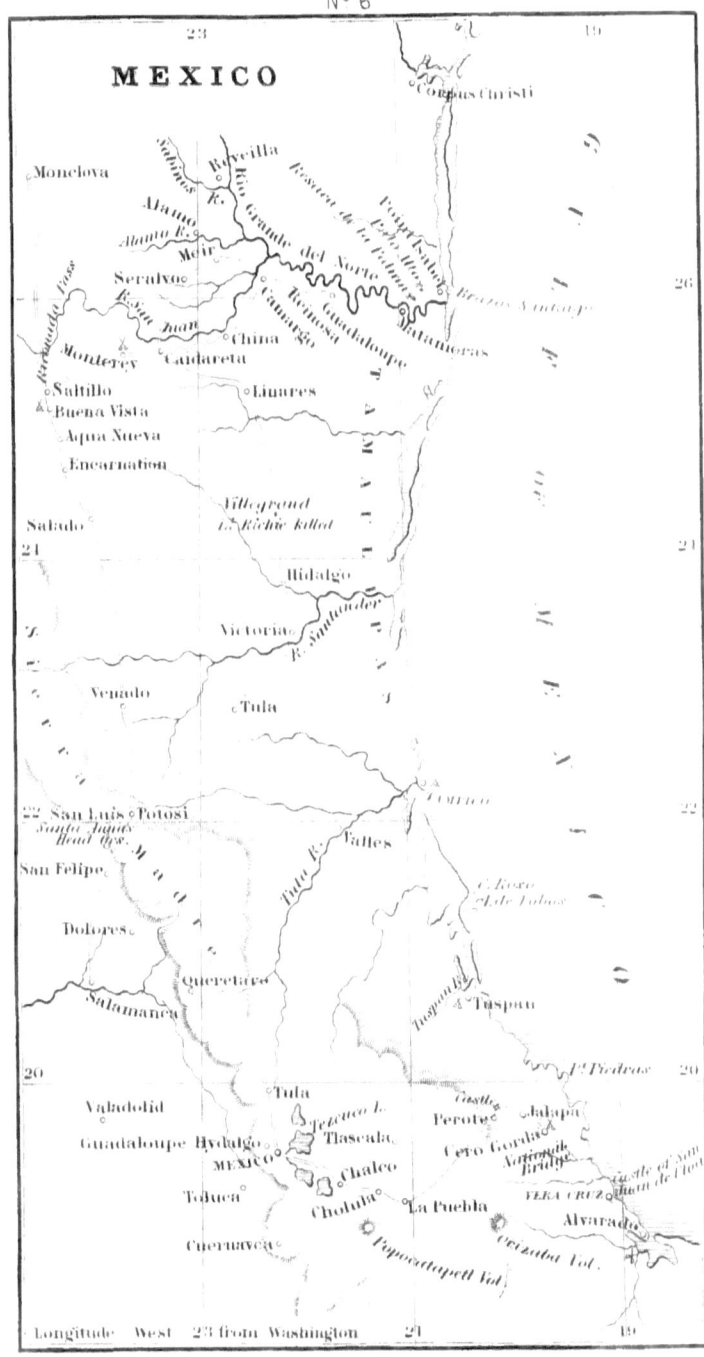

MEXICO

Monclova

Reveilla
Rio Grande del Norte
Corpus Christi

Alamo
Alamo R.
Meir
Seralvo
R. Sua Juan
China
Camargo
Reinosa
Guadaloupe
Matamoras
Brazos Santiago

Monterey
Candareta
Saltillo
Buena Vista
Aqua Nueva
Encarnation
Linares

Salado
Villegrond
L. Richie killed

Hidalgo

Victoria
R. Santander

Venado
Tula

San Luis Potosi
Santa Anas
Head Qrs.
San Felipe
Valles

Dolores
Tula R.

Queretaro
Tuspan R.
Tuspan

Salamanca
P. Piedras

Valadolid
Tula
Guadaloupe Hydalgo
Tezcuco L.
Tlascala
Castle
Perote
Jalapa
MEXICO
Cero Gordo
National Bridge
Toluca
Chalco
Castle el San
Juan de Flou
VERA CRUZ
Cholula
Cuernavaca
La Puebla
Popocatapetl Vol.
Orizaba Vol.
Alvarado

Longitude West 23 from Washington

His accompanying force amounted to ten thousand seven hundred and twenty-eight men; three thousand were left in the hospital, and as a garrison, under Colonel Childs.

2. On the 3d day after leaving Puebla, the army reached the summit of the Cordilleras, when the grand valley of Mexico burst upon their gaze in all its glory. Lakes, plains, cities and cloud-capped mountains, spreading around and beneath, rendered the prospect enchanting. "Far to the left was descried the giant peak of Popocatapetl; before them lay the Lake Tezcuco; and beyond, the domes and towers of the Montezumas."

3. On the 11th, the advance, under command of General Twiggs, reached Ayotla, north of Lake Chalco, fifteen miles from the capital. Between this and the city, by the Vera Cruz road, was a strong fortification, called El Penon, eight miles from Mexico, and which was deemed impregnable. Taking advantage of a concealed road, this fortification was avoided, and the army at length encamped at St. Augustine, on the Acapulco road. Between this point and the city was the fortress of Antonia, and a mile and a half further north, the strongly fortified hill of Churubusco. In the neighborhood of the encampment was Contreras, which was occupied by General Valencia with six thousand Mexican troops, and defended by twenty-two heavy guns. A little past midnight, on the morning of the 20th, a portion of the American army, four thousand five hundred, engaged the Mexican force.

4. The contest was brief, but the Americans were the victors. Three thousand prisoners fell under their power, and more than thirty pieces of artillery, of which two were brass six-pounders which the Mexicans had taken at the battle of Buena Vista.

5. The victory of Contreras was followed, the same day, by other brilliant achievements, — the forcing of San Antonia, the capture of the enemy's citadel, the battle of Churubusco, a hamlet bearing this name, and a second engagement in its rear.

6. All these defences were successively carried, notwithstanding that the Mexicans fought with a bravery and determination proportioned to the magnitude of their cause. In these several battles, thirty-two thousand Mexicans had been engaged and defeated. Three thousand prisoners, including eight generals, had been taken, and two hundred and five other officers. Four thousand of all ranks had been killed or wounded, and thirty-seven field-pieces had been captured. The loss of the Americans was one thousand and fifty-three in killed and wounded. Of the killed, sixteen were officers; and of the wounded, sixty.

XVIII. Attempts at Peace. — 1. The victories thus achieved

presented an easy access to the capital, which might have been occupied the same evening; but, at this point, General Scott decided to halt, for the purpose of effecting a peace, if practicable, before entering the imperial city. Some time previously, the president had commissioned Nicholas P. Trist, Esq., to proceed to Mexico, and negotiate a treaty with the Mexican government, if practicable. The present was considered a favorable time for the accomplishment of that object; and, with this view, an armistice was agreed upon.

2. These negotiations, however, failed; and, as the terms of the armistice had been repeatedly violated, General Scott entered upon a more spirited prosecution of the war. And the first object was an attack upon a fortified building of stone, called El Molinos del Rey, or the King's Mill. This was situated about a mile from Tacubaya, the head-quarters of General Scott, from which, nine miles distant, Mexico was in full view.

3. The battle of Molinos del Rey occurred on the 8th of September, and a melancholy victory was then won. Santa Anna commanded in person, at the head of fourteen thousand men, — five times the number of the assailing party. One brigade lost its three senior officers, — Colonel McIntosh and Major White, wounded, and Colonel Martin Scott killed.

XIX. REDUCTION OF CHEPULTEPEC. — 1. One further object only remained to be secured, in order to an easy access to the capital, — the reduction of Chepultepec. This is a natural and isolated mound, of great elevation; and was strongly fortified at its base, and on its acclivities and heights. Here was the military school of Mexico.

2. On the night of the 11th of September, General Scott erected four heavy batteries, bearing on the fortress. On the morning of the 12th, the bombardment was commenced, and continued on the 13th. The Mexicans resisted with stubborn obstinacy, and yielded, at length, only from dire necessity. The officer who had the honor of striking the Mexican flag from the walls, and planting the American standard, was Major, afterwards Colonel Seymour, of the New England regiment, soon after he had succeeded the gallant Colonel Ransom, who fell while leading his troops up the heights of Chepultepec. Thus the fate of this fortress was sealed, and access to the city opened to the American army.

XX. OCCUPATION OF MEXICO. — 1. The day following the fall of Chepultepec, September 14th, the American army realized the object of their long and eventful march, — the occupation of the capital of the Mexican empire.

2. As early as four o'clock of the 14th, a deputation from the city council waited upon General Scott, demanding terms of capitulation in favor of the church, the citizens, and the municipal authority. These demands were promptly met and denied. Generals Worth and Quitman were directed to move forward, — the one to the Alameda, and the other to the Grand Plaza, where were now reared, above the national palace of Mexico, the stars and stripes of the American republic. Soon after, the commander-in-chief made his grand entrance, with a suitable escort of cavalry. He was welcomed on the Plaza by the victorious army; and here, with his companions in arms, took formal possession of the now conquered city of the Aztecs. On the 16th, the army was directed to offer public and private thanks to God for victory. On the 19th, martial law was proclaimed, in consequence of disturbances occasioned by two thousand convicts, liberated by the flying government, the night before.

XXI. TREATY. — 1. The occupation of Mexico by the American army may be considered as essentially terminating the war. A few other engagements occurred, as at Huamantla and Atlixco, — the desperate efforts of Santa Anna to retrieve his waning fortunes, — but it was all in vain. The proud city of the Aztecs was in possession of the Americans. The Mexican empire was subjugated.

2. To the Mexicans this event was most humiliating. It crushed their hopes, and paralyzed their efforts, leaving them no rational prospect of longer successfully continuing the struggle. They were prepared, therefore, to treat with Mr. Trist, who, on the 2d of February, 1848, signed, with the Mexican commissioners, the treaty of Guadalupe Hidalgo. This treaty, twenty days after, was adopted, with alterations, by the President and Senate. On the 4th of July, these alterations having been confirmed by the Mexican government, the president, by his proclamation, announced the treaty as in full force.*

* Antecedently to the signing of this treaty by Mr. Trist and the Mexican commissioners, the powers of the former had been revoked by the American executive. Notwithstanding this revocation, and his recall, Mr. Trist presumed to act in the existing emergency, and had the approbation of General Scott. As the treaty had undergone important modifications by the American government, President Polk appointed Mr. Sevier, of the Senate, and Mr. Clifford, Attorney General, to proceed to Queretaro, the seat of the Mexican Congress, to explain the modifications made, and to procure the ratification, in which they were successful.

The most important stipulations of this treaty were the following: — 1st. That the American armies should evacuate Mexico within three months. 2d. That, for territory gained, the American government should pay to Mexico three millions of dollars in hand, and twelve millions in four annual

26*

XXII. Death of Mr. Adams. — On the 23d of February, 1848, John Quincy Adams, a former President of the United States, greatly distinguished for his learning, philanthropy, and patriotism, expired, at Washington, at the advanced age of eighty-one years, while attending to his duties in the national legislature, of which he was a member. Mr. Adams was suddenly struck by a fatal paralysis, during the debates in the House of Representatives. He was removed to the speaker's room, where, on the 23d, he expired, uttering, shortly before his death, in the presence of relatives and several congressional associates, the brief but impressive sentence, "This is the last of earth!" He had long been characterized as "the old man eloquent." For more than sixty years he had been employed in the service of his country; and in the various important stations which he had filled, whether at home or abroad, he had honored himself and honored his country.

XXIII. Admission of Wisconsin. — Wisconsin derives its name from the river of that name, which flows through the territory. On the 29th of May, 1848, it was admitted into the Union, as an independent state.

XXIV. Election of General Taylor. — The administration of Mr. Polk was signalized by many interesting and important events. Yet it cannot be said to have been popular, even with the party to which he owed his elevation. Towards the close of his term, few, if any, seriously advocated his reëlection. The Democratic party proposed Lewis Cass, of Michigan, as their candidate; but a majority of electors were in favor of Zachary Taylor, of Louisiana, the "hero of Buena Vista." Millard Fillmore, of New York, was elected vice-president.

---

instalments, besides assuming her debts to American citizens to the amount of three millions and a half more. 3d. That the limits, as relate to Mexico, should begin at the mouth of the Rio Grande, thence to proceed along the deepest channel of that river, to the southern boundary of New Mexico; thence they should follow the river Gila to the river Colorado; thence straight to the Pacific, at a point ten miles south of San Diego.

UNITED STATES.

PERIOD XVI.

ZACHARY TAYLOR, President.

Inaugurated March 5th, 1849; died July 9th, same year.

MILLARD FILLMORE, Vice-President.

HEADS OF DEPARTMENTS.

John M. Clayton,	Delaware,	March 6, 1849,	Secretary of State.
William M. Meredith,	Penn.,	March 6, 1849,	Sec'y of the Treasury.
Thomas Ewing,	Ohio,	March 6, 1849,	Sec'y of Home Depar't.*
George W. Crawford,	Georgia,	March 6, 1849,	Secretary of War.
William B. Preston,	Virginia,	March 6, 1849,	Secretary of the Navy.
Jacob Collamer,	Vermont,	March 6, 1849,	Postmaster General.
Reverdy Johnson,	Maryland,	March 6, 1849,	Attorney General.

* A new office, embracing certain portions of business heretofore transacted in the departments of state, treasury, &c.

SPEAKERS OF THE HOUSE OF REPRESENTATIVES.

Howell Cobb,	Georgia,	Thirty-first Congress,	1849.
Linn Boyd,	Kentucky,	Thirty-second do.	1851.

IT was an occasion of great rejoicing, on Monday, the 5th of March, — the 4th falling on the Sabbath, — when the hero of Buena Vista stood on that spot, at the eastern portico of the national capitol, where had stood Jefferson, Madison, and others, and, baring his head, took the oath prescribed, to support the constitution, which was administered to him by Chief-justice Taney. The inaugural address of General Taylor, like all his official communications to government while in the field, was brief, — shorter than any similar address, by any other president, except Mr. Madison's. To a majority of the people it proved quite satisfactory, and even in England was pronounced an eloquent production. Previous to his election, General Taylor had declined all pledges, excepting the assurance to the nation that he would never be the president of a party; but, if elected, would endeavor to bring back the government to the spirit of the constitution, as understood and administered by

Washington.   Other pledges than this he now declined, standing, as he did, before God and the nation; but this pledge he
was ready to renew.   "In the discharge of these duties," said
he, "my guide will be the Constitution, which I this day swear
to preserve, protect, and defend."   Few measures or events of
national importance signalized the brief administration of General Taylor.   The death of two eminent civilians preceded his
own.

I. Death of Mr. Polk. — This late incumbent of the presidential chair died, at his residence, in Nashville, Tennessee, on
the 15th of June, 1849.   He was a native of Mecklenburg
county, North Carolina, where he was born, on the 2d of
November, 1795.   His father was an enterprising farmer.   At
the early age of thirty, Mr. Polk became a member of Congress.
He was a warm supporter of Mr. Jefferson, and, through life, a
firm and undeviating Democrat.   He was cut off just at the
close of an administration replete with toil and anxiety, and
when he was naturally looking forward to the enjoyment of
repose, in the bosom of his family.

II. Death of Mr. Calhoun. — The death of this distinguished
statesman occurred at Washington, on the 31st of March, 1850,
while a senator in Congress from South Carolina.   There are
few whose names have been more intimately connected with
the political history of the country than Mr. Calhoun.   His
career of public service extended over nearly half a century, —
an eventful period, during which he exerted a powerful influence over the policy of the nation.   He entered Congress previous to the last war with Great Britain, as representative from
South Carolina; since which time, he had been almost uninter-
ruptedly connected with public affairs and measures, having successively filled the offices of representative, senator, secretary of
war, vice-president, and secretary of state, — the duties of which
offices he performed with ability and stern integrity.   The highest honors were paid to his memory.

III. Death of General Taylor. — 1. On the 9th of July, the
death of this distinguished individual — able and brave as a soldier,
upright and honorable as a statesman and a man — occurred in
the national mansion, at Washington, — the result of exposure
and fatigue, on the day of our national independence.   He met
death with the calmness and fortitude of the Christian, uttering,
as his last words, — "I am prepared to meet death.   I have
always endeavored to do my duty.   I am sorry to leave my
friends."

2. The news of the death of President Taylor was known,

thousands of miles from the seat of government, within a few hours of its occurrence, wherever the wires of the magnetic telegraph extended; and the national bereavement was received with sorrow, and every manifestation of regret, by people of all political parties. One of the latest acts of his administration was signing a treaty with Great Britain, called the Nicaragua Treaty, designed to secure the constructing of a canal from the Atlantic to the Pacific Oceans, open, with certain stipulations, to all nations.

3. On the following day, Mr. Fillmore assumed the duties of president, as provided by the constitution.

MILLARD FILLMORE, PRESIDENT.

Assumed the government July 10th, 1850 ; retired ——.

[Immediately upon the death of President Taylor, the members of the Cabinet tendered their resignation to Mr. Fillmore; but, at his request, they retained their offices till the 15th, when the following cabinet was formed :]

Daniel Webster,	Mass.,	July 15, 1850,	Secretary of State.
Thomas Corwin,	Ohio,	July 15, 1850,	Sec'y of Treasury.
Alexander H. H. Stuart,	Virginia,	1850,	Sec'y of the Interior.
Charles M. Conrad,	Louisiana,	1850,	Sec'y of War.
William A. Graham,	N. Carolina,	July 15, 1850,	Sec'y of the Navy.
John J. Crittenden,	Kentucky,	July 15, 1850,	Attorney General.
Nathan K. Hall,	New York,	July 15, 1850,	Postmaster General.

It is an admirable feature of the Constitution of the United States, that it provides, in case of the death of a president, for the ready and quiet transfer of all his powers to the vice-president, as his constitutional successor; and a most interesting hour was that, when, on the day following the death of General Taylor, and while his remains were still reposing in the national mansion, Mr. Fillmore took the oath of the presidential office, in the presence of both houses of Congress. It was a service which occupied but a brief space; but, in that short time, a transfer of all executive power was quietly effected, and the machinery of government was again moving, with its accustomed regularity and harmonious action.

A RETROSPECTIVE VIEW

OF THE

GENERAL PROGRESS OF THE UNITED STATES,

DURING THE LAST HALF-CENTURY.*

I. STATES. — 1. Thirteen colonies existed at the commencement of the Revolutionary struggle, all of which contributed to achieve the independence of America. These became independent states, and severally adopted the federal constitution, in the order indicated at page 216.

2. Three states were admitted during the administration of Washington, namely:

Vermont, March 4, 1791.   Kentucky, June 1, 1792.
Tennessee, June 1, 1796.

3. Fifteen states have been admitted during the present century, namely:

Ohio,	Nov.	29, 1802.	Arkansas,	June	15, 1836.
Louisiana,	Apr.	30, 1811.	Michigan,	June	15, 1836.
Indiana,	Dec.	11, 1816.	Florida,	May	3, 1845.
Mississippi,	Dec.	10, 1817.	Iowa,	May	3, 1845.
Illinois,	Dec.	3, 1818.	Texas,	Dec.	29, 1846.
Alabama,	Dec.	14, 1819.	Wisconsin,	May	29, 1848.
Maine,	March	16, 1820.	California,	Sept.	7, 1850.
Missouri,	Aug.	10, 1821.			

4. To the thirty-one states now forming the Federal Union, may be added five territories: MINESOTA (organized in 1849), lying east of the Rocky Mountains; OREGON (organized August 2—13, 1848), west of the Mountains; NEW MEXICO and UTAH (organized in September, 1850), and the DISTRICT OF COLUMBIA.

---

* The author has derived essential aid, in the preparation of portions of this "Retrospective View," from two works recently published, namely: "The Half-century," by Rev. Dr. Davis, and "Christian Retrospect and Register," by Rev. Dr. Baird.

5. The limits of the country, in 1800, were: The British Possessions, on the north; the province of New Brunswick and the Atlantic, on the east; the Floridas and Louisiana, on the south; and the Mississippi, on the west. At the present time, the western boundary is the Pacific Ocean, and the southern the Gulf of Mexico. Then, the superficial area was one million of square miles; now, three millions and a quarter, — equal, within four hundred thousand square miles, to the entire continent of Europe; and, in point of extent, second only to the great Russian empire. It has been computed that ninety such islands as that of England might be put within the territory of the United States, and still leave a good ship-channel between each island.

6. Since the commencement of the present century, there have been added to the United States that vast tract of territory formerly known as LOUISIANA, purchased of France for fifteen millions of dollars (p. 232); FLORIDA, purchased of Spain for five millions of dollars (p. 263); TEXAS, which had achieved her independence of Mexico (p. 289); and NEW MEXICO and UPPER CALIFORNIA, ceded by Mexico to the United States, at the close of their war with that power, for fifteen millions of dollars (p. 305).

II. GOVERNMENT. — The government under the constitution has existed since 1798. There have been thirty-two Congresses, each elected for two years. Since 1800, Congress has held twelve extra sessions: three during the administration of Mr. Jefferson; five during that of Mr. Madison; two during that of Mr. Monroe; one during that of Mr. Van Buren; and one during that of Mr. Tyler.

III. PRESIDENTS. — There have been thirteen presidents, ten of whom have died.

	Born.	Died.	Aged.
George Washington,	Feb. 22, 1732.	Dec. 14, 1799.	68.
John Adams,	Oct. 19, 1735.	July 4, 1826.	91.
Thomas Jefferson,	Apr. 2, 1743.	July 4, 1826.	83.
James Madison,	Mar. 5, 1751.	June 28, 1836.	79.
James Monroe,	Apr. 2, 1759.	July 4, 1831.	73.
William H. Harrison,	Feb. 9, 1772.	Apr. 4, 1841.	68.
Andrew Jackson,	Mar. 15, 1767.	June 8, 1845.	78.
John Quincy Adams,	July 11, 1767.	Feb. 23, 1848.	81.
James K. Polk,	Nov. 2, 1795.	June 15, 1849.	54.
Zachary Taylor,	Nov. 24, 1784.	July 9, 1850.	66.
Martin Van Buren,	Dec. 5, 1782.		
John Tyler,	Mar. 29, 1790.		
Millard Fillmore,	Jan. 7, 1800.		

IV. Population. — 1. By the census of 1800, the population of the United States was, in round numbers, five millions three hundred thousand; by the census of 1850, it exceeds twenty-three millions, or more than quadruple what it was in 1800.

2. The aborigines within the United States are supposed to be between four and five hundred thousand. Most of those who formerly resided in the States of Mississippi, Alabama, Florida, Georgia, and Tennessee, have been removed to lands west of the States of Arkansas and Missouri. They have organized governments of their own; schools, academies, churches, &c.

3. The immigration into the United States, from other countries, has been very great. From 1820 to 1840, about one million; from 1840 to 1850, more than one million and a half.

V. Personal Appearance. — 1. The inhabitants of the United States bear a strong resemblance to the inhabitants of the countries whence they originated. Time, however, has effected some changes, as have different climates and different modes of living. In New England, the English blood greatly predominates. The people here have, generally, fair complexions. They are also robust, and capable of enduring great hardships and fatigue. They are somewhat taller, and more slender in form, than the inhabitants of Great Britain.

2. In the Middle and Western States, those who partake of English blood have a similar appearance. But there is a far greater mixture of races there than in New England. People of Dutch and German descent constitute no small part of the Middle States, particularly in New York and Pennsylvania. These, in person, strongly resemble the nations from which they have descended. This is true, also, of the Irish population, of whom great numbers have emigrated, within the last half-century, to these shores, and are scattered over all New England, and west of it. There are, also, numbers of French, Swiss, and Swedes, with their characteristic differences of personal appearance.

3. The citizens of the southern portion of the country who are of English descent — and these constitute a very large proportion — show the effects of a warmer climate, in the sallow complexion by which they are distinguished. The negro population, throughout the entire country, strongly resemble the natives of Africa in form, features, and complexion, with some variety in respect to those in whom exists a mixture of blood.

VI. Character. — 1. Nearly the same may be said, respecting the character of the people of the United States, as was said respecting their personal appearance, as a whole. They differ as their ancestors did, with such modifications as time and peculiar circumstances have effected. They have no national character, as have the French, Germans, and other European nations. They are yet too mixed and various; but, when years shall have elapsed, — perhaps centuries, — and emigration shall have ceased, we may have a homogeneous people, and then a thoroughly national character.

2. Yet there are some general traits of character which we may here mention. 1. A great spirit of enterprise. 2. A large share of personal independence and resolution. 3. An enlightened and cordial attachment to liberty, civil and religious. 4. Great inquisitiveness, and a strong capacity for mechanical inventions and improvement. This is more particularly true of the people of New England. 5. A love of general intelligence. 6. A marked regard to the dictates of humanity. This is shown in our laws regarding the descent of property, provision for widows and orphans, the non-impressment of seamen, and the simplicity and mildness of our penal codes. 7. A toleration of all religious sects.

3. If we look at separate divisions of the country, the above characteristics may, perhaps, be somewhat varied and extended. The enterprise of New England has long been proverbial, as have been her general intelligence, morality and piety. No people enjoy greater means of mental culture and improvement. None are more inquisitive, shrewd, calculating, or economical. If not ardent and sanguine, they are resolute and persevering.

4. The morality and piety of New England have been visible throughout their history. With much that is wrong, doubtless, the people, as a whole, are known for their general sobriety and decorum, their veneration for sacred things, their regard for the Sabbath, their respect for the ministry, their devout attendance upon religious worship, and the religious care and education of their children.

5. In the Middle States, there is not much that is peculiar. The traits of the New Englander appear, wherever New England has supplied the population. The people are active and enterprising in trade, commerce, agriculture, mechanic arts, education, morals and religion. The Dutch still exhibit their regard for economy, neatness, and a plodding industry. In Pennsylvania, the Friends and Germans, — in Maryland, the Catholics, and so far as the Irish extend, — all have their peculiar views, habits, customs, and religious forms and ceremonies.

6. The southern people are fond of society, and cultivate social intercourse more than the citizens of the north, although

27

they live much less compactly. Their hospitality is everywhere celebrated; and the more freely their guest partakes of their bounties, the more is he welcome. They are, doubtless, more haughty in their bearing; but none excel them in the courtesies and proprieties of life. "A planter," it has been said, "would be more apt to do what he would be sorry for, than what he would be ashamed of."

7. The inhabitants of the Western States have few peculiarities. The people bear strong resemblances to those of New England and the Southern States, whence their population has been chiefly derived. In the northern portion, including particularly Ohio, the New England character predominates. In the southern portion, the southern character, more especially that of Virginia, prevails. Kentucky, the leading state of the great western valley, was settled principally from Virginia; while Ohio, the leading state in the northern section, received its early population from New England. The character of the men of the Western States may be described, therefore, as a compound of the New England and Virginia character. A noble parentage; and most fruitful has it been in producing a generation of men distinguished for a firmness, a love of freedom, an independence, a patriotism, a generosity, unknown to people living in greater ease, and under established institutions.

VII. DRESS. — 1. At the opening of the present century, the families of farmers, and, indeed, of other classes, manufactured, to a great extent, their own garments. The hand-card and spinning-wheel were in nearly every habitation. The good wife could show a large amount of yarn, every spring, ready for the loom; and no young lady was thought fit to be married, who had not fitted herself out with a fair complement of linen fabrics, for the various uses of housekeeping, as well as for her own person.

2. Under the reign of machinery, the family manufacture has been generally superseded. Clothing has been wonderfully cheapened. In general, the people of the United States are better clothed than the people of any other country. Indeed, it is not uncommon to see persons, — especially females, — in the common walks of life, and those in service, dressed in a style which, fifty years since, would have been considered extravagant in the more wealthy classes.

3. The modes of dress do not vary greatly, in the different sections of the country. Those most prevalent are the French and English. London and Paris give law to fashion in Boston and New York, as well as to the inhabitants of those cities. The

Germans of the Middle States yet wear broad hats and purple breeches. In Philadelphia, "there is still the drab bonnet, and the drab gown and the frill, and the neckerchief and apron to correspond." Here and there is yet to be seen the cocked hat, and the white-topped boots, and the light breeches ; but they are worn by a race of men fast disappearing from among us, as are the men who once wore the capacious wig.

VIII.   DWELLINGS. — 1. The mode of building in the United States is accommodated very much to the external condition of the people.   In all our new settlements, the first dwellings are log or mud houses.   Elegance, proportion, taste, are not consulted.   The first object is shelter; the next, comfort ; and, as the lands are cleared up, and the settlers become more thriving, the huts and hovels give place to more substantial tenements. This, however, is the work of time.

2. In the older portions of the country, though the houses of the citizens are not distinguished for beauty and elegance, many of them, even in the country, are neat and handsome structures. Individual habitations there are in fine and imposing situations, which add to the charms of our natural scenery.   These residences of gentlemen — particularly merchants, professional men, head manufacturers, and wealthy farmers — are multiplying every day.   In the vicinity of cities, they are becoming even numerous ; and indicate a great increase of taste, wealth and luxury, since the opening of the present century.

3. The greater proportion of good dwellings in the country are grouped together in villages, where, with their out-houses, and front and garden fences, they make a neat and pretty appearance.   Indeed, no collection of houses in any country are said to strike the eye with greater effect, as objects of beauty, than many American villages, — particularly those in New England and the Middle States.

4. In general, our dwellings are composed of less substantial materials than are used in European countries.   In New England, the houses, in the country villages, are chiefly of wood.   In the Middle States, there are still ancient houses of the Flemish model, tiled, with gables on the street, and huge weathercocks on the top, as described in our notes appended to the Period of Settlements.   In Western New York, the villages are built in an exceedingly neat manner.   They are of wood, painted white, with green blinds, and often verandas, as in New England.   In Maryland and Pennsylvania are many stone houses and barns, the latter often of vast size.

5. In the Southern States the manner of building is less

substantial than in the Middle and Northern States. Few houses are of brick, and the low country is without stone. Those inhabited by the planters have much uniformity. They are of one or two stories, and have a veranda in front and chimneys at the end, on the outside. The residences of the wealthy are often in good taste, and commodious. They are generally placed at a considerable distance from the public roads.

6. In the West, we occasionally see structures like those of the East. Some towns are built of brick ; but, except in the cities, there is little good architecture. The log house still abounds ; but this kind of habitation gradually disappears, and habitations more like those of New England take their place.

7. There is yet ample room for improvement in our architecture. We do not compare with England, France, Germany, in the number or architectural taste of their magnificent structures. Among the causes for this, may be mentioned our recent origin, our want of means, and our republican simplicity. Still, our cities exhibit fine specimens of architectural beauty, both public and private ; and the taste for them, and the ability to create them, are fast increasing.

IX. Food. — 1. The people of no country on the globe are better, or so well fed, as the Americans. It is emphatically a land of plenty. In European countries, starvation is not uncommon : in the United States, it is a rare event.

2. With some nations the culinary art has attained to great perfection ; and, in the United States, a marked advance has been made, within a few years. The employment of European cooks is not uncommon. The bills of fare on the tables of many of our principal hotels, in New York, Boston, Baltimore, Cincinnati, — especially on great occasions, — would compare well with those in London, Paris, and other trans-atlantic cities. Our beef is said still to be inferior to the "roast beef of old England ;" but it is a distinction, in some cases, it is believed, without a difference.

3. The Americans generally eat fast. They are too busy otherwise to enjoy their meals. Even the dinner, which is the great meal of the day, and altogether so with the English, and to which they give time, the Americans despatch often in a few minutes. Our breakfasts are much richer and more substantial than theirs. Our suppers are various. With some classes, it is a light concern : with the laboring classes, it often consists of the most substantial food.

4. In New England, in the country towns, breakfast is usually at an early hour ; often at sunrise, or before. In a farmer's

family, it consists of ham, beef, sausages, pork, bread, butter, boiled or fried potatoes, pies, and coffee.

5. The use of coffee in the morning, and often at night, is almost universal. At hotels and boarding-houses, there is often a greater variety of dishes. In cities, the usual bread is made of wheat flour; on the other hand, in the country, until within a few years, the common bread was made of rye, or a mixture of rye and Indian corn. Wheat, however, has been substituted, to a great extent, especially in manufacturing districts. Hasty pudding was formerly a favorite dish, and most commonly prepared on Saturday evening. It was eaten with milk when warm, and fried when cooled. The Indian pudding, also, was once a very favorite dish throughout New England.

6. In the Middle States, the diet is much as in New England. More use, however, is made of the sweet potato, which is raised in New Jersey, and in states south of it. It is cooked variously, though it is generally preferred boiled or baked. Buckwheat is extensively used in the Middle States, though not peculiar to any one section. Hominy — coarse Indian meal — is much used.

7. In the Southern States, the food differs considerably from what it is at the North. Garden vegetables are not extensively cultivated; the Irish potato does not thrive; the sweet potato abounds. Rice, generally boiled, is a substitute for vegetables, and even for bread. Hominy is found at all tables. Hoe-cake, — the johnny-cake of New England, — and ashpone, — a coarse cake, baked under the ashes, — are in as common use as bread. Ham is a general article, and often found on the table three times a day. In Virginia, it is commonly, in the season, accompanied by greens. In Louisiana, gumbo, a compound soup, is much used: in New Orleans, it is sold in the streets.

8. In the Western States, the two great articles of food are bacon and Indian corn. Fish abound in the rivers; but they are coarse. Game is plenty. Rice is used: it is commonly boiled hard, and eaten with gravy. Coffee is very common, as are maple and other sugars. In the western cities and larger towns, however, within a few years, nearly all the varieties and delicacies of living are to be found which exist in any part of the country. The facilities for rapid transportation have so increased, that, in a few days, the finest fish, oysters, lobsters of the east, and other delicacies, can be furnished at Buffalo, Cleveland, and even Cincinnati, in the greatest perfection.

X. MEANS OF INTERCOMMUNICATION. -- The facilities for intercommunication, within the last half-century, are, doubtless,

27*

far more valuable than all others, since the commencement of
the Christian era. In many parts of the country, so great
has been the change, that the use of vehicles, and particularly
riding on horseback, for the purpose of extended journeys,
is almost unknown. Even the era of turnpikes has gone
by. Common roads are greatly neglected. In some of the
interior portions of the country, the stage-coach goes lumbering
along; but a few years hence, and even that will be as uncommon as it once was frequent. The joyous post-horn will be
heard among the hills no more. Other modes of conveyance are
taking the place of the old and social modes. Some of these we
proceed to specify.

1. CANALS. — 1. Few canals existed in the United States
prior to 1800. Their number is not destined to increase. They
will be superseded, for travelling purposes, by railroads, which
are not exposed to long or serious interruption, on the occurrence of winter. The last half-century may, therefore, be
regarded as the era of canals in the United States.

2. The Erie Canal, which is three hundred and sixty-three
miles in extent, was first opened in 1825. Except one in China,
it is the longest in the world. It connects Hudson's river and
Lake Erie. New York has more miles of canals than any other
state in the Union, and they produce a larger income. The
great promoter of this canal system in New York — though not
the projector — was the late distinguished De Witt Clinton. It
was, doubtless, mainly owing to his enterprise and perseverance,
that the above great work was ultimately completed.

3. The Ohio Canal is the next longest in the United States,
being three hundred and nine miles long, and connects Lake Erie
and Ohio. It was opened in 1832. Comparatively few canals
have been constructed, since 1830. In one respect, the canal
has the advantage of the railroad; — heavy freight can be conveyed through the interior of a country, at a less cost, though at
less speed. Those already constructed will be likely to be
employed, for certain descriptions of goods, in preference to railroads.

2. STEAM NAVIGATION. — 1. Since the commencement of the
century, a most remarkable change has taken place in the navigation of rivers, lakes, and even the ocean, by means of boats and
packets propelled by steam.

2. The first successful effort by this mode was a trip from
New York to Albany, one hundred and fifty miles, in August,
1807, in thirty-two hours, by Robert Fulton. His return was
accomplished in thirty hours, or at the rate of five miles per

hour.   Fulton died in 1815, at the age of fifty.   Soon after his death, boats attained the speed of nine miles per hour ; now, from fifteen to twenty.

3. The first steamboat that run upon the western waters was built at Pittsburg, in 1811.   In 1817, a boat ascended from New Orleans to Louisville, one thousand two hundred and seventy-five miles, in twenty-five days.   In 1827, the same distance was accomplished in eight days and two hours.   Western commerce has been revolutionized.   The number of boats on the Mississippi and its tributaries, in 1818, was twenty-three ; in 1848, one thousand three hundred.

4. For years after the experiment had succeeded in regard to river steam navigation, it was still a problem whether the ocean could be safely navigated by the same means.   The size of the boat, the weight of the machinery, the quantity of fuel required for the voyage, were thought insuperable objections ; and, in addition to being too hazardous, any such project, it was thought, would prove unprofitable.   But the experiment has shown a widely different result.

5. The first steam-propelled vessel that crossed the Atlantic was American built, and called the Savannah.   She was three hundred and eighty tons.   She sailed first to Savannah, in 1819, from New York, and thence directly to Liverpool, where she arrived after a passage of eighteen days, seven of which she used steam.   When first seen on the other side, she was supposed to be a ship on fire.   From Liverpool she proceeded to Copenhagen, and thence to St. Petersburg.   On her return to Savannah, she was divested of her steam apparatus, and used as a packet between Savannah and New York.

6. Two ocean steamers left, the one from Cork, April 4th, 1838, and the other from Bristol, the 8th of the same month, for New York.   These were the Sirius and the Great Western.   Both arrived on the 23d.   This event formed a new era in navigation.   From this time, steam packets have continued to run between New York and Liverpool.   In 1840, the British and North American line, commonly called the Cunard line, was established.   Subsequently, the celebrated line between New York and Liverpool, usually called the Collins line, has commenced running.   And, still later, lines have been established between New York and Bremen, Havre, Chagres, and several other places.

7. In 1620, the Mayflower, which brought the Pilgrim Fathers to the shores of New England, was sixty-five days in accomplishing the voyage to Plymouth : the ocean steamers

often accomplish the same voyage in a little more than ten days. In short, England is brought as near the United States as New York and Boston were, a century ago.

3. RAILROADS. — 1. The first railroad ever constructed in the United States was one, four miles in length, for the purpose of conveying granite from Quincy, in Massachusetts, to navigable water on the Neponset river. It was finished in 1827. Horse-power only was employed. Steam-power was first used in 1833, on the Mohawk and Hudson Railroad.

2. The average cost of the railroads in the United States is about thirty-two thousand dollars per mile. In England, the cost is far higher; but railroads there are not as much superior to ours as the difference in the cost might seem to indicate.

3. The extreme speed of the fastest trains in England is said to be seventy-five miles per hour: in the United States, the greatest speed is less than fifty. According to the experiments of Dr. Hutton, the velocity of a cannon-ball is three hundred miles — only four times greater than the extreme speed attained in England, and six times greater than that attained in the United States.

4. At the close of 1849, there were in operation eight thousand seven hundred and ninety-seven miles of railroad, at an aggregate cost of two hundred and eighty-six million five hundred thousand dollars. The number of passengers transported in 1850, on the various railroads, was sixty millions, or about one hundred and sixty thousand per day. Boston is connected with Ogdensburg, on the St. Lawrence, a distance of some four hundred miles; and by Albany, with Lake Erie, at Buffalo, a distance of five hundred and twenty-five miles. New York is connected with Lake Erie at Dunkirk, and will soon be connected with Montreal, and, at no distant day, with New Orleans, by the way of Charleston and Savannah, or other routes.

5. A magnificent project has, within a few years, been proposed by Mr. Whitney, a wealthy and enterprising gentleman of New York, for constructing a road from Lake Michigan to Columbia river, on the Pacific; and, still later, a Mr. Degrand has proposed the plan of a railroad from St. Louis to San Francisco, California. While these great projects are maturing, — one of which will, probably, in time, be accomplished,— a railroad is in actual process of construction across the Isthmus from Chagres to the Pacific, the estimated cost of which is one million of dollars.

4. ELECTRO-MAGNETIC TELEGRAPH. — 1. Prior to the invention of the electro-magnetic telegraph, the best mode of conveying

intelligence by signals was the system of Colonel Paisley, of France, adopted in 1822. Signal stations were placed from three to five miles apart, each of which was visible to the two nearest to it. It could be used, however, only by daylight. It was used between Paris and Brest, a distance of three hundred and twenty-five miles. But the progress of communication was slow; a sentence of ten words requiring a half-hour for transmission, and the employment of eighty men at the different signal stations. This line cost the French government annually more than two hundred thousand dollars.

2. In 1832, Prof. Samuel F. B. Morse, while on a voyage from Europe to the United States, had his attention directed to a remark of Franklin; namely, that, inasmuch as the electric fluid passes instantaneously upon wires of any length, it might be made the means of conveying information. This led to the construction of the electro-magnetic telegraph.

3. In 1848, Congress made an appropriation of thirty thousand dollars to test the practicability of Mr. Morse's discovery. Posts were first set up between Washington and Baltimore, a distance of forty miles; and the telegraph put in successful operation between those two cities. There are now (1852) more than fifteen thousand miles of telegraph in the United States, worked under Professor Morse's patent.

4. There are three rival telegraphs in the United States, — the inventors of each of which have secured patent rights, — Morse's, Bain's, and House's. Morse's is, as yet, more extensively used; but House's is an elegant invention, — all communications being printed in small-capitals, — and, when working at the maximum rate, can transmit three thousand words in an hour. Morse's system is in extensive operation on the continent of Europe.

5. It may be stated, in evidence of the rapidity with which communications are made by means of this invention, that President Polk's last message, in December, 1848, was telegraphed to St. Louis, and other western cities; the paper on which the signs were written was seven thousand two hundred feet in length. More recently, a communication was transmitted directly from New York to New Orleans, and an answer returned, in the space of five minutes, — making a distance of nearly three thousand miles.

6. The cost, in England, of erecting telegraphs, is about seven hundred and fifty dollars per mile; in the United States, only one-fifth of that sum, or one hundred and fifty dollars. The cost of messages in the former is from eight to sixteen cents per word;

In America, the cost is only from two to ten cents a word. This maximum rate pays for the transmission of messages from New York to New Orleans.

5. POST-OFFICE. — 1. In the early history of the country, frequent communications between the new settlements was difficult. Special messengers were employed in cases of necessity. A single fact will serve to show at what trouble and expense intercommunication was had. On the 10th of December, 1672, Governor Lovelace, of the colony of New York, issued his formal proclamation, that, on the first of January following, a " sworn " messenger, or post, would start from New York city for Boston, and accomplish the journey there and back, within the month. Persons, therefore, who had letters, or " small portable goods," for Hartford or Boston, must lodge them at the secretary's office by a given day. The post was to be paid before the " bagg bee seald up." And all this " was for the more speedy Intelligence and Dispatch of Affayres."

2. What a change has been effected in relation to the transmission of letters, newspapers, and periodicals! Now, several mails are despatched, by various routes, each way, and every day, between these two important points. In 1800, there were nine hundred post-offices; now, 1852, about twenty thousand. In 1800, there were twenty thousand miles of post-routes; now, one hundred and ninety-six thousand, and the amount of transportation fifty-three millions of miles. In 1800, the income was nearly three hundred thousand dollars; in 1851, more than six millions.

3. In 1800, the rates of postage were eight cents, ten cents, twelve and a half, seventeen, and twenty-five, — according to the distance; in 1852, three cents for each half-ounce letter for all distances under three thousand miles, and six cents for all over. Letters transmitted are yearly multiplying, by millions on millions.

6. NEWSPAPERS. — More than eighty years elapsed from the landing of the Pilgrims, in 1620, before a newspaper was established in America. It was called " The Boston Weekly News-Letter." Its circulation was exceedingly limited. In 1800, the number of newspapers had increased to two hundred. In 1850, the newspapers and periodicals had reached the number of two thousand eight hundred; of which the annual number of copies printed was four hundred and twenty-two millions. No people on the globe are so well supplied with reading of this kind as the people of the United States. The first religious newspaper ever published in the United States was the Boston

Recorder. It appeared at Boston in January, 1816. The second was the Religious Intelligencer, at New Haven, June, 1816.

XI. INVENTIONS — ARTS — MANUFACTURES. — 1. No people on the globe are more distinguished for their inventive genius than the Americans. To the contrivance and perfection of all kinds of machinery they have been compelled, in order to compete with the manufactures of those countries where labor is cheap. In addition to this, annual fairs and industrial exhibitions, especially where rewards have been offered, have stimulated the exercise of mechanical skill, and led to numerous useful and ingenious inventions.

2. The patent-office of the United States was opened in 1789 : since which era, the patents in Massachusetts have been one to every three hundred and ninety-four of its inhabitants; in Connecticut, one to two hundred and eighty-five; while in South Carolina, but one to four thousand seven hundred and thirty-three; and in Georgia, but one to ten thousand seven hundred and six, — facts which show how much more favorable the pursuits of the North have been to the development of enterprize and genius than the South. The whole number of patents issued within the last half-century may be estimated at sixteen thousand; and it is interesting to know, that the greatest number of any particular class relate, according to Dr. Baird, to agriculture, and the smallest number relate to war.

3. Perhaps the three most important inventions of the last half-century are those of Whitney, Fulton, and Morse. The cotton-gin, the invention of the first-named, was patented in 1793; but it remained for the present century to develop its immense benefits. Mr. Whitney died at New Haven, in 1825. Before the cotton-gin came into use, not more than one thousand bales of cotton were annually shipped to England. Now, the annual product exceeds two millions of bales, of which a considerable part finds a market abroad. Of the inventions of Fulton and Morse we have spoken in another place.

4. The use of steam-power for printing belongs to the present century, and has greatly aided in the multiplication of newspapers, pamphlets, and books. Until within a few years, the only printing-press was the hand-press, which gave two hundred and fifty or three hundred impressions an hour. The most celebrated press of modern times is one recently invented by Mr. Hoe, of New York, which prints from cylinders at the rate of twelve thousand, and even, it is alleged, twenty thousand

per hour. .Sheets for books, however, are printed less rapidly, as the impressions require to be more perfect than for news-papers.

5. Anterior to the Revolution, the colonies were not permit-ted to manufacture, even for themselves; the object of Eng-land being to keep them in a state of dependence. Even Lord Chatham, the friend of American liberty, said that they should not be allowed to manufacture a hob-nail. During the Rev-olutionary struggle, the people were in no condition to turn their thoughts to manufactures; and, indeed, it is only since the commencement of the present century, that the genius of the people has had full scope. But, since that era, manufactures have been multiplied to an extent, and in a variety, difficult to realize. We cannot even name them.

6. Yet, it may be mentioned, that the power-loom, for weav-ing cotton fabrics, was first introduced at Waltham, in 1815. The jenny, and the broad loom, for weaving woollens, at Pitts-field, in 1807. The discovery of the application of India rubber to cloth, by which it is rendered impervious to water, was first announced by Dr. Comstock, of Hartford, in 1828. It is now used to a great extent in that form, and for numerous other pur-poses.

7. Another important discovery belongs to the latter part of the last half-century. It was ascertained that the inhaling of the vapor of ether would produce insensibility to such a degree, that a person under its effects might be subjected to the most diffi-cult surgical operation without experiencing the least degree of pain. A controversy, as to the honor of the discovery, has arisen between Drs. Jackson and Morton, of Boston, and Dr. Wells, of Hartford; but it is not within the scope of this work to decide the merits of it.*

8. The respiration of sulphuric ether, since its first application as above, or of chloroform, another substance used for a similar purpose, has been resorted to in thousands of cases; and during the insensibility which succeeds, operations otherwise past en-durance have been safely performed. This, doubtless, is one of the most remarkable alleviating discoveries of the age. It should be observed here, however, that ether is now greatly pre-ferred to chloroform. The latter puts the patient into the power of the operator; ether, on the contrary, while it renders the

---

* The French Academy conferred rewards of merit on Messrs. Jackson and Wells. In 1848, the American Congress awarded to Morton the honor of the discovery. See Davis' "Half-century," p. 295.

patient insensible to pain, leaves him a free agent, having the power of choice.

9. In this connection, it may be observed that no arts have made greater progress than engraving, sculpture, and painting. The names of Greenough, Powers, Brown and Crawford, as sculptors, are familiar to the lovers of art, and will ever be held in remembrance.

10. Several eminent painters, says Dr. Davis, have flourished and departed, during the last half-century. Among them, we may mention Benjamin West, who, though he spent the most of his life in England, was American born. He died in 1820, aged eighty. Washington Allston, a painter of great merit, especially in Scripture subjects, was a native of South Carolina. He died at Cambridge, Massachusetts, in 1842, at the age of sixty. To these we may add the names of Trumbull, Inman, Stuart, Cole, all of whom will be long remembered, as artists of superior attainments.

XII. AGRICULTURE. — 1. A new era has recently commenced in relation to agriculture, which, as a science and an art, is receiving that degree of attention which its importance demands. It is beginning to be regarded, as it should be, not only as the basis of population and subsistence, but as the parent of individual and national opulence. The states most devoted to planting and farming, or whose products are chiefly agricultural, are the Southern and Western. All the New England and Middle States, as also Ohio, are very considerably manufacturers, and the most of them have a large commercial and navigation interest, — causes which operate to draw away hands from agriculture. The proportion of the inhabitants of the United States devoted to agricultural pursuits is large, probably exceeding one-fifth of the whole population; or, excluding children and females, about two-thirds of all the males over ten years of age.

2. Great attention has been paid, within a few years, to agricultural chemistry, by which the nature of soils and the constituents of plants have been developed. The value of different kinds of manures has also been determined. Two individuals have done the agricultural world vast good, by their experiments: namely, Davy and Liebig. Similar investigations have also recently been made by Boursingault and Payen, in France; Malda, in Holland; and Johnston, Kane, and Anderson, in England.

3. Almost every European country has its established school of instruction in scientific and practical agriculture. New York and Massachusetts have under consideration plans for efficient agricultural institutions, to be supported by the state. A few

of our colleges have professorships of agriculture already established.

XIII. TRADE AND COMMERCE. — 1. The commerce of the United States, during the last half-century, has expanded to an immense extent, and is still yearly increasing, with the progress of population, and the still increasing spirit of enterprise. It consists, principally, in the exchange of agricultural produce, and, within a few years, of manufactured articles, for the manufactures of other parts of the world, and the productions of the tropical climates. The principal articles of domestic produce exported are cotton, wheat, flour, biscuit, tobacco, lumber, rice, pot and pearl ashes, Indian corn and meal, dried and pickled fish, beef, rye, pork, &c.

2. Of these exports, New England and New York are the great carriers. To them belong nearly two-thirds of all the shipping of the United States. The states south of the Potomac own only about one-eighth part. Our staple articles are principally the growth of the Southern and Western States; and are carried coastwise from the Southern to the Middle States, whence they are sent to foreign countries, almost entirely in ships owned by northern merchants, and navigated by northern seamen. Within a few years, cotton, in considerable quantities, has been shipped directly from New Orleans, and some few other ports. This mode of transportation is on the increase. The exports from the United States are sent to various countries; but the British dominions always receive the largest portion of our domestic produce, particularly cotton. The Spanish, Portuguese, and French dominions have usually received the most, next to the British.

3. The goods received in return for exports are, generally, the manufactures of those countries to which the exports are carried. From Great Britain are imported vast quantities of woollen and cotton goods, and manufactures of iron, steel, brass, copper, glass, earthen ware, silk, &c. France furnishes a large amount of silk goods, and fancy articles. From China, we receive tea and silk; from Russia, iron and hemp. Coffee comes from the colonies of the European powers in America and the East Indies; sugar, from the East and West Indies; rum, from the British and Danish West Indies. Wines are, principally, from France, Spain, Portugal, Madeira, and the Canary Isles; brandy, from France, Spain, Italy, &c.

4. Since the acquisition of California, large amounts of gold have been imported into the country; which, however, after having been coined, have gone abroad to pay the balance of trade

against us; which, at least, in respect to Great Britain, is, and always has been, against us.

5. Within the half-century, a new trade has sprung up, of which some account belongs to this place, — the ice trade. The first shipment of ice was made in 1805, by Frederick Tudor, of Boston, of one hundred and thirty tons, to Martinique, a West India Island. He lost four thousand five hundred dollars by the experiment. In 1815, he made profitable shipments to Havana. In 1833, he made his first shipment of ice to the East Indies.

6. Within a few years the shipments of ice have greatly increased. In 1847, the amount shipped from Boston to southern ports was fifty-one thousand eight hundred and eighty-seven tons; to foreign ports, twenty-two thousand five hundred and ninety-one; total, seventy-four thousand four hundred and seventy eight, requiring three hundred and fifty-three vessels, . and yielding five hundred and seven thousand six hundred and fifty-one dollars. The ice is taken from ponds in the vicinity of Boston. It is packed in saw-dust, of which, in 1847, there were used four thousand six hundred cords, from Maine, costing two dollars and fifty cents per cord.

7. The price in Havana is six and a quarter cents per pound, or one hundred and twenty-five dollars per ton; in Calcutta, it has receded from six cents to two and a half; at New Orleans, sometimes from three cents to half a cent; and the amount used at this last place is twenty-eight thousand tons, annually.

XIV. EDUCATION. — 1. Attention to the education of children and youth was coëval with the settlement of the country, as we have had occasion to show, page 126. But, within the present century, the subject has received still greater attention, and the principle is being adopted, throughout the country, of having common or public schools supported by state provision.*

2. Infant schools, Lancasterian and manual labor schools, once popular, have generally ceased to be patronized. Female seminaries, of a high order, are becoming common. Of Normal schools, Massachusetts has three, — at West Newton, Westfield, and Bridgewater; Connecticut one, — at New Britain, estab-

---

* Several states have funds, — some, large funds, — for the support of common schools, namely : Massachusetts, Connecticut, Maine (small), New York, New Jersey, Ohio, Michigan, Kentucky, and Wisconsin Vermont, New Hampshire and Rhode Island, depend upon taxation. Pennsylvania makes an annual appropriation. Virginia, Delaware, the Carolinas, and almost all the other Southern States, have no school system, but do more or less for the education of the poor.

lished 1850 ; but the largest in the United States is at Albany, established in 1844.

3. COLLEGES. — At the opening of the present century, the colleges of the United States were twenty-five ; now, one hundred and twenty. Those who have the most extensive or valuable libraries are Harvard, Yale, New Jersey, and the University of Virginia. The advance in the preliminary studies, before entering college, has been great within a few years; and the system of studies pursued is far more complete.

4. Of theological institutions, there are forty-two ; law schools, twelve ; medical schools, thirty-seven. The United States supports two schools. The Military Academy, at West Point, was established there in 1802, but went into operation in 1794 ; it was projected by Gen. Knox. It costs the United States one hundred and fifty thousand dollars per annum. The Naval Academy, founded, in 1842, at Annapolis, costs, per annum, nearly thirty thousand dollars.

XV. CHARITABLE EDUCATIONAL INSTITUTIONS. — 1. These are numerous ; and nearly all have had their origin in the present century, — at least, in the United States. We can do little more than name them. At the head of these we place Sabbath-schools. The founder of these was Robert Raikes, of Gloucester, England. The first school of the kind he commenced in his native town, in 1781. Raikes died in 1811, aged seventy-six.

2. A similar school, it is said, was gathered in Philadelphia, in 1791 ; but it was not until the present century commenced that these schools began to be extensively organized. The first is said to have been collected by two young ladies, in Beverly, Massachusetts, in 1810. Now, they exist in all parts of the land ; and are, doubtless, the means of good which no one can estimate.

3. INSTITUTIONS FOR DEAF MUTES. — The first institution of this kind was opened at Hartford, Connecticut, April 15, 1817. It is called the " American Asylum." It had its origin in the efforts of Dr. Mason Coggswell, of Hartford, who, having a daughter deaf and dumb, employed the late Rev. Thomas H. Gaulladet to instruct her. Subsequently, Mr. G. was employed by a number of gentlemen to proceed to Europe, and qualify himself for the superintendence of an institution for the benefit of deaf mutes in this country. After spending some time in Europe, with the above object in view, — especially in Paris, with the Abbé Sicard, — Mr. G. returned, and, soon after, the " American Asylum " went into operation. Similar institutions

have since been established in the United States, to the number of eleven.*

4. INSTITUTIONS FOR THE BLIND. — There are three already established in the country. The first, called the " New England Institution for the Blind," was incorporated in 1829. A course of instruction was begun by Dr. S. G. Howe, the superintendent, after having visited Europe, in 1832. In 1834, the institution was presented with a font of types, adapted to printing with raised characters, by citizens of New Bedford and Nantucket.†

5. LUNATIC ASYLUMS. — The oldest institutions, exclusively for the insane, in the United States, — excepting, perhaps, one at Williamsburg, Virginia, in 1773, — are the Maryland Asylum, founded in 1816, and the Friends' Asylum, at Frankford, seven miles from Philadelphia, established in 1817. The number now exceeds twenty. To the establishment of insane institutions, Miss D. L. Dix, a native of Boston, has greatly contributed, by visiting legislatures of different states, and presenting facts bearing upon the condition of this suffering portion of the community, and pleading for their relief.

6. INSTRUCTION OF IDIOTS. — This has been commenced in Massachusetts, in which state alone the number of idiots exceeds one thousand two hundred ; and the experiment thus far made has produced the conviction, in the minds of those interested in the subject, that they are " capable of improvement, and can be raised, from a state of low degradation, to a higher condition."

XVI. RELIGION. — 1. The principal religious denominations in the United States are, — and in the order of their numbers, — Baptists, Methodists, Presbyterians, Congregationalists,

---

* " The most remarkable pupil in any of these asylums," says Dr. Davis, " is Julia Brace, of Hartford, Connecticut, Asylum. She was born January, 1807. When four years old, she had the typhus fever, and, on the twenty-fourth day, lost her sight and hearing, which she has never recovered. She continued to talk for a while, and did not lose her speech entirely for a year. The word she continued to articulate longer than any other was MOTHER. She is still a resident of the asylum, where she has remained since 1821. When nine years old, she learned to sew and knit."

† The same writer quoted above says : " The most remarkable pupil, in any of the asylums of the blind, is Laura Bridgman, who, like Julia Brace, is deaf, dumb, and blind ; and, indeed, no sense is perfect, except that of touch ; and yet she is made the recipient of knowledge. She was born in Hanover, N. H., in 1829. She was so puny and feeble, until she was a year and a half old, that her parents hardly expected to raise her. When two years old, she had a fit of sickness, during which she lost both her sight and hearing, and by which the sense of taste and smell were much impaired. Her propensity to imitate was very strong, and she learned much of the things about her. In 1837, she was placed under the instruction of Dr. Howe, in the Perkins Institution for the Blind, where she has continued ever since."

28*

and Episcopalians.   Besides these, the Unitarians, Universalists, Catholics, and Dutch Reformed, have numerous congregations.

2. It is not to be disguised that much irreligion and vice prevail, and that a spirit of infidelity exists, though in a form more concealed than formerly, and under more decent names.   Nor does it become us to deny, that, in a time of so much religious action and religious news, by which attention is occupied, there is danger of a superficial acquaintance with the doctrines of the Bible, among the mass of professors.   Yet, whatever may be the danger from this source, we are persuaded that such exertions are altogether congenial with the precepts of the Gospel, and will, in the end, produce a vastly counterbalancing good.   The exigencies of the church, and of the times, require precisely such a spirit of benevolent enterprise, to be increased, we trust, with the growth of the nation.

THE

CONSTITUTION

OF THE

UNITED STATES OF AMERICA;

FRAMED by a convention of delegates, of which Washington was the president, which met at Philadelphia, from the States of New Hampshire, Massachusetts, Connecticut, New York, New Jersey, Pennsylvania, Delaware, Maryland, Virginia, North Carolina, South Carolina, and Georgia ; and adopted 17th September, 1787.

PREAMBLE.

We, the people of the United States, in order to form a more perfect union, establish justice, insure domestic tranquillity, provide for the common defence, promote the general welfare, and secure the blessings of liberty to ourselves and our posterity, do ordain and establish this Constitution for the United States of America. *Objects.*

ARTICLE I.

SECTION I.

1. All legislative powers herein granted shall be vested in a Congress of the United States, which shall consist of a Senate and House of Representatives. *Legislative powers.*

SECTION II.

1. The House of Representatives shall be composed of members chosen every second year, by the people of the several states; and the electors in each state shall have the qualifications requisite for electors of the most numerous branch of the state legislature. *House of Rep.*

2. No person shall be a representative who shall not have attained to the age of twenty-five years, and been seven years a citizen of the United States, and who shall not, when elected, be an inhabitant of that state in which he shall be chosen. *Qualifications of rep.*

3. Representatives and direct taxes shall be apportioned among the several states which may be included within this Union, according to their respective numbers, which shall be determined by adding to the whole number of free persons, including those bound to service for a term of years, and excluding Indians not taxed, three-fifths of all other persons. The actual enumeration shall be made within three years after the first meeting of the Congress of *Apportionment of rep.*

the United States, and within every subsequent term of ten years, in such manner as they shall by law direct. The number of representatives shall not exceed one for every thirty thousand, but each state shall have at least one representative; and until such enumeration shall be made, the State of *New Hampshire* shall be entitled to choose three ; *Massachusetts*, eight ; *Rhode Island and Providence Plantations*, one ; *Connecticut*, five ; *New York*, six ; *New Jersey*, four ; *Pennsylvania*, eight ; *Delaware*, one ; *Maryland*, six ; *Virginia*, ten ; *North Carolina*, five ; *South Carolina*, five ; and *Georgia*, three.

Vacancies, how filled.
4. When vacancies happen in the representation from any state, the executive authority thereof shall issue writs of election to fill up such vacancies.

Speaker, how appointed.
5. The House of Representatives shall choose their speaker and other officers, and shall have the sole power of impeachment.

SECTION III.

No. of sen. from each state.
1. The Senate of the United States shall be composed of two senators from each state, chosen by the legislature thereof, for six years; and each senator shall have one vote.

Classification of sen.
2. Immediately after they shall be assembled in consequence of the first election, they shall be divided, as equally as may be, into three classes. The seats of the senators of the first class shall be vacated at the expiration of the second year ; of the second class, at the expiration of the fourth year; and of the third class, at the expiration of the sixth year, so that one-third may be chosen every second year; and if vacancies happen, by resignation or otherwise, during the recess of the legislature of any state, the executive thereof may make temporary appointments until the next meeting of the legislature, which shall then fill such vacancies.

Qualifications of sen.
3. No person shall be a senator who shall not have attained to the age of thirty years, and been nine years a citizen of the United States; and who shall not, when elected, be an inhabitant of that state for which he shall be chosen.

Presiding officer of Sen.
4. The Vice-president of the United States shall be President of the Senate; but shall have no vote, unless they be equally divided.

5. The Senate shall choose their other officers, and also a president pro tempore, in the absence of the vice-president, or when he shall exercise the office of President of the United States.

Senate a court for trial of impeachments.
6. The Senate shall have the sole power to try all impeachments. When sitting for that purpose, they shall be on oath or affirmation. When the President of the United States is tried, the chief justice shall preside; and no person shall be convicted without the concurrence of two-thirds of the members present. ·

Judgment in case of conviction.
7. Judgment, in case of impeachment, shall not extend further than to removal from office, and disqualification to hold and enjoy any office of honor, trust or profit, under the United States ; but the party convicted shall, nevertheless, be liable and subject to indictment, trial, judgment, and punishment, according to law.

SECTION IV.

Elections of sen. and of rep.
1. The times, places, and manner of holding elections for senators and representatives, shall be prescribed in each state by the legislature thereof ; but the Congress may, at any time, by law, make or alter such regulations, except as to the places of choosing senators.

Meeting of Congress.
2. The Congress shall assemble at least once in every year ; and

such meeting shall be on the first Monday in December, unless they shall by law appoint a different day.

SECTION V.

1. Each house shall be the judge of the elections, returns, and qualifications of its own members ; and a majority of each shall constitute a quorum to do business; but a smaller number may adjourn from day to day, and may be authorized to compel the attendance of absent members, in such manner and under such penalties as each house may provide. *Organization of Congress.*

2. Each house may determine the rules of its proceedings, punish its members for disorderly behavior, and, with the concurrence of two-thirds, expel a member. *Rules of proceeding.*

3. Each house shall keep a journal of its proceedings, and from time to time publish the same, excepting such parts as may in their judgment require secrecy ; and the yeas and nays of the members of either house, on any question, shall, at the desire of one-fifth of those present, be entered on the journal. *Journal of Congress.*

4. Neither house, during the session of Congress, shall, without the consent of the other, adjourn for more than three days, nor to any other place than that in which the two houses shall be sitting. *Adjournment of Congress.*

SECTION VI.

1. The senators and representatives shall receive a compensation for their services, to be ascertained by law, and paid out of the treasury of the United States. They shall, in all cases, except treason, felony, and breach of the peace, be privileged from arrest during their attendance at the session of their respective houses, and in going to or returning from the same ; and for any speech or debate in either house they shall not be questioned in any other place. *Compensation and privileges of members.*

2. No senator or representative shall, during the time for which he was elected, be appointed to any civil office, under the authority of the United States, which shall have been created, or the emoluments whereof shall have been increased, during such time ; and no person holding any office under the United States shall be a member of either house during his continuance in office. *Plurality of offices prohibited.*

SECTION VII.

1. All bills for raising revenue shall originate in the House of Representatives ; but the Senate may propose or concur with amendments, as on other bills. *Bills; how originated.*

2. Every bill which shall have passed the House of Representatives and the Senate shall, before it become a law, be presented to the President of the United States. If he approve, he shall sign it; but if not, he shall return it, with his objections, to that house in which it shall have originated, who shall enter the objection at large on their journal, and proceed to reconsider it. If, after such reconsideration, two-thirds of that house shall agree to pass the bill, it shall be sent, together with the objections, to the other house, by which it shall likewise be reconsidered, and if approved by two-thirds of that house, it shall become a law. But, in all such cases, the votes of both houses shall be determined by yeas and nays, and the names of the persons voting for and against the bill shall be entered on the journal of each house respectively. If any bill shall not be returned by the president within ten days (Sundays excepted) after it shall have been presented to him, the same shall be a law in like manner as if he had signed it, unless *How bills become laws.*

the Congress, by their adjournment, prevent its return, in which case it shall not be a law.

Approval and veto powers of president.

3. Every order, resolution or vote, to which the concurrence of the Senate and House of Representatives may be necessary (except on a question of adjournment), shall be presented to the President of the United States; and, before the same shall take effect, shall be approved by him, or, being disapproved by him, shall be repassed by two-thirds of the Senate and House of Representatives, according to the rules and limitations prescribed in the case of a bill.

SECTION VIII.

Powers vested in Congress.

The Congress shall have power —

1. To lay and collect taxes, duties, imposts, and excises; to pay the debts and provide for the common defence and general welfare of the United States; but all duties, imposts, and excises, shall be uniform throughout the United States :

2. To borrow money on the credit of the United States :

3. To regulate commerce with foreign nations, and among the several states, and with the Indian tribes :

4. To establish a uniform rule of naturalization, and uniform laws on the subject of bankruptcies, throughout the United States:

5. To coin money, regulate the value thereof, and of foreign coin, and fix the standard of weights and measures :

6. To provide for the punishment of counterfeiting the securities and current coin of the United States :

7. To establish post offices and post roads :

8. To promote the progress of science and useful arts, by securing for limited times, to authors and inventors, the exclusive right to their respective writings and discoveries :

9. To constitute tribunals inferior to the Supreme Court : to define and punish piracies and felonies committed on the high seas, and offences against the law of nations :

10. To declare war, grant letters of marque and reprisal, and make rules concerning captures on land and water :

11. To raise and support armies; but no appropriation of money to that use shall be for a longer term than two years :

12. To provide and maintain a navy :

13. To make rules for the government and regulation of the land and naval forces :

14. To provide for calling forth the militia to execute the laws of the Union, suppress insurrections, and repel invasions :

15. To provide for organizing, arming, and disciplining the militia, and for governing such part of them as may be employed in the service of the United States, reserving to the states respectively the appointment of the officers, and the authority of training the militia according to the discipline prescribed by Congress :

16. To exercise exclusive legislation, in all cases whatsoever, over such district (not exceeding ten miles square) as may, by cession of particular states, and the acceptance of Congress, become the seat of government of the United States; and to exercise like authority over all places purchased, by the consent of the legislature of the state in which the same shall be, for the erection of forts, magazines, arsenals, dock-yards, and other needful buildings : — and,

17. To make all laws which shall be necessary and proper for carrying into execution the foregoing powers, and all other powers vested by this constitution in the government of the United States, or in any department or officer thereof.

SECTION IX.

1. The migration or importation of such persons as any of the states now existing shall think proper to admit shall not be prohibited by the Congress prior to the year one thousand eight hundred and eight, but a tax or duty may be imposed on such importation, not exceeding ten dollars for each person. *Emigrants, how admitted.*

2. The privilege of the writ of habeas corpus shall not be suspended, unless when, in cases of rebellion or invasion, the public safety may require it. *Habeas corpus.*

3. No bill of attainder, or ex post facto law, shall be passed. *Attainder.*

4. No capitation or other direct tax shall be laid, unless in proportion to the census or enumeration herein before directed to be taken. *Capitation.*

5. No tax or duty shall be laid on articles exported from any state. No preference shall be given, by any regulation of commerce or revenue, to the ports of one state over those of another ; nor shall vessels bound to or from one state be obliged to enter, clear, or pay duties, in another. *Regulations regarding duties.*

6. No money shall be drawn from the treasury but in consequence of appropriations made by law ; and a regular statement and account of the receipts and expenditures of all public money shall be published, from time to time. *Moneys, how drawn.*

7. No title of nobility shall be granted by the United States, and no person holding any office of profit or trust under them shall, without the consent of the Congress, accept of any present, emolument, office, or title of any kind whatever, from any king, prince, or foreign state. *Titles of nobility prohibited.*

SECTION X.

1. No state shall enter into any treaty, alliance or confederation ; grant letters of marque and reprisal ; coin money ; emit bills of credit ; make anything but gold and silver coin a tender in payment of debts ; pass any bill of attainder, ex post facto law, or law impairing the obligation of contracts ; or grant any title of nobility. *Powers of states defined.*

2. No state shall, without the consent of the Congress, lay any imposts or duties on imports or exports, except what may be absolutely necessary for executing its inspection laws ; and the neat produce of all duties and imposts, laid by any state on imports or exports, shall be for the use of the treasury of the United States, and all such laws shall be subject to the revision and control of the Congress. No state shall, without the consent of Congress, lay any duty of tonnage, keep troops or ships of war in time of peace, enter into any agreement or compact with another state, or with a foreign power, or engage in war, unless actually invaded, or in such imminent danger as will not admit of delay. *Powers further defined.*

ARTICLE II.

SECTION I.

1. The executive power shall be vested in a President of the United States of America. He shall hold his office during the term of four years, and, together with the vice-president, chosen for the same term, be elected as follows : *Executive power, in whom vested.*

2. Each state shall appoint, in such manner as the legislature thereof may direct, a number of electors equal to the whole number of senators and representatives to which the state may be entitled in the Congress ; but no senator, or representative, or per- *How elected.*

son holding an office of trust or profit under the United States, shall be appointed an elector.

Proceedings of electors and of House of Rep.   3. The electors shall meet in their respective states, and vote by ballot for two persons, of whom one, at least, shall not be an inhabitant of the same state with themselves. And they shall make a list of all the persons voted for, and of the number of votes for each ; which list they shall sign and certify, and transmit sealed to the seat of the government of the United States, directed to the President of the Senate. The President of the Senate shall, in the presence of the Senate and House of Representatives, open all the certificates, and the votes shall then be counted. The person having the greatest number of votes shall be the president, if such number be a majority of the whole number of electors appointed ; and if there be more than one who have such majority, and have an equal number of votes, then the House of Representatives shall immediately choose, by ballot, one of them for president ; and if no person have a majority, then, from the five highest on the list, the said house shall, in like manner, choose the president. But, in choosing the president, the votes shall be taken by states, the representation from each state having one vote ; a quorum from each state shall consist of a member or members from two-thirds of the states, and a majority of all the states shall be necessary to a choice. In every case, after the choice of the president, the person having the greatest number of votes of the electors shall be the vice-president. But, if there should remain two or more who have equal votes, the Senate shall choose from them, by ballot, the vice-president.

Time of choosing electors.   4. The Congress may determine the time of choosing the electors, and the day on which they shall give their votes ; which day shall be the same throughout the United States.

Qualifications of the president.   5. No person, except a natural-born citizen, or a citizen of the United States at the time of the adoption of this constitution, shall be eligible to the office of president ; neither shall any person be eligible to that office who shall not have attained to the age of thirty-five years, and been fourteen years a resident within the United States.

Resort in case of his disability.   6. In case of the removal of the president from office, or of his death, resignation, or inability to discharge the powers and duties of the said office, the same shall devolve on the vice-president; and the Congress may, by law, provide for the case of removal, death, resignation, or inability, both of the president and vice-president, declaring what officer shall then act as president; and such officer shall act accordingly, until the disability be removed, or a president shall be elected.

Salary of president.   7. The president shall, at stated times, receive for his services a compensation, which shall neither be increased nor diminished during the period for which he shall have been elected; and he shall not receive within that period any other emolument from the United States, or any of them.

Oath required.   8. Before he enter on the execution of his office, he shall take the following oath or affirmation :

9. "I do solemnly swear (or affirm) that I will faithfully execute the office of President of the United States, and will, to the best of my ability, preserve, protect, and defend, the constitution of the United States."

SECTION 11.

Duties of president.   1. The president shall be commander-in-chief of the army and navy of the United States, and of the militia of the several states, when called into the actual service of the United States ; he may require the opinion, in writing, of the principal officer, in each of the executive departments, upon any subject relating to the duties of their respective offices; and he shall have power to grant reprieves and pardons for offences against the United States, except in cases of impeachment.

2. He shall have power, by and with the advice and consent of the Senate, to make treaties, provided two-thirds of the senators present concur; and he shall nominate, and by and with the advice and consent of the Senate shall appoint, ambassadors, other public ministers and consuls, judges of the Supreme Court, and all other officers of the United States, whose appointments are not herein otherwise provided for, and which shall be established by law. But the Congress may, by law, vest the appointment of such inferior officers as they think proper in the president alone, in the courts of law, or in the heads of departments. *May make treaties, appoint ambassadors, judges, &c.*

3. The president shall have power to fill up all vacancies that may happen during the recess of the Senate, by granting commissions which shall expire at the end of their next session. *May fill vacancies.*

SECTION III.

1. He shall, from time to time, give to the Congress information of the state of the Union, and recommend to their consideration such measures as he shall judge necessary and expedient; he may, on extraordinary occasions, convene both houses, or either of them, and, in case of disagreement between them, with respect to the time of adjournment, he may adjourn them to such time as he shall think proper ; he shall receive ambassadors and other public ministers ; he shall take care that the laws be faithfully executed ; and shall commission all the officers of the United States. *May convene Cong.*

SECTION IV.

1. The president, vice-president, and all civil officers of the United States, shall be removed from office on impeachment for, and conviction of, treason, bribery, or other high crimes and misdemeanors. *How officers may be removed.*

ARTICLE III.

SECTION I.

1. The judicial power of the United States shall be vested in one Supreme Court, and in such inferior courts as the Congress may, from time to time, ordain and establish. The judges, both of the supreme and inferior courts, shall hold their offices during good behavior ; and shall, at stated times, receive for their services a compensation which shall not be diminished during their continuance in office. *Judicial power, how vested.*

SECTION II.

1. The judicial power shall extend to all cases in law and equity, arising under this constitution, the laws of the United States, and treaties made, or which shall be made, under their authority ; to all cases affecting ambassadors, other public ministers and consuls; to all cases of admiralty and maritime jurisdiction; to controversies to which the United States shall be a party ; to controversies between two or more states ; between a state and citizens of another state ; between citizens of different states; between citizens of the same state claiming lands under grants of different states ; and between a state, or the citizens thereof, and foreign states, citizens, or subjects. *To what cases it extends.*

29

Jurisdiction of the Supreme Court.

2. In all cases affecting ambassadors, other public ministers and consuls, and those in which a state shall be a party, the Supreme Court shall have original jurisdiction. In all the other cases before mentioned, the Supreme Court shall have appellate jurisdiction, both as to law and fact, with such exceptions, and under such regulations, as the Congress shall make.

Rules respecting trials.

3. The trial of all crimes, except in cases of impeachment, shall be by jury, and such trial shall be held in the state where the said crimes shall have been committed; but when not committed within any state, the trial shall be at such place or places as the Congress may by law have directed.

SECTION III.

Treason defined.

1. Treason against the United States shall consist in levying war against them, or in adhering to their enemies, giving them aid and comfort. No person shall be convicted of treason, unless on the testimony of two witnesses to the same overt act, or on confession in open court.

How punished.

2. The Congress shall have power to declare the punishment of treason ; but no attainder of treason shall work corruption of blood, or forfeiture, except during the life of the person attainted.

ARTICLE IV.

SECTION I.

Rights of states defined.

1. Full faith and credit shall be given in each state to the public acts, records, and judicial proceedings, of every other state. And the Congress may, by general laws, prescribe the manner in which such acts, records, and proceedings, shall be proved, and the effect thereof.

SECTION II.

Privileges of citizens.

1. The citizens of each state shall be entitled to all privileges and immunities of citizens in the several states.

Executive requisitions.

2. A person charged in any state with treason, felony or other crime, who shall flee from justice, and be found in another state, shall, on demand of the executive authority of the state from which he fled, be delivered up, to be removed to the state having jurisdiction of the crime.

Law regulating service, or labor.

4. No person held to service or labor in one state, under the laws thereof, escaping into another, shall, in consequence of any law or regulation therein, be discharged from such service or labor; but shall be delivered up on claim of the party to whom such service or labor may be due.

SECTION III.

New states, how formed and admitted.

1. New states may be admitted by the Congress into this Union; but no new states shall be formed or erected within the jurisdiction of any other state, nor any state be formed by the junction of two or more states, or parts of states, without the consent of the legislatures of the states concerned, as well as of the Congress.

Power of Congress over public lands.

2. The Congress shall have power to dispose of, and make all needful rules and regulations respecting, the territory or other property belonging to the United States; and nothing in this constitution shall be so construed as to prejudice any claims of the United States, or any particular state.

SECTION IV.

Republican government guaranteed.

1. The United States shall guarantee to every state in this Union a republican form of government, and shall protect each of

them against invasion ; and, on application of the legislature, or of the executive (when the legislature cannot be convened), against domestic violence.

ARTICLE V.

1. The Congress, whenever two-thirds of both houses shall deem it necessary, shall propose amendments to this constitution ; or, on the application of the legislatures of two-thirds of the several states, shall call a convention for proposing amendments, which, in either case, shall be valid to all intents and purposes, as part of this constitution, when ratified by the legislatures of three-fourths of the several states, or by conventions in three-fourths thereof, as the one or the other mode of ratification may be proposed by the Congress; provided, that no amendment which may be made prior to the year one thousand eight hundred and eight shall in any manner affect the first and fourth clauses in the ninth section of the first article ; and that no state, without its consent, shall be deprived of its equal suffrage in the Senate. *Constitution ; how to be amended.*

ARTICLE VI.

1. All debts contracted and engagements entered into, before the adoption of this constitution, shall be as valid against the United States under this constitution as under the Confederation. *Validity of debts recognized.*

2. This constitution, and the laws of the United States which shall be made in pursuance thereof, and all treaties made, or which shall be made, under the authority of the United States, shall be the supreme law of the land ; and the judges in every state shall be bound thereby, anything in the constitution or laws of any state to the contrary notwithstanding. *Supreme law of the land defined.*

3. The senators and representatives before mentioned, and the members of the several state legislatures, and all executive and judicial officers, both of the United States and of the several states, shall be bound by oath or affirmation to support this constitution; but no religious test shall ever be required as a qualification to any office or public trust under the United States. *Oath ; of whom required, and for what.*

ARTICLE VII.

1. The ratification of the conventions of nine states shall be sufficient for the establishment of this constitution between the states so ratifying the same. *Ratification.*

Done in convention, by the unanimous consent of the states present, the seventeenth day of September, in the year of our Lord one thousand seven hundred and eighty-seven, and of the independence of the United States of America the twelfth. In witness whereof, we have hereunto subscribed our names.

GEORGE WASHINGTON, *President,*
and Deputy from Virginia.

The constitution was ratified by the prescribed number of states in 1788, and went into operation in 1789. Vermont, the first of the new states which joined the Union, gave her assent early in 1791. The number of delegates chosen to the convention was sixty-five ; ten did not attend ; sixteen declined signing the *Constitution, when ratified.*

constitution, or left the convention before it was ready to be signed Thirty-nine signed, as follows :

NEW HAMPSHIRE.
John Langdon,
Nicholas Gilman.

MASSACHUSETTS.
Nathaniel Gorman,
Rufus King.

CONNECTICUT.
Wm. Samuel Johnson,
Roger Sherman.

NEW YORK.
Alexander Hamilton.

NEW JERSEY.
William Livingston,
David Bearley,
William Paterson,
Jonathan Dayton.

PENNSYLVANIA.
Benjamin Franklin,
Thomas Mifflin,
Robert Morris,
George Clymer,
Thomas Fitzsimons,
Jared Ingersoll,
James Wilson,
Governeur Morris.

DELAWARE.
George Read,
Gunning Bedford, Jr.,
John Dickinson,
Richard Bassett,
Jacob Broom.

MARYLAND.
James M'Henry,
Daniel of St. Thomas Jenifer,

Daniel Carroll.

VIRGINIA.
John Blair,
James Madison, Jr.

NORTH CAROLINA.
William Blount,
Rich'd Dobbs Spaight,
Hugh Williamson.

SOUTH CAROLINA.
John Rutledge,
Charles   Cotesworth
Pinckney,
Charles Pinckney,
Pierce Butler.

GEORGIA.
William Few,
Abraham Baldwin.

Attest,   WILLIAM JACKSON, *Secretary.*

AMENDMENTS TO THE CONSTITUTION.

AT the first session of the first Congress, twelve amendments to the constitution were recommended to the states, ten of which were adopted; the others have since been adopted.

Freedom in religion — speech — press.

Art. 1. Congress shall make no law respecting an establishment of religion, or prohibiting the free exercise thereof ; or abridging the freedom of speech, or of the press; or the right of the people peaceably to assemble, and to petition the government for a redress of grievances.

Militia.

Art. 2. A well-regulated militia being necessary to the security of a free state, the right of the people to keep and bear arms shall not be infringed.

Soldiers.

Art. 3. No soldier shall, in time of peace, be quartered in any house, without the consent of the owner; nor in time of war, but in a manner to be prescribed by law.

Search-warrant.

Art. 4. The right of the people to be secure in their persons, houses, papers, and effects, against unreasonable searches and seizures, shall not be violated ; and no warrants shall issue but upon probable cause, supported by oath or affirmation, and particularly describing the place to be searched, and the persons or things to be seized.

Capital crimes.

Art. 5. No person shall be held to answer for a capital or otherwise infamous crime, unless on a presentment or indictment of a grand jury, except in cases arising in the land or naval forces, or in the militia, when in actual service, in time of war or public danger; nor shall any person be subject for the same offence to be twice put in jeopardy of life or limb; nor shall be compelled, in any criminal case, to be a witness against himself ; nor be deprived of life, liberty or property, without due process of law; nor shall private property be taken for public use, without just compensation.

Trial by jury.

Art. 6. In all criminal prosecutions the accused shall enjoy the right to a speedy and public trial by an impartial jury of the state and district wherein the crime shall have been committed, which district shall have been previously ascertained by law, and to be informed of the nature and cause of the accusation ; to be confronted with the witnesses against him ; to have compulsory process for obtaining witnesses in his favor; and to have the assistance of counsel for his defence.

Art. 7. In suits at common law, where the value in controversy *Suits at common law.* shall exceed twenty dollars, the right of trial by jury shall be preserved; and no fact tried by a jury shall be otherwise reëxamined, in any court of the United States, than according to the rules of the common law.

Art. 8. Excessive bail shall not be required, nor excessive fines *Bail.* imposed, nor cruel and unusual punishments inflicted.

Art. 9. The enumeration in the constitution of certain rights *Certain rights defined.* shall not be construed to deny or disparage others retained by the people.

Art. 10. The powers not delegated to the United States by the *Rights reserved.* constitution, nor prohibited by it to the states, are reserved to the states respectively, or to the people.

Art. 11. The judicial power of the United States shall not be *Judicial power limited.* construed to extend to any suit in law or equity, commenced or prosecuted against one of the United States, by citizens of another state, or by citizens or subjects of any foreign state.

Art. 12. § 1. The electors shall meet in their respective states, *Amendment to Art. II., Sect. 4, respecting election of president and vice-president.* and vote by ballot for president and vice-president, one of whom, at least, shall not be an inhabitant of the same state with themselves; they shall name in their ballots the person voted for as president, and in distinct ballots the person voted for as vice-president; and they shall make distinct lists of all persons voted for as president, and of all persons voted for as vice-president, and of the number of votes for each, which lists they shall sign and certify, and transmit, sealed, to the seat of the government of the United States, directed to the President of the Senate; the President of the Senate shall, in the presence of the Senate and House of Representatives, open all the certificates, and the votes shall then be counted; the person having the greatest number of votes for president shall be the president, if such number be a majority of the whole number of electors appointed; and if no person have such majority, then from the persons having the highest numbers, not exceeding three, on the list of those voted for as president, the House of Representatives shall choose immediately, by ballot, the president. But, in choosing the president, the votes shall be taken by states, the representation from each state having one vote; a quorum for this purpose shall consist of a member or members from two-thirds of the states, and a majority of all the states shall be necessary to a choice. And if the House of Representatives shall not choose a president, whenever the right of choice shall devolve upon them, before the fourth day of March next following, then the vice-president shall act as president, as in the case of the death or other constitutional disability of the president.

2. The person having the greatest number of votes as vice-president shall be the vice-president, if such number be a majority of the whole number of electors appointed; and if no person have a majority, then from the two highest numbers on the list the Senate shall choose the vice-president: a quorum for the purpose shall consist of two-thirds of the whole number of senators, and a majority of the whole number shall be necessary to a choice.

3. But no person constitutionally ineligible to the office of president shall be eligible to that of vice-president of the United States.

DECLARATION OF INDEPENDENCE.

In Congress, July 4, 1776.

THE UNANIMOUS DECLARATION OF THE THIRTEEN UNITED STATES OF AMERICA.

WHEN, in the course of human events, it becomes necessary for one people to dissolve the political bands which have connected them with another, and to assume, among the powers of the earth, the separate and equal station to which the laws of nature and of nature's God entitle them, a decent respect to the opinions of mankind requires that they should declare the causes which impel them to the separation.

We hold these truths to be self-evident: — That all men are created equal; that they are endowed by their Creator with certain unalienable rights; that among these are life, liberty, and the pursuit of happiness. That, to secure these rights, governments are instituted among men, deriving their just powers from the consent of the governed; that, whenever any form of government becomes destructive of these ends, it is the right of the people to alter or to abolish it, and to institute a new government, laying its foundation on such principles, and organizing its powers in such form, as to them shall seem most likely to effect their safety and happiness. Prudence, indeed, will dictate, that governments long established should not be changed for light and transient causes; and accordingly all experience hath shown that mankind are more disposed to suffer while evils are sufferable, than to right themselves by abolishing the forms to which they are accustomed. But when a long train of abuses and usurpations, pursuing invariably the same object, evinces a design to reduce them under absolute despotism, it is their right, it is their duty, to throw off such government, and to provide new guards for their future security. Such has been the patient sufferance of these colonies; and such is now the necessity which constrains them to alter their former systems of government. The history of the present King of Great Britain is a history of repeated injuries and usurpations, all having in direct object the establishment of an absolute tyranny over these states. To prove this, let facts be submitted to a candid world.

He has refused his assent to laws the most wholesome and necessary for the public good.

He has forbidden his governors to pass laws of immediate and pressing importance, unless suspended in their operation till his assent should be obtained ; and when so suspended, he has utterly neglected to attend to them. He has refused to pass other laws for the accommodation of large districts of people, unless those people would relinquish the right of representation in the legislature, — a right inestimable to them, and formidable to tyrants only.

He has called together legislative bodies at places unusual, uncomfortable, and distant from the repository of their public records, for the sole purpose of fatiguing them into compliance with his measures.

He has dissolved representative houses repeatedly, for opposing, with manly firmness, his invasions on the rights of the people.

He has refused, for a long time after such dissolutions, to cause others to be elected; whereby the legislative powers, incapable of annihilation, have returned to the people at large, for their exercise, the state remaining, in the mean time, exposed to all the dangers of invasion from without, and convulsions within.

He has endeavored to prevent the population of these states; for that purpose, obstructing the laws for naturalization of foreigners, refusing to pass others to encourage their migration hither, and raising the conditions of new appropriations of lands.

He has obstructed the administration of justice, by refusing his assent to laws for establishing judiciary powers.

He has made judges dependent on his will alone for the tenure of their offices, and the amount and payment of their salaries.

He has erected a multitude of new offices, and sent hither swarms of officers, to harass our people, and eat out their substance.

He has kept among us, in times of peace, standing armies, without the consent of our legislatures.

He has affected to render the military independent of, and superior to, the civil power.

He has combined with others to subject us to a jurisdiction foreign to our constitution, and unacknowledged by our laws ; giving his assent to their acts of pretended legislation,—

For quartering large bodies of armed troops among us :

For protecting them, by a mock trial, from punishment for any murders which they should commit on the inhabitants of these states :

For cutting off our trade with all parts of the world :

For imposing taxes on us without our consent :

For depriving us, in many cases, of the benefits of trial by jury :

For transporting us beyond seas to be tried for pretended offences :

For abolishing the free system of English laws in a neighboring province, establishing therein an arbitrary government, and enlarging its boundaries, so as to render it at once an example and fit instrument for introducing the same absolute rule into these colonies :

For taking away our charters, abolishing our most valuable laws, and altering, fundamentally, the forms of our governments :

For suspending our own legislatures, and declaring themselves invested with power to legislate for us in all cases whatsoever.

He has abdicated government here, by declaring us out of his protection, and waging war against us.

He has plundered our seas, ravaged our coasts, burnt our towns, and destroyed the lives of our people.

He is at this time transporting large armies of foreign mercenaries, to complete the works of death, desolation, and tyranny, already begun with circumstances of cruelty and perfidy scarcely paralleled in the most barbarous ages, and totally unworthy the head of a civilized nation.

He has constrained our fellow-citizens, taken captive on the high seas, to bear arms against their country, to become the executioners of their friends and brethren, or to fall themselves by their hands.

He has excited domestic insurrections amongst us, and has endeavored to bring on the inhabitants of our frontiers the merciless Indian savages, whose known rule of warfare is an undistinguished destruction of all ages, sexes, and conditions.

In every stage of these oppressions, we have petitioned for redress in the most humble terms ; our repeated petitions have been answered only by repeated injury. A prince, whose character is thus marked by every act which may define a tyrant, is unfit to be the ruler of a free people.

Nor have we been wanting in attentions to our British brethren. We have warned them, from time to time, of attempts by their legislature to extend an unwarrantable jurisdiction over us. We have reminded them of the circumstances of our emigration and settlement here. We have appealed to their native justice and magnanimity; and we have conjured them, by the ties of our common kindred, to disavow these usurpations, which would inevitably interrupt our connections and correspondence. They, too, have been deaf to the voice of justice and of consanguinity. We must, therefore, acquiesce in the necessity which denounces our separation, and hold them, as we hold the rest of mankind, enemies in war, in peace friends.

We, therefore, the Representatives of the United States of America, in General Congress assembled, appealing to the Supreme Judge of the world for the rectitude of our intentions, do, in the name and by the authority of the good people of these colonies, solemnly publish and declare, that these united colonies are, and of right ought to be, free and independent states; that they are absolved from all allegiance to the British crown, and that all political connection between them and the state of Great Britain is, and ought to be, totally dissolved; and that, as free and independent states, they have full power to levy war, conclude peace, contract alliances, establish commerce, and to do all other acts and things which independent states may of right do. And, for the support of this declaration, with a firm reliance on the protection of Divine Providence, we mutually pledge to each other our lives, our fortunes, and our sacred honor.

JOHN HANCOCK.

NEW HAMPSHIRE.
Josiah Bartlett,
William Whipple,
Matthew Thornton.

MASSACHUSETTS BAY.
Samuel Adams,
John Adams,
Robert Treat Paine,
Elbridge Gerry.

RHODE ISLAND, ETC.
Stephen Hopkins,
William Ellery.

CONNECTICUT.
Roger Sherman,
Samuel Huntingdon,
William Williams,
Oliver Wolcott.

NEW YORK.
William Floyd,
Philip Livingston,
Francis Lewis,
Lewis Morris.

NEW JERSEY.
Richard Stockton,
John Witherspoon,
Francis Hopkinson,
John Hart,
Abraham Clark.

PENNSYLVANIA.
Robert Morris,
Benjamin Rush,
Benjamin Franklin,
John Morton,
George Clymer,
James Smith,
George Taylor,
James Wilson,
George Ross.

DELAWARE.
Cæsar Rodney,
George Read,
Thomas M'Kean.

MARYLAND.
Samuel Chase,
William Paca,

Thomas Stone,
C. Carroll, of Carrolton.

VIRGINIA.
George Wythe,
Richard Henry Lee,
Thomas Jefferson,
Benjamin Harrison,
Thomas Nelson, Jr.,
Francis Lightfoot Lee,
Carter Braxton.

NORTH CAROLINA.
William Hooper,
Joseph Hewes,
John Penn.

SOUTH CAROLINA.
Edward Rutledge,
Thomas Heyward, Jr.,
Thomas Lynch, Jr.,
Arthur Middleton.

GEORGIA.
Burton Gwinnett,
Lyman Hall,
George Walton.

QUESTIONS.

The figures 1, 2, 3, 4, 5, 6, which occur in the following questions, and which are enclosed in parentheses ( ), refer to the MAPS; and the pupil is requested to consult the map to which reference is at any time thus made.

Map No. 1 faces page 14.   Map No. 4 faces page 134.
  "   "   2   "   "   36.   "   "   5   "   "   172.
  "   "   3   "   "   66.   "   "   6   "   "   302.

INTRODUCTION.

1. OF what does history set before us striking instances? By what does it incite us to imitate such noble examples? With what pictures does history present us? Against what does it warn us?

2. What is history the school of? What springs does it open? What influences does it point out? What blessings does it illustrate? What miseries? What dangers? What mischiefs?

3. What dealings does history display? What does it call upon us to regard with awe? What emotions does it awaken? On whom does it lead us to depend? What does it strengthen? With what conviction does it impress us?

4. How does the study of history affect the imagination? The taste? For what does it furnish matter? Of what does it enlarge the range? What does it strengthen and discipline?

5. What is the first reason why the history of the United States should be studied? What the second? third? fourth? fifth?

GENERAL DIVISION.

Into how many periods may the history of the United States be divided?

For what is Period I. distinguished? When did it commence? When did it end? How long is it?

NOTE. Questions similar to the four last may be asked on each of the following Periods.

PERIOD I., p. 9.

For what is Period I. distinguished? When did it commence? When terminate? Length?

I. COLUMBUS. 1. To what nation belongs the honor of making known to the Europeans the existence of a Western Continent? To what individual? Of what nation was Columbus a native?

2. Where was Columbus born? When? Who was his father? How many brothers and sisters had he? What is said of his early education? At what age did he first go to sea?

3. To what city did he repair? What was his age? What is said

of him at this time? Whom did he marry? Where did he fix his residence?

4. With whom did he reside? What privilege was he allowed? With what did he thus become acquainted?

5. What belief did he adopt?

6. What discoveries confirmed his belief? What well-established fact?

7. Under whose patronage did he first offer to sail? With what success? To whom did he next apply? How was he treated by the Portuguese king and his advisers? Whom did he send to England? What was the result? To what country did he next repair?

8. By what route? In Spain, where do we find him? Who was with him? What did he want? What took place between him and the prior of the convent? How did the latter assist Columbus?

9. How did these sovereigns treat his application? What, at length, did the queen decide to do? How did she propose to defray the expense of the voyage? How many vessels were provided? Names of these vessels? Of which had Columbus command? Describe them. Number of mariners? Number in all?

10. Time of sailing? Port? To what islands did they first sail?

11. What incidents shall we pass over? What took place Oct. 20? What reward was promised? To whom? For what? Who made this offer?

12. Where did Columbus take his station? What was his state of mind? What did he think he saw? At what hour? Whom did he call? For what?

13. Whom did he next call? What did they see? What did Columbus consider these indications of?

14. What signal did the Pinta give? When? Who first discovered land? To whom, however, was the award adjudged? Why?

15. On the following morning, what did they see before them? When was this? What did the natives call the island? What name did Columbus give it? What is this island called in English maps? With what was it covered? Latitude and longitude of this island? (1.) Which way is it from Cuba? Which way from Washington city?

16. Describe the landing of Columbus. By whom was the island inhabited? What was their appearance? How did they regard the English? What did they think of the ships?

17. What large island did Columbus next discover? Present capital of Cuba? What other large island did Columbus discover? What other name has St. Domingo? (1.) Which way is St. Domingo from Cuba? What island lies nearly west of Hayti? What island nearly east? (1.)

18. What befell Columbus during his return voyage? What did he enclose in a cask? Why? When did he arrive in Spain?

19. To what was Columbus entitled? By whom was he robbed of this honor? Who was Vespucius? By what means did he give name to America?

20. Did Columbus make other voyages? Did he ever discover the continent? At what point? When? Did he know it?

21. What took place on his third voyage? What did his enemies induce the king to do? How was this order executed?

22. What is said of Columbus on his return? What had become

of Isabella? What effect had her death upon him? When did he die? Where? What were his last words?

23. Where was his body deposited? To what place was it removed? Where were the remains of his son Diego? To what place were their bodies removed? Where do they now repose?

24. Ignorant of what did Columbus die? What idea did he entertain? What did he think Hispaniola was? What Cuba?

II. JOHN CABOT. What followed the announcement of Columbus' discovery? Who was John Cabot? Where did he reside? When did he sail for America? Under whose patronage? By whom accompanied? When did he fall in with land? What did he call it? What was this land? What island did he probably discover? Where is the coast of Labrador? Where is Newfoundland? (3.) Which way from Boston is Labrador? Which way from Labrador is Newfoundland?

III. SEBASTIAN CABOT. When did Sebastian Cabot make a second voyage? In company with whom? What did he explore? In what direction did he sail? What reward had he for his services? Who bestowed this reward?

IV. JOHN VERRAZANI. 1. When did the French attempt discoveries? Who was employed to make them? By what king? Of how many did his squadron consist? What is said of his ships?

2. Where did he strike the coast? (1.) In what latitude is Wilmington? (5.) After proceeding south, along what coast did he sail? At what point did he land? In what harbor did he anchor? What coast did he explore? In what direction must he have sailed? (3.) What name did he give to the country? How long was this name applied to the country? To what territory was it afterwards restricted?

3. What became of Verrazani?

V. JAMES CARTIER. 1. When did Cartier make a voyage to America? Under whose patronage? What island did he visit? What gulf discover? (3.) During a second voyage, what places did he visit? Point them out. (3.) Whence had Montreal its name? What Indian settlement existed there? Where did Cartier spend the winter? Which way from Quebec is the Island of Orleans? (3.) What is the course of the river St. Lawrence?

2. What is said of Cartier in 1540? Where did he build a fort? What became of his colony? What became of Cartier? What became of the party he met at Newfoundland?

VI. FERDINAND DE SOTO. 1. When, and by whom, was the Mississippi discovered? Who was De Soto? How long after the discovery of the St. Lawrence was the Mississippi discovered? From what island did De Soto come? In what year? For what purpose? When did he first discover the river? At what point? Where does the Mississippi empty? What is its general direction? (5.)

2. What was Soto's object in traversing the country? Where did he spend the summer of 1539? Where did he go in 1540? What rivers did he cross? What places did he visit? Where are Mobile and Pensacola? (1.) (5.) When did De Soto die? Where? Where did his followers attempt to go? Where did they encamp? What is Red river a branch of? What did they here construct? Whence did they proceed? Where, at length, did they arrive?

VII. SIR WALTER RALEIGH. Whom did Raleigh despatch to America? When? Under commission of whom? How many vessels?

What sound did they enter? On what coast? To what island did they proceed? What did they do here? Who gave name to Virginia? Why this name?

VIII. BARTHOLOMEW GOSNOLD. 1. In what year did Gosnold make a voyage to America? To what part? What discoveries did he make? Origin of Cape Cod? Where is this cape? (2.)

2. Who was Gosnold? By what route did he reach America? Length of his voyage? What islands did he discover? Where are these islands? (2.) Where did he form a settlement? What became of it? Length of his return voyage?

IX. STATE OF THE COUNTRY. What was the aspect of North America on the arrival of the first settlers? What wild beasts inhabited the forest? What is said of the grapes? Natural productions in the South? In all parts of the land?

X. ABORIGINES. 1. By whom was the country inhabited? Probable number?

2. What can you say of their personal character? What of their personal appearance? What of their complexion? What of their constitution?

3. What was their general character? What was their disposition? For what distinguished in council? For what in war? What is said of their revengeful feelings? If captured, what was their conduct?

4. What is said of their books? To what was their education confined? What was their language? To what were their arts and manufactures confined?

5. What is said of their agriculture? What articles of food did they raise? To what was their skill in medicine confined? To what did they resort, when they knew no remedy for a disease? By what means did the powow attempt a cure? What is said of diseases among the Indians?

6. Employments of the men? Of the women?

7. Amusements of the men? What did they do during their war-dances? What were the amusements of the females?

8. What was their dress in summer? What in winter? What is said of their regard for ornaments? What did their sachems wear on days of festivity and show? What object did they aim at in painting themselves? What was their sign for royalty?

9. What were their habitations called? How constructed?

10. Mention some of their domestic utensils. On what did they sit, eat and lodge? What did they use instead of knives? What instead of twine? What for fish-hooks?

11. What did their food consist of? How did they cook it? How did they cook corn?

12. What was their money? What was it called? How did the wampum of the New England Indians and that of the Six Nations differ? What was a belt of wampum a token of?

13. What is said of society among them? What is said of the men? What was the condition of the women? Why did they form few local attachments?

14. What was their favorite employment? What were their offensive weapons? What their defensive? In what manner did they attack their enemies? How did they treat prisoners? How were treaties ratified?

15. What was their government? Whose decisions were final? Whom, however, did he consult?

16. By what means were they able to remember the speeches they had heard?

17. How many principal gods did they acknowledge? Which did they consider the superior? Which did they worship? Of what did they form images of these? What else did they worship? Manner of worship? What offerings did the Virginia Indians make to their gods? Of what events had they traditions?

18. What is said of marriage among them? What of polygamy? What was their treatment of females? How were they considered? What were they required to perform?

19. What is said of their burials? How were their graves dug? What did they bury with their friends? What did they raise over their graves? In what posture did some tribes bury their dead? Toward what point were their faces placed? What took place during the burial service? What is said of the origin of the Indians? Whence did the Indians probably come to America? Why is this opinion probable? Could they have emigrated from the Eastern Continent?

XI. REFLECTIONS. 2. What in the conduct of Columbus should we emulate? What may we hope to accomplish by these? In what career should we press forward? What, however, should moderate our expectations of reward on earth?

3. To what results do small actions sometimes lead? For what will the name of Americus Vespucius ever be stigmatized?

MISCELLANEOUS QUESTIONS ON GENERAL DIVISION AND PERIOD I.

1. Into how many periods may the history of the United States be divided? How may each be distinguished? For what is Period I. distinguished? second? third? &c. Which is the longest period? Which next? What five periods were each eight years? What two periods were four years each? How long was it from the discovery of America to the battle of Lexington?

2. To what countries did the discoverers of the principal parts of America belong? Ans. Spain, England and France. Of what nation were the leaders of the discoveries? Ans. The Italian. What was the Italian name of Columbus? Ans. Cristoval Colon. Under what captain did he serve for several years? Ans. Captain Colon. What part of the New World did Columbus first discover? Did he ever discover the continent? What part of it? Had any one previously discovered it? Who? What part? Who patronized the voyage of Columbus? Why did not Ferdinand take any part in the enterprise? Ans. He had no confidence in the project of Columbus. From what port did Columbus sail? Where is Palos? Ans. In Spain, near the south-east corner of Portugal. Which way from Jamestown? Ans. Exactly east. Where did Columbus expect to land? Ans. In India.

3. Who discovered Cape Cod? Where is Cape Cod? Who discovered the Gulf of St. Lawrence? Whence did Virginia derive its name? What islands did Columbus discover? What other name is given to the island of Hayti? Meaning of Hispaniola? Ans. Little Spain. At what place did Columbus die? What was the whole expense of the first outfit of Columbus? Ans. About four thousand pounds sterling. Value of a pound sterling? Ans. Four dollars and forty-four cents. Value of

his outfit in dollars ? Did Isabella actually part with her royal jewels ? ANS. No. She offered to do so, but the money was advanced by St. Angel.

4. From what port did Cabot sail ? ANS. Bristol. What part of the continent did he first discover ? Who discovered the Mississippi ? Who was Americus Vespucius ? What was his occupation ? ANS. He was a merchant.

5. What is meant by the aborigines of a country ? What were the aborigines of America called ? Whence did the Indians come to America ? What was their appearance ? What was their money called ? What gods did they worship ? Amusements ? Habitations ? Domestic utensils ? Agriculture ? When sick, to whom did they apply ? Arts and manufactures ? Dress ? Favorite employments ?

PERIOD II., p. 25.

1. For what is Period II. distinguished ? When did it commence ? When terminate ? Length ?

I. VIRGINIA.

1. How long was it from the discovery of San Salvador to the settlement of Jamestown ? What is said of attempts to settle the country during that time ? Of how many did the Jamestown colony consist ? Where is Jamestown ? (5.) When did the colony leave England ? What is said of this settlement ?

2. Why was it called Jamestown ? What two companies were formed in England ? What lands did James I. give to these two companies ?

3. Under which company was Virginia settled ? Who commanded the expedition ? Where was the government of the colony framed ? Of whom did it consist ?

4. Where did the colony intend to settle ? Where is Roanoke ? (5.) Why did they not settle there ? What bay did they enter ? What are its capes ? (5.) Names of the council ? Who was president ?

5. What enterprising magistrate can you mention ? What is said of his patriotism and self-denial ? What became of him during the voyage ? Why ?

6. What took place in regard to him after their arrival ?

7. Condition of the colony soon after its commencement ? On what account did it suffer ? What distinguished man soon died ?

8. When and by what means was the condition of the colony improved ? What accessions were made to it ?

9. When did the London Company obtain a new charter ? Why ? Who was appointed governor ? Title of the company, under their new act of incorporation ? What territory was granted them ? Where is Point Comfort ? (5.)

10. Why did not Lord de la War come to America ? Whom did he despatch ? With how many ships and men ? How many of these ships arrived, and when ? What became of one of them ?

11. Condition of the colony, on the arrival of Sir Thomas ? Where was Captain Smith ? What took place after his departure ? How much had the colony become reduced ? What took place at this juncture ? What was proposed ? How was their return to England prevented ?

12. When did Lord de la War leave the administration, and why ? Who succeeded ? What change took place in regard to the ownership of lands ? How did this operate ?

13. What memorable event took place in Virginia in 1609? What is said of this colonial assembly? Who convened it, and where? Before this, how had the colonies been ruled? With what were they now invested? How divided?

14. What is said of accessions to the colony in 1620? Number of colonists before this accession? What was done to attach them still more to the country? Price of a wife? How much was this tobacco worth per pound? What, then, did a wife cost?

15. What other accessions were made, and by whose order? When was slavery introduced? By whom?

16. Who was the successor of Powhatan? What did he attempt? In what year? How far was his plan put in execution?

17. When was the London Company dissolved? By whom? Under what pretext? Who assumed the government? What did it consist of?

18. Of whom did the London Company consist? Amount they had expended? Number of persons sent over? Number of survivors at the dissolution of the company?

19. What is said of the dissolution of the charter? What of the subsequent regulations of the king? Whom did the people at length send prisoner to England? When, and why? What did the king do with Harvey? Who, however, succeeded him? When, and with what instructions? What effect had the granting of this privilege? What took place in 1652? What became of Berkley?

20. When was Berkley invited back? What did Charles II. do, on his accession? What was the conduct of Berkley from this time? What rebellion resulted from the discontent of the people?

21. Who was Bacon? For what was he distinguished? What commission did he ask of Berkley? How did Berkley treat him? What did Bacon do? What became of Berkley?

22. What was done to Jamestown by Bacon's followers? What other outrages were committed? What became of Bacon himself? After this, what did Berkley do? What is said of this rebellion in Virginia? How long did its effects last? During its continuance, what was neglected? How long was Berkley Governor of Virginia? Where did he die?

23. What is thought of Bacon by some historians? What was the character of Berkley's administration? What would he not allow in the province? By whom was Bacon's conduct condemned, and what was he declared?

24. Who succeeded Berkley? What laws did Culpepper bring with him? What is said of one particular law? What dishonest act of Culpepper can you mention? On presenting the laws to the assembly, what did Culpepper inform them? What did the assembly do? What is said of further events in the history of Virginia?

II. MASSACHUSETTS, p. 35.

1. Derivation of the name Massachusetts?

2. What was Massachusetts originally a part of? To what company had it been conveyed? By whom, and when?

3. Under whom did the company send a colony? Where did they land? (2.) What became of this colony?

4. What is said of Captain John Smith, in 1614? What coast did he explore? (2.) To whom did he present a map of the country? What did Charles call it?

5. What effect had the representations of Captain Smith on the Plymouth Company? What became of the old company? What was the title of the new company? What territory was granted to this company?

6. Date of their charter? What was it the basis of? Had the first settlement of the territory been begun with or without any patent?

I. PLYMOUTH COLONY. 1. When did the Plymouth Colony arrive on the coast of America? Of how many did it consist? Where did they land, and when? What did they call their settlement? (2.)

2. Where were these settlers principally from? Where had they sometimes lived, before embarking for America? Why? Who was their leader? How early did they attempt to remove to Amsterdam? Did they succeed? Why not?

3. When did they succeed? What part, however, were detained, and why?

4. On what coast were they driven? What did the sailors exclaim? What did the Pilgrims do? What was the effect of their prayers?

5. How long did they remain in Holland? At what two places? On what account was their situation unpleasant? Where did they decide to remove? Of whom did they seek direction? By what service?

6. Where did they originally contemplate settling? With whom did they form a partnership? Why with them? What is said of the terms of this partnership?

7. What two vessels did they procure? Which did they purchase, and which hire? Tonnage of these vessels?

8. Before departing, what religious service did they observe? From Leyden where did they repair? To what place did they sail? Where were they joined by the Mayflower? When did both vessels set sail? What became of the Speedwell?

9. When did the Mayflower sail from Plymouth? With how many passengers? When did they first descry the coast of America? What cape? (2.) How long had their voyage been? Where did they design to settle? Why did they relinquish it? In what harbor did they anchor?

10. Before landing, what did they do? Who was chosen governor? Whom did they send out to make discoveries? With what effect?

11. What is said of Miles Standish and his party? Whom did they see? What did they discover? What did they do with this corn? How did it serve them afterward? Who was the first-born European child in New England?

12. How were they employed for several days from the 16th of December? Where did they land? On what rock?

13. What is said of the Mayflower? Where did they station their ordnance? Into how many families were they divided? What was assigned to each one? What common house was erected? What did this serve for? What is said of a fort, afterwards erected?

14. What presently was the condition of the Pilgrims? Why did they so suffer? Number of deaths before the middle of March? How many of these had signed the compact on board the Mayflower? Where was their burial-place? What is said of those early graves?

15. What is said of the neighboring Indians? When was the first treaty made with the Indians? Through whom, and with what chief? How long was this treaty kept inviolate?

16. Who was Canonicus? What did he do? How did Governor Bradford retort upon him? What was the result?

17. In what year did the colony anticipate a famine? Why? What did the Indians prophesy? What day did the colonists observe? What is said of this day? What change took place toward evening? In token of gratitude, what did the colonists do? Was this the first or second Thanksgiving? When was the first?

18. Was this Plymouth Colony a profitable enterprise to the London adventurers? Why did they grow discouraged? How did they act in opposition to the interest of the colony?

19. When did this partnership end? By what means? Who became sole proprietors of the land? What patent had been procured? What division now took place?

20. Was the colony ever incorporated by the king? How was the government at first formed and conducted? What did it consist of till 1624? What change then took place? When did the towns send deputies? How long did the colony continue distinct? With what was it united? When? and by whom?

II. COLONY OF MASSACHUSETTS BAY. 1. What was the second colony of New England called? When was it founded? By whom? Who was sent over by the purchasers? Where did they settle? Indian name? Number of colonists?

2. Object of these colonists? What two men were most active in this enterprise?

3. What tract of land did they purchase?

4. When did they obtain a charter? By what title? First governors? When did additional settlers arrive? What did they bring with them? What settlement did they commence?

5. What took place in 1630 in regard to the charter and powers of government? Where were the officers of government first chosen? First governor? Who were the other magistrates?

6. Who came over with Governor Winthrop? Where did they design to settle? Where did they settle? and why? (2.) Where did Governor Winthrop settle? What was Boston first denominated?

7. What is said of Governor Winthrop? In what condition did he find the colony?

8. What other evils were troubling them? What number of deaths occurred, by the close of the year? What venerable minister died? What is said of his colleague? What is said of Mr. Johnson and his lady?

9. Character of the succeeding winter? Why did the colonists suffer so severely? What is said of their stock of provisions? What of a poor man and the governor? Upon what did many subsist?

10. What was done, in this state of calamity? What occurred the day before the Fast? What change took place in consequence?

11. What two rules were adopted by the electors in 1631? Would such a rule as the latter be now tolerated? When was it repealed? What was the design of it?

12. What more important change took place in 1634? Why was this change expected? What does Mr. Bancroft observe upon this?

13. What is said of the next ten years from this time? What did the assistants claim over the freemen of the colony? What remedy was found for this evil? and when? What thus commenced?

14. When was Roger Williams banished? Why? What did he

30*

deny? What did he maintain? What, however, was the chief cause of his banishment? What is said of his doctrine?

15. What is said of the banishment of Mr. Williams? What is said of the Pilgrim Fathers in so acting in reference to him? What colony did Mr. Williams found?

16. What accessions were made in 1635? What two distinguished personages were among the number? What office was conferred on Sir Harry Vane? Why? What does Mr. Bancroft say of this appointment?

17. Who was Anne Hutchinson? What monstrous doctrine did she advance? Who embraced her views? Who deemed her sentiments heretical? How were the people affected? By whom were her opinions condemned? What became of her? What is said of Governor Vane?

18. What was done for education as early as 1636? Who was John Harvard? What benefaction did he leave? What college was named after him? What was done in 1647 for schools?

19. What do you mean by the union of the colonies? What colonies were these? What articles did they sign? and when? Why were they urged to such a union?

20. What were some of the articles of this confederacy?

21. How long did this union last? What colony petitioned to be admitted? When? Why was she refused? What were some of the effects of this union?

22. What two men enlisted themselves in behalf of the Indians? What was their object? How did they attempt to convert the Indians? What society was formed in England with reference to this object? How did the Indians regard Christianity? What success had Mayhew and Eliot? What is said of Indian converts? Where are Martha's Vineyard and Nantucket? (2.)

23. What other history is connected with the history of Massachusetts? What is said of the settlements of New Hampshire in 1641? What of the inhabitants of Maine in 1652? When did the coast of Maine begin to be settled? What took place before they had gathered much strength? Where are the Piscataqua and Penobscot? (2.) What did these conflicting patents give rise to?

24. Where is Saco? (2.) What court was held there? When? By whom? and why? Death of Gorges? What took place after his death?

25. When did a royal fleet arrive for the reduction of the Dutch? Where did it arrive? What commissioners were on board? What were they authorized to do? How did King Charles regard the colonies?

26. Conduct of the commissioners? What did they receive? What did they require? What did they hear and decide? What is said of their recall?

27. When did King Philip's War commence? What is said of it? How had the Indians regarded the English? Why?

28. Who was the principal exciter of the Indians? Who was Philip? What is said of a treaty made with Masassoit at page 41? Residence of Philip? Where was Mount Hope? Immediate cause of the war? Upon whom was the first attack made? and when? What were the people about? Where is Swanzey? (2.)

29. What took place in consequence of this attack? What became

of Philip? Who favored Philip? Where did the Narragansets live? (2.) By whom was a treaty made with them?

30. Where was Philip next found? What did the English forces do? What did the English attempt to do? What became of Philip? Who were the Nipmucks? Who were sent to treat with them? How did the Indians treat those sent? Who was killed?

31. Where did the rest flee to? Where is Brookfield? (2.) What is said of the burning of Brookfield? Who raised the siege?

32. What towns were next attacked? Where are Hadley, Deerfield and Northfield? (2.) What is said of Captain Lathrop? What of Captain Mosely?

33. Give an account of the attack on Springfield. Who were the Tarrenteens? What towns in Maine did they burn and plunder? Where are Saco, Scarborough and Kittery? (2.)

34. What towns did they next attack? Where are Oyster River, Salmon Falls, Dover and Exeter? (2.)

35. How did the Narragansets regard their treaty? Upon this, what did Governor Winslow do? What is said of this swamp fight of December 29th?

36. What is said of the conduct of some Connecticut men? What number of wigwams were fired? Number of Indians killed? Number taken prisoners? What is said of the victory? English captains who fell? Number of English killed? Number wounded?

37. What is said of this defeat? What towns in Massachusetts were assaulted? What towns in Rhode Island?

38. What gave the finishing stroke to the war? When? Where did the death of Philip occur? Who conducted the expedition against him?

39. Who killed Philip? What epitaph did the Indian pronounce over him?

40. What is said of Philip? What is said of the war after his death? What of this melancholy period in the annals of New England?

41. What controversy terminated in 1677? Upon this, what did Massachusetts do? How long did Maine continue annexed to Massachusetts? Upon what did Massachusetts found her claim to Maine? Upon what did Gorges' heirs found their claim? When was the province taken under the jurisdiction of Massachusetts? What county did it constitute? When was the territory incorporated with Massachusetts? and how long did it continue?

42. When was New Hampshire separated from Massachusetts? When and where was the first royal government in New England? What did this form of government prescribe? How long had the colony been under the jurisdiction of Massachusetts?

43. What important event took place in England in 1684? Who succeeded King Charles? What did James do? What is said of Rhode Island? What of Plymouth? What of Connecticut?

44. Of what avail were these petitions and remonstrances? Who was appointed Governor of New England?

45. When did Andros arrive? What is said of his administration?

46. Condition of the New England colonies? In what event did they find relief?

47. What did the people of Boston do with Andros and his associates?

48. Where did James flee from England? What was the consequence? By what name is this war known? How long did it last?

49. How was the opening of this war signalized? Who was surprised and murdered at New Hampshire? What village on the Mohawk was burnt? Where is Schenectady? (4.) What other settlements were burnt? What expedition was fitted out by way of retaliation? By what colony, and under whose command? What was the result of this expedition? Where was Port Royal? (3.)

50. What other expedition was planned? By what colonies? Against what cities? (3.) How many troops were furnished by New York? By what lake were they to proceed? Where is Lake Champlain? (4.) Who was to invest Quebec? What was the result of this expedition? What sort of bills did Massachusetts issue? Why?

51. What did King William do for Massachusetts? When was this charter granted? What one privilege only did it allow? What did it do in regard to limits?

52. How was this new charter rendered more acceptable to the colony? When did Phipps arrive in Boston?

53. What was among his first acts? What law existed in England against witchcraft?

54. Where did the first suspicion of witchcraft begin? When? What is said of trials and executions in Massachusetts? How long after this did the subject rest? When was it revived, and in respect to whom? In what year did it appear in Danvers? Where is Danvers? (2.) Who were first affected? How were they affected?

55. What did they, at length, begin to do? Where did the mania spread? Against whom were accusations made? Who was pressed to death, and why? How many were executed? How many imprisoned?

56. What, at length, began to prevail? What special court was held? What was the result? Remarks of President Dwight?

57. What is said of the war of the French and Indians? What towns suffered? Where is Haverhill? (3.) When was an end put to hostilities? By what treaty?

58. What soon followed the peace of Ryswick? What was the first cause which produced hostilities? What a second? What a third? When did England declare war against France? How long did it last? What was this war called?

59. Upon whom did the weight of this war fall? What colony particularly was unmolested? What two colonies bore the chief burden?

60. What was the declaration of war followed by?

61. What expedition was planned in the spring of 1707? What did the expedition consist of? What was the result of it?

62. What other attempt was made upon the place, and when? Who furnished the fleet, and who the troops? What was the result? What change of names took place?

63. The following year, what plan was projected? What forces were employed in the expedition?

64. What disaster happened to the fleet? In consequence of this, what took place?

65. When did Queen Anne's War terminate? By what treaty?

66. How long did peace last? When were hostilities again commenced? What was this war called? What did it originate in?

67. Most important event of this war in America? Where was Louisburg? (3.) On what island? What is said of its fortifications?

68. Who planned its reduction? What reason was there for reducing it? Who raised troops? Who artillery? and who provisions? Number of troops? Naval force?

69. Whose coöperation was expected? Where did he join the expedition? When did the forces appear off Louisburg?

70. What is said of the batteries erected? What of the labor of their erection?

71. What did Commodore Warren do? What took place soon after this? How long was the siege? When did Louisburg surrender?

72. What is said of this daring expedition? What of the acquisition? Estimated value of the stores and prizes? To whom was security given, and for what?

73. What did the court of France do, by way of revenge? What was the object of this expedition? What was the fate of it? How many ships arrived at Halifax? (3.) What was the former name of Halifax? What took place here?

74. When were the preliminaries of peace signed? Where? Provisions of the treaty?

III. MAINE. 1. Whence did Maine derive its name? How early so called? With whose history did her history long blend?

2. When was the coast of Maine first settled? What took place before they had gathered much strength? Consequence of these grants?

3. Who secured to himself a distinct charter? Of what land, and when? What did Gorges form? What did he incorporate? (3.) When was the province taken under the jurisdiction of Massachusetts? When did it become an independent state?

4. What county did it become in 1652? What privilege had it? Why did Massachusetts lay claim to it? When was the territory incorporated with her? When were efforts made to separate from Massachusetts? When was it effected?

5. What is said of the sufferings of the early settlements in Maine? What towns in different years were laid waste?

III. NEW HAMPSHIRE, p. 68.

1. Whence has New Hampshire her name? When was it first applied to the territory?

2. Who obtained the first grant of New Hampshire? From whom? When? What was it called? When and where were settlements first made? (2.)

3. Who was Reverend John Wheelright? What territory did he purchase, and of whom? What town did he found? (2.) To whom was this tract of country conveyed, the same year? Where did he erect the first house?

4. What coalition took place in 1641? What change in the government took place in 1680?

5. First legislative assembly held? Of whom did it consist? What famous declaration was made by this assembly? How long before a similar enactment in Massachusetts? To whom did the declaration give great umbrage?

6. Who was Robert Mason? What appointment had he? What demands did he make? What is said of the judgment he obtained?

7. What power had the Massachusetts governor over New Hampshire? When Andros was seized in 1689, what did the people of New Hampshire do? Under whose jurisdiction did they place themselves? When was this? What took place in 1692? What in 1699?

8. What did Samuel Allen do in 1691? What did his heirs do in 1715? Upon this, who revived claims to lands in the province? Why? How was this long controversy at length terminated? When did a final separation between New Hampshire and Massachusetts take place?

IV. CONNECTICUT, p. 71.

I. COLONY OF CONNECTICUT. 1. Whence has Connecticut her name?

2. Who was the first proprietor of the soil? Under grants from whom? To whom did he transfer it? What did the patent include?

3. Who first visited Connecticut river? At whose instance? What did Governor Winslow decide to do?

4. Meanwhile, what is said of the Dutch at New York? In what year was this? What is said of William Holmes? What did the Dutch forbid Holmes to do? Where did Holmes erect his house? Where are Hartford and Windsor? (2). What did the Dutch attempt, the following year?

5. When were Windsor, Wethersfield and Hartford, settled? By whom? What is said of their journey?

6. When did they arrive on the Connecticut? In what state did they find the river? What is said of the loss of cattle? What of the sufferings of the new settlers?

7. Who was John Winthrop? When did he arrive at Boston? With what commission? What fort did he erect? How long did the Saybrook colony continue independent? Who attempted to take possession of the river? Why did they not succeed?

8. Who removed to Connecticut in June, 1636? What is said of their journey? Where did they settle? What is said of Mr. Hooker and Mr. Stone?

9. What is the year 1637 remarkable for? Who were the Pequots? What assaults had they made? What did the court at Hartford decide to do? How many men were raised? What number did Hartford furnish? Windsor? Wethersfield?

10. Who conducted the expedition? What Indians assisted? Where was their principal fort? What gave the alarm, as the English troops approached?

11. What is said of the conflict? What was Captain Mason, at length, obliged to resort to? What destruction was caused?

12. Why were the troops now in so great distress? What providential relief did they receive?

13. Who was Sassacus? What became of him? Where was there another fight? Result of this? What became of the Pequots? How was the event of peace celebrated?

II. NEW HAVEN COLONY. 1. What was the Indian name of New Haven? How came the English acquainted with it? When was the town begun?

2. Who was one of the principal founders of New Haven? Why did

he flee first to Holland and afterwards to New England ? Who accompanied him ?

3. Who made advantageous offers to Mr. Davenport and his associates ? When and where at New Haven did they keep their first Sabbath ? Who preached ?

4. When did the freemen of Hartford adopt a constitution ? Why ? What did it ordain ? Officers of the government ? Who sent deputies ? First governor ?

5. When did New Haven adopt a constitution ? Where did the planters assemble ? What singular rules did they adopt ?

6. Who was chosen governor ? How long did he continue to be elected ? What is said of the people of this colony ? What pursuits were they inclined to ? What event discouraged their commercial enterprise ?

7. Who proved troublesome neighbors ? What did the Dutch claim ? What did these disturbances induce the colonists to adopt ?

8. What became of the little colony of Saybrook ? When did she lose her independence ?

9. What treaty was concluded in 1650 ? Provisions of the treaty ?

10. Notwithstanding his pledge, what did Stuyvesant do ? What famous chief did he entertain, and for what purpose ?

11. What did the commissioners decide upon ? Why were hostilities permitted ? Who was applied to for aid ? What did Cromwell do ? What did the Legislature of Connecticut do, this year ?

12. When was Charles II. restored ? What did Connecticut apply for ? Who succeeded in obtaining a charter ? By what means ? Date of it ? How long did the people live under it ?

13. What did this charter include ? How did New Haven relish this ? When were New Haven and Connecticut united ? What charter did Charles confer in 1663 ?

14. How was Connecticut affected by Philip's war ? What is said of her troops in the swamp-fight with the Narragansets ?

15. When did Sir Edmund Andros land in Boston ? In what capacity ? For what purpose did he go to Hartford, in the autumn of 1687 ? What did he demand ? By whom was the charter seized, and where concealed ? How long did Sir Edmund administer the government ?

16. When was the secreted charter taken from its hiding-place ? What is said of the assembly and the colonial records ?

17. What other encroachment was soon after attempted ? By whom ? What did he attempt to do ? When did he repair to Hartford ? What did he demand of the assembly ? Before whom did Fletcher direct his commission to be read ?

18. What dialogue ensued between Captain Wadsworth and Fletcher ? What did Fletcher think best to do ? What did the king decide about the militia ?

v. RHODE ISLAND, p. 79.

1. Why so called ?

2. Whom did Roger Williams visit, after his banishment ? Who was Ousamequin ? Where was his residence ? What grant of land did Williams obtain ? Why did he move from this ? Where did he move to ? What did he call his settlement ? Why ?

3. Within whose jurisdiction was this? From whom did he receive a deed of land?

4. By whom was Mr. Williams joined? What did he share with them?

5. What example was presented in this community?

6. Nevertheless, what did Mr. Williams provide for? What covenant were the settlers required to sign? What was this the basis of?

7. How was the government of the town exercised? Who were appointed, and for what purpose?

8. What others followed Mr. Williams to Providence? When? Why? What did they purchase? Of whom? What settlement did they begin? Where? (2.) What other settlement did they commence?

9. What form of government was adopted? When was the government changed? Who was chosen governor? What other officers?

10. What did Providence and Rhode Island Plantations wish in 1648? Why were they refused? Whereupon, what did Mr. Williams do? What was granted in 1663? What government did this charter constitute? Who was made Governor of New England in 1686? What did he do in respect to Rhode Island? What happened three years afterward?

VI. NEW YORK, p. 81.

1. What was it originally called? Why called New York?

2. Where is Sandy Hook? What vessel cast anchor there? In what year? Was it the first vessel? What does the note say? Who was the commander of the Crescent? In whose service? On what voyage? What shores did he sail along, and how far south? What was Hudson looking for, on his return? What did he pass through? How far up the river did the ship proceed? How far the boat? (4.)

3. On arriving in England, what did King James forbid Hudson to do? Why?

4. What did the Dutch do? What did the Dutch or East India Company do, the following year? What did the natives call the island? What is said of Captain Argall in 1613?

5. What demand did he make? What took place on his retirement? When was New York first begun? What was it called? When was Albany begun? What was it first called? What name did the country receive?

6. How long did the Dutch hold possession of New Netherlands?

7. What grant did the Dutch republic of Holland make in 1621? What lands was this construed as including? What present states did it include?

8. What other settlements did the Dutch make? When? What does Bancroft say of the Dutch?

9. Who was the first Governor of New Netherlands? By whom appointed? When did he arrive? What officers were under him?

10. What is said of the manors of New York? What did the West India Company allow in 1629? What were those called who availed themselves of the privilege? What agent did the patroons despatch, and for what purpose?

11. Who succeeded Minuits as governor? What took place a few months before his arrival? What is said of the interests of the colony under Van Twiller?

12. Who succeeded him ? When ? What is said of Kieft?

13. What colony arrived about this time ? Under whom ? Where did they settle ? How did Kieft regard this movement ? Where did the Swedes extend their settlements ? (4.) What was the territory called ?

14. To what more serious troubles were the Dutch destined ? What expedition did the Dutch fit out? What was its success ? Who was killed ? What did the Indians refuse to do ? What was Kieft resolved upon ?

15. Give an account of this expedition. What celebrated woman was killed on this occasion ? What were the Dutch compelled to do ? Who was peace-maker between the Dutch and Indians ?

16. Were the Indians pacified ? What is said of the war ? Whom did the Dutch engage in their service ? What was his force ? Whom did he rout ?

17. How long did the war continue ? What did the Mohawks now claim ? Through their influence what took place ?

18. What is said of the conduct of Kieft ? What became of him ?

19. Who was the last Dutch governor ? When did he succeed Kieft ? What is said of him ? What was his policy toward the Indians ?

20. When and for what did Stuyvesant go to Hartford ? What did the Dutch claim ? How was the controversy settled ?

21. What is said of the Swedes on the Delaware ? When was their power annihilated ? By whom ? What became of the colonists ?

22. Where was the village of Esopus ? What is it now called ? (4.) When and by whom was it attacked ? How many of the inhabitants were killed, or made prisoners ? How were the Indians rebuked ?

23. On what ground did the English claim New Netherlands ? What grant did Charles II. make to the Duke of York ? In what year ?

24. How did the duke assert his claim ? Who commanded the expedition? What was Stuyvesant obliged to do ? What did Nichols promise the inhabitants ?

25. What change of names took place ? What is said of the Swedes on Delaware Bay ? What of the duke's conveyance of New Jersey ? What of the purchase of Long Island ?

26. Who assumed the government ? How long did he continue in office ? What is said of his administration ? What wrong act was he guilty of ?

27. Who succeeded Nichols ? Character of his administration ?

28. When was New York retaken by the Dutch ? Under what circumstances ? What became of Manning ? When was New York restored to the English ?

29. To remove all controversy about titles, what did the Duke of York do ? Whom did he appoint governor ? What is said of his administration ?

30. What other colony experienced the weight of his oppression ? In what way ? Circumstances of the interview between Andros and Captain Bull ?

31. What important change was effected, in 1682, in respect to the " Territories " ?

32. Who succeeded Andros in the government ? When did he arrive in the colony ? With what instructions ? What did James II. refuse to confirm ? What is said of printing-presses ? What of important provincial offices ?

31

33. To what jurisdiction were New York and New Jersey added in 1688 ? Who was made captain-general ? Who was governor under Andros ?

34. On the flight of James II., in 1689, what is said of the people of New York ?

35. Who seized the fort of New York ? For whom did they hold it ? What did Nicholson and his officers do ? Where did they retire ? At this juncture, what letter was received ? How did Leisler construe this letter ? What did he assume ? What part of New York submitted to him ? What is said of Albany ?

36. Who, in 1691, came out as king's governor ? Who was now released, and who tried and condemned ? What did the people urge ? Why did the governor defer their execution ? By what means did the people effect their purpose ? What privileges did Governor Sloughter confer on the people ?

37. Who were the governors who succeeded Sloughter, to the French and Indian War ? What is said of these governors ?

VII. NEW JERSEY, p. 89.

1. When was New Jersey so named ? In honor of whom ?

2. When did the jurisdiction of the Dutch over New Jersey cease ? To whom did Charles II. convey the territory ? To whom did the Duke of York sell it ?

3. When was New Jersey first settled ? Where is Bergen ? What fort was soon after built ? Where ? Where is Camden ? Where is Elizabethtown ? What is said of it ? (4.)

4. Who was appointed governor ? When ? What did he bring with him ? What did this constitution ordain ? How were the officers chosen ?

5. What was the effect of this liberal constitution ?

6. When were New Jersey and Delaware recaptured by the Dutch ? On what occasion ? When restored ?

7. What conveyance was made in 1674 ? By whom, and to whom ? What did Billinge do ?

8. What division of New Jersey was made ? When ? Who took East Jersey ? who West ? Who laid claim to West Jersey ? Was this just ? Why not ? What did Andros attempt ? What was the issue of this contest ?

9. To whom did Carteret sell his right to East Jersey ? When ? What did Penn do ? Who was made Governor of East Jersey ? When were the Jerseys annexed to New England ? How long did they continue so ? When were the Jerseys surrendered to the crown ?

10. What is said of the two provinces now ? What were the people allowed ?

11. How long did the province continue under the Governors of New York ? Who was the first royal governor ?

VIII. DELAWARE, p. 91.

1. On what bay does Delaware lie ? (4.) After whom was it named ?

2. Who first settled Delaware ? When did they arrive ? Under whose charge ? What place did Minuits build ? Near what town ? (4.) What name was given to the territory ? (4.) Extent of it ? (4.)

3. Who laid claim to the territory? How did Governor Kieft attempt to keep him in check? Who was John Printz? What did he do? Why?

4. Proceedings of Stuyvesant in 1651? Who protested? What did Governor Rising do?

5. How did Governor Stuyvesant rebuke this outrage? What became of the Swedes and their forts?

6. When was the territory surrendered to New York? Who commanded the expedition? To whom was it sold in 1682? How were these tracts then known? How were they governed until 1703? What then took place?

7. What is said of Delaware during the Revolution? What of the Delaware regiment?

IX. MARYLAND, p. 93.

1. After whom so called?

2. Who was Sir George Calvert? To what place did he emigrate? Why? When? What was he compelled to seek?

3. Of what territory did he procure a patent? From whom?

4. To whom was the patent made out? Why to him? What land did this grant cover? What contentions arose in consequence?

5. First governor of the province? When did he arrive? Whom did he bring with him? What was their religion? Where did they settle? At the mouth of what river? (4.)

6. What circumstances contributed to the rapid growth of Maryland? What is said of its charter? What did it secure to emigrants? What privilege did it grant? What is said of taxes?

7. Who at first enacted the laws? When was a house of assembly constituted? What did this consist of? What change took place in 1650? How were the members of these houses appointed?

8. What rebellion broke out in 1635? Who was Clayborne? What became of his followers? What of himself and estate?

9. What is said of Clayborne in 1645? What became of the governor? What is said of this revolt?

10. What did the assembly of the colony reiterate in 1649? By this act, what might every one enjoy? What was the effect of this religious toleration?

11. What is said of commissioners appointed in 1651? Who was one of these? What were they to do? What war did this give rise to? Between whom? What is further said about this matter?

12. What did the next assembly ordain? When did the war commence? What did Stone, the lieutenant, do? Which party was victorious? What became of Stone and others?

13. When was Lord Baltimore restored to his rights? Who was appointed governor? To whom was pardon extended?

14. When did Lord Baltimore, the founder of Maryland, die? Who succeeded him? What is said of Cecil Calvert? What of Charles?

15. When was the tranquillity of Maryland again interrupted? Why? Which party, Protestant or Catholic, obtained the government?

16. How long did they hold it? What did the king then do? Whom did he send over as governor? Under Copley, what took place?

17. When was this wrong rectified? In what way? What government was restored?

X. PENNSYLVANIA, p. 96.

1. Whence her name ?
2. Who was this William Penn ? On what account did he receive the territory of Pennsylvania ? From whom ?
3. Upon what territory did this patent encroach ? To what extent ? Between whom did contentions hence arise ? What other conveyances were made to Penn ? What did these grants embrace ?
4. Religious views of Penn ? What was his object in founding a colony ?
5. What assurances did he give to his Swedish settlements ?
6. What offers did Penn make to settlers ? Who took advantage of these offers ? Who was William Markham ? What letter did Penn write ?
7. What form of government did he publish ? Who might be a freeman ? What latitude of conscience was given ?
8. Did Penn come to America ? With whom ? Where did he land ? What did he find upon the territories ? To what place did he proceed ? What did he convoke ? What did he order ? What did this assembly do ?
9. Who engaged the Indians to form a treaty ? Where was this treaty negotiated ? Near what city ? (4.) What did Penn say to the Indians ?
10. How did the Indians act ? What did they say ? What did Mr. Bancroft say of the Indians ? What was the result of this kindness of Penn ?
11. Meaning of the word Philadelphia ? Who commenced the city ? Of whom did Penn purchase the territory ? What is said of the growth of the city ?
12. What is said of the rapid settlement of Pennsylvania ? To what was this owing ?
13. When did Penn convene a second assembly ? Where did it meet ? For what purpose ? What at this time was ordained ? Effect of these wholesome regulations ?
14. When did Penn return to England ? To whom did he leave the care of the government ? What is said of James II., soon after ? How did Penn regard this monarch ? What became of Penn ? Why imprisoned ? What, at length, was he permitted to resume ? Who was his deputy-governor ?
15. Did Penn visit Pennsylvania a second time ? When ? What did he find ? What, upon this, did he do ? When was this charter accepted by the people ? Who dissented ?
16. What is said of Penn after this ? What took place after his departure ? What is said of the colony ? When did the people form a new constitution ? What did they allow the proprietor ?

XI. CAROLINAS, p. 100.

1. In honor of whom was Carolina so called ? Meaning of Carolus in Latin ?
2. What did this territory include ? To whom was it conveyed ? By whom ?
3. When was a settlement begun ? By whom ? Near what sound ? What name did this colony receive ?

4. When was a second permanent settlement effected? Near the mouth of what river? (5.) By what emigrants? Name of this colony? First governor? In what state were both these colonies?

5. When was a third colony founded? What was it called, and after whom? Who came over with the colonists? What harbor did they first enter? To what river did they remove? What city did they found? What is said of the present city of Charleston? Of what state was this the commencement?

6. Who prepared a constitution of government for these colonies? What did it propose? What is said of the plan? What did it cause in Abemarle county?

7. Who succeeded Governor Sayle? Under him, what two colonies were united? What began now to be used in respect to the two remaining colonies?

I. NORTH CAROLINA COLONY. 1. What is said of the progress of North Carolina? What took place in 1677?

2. Who was Seth Sothel? When was he sent over, and why? How long did the inhabitants bear with him? What did they then do? Remark of an historian?

3. Who succeeded Sothel? What did he do? What is said of Sir John Archdale, successor of Ludwell? What is said of emigrants and assignments of land? Who were a great accession of strength and numbers to the colony?

4. How did the neighboring Indian tribes regard the colony? For what purpose did they combine? What massacre took place? When?

5. Who came to their relief, and what did Barnwell do?

6. What did the Indians, soon after, again do? Who interfered? The fort of what tribe was reduced? Number of prisoners? What became of the Tuscaroras? With whom was a treaty concluded, and when?

7. When did the proprietary government cease in Carolina? Why? What became of their charter? When did the proprietors surrender their rights?

II. SOUTH CAROLINA. 1. Who laid the foundation of the southern colony in Carolina? In what settlement? When? Who succeeded Sayle? What colony was incorporated with it?

2. Which colony flourished the most? Why? What accessions were made from New York? Where did they chiefly concentrate? What is said of Puritan refugees?

3. When was the present city of Charleston founded? (5.) By whom?

4. How were the people soon after annoyed? What was done with these Indians?

5. What is said of the accession of French Protestants? When did they come over? To whom were they not welcome?

6. Who, about this time, was appointed governor? Why? What was the effect of his measures?

7. What notable person now appeared in the province? What was he allowed to do? What became of him? Who succeeded him? Why was he glad to retire?

8. Who succeeded Ludwell? When? What is said of the people? How did he manage?

9. What one difficulty still remained? What did the English Episcopalians deny to the French Protestants?

31*

10. By what means were these animosities at length healed?

11. What proposal did Governor Moore make to the assembly? During whose war was this? What did the assembly think of it? Troops raised for the expedition? What was the plan of the expedition?

12. Why could the governor effect nothing? What was Daniel despatched for? What took place during his absence? What is said of Daniel on his return? Consequences of this unfortunate enterprise?

13. How was the failure of this expedition compensated? What expedition did Governor Moore undertake? What was its success?

14. Who succeeded Moore? When? What forms of worship were established? From what were dissenters excluded? When were these laws of exclusion repealed? Why? What acts, however, continued in force?

15. What design was attempted in 1706? By whom? During whose war? How was it defeated?

16. What combination of Indians was formed in 1715? What was the extent of this combination? (5.) What day was assigned for the destruction of the colony? How was the calamity averted? What became of the Yamassees?

17. What, at length, did the people of Carolina resolve to do? Whom did they request to accept the government? Upon his refusal, whom did they appoint?

18. To whom did the Carolinians complain? What did the privy council decide? Under whose protection was the colony taken? What agreement between the proprietors and the crown followed?

XII. GEORGIA, p. 107.

1. Whence its name?

2. In what patent was the territory of Georgia originally included? What is said of the territory? Why had the king a right to re-grant it? Who laid claim to it?

3. Who was James Oglethorpe? What plan did he and others concert? When?

4. What did King George do in furtherance of this plan? What did the charitable do?

5. When did the colony arrive? How many, and under whom? Where did they first touch? To what place did they then proceed? (5.) Where did they begin a settlement? What was Oglethorpe's next object?

6. How many chiefs did he collect? What did he ask of them? What was the reply of the Creek chief?

7. By whom was Oglethorpe assisted? What is said of this Mary Musgrove?

8. Why did not the colony flourish?

9. What inducements were held out to new settlers? Who availed themselves of these offers? Number of planters who arrived? What did Parliament do for the settlers? What did individuals do? Why did not the colony flourish?

10. What country did Oglethorpe visit? Whom did he take with him? When did he return? By whom was he accompanied? What was the object of Wesley? What is said of him? When did he go back? What denomination did he found?

11. By whom was Wesley succeeded? Object of Whitefield? What is said of him? What of his orphan asylum? Where did he die?

12. What expedition did Oglethorpe project? When? Where is St. Augustine? (5.) By whom was he aided? What forts did he take? What naval force aided? Result of the expedition?

13. What took place two years after? What did the Spanish armament consist of? Where did it sail from? What river did it enter? Where is the river Altamaha? (5.) Where was Oglethorpe? What did he do? To whom had Oglethorpe applied for assistance? Why did the Carolinians refuse?

14. What stratagem did Oglethorpe resort to? What letter did he write? What was the import of this letter?

15. What became of the above letter? What did the Spanish general do to the French deserter? What mistake did the Spanish council of war make in reference to three supply-ships? What did the Spaniards do, in consequence?

16. What became of Oglethorpe, the founder of the colony? In what state did he leave it? What is said of the emigrants? What, at length, did the trustees do?

NOTES.

1. Extent of the period of settlements? How many colonies were planted in America? What were they?

2. Date of the settlement of Virginia? Date of the commencement of the Carolinas? Years between? Colonies settled within those years? When was Georgia settled? How many years after the Carolinas?

3. What colonies were early united? What names did they take? How many colonies at the close of the period of settlements? Age of the oldest? Age of the youngest?

4. By whom were these colonies settled? By whom was New York? Maryland? Pennsylvania? Delaware? What is said of emigrants and others?

5. What is said of the inhabitants of these colonies for many years? How did they live among themselves? Why?

MANNERS OF THE COLONISTS, &c. 1. What is said of the manners of the Virginians? What does Stith say? Yet at the close of this period what is said of many in regard to frankness, &c.?

2. What does Beverly say touching the courtesy of poor planters to travellers?

3. What were the circumstances of the earliest emigrants? Of what was there a great dearth? How was that dearth supplied?

4. Why did not the Virginians suffer from want? What story does a writer tell about five pounds?

5. Habitations of the first settlers? Before the close of the period, how were they?

6. What is said of the living of the Virginians? What of their beef and mutton? What inducement had the people to be lazy? What was the price of some articles of living? What is said of bread?

7. Whence did the colonies get their clothing? What does a writer say of their sheep? What of bowls and birchen brooms? What, however, should be remembered?

8. What is said of the New England colonists? What is said of their notions? What of their manners? What of their government and

morals ?   What did they study ?   What were some of their characteristics ?

9. What will throw great light on the views and manners of the
people of that age ?   Mention some of these laws.   How was Mr. Josias
Plaistowe punished ?   How Sergeant Perkins ?   How Robert Shorthose ?

10. In 1655, what did the town of Hartford order ?   What was the
penalty for not attending town-meeting ?   How were boys punished
for playing during public service ?   What order was made in 1643
about ringing a bell ?

11. What did the colony of Connecticut order, in 1647, about tobacco ?
What were the Virginians doing at this time ?

12. What did the colony of New Haven resolve, in 1639 ?   How was
one Broomfield punished, and for what ?   What other punishments
were inflicted ?

13. How are these matters sometimes referred to ?   Why is there little
just cause for the censure of the present generation ?   What was the
object of these regulations ?   What were they really the dictates
of ?

14. What is said of the early manners of the colony of New York ?
In what respect did they pattern after the Dutch ?   What is said after
the conquest of the English ?

15. What is said of the gable end of their houses ?   How was the
date of their erection designated ?   What had they always on the top
of the roof ?

16. Where did the family enter ?   Where did they live ?   What is
said of the front door ?   What of the grand parlor ?   What of the sand
on the floor ?

17. How did the old burgher dispose of himself?   How his good
wife ?   What did the young folks do ?

18. When did a well-regulated family rise ?   Dine ?   Go to bed ?
What is said of their tea-parties ?   How was their tea-table crowned ?
What other articles graced it ?

19. What story does the author tell about a Dutch custom ?

20. What is said of other colonies ?   What of peculiarities before the
close of the period ?

RELIGION. 1. To what church was the colony of Virginia devoted ?

2. What provisions were made for the support of ministers ?   How
was this stipend settled ?   What law passed the assembly in 1642 ?

3. What is said of the religion of the Church of England in 1650 ?
How many pounds of tobacco were granted a minister ?   What had he
in addition ?   How was the tobacco prepared ?

4. What was the special object of the New England planters ?   Of
what sect were they in doctrine ?   In discipline ?   And what right did
each church maintain ?   What did they hold to the validity of ?   When,
and for what purpose, did they convene councils ?   What officers were
there generally in each church ?   What was the pastor's office ?
Teacher's ?   Ruling elder's ?

5. What provision was made by the colonists of Massachusetts Bay
for ministers ?   Who was obliged to contribute to the support of the
church ?   What is said of persons attending public worship ?   What
were the Connecticut laws touching the subject ?

6. When and where was the first synod convened in America ?
What was the object of it ?   What did the synod do ?

7. Where was the Dutch Reformed Church first introduced ?   What

is said of their first meeting-house? . Cost of it? How covered? What is said of the town-bell?

8. When did the Roman Catholics first come to America? Where did they settle? Where was the first Baptist church formed? When, and by whom? What law did Massachusetts pass, in 1651, against their doctrines?

9. When did Quakers make their appearance in Massachusetts? What laws were passed against them? What severe penalties were enacted against them in 1657? What took place in 1659? What is said of the conduct of Baptists, Quakers, &c.? What did our forefathers seek to avert? What had they not yet learned?

10. What can you say of the synod at Cambridge? What platform did they adopt? What ministers and churches were present? How long was this platform the religious constitution of Connecticut?

11. What were Penn's religious views and tenets? What worship did he institute? What was a fundamental principle of Penn? When was Episcopacy introduced into New York? New Jersey? Rhode Island? South Carolina? Connecticut?

12. When was the Saybrook platform formed? By whom? Under whose authority? What is said of the revival of 1737? When did Whitefield come to America? What is said of him? What sect did he give rise to?

13. What is said of religious persecution before the close of this period? What of rights of conscience?

TRADE AND COMMERCE. 1. What is said of the early trade of the colonies? What did they import? What did they return?

2. What were the first exportations of the colony of Virginia? How did the price fall? What was the consequence? What did they receive from the Indians? What did they do with these furs? In what vessels was the export trade carried on? What other trade had the Virginians?

3. First vessel from the West Indies? First American vessel from the West Indies? What is said of the ship Desire, of Salem? First introduction of African slaves into New England?

4. What, at length, excited the jealousy of the mother country? What was forbidden by the mother country? What did the colonies export to England? What did they build and sell?

5. On which side was the balance of trade? How was this balance paid?

AGRICULTURE. 1. What was the first business of the settlers? How did they clear the land? What was early cultivated in Virginia? What is said of Indian corn? What of vineyards? When was rye first raised in Massachusetts?

2. Who first introduced neat cattle into New England? What is said of the importation in 1629? What of cattle in Virginia in 1623? What did New York begin to export in 1678? What were the principal productions of the middle colonies? Of the northern colonies? Of the southern colonies?

ARTS AND MANUFACTURES. 1. What is said of early arts and manufactures? Why did they not flourish?

2. What manufactures were begun in Virginia in 1620? What does Chalmers say of New England in 1673?

3. First buildings of the settlers, what made of? When were brick and framed houses erected? Where were the frames and brick pro-

cured? First windmill in New England? First vessel built in Massachusetts? What was it called?

4. First printing in New England? Who was the proprietor of the press? First article printed? Second? Third? What Bible was printed? When, and where? Mode of travelling? Why?

5. Progress of the arts and manufactures? Mention some articles. Were they sufficient for the inhabitants?

6. First newspaper in North America? How many before the close of the period? General character of the books published?

POPULATION. 1. Population of the colonies in 1701?

2. Population in 1755? How many of these were foreigners?

EDUCATION. 1. What is said of attention to education? In what colony and where was a college established? For whose education? What appropriation did the Virginia Company make for education? When was William and Mary's College established?

2. What is said of education in the northern colonies? What appropriation did the General Court of Massachusetts make, in 1636? When was Cambridge college established? Where, at first, located? Who endowed it? What legacy did he leave it? When was the first commencement? Graduates? What other colonies contributed to its funds?

3. What is said of common schools? What specimen can you mention of the arrangements for common schools?

4. When was Yale College commenced? By whom? Who chartered it? Where begun? First commencement? When and where removed? After whom called, and why? Who founded Nassau Hall? Where is this located? When? By whom was it enlarged?

REFLECTIONS. 1. What is said of the continent at the commencement of this period? What change do we find at the close? What do we now see?

2. How has this change been effected?

3. If you look at our fathers, in what circumstances do you see them?

4. For what should we be thankful in regard to our lot, compared with our ancestors?

5. What does the delusion regarding the Salem witchcraft warn us against?

6. What does our account of the Salem witchcraft still further suggest? What should we exercise towards those who fall into occasional error?

MISCELLANEOUS QUESTIONS ON PERIOD II.

1. When was Jamestown settled? How long is Period II.? How long from the discovery of America to settlement of Jamestown? Who was the most efficient man among those who settled Jamestown? How far is Jamestown from the mouth of the river? ANS. About thirty-two miles. To what two companies were letters patent granted in 1606? By whom?

2. When was Plymouth in Massachusetts settled? By whom? How long after Jamestown? When, and by whom, was laid the foundation of Massachusetts colony? When was Connecticut settled? Colony of New Haven? Georgia? New Hampshire? New York? By whom was New York settled? When was New York surrendered to the English? When was New Jersey settled? Delaware? Pennsylvania? What people generally settled Pennsylvania? Who settled Maryland?

When was it first settled? Who was Roger Williams? What colony did he found? When were North and South Carolina settled? When were they divided?

3. Who was John Holmes? What do you recollect about him? What about Wahquimicut? What two Indian wars occurred during this Period? About what year was Philip's War? Who killed Philip? Who conducted the war against the Pequots? What town did Roger Williams found in Rhode Island? What were the principal forts of the Pequots? Where was the principal residence of Philip? Who was the great sachem of the Pequots? What was the Indian name of New Haven? Of Boston? Of New York? Of Savannah?

4. What two ministers accompanied the first settlers of Connecticut? Who was the principal founder of New Haven? When were New Haven and Connecticut colonies united? Date of the union of the New England colonies? Why was this union formed? How many colonies formed it? Who was John Eliot? What do you recollect about him?

5. Who were the Narragansets? In what wars did they act a distinguished part? Whom did the Duke of York appoint his governor? What was the character of his administration? Relate the story of his coming to Hartford and demanding the charter. What rebellion occurred in Virginia? When? Who headed it? Who was at that time governor? Issue of it?

6 Who founded Philadelphia? When? How long after the settlement of Jamestown? Plymouth? What is the meaning of Philadelphia? Who was Masassoit? With whom did he make a treaty? Who was the first Governor of Plymouth Colony? Of New Haven Colony? Of Massachusetts Colony? Who was Lord Baltimore? Who was considered the father of the Puritans? Did he ever remove to America? Who was Samoset? Who was Squanto? What day of what month is celebrated as the landing of the Pilgrims? In what vessels did the Pilgrims come to America? Who was Miles Standish?

7. Where was the first representative legislature in this country? When? When did the towns in Connecticut first establish a constitution? When were East and West Jersey united? Who settled Delaware?

8. Tell the date of the settlement of every state mentioned in this Period. What towns suffered much in Philip's War? What was the occasion of Philip's War? What scene opened this war? To whom did James I. grant a patent of New England in 1620? Where did Endicott settle?

9. In what town did the Indians murder nine persons in 1637? When, and by whom, was Salem settled? What colony was settled mostly by Roman Catholics? What by Quakers? What two colonies were founded on very liberal principles?

10. What colony was refused admittance into the New England Confederacy, formed in 1643? Why? Who was a distinguished minister of Roxbury? Who was Sassacus?

11. When was Roger Williams banished from Salem? Who were the Mohawks? From what town in Massachusetts came the first settlers of Hartford? What was the Indian name of Rhode Island? Who was William Coddington? What patent was granted to Lords Say and Seal, &c., in 1631?

12. What event most interesting to Massachusetts occurred in 1684?

What other charters were soon vacated? Meaning of this term? When was the condition of New England distressing, in consequence of the arbitrary acts of Andros? What event brought them relief? When was William, Prince of Orange, proclaimed?

13. What wars occurred during this period? When did King William's war begin? When end? In what treaty? When did Anne's war begin? How long was it? In what treaty did it end? Date of this treaty? When did the war of George II. begin? When end? In what treaty? Which was the longest of these wars? Which the most severe?

14. When was Georgia settled? By whom? Who was the leader of the colony? How long after the settlement of Jamestown? When did William ascend the throne? What was done with Andros? What colonies resumed their charters? What colony obtained a new charter?

15. What insurrection occurred in New York in 1689-90? Cause of it? Head of it? Issue of it? Who was Seth Sothel? History of his proceedings? When did the infatuation about witchcraft begin? Where? What distinguished persons were accused? Who was Sir William Phipps? What expedition did he lead? In what war? With what success?

16. When was the first printing-press established in the country? Where? What kind of mill was the first in New England? In what year was built the first vessel in Massachusetts? Name? What was first printed? Whose version of the Bible was first printed? In what language?

17. Population of the colonies at the close of the Period of Settlements? With what country did the colonies principally trade during the Second Period? When were slaves first introduced into New England? What college was first founded in the colonies? Which was the second? Where was the Cambridge platform composed and adopted? When? By whom?

18. What newspaper was first printed in North America? Where? In what year? What were the provisions of the treaty of Ryswick? Who settled in Carolina in 1707 and 1710? Who plotted their destruction, two years after?

19. Where is Louisburg? How was this fortified? What was it called? How long was it besieged before it was taken? When did it surrender? What colonies were engaged in the expedition?

PERIOD III., p. 129.

For what is Period III. distinguished? When did it commence? When terminate? Length?

1. What is said of the history of the colonies to this date?

2. What is said of their history for years from this time? What had the American colonies to do with reference to England? How long did they enjoy peace? When did England declare war against France? When was it reciprocated by France?

3. What is this war called? What were the principal events of 1754? 1755? 1756? 1757? 1758? 1759? 1760? 1763?

4. What was the general cause of the French and Indian War? Where were these English settlements? Where had the French

extended themselves ? What had they decided to connect ? By means of what ? What object had they ? What was the English claim founded upon ? Upon whom fell the severity of the war ?

5. What circumstance opened the war ? Of whom did the Ohio Company consist ? What purchase had they made, and for what purpose ? Who had intelligence of these transactions ? What did he fear ? What did he do ?

6. To whom did the Ohio Company appeal ? What did Dinwiddie do ? What did the assembly order ?

7. To whom was this service intrusted ? How old was Washington ? What is said of the service assigned him ? How did he perform the service ? What reply did he bring back ?

8. What did the British ministry direct to be done ? What force was raised ? To whose command was it intrusted ? When did Washington march, and whither ?

9. What fort did he erect ? Towards what French fort did he proceed ? What was it the present site of ? (4.) Whither did he retire ? Why ? What befell him at Fort Necessity ? What was he obliged to surrender ? How long after this was the formal declaration of war ?

10. What did the British ministry recommend to the American colonies ? Why ? What convention was accordingly held ? Where ? When ? What was adopted ? What did it resemble ? Why was it not adopted ?

CAMPAIGN OF 1755. 1. How many expeditions were planned for this campaign ? (3.) (4.)

2. By whom was the expedition against Nova Scotia conducted ? Of what did it consist ? From what did it sail ? By whom was it joined ? What port was taken ? To what name was it changed ? What is said of the whole of Nova Scotia ? (3.)

3. What difficult question arose, in relation to the inhabitants of Nova Scotia ? How were they disposed of ? Why ?

4. Who conducted the expedition against the French on the Ohio ? Who was Braddock ? Force ? Against what fort did he proceed ? (4.) Whom did he leave to follow ? With what troops press on ? Against what was he warned ? Where was he surprised ? When ? Number of the enemy ? What became of Braddock ? Loss of soldiers and officers ?

5. To what was the defeat of Braddock to be ascribed ? In what estimation did he hold the provincial troops ? Whose retreat did they cover ? Who commanded ? To what fort did the army proceed ? What might they here have done ? What course did Colonel Dunbar pursue ?

6. Who conducted the expedition against Crown Point ? What was the success of this ? To what point did the army of Johnson proceed ? What intelligence was here received ? Where was Fort Edward ? (4.) What did a council of war resolve to do ? Who commanded the party detached ? By whom was it surprised ? Who were killed ?

7. Where was the firing heard ? What was inferred ? What was done ? Who was defeated ? What distinguished French gentleman fell ?

8. Who led the expedition against Niagara ? Force employed ? How far did the expedition proceed ? Why was it abandoned ?

CAMPAIGN OF 1756. 1. Who succeeded Governor Shirley ? Who

32

commanded until the arrival of Abercrombie? How had the war been carried on till this time? When was war declared?

2. What was the plan of operation for 1756? What is said of these places? What of the former? What of the latter? Why did the plan fail?

3. Who succeeded Dieskau? What fort did he invest in August? Where was this fort? (4.) With what success? What is said of the fall of Oswego?

4. Of what lakes did the capture of this fort give the enemy command? Of what country? What losses did the English experience, in men and stores? What is said of further extensive operations? To what was this suspension attributed?

CAMPAIGN OF 1757. 1. What did the British Parliament do for the campaign of 1757? The reduction of what place was planned? On what account were the colonies disappointed? On what account was the expedition abandoned?

2. What is said of the indecision of the English, and the victories of the French? What fort did Montcalm reduce, on the north shore of Lake George? Number of the garrison? Number of Montcalm's forces? Continuance of the siege?

3. Defender of the fort? How was the capitulation shamefully broken? What is said of a New Hampshire corps? Why were not the Indians restrained?

CAMPAIGN OF 1758. 1. What change was made in the British administration in 1758? What is said of Pitt? In whose favor did the tide of success now turn? Import of a circular, addressed by Pitt to the colonial governors? What three colonies responded? How?

2. How many expeditions were planned?

3. What force was sent against Louisburg? (5.) What admiral commanded the fleet? Who commanded the army? Who was under him? When did the fortress surrender? How many prisoners? What other places fell into the hands of the English? What is said of this loss to France?

4. Who succeeded Lord Loudon as commander-in-chief? What expedition did Abercrombie conduct? How many followed his standard? What was the success of an attack upon Ticonderoga? What was the English loss? To what was this ill success attributed? What is said of the retreat? How might a different result have been reached?

5. Where did Abercrombie retire? What fort was soon after taken by the English? Where was this fort? ANS. Where Kingston now stands. (4.) Who conducted the expedition? What fell into his hands?

6. What third expedition was contemplated this year? Where was Fort Du Quesne? (4.) Why was this fort so important? Who commanded the enterprise? Force employed? When did they reach the fort? Why was an attack needless? To what was the name of the place changed?

7. What other event bore upon the fortunate issues of the next year? Where was this treaty concluded?

CAMPAIGN OF 1759. 1. What had the campaign of 1759 for its object? How was it proposed to accomplish this? What were the strong-holds of the French in Canada? Who led the enterprise against Ticonderoga? What other place soon after surrendered? Who proceeded against Niagara? Result of that expedition?

2. Who commanded the expedition against Quebec? At what place did he embark? With what force? Under what convoy? Where did he land? (5.) Which way from Quebec? What project did he at length decide upon? Whose suggestion was this?

3. Where were the troops transported? What did Wolfe do, on leaving the ships? Did he land at the place he intended? Why not?

4. What was the perpendicular ascent which they climbed? On what plains was the army formed? Who commanded the French?

5. Where was the battle fought? Describe it.

6. What two generals fell? Where was Wolfe wounded? Who succeeded him? Who succeeded Monckton, and why? Where was Montcalm when he fell? Who fell near his side?

7. Where did Wolfe die? Before dying, what did he hear, and what did he say? Which cause was victorious? Loss of the French? Loss of the English? Terms of capitulation? The capture of what place soon followed? Why did it not terminate the war?

CAMPAIGN OF 1760. 1. When did the French attempt to re-take Quebec? Who commanded the French? Who the English forces? Where was the battle fought? Which was victorious? Where did the English retreat to? How came the French to raise the siege?

2. What important fortress still remained in possession of the French? What plan was adopted to take possession of it? Under what circumstances was it surrendered? The surrender of what other places followed?

3. How long had this war lasted? How did the colonies express their joy at its termination?

4. What is said of Indian outrages, about this time, at the south? Who were these Indians? What colonies suffered? When were they defeated, and by whom? When was the treaty signed that closed the war? At what place? What cessions were made to the British crown?

MISCELLANEOUS QUESTIONS ON PERIOD III.

1. For what is Period III. distinguished? With what event does it begin? How long was this after the settlement of Jamestown? How long from the treaty of Aix-la-Chapelle? General cause of this war? In what year did it end? In what treaty? What were the provisions of the treaty of Paris?

2. Between whom was a plan of union adopted, in 1754? Where? What did it resemble? On what day of what month was this plan signed? How long before the Declaration of Independence? What fort was, on that day, surrendered? How old was Washington when first called to public service? What duty was assigned him? How did he perform it?

3. Where was Braddock defeated? Year, month, and day, of his defeat? How long after the accession of William, Prince of Orange, to the throne of England? after the settlement of Jamestown? What four expeditions were planned in 1755? Which were successful? Which otherwise? Who commanded in that against Nova Scotia? that against the French on the Ohio? against Crown Point? against Niagara? What was the principal expedition of the campaign of 1758? What was its issue? What fort was surrendered to the French? Who commanded the French? Who gallantly defended Fort William Henry?

4. What change was made in the ministry of England in 1758? What expeditions were planned in 1758? Which were successful? Which otherwise? Commander of the expedition against Louisburg? against Ticonderoga? Du Quesne? What treaty was formed in 1758? Where? Influence of it?

5. Great object of the campaign of 1759? What were the strong-holds of the French in Canada? Which of these was surrendered without a battle? To whom did Niagara surrender? Who commanded the expedition against Quebec? What do you understand by the Heights of Abraham? For what will these ever be memorable? What two gen-erals here lost their lives? When was the battle fought? What did this battle decide? How long was this battle after the Pequot war? after the settlement of Plymouth?

PERIOD IV., p. 145.

For what is Period IV. distinguished? When did it begin? When terminate?

1. In what year did the war of the Revolution begin? When was the first blood shed? What is said of the occurrence of the Revolution? What did the English statesmen suppose?

2. What feelings had the colonists towards the mother country? Might the event have probably been avoided? By what means? How was it hastened? Remote and proximate causes of the Revolution? Mention the first. Second, &c. &c.

3. How many colonies had been planted? Which were they? Objects proposed in the establishment of these colonies?

4. What is said of the love of liberty which prevailed?

5. How many forms of government existed? Which were the char-ter governments? Which were the proprietary?

6. What can you mention as evidence that the forms of government conduced to independence?

7. What did the first principles of the colony then favor? What is said of this early spirit of liberty?

8. What is said of the neglect of Britain? What did Parliament pay for the colonies? What did Massachusetts Bay pay? What Lord Baltimore? What other settlers?

9. Conduct of England during her colonial wars? What did the colonists learn from this neglect?

10. What hastened the Revolution more than all other causes? What did these consist of?

11. What were writs of assistance? First application of the kind? What question was raised? Who appeared for the crown? Who for the merchants? Judges?

12. Who opened the cause? What did he maintain? Who followed? Who succeeded him? Who was present? What did he say of Otis? What did Otis say?

13. What was thought? What was the decision of the court? What is said of these writs afterwards?

14. What is said of taxation before 1763? What, if money was wanted? When was the first revenue act passed by Parliament? What duty was laid?

15. Why did not the colonies approve this? What fundamental law

did the colonies hold ? What was the hinge upon which the Revolution turned ?

16. In what year was the stamp act passed ? What did this act ordain ?

17. How was the news of its passage received in America ? What did Massachusetts recommend ? Who acceded to this ? When did these commissioners meet ? Where ? President ? What was their declaration ? What did they say of the stamp act ? When did this Congress adjourn ? Who approved of their proceedings ?

18. What is said of stamps when the act came into operation ? What had become of them ? What is said of business ? What did printers do ? What is said of Canada papers ? Of courts of justice ? Of marriages ?

19. What were sons of liberty ? What was their object ? What is said of other societies ? What did these societies deny themselves ? What did women betake themselves to do ? What effect had this in England ?

20. What fortunate change took place in England, about this time ? What was apparent to Mr. Pitt and his friends ? What act was repealed ? What is understood by the declaratory act ?

21. What famous speech did Mr. Pitt deliver ? What did he declare ? How did the people regard him ? How, in the House of Peers, did some members wish to do ?

22. What is said of the repeal of the stamp act ? What, in consequence of this satisfaction, was revived ? What vote did Massachusetts pass ? What action did Virginia take ?

23. What did the enemies of American liberty intend ? When was another plan of taxation introduced ? What other two acts were passed ?

24. When did these three acts reach America ? What is said of them ? How did several of the colonies regard them ?

25. How was the public excitement soon increased ? What was the object of sending these regiments ? Where was the fleet stationed? How were the troops disposed of?

26. What was done the next day ? Where were two field-pieces stationed ? How was the state-house occupied ? What other places ? What is said of the common ? What of the Lord's day ?

27. What action was taken by Parliament in regard to those guilty of treason ? When was this ? What is said of this measure ?

28. What bill was introduced into Parliament in 1770 ? Why was tea excepted in that bill ?

29. What affray occurred in Boston, March 5th, 1770 ? When did this quarrel commence ? Between whom ? Who gave the provocation ? What took place on the fifth ? How many citizens were killed ? How many wounded ? What took place in the town ? How was the commotion settled ? Who was imprisoned ? Result of their trial ? What is said of the evening of that day in subsequent years ?

30. What fresh obstacle to a reconciliation occurred in 1772 ? Why was this vessel destroyed ? What order was made upon a Providence packet ? Upon refusal, what was done ? How did the master of the packet manage ? What took place the following night ? For what did the governor offer a reward ? What sum ? What was the report of commissioners appointed to investigate the offence ?

31. When were committees of correspondence and inquiry instituted ? For what purpose ? Where had this measure its origin ? By means

32*

of what meeting ? On learning the proceeding of the house of Massa-
chusetts, what resolution did the Virginia House of Burgesses adopt ?
How did the other colonial assemblies act, upon the recommendation of
Virginia ?

32. Why had little tea been brought into the country for some time
before 1773 ? Where was the tea of the East India Company ? What
bill was introduced into Parliament for their relief ? How would this
bill affect the price of tea in the colonies ? What duty was paid on this
tea ? Why ? To what places was tea shipped ? Before its arrival,
what resolutions had been formed by the inhabitants of those places ?
What became of the cargo destined for Charleston ? What is said of
the vessels which brought tea to Philadelphia and New York ?

33. What was designed by the leading patriots of Boston ? Why
could they not effect their purpose ? What resolutions were passed in
several town-meetings ? What orders were given to the captains of the
vessels ?

34. During another meeting of the citizens, what request was made
of the governor ? What did the governor do ? What secret purpose,
upon this, was formed ? By whom was it executed ? What is said of
the conduct of the citizens, meanwhile ?

35. What effect had the intelligence of these proceedings in Parliament ? What bill was passed, by way of revenge ? Of what privilege
did this bill deprive the citizens ? What did the second bill essentially
alter ? What did a third direct the governor to do ?

36. On the arrival of these acts, what vote did the town of Boston
pass ? How did the House of Burgesses, of Virginia, express their sympathy for the people of Boston ?

37. Where did the Continental Congress of 1774 convene ? How
many colonies were represented ? Who was elected president ? who
secretary ? What was agreed upon ? what recommended ? what voted ?

38. When was an assembly ordered by Governor Gage, of Massachusetts, to convene ? Why did he countermand this order ? Where
did they meet, and to what place adjourn ? Whom did they choose
president ? To what place did they adjourn, and what did they do ?
When did this assembly again meet ? What force did they resolve to
equip ? Whom to enlist ? To what colonies did they send a request,
and what was it ?

39. What is meant by the conciliatory bill ? Who introduced it into
the House of Lords ? When ? What was its fate ? What bill was
passed, the following day ? What restrictions were soon after imposed ?

40. What is said of the measures of which we have given a succinct
account ? To what were the colonies loudly summoned ? What event
opened the scene ?

PRINCIPAL EVENTS OF 1775.

What were they ?

1. Who was the royal governor of Massachusetts at this time ? Why
did he send a body of soldiers to Concord ? Their number ? Principal
officers ? What measures were taken to prevent the intelligence of this
expedition reaching the country ? Were these successful ?

2. When did the enemy reach Lexington ? (2.) Who were assembled ? What did Pitcairn say to them ? What did he then do ? From
Lexington, whither did the British troops proceed ? What did they
do at Concord ? (2.) Whither did they now retreat ? What was the
conduct of the Americans ?

3. When were the British reinforced, and by whom ? Where, however, did they retreat ? Loss of the British ? Loss of the Americans ? Effect of the intelligence, as it spread ?

4. What fortresses was it now deemed important to secure ? Who conducted the expedition against these fortresses ? What was their success ? At what time was Ticonderoga taken ? Who demanded its surrender ? In what name ?

5. What memorable battle soon followed ? Month and day on which the battle was fought ? Where was the battle actually fought ? Where is that hill ? How many men were sent to fortify Bunker Hill ? (2.) What was the result of their labors, by the dawn of day ? When did the British discover the redoubt ? How did they attempt to annoy them ? From what hill did the British fire ? What was the conduct of the Americans while thus cannonaded ? Their loss during the forenoon ? How many British were sent to attack them ? Under whose command ? Which commenced firing ? At what distance did the Americans return the fire ? Effect of it ? How near did the Americans suffer the British to approach, before they fired the second time ? What was the effect of this fire ? What took place on the third charge of the British ?

6. Why were the Americans compelled to retire ? Loss of the British ? Loss of the Americans ? What distinguished British officer fell ? What distinguished American ?

7. How were the horrors of the scene greatly increased ? By whose orders ? How many persons became houseless by this conflagration ? Amount of property destroyed ? Number of houses burnt ? Consequences of this battle to the Americans ? What did they learn about their enemies ? Of what else did they learn the importance ? What was the effect of this battle upon the nation ?

8. When did the second Continental Congress meet? Where? Whom did Congress choose as commander-in-chief of the armies ? How many major-generals were appointed ? Names ? How many brigadier-generals ? Names ?

9. Where and when did Washington take command of the army ? (2.) How was he received ? Number of the American army ? Over what region were they spread ? What places did the British forces occupy ?

10. To what was the attention of the American commander directed ? What expedition was planned against Canada ? To whom assigned ? Where is St. Johns ? (2.) Who captured it ? What other city did Montgomery take ? (2.) Whither did he now proceed ? Who was waiting to aid him ? Who had sent Arnold ? With how many men ? By what route ? (2.) What had Arnold done before Montgomery's arrival ?

11. What plan was laid for the reduction of Quebec ? Was the siege successful ? What attacks were then made ? Issue of these attacks ? What officers fell ? Whither did Arnold retire ? When did Arnold leave Canada ? When did the Americans evacuate Canada ?

12. Who was the royal Governor of Virginia in 1775 ? What was the result of his indiscretion ? What is said of the Virginians, in respect to the controversy with Great Britain ? How did Dunmore attempt to thwart their measures of defence ? What did this conduct occasion ? Where did Dunmore retire ? Why ? What was the import of his proclamation ? What town did he burn ? Why ? Estimated

loss of property? Number of persons deprived of habitations? Whither did the royal Governors of North and South Carolina retire? When did the royal government generally terminate?

PRINCIPAL EVENTS OF 1776.

What were they?

1. In the spring of what year did General Washington attempt to expel the British from Boston? What heights were taken possession of and fortified? What did these heights command? How many Americans were engaged to fortify the heights? How were the British affected when they discovered the works? What did the English admiral declare? What did the British determine upon? When did they evacuate Boston? Whither did they retire? Under whose command?

2. The reduction of what southern city was now devised? (2.) By what forces? What is said of Charleston? What fort had been erected? Who commanded it? What was its force? When was this fort attacked? By what force? Length of the bombardment? Who were repulsed? Loss of the British? Loss of the Americans? By means of this repulse what states enjoyed a respite from war, and how long?

3. Who made the motion for the Declaration of Independence in Congress? When? For what purpose was a committee raised on the eleventh?

4. Who stood first on this committee? Who second? Who were requested to prepare a draft of the declaration? Who drew up the paper? What alterations were made in it? To whom belongs the honor of having prepared this declaration? Who was its great supporter on the floor of Congress? What did Mr. Jefferson say of Mr. Adams, on one occasion? What at another time?

5. When was the important declaration made? How was it received abroad? What is said of the ensigns of royalty? What of public processions, &c.?

6. What did Washington do, on taking possession of Boston? Whither did he next remove? Why? Where did he station his forces? Number of his troops?

7. When did the British army return from Halifax? What island did they take possession of? By whom was General Howe joined? Number of the combined forces? Where did they land? What was their object?

8. What communication did General and Admiral Howe make to Washington? Why did the latter decline it? What were their powers?

9. Whom did the British generals next decide to attack? Who commanded the Americans? Date of the battle? Loss of the Americans? Loss of the British? American generals made prisoners? Where was Washington? What is said of him on beholding the slaughter of his troops? Why did he not call in his forces at New York?

10. Why did Washington evacuate the city of New York? When did the British enter it? What is said of the retreat of the American troops from Long Island? When was it made? What circumstances prevented the passage? What change, fortunate for the Americans, took place? What other remarkable circumstance can you mention? When did the English first discover the retreat of the Americans?

11. What place did Washington occupy, on retiring from New York? Where did he next take post? What took place at White Plains? Issue of the engagement?

12. Who was Captain Nathan Hale? For what purpose did he volunteer his services? On being taken, who ordered him to execution? What was he not allowed? Last observation?

13. Whither did Washington retire from White Plains? What was now the design of the British general? How did Washington garrison Fort Washington and Fort Lee? Where were these forts? Who commanded them? What became of Fort Washington? What became of Fort Lee? What became of the garrison? Whither had Washington retired?

14. From Newark, where did Washington retreat? Why? To what other places was his retreat continued? What river did he cross, and into what state?

15. What circumstances rendered this retreat from New Jersey peculiarly trying? To what number was the American army reduced? What were the accommodations of the soldiers? What was the conduct of leading characters in New Jersey and Pennsylvania? What prospect presented itself on all sides? What is said of Washington during these times of trial?

16. What was the next object aimed at by the British general? What prevented? How did the British general dispose of four thousand German troops? Where was the remainder of the British army? What was he waiting for?

17. What plan did Washington now decide upon? How many American troops were detached for the service? When was the Delaware crossed? What obstructed the passage? What further retarded their march? What is said of their surprise of the Hessians? Number of prisoners? Number killed? What German officer?

18. What is said of the success at Trenton? (4.) What did Cornwallis do to regain the ground lost? When did he march out to attack Washington? Where was Washington? Where did the British encamp?

19. In the morning, what had become of Washington and his troops? What enterprise had he projected? What contest ensued? When did Washington leave the main body of the enemy, and whom did he hasten forward to attack? Success at Princeton? (4.) What general was killed? What lieutenant was wounded?

20. What is said of the victories at Trenton and Princeton? To what winter quarters did the British army retire? Where the Americans? (4.)

What were they?

1. When did the Marquis de Lafayette arrive? What was his object? What is said of him? Through whose influence did the French government favor the Americans? What did it allow them to do?

2. What is said of the people of France? Of several French officers? At whose expense did the marquis come? What commission was given him?

3. What stores were destroyed in Connecticut? When? In what town? Number of houses burnt? Number of persons murdered? By

whom was this party attacked? Who was mortally wounded? Where
did Arnold attack them? Whither did they retreat? The loss of the
British during this excursion? How did Congress resolve to honor the
memory of Wooster? In what manner was Arnold rewarded?

4. Strength of the American army in the spring of 1777? On leaving Morristown, where did Washington take post? How near to the
British? What did General Howe seem intending to do? Why did he
not attack Washington? Instead of this, where did he embark? With
what force?

5. What was the design of Howe? What movement did Washington
make to prevent it? To what point did he advance? Where did the
British land? What did Washington think wise to do?

6. Where did the armies meet? Which was obliged to retreat? To
what places? What officers distinguished themselves? Which was
wounded?

7. What did Congress recommend to Washington? What prevented? Where did Washington retire from Philadelphia? Where
is Pottsgrove? Who entered Philadelphia? Where were the rest
of the British stationed? (2.) To what place did Congress adjourn? (2.)

8. What is said of the reduction of some forts on the Delaware?
Why was this reduction attempted? What, meanwhile, did Washington attack? Where?

9. Date of this action? Issue of it? Whither did the British
remove? Where did Washington retreat? Why was he so chagrined
at the defeat at Germantown? To what chiefly was this defeat owing?
What did Congress express?

10. What has been said of Ticonderoga and Crown Point? What of
St. Johns? What of Montreal? Of Quebec? What is said of the
evacuation of Canada?

11. What plan was adopted in England, in 1777? What would the
success of such a plan preclude? To whom was the execution of this
plan committed? Force of Burgoyne? What important fortress did
Burgoyne invest, and when? Number of the garrison?

12. What did St. Clair abandon? Why? Whither did he retreat?
Whom did he join? After this junction, what followed?

13. Where did Burgoyne destroy a quantity of military stores?
How long did he stay at this place? To what fort did he then proceed?
By whom was his progress impeded? In what manner?

14. In what state is Bennington? (2.) Whom did Burgoyne send to
seize stores at that place? Who commanded them? Who attacked
them? What was the result? On his arrival at Bennington, what
did Baum learn? For what did he send to Burgoyne? Whither was
Stark marching when he heard of Baum's approach? When did the
battle occur? Who arrived at a most critical moment? Was the
battle now renewed? How did it end? Loss of the British? Loss
of the Americans? Effect of the battle at Bennington on the Americans? Upon Burgoyne?

15. What was now the situation of Burgoyne? What question did
he find it difficult to settle? When did he pass the Hudson? Upon
what did he advance? (4.) What engagement occurred on the nine-
teenth? What is said of it?

16. When was the battle renewed? What was the design of Bur-

goyne ? What is said of the battle ? What ended it ? What attempt did the royal army make to retreat ? Why did they not proceed ? What decision was then formed by a British council of war ? How many men were surrendered ? When was this surrender made ?

17. Whom did Gates depute to carry the tidings to Congress? What did he say on being introduced into the hall of Congress ?

18. How were the Americans affected by the surrender of Burgoyne? How was this joy soon after increased ? What treaty was formed, and when ?

19. What is said of the Declaration of Independence? Did that declaration form any real bond of union between the states ? What held them together ? What articles did Congress adopt, and when ? By whom was this confederation ratified ? What did it authorize Congress to do ? What could Congress not do ? What did the states reserve ? Consequence of these reservations ?

20. Where did the British continue, the following winter ? Where were the winter quarters of the Americans ? Where is Valley Forge ? How did the royalists pass the winter ? How the patriots ?

PRINCIPAL EVENTS OF 1778.

What were they ?

1. What orders were issued to the British in the spring of 1778 ? Why ? What did Sir Henry Clinton do, pursuant to this order ?

2. What did Washington do ? What was his object ? Where did the British army encamp ? Where is Monmouth ? (4.)

3. What order was issued to General Lee ? Upon his declining, to whom was the honor tendered ? What, at length, did Lee decide to do ? What is said of the morning ? What was greatly needed ? What day was it ?

4. What was the strange conduct of Lee ? On learning the flight of Lee, what did Washington do ? What did he demand of Lee ? Who rallied the forces ? What did Washington then ask Lee ? What did Lee reply ?

5. Who now did their duty ? How long were the armies engaged ? Why did the soldiers greatly suffer ? From what causes did many die ?

6. Where did the armies sleep, that night ? What did Washington decide to do ? How was he disappointed ? Where did the British proceed to ? Where did Washington lead his army ?

7. Where is Wyoming ? (4.) What took place there in July ? Who led the Tories, and who the Indians ? How many inhabitants were slain ? What became of the wives and children ? What is said of other settlements ?

PRINCIPAL EVENTS OF 1779.

What were they ?

1. When did the Southern States become the principal theatre of war ? Which state was attacked first, and why ?

2. Who, at this time, held possession of Savannah ? What was his garrison ? Who was sent from New York to reduce him ? By whom ? With how many men ? What month ? When were the troops landed, and what was Howe compelled to do ?

3. Who commanded an expedition against Connecticut? When? How far did Tryon proceed? What did he do? Who opposed him? Where? Relate the story of Putnam's escape.

4. What other predatory expedition of Tryon can you mention? Where was this? What city was plundered? What towns were reduced to ashes?

5. Where is Stony Point? (4.) When was this place reduced?

6. What is said of this place? Who conducted the enterprise? What is said of his march? When did he arrive?

7. Where did Wayne form his men? What did he direct them to do? On their arrival, what unexpected obstacle presented itself? What did the English do? How did the Americans act? Loss of the English? Worthy conduct of the Americans?

8. What fleet arrived on the coast of Georgia? When, and for what object? Who was in command at Savannah? What had he already done? What unwise grant was made by Lincoln?

9. How long did the siege last? When was an assault made? Result of it? Who was wounded? Who mortally? Loss of the Americans? Story of Jasper? Where did D'Estaing retire? Where Lincoln retreat?

10. For what was the campaign of 1779 remarkable? What is said of almost every scheme? Why? What is said of the French fleet?

11. What more powerful cause existed for their feeble exertions? When were bills of credit first issued by Congress? What was the amount of these bills in 1780? What was the progress of their depreciation? How great was the final depreciation of paper money? Causes of this depreciation?

12. What is said of such a currency? What influence had this currency? On the other hand, what is said of Great Britain? What did Parliament do?

PRINCIPAL EVENTS OF 1780.

What were they?

1. For what object did Clinton embark for the south, towards the close of 1779? With how many troops? Who, at this time, was the American commander at Charleston? When did Clinton commence the siege?

2. What British fleet aided? Who urged Lincoln forward? What was the result of the siege? To what humiliation were the Americans subjected? When and how was this retaliated?

3. What measures were now taken to reëstablish royal authority? To what city did Clinton return, after the surrender of the city of Charleston? Whom did he leave in command?

4. Who superseded General Lincoln? Amount of his force? Of whom composed?

5. Who, at this time, commanded on the frontier? Where did he concentrate the royal forces? Who joined them at Camden? (5.) Where did the hostile forces meet? When?

6. What decided the fate of the battle? What militia threw down their arms, and fled? Who followed their example? What was the conduct of the continental troops? What brave officer fell? Who was De Kalb? How did Congress honor his memory? What is said of the battle of Camden? What is added about the British cause? What about the Americans?

7. Who invaded New Jersey in June? With what force? What was their conduct? What bloody act was committed at Connecticut Farms? How was it attempted to be excused?

8. How did the inhabitants suffer, in addition to these predatory incursions? Where had Washington encamped, the preceding winter? What name was given to that winter? What prospect was often before Washington?

9. What is said of the return of spring? What report of the state of the army did a committee from Congress make to that body?

10. What is said of the Americans in the midst of their distresses?

11. What force arrived from France, in Rhode Island, in July? Who was the naval commander? What land force was brought out? Commander of these? Feelings of the Americans, on this event? Why did not the French assist the Americans?

12. Where is West Point? (4.) How far from New York? Who obtained the command of this fortress in 1780? With whom did Arnold enter into negotiations to deliver it up?

13. Who was the British agent in this negotiation? What was the military rank of Andre? In what vessel did he ascend the North river? Whom did he meet? After his interview with Arnold, why did he not return in the Vulture? How was he compelled to return?

14. What name did Andre assume? What passport did he receive? What place did he reach? (4.) Who arrested him? What conversation ensued?

15. What did he declare himself to be? What did he offer, to be released? To whom did they conduct him? How did Arnold effect his escape? Where did he take refuge? By whom was Andre tried? Who was president? What was their decision?

16. How was Andre regarded by the American army? What British officer endeavored to save him? What request did Andre make of Washington? Why did Andre prefer being shot to being hung? What effect had Andre's letter upon Washington? Was his request granted? When did he suffer?

17. How were his captors rewarded?

18. How was Arnold rewarded?

PRINCIPAL EVENTS OF 1781.

What were they?

1. What afflicting event occurred early in 1781? What was the cause of this mutiny? Where did it occur? Who inquired into their grievances? What was their report? What did the mutineers do, upon being redressed?

2. Who commanded these troops? In his ardor, what did Wayne do? What did the troops do? What did they say? Whither did they withdraw? Who sent agents to induce them to join the British? How did they treat the proposal? How did they treat the agents?

3. In what Southern State did Arnold commit great depredations? What were some of the outrages of his troops? What squadron was sent to cut off Arnold's retreat? Success of their enterprise?

4. Who superseded Gates, after the battle of Camden? What is said of Greene as a commander? How did he compare with Washington? State of the army at this time? Who were Greene's officers? What is said of them?

5. First measure of Greene? What has been said of it? Whom did it serve to perplex?

6. Whom did Cornwallis begin with? Where was Morgan stationed? (5.) Who was sent to attack him? With how many men? What was Cornwallis to do?

7. What is said of a contest between Morgan and Tarleton? What is said of the Americans, on the first onset? What was done at this critical moment? What had Morgan time to do? What is said of the achievement?

8. On the defeat of Tarleton, what did Cornwallis do? What did Greene do, as a counter movement? Toward what court-house did he march? (5.)

9. What is said of this undertaking? Why was it perilous? What rivers did Greene pass in his retreat? During what month was this retreat effected? With what remarkable interpositions were the Americans favored?

10. From Guilford court-house, where did Greene proceed? By whom pursued? What river must they pass? Who was near at hand?

11. On reaching the banks, what were rolling before them? Who were stationed in the rear? Why? What was announced, about noon? Why had Greene delayed crossing?

12. What is said of the last boat? What of the disappointment of the British? Length of this retreat? What did Cornwallis here do? Where is Hillsborough? (5.)

13. What is said of the strength of Greene's army? Where did he proceed? When did an engagement take place? What is said of the Carolina militia? What was Greene compelled to do? What is said of the result? What did Fox say of the victory?

14. Where did Cornwallis retire? Whence then did he proceed? Meanwhile, what did Greene decide to do? What is said of this experiment? Where did he encamp? Where was Hobkirk's Hill? Where were the British strongly intrenched?

15. What engagement soon after took place? Who was the British commander? How were the Americans engaged when attacked? What did they do? What is said of the Gunby regiment?

16. What is said of Greene's attempt to rally them? With what success? Issue of the battle?

17. By what other name is this battle known? Where, after it, did Greene proceed? Where was Ninety-Six? How long did he lay siege to it? Why did he assault it? When? With what success?

18. Who followed Greene on his retreat? What did Rawdon then do? Where did the British army take post? (3.) What became of Rawdon? Whom did he leave in command?

19. What American was executed, about this time? Where? By whom? Under what circumstances?

20. Where did General Greene spend the hot season? (5.) In September, what did he do? What battle occurred? Who claimed the victory? At the close of the battle, what took place?

21. What is said of the battle of Eutaw Springs? What became of the British? When did they evacuate the city of Charleston? Who entered? What did the people say?

22. What is said of the merit of Greene? What did Washington say of him?

23. What is said of Cornwallis, at page 198 ? What place did he reach ? (5.) Whose troops were at Petersburg ? What had become of Phillips ?

24. Whom had General Washington sent to Virginia ? With what force ? For what object ? What orders had been given to Lafayette ? What did Lafayette attempt to do ? Did he succeed ?

25. What was the object of Cornwallis ? What did Lafayette do ? Why did he not hazard a contest ? How did Cornwallis employ himself ? Where, at length, did he concentrate his forces ? (5.) What did he here do ? (5.) What is said of Gloucester Point ?

26. What was the object of the campaign of 1781 ? To be aided by whom ? In prosecution of this plan, what did the French troops do ? Where were Washington's forces concentrated ? (4.)

27. Why was this plan suddenly changed ? Who now became Washington's object ? Where did the combined troops now march ? When did they appear before Yorktown ?

28. What is said of the Count de Grasse ? What had he done ? What is said of the French troops ?

29. What excursion did Arnold make, meanwhile ? Object of this expedition ? How was this expedition signalized ? What forts were taken and burnt ? (2.)

30. What is said of the defence of Fort Trumbull ? What of that of Fort Griswold ? Who was inhumanly murdered ? What is said of the burning of New London ?

31. Why did not Washington send an expedition after Arnold ?

32. When did the siege of Yorktown commence ? How was it pursued ? What is said of the sixteenth instant ?

33. What attempt at retreat did Cornwallis make ? Issue of this attempt ? When did the capitulation take place ?

34. How long after the surrender of Cornwallis did Clinton appear in view ? Amount of his reinforcement ? Whither did he return, on learning the fate of Cornwallis ? To what did Cornwallis impute his fall ? What had Clinton promised him ? Cause of the delay ?

35. How were the Americans affected by the victory over Cornwallis ? What did Congress appoint, on the occasion ?

36. What event substantially closed the war ? What posts were still held by the British ? After the capture of Cornwallis, what indicated the continuance of the war ? What became of the French army ? Where did Rochambeau, with his army, spend the winter ? To what place did the American army retire ?

PRINCIPAL EVENTS OF 1781–3.

What were they ?

1. What resolution passed Parliament, 1782 ?

2. Who succeeded Clinton in command ? What instructions were given to Carleton ? Why did Congress refuse to correspond with Carleton ?

3. What did the French court now press upon Congress ? Who were appointed ? Who were appointed on the part of Great Britain ? Where did they meet ? Date of the provisional articles of peace ? Date of the definitive treaty ? From what time had there been no acts of hostility ? When was the cessation of hostilities proclaimed to the American army ? When was Savannah evacuated ? When New York ? Charleston ?

4. When was the American army disbanded ?   To whom did Washington bid an affectionate adieu ?   In what words did he bid the army adieu ?

5. To what still more painful separation was Washington soon called ? Where did they assemble for this purpose ?   With what did he say his heart was full ?   What wish did he express for them ?   In what manner did he treat each one ?   Whither did they follow him ?   What was his last adieu ?

6. When did Washington resign his commission ?   Whom did he commend to Congress ?   To whose protection did he commend the interests of his country ?

7. How did Congress express their sense of his wisdom and energy ? To whom did President Mifflin, in behalf of Congress, commend the interests of the country ?   To whom did he commend Washington ?

8. Whither did Washington retire ?   In what character ?

NAVAL OPERATIONS.

1. What is said of the naval force of the colonies at the beginning of the Revolution ?   What soon after did the brave and patriotic do ?

2. When did the news of the battle of Lexington reach Machias ? (2.) What schooner was lying there ?   What plan was devised ?   What did the captain of the schooner do ?

3. What is said of the sloop ?   What took place ?   How many were killed ?   What is said of this engagement ?

4. What colonies had provided vessels before the action of Congress ?

5. When did Congress authorize a regular marine ?   Where were they to be built ?   What were some of their names ?   How many thirty-two's ?   How many twenty-eight's ?   How many twenty-four's ?

6. How many of these got to sea ?   Why not all ?   What became of those which were built ?

7. What was the title of the commander-in-chief of the navy ?   Who was he ?   What was his pay ?   How many captains ?

8. Describe the flag used.   When were our present national colors adopted ?

9. What is said of our naval officers ?   Mention some, of the greatest reputation.

10. What is said of the commanders of privateers ?   How many vessels did they capture ?

11. What spirited naval actions can you mention ?   Which was the most remarkable ?

12. Who commanded the Richard ?   Who the Serapis ?   When and where did the action occur ?   By what was it commenced ?   What is said of the Bon Homme and Serapis, and of the action between them ?

13. What fire occurred, and which vessel began to sink ?   What mistake occurred ?   Which vessel surrendered ?   Loss of the Richard ?   Loss of the Serapis ?   What became of the vessels ?

14. Describe the Torpedo.   Whose invention was it ?   In what year ? What was its object ?

15. What did Bushnell attempt by means of a torpedo ?   What was his success ?   What was the single instance in which he succeeded ? What is said of this mode of warfare, and what is said of Bushnell ?

NOTES.

MANNERS. 1. What were the employments of the Americans at the commencement of the war? What was their character? What control had repressed every attempt on their part to rise?

2. What soon wrought in them a great expansion of character? With whom were they soon qualified to cope?

3. What effect had the war upon their morals? What does an army always carry in its train? What effect had the failure of public credit? What became of a high sense of integrity?

4. When did Dr. Ramsay write? What was his declaration? What did he think the friends of public order should do?

RELIGION. 5. What effect had the war upon local prejudices? Upon religious controversies?

6. What unhappy principles were sown in the American army, by the French? What was the effect of these principles upon religion? What is said of religious institutions? What of churches? What of public worship? What of the clergy?

TRADE AND COMMERCE. 7. What was the effect of the war upon commerce? What became of the shipping?

AGRICULTURE. 8. What was the effect of the war upon agriculture?

ARTS AND MANUFACTURES. 9. What is said of the trade with England? What of manufactures?

POPULATION. 10. Number of inhabitants in 1784? What is said of the increase of the population during the war? Why was it so small?

EDUCATION. 11. Effects of the war upon education? What is said of instruction in several colleges? Number of colleges and academies at the close of this period?

REFLECTIONS. 12. What is the most interesting event of modern times? Have not changes equally violent often taken place? But what, in the achievement of the American Revolution, is worthy of special notice? What sprang from the blood which was then spilt?

13. What has been the general foundation of most governments? How was our independence won? With what do our annals shine?

14. What do we owe to Providence? What has the American Revolution taught the world?

MISCELLANEOUS QUESTIONS ON PERIOD IV.

1. For what is Period IV. distinguished? When does it begin? When end? Length? What battle may be said to have opened the war? What closed it? How long between the battles of Lexington and Yorktown?

2. What were some of the causes of the Revolution? How many colonies had been planted? Mention some of the battles fought, between those of Lexington and Yorktown. In which battles were the Americans victorious? When was the battle of Lexington fought? Was the battle of Bennington before or after the taking of Burgoyne?

3. What two fortresses were taken by the Americans in less than a month after the battle of Lexington? When were committees of correspondence and inquiry appointed in various parts of the country? Object of these? What event happened March 5th, 1770, which helped to bring on the war?

4. Who commanded the Americans in the battle of Bennington?

33*

What do you understand by the Boston Port-bill? When did the Congress of 1774 meet? Who was president of it? Who secretary? What were the proceedings of that body?

5. What act of great heroism do you recollect of General Putnam? Was Washington appointed to the command of the army before or after the battle of Lexington? When and where did the first Continental Congress meet? How many colonies were reported? At the time of the battle of Bunker Hill, what added greatly to the horror of the scene? In what battle did General Montgomery fall? Date of the evacuation of Boston by the British? Was this before or after the Declaration of Independence? When was Philadelphia evacuated by the British?

6. When was the battle of Bunker Hill? For what was the campaign of 1779 distinguished? Who was Benedict Arnold? What fortress did he conspire to deliver up to the British? What events of his life do you remember, before this time? What after it?

7. During the famous retreat of Washington following the battle of Long Island, through what plains did he pass? During this retreat what two American forts fell into the hands of the British? Where were these forts? What can you relate about him? What two victories soon followed the retreat through New Jersey?

8. Where was Stony Point? What can you relate about an attack upon that? In what year was this? Who were the principal English generals in the American army during the Revolutionary War? What nation assisted the Americans? What French generals do you recollect? What distinguished American generals?

9. Of all the American generals, which was the most firm and enduring? Which were characterized for great boldness and courage? Of what general is it said that he managed so well, even when defeated, that he reaped nearly the advantage of a victory? How many turned traitors to our country during the Revolutionary War?

10. What general was killed in the battle of Camden? Where is Camden? Who was the American general in the south when Charleston surrendered? What two similar transactions took place after the surrender of Charleston and after the battle of Yorktown?

11. What event substantially closed the Revolutionary War? In what year was there a serious revolt among the American troops? Where? How many revolted? What general attempted to quiet them? How was he treated? Of what remarkable enterprise had this general the command?

12. When was the American army disbanded? How long after Washington took command of it? When did Washington resign his commission? Who were the American commissioners who signed the treaty of peace? When was this signed?

13. Who supported the Declaration on the floor of Congress with more power than any other? What did Mr. Jefferson say of Mr. Adams? In what way might Great Britain have prevented the Revolution? What was the population of the United States at the close of the war? What effect had the Revolution upon religion? What infidelity was spread abroad?

14. Who were the Hessians? When and where was a large body of these taken by the Americans? What victory seemed to turn the tide of prosperity in our favor in August, 1777? Who was Sergeant Jasper? Tell his story. In what battle was the heat so great that the

tongues of the soldiers became so swollen that they could not retain them in their mouths?

15. What do you recollect of Gloucester Point? On what occasion was General O'Hara the representative of Cornwallis? What is said of our prospects after the first battle of Camden? Who were Paulding, Williams and Van Wert? Who Count de Grasse? Who was Colonel Ledyard? What American committed great depredations in Virginia, in 1781? Who was D'Estaing?

16. What outrages did the British commit at Danbury, in 1777? Who was Charles Townsend? Where was General Montgomery killed? Where General Wooster? Baron de Kalb? General Warren? General Mercer? Which was the first general who fell?

17. Relate the particulars of the massacre at Wyoming. When was the hard winter, and what is said of the sufferings of the American army? What two Americans were executed as spies? When? What as a commander was the character of General Greene? What was the character of General Wayne? Who superseded General Lincoln, on the fall of Charleston?

18. What generals were taken prisoners at the battle of Long Island? Who were the principal generals at the south, under General Greene? Who was General Kniphausen? Which was the last general engagement at the south? In respect to what engagement was it that Fox said "another such engagement will ruin the British army"?

19. Where was Fort Edward? Who commanded the English at the battle of Bennington? What two officers were wounded at the battle of Brandywine? What towns in Connecticut suffered during the expedition of Arnold? In what year was this? When did royal government, generally, cease in America? What were writs of assistance?

20. Who was principally instrumental in procuring the aid of France? What do you understand by the articles of confederation? Which was the most noted naval action during the Revolutionary War?

PERIOD V., p. 214.

For what is Period V. distinguished? When did it commence? When did it terminate? Length?

1. What is now said of the Revolution? Of the British troops? Of the American army? What great object had the colonies accomplished?

2. To what had they been looking forward, during the war? What did they soon perceive? What had they not?

3. What had they? What did the confederation prove? What powers had Congress? What powers were withheld? Amount of public debt? What could Congress do, in regard to this debt?

4. What was proposed? What colonies refused assent? What was the consequence?

5. What did Congress do? What did some of the states attempt to do? What did this produce in Massachusetts? What did the insurgents demand? By what force was it suppressed?

6. At length, what conviction was general?

7. When did Virginia recommend a convention? Where? For what purpose? Why did it adjourn? When? What did it recommend? How did the colonies respond? What state refused to appoint

commissioners? How many members did the convention consist of? Who was president? How did the convention proceed?

8. What was the first question discussed? How was this decided? How long did the session of the convention last? What was agreed on? To whom was this constitution submitted? How many ratified it? In what manner? What three in 1787? What nine in 1788? Which was the last to ratify it? In what year?

9. What did Congress do, at its first session, in regard to amendments? To what did these amendments relate? How many were adopted? By whom? How many were subsequently added?

10. Who was at once thought of for president? What were Washington's wishes? What do you understand by Federalists and Anti-Federalists? Which of these elected Washington? Who was elected vice-president?

PERIOD VI., p. 218.

For what distinguished? When was Washington inaugurated? When did he retire? Length of his administration? Who was the first Secretary of State? Who the first Secretary of the Treasury? Who the first Secretary of War? Who the first Postmaster-general? Who the first Attorney-general? Who the first Speaker of the first Congress under the constitution?

1. Where was General Washington inaugurated? In whose presence? Who administered the oath? What did Washington then deliver? What religious sentiment did he introduce into his speech? What religious worship did he and Congress then attend? What example did he set?

2. What did the acts and events which signalized his administration relate to?

I. System of Revenue. What was the first duty of Congress, under the constitution? What duties were laid? What encouragement given to American shipping?

II. Regulations of Departments. How many departments were created? Design of them? How were they styled? What were their heads called? What did they constitute? What might the president require?

III. Establishment of a Judiciary. When was such judiciary established? What did it consist of? What did the Supreme Court consist of? District Courts? Circuit Courts? What is said of this system? Who was first chief justice?

IV. Assumption of Debts. Amount of foreign and domestic debt? Debts of the states? What did Mr. Hamilton propose, in respect to these debts? What is said of the assumption of foreign debt? Why was the assumption of the domestic debts and state debts opposed? What became of the plan of Mr. Hamilton?

V. Removal of Seat of Government. What is said of the debates on this subject? What compromise was effected? What did it lead to? What was understood? What did this assumption of debts lay the foundation of? What did individuals realize? What is added?

VI. National Bank. What was the next public measure adopted? Who recommended it? Who opposed it, and why? Who approved of it? Capital stock? Duration of its charter? Location? What did this bill and other measures contribute to?

VII. ADMISSION OF VERMONT. 1. When was Vermont admitted?
Derivation of the name?
2. When was Vermont settled? Who laid claim to the territory?
Who denied the New Hampshire claim? What did they do in regard
to the New York claim? What is the date of the act of admission?
VIII. INDIAN WAR. 1. When did a war break out, and where?
Whom did the president send into that country, and for what purpose?
When and where was Harmar routed? (5.)
2. Who succeeded Harmar? When and where was St. Clair defeated?
Loss?
3. Who was successor to St. Clair? What fort did he build, and
near what spot? What fort did he erect in 1794? (5.) What victory
did he obtain, that summer? When was this war brought to a close?
By what treaty? What was ceded to the United States?
IX. ADMISSION OF KENTUCKY. When was Kentucky admitted?
Origin of her name? First permanent settlement? When and where?
(5.) What is said of the inhabitants during the Revolutionary War?
After what time did they enjoy more peace?
X. REELECTION OF WASHINGTON. When was Washington reëlected?
What determination had he previously formed? Who was elected vice-
president?
XI. DIFFICULTIES WITH FRANCE. 1. What is said of the reëlection
of Washington? What revolution was in progress? When? What
is said of Louis XVI.? What had the national convention done? How
was this revolution regarded in America?
2. What was the wish of many Americans in regard to France?
What did the cabinet decide? What proclamation was issued? What
did the republic of France do? What minister did they send? What
was the object of Genet? What did he attempt to do? What did the
president solicit of the French republic? Who succeeded Mr. Genet?
XII. INSURRECTION IN PENNSYLVANIA. When was this insurrection?
Origin of it? How was opposition manifested to this taxation? What
did the president do? What became of the insurgents?
XIII. PROHIBITION OF THE SLAVE-TRADE. 1. When did Congress
prohibit the slave-trade from American ports? How long had England
been engaged in the slave-trade? When were the first slaves introduced? How many? By what ship? What is said of their increase?
Where were they soon found? Number in 1784? Number in 1790?
Who fastened this evil upon the colonies?
2. What law was passed in Massachusetts in 1645? What in 1703?
What did Virginia attempt as early as 1699? What do these acts
show?
3. When did Virginia abolish the traffic by law? What other states
before 1789? What resolution did the Continental Congress pass?
What did the third Congress do?
XIV. JAY'S TREATY. 1. What is said of the relation between the United
States and Great Britain? What were the principal complaints? What
other sources of trouble were there? What became, therefore, more
probable?
2. Who was despatched to the court of St. James? What did he
negotiate? What were the main features of this treaty? When was
this treaty submitted to the Senate?
3. What did the Senate advise? How did the cabinet stand? How
the country? How did the friends of England regard the treaty?

What is said of Boston ? What of other cities ? How were Mr. Jay and Mr. Hamilton and others treated ? What did the president do, notwithstanding ? How did the treaty work ?

XV. ADMISSION OF TENNESSEE. When was Tennessee admitted ? Origin of its name ? In what was it originally included ? To whom did it fall ? What did North Carolina do with it ? When was it made a territorial government, and by what title ? When first settled, and by whom ?

XVI. ELECTION OF MR. ADAMS. What political parties sprang up during Washington's administration ? Who were at the head of these parties ? What is said of the election ? Upon whom did the choice fall ?

XVII. FAREWELL ADDRESS. 1. When did Washington's administration end ? What is said of his last levee ?

2. What did his farewell address embody ? What is said of it ? What is Washington's remark about the union of government ?

PERIOD VII., p. 227.

For what is Period VII. distinguished ? When was Adams inaugurated ? When did he retire ? Length of his administration ?

1. What is said of the country on the accession of Mr. Adams ? What had been done at home ? What is said of the agricultural and commercial interests of the country ? What of the western Indians ? What of England ? What of France ?

2. What were the principal events of Mr. Adams' administration ?

I. DIFFICULTIES WITH FRANCE. 1. What is said of these difficulties after Mr. Adams' accession ? What is said of the successors of Mr. Genet ? What attempts were made to settle the existing difficulties ? What did the French Directory refuse, and what order ?

2. Whom did Mr. Adams summon, and what did he urge Congress to do ? What specific measures, however, were taken ?

3. What warlike measures did Congress adopt ? Who was appointed commander ? What captures were authorized ? What hostile acts were committed ?

II. TREATY WITH FRANCE. Consequence of the bold and decided tone of the Americans ? Measures on the part of the president ? What did these envoys find, on their arrival at Paris ? What did Bonaparte do ? Date of the treaty ? What became of the provisional army ?

III. DEATH OF WASHINGTON. 1. When did the death of Washington occur ? Where ? At what age ? What was his complaint ? What did he say, in view of death ?

2. What did Congress do, on the news of his death ? What action did they subsequently take, expressive of the national feeling ?

3. What funeral solemnities took place in Philadelphia ? Who pronounced an oration ? What was done in other places ?

IV. REMOVAL OF THE SEAT OF GOVERNMENT. When was the seat of government removed to Washington ?

V. ELECTION OF MR. JEFFERSON. 1. What is said of the administration of Mr. Adams ? What two measures injured his popularity ?

2. What did the alien law authorize ? Design of the sedition law ? What did it impose ?

3. How did the votes of the electors stand ? Upon whom did the election devolve ? Why ? How did the members of Congress vote ?

4. How did they proceed? How did the vote stand, on the first ballot? How long did this result continue? What was the result of the thirty-sixth balloting? Who, of course, was vice-president?

PERIOD VIII., p. 231.

For what is Period VIII. distinguished? When was Mr. Jefferson inaugurated? When did he retire? Length of his administration?

1. What is said of Mr. Jefferson's transfer of lucrative offices? What alterations were made as to internal taxes and the judicial system?

2. What were the leading events of Mr. Jefferson's administration?

I. Admission of Ohio. When was Ohio admitted into the Union? Derivation of its name? Her territory, by whom claimed? What is said of the cession of Virginia in 1781? Who first began the settlement of Ohio? Where and when? (5.) What retarded the settlement? What, at length, gave a spring to this settlement?

II. Purchase of Louisiana. What right had the United States to navigate the Mississippi? What right to the use of New Orleans? When were these rights violated, and by whom? Consequence of this violation? How was the difficulty settled? Cost of Louisiana? When transferred?

III. Murder of Hamilton. When did the death of Hamilton occur? What caused it? Why was this duel fought? What is said of Hamilton?

IV. Re-election of Mr. Jefferson. When was Mr. Jefferson reëlected? Who became vice-president?

V. War and Peace with Tripoli. When did this war terminate? In what? Conditions of the treaty?

VI. Conspiracy and Trial of Burr. What project was Colonel Burr detected in? When? By whom arrested? Where tried? On what charge? Result?

VII. France and England. 1. What do you understand by the carrying trade? Who enjoyed this trade, and why? British order in council, 1806? What effect had this order upon American vessels? Decree of Bonaparte, by way of retaliation?

2. How did the British government retaliate? Effect of this contention upon American commerce? What do you understand by the right of search? Who claimed this right?

VIII. Attack on the Chesapeake. 1. When was this attack made? By whom? Occasion of it? What did it rouse?

2. Why did the Chesapeake strike her colors? How much damage? What was done with the men claimed? What proved to be the facts?

3. What did the president do, in consequence of this outrage? What instructions were sent to Mr. Monroe? What further negotiations took place?

IX. Embargo. When did Congress meet? What was done by that body for defence? What is said of an embargo?

X. Orders in Council. What orders were issued by Great Britain to retaliate the French decree of November, 1806?

XI. Milan Decree. What is meant by the Milan Decree?

XII. Non-Intercourse. What effect had the embargo? What substitute was recommended for it? With what proviso?

XIII. Election of Mr. Madison. Who succeeded Mr. Jefferson as president? Who was appointed vice-president?

*

PERIOD IX., p. 238.

For what is Period IX. distinguished? When was Mr. Madison inaugurated? When did he retire? Length of his administration?

1. Condition of the United States? What two powers were still at war? What was the effect of their commercial edicts? From what else was America suffering?

2. Why did the president issue his proclamation renewing intercourse with Great Britain? Effect of this measure upon the people? On what account were they soon disappointed? What proclamation did the president soon issue?

3. When did Bonaparte issue his Rambouillet decree? Why? What did it order? What act passed Congress, May 1st? What did it provide? When was intercourse with France renewed? By what act?

4. Between what vessels did an engagement take place, in 1811? Which commenced the attack? What was the decision of a court of inquiry, appointed to investigate the affair? What events signalized the year 1811? 1812? 1813? 1814? 1815 and 1816?

I. ADMISSION OF LOUISIANA. When was Louisiana admitted into the Union? Origin of its name? Who first discovered it? When? Of whom did the United States purchase it, and for how much?

II. BATTLE OF TIPPECANOE. 1. When was this battle fought? What is said of it? What is said of Tecumseh and his brother?

2. Who was General Harrison? What treaty did he negotiate? When? How did Tecumseh like it?

3. Where did General Harrison meet these Indians? What took place?

III. DECLARATION OF WAR. When was war declared? Principal grounds of the war? Who protested against the war? On what grounds? Force ordered to be raised? Who was appointed commander-in-chief? Brigadiers?

IV. SURRENDER OF HULL. 1. Who was General Hull? Where was he stationed? Where is Detroit? (5.) Against what British post was he sent? With what force? Where was Malden? (5.)

2. What time did he here waste? Meanwhile, how was Malden reinforced? What is said of Mackinaw? When was this?

3. What report served to terrify General Hull? In consequence of this, what did Hull do?

4. Who commanded at Malden? What did General Brock do? To whom did Hull capitulate?

5. Reason assigned for this by Hull?

6. What became of Hull? Charges brought against him? Where was he tried? What was the decision of the court-martial? What did the president remit?

V. CAPTURE OF THE GUERRIERE. For what achievements was this war distinguished? By whom were they commenced? What frigate did Hull capture? Which was superior in force? What was the loss of each vessel? Damage each vessel sustained?

VI. BATTLE OF QUEENSTOWN. 1. Who was commander-in-chief of our army? Towards the invasion of what province did he turn his attention? Forces collected for this purpose? How were the American troops distributed ? What division did Harrison command ? What Van Rensselaer ? What Dearborn ?

2. Where did a detachment of American troops attack the British, October 13th ? Who commanded them ? How were the American forces divided ? Who was early wounded ? Who took the command ? Of what did they gain possession ? Who reinforced the fort ? What prevented the Americans keeping possession of it ?

3. Why would not the militia cross the river ? What is said of the probable result, if they had done so ?

VII. CAPTURE OF THE FROLIC. What is said of an engagement between the Wasp and Frolic ? How long did the action last ? Off what coast was it ? Why was the fire of the Americans so much more destructive than that of the British ? By what ship were both captured, the same day ?

VIII. CAPTURE OF THE MACEDONIAN. 1. What was the next naval achievement ? Off what isles ? Comparative damage ?

2. What act of kindness distinguished the crew of the United States ?

IX. CAPTURE OF THE JAVA. What was the second naval victory of the Constitution ? Where was the action fought ? Comparative loss ? What was done with the Java ?

X. END OF THE CAMPAIGN. What is said of the campaign of 1812 ?

XI. CAMPAIGN OF 1813. Principal events of this campaign ? What is said of the military operations of the campaign ? Location of the army of the west ? Commander ? Location of the army of the centre ? Commander ? Army of the north ? Commander ? Generals of the British forces in Canada ?

XII. BATTLE OF FRENCHTOWN. 1. Who held possession of Michigan, in 1813 ? In order to recover it, what did General Harrison determine to do ? In pursuance of this plan, where did General Winchester advance ? Number and character of his troops ? Where is Frenchtown ? (5.) Whom did Winchester here rout ?

2. When, and by whom, was Winchester here attacked ? Result ?

3. What inhuman butchery was afterwards perpetrated ?

4. What became of the remains of those who fell ?

XIII. CAPTURE OF THE PEACOCK. What was the result of the action between the Hornet and Peacock ? Where was it fought ? Captains of these vessels ? What became of the Peacock ? Seamen sunk with her ? Generous conduct of the crew of the Hornet ?

XIV. RE-ELECTION OF MR. MADISON. When was Mr. Madison reëlected ? Over what competitor ? Vice-president ? Who succeeded, on the death of Clinton ?

XV. CAPTURE OF YORK. 1. What is York the capital of ? What was it the great depository of ? When was an attack made upon it by the Americans ? Who commanded the land forces ? Who the flotilla ? Who opposed the landing ?

2. Who was intrusted with the command ? What befell him ? What was his dying order ? Number killed by the explosion ? Result ?

XVI. SIEGE OF FORT MEIGS. 1. Who constructed Fort Meigs ? Where situated ? After whom called ? By whom was it besieged, in May ? The length of the siege ? Issue of it ? Whither did Harrison go ? Under whose care did he leave the fort ? What demand was made on the third day of the siege ? What did Harrison reply ?

2. By whom was Harrison reinforced? Aided by these, what sortie was made? Result of it? Why did the British general raise the siege?

3. Who again appeared at Fort Meigs? When, and with what number of troops? Why did they retire? Against what fort did they proceed? How was this garrisoned, and who was the commander? To the command to surrender, what did he reply? What did the enemy attempt to do? What is said of their reception?

XVII. LOSS OF THE CHESAPEAKE. What American frigate was captured off Boston harbor? By what frigate? Who was the commander of the Chesapeake? What was his fate? Under what circumstances did Lawrence fight? What accident decided the contest? Last heroic order of Lawrence?

XVIII. LOSS OF THE ARGUS. When, and by whom, was the Argus captured? How had she been employed? Fate of Captain Allen?

XIX. CAPTURE OF THE BOXER. By whom was the Boxer captured? Off what coast? Fate of the captains? Where were they interred?

XX. PERRY'S VICTORY. When was the naval action on Lake Erie, between Commodore Perry and a British fleet? Force of the Americans? Force of the British? Heroic conduct of Perry? How many vessels did he capture? In what words did he announce his victory?

XXI. BATTLE OF THE THAMES. 1. Why was the victory of Perry welcome? For what was the way now prepared? What was now the first object of Harrison? What force had he assembled? On reaching Malden, what did they find? Whom did they pursue? What place did they take possession of?

2. Leaving Detroit, whither did they next proceed? With what force? What battle ensued? What Indian chief was slain? What did this lead to? What were retaken? What is said of Tecumseh?

XXII. PROPOSED INVASION OF CANADA. 1. What did the fall of Detroit put an end to? Whom did Harrison leave at Detroit? Whither did Harrison go, with the remainder of his force? What prepared the way for the invasion of Canada?

2. Commander-in-chief at this time? What was the chief object of his instructions? Forces destined for the accomplishment of these purposes?

3. What change of plan was ordered by General Armstrong? What prevented its execution? What is said of Wilkinson and his force? Of Hampton and his force? Of Harrison and his force?

XXIII. END OF THE CAMPAIGN OF 1813. What did the end of this campaign give rise to? What is said of public opinion about it?

XXIV. CAMPAIGN OF 1814. CREEK WAR. 1. What Indian war distinguished the year 1813 and a part of 1814? Who instigated the Creeks? Character of the war? Commander of the Americans? Battles fought? (5.) Treaty? What is said of General Jackson? Whom did he succeed at New Orleans?

2. What was the commencement of the Creek war? What did General Jackson and General Coffee do? What place did the Creeks fortify? What is said of its reduction?

3. What put an end to the war? What is said of the remnant of the nation? What did Weatherford, their leader, say?

XXV. CHIPPEWA AND BRIDGEWATER. 1. What is said of General Wilkinson, in the spring of 1814? Where did General Brown go? 2. What is said of Wilkinson's attack of a stone mill at La Cole? By whom was he tried? What did the court-martial do with him? Who succeeded him? 3. What is said of the inactivity of the armies subsequently, and why were they inactive? 4. In what way was the contest renewed? What happened at Chippewa? (4.) 5. Where did General Riall retire to? By whom was he joined? What movement did they make? Where did the hostile armies meet? What was the result of the battle of Bridgewater? What generals were wounded? What did they abandon? 6. To what fort did General Ripley return? Who besieged it? When? Length of the siege? Result?

XXVI. CAPTURE OF WASHINGTON. When was an attack made upon the city of Washington? By what British force? By whom commanded? Of what disgraceful conduct was Ross guilty? What was burnt with the capitol?

XXVII. DEFENCE OF BALTIMORE. By what attack was the capture of Washington followed? Issue of it? What British general was killed?

XXVIII. WAR ON THE COAST OF NEW ENGLAND. What is said of movements in other quarters? What of a British fleet on the coast? What is said of Commodore Hardy?

XXIX. ENGAGEMENT ON LAKE CHAMPLAIN. 1. When did this engagement take place? What battle at the same time occurred? (4.) Between whom were these contests? Who were the several commanders? 2. Which naval force was the superior? 3. Length of the engagement? What fell into the hands of the Americans?

XXX. HARTFORD CONVENTION. 1. How did the people of New England regard the war? Which state recommended a convention? Which were represented? 2. Where did this convention meet? Length of their session? What did they suggest?

XXXI. BATTLE OF NEW ORLEANS. 1. Date of this battle? (5.) Forces employed? Commanders? 2. Result of the attack? What British generals were killed? What one was wounded? Loss of the Americans? Loss of the British?

XXXII. TREATY OF GHENT. By what was the news of the victory of New Orleans soon followed? When and where was the treaty signed? When ratified? Upon what subjects was it silent? For what did it provide?

XXXIII. TREATY WITH ALGIERS. 1. What other war was terminated by treaty, soon after the war with Britain? Where was it negotiated? Agents of the United States? Who commenced this war? How had peace been preserved with the dey? 2. In 1812, what became of the American consul? Why was Mr. Lear dismissed? What became of several American vessels? 3. What action did Congress take upon this? What squadron was despatched? What was the result of this demonstration? Who dictated the treaty? What were the important articles of it?

XXXIV. NATIONAL BANK. When did the former national bank expire? When was a new bank chartered? Capital? Length of its charter?

XXXV. ADMISSION OF INDIANA. When was Indiana admitted into the Union? Derivation of its name? Who first settled it? What is said of it during the war of 1812?

XXXVI. Who succeeded Mr. Madison? Who was elected vice-president?

PERIOD X., p. 259.

For what is Period X. distinguished? When was Mr. Monroe inaugurated? When did he retire?

1. What is said of the elevation of Mr. Monroe to the presidency? In what respects was he well qualified for his station?

2. What was the condition of the country? What is said of commerce and manufactures? What of other departments of industry?

3. Principal measures and events of Mr. Monroe's administration?

I. ADMISSION OF MISSISSIPPI. Who first visited the State of Mississippi? What was the region round about called? Who gave it that name? Who claimed the country? Where did they begin a settlement? When and to whom did the French cede the country of Mississippi? Who were its owners subsequently? Who claimed this territory afterwards? What was it called? When was it erected into a territorial government? When was the Mississippi Territory divided, and how?

II. PROVISION FOR INDIGENT OFFICERS AND SOLDIERS. Why were they left without adequate compensation? What did they receive? What did they do with these certificates? What is said of the purchasers? When did Congress first make provision for these officers and soldiers? What is said of the subsequent action of Congress on this subject?

III. ADMISSION OF ILLINOIS. When was Illinois admitted into the Union? Derivation of its name? First settlements, and when? By whom? What is said of the territory, in 1763? What in 1783? What was Illinois originally a part of?

IV. SEMINOLE WAR. 1. Where did the Seminoles live? (5.) Of whom did they consist? Why were they dissatisfied? Who fanned their resentments? What order was given to General Gaines? Effect of this order?

2. What order was given to General Jackson? How did he observe this order?

3. What territory did General Jackson enter? Upon what Spanish fort did he march? (5.) What did he do here? Whom did he find at St. Marks? What was done with these men? What decision did General Jackson reverse?

4. What did General Jackson next seize? (1.) What government did he establish? What was thought by the American people of General Jackson's conduct? What action was taken in Congress about it?

V. CONVENTION WITH GREAT BRITAIN. When was this convention concluded? When ratified? What was the first article? What did the second establish? What did the fourth article provide for?

VI. CESSION OF FLORIDA. When was Florida ceded to the United

States? By whom? What sum was to be paid to the citizens of the United States, and why?

VII. ADMISSION OF ALABAMA. 1. When was Alabama admitted into the Union? Origin of her name? By whom visited, and when? When settled?

2. By whom was Alabama claimed? To whom did Georgia cede it, and for what sum? When was Alabama separated from Mississippi?

VIII. ADMISSION OF MAINE. When was Maine admitted into the Union? Under whose jurisdiction had she been?

IX. RE-ELECTION OF MR. MONROE. When did Mr. Monroe enter upon his second term? Vice-president?

X. ADMISSION OF MISSOURI. 1. Origin of the name? When admitted into the Union?

2. First permanent settlements? What is the capital of the state? (5.) When begun? Of what was Missouri a part? To whom was it ceded by France? To whom was it ceded by Spain? To whom was it ceded by this latter power, and when?

3. What do you understand by the territory of Orleans? What did that territory become in 1811? What did the remaining part of the original province of Louisiana become? What application did Missouri make to Congress in 1818–19? What bill, growing out of this application, was introduced into Congress? Which house passed this bill? Which rejected it? When was the bill revived? What compromise was effected? What was Missouri obliged to do, if admitted into the Union?

XI. APPORTIONMENT OF REPRESENTATION. What does the constitution provide about representatives? What has public opinion decided? Number of members of the Congress of 1776? Number of that which formed the Confederation? Number of that which formed the constitution? Number after the first census? Number after the second census? Number after the third census? What was the ratio fixed by Congress, of 1822–3? Number under this ratio?

XII. VISIT OF LAFAYETTE. 1. When did the marquis arrive? Why was he so joyfully greeted? What is said of him at page 176?

2. Length of his visit? Number of states visited? How did he return to France?

3. Who addressed him, on his departure? Reply of Lafayette? What is said when he left the mansion of the president? Where did he land, and for what purpose?

5. What appropriation did Congress make for him, and why?

XIII. ELECTION OF MR. ADAMS. 1. State of the country during the presidency of Mr. Monroe?

2. What is said on the subject of his successor? Who were the candidates, beside Mr. Adams?

3. What is said of a choice by the electors? Who were the candidates in the House of Representatives? Through whose supposed influence was Mr. Adams elected?

PERIOD XI., p. 267.

For what distinguished? When was Mr. Adams inaugurated? When did he retire? Vice-president?

34*

1. Policy and views of Mr. Adams? What is said of him? With what was he charged? What is said of such a bargain? What was unfortunate for Mr. Adams? Principal measures and events?

I. CONTROVERSY ABOUT CREEK LANDS. Between whom was this controversy? What was the agreement of the United States with Georgia? What did Georgia demand? Why did not the United States purchase the lands? What, upon this, did the Governor of Georgia do? What did the general government do? How was the controversy at length settled?

II. FIFTIETH ANNIVERSARY OF INDEPENDENCE. 1. For what was it rendered remarkable?

2. What remarkable coincidences in their lives can you mention?

III. AMERICAN SYSTEM. What do you understand by this phrase? When first employed? Who has generally opposed the principle of protection? Who favored it? What is said of the tariff of 1828?

IV. ELECTION OF GENERAL JACKSON. What is said of the administration of Mr. Adams? What were the grounds of complaint against him, by his opponents? How were the candidates treated by their opposers? Which was elected?

PERIOD XII., p. 270.

For what is Period XII. distinguished? When was General Jackson inaugurated? When did he retire? Vice-presidents during his presidency?

1. Condition of the United States on the accession of General Jackson? What can you mention as evidence of this?

2. Prominent measures and events of General Jackson's administration?

I. REMOVALS FROM OFFICE. 1. What work did General Jackson soon commence? Number of removals, compared with those of his predecessors? What did the opposers of his administration say about these removals?

2. How did the friends of the president justify his course?

3. What did Congress do in relation to these removals?

II. NATIONAL BANK. 1. What did General Jackson say about the bank, in his first message? To whom was the subject referred? What did the committee report?

2. When did the friends of the bank ask for a renewal of their charter? What did Congress do about it? What did the president do with the bill?

3. How was the president's veto regarded? What was predicted?

III. GEORGIA AND THE CHEROKEES. 1. What embarrassing subject early engrossed the attention of the administration? What did Georgia do in regard to the Cherokee lands? What encouraged her in so doing? How did she attempt to enforce her state laws? Who were imprisoned?

2. What did the Supreme Court decide, as to the claims of Georgia? What did they order in regard to the missionaries? What, upon this, did Georgia do?

3. When and how was this unpleasant controversy ended? When and by whom, and where to, were the Cherokees removed?

IV. INTERNAL IMPROVEMENTS. 1. When were appropriations first made for internal improvements? For what objects? Under what administrations was the policy pursued? How did General Jackson regard such appropriations? How did he prove his opposition? What did Congress do, notwithstanding his vetoes?

V. INDIAN HOSTILITIES. What war occurred in the spring of 1832? In what territory? Under what chief? Who were sent into the field? Issue of the contest? What is said of Black Hawk and other chiefs?

VI. DISCONTENTS IN SOUTH CAROLINA. 1. What were these discontents, and what did they arise from? How did South Carolina regard the tariff of 1832? What is said of her convention at Columbia? Who were forbidden to force the tariff acts?

2. What effect had this upon General Jackson? What did he do? What is said of his proclamation? What effect had it upon South Carolina? What did her legislature do?

3. What two events occurred which served to allay the rising storm? What did the bill of Mr. Clay provide for?

VII. RE-ELECTION OF GENERAL JACKSON. When was General Jackson reëlected? Rival candidate? Vice-president?

VIII. REMOVAL OF THE DEPOSITS. 1. What did the law of 1816 direct as to the public moneys? What power, however, did the president assume? On what ground? What did Mr. Duane refuse? Who acceded to the wishes of the president?

2. When did Congress take action on the subject of these removals? What two resolutions were adopted in the Senate? How did the president regard the latter resolution? How long did it remain on the Senate's journal? What was then done with it?

IX. DEATH OF LAFAYETTE. When and where did the death of Lafayette occur? How did Congress notice the event?

X. DEPOSIT AND DISTRIBUTION ACT. With whom did Congress order the deposit of the public funds? What did this enable the banks to do? What were these deposit banks called? How did they promote a spirit of speculation? In what way did the government suffer?

XI. FLORIDA WAR. 1. Residence of the Seminoles? (5.) When did they commence hostilities? What incited them to these? Who was their king? Who their chief warrior? What did they think of removal?

2. What is said of this war? What is said of Osceola? On what account was he exasperated? On getting his liberty, what did he do?

3. Where is St. Augustine? (5.) Where Fort Doane? What happened here in December, 1835? What happened at Fort King, about the same time?

4. Who joined the Seminoles in 1836? What took place after this?

5. What became of the Creeks? What is said of the continuance of the war?

XII. ADMISSION OF ARKANSAS AND MICHIGAN. 1. When were these admitted into the Union?

2. Origin of their names? Of what was Arkansas originally a part? Of what subsequently? When Missouri was divided, which part took the name of Arkansas?

3. Upon what condition was Michigan received into the Union? Between whom had there existed a controversy, and as to what?

XIII. TREASURY CIRCULAR. What was the date of this circular?

By whom issued ?   What did it require ?   How was it regarded by the people ?

XIV.   ELECTION OF MR. VAN BUREN.   When was Mr. Van Buren elected president ?   Who became vice-president ?

PERIOD XIII., p. 279.

For what is Period XIII. distinguished ?   When was Mr. Van Buren inaugurated ?   When did he retire ?   Length ?

1. What is said of Mr. Van Buren, prior to his elevation ?   How had he been honored ?   When was he born ?   What is said of General Jackson's address, on retiring ?

2. Principal topics to be noticed in Mr. Van Buren's administration ?

I.   CONDITION OF THE COUNTRY.   What was the state of the pecuniary affairs of the country, after Mr. Van Buren's accession ?   What is said of failures in the city of New York ?   What of confidence ?

II.   SUSPENSION OF SPECIE PAYMENTS.   What was Mr. Van Buren solicited to do ?   Did he comply ?   What befell the bank, soon after ?

III.   EXTRA SESSION OF CONGRESS.   When did Congress meet ?   What did they do for the general relief ?   What did they postpone ?   What did they order to be issued ?

IV.   RESUMPTION OF SPECIE PAYMENTS.   When were specie payments resumed ?   What banks again suspended, and when ?   Who began the suspension, 1836 ?   What was required of the banks in 1837 ?   What did these banks induce others to do ?   What did some, however, predict ?   What banks continued the payment of specie ?

V.   SEMINOLE WAR.   1. What is said of the continuance of this war ?

2. What treaty was effected with the Seminoles ?   By whom ?   What did they stipulate ?   Through whose influence was it broken ?   What was done with the chief ?   Why was General Jessup censured for this ?   What did he plead in justification ?   What is said of Osceola ?

3. What is said of the continuance of this war ?   Movements of Colonel Harney ?

VI.   INTERNAL IMPROVEMENTS.   What appropriations were made for these ?   What were Mr. Van Buren's views of the appropriations ?   What were these expenditures for ?

VII.   DIFFICULTIES IN MAINE.   What were these difficulties about ?   What seemed likely to result ?   Who preserved the public peace ?   What further measures were taken by Congress ?

VIII.   NORTHERN BORDER TROUBLES.   1. When did the Canada rebellion break out ?   Whose sympathies were enlisted ?   What name did they assume ?   What associations form ?   Object of these ?

2. What did a daring party do ?   Their number ?   With what were they supplied ?   Upon what did they fire ?

3. What was the Caroline ?   By whom hired ?   For what object ?   What befell this steamboat ?   What befell several men ?   How were the Americans affected by these movements ?

IX.   SUB-TREASURY BILL.   What do you understand by the sub-treasury ?   What did Mr. Van Buren think of this ?   When did Congress adopt it ?

X. ELECTION OF GENERAL HARRISON. Who were the candidates in the canvass of 1840? What is said of the friends of Mr. Van Buren? What was thought of his measures regarding banks and currency? Who, at length, was elected president? Who vice-president?

PERIOD XIV., p. 284.

For what is Period XIV. distinguished? When was General Harrison inaugurated? When did he die?

1. What is said of General Harrison's inaugural address? In conclusion, what did he say?

2. What is said of his death? How did the public regard his death? What honors were paid his memory?

3. Who succeeded General Harrison?

When did Mr. Tyler assume the government? When did he retire?

1. What religious service did President Tyler propose, on the death of General Harrison?

2. What did Mr. Tyler next do by way of indicating his course of policy? Principal measures and events of his administration?

I. EXTRA SESSION OF CONGRESS. 1. Who had convened Congress? When did it meet? First measure adopted? Second? Third?

2. Great object of the session? What did the president do in regard to two bills? Consequence of his vetoes?

II. APPORTIONMENT OF REPRESENTATIVES. What is said of the census of 1840? What number of inhabitants did it show? What increase over the census of 1830? What ratio of increase? What act passed? Ratio adopted?

III. EXPLORING EXPEDITION. When did this expedition return? How long absent? Distance sailed? What did they discover? Sketches of natural history brought home?

IV. NORTH-EASTERN BOUNDARY. When and by whom was the north-eastern boundary question settled?

V. MODIFICATION OF THE TARIFF. 1. When was the tariff of 1836 altered? Whence are the revenues of government derived? What is necessary, therefore? How would one portion of the people limit the tariff? How another portion fix it?

2. What was the design of the tariff of 1842? What did Congress do with the bill? What the president? The fate of a second bill?

VI. REPEAL OF THE BANKRUPT LAW. What is said of this law at the time it was passed? Who took advantage of it? What did this abuse of the law lead to?

VII. BUNKER HILL MONUMENT. 1. When was this monument completed? How was the event celebrated? Who was present? Who was the orator? What is said of the scene?

2. What sad event soon followed? Who was Mr. Legaré? What is said of his sickness? What of his reputation?

VIII. EXPLOSION ON BOARD OF THE PRINCETON. When did this explosion occur? What distinguished personages were killed?

IX. TREATY WITH CHINA. When was this treaty negotiated? By whom? When ratified? What is said of it?

X. ANNEXATION OF TEXAS. How was Texas annexed? How had it been attempted before? Why not by treaty? Who favored the mode by joint resolution? Who opposed it? What was said of it in respect to Mexico? What was predicted as a consequence?

XI. ADMISSION OF FLORIDA AND IOWA. When were these admitted? Why and by whom called Florida? Whence the name Iowa?

XII. Who were the candidates for the presidency in 1845? Who was elected? Who vice-president?

PERIOD XV., p. 291.

For what is Period XV. distinguished? When was Mr. Polk inaugurated? When did he retire? Length? What events and measures signalized the administration of Mr. Polk?

I. DEATH OF GENERAL JACKSON. 1. When did his death occur? Where? What was his religious belief?

2. What is said of him? What merit was generally accorded him? Who paid a tribute to his memory?

II. ADMISSION OF TEXAS. 1. What did President Polk inform Congress in relation to Texas? What did he say remained to be done?

2. What action did Congress take in relation to the admission of Texas? What privilege had Texas?

III. DIFFICULTIES WITH MEXICO. 1. What steps did the Mexican minister take in consequence of the admission of Texas? How was the American minister treated by Mexico?

2. Whose act precipitated the war? What was this act? Who claimed the Nueces as their boundary? Where was Taylor to take post? (6.)

IV. DIVISION OF OREGON. 1. Who claimed Oregon? What attempts had been made to settle these claims? What agreement was made in 1818? What in 1827? What did the president recommend in 1845?

2. When was notice given? What took place before the notice was delivered? Where and by whom were the difficulties settled?

3. Northern boundary of Oregon? How fixed? What was ceded to Great Britain? How was the settlement of this question regarded?

V. COMMENCEMENT OF HOSTILITIES. 1. When did General Taylor move from Corpus Christi, and to what point? (6.) When did he proceed from this point? (6.) What did he leave at Point Isabel?

2. What did he do at Matamoras? What fort did he erect? Who was the Mexican general at Matamoras? What notice did he give General Taylor?

3. Who succeeded Ampudia? What did Arista communicate to Taylor? What is said of Captain Thornton and his party? What of Captain Thornton himself?

VI. SIEGE OF FORT BROWN. 1. What intelligence did Taylor receive respecting Point Isabel? What did he deem necessary?

2. Who was left in command of the fort? What instructions did he leave behind?

3. What is said of an attack upon the fort? Who was killed? Who was mortally wounded? Whereupon, what was done?

VII. BATTLES OF PALO ALTO AND RESACA DE LA PALMA. 1. When did General Taylor leave Point Isabel? Why? With what force? Where did he encamp? When resume his march?

2. What did the army, at length, reach? Meaning of Palo Alto? What were on either side of the American army? What beyond? Where were the Mexicans drawn up?

3. What soon occurred? What batteries did great execution?

4. What two brave men were mortally wounded? What put an end to the contest? How did the Mexicans leave the field?

5. When did the American army resume its march? Where did they discover the Mexican army a second time? Meaning of Resaca de la Palma?

6. What is said of this battle? What was captured? What general? When was Matamoras taken possession of?

7. When did the Mexican government declare war against the United States? Instead of such declaration, what did Congress declare? What did Congress authorize?

VIII. FALL OF MONTEREY. 1. What order did the American government give General Taylor? What place did he take possession of? (6.)

2. Capital of New Leon? (6.) Distance from Matamoras? What is said of the march of the American army towards it?

3. How was Monterey fortified? Who attacked it? Progress of the siege?

4. When was it surrendered? Number of prisoners? What was permitted them?

5. What is said of an armistice? Why did Taylor accede to it? Length of it? Who terminated it?

IX. PROCEEDINGS IN CONGRESS. 1. What important bill in 1845–46? What other? A third? A fourth?

2. Until now, how had the tariff been adjusted? What alteration was effected by the tariff of 1846? What was prognosticated?

X. BATTLE OF BUENA VISTA. 1. Following the capture of Monterey, what was done? What did General Taylor take possession of? (6.) Where did General Worth march? (6.) What did General Wool do? (6.)

2. What intelligence reached General Worth? Why did he not send to General Taylor? To whom did he send?

3. What order was communicated to General Taylor at Victoria? What to General Wool? What is said of their compliance?

4. Whither did General Taylor next move? Amount of their combined force?

5. When did the army take post? In whose charge was it? To what point did General Taylor proceed? For what purpose? What is said of Santa Anna?

6. What is the 22d of February memorable for? What is said of the American army? What summons did Santa Anna send to Taylor? What was the reply of the latter?

7. When did the battle of Buena Vista occur? What is said of the contest? What batteries seem to have decided it?

8. What did the Americans intend to do, the next morning? What became of the Americans? What did they leave behind? Distinguished American officers who were killed?

9. What did the victory of Buena Vista secure? What became of General Taylor? Whom did he leave in command?

XI. NAVAL OPERATIONS. 1. Movement of Commodore Sloat in the Pacific? Movement of Commodore Montgomery? In what year and what months were these movements? What is said of Commodore Stockton and Col. Frémont? In whose name did Com. Stockton establish a government there? (6.)

2. Operations of the home squadron? What places were taken? By whom?

XII. ARMY OF THE WEST. 1. By whom was this army organized? What was it to undertake?

2. What fort did General Kearney leave, and when? Course pursued? To what point? (7.) What is Santa Fé the capital of? When did he reach it? Distance marched? Space occupied?

3. What did he do at New Mexico? Whence then did he proceed? What information did he soon after receive? Whose return did he order? What did he then do? What place did he reach? Whom did he meet?

4. What did Kearney now claim? Whose claims did Stockton advocate? What did Kearney now do?

5. What is said of the arrest of Frémont, subsequently? When was he tried? Sentenced? What did the president offer?

XIII. EXPEDITION OF COLONEL DONIPHAN. 1. What order did General Kearney give to Doniphan? What was Kearney's second order to him? Why this expedition against these Indians?

2. How did Doniphan divide his regiment? What is said of this enterprise? What was his success?

3. Towards what did Doniphan next proceed? Whom did he expect to find? Whom did he encounter? When and where did he plant his standard? (6.)

4. To what point did Doniphan next march? When did he reach Saltillo? Why did he proceed to New Orleans? By what way? What distance did he march?

XIV. REDUCTION OF VERA CRUZ. 1. Where is Vera Cruz? (6.) Distance from the city of Mexico? What fortress opposite? To whom was the reduction of these intrusted?

2. Force employed? Rendezvous of the invading army? When was the city invested?

3. When was the bombardment begun? What naval battery was employed? Distance it was transported?

4. When was the city surrendered? Prisoners taken? American officers killed?

5. Number of shot and shells thrown by the American batteries? Aggregate weight? What does a writer say?

XV. BATTLE OF CERRO GORDO. 1. What and where is Cerro Gordo? When did the army reach this pass? What had Santa Anna here done? His force? Force of the Americans?

2. How did General Scott proceed? When did the battle occur? Number of Mexicans who fell? Number taken prisoners?

3. Boast of Santa Anna previous to the battle? What became of him?

XVI. PROGRESS OF THE ARMY. 1. After the battle of Cerro Gordo, what did the army do? What places were taken possession of? What is said of the fortress of Perote?

2. What city next reached? (6.) Number of its inhabitants? What did General Scott here do?

XVII. CONTRERAS — CHURUBUSCO. 1. Whither did General Scott next move? When? Accompanying force? Numbers left in the hospital, and as a garrison?

2. What is said of the army the third day after leaving Puebla? What sight burst upon them? What did they descry to the left? What before them? What beyond?

3. What place did General Twiggs reach on the 11th? What fortifi-

cation was between this and the city? Of what did the army take advantage? Where was Antonio? Where Contreras? Who occupied the last point, and with what force? When did an engagement here take place, and between whom?

4. What is said of the contest? Number of prisoners taken? Number of pieces of artillery? What is said of two brass six-pounders?

5. By what was the victory of Contreras followed?

6. What is said of the bravery of the Mexicans? How many Mexicans were engaged? How many prisoners taken? How many generals? How many other officers? Numbers killed and wounded? Field-pieces captured? Loss of the Americans?

XVIII. ATTEMPTS AT PEACE. 1. Why did General Scott here halt? Who was commissioned to negotiate a peace? What was agreed upon?

2. Who resumed the prosecution of the war, and why? What was the first object of General Scott?

3. When did the battle of Molinos del Rey occur? Who commanded the Mexicans? How did the armies compare as to numbers? American officers killed or wounded?

XIX. REDUCTION OF CHEPULTEPEC. 1. What now remained to be secured? What was Chepultepec?

2. What measures did General Scott take to reduce it? Who struck the Mexican flag from the walls, and planted the American standard?

XX. OCCUPATION OF MEXICO. 1. What followed, the next day? When was this?

2. When and by whom were terms of capitulation demanded? How were these demands met? Who were ordered to move into the city? When did General Scott take formal possession of it? What took place on the 16th? What on the 17th, and why?

XXI. TREATY. 1. What essentially terminated the war? What other engagements occurred?

2. What is said of the Mexicans, following the occupation of their city? What treaty followed? When was this treaty adopted by the American government? When was the treaty announced by proclamation?

XXII. DEATH OF MR. ADAMS. When and where did the death of this eminent man occur? What were the circumstances of his death? How long had he been employed in the service of his country? What was he often denominated?

XXIII. ADMISSION OF WISCONSIN. When was Wisconsin admitted into the Union?

XXIV. ELECTION OF GENERAL TAYLOR. What is said of the administration of Mr. Polk? Who were the candidates in the canvass of 1848? Who were elected president and vice-president?

PERIOD XVI.

For what is Period XVI. distinguished? When was General Taylor inaugurated? When did he die?

Why was General Taylor inaugurated on the 5th of March? What is said of his inaugural address? What in that did he pledge himself to do? What is said of the measures of his brief administration?

I. DEATH OF MR. POLK. When and where did this event occur? When was he born? How early was he a member of Congress? What were his politics?

II. Death of Mr. Calhoun. When and where did this distinguished individual die? What is said of his career of public service? How long had he been connected with public affairs? What offices had he held, and how had he performed his duty?

III. Death of General Taylor. 1. When and where did this able soldier and statesman die? To what was his last sickness owing? How did he meet death? What were his last words?

2. How was this national bereavement received? What was one of the last acts of his administration? When did Mr. Fillmore assume the government?

I. What does the constitution provide? When did Mr. Fillmore take the oath of office? What is said of the transfer made in the brief space which that service occupied?

GENERAL PROGRESS.

I. States. 1. Number of colonies at the commencement of the Revolution? What did these become? What adopt?

2. What states were admitted during the administration of Washington?

3. How many states since?

4. How many territories had been organized?

5. Limits of the country in 1800? Limits at the present time? Superficial area then? What is it now? How does it compare with the continent of Europe? How compare with the Russian empire? How with England?

6. What tracts of territory have been added during the present century? How were they obtained?

II. Government. Since when has a government existed? Number of Congresses? Extra sessions?

III. Presidents. How many presidents have there been? Name them in their order. How many have died? Which was the oldest? Which the youngest? How many served eight years? How many four? Who died in office?

IV. Population. 1. Population in 1800? In 1850?

2. Number of Indians? From what states have the Indians been removed, and where? What is said of them?

3. Immigration from 1820 to 1840? From 1840 to 1850?

V. Personal Appearance. 1. Whom do the inhabitants resemble? What blood predominates in New England? What is said of them? What of their stature?

2. What is said of the people of the Middle and Western States? What people predominate there? What other sorts of people are to be found in these states?

3. What is said of the people of the South? What of the negro population?

VI. Character. 1. What may be said of the character of the people? What of national character?

2. Of general traits, what is the first mentioned? 2? 3? 4? 5? 6? 7?

3. What is said of these characteristics as applied to New England?

4. What is said of her morality and piety? How is the Sabbath regarded?

5 What is said of the Middle States ? In what are the people active and enterprising ? What is said particularly of the Dutch ? What of Friends, Germans, Catholics, &c. ?

6. What is said of the hospitality and courtesy of the southern people ?

7. Whom do the inhabitants of the Western States resemble? What portion resembles New England ? What portion Virginia ? From what was Kentucky settled ? From what Ohio ? Of what compound, then, is the character of the Western States ? What has this parentage produced ?

VII. DRESS. 1. Who formerly manufactured their own garments ? What is said of the hand-card and spinning-wheel ? What is said of the manufacture of yarn ?

2. How has this family manufacture been superseded ? How are the people of the United States clothed ? How are they dressed compared with persons fifty years ago ? The fashions of what cities are the most prevalent ? What do the Germans wear ? What the Quakers ?

VIII. DWELLINGS. 1. What of the mode of building ? First dwellings in new settlements ? Progress in respect to dwellings ?

2. Where are neat and handsome structures to be found ? What is said of the residences in the neighborhood of cities ?

3. What is said of American villages ?

4. What is said of materials used for dwellings ? Where is wood chiefly used ? Where is the Flemish model to be found ? What is said of villages in western New York ? Where are stone houses and barns to be found ?

5. Manner of building at the South ? What are the houses composed of ?

6. What is said of structures at the West ? How are some towns built ? What abounds ? Where does the log-house disappear ? What is said of our architecture as compared with England, France and Germany ? Causes for this ?

IX. FOOD. 1. How are the Americans fed ? What is said of starvation ?

2. What is said of the culinary art ?

3. What is said of fast eating ?

5. What is said of wheat ?

6. What is said of the diet of the Middle States ?

7. What is said of food used in the Southern States ? What of garden vegetables ?

8. What are the two great articles of food in the Western States ?

X. MEANS OF INTERCOMMUNICATION. What is said of facilities for intercommunication ? What of the use of vehicles ? What of turnpikes ? What of the stage-coach ?

1. CANALS. 1. What is said of canals prior to 1800 ? By what will they be superseded ? Era of canals in the United States ?

2. Length of the Erie Canal ? When first opened ? What does it connect ? Which state has the greatest number of miles in canals ? Who was the great promoter of the canal system ?

3. Length of the Ohio Canal ? What does it connect ? When opened ? In what respect has the canal the advantage of the railroad ?

2. STEAM NAVIGATION. 1. In what respect has a change taken place in the navigation of rivers, &c. ?

2. First successful trip of a steamboat ? By whom ? Between what

places ? Distance ? When ? Time consumed ? What is said of his return ? When did Fulton die ? Age ? Speed soon after attained ?

3. First steamboat on the western waters ? Length of a voyage of a boat from New Orleans to Louisville, in 1817 ? In 1827 ? Distance ? Number of boats at the West in 1818 ? Number in 1848 ?

4. Why was it thought that the ocean could not be safely navigated by steamboats ?

5. First steam vessel that crossed the Atlantic ? Give an account of her voyage.

6. Give an account of a voyage of the Sirius and Great Western. What lines of ocean steamboats are now established ?

7. Length of the voyage of the Mayflower ? Ordinary length of the voyage of ocean steamers ? How near now is England to the United States ?

3. RAILROADS. 1. First railroad in the United States ? Where ? When finished ? Object of it ? When and where was steam-power first used ?

2. Average cost of railroads in the United States ? In England ?

3. Extreme speed in England ? In the United States ? How does this speed compare with the velocity of a cannon-ball ?

4. Number of miles of railroad in 1849 ? Aggregate cost ? Number of passengers transported in 1850 ? With what is Boston connected ? With what is Albany ? With what is New York ?

5. What is the project of Mr. Whitney ? What plan has Mr. Degrand ? What is said of a railroad across the isthmus ?

4. ELECTRO-MAGNETIC TELEGRAPH. 1. Prior to this invention, by what system was intelligence conveyed ? When adopted ? Distance of stations ? When only used ? Where used ? Progress of communication ? Annual cost ?

2. Who constructed the electro-magnetic telegraph ? How came his attention directed to the subject ?

3. When was the practicability of Morse's discovery tested ? Through what appropriation ? When ? How ? Number of miles of Morse's telegraph in 1852 ?

4. Rival telegraphs in the United States ? Which is most used ? What is said of House's ?

5. What evidence can you give of the rapidity of transmission ? What is said of communication between New York and New Orleans ?

6. Cost of erecting telegraphs in England ? Cost in the United States ? Cost of messages in England ? Cost in America ?

5. POST-OFFICE. 1. By whom were communications sent, in our early history ? What fact shows the trouble and expense of early intercommunication ?

2. What is said of mails between Boston and New York ?

3. Rates of postage in 1800 ? Rates in 1852 ?

6. NEWSPAPERS. First newspaper after the landing of the Pilgrims ? First religious newspaper in the United States ? Second ?

XI. INVENTIONS — ARTS — MANUFACTURES. 1. What is said of the inventive genius of the Americans ? How has this genius been stimulated ?

2. Patent office, when opened ? Number of patents in Massachusetts ? Number in Connecticut ? Number in South Carolina ? In Georgia ? What do these facts show ? Whole number issued ? What do the greatest number relate to ? And what the least ?

3. The three most important inventions of the last half-century ? When was the cotton-gin patented ? When did Mr. Whitney die ? Bales of cotton shipped before the cotton-gin came into use ? Annual product now ?

4. Hourly number of impressions on the hand-press ? Number by Mr. Hoe's recently invented cylinder press ?

5. Manufactures prior to the Revolution ? Saying of Lord Chatham ? Manufactures during the Revolution ? Since ?

6. Power-loom, where and when introduced ? When and where the jenny and broad-loom ? Who discovered the application of India rubber to cloth ? When ?

7. What other important discovery is here alluded to ? What effect has ether, when inhaled ?

8. What is said of the use of sulphuric ether or chloroform ? Which of these is to be preferred ? Why ?

9. What is said of engraving, sculpture and painting ? What names of eminent sculptors can you mention ?

10. Eminent painters, during the last half-century ? What is said of West ? What of Allston ?

XII. AGRICULTURE. 1. What is said of agriculture ? Which states are chiefly agricultural ? Which are considerably manufacturing ? Proportion of inhabitants who follow agricultural pursuits ?

2. What is said of agricultural chemistry ? What two individuals have done vast good by their experiments ? Who have made similar investigations ?

3. What has been done in Europe and America by way of agricultural education ?

XIII. TRADE AND COMMERCE. 1. What is said of trade and commerce in the United States during the last half-century ? What does it consist in ? Principal articles of exportation ?

2. Who are the great carriers of these exports ? Proportion of shipping belonging to them ? What part owned by states south of the Potomac ? Staple articles, the growth of what states ? How are they carried ? How sent to foreign countries ? What is said of cotton shipped from New Orleans ? What country receives the largest shipments ? What countries next the British dominions ?

3. Goods received in return ? What from Great Britain ? What from France ? From China ? From Russia ? From the East and West Indies ? From whence do wines come ? Brandy ?

4. What is imported from California ? What, however, has become of this gold ?

5. When was the first shipment of ice made ? By whom ? To what place ? First profitable shipments, when and where to ? First shipment to the East Indies ?

6. Amount shipped in 1847 to southern ports ? To foreign ports ? How many vessels did it require ? Aggregate value ? In what is it packed ?

XIV. EDUCATION. 1. What is said of early attention to the education of children and youth ? What principle is being adopted in reference to schools ?

2. What is said of infant, Lancasterian and manual-labor schools ? What of female seminaries ? Where are normal schools established ? Where is the largest ?

3. Colleges ? Number of colleges in the United States in 1800 ?

35*

Number now ?   Which have the most extensive libraries ?   What is said of the preliminary studies ?

4. Number of theological institutions ?   Law schools ?   Medical schools ?   What is said of the military academy ?   What of the naval academy ?

XV. CHARITABLE EDUCATIONAL INSTITUTIONS. 1. What is said of them ?   Who was the founder of Sabbath-schools ?   When and where did Raikes found the first Sabbath-school ?   When did he die ?

2. When was a similar school gathered in Philadelphia ?   What is said to have been the first Sabbath-school in America ?   In what state ?

3. INSTITUTIONS FOR DEAF MUTES. When and where was the first institution of the kind opened ?   What is it called ?   In what did it have its origin ?   Where did Mr. Gallaudet qualify himself ?   Number of such institutions now ?

4. INSTITUTIONS FOR THE BLIND. Number of these established ?   What was the first called ?   Superintendent ?

5. LUNATIC ASYLUMS. Oldest institutions of this kind ?   Number now existing ?   What lady has contributed much to the establishment of insane institutions ?   In what way ?

6. INSTRUCTION OF IDIOTS. Where has such instruction been commenced ?   Number of idiots in Massachusetts ?   Result of the experiment thus far ?

XVI. RELIGION. 1. Principal religious denominations in the United States ?   What is said of other denominations ?

2. What is said of irreligion and infidelity ?   What are we in danger of ?   What do the exigencies of the church require ?

QUESTIONS ON THE CONSTITUTION.

PREAMBLE.

For what objects did the people of the United States adopt a constitution ?

ARTICLE I.

Section I. In whom does the constitution vest all legislative powers ? Of whom does this Congress consist ?

Section II. 1. Who chooses representatives ? How often ? Qualifications of electors of representatives ?

2. Age of a representative ? How long must he have been a citizen of the United States ? Of what state an inhabitant ?

3. How are representatives and direct taxes to be apportioned among the several states ? How are their respective numbers to be determined ? When was the first census or enumeration to be made ? How often afterwards ? How many inhabitants could send one representative ? Suppose a state had less than thirty thousand ? Which state at first sent the greatest number of representatives ? How many ? Which states sent eight ? Which six ? Which five ? Which four ? Which three ? Which two ? Which one ?

4. How are vacancies filled ?

5. Speaker and other officers of the house, by whom chosen ? Who has the sole power of impeachment ?

Section III. 1. Of whom is the Senate composed ? How chosen ? For what time ? How many votes has each senator ? Have not the large states more senators than the small states ? Have the small states, then, the same power, in passing or rejecting a bill, as the large states ?

2. Into how many classes are the senators divided ? When are the seats of the first class vacated ? When those of the second ? When those of the third ? How often, then, is one-third chosen ? What advantage is there in this arrangement ? How are vacancies which occur during the recess of a legislature filled ? How long does such senator hold his office ?

3. Age of a senator ? How long a citizen of the United States ? How long an inhabitant of the state ?

4. Who presides in the Senate ? What vote has he ?

5. Other officers of the Senate, by whom chosen ? What is a president pro tempore ? What duties may devolve upon him ?

6. Who tries impeachments ? Who would preside, were the President of the United States to be impeached ? Majority necessary to a conviction ?

7. Suppose a person convicted, to what might the penalty extend ? To what the convicted party be further liable ?

Section IV. 1. Who prescribes the times, places and manner, of holding elections for senators and representatives? But what power has Congress in relation to such regulations?

2. How often does Congress assemble? When?

SECTION V. 1. In respect to what does each house judge? What number makes a quorum? Meaning of quorum? Who may adjourn from day to day? What else may they do?

2. What rules may each house adopt? How many members can expel a member?

3. What is said of a journal of proceedings? What of publishing it? When are the yeas and nays to be entered on the journal?

4. What is said of adjournment?

SECTION VI. 1. What compensation do members of Congress receive? How paid? In what cases are they exempted from arrest? For what may they not be questioned?

2. What is said of members of Congress holding any civil office? Suppose a person holds an office under the United States, what then?

SECTION VII. 1. In which house must revenue bills be originated? But what may the Senate do?

2. What must the President of the United States do, in order that a bill may become a law? Suppose he does not approve of it, what does he do? What does the house then do? In order to pass the bill, what number is required? To whom is it then sent? When does it become a law? What further must be done? Within what time must a president return a bill? Suppose he does not return it within ten days?

3. What is necessary that an order, resolution or vote, of the two houses, may take effect? Suppose the president disapproves of such order, resolution, or vote?

SECTION VIII. What power has Congress in regard, 1. To taxes, duties, imports and excises? To payment of debts? But what must be uniform? 2. As to borrowing money? 3. Regulating commerce? 4. Naturalization? Bankruptcies? 5. Coining money? 6. Counterfeiting? 7. Post-offices? 8. Progress of science and useful arts? 9. Piracies? 10. Declaring war? 11. Armies? 12. Navy? 13. Land and naval forces? 14. Suppression of insurrections? Repelling invasions? 15. Organizing armies and disciplining the militia? 16. Exercising exclusive legislation over seat of government, and all places purchased for the erection of forts, &c.?

SECTION IX. 1. What power had Congress in regard to immigrants into the country, prior to 1808? What tax might be imposed?

2. What is said of the writ of habeas corpus?

3. What of bills of attainder or ex post facto law?

4. Capitation or direct taxes, how to be laid?

5. What is said of duties on articles exported from any state? What of preferences? What of vessels from one state to another?

6. When may money be drawn from the treasury? What statement must be published?

7. What is said of titles of nobility? What of persons holding offices of trust accepting presents?

SECTION X. 1. What may individual states not do?

2. What are individual states prohibited, as to imposts or duties? What exception is made? To whom does the real produce of all duties and imposts belong? What further are the states prohibited?

ARTICLE II.

SECTION I. 1. In whom is the executive power vested ? Duration of his office ?

2. By whom chosen ? Who chooses the electors ? Number in each state ? Who may not be an elector ?

3. When do they meet ? Number of persons voted for ? What list do they make out ? To whom are they transmitted ? By whom, and before whom, are these votes counted ? What number elects ? When must the House of Representatives choose a president ? How ? Suppose no one has a majority, what is done ? How many votes has each state ? What constitutes, in this case, a quorum ? How many states are necessary to a choice ? Who is vice-president ? When does the Senate choose a vice-president ? *

4. What is said as to the time of choosing the electors, and of the day on which the latter shall give their votes ?

5. Qualifications of a president ? Age ? How long a resident in the United States ?

6. What are the causes of the disability of a president ? Upon whom, in such a case, do his duties devolve ? What power has Congress in relation to some one who shall act as president ?

7. What does the constitution provide in regard to a president's salary ? What oath must he take ?

SECTION II. 1. How does the president stand related to the army, navy and militia ? Whose opinion may he require in writing, and on what subjects ? What power has he in respect to reprieves and pardons ? With what exception ?

2. What power has he in respect to treaties ? To ambassadors ? Consuls ? Judges ?

3. What vacancies can he fill ? Length of such commissions ? ·

SECTION III. Duties of the president in respect to Congress ? When may he convene that body ? When adjourn it ? His duty in respect to ambassadors ? The execution of the laws ? Whom is he to commission ?

SECTION IV. How may all officers of the government be removed ? For what crimes ?

ARTICLE III.

SECTION I. How is the judicial power of the United States vested ? Tenure of the judges' office ? Compensation ?   •

SECTION II. 1. To what cases does the judicial power extend ? To what controversies ? To what persons ?

2. In what cases has the Supreme Court original jurisdiction ? In what cases has it appellate jurisdiction ? Meaning of appellate ?

3. Before whom are trials to be held ? Where ? But when the crime is not in any State ?

SECTION III. 1. What is treason ? How may a person be convicted of treason ?

2. Who may punish treason ? With what limitation ?

---

* See Art. 12, Sec. I., of amendments, where the mode of choosing a president and vice-president is somewhat altered.

ARTICLE IV.

Section I. How are public acts, records, and judicial proceedings, of the states, to be treated? How are they to be proved?

Section II. 1. What is said of the privileges of citizens of one state in other states?

2. Suppose a person charged with crime flees into another state, how may he be taken?

3. What is provided, in regard to those held to service, who escape from one state into another?

Section III. 1. What is said of the admission of new states? What of the formation of new states?

2. What power has Congress in respect to the territory or other property belonging to the United States?

Section IV. What guarantees does the constitution make to the several states?

ARTICLE V.

1. Amendments to the constitution, how proposed? By whom ratified? With what proviso?

ARTICLE VI.

1. What debts does the constitution recognize?

2. What constitutes the supreme law of the land?

3. Who are specially bound to support the constitution? How? What is said of religious tests?

ARTICLE VII.

1. How many states were required to ratify the constitution, in order to its establishment? Where did the convention meet which framed the constitution? Who was president of it? When was it adopted? What states ratified it? Year? When did it go into operation? What new state joined? When? Number of delegates to the convention? How many signed? Why not all?

AMENDMENTS.

When were amendments proposed? How many? Number adopted?

Art. 1. What is said of an established religion? What of freedom of speech? Of the press? Of the right of petition?

Art. 2. What is said of the right of the people to keep and bear arms?

Art. 3. What of quartering soldiers?

Art. 4. What of warrants and seizures?

Art. 5. What is said of capital or other infamous crimes? Except in what cases? What of double trial for the same offence? What other provisions are made for the protection of citizens?

Art. 6. What right shall a person accused of crime enjoy? Where? What shall he be informed of? With whom confronted? How obtain witnesses? And by whom aided?

Art. 7. In what suits shall the right of trial by jury be preserved? What is said of the reëxamination of facts tried by a jury?

Art. 8. What is said of excessive bail, fines, or punishments?

Art. 9. What is said of rights retained by the people?

Art. 10. What is further said of powers not delegated?

Art. 11. How is the judicial power limited?

ART. 12. 1. Who elect the president and vice-president? Where must they meet? May both belong to the same state with themselves? How must they vote? What lists must be made? To whom must these lists be sent? Who opens these certificates, or lists? In whose presence? Who is declared president? But suppose no one has a majority, what number is selected? Who chooses from these three? How are the votes taken? How many votes has each state? How many constitutes a quorum for this purpose? What majority is necessary to a choice? Suppose no choice is made by the house before the 4th of March, who acts as president?

2. Who is declared vice-president? Suppose no one has a majority, who elects a vice-president? From whom? What constitutes a quorum for this purpose? What majority is necessary?

3. Who is not eligible to the vice-presidency?

QUESTIONS ON THE DECLARATION OF INDEPENDENCE.

NOTE. — This memorable Declaration, the patriotic work of the Congress of 1776, was signed by that body on the 4th of July of that year. The signers were fifty-six in number. Richard Henry Lee, of Virginia, first moved the question. Mr. Jefferson, John Adams, Dr. Franklin, Mr. Sherman, and R. R. Livingston, were appointed a committee to prepare the Declaration. The original draft was by Mr. Jefferson. John Adams was its great supporter on the floor of Congress. John Hancock's signature stands first. Not a single individual of this patriotic band now survives. In the order of history, the Declaration should precede the Constitution; but it was deemed better that it should be inserted here, to be learned by the pupil or not, as the teacher may decide. The author, however, is of opinion that every child should become acquainted with the reasons which induced our ancestors to separate themselves from Great Britain.

When was the Declaration of Independence signed? By whom? What was their number? Who moved the question? Who were appointed to prepare a declaration? Who drafted it? Who was its great supporter? Whose signature stands first? Are any of these patriotic men now living? With what should every child become acquainted?

When are a people justified in dissolving their political connection with another people? ANS. When that people, or their rulers, oppress them by manifestly unjust and long-continued abuses and usurpations. What, in that case, does a decent respect for the opinions of mankind require them to do?

What two great truths did the Congress of 1776 hold to be self-evident? What among these rights did they specify? What is the design of government? From whom are the just powers of government derived? When is it right to alter or to abolish governments? On what principle should a new government be framed, and its powers organized? Yet what will prudence dictate? What hitherto has experience shown? But when is it the right and duty of a people to throw off their government? What is said of the forbearance of the colonies? What of the necessity of a change of government? What did Congress declare concerning the history of the then King of Great

Britain? Who was he? Ans. George III. By an appeal to what did the Congress attempt to prove their assertion?
To what laws had he refused assent?
What laws had he prohibited his governors to pass?
What other laws had he refused to pass?
What had he done in respect to convening legislative bodies? Why?
What had he repeatedly dissolved? Why?
What, after such dissolution, had he refused? What had resulted? And to what dangers had the state been exposed?
What had he endeavored to prevent? By what means?
The admission of what had he obstructed? How?
Upon whom had he made judges dependent?
What in respect to new offices and new officers had he done?
What in respect to standing armies?
What in respect to the military?
To a foreign jurisdiction?
Bodies of armed troops?
How protecting them, and for what?
What had he done in regard to trade?
In regard to taxes?
In regard to trial by jury?
Transportation of American citizens?
What had been his conduct toward a neighboring province?
What had he done in regard to the colonial charters? Their most valuable laws? Their powers of government?
What in regard to the colonial legislatures?
What had he abdicated here, and what had he declared respecting the people?
What had he done on our seas? Coasts? To our towns? To our citizens?
What was he then doing in respect to large armies? And for what purpose? And in what manner?
What had he done with those taken captive on the high seas?
What insurrections had he excited? What had he excited the frontier Indians to do?
What, meanwhile, had the people done by way of redress? How? How had these petitions been answered? What was such a prince unfit for?
How had the colonists treated their British brethren? Of what had they warned them? Of what had they reminded them? To what appealed? How conjured them? To what had they been deaf? To what necessity, therefore, were they driven?
To whom, therefore, did they appeal? What did they publish and declare? In whose name, and by whose authority? From what absolved? And for what had they full powers? Upon whom did they rely? What did they mutually pledge? And in support of what?

INDEX OF TOPICS.

36*

WORCESTER'S

SERIES OF
AMERICAN
SCHOOL DICTIONARIES.

DESCRIPTION OF THE SERIES.
WORCESTER'S COMPREHENSIVE DICTIONARY.

A Comprehensive Pronouncing and Explanatory Dictionary of the English Language, with Pronouncing Vocabularies of Classical, Scripture, and Modern Geographical
Names. By JOSEPH E. WORCESTER, LL. D. Enlarged
Revised Edition, with important additions. 526 pp.,
large 12 mo., containing 67,000 words.

This Dictionary combines, in a very condensed and cheap form,
a greater amount of valuable matter than any other similar work.
It contains, in its various vocabularies, upwards of sixty-seven
thousand words, many *technical terms*, and a copious list of such
words and phrases from foreign languages as are often found in
English books. — It comprises very full pronouncing vocabularies of Classical and Scripture Proper Names, and upwards of
four thousand *Modern Geographical Names*. The additions
which have recently been made consist of Abbreviations used in
Writing and Printing ; Phrases and Quotations from the Latin,
French, Italian, and Spanish Languages, in general use ; and a
description of the Principal Deities, Heroes, &c., of the Fabulous
History of the Greeks and Romans. This additional matter is not
only very useful to the general reader, but is of the highest
importance to children in schools, who have no Classical Dictionaries to consult.

As a PRONOUNCING Dictionary, it possesses decided advantages
over all others, the pronunciation of every word being plainly
marked, not only in the *accent*, but in the *sounds of the vowels*, — a
most important feature in the plan of the work. Every difference

of pronunciation in our language is presented according to the respective and most eminent authorities.

The ORTHOGRAPHY in the work is that which is authorized by the best usage. Innovations which have no sanction from English usage, or the prevailing and best usage of this country, have been avoided. *The vocabulary of words of doubtful or various orthography*, together with the rules and remarks which accompany them, comprises nearly all the difficult and doubtful cases in English orthography.

WORCESTER'S ELEMENTARY DICTIONARY.

An English Dictionary for Common Schools, with Pronouncing Vocabularies of Classical, Scripture, and Modern Geographical Names. By JOSEPH E. WORCESTER, LL. D. Revised and Enlarged. 360 pp., 12mo., containing 44,000 words.

This work is a reduced form of the *Comprehensive Dictionary*, and is especially adapted to the use of common schools. It contains, in its several vocabularies, upwards of 55,000 words. In addition to the Dictionary proper, it comprises the following matters or divisions :—

1st. A list of such *Words and Phrases from Foreign Languages* as are often found in English books. This is a class of words for the definition and pronunciation of which an English reader often wants assistance.

2d. A short list of *Americanisms*, or words which are reputed as peculiar to America, and English words which are used in America in a peculiar manner.

3d. *Remarks on Orthography*, with a copious vocabulary of *Words of doubtful or various Orthography*.

4th. Walker's Vocabulary of *Greek and Latin Proper Names*, with large additions from *Trollope* and *Carr*.

5th. *Scripture Proper Names*, with the pronunciation according to Walker and other orthoëpists.

6th. A *Vocabulary of Geographical Names*, with the pronunciation given according to the best authorities.

WORCESTER'S PRIMARY DICTIONARY.

A Primary Pronouncing Dictionary of the English Language ; with Vocabularies of Classical, Scripture, and

Modern Geographical Names. By JOSEPH E. WORCES-
TER, LL. D. 352 pp., 18mo., containing 41,000 words.

This little work contains a vocabulary of the common and well-
authorized words in the English language. Technical terms, and
words which are obsolete, provincial, vulgar, or not well authorized, and also a great portion of the compound and derivative
words of the language, have been omitted, as not necessary or
suitable in a manual of this kind, which is designed to exhibit the
correct orthography and pronunciation, together with a concise
definition, of the common words of the language, such as are
usually found in the standard works of English literature.

RECOMMENDATIONS.

Dr. Worcester's Universal and Critical Dictionary of the English Language, of which the three works severally designated as
the Comprehensive, Elementary, and Primary Dictionaries are
abstracts, has been commended in unqualified terms, by the highest
literary authority of our country, as follows : —

The DEFINITIONS are clear and exact, and those pertaining to
technical and scientific terms are specially valuable to the general
reader.

The author has evidently bestowed great labor on PRONUNCIA-
TION. His system of notation, which is easily understood, and
founded on a more complete analysis of the vowel sounds than we
have elsewhere met with, together with his plan of exhibiting all
the best English authorities in relation to words differently pronounced by different orthoëpists, gives to this work important
advantages as a Pronouncing Dictionary.

In ORTHOGRAPHY he has made no arbitrary changes ; but, where
usage is various and fluctuating, he has aimed to be consistent,
and to reduce to the same rules words of similar formation.

We confidently recommend it as containing an ample and careful view of the present state of our language.

JARED SPARKS, LL. D., President of Harvard University.
SIDNEY WILLARD, A. M., late Professor of Hebrew, &c., Har-
vard University.
MOSES STUART, D. D., Professor Sacred Literature, Andover,
Mass.
EDWARDS A. PARK, D. D., Abbott Professor of Christian The-
ology, Andover, Mass.

LEONARD WOODS, Jr., D. D., President of Bowdoin College, Maine.

N. LORD, D. D., President of Dartmouth College, New Hampshire.

EDWARD HITCHCOCK, D. D., LL. D., President of Amherst College, Mass.

MARK HOPKINS, D. D., President of Williams College, Mass.

EDWARD T. CHANNING, LL. D., Boylston Professor of Rhetoric and Oratory, Harvard University.

HENRY W. LONGFELLOW, A. M., Professor of Belles Lettres, Harvard University.

BENJAMIN ·HALE, D. D., President of Geneva College, New York.

ALONZO POTTER, D. D., LL. D., Bishop of Pennsylvania.

ROBLEY DUNGLISON, M. D., Professor in Jefferson Medical College, Philadelphia.

FRANCIS BOWEN, A. M., Editor of the North American Review.

CHARLES FOLSOM, A. M., Librarian of the Boston Athenæum.

HECTOR HUMPHREY, D. D., President of St. John's College, Maryland.

DAVID L. SWAIN, LL. D., President of University of North Carolina.

JOHN McLEAN, LL. D., Justice United States Supreme Court, Ohio.

PHILIP LINDSLEY, LL. D., President of the University of Nashville, Tenn.

N. LAWRENCE LINDSLEY, A. M., Professor of Ancient Language and Literature, Cumberland University, Tenn.

We concur fully in the leading portions of the above recommendation, — not having had leisure to examine all the particulars referred to.

LEVI WOODBURY, LL. D., Justice of United States Supreme Court, Mass.

ELIPHALET NOTT, D. D., LL. D., President Union College.

From a general and frequent reference to this Dictionary, in constant use, I fully concur in the general merits of the work, and regard it as a very valuable aid to science.

THEODORE FRELINGHUYSEN, LL. D., Chancellor of the University of New York.

I have used "Worcester's Universal and Critical Dictionary of the English Language," in preference to any other, for constant reference.

JOHN WHEELER, D. D., President of University of Vermont.

The Comprehensive Dictionary is used in the public schools of Boston, the Free Academy of New York city, and many other places. The Board of Education of New Hampshire have recently adopted it for the schools throughout that state.

Attention is particularly invited to the following recommendations from gentlemen who do not lend their names or influence to indifferent publications.

" This Dictionary exhibits, in its different parts, ample evidence of inquiry, careful comparison, and sound judgment. It combines, in a very condensed, yet intelligible form, a greater quantity of valuable matter than any other similar work ; and as a Pronouncing Dictionary, it possesses decided advantages over all others, by its superior system of notation, and by its exhibition of all the principal authorities respecting words of doubtful and various pronunciation. We do not hesitate to pronounce it, in our judgment, *the most comprehensive, accurate, and useful compendium within our knowledge.*"

JOSEPH STORY, LL. D., Professor Law, Cambridge, Mass.

SIDNEY WILLARD, A. M., Professor Hebrew, Latin, &c., Cambridge, Mass.

E. T. CHANNING, A. M., Professor Rhetoric and Oratory, Cambridge, Mass.

JOHN PICKERING, LL. D., Boston.

WM. ALLEN, D. D., President Bowdoin College, Maine.

J. L. KINGSLEY, LL. D., Professor Latin, Yale College, Conn.

ALONZO POTTER, Professor Rhetoric, Union College, N. York.

C. ANTHON, LL. D., Professor Greek and Latin, Columbia College, New York.

J. P. CUSHING, A. M., President Hampden Sidney College, Va.

JASPER ADAMS, D. D., President Charleston College, S. C.

ALONZO CHURCH, D. D., President University of Georgia.

PHILIP LINDSLEY, D. D., President Nashville University, Tenn.

EDWARD BEECHER, A. M., President Illinois College.

DAVID PRENTICE, LL. D., Professor of Languages, Geneva College, New York.

PETER S. DUPONCEAU, LL. D., Philadelphia, says : — Worcester's Pronouncing and Explanatory Dictionary contains many valuable improvements on other works of the same kind, which makes me consider it as the best Parlor Dictionary now extant. I have introduced it into my family, and will not fail to recommend it to my friends on every occasion.

HECTOR HUMPHREY, D. D., President of St. John's College, Annapolis, Md., remarks : — Worcester's Dictionary is in our schools, and I should be glad to see it adopted everywhere. I find it exceedingly convenient and useful.

1*

ROBLEY DUNGLISON, M. D., Professor in the University of Maryland, observes : — l have examined this Dictionary with care, and am much pleased with the plan and execution. I can have no hesitation in awarding to it the merit of being the best adapted to the end in view of any that I have examined. It is, in other words, the best portable " Pronouncing and Explanatory Dictionary " that I have seen, and as such is deserving of extensive circulation.

THE AMERICAN MONTHLY REVIEW remarks : — That a work of this kind was needed, no one who has attended to the subject can doubt ; and all who have examined Mr. Worcester's Dictionary, and are competent judges of its merits, must be satisfied that much has been done to supply a well-known deficiency in regard to books of this class.

TAIT'S EDINBURGH MAGAZINE says, in a notice of a specimen of this Dictionary, which was republished in London : — If the work possesses the sterling merit of the specimen before us, it will go far to supersede most others at present in common use.

THE SELECT JOURNAL OF FOREIGN PERIODICAL LITERATURE remarks : — No specimen, as is well known by all who have used this Dictionary, would give too favorable an impression of its completeness and correctness.

THE BOSTON DAILY ADVERTISER says: — This work has been so long before the public, that it has assumed in many circles the character of a standard book of reference. Mr. W.'s name is a sufficient warrant that the accuracy of the book will be fully maintained by the closest examination.

THE BOSTON SCHOOL COMMITTEE, in their Report for 1851, say: " Instances of mispronunciation also occurred ; and on calling for a Dictionary, none was at hand. A fine edition of Webster's large work lay on the master's table in another story, but, for all practical uses, where it was then wanted, it might as well have been in Texas. It is recommended that all the teachers be required to have Dictionaries in their several rooms. It is also proposed that all the younger pupils be required to have Worcester's Primary Dictionary, and the more advanced pupils his Comprehensive Pronouncing and Explanatory Dictionary. These books are very cheap, and, for the price, are the most valuable School Books in the English language."

Mr. William H. Wells, Principal of the Putnam Free School, and author of a popular Grammar of the English Language, says : — " As a standard of orthography and pronunciation, the compilation of Mr. Worcester is far in advance of all other works of its class. His exhibition of the elementary sounds of the language surpasses even the masterly analysis of Smart. The definitions are copious and accurate, and every portion of the work affords evidence of the most careful and exact discrimination, and the profoundest research."

Mr. William Russell, formerly editor of the American Jour nal of Education, and author of a Series of Reading Books, says : — " You are aware that I have, in my compilations on elocution, and in my instructions on that subject, uniformly referred to the previous Dictionaries of Mr. Worcester as the most accurate and satisfactory sources of information in their department. The new Dictionary I have examined closely, and am daily using it as a standard for reference ; and it seems to me the most valuable work of the kind ever produced in this country. To teachers and students it commends itself by its comparative *completeness*, its *perfect fidelity* in observing the authority of *the best standards*, and its *exactness* in detail. Its style, both in orthography and orthoëpy, conforms strictly to *actual living usage*, both in this country and in England, with the single exception of words of more than one syllable terminating in the letters *or* or *our*, in which Mr. Worcester gives the preference to American usage. In my communications with teachers, I have been accustomed, for many years, to hear an earnest wish expressed for an American Dictionary, free from the peculiarities of Webster, and the obsolete extremes of Walker. Such a work Mr. Worcester seems to have furnished, and it bids fair to be generally adopted as a standard in instruction."

Mr. D. S. Rowe, Principal of Massachusetts State Normal School, Westfield, says : — " I know of no author who has so uniformly exhibited so much good taste and accurate discrimination in respect to all the departments of lexicography as Dr. Worcester. His book is truly a splendid production."